T0210543

Lecture Notes in Computer Science 9202

Commenced Publication in 1973
Founding and Former Series Editors:
Gerhard Goos, Juris Hartmanis, and Jan van Leeuwen

More information about this series at http://www.springer.com/series/7408

Nick Bassiliades · Georg Gottlob
Fariba Sadri · Adrian Paschke
Dumitru Roman (Eds.)

Rule Technologies: Foundations, Tools, and Applications

9th International Symposium, RuleML 2015
Berlin, Germany, August 2–5, 2015
Proceedings

 Springer

Editors
Nick Bassiliades
Aristotle University of Thessaloniki
Thessaloniki
Greece

Georg Gottlob
University of Oxford
Oxford
UK

Fariba Sadri
Imperial College London
London
UK

Adrian Paschke
Freie Universität Berlin
Berlin
Germany

Dumitru Roman
SINTEF/University of Oslo
Oslo
Norway

ISSN 0302-9743   ISSN 1611-3349   (electronic)
Lecture Notes in Computer Science
ISBN 978-3-319-21541-9   ISBN 978-3-319-21542-6   (eBook)
DOI 10.1007/978-3-319-21542-6

Library of Congress Control Number: 2015943822

Springer Cham Heidelberg New York Dordrecht London

Printed on acid-free paper

Springer International Publishing AG Switzerland is part of Springer Science+Business Media
(www.springer.com)

Preface

The annual International Web Rule Symposium (RuleML) is an international conference on research, applications, languages, and standards for rule technologies. It has evolved from an annual series of international workshops since 2002, international conferences in 2005 and 2006, and international symposia since 2007. RuleML 2015 was the ninth symposium of this series, collocated in Berlin, Germany, with the 25th jubilee edition of the International Conference on Automated Deduction (CADE-25), the 9th International Conference on Web Reasoning and Rule Systems (RR 2015), the 11th Reasoning Web Summer School (RW 2015), and the 7th Workshop on Formal Ontologies Meet Industry (FOMI 2015).

RuleML is a leading conference aiming to build bridges between academia and industry in the field of rules and their applications, especially as part of the semantic technology stack. It is devoted to rule-based programming and rule-based systems including production rule systems, logic programming rule engines, and business rule engines and business rule management systems, Semantic Web rule languages and rule standards (e.g., RuleML, SWRL, RIF, PRR, SBVR, DMN, CL, Prolog), rule-based event processing languages (EPLs) and technologies, and research on inference rules, transformation rules, decision rules, and ECA rules.

This annual symposium is the flagship event of the Rule Markup and Modeling Initiative (RuleML). The RuleML Initiative (http://ruleml.org) is a nonprofit umbrella organization of several technical groups from academia, industry, and government working on rule technology and its applications. Its aim is to promote the study, research, and application of rules in heterogeneous distributed environments such as the Web. RuleML maintains effective links with other major international societies and acts as intermediary between various specialized rule vendors, applications, industrial and academic research groups, as well as standardization efforts from, e.g., W3C, OMG, OASIS, and ISO. One of its major contributions is the Rule Markup Language, a unifying family of XML-serialized rule languages spanning across all industrially relevant kinds of Web rules.

The technical program of RuleML 2015 included presentations of novel rule-based technologies, such as Semantic Web rule languages and standards, rule engines, formal and operational semantics, and rule-based systems. Besides the regular research track, RuleML 2015 included four special research tracks: a track on Complex Event Processing, with the main theme of Uncertainty Handling in Complex Event Processing, a track on Existential Rules and Datalog+/-, a track on Legal Rules and Reasoning, and a track on Rule Learning. These tracks reflect the significant role of rules in several research and application areas, which include: the relation between databases and rules, reasoning over actions and events and developing reactive systems, aspects related to using rules in legal applications, and automatically discovering rules from mining data.

A new feature of RuleML 2015 was the inclusion of an Industry track, describing practical applications of rules and the state of the art of rule-based business cases.

Special highlights of this year's symposium included two keynote talks:

- Michael Genesereth, from Stanford University, USA, presenting the Herbrand Manifesto
- Thom Fruehwirth, from the University of Ulm, Germany, presenting an overview of Constraint Handling Rules

There was also one invited talk:

- Avigdor Gal, from the Technion - Israel Institute of Technology, presenting a framework for mining the rules that guide event creation.

In addition, the program included the 9th International Rule Challenge, dedicated to practical experiences with rule-based applications, a special challenge (RecSysRules 2015) focusing on rule learning algorithms applied to recommender problems using the linked open data cloud for feature set extension, the 5th RuleML 2015 Doctoral Consortium, which focused on PhD research in the area of rules and markup languages, and finally, a poster session.

The contributions in this volume include a set of invited papers, research track papers, and industry track papers. Invited papers included two full papers for the keynote talks, one full paper and one abstract for the invited talks, and two track papers. The research papers included a selection of 22 full papers and one short research paper, which were presented during the technical program of RuleML 2015. The research papers were selected from 54 submissions through a peer-review process. Each paper was reviewed by at least three members of the Program Committee and the Program Committee chairs. For the papers submitted to one of the four special research tracks, the track chairs were also involved in the reviewing phase. Industry track papers included a selection of three papers (out of nine submissions, which underwent a peer-review process).

Owing to the above efforts, RuleML 2015, like its predecessors, offered a high-quality technical and applications program, which was the result of the joint effort of the members of the RuleML 2015 Program Committee.

A special thanks is due to the track chairs, the excellent Program Committee, and the additional reviewers for their hard work in reviewing the submitted papers. Their criticisms and very useful comments were instrumental in achieving a high-quality publication. We also thank the authors for submitting high-quality papers, responding to the reviewers' comments, and abiding by our production schedule. We further wish to thank the keynote and invited speakers for their inspiring talks. We are very grateful to the organizers of all the collocated events, CADE, RR, RW, and FOMI, for enabling this fruitful collocation with RuleML 2015. RuleML 2015 was financially supported by industrial companies and scientific journals and was technically supported by several professional societies. We wish to thank our sponsors, whose financial support helped us offer this event, and whose technical support allowed us to attract many high-quality submissions. Last, but not least, we would like to thank the development team of the EasyChair conference management system and our publisher, Springer, for their support in the preparation and publication of this volume of proceedings.

May 2015

Nick Bassiliades
Georg Gottlob
Fariba Sadri
Adrian Paschke
Dumitru Roman

Organization

General Chair

Adrian Paschke Freie Universität Berlin, Germany

Scientific Program Co-chairs

Nick Bassiliades Aristotle University of Thessaloniki, Greece
Georg Gottlob University of Oxford, UK
Fariba Sadri Imperial College London, UK

Track Chairs

Rule Learning Track

Johannes Fürnkranz Technical University of Darmstadt, Germany
Tomas Kliegr University of Economics, Prague, Czech Republic

Existential Rules and Datalog+/- Track

Georg Gottlob University of Oxford, UK

Complex Event Processing Track

Alexander Artikis National Center for Scientific Research Demoktrios,
 Athens, Greece
Mathias Weidlich Imperial College London, UK

Legal Rules and Reasoning Track

Monica Palmirani Università di Bologna, Italy
Ken Satoh NII (National Institute of Informatics), and Sokendai
 (The Graduate University of Advanced Studies),
 Japan

Industry Track

Marc Proctor Redhat, UK
Dumitru Roman SINTEF, Norway
Nenad Stojanovic Nissatech Innovation Centre, Serbia

Proceedings Chair

Dumitru Roman   SINTEF, Norway

Doctoral Workshop Chairs

Grzegorz J. Nalepa   AGH University of Science and Technology, Krakow,
                             Poland
Monica Palmirani   Università di Bologna, Italy

9th International Rule Challenge Co-chairs

Paul Fodor   Stony Brook University, USA
Adrian Giurca   Brandenburg University of Technology
                             Cottbus–Senftenberg, Germany
Tomas Kliegr   University of Economics, Prague, Czech Republic

RecSysRules 2015 Challenge Track Co-chairs:

Jaroslav Kuchař   Czech Technical University, Prague, Czech Republic
Tommaso di Noia   Politecnico di Bari, Italy
Heiko Paulheim   University of Mannheim, Germany
Tomas Kliegr   University of Economics, Prague

RuleML Rulebase Competition Co-chairs:

Paul Fodor   Stony Brook University, USA
Adrian Giurca   Brandenburg University of Technology
                             Cottbus–Senftenberg, Germany

Sponsoring, Publicity and Social Media Chair

Patrick Hung   University of Ontario Institute of Technology, Canada

Local Organization Chair

Adrian Paschke   Freie Universität Berlin, Germany

Financial Chair

Sebastian Fuß   InfAI e.V., Germany

Web Chair

Shashishekar Ramakrishna   Freie Universität Berlin, Germany

Program Committee

Mario Alviano
Darko Anicic
Grigoris Antoniou
Marcelo Arenas
Alexander Artikis
Tara Athan
Martin Atzmueller
Ebrahim Bagheri
Nick Bassiliades
Meghyn Bienvenu
Antonis Bikakis
Henrik Bostrom
Pierre Bourhis
Lars Braubach
François Bry
Federico Chesani
Horatiu Cirstea
Claudia D'Amato
Célia Da Costa Pereira
Christian De Sainte Marie
Juergen Dix
Vadim Ermolayev
David Eyers
Wolfgang Faber
Jacob Feldman
Michael Fink
Sergio Flesca
Giorgos Flouris
Paul Fodor
Enrico Francesconi
Fred Freitas
Johannes Fürnkranz
Avigdor Gal
Aldo Gangemi
Adrian Giurca
Thomas F. Gordon

Georg Gottlob
Guido Governatori
Christophe Gravier
Ioannis Hatzilygeroudis
André Hernich
Stijn Heymans
Martin Hirzel
Aidan Hogan
Markus Krötzsch
Jaroslav Kuchař
Evelina Lamma
Florian Lemmerich
Francesca Alessandra Lisi
Michael Maher
Marco Manna
Alessandro Margara
Maria Vanina Martinez
Thorne Mccarty
Loizos Michael
Alessandra Mileo
Cristian Molinaro
Michael Morak
Grzegorz J. Nalepa
Giorgio Orsi
Monica Palmirani
Jose Ignacio Panach
   Navarrete
Jeffrey Parsons
Adrian Paschke
Theodore Patkos
Heiko Paulheim
Andreas Pieris
Alexandra Poulovassilis
Cristian Prisacariu
Marc Proctor
Jan Rauch

Fabrizio Riguzzi
Dumitru Roman
Fariba Sadri
Ken Satoh
Vadim Savenkov
Erich Schweighofer
Gerardo Simari
Mantas Simkus
Davide Sottara
Ahmet Soylu
Giorgos Stamou
Giorgos Stoilos
Nenad Stojanovic
Umberto Straccia
Michaël Thomazo
Ioan Toma
Irina Trubitsyna
Martin Holena
Yuh-Jong Hu
Patrick Hung
Frederik Janssen
Tomas Kliegr
Boris Koldehofe
Roman Kontchakov
Efstratios Kontopoulos
Robert Kowalski
Wamberto Vasconcelos
George Vouros
Jian Wang
Renata Wassermann
Matthias Weidlich
Adam Wyner
Bernard Zenko
Albrecht Zimmermann
Thomas Ågotnes

External Reviewers

Mario Fusco
Nikos Katzouris
Cleyton Rodrigues

RuleML 2015 Sponsors

When Processes Rule Events

Avigdor Gal

Technion – Israel Institute of Technology
avigal@ie.technion.ac.il

Abstract. Big data, with its four main characteristics (Volume, Velocity, Variety, and Veracity) pose challenges to the gathering, management, analytics, and visualization of events. These very same four characteristics, however, also hold a great promise in unlocking the story behind data. In this talk, we focus on the observation that event creation is guided by processes. For example, GPS information, emitted by buses in an urban setting follow the bus scheduled route. Also, RTLS information about the whereabouts of patients and nurses in a hospital is guided by the predefined schedule of work. With this observation at hand, we thoroughly seek a method for mining, not the data, but rather the rules that guide data creation and show how, by knowing such rules, big data tasks become more efficient and more effective. In particular, we demonstrate how, by knowing the rules that govern event creation, we can detect complex events sooner and make use of historical data to predict future behaviors.

Contents

Complex Event Processing Track

Existential Rules and Datalog+/- Track

Legal Rules and Reasoning Track

Rule Learning Track

Industry Track

Invited Papers

The Herbrand Manifesto
Thinking Inside the Box

Michael Genesereth[(⊠)] and Eric Kao

Computer Science Department, Stanford University, Stanford, USA
genesereth@stanford.edu, erickao@cs.stanford.edu

Abstract. The traditional semantics for relational logic (sometimes called *Tarskian* semantics) is based on the notion of interpretations of constants in terms of objects external to the logic. *Herbrand* semantics is an alternative that is based on truth assignments for ground sentences without reference to external objects. Herbrand semantics is simpler and more intuitive than Tarskian semantics; and, consequently, it is easier to teach and learn. Moreover, it is stronger than Tarskian semantics. For example, while it is not possible to finitely axiomatize integer arithmetic with Tarskian semantics, this can be done easily with Herbrand semantics. The downside is a loss of some common logical properties, such as compactness and inferential completeness. However, there is no loss of inferential power—anything that can be deduced according to Tarskian semantics can also be deduced according to Herbrand semantics. Based on these results, we argue that there is value in using Herbrand semantics for relational logic in place of Tarskian semantics. It alleviates many of the current problems with relational logic and ultimately may foster a wider use of relational logic in human reasoning and computer applications.

1 Introduction

One of the main strengths of relational logic is that it provides us with a well-defined language for expressing complex information about objects and their relationships. We can write negations, disjunctions, implications, quantified sentences, and so forth. Logic also provides us with precise rules for deriving conclusions from sentences expressed within this language while avoiding the derivation of sentences that are *not* logical conclusions.

What makes it all work is that the language has a clearly defined semantics, which gives meaning to logical connectives and quantifiers. This allows us to know that we are using those connectives and quantifiers correctly; and it allows us to know that, in our reasoning, we are deriving conclusions that follow from our premises and avoiding those that do not.

The basis for almost all treatments of logical semantics is the notion of a model. A *model* is a mathematical structure that tells us which sentences are true and which are false. And this is the basis for logical entailment. We say that a set of premises *logically entails* a conclusion if and only if every model that

N. Bassiliades et al. (Eds.): RuleML 2015, LNCS 9202, pp. 3–12, 2015.
DOI: 10.1007/978-3-319-21542-6_1

satisfies the premises also satisfies the conclusion. In other words, the conclusion must be true whenever the premises are true.

Tarskian semantics is the traditional approach to defining models in relational logic. In Tarskian semantics, a model consists of an arbitrary set of objects (called the universe of discourse) and an interpretation function that (1) maps object constants into elements of this set, (2) maps function constants into functions on this set, and (3) maps relation constants into relations on this set.

As an example, consider the model defined below. Our language in this case consists of the object constants a and b, the unary function constant f and the binary function constant r. Our universe of discourse consists of the natural numbers. Our interpretation maps a into 1 and b into 2; it maps f into a function on these numbers; and it maps r into a set of 2-tuples.

Vocabulary:
$$\{a, b, f, r\}$$
Universe:
$$\{1, 2, 3, 4, \ldots\}$$
Interpretation:
$$i(a) = 1$$
$$i(b) = 2$$
$$i(f) = \{1 \mapsto 2, 2 \mapsto 4, \ldots\}$$
$$i(r) = \langle 1, 2 \rangle, \langle 2, 3 \rangle, \langle 3, 4 \rangle, \ldots$$

A model of this sort completely determines the truth or falsity of all sentences in the language. And it gives us a definition of logical entailment. Note, however, that there are unboundedly many interpretations for any language, and entailment is defined over all conceivable universes—finite, countably infinite, and beyond. It also requires an understanding of relations as set of tuples of objects.

Herbrand semantics is simpler. We start out with the notion of a Herbrand base, i.e. the set of ground atoms in our language. A model is simply a subset of the Herbrand base, viz. the elements that are deemed to be true.

As an example, consider the model defined below. Our language here consists of the object constants a and b, the unary relation constant p, and the binary relation constant q. The Herbrand base corresponding to this vocabulary has just six elements, as shown. Any subset of these elements is a model.

Vocabulary: $\{a, b, p, q\}$

Herbrand Base: $\{p(a), p(b), q(a, a), q(a, b), q(b, a), q(b, b)\}$

Herbrand Model: $\{p(a), q(a, b)\}$

As with Tarskian semantics, a Herbrand model completely determines the truth or falsity of all sentences in the language, not just the ground atoms. And it gives us a definition of logical entailment. One important difference from Tarskian semantics is that Herbrand semantics is less open-ended. There is no external universe, only symbols and sentences in the language. In a sense, it is thinking inside the box.

In much of the literature, Herbrand semantics is treated (somewhat under-standably) as a special case of Tarskian semantics—the case where we look at so-called Herbrand interpretations [4]. One downside of this is that Herbrand semantics has not been given as much theoretical attention as Tarskian seman-tics. In this paper, we turn things upside down, focussing on Herbrand semantics in its own right instead of treating it as a special case of Tarskian semantics. The results are interesting. We no longer have many of the nice features of Tarskian semantics—compactness, inferential completeness, and semidecidability. On the other hand, there are some real benefits to doing things this way. Most impor-tantly, Herbrand semantics is conceptually a lot simpler than Tarskian semantics; and, as a result, Herbrand semantics is easier to teach and learn. It has equiva-lent or greater inferential power. And more things are definable with Herbrand semantics than with Tarskian semantics. In the remainder of this paper, we demonstrate with examples some of the power and the properties of Herbrand semantics; each point is explained in detail in a companion paper [3].

2 Nuts and Bolts

Let's start with the basics. As mentioned earlier, a Herbrand base is the set of ground atoms in our language; and a model is an arbitrary subset of this set.

Given a model Δ, we say that a ground atom φ is true iff φ is in Δ. Here, h is the truth assignment corresponding to Δ. We use 1 to represent truth and 0 to represent falsity.

$h(\varphi) = 1$ iff $\varphi \in \Delta$

The truth values of logical sentences are defined the same as with Tarskian semantics. A negation is true iff the negated sentence is false. A conjunction is true iff the conjuncts are both true. And so forth.

$h(\neg\varphi) = 1$ iff $h(\varphi) = 0$

$h(\varphi \wedge \psi) = 1$ iff $h(\varphi) = 1$ and $h(\psi) = 1$

$h(\varphi \vee \psi) = 1$ iff $h(\varphi) = 1$ or $h(\psi) = 1$

$h(\varphi \Rightarrow \psi) = 1$ iff $h(\varphi) = 0$ or $h(\psi) = 1$

$h(\varphi \Leftrightarrow \psi) = 1$ iff $h(\varphi) = h(\psi)$

Finally, a universally quantified sentence is true if and only all of the instances are true.

$h(\forall x.\varphi(x)) = 1$ iff $h(\varphi(\tau)) = 1$ for every ground term τ

Despite many similarities, this definition does *not* produce the same results as Tarskian semantics. To illustrate this point, let's look at an example that illustrates the difference.

Here is a popular question from Stanford 's doctoral comprehensive exam. Suppose we are given a set Δ of sentences in the language of relational logic such that Δ logically entails $\varphi(\tau)$ for every ground term τ in the language. Is it the case that Δ logically entails $\forall x.\varphi(x)$?

The question is not difficult if one understands Tarskian semantics, but apparently not everyone does. The most common answer to this question is 'yes'; people seem to think that, if Δ logically entails every ground instance of

φ, it must entail the universally quantified version. Of course, under Tarskian semantics, that answer is wrong. There can be some unnamed element of the universe of discourse for which the sentence is false.

However, the popularity of the "incorrect" answer suggests that perhaps our semantics does not capture our intuitions about logic. Maybe it should. The good news is that, with Herbrand semantics, the answer to this question is 'yes'. (See the definition of satisfaction for universally quantified sentences above.)

As another example of a difference between Tarskian semantics and Herbrand semantics, consider the problem of axiomatizing Peano Arithmetic. As we know from Gödel, a finite axiomatization is not possible in relational logic with Tarskian semantics. Interestingly, with Herbrand semantics there is such a finite axiomatization.

Since there are infinitely many natural numbers, we need infinitely many terms. A common approach is to represent numbers using a single object constant (e.g. 0) and a single unary function constant (e.g. s). We can then represent every number n by applying the function constant to 0 exactly n times. In this encoding, $s(0)$ represents 1; $s(s(0))$ represents 2; and so forth.

Unfortunately, even with this representation, axiomatizing Peano Arithmetic is a bit challenging. We cannot just write out ground relational sentences to characterize our relations, because there are infinitely many cases to consider. For Peano Arithmetic, we must rely on logical sentences and quantified sentences, not just because they are more economical but because they are necessary to characterize our relations in finite space.

Let's look at equality first. The axioms shown here define equality in terms of 0 and the s function. For all x, equal(x, x). For all x, 0 is not equal to $s(x)$ and $s(x)$ is not equal to 0. For all x and for all y, if x is not equal to y, then $s(x)$ is not equal to $s(y)$.

$\forall x.\text{equal}(x, x)$
$\forall x.(\neg\text{equal}(0, s(x)) \land \neg\text{equal}(s(x), 0))$
$\forall x.\forall y.(\neg\text{equal}(x, y) \Rightarrow \neg\text{equal}(s(x), s(y)))$

It is easy to see that these axioms completely characterize equality. By the first axiom, the equality relation holds of every term and itself. The other two axioms tell us what is not true. The second axiom tells us that 0 is not equal to any composite term. The same holds true with the arguments reversed. The third axiom builds on these results to show that non-identical composite terms of arbitrary complexity do not satisfy the equality relation. Viewed the other way around, to see that two non-identical terms are not equal, we just strip away occurrences of s from each term till one of the two terms becomes 0 and the other one is not 0. By the second axiom, these are not equal, and so the original terms are not equal.

Once we have the equal relation, we can define the other relations in our arithmetic. The following axioms define the plus relation in terms of 0, s, and equal. Adding 0 to any number results in that number. If adding a number x to a number y produces a number z, then adding the successor of x to y produces the successor of z. Finally, we have a functionality axiom for plus.

$\forall y.\mathsf{plus}(0, y, y)$

$\forall x.\forall y.\forall z.(\mathsf{plus}(x, y, z) \Rightarrow \mathsf{plus}(s(x), y, s(z)))$

$\forall x.\forall y.\forall z.\forall w.(\mathsf{plus}(x, y, z) \wedge \neg\mathsf{same}(z, w) \Rightarrow \neg\mathsf{plus}(x, y, w))$

The axiomatization of multiplication is analogous. Multiplying any number by 0 produces 0. If a number z is the product of x and y and w is the sum of y and z, then w is the product of the successor of x and y. As before, we have a functionality axiom.

$\forall y.\mathsf{times}(0, y, 0)$

$\forall x.\forall y.\forall z.\forall w.(\mathsf{times}(x, y, z) \wedge \mathsf{plus}(y, z, w) \Rightarrow \mathsf{times}(s(x), y, w))$

$\forall x.\forall y.\forall z.\forall w.(\mathsf{times}(x, y, z) \wedge \neg\mathsf{same}(z, w) \Rightarrow \neg\mathsf{times}(x, y, w))$

Under Herbrand semantics, this axiomatization is complete since we have defined truth for all ground atoms and thus all sentences. By contrast, Gödel's incompleteness theorem tells us that these axioms are not complete under Tarskian semantics. Note that the Incompleteness Theorem assumes semi-decidability of logical entailment. Relational logic with Tarskian semantics is semi-decidable; with Herbrand semantics, it is not semi-decidable, as we shall see shortly. So, there is no contradiction here.

3 No Free Lunch

Unfortunately, the additional expressive power of Herbrand semantics comes with a price. We lose some nice features that we have with Tarskian semantics.

First of all, there is compactness. A logic is *compact* if and only if every unsatisfiable set of sentences has a finite subset that is unsatisfiable.

Relational logic with Tarskian semantics turns out to be compact. The upshot is that it is possible to demonstrate unsatisfiability in finite space; alternatively, all proofs are finite.

By contrast, relational logic with Herbrand semantics is not compact—there are infinite sets of sentences that are unsatisfiable while every finite subset is satisfiable. Consider the set of sentences shown here. It is clearly unsatisfiable under Herbrand semantics; but, if we remove any one sentence, it becomes satisfiable.

$$\{p(0), p(s(0)), p(s(s(0))), ..., \exists x.\neg p(x)\}$$

The upshot is that relational logic with Herbrand semantics is not compact. Fortunately, this does not cause any practical difficulties, since in all cases of practical interest we are working with finite sets of premises.

More disturbing is that there is no complete proof procedure for relational logic with Herbrand semantics. Gödel's incompleteness theorem tells us that the set of all true sentences of Peano Arithmetic is not computably enumerable. Our axiomatization is complete using Herbrand semantics. If Herbrand entailment were semi-decidable, the set of all true sentences would be enumerable. Consequently, there is no complete (semi-decidable) proof procedure for relational logic with Herbrand semantics.

However, this is not as bad as it seems. It turns out that everything that is true under Tarskian semantics is also true under Herbrand semantics, so we can use the same rules of inference. The upshot here is that we lose nothing by switching to Herbrand semantics. In fact, we can add some additional rules of inference. It is not that relational logic with Herbrand semantics is weaker. In fact, it is stronger. There are more things that are true. We cannot prove them all, but we can prove everything we could prove before.

Some may be disturbed by the fact that Herbrand entailment is not semi-decidable. However, Tarskian semantics is not perfect either. Although it is semi-decidable, it is not decidable; a proof procedure might still run forever if a proposed conclusion does not follow from a set of premises.

There is one other limitation that some may find even more disturbing. Since Herbrand semantics is effectively limited to countable universes, it would appear that we can no longer use the logic to axiomatize uncountable sets, such as the real numbers. This is true. However, it is not that much of a limit. For one, most CS applications involve finite or countably infinite domains. Remember that there are at most countably many floating point numbers.

Arguably one might want to axiomatize the reals even without converting to floating point numbers. However, even here, Tarskian semantics is limited because of the Löwenheim-Skolem theorem. This theorem states that, under Tarskian semantics, if a set of sentences has an infinite model of any cardinality, then it has a countable model. In particular, any theory of the real numbers has a countable model—everything one can say about the real numbers in relational logic is also true of some countable model.

4   Curiouser and Curiouser

The power of Herbrand semantics is, in large part, due to the implicit property of domain closure—there are no objects in the universe except for ground terms. This allows us to give complete definitions to things that cannot be completely defined with Tarskian semantics. We have already seen Peano Arithmetic. It turns out that, under Herbrand semantics, we can also define some other useful concepts that are not definable with Tarskian semantics, and we can do so without resorting to more complex logical mechanisms, such as negation as failure.

Let's look at transitive closure first[1]. Let's say that we have a binary relation p and we want to axiomatize its transitive closure q. The typical approach in relational logic would be to write the definition shown here.

$$\forall x.\forall z.(q(x,z) \Leftrightarrow p(x,z) \lor \exists y.(p(x,y) \land q(y,z)))$$

It is easy to see that q contains the transitive closure of p. The problem is that, in general, it can contain additional elements as well, corresponding to various non-standard models. For example, the universe of discourse might contain an

---

[1] Uwe [5] offers a more detailed explanation of why transitive closure is not axiomatizable in (first-order) relational logic with Tarskian semantics.

object that does not have any p relationships at all. However, if we link all other objects to this object via q, this satisfies our definition. The upshot is that we have a model of our sentence that is a proper superset of the transitive closure of p. Not good.

By contrast, we *can* define the transitive closure of a relation in relational logic with Herbrand semantics. It is not as simple or intuitive as the definition above, but it is theoretically possible. The trick is to exploit the enumerability of the Herbrand universe. Suppose we have the object constant 0, an arbitrary unary relation constant s; and suppose our job is to define q as the transitive closure of p.

We start by defining a helper relation q_h as shown below. The basic idea here is that $q_h(x, z, n)$ is the (partial) transitive closure in which no intermediate variable is bigger than n. Once we have q_h, we can easily define q in terms of q_h. q is true of two elements if and only if there is a level at which q_h becomes true of those elements.

$$q_h(x, z, 0) \Leftrightarrow p(x, z) \lor p(x, 0) \land p(0, z)$$
$$q_h(x, z, s(n)) \Leftrightarrow q_h(x, z, n) \lor (q_h(x, s(n), n) \land q_h(s(n), z, n))$$

It is easy to see that q is exactly the transitive closure of p. The only disadvantage of this axiomatization is that we need the helper relation q_h. But that causes no significant problems.

$$\forall x. \forall z. (q(x, z) \Leftrightarrow \exists n. q_h(x, z, n))$$

But wait. There's more! As we know, it is possible to encode some relations in rule systems that cannot be encoded in relational logic with Tarskian semantics. Rule systems get this power from the use of negation as failure to minimize those relations. The cool thing is that, even without any form of negation as failure, it is possible to encode those relations in relational logic with Herbrand semantics. Moreover, various minimization policies can result from different axiomatizations.

Consider a logic program like the one shown here. There are two rules defining p and one rule defining q.

$$p(0, 1)$$
$$p(X, Y) \;:\!-\; q(X, 0), p(Y, Z)$$
$$q(X, Y) \;:\!-\; p(X, 0), q(Y, Z)$$

The first step of our conversion is to normalize the program so that the head of every rule consists of distinct variables. This is easy to do using equality (defined as we did earlier in Peano Arithmetic). We then combine the bodies of the resulting rules using the disjunction operator.

$$p(X, Y) \;:\!-\; X = 0, Y = 1$$
$$p(X, Y) \;:\!-\; q(X, 0), p(Y, Z)$$
$$q(X, Y) \;:\!-\; p(X, 0), q(Y, Z)$$

Next we transform the normalized program as follows. The first two sentences here are the result of transforming the original axioms using our helper relations. The other axioms are the additional axioms defining the helper relations and defining the target relations in terms of these helper relations. For each rule defining an n-ary relation in the normalized program, we define an $(n + 1)$-ary auxiliary relation as shown here. p_h is true of x and y and 0 iff $x=0$ and $y = 1$. p_h is true of x and y and $s(n)$ iff there is a z that the definition holds of elements on step n. Finally, if p_h is true of x and y on step n, then it is also true on step $s(n)$. Ditto for q_h.

$$p_h(x, y, 0) \Leftrightarrow x = 0 \wedge y = 1$$
$$p_h(x, y, s(n)) \Leftrightarrow \exists z.(q_h(x, 0, n) \wedge p_h(y, z, n))$$
$$p_h(x, y, s(n)) \Leftarrow p_h(x, y, n)$$

$$\neg q_h(x, y, 0)$$
$$q_h(x, y, s(n)) \Leftrightarrow \exists z.(p_h(x, 0, n) \wedge q_h(y, z, n))$$
$$q_h(x, y, s(n)) \Leftarrow q_h(x, y, n)$$

Finally, we define p and q in terms of p_h and q_h, as we did in the transitive closure example.

$$p(x, y) \Leftrightarrow \exists n.p_h(x, y, n)$$
$$q(x, y) \Leftrightarrow \exists n.q_h(x, y, n)$$

Now, the interesting thing is that it turns out that we can do this transformation in general (for arbitrary logic programs so long as they are safe and stratified). Let P be an arbitrary safe, stratified program over R. Let M be the unique minimal model of P under stratified semantics [1,6]. Then, this transformation has a unique model M' under Herbrand semantics such that $M' = M$ over R. Voila—minimization without negation as failure.

One consequence of this result is that we can treat :- as syntactic sugar for definitions requiring minimization. There is no need for a different logic. Which does not mean that :- is useless. In fact, the oddity of our definitions makes clear the value of :- in expressing definitions intuitively.

I think there is also another, more subtle benefit of this theorem. One possible practical consequence of this work concerns the relationship between rule systems and ordinary logic. Rules and ordinary logic are often seen as alternatives. Herbrand semantics has the potential to bring these two fields closer together in a fruitful way. This upshot could be a possible re-prioritization of research in these two areas.

The power and beauty of rule systems is their suitability for writing complete definitions. We start with some completely specified base relations and define other relations in terms of these base relations, working our way up the definitional hierarchy. At every point in time we have a complete model of the world.

Unfortunately, complete theories are not always possible; and in such situations we need to provide for expressing incomplete information. In an attempt to deal with incomplete information, researchers have proposed various extensions to rule systems, e.g. negations, disjunctions, and existentials in the heads of rules, unstratified rules systems, and so forth. Unfortunately, extensions like these mar the beauty of rule systems and ruin their computational properties.

The alternative is to switch to relational logic in such situations. Unfortunately, relational logic with Tarskian semantics is more complex and fails to provide minimization or negation as failure.

Our argument is that Herbrand semantics for ordinary logic gives us an ideal middle ground between rules and relational logic, allowing us to combine rules with relational logic without losing the benefits that each brings to the table. We can use rules for definitions and ordinary logical operators for constraints. The two can co-exist. In fact, as I have suggested, we can even formalize negation as failure and various minimization policies within relational logic, so long as we are using Herbrand semantics.

Now, I do not know whether this is practically possible or not. However, I think it is an idea worthy of study, considering the lack of a unifying semantics today.

5   Conclusion

In conclusion, let's return to the theme of simplicity. The fact is that Tarskian semantics is more difficult to understand than Herbrand semantics.

First of all, in Tarskian semantics, there are unboundedly many interpretations for any language, and entailment is defined over all conceivable universes—finite, countably infinite, and beyond.

Second, Tarskian semantics requires an understanding of relations as sets of tuples, which is a novel concept for many students. In Herbrand semantics, everything is defined in terms of sentences, which are more concrete and which students already understand.

Finally, in Tarskian semantics, there is also greater complexity in the definition of satisfaction. Here is the definition in Tarskian semantics. "An interpretation i and a variable assignment s *satisfy* a universally quantified sentence if and only if i and s satisfy the scope of the sentence for every version of the variable assignment. A *version* $s[v \mapsto x]$ of a variable assignment s is a variable assignment that assigns v the value x and agrees with s on all other variables." That's a mouthful. Now, compare the definition in Herbrand semantics. "A model *satisfies* a universally quantified sentence if an only if it satisfies every instance." That's it. Shorter and easier to understand.

These ideas confuse students. As a result, they feel insecure and are all too often turned off on logic. This is sad because we should be teaching more logic and not turning people away. In Greek times, logic was one of the three basic disciplines that students learned. Today, it is taught in only a very small percentage of schools. Instead, we are taught geometry. We are taught how to bisect angles in high school, but we are not taught logic. Only few of us need to bisect angles in our daily lives, but many of us use logic in our professional lives and in our private live, e.g. to understand political arguments, court cases, and so forth. Perhaps, if we could make logic more useful and easier to teach, this could change.

To test the value of Herbrand semantics in this regard, we recently switched Stanford's introductory logic course from Tarskian semantics to Herbrand semantics. The results have been gratifying. Students get semantics right away. They do better on quizzes. And there are fewer complaints about feeling lost. It is clear that many students come away from the course feeling empowered and intent on using logic. More so than before anyway.

The logic course is now available as a MOOC [2] (and an associated book [2]). It was one of the first MOOCs taught at Stanford. We teach it each year in the Fall. Typical enrollment is now almost 100,000 students per session. To date, more than 500,000 students have enrolled in all. As is typical with MOOCs, only a fraction of these students finish. Even so, more students have seen this than have graduated from Stanford's math program in its entire history.

In a previous keynote address at RuleML, we talked about Logical Spreadsheets. On that occasion, we mentioned the goal of popularizing logic and suggested that what we need is a way to make logic more accessible and we need tools that make it clear that logic is useful, not just as an intellectual tool but as a practical technology as well.

This time, we have talked about a way to make logic more accessible—a way to teach people enough logic so that they can use logical spreadsheets and other logic-based technologies. If logic is easy to learn, our hope is that we can make it more popular. Not just to promote our interests as researchers but also to benefit society with the fruits of our research.

References

1. Chandra, A.K., Harel, D.: Horn clause queries and generalizations. The Journal of Logic Programming **2**(1), 1–15 (1985)
2. Genesereth, M., Kao, E.: Introduction to Logic, Synthesis Lectures on Computer Science, vol. 4. Morgan & Claypool Publishers, 2 edn. January 2013. http://www.morganclaypool.com/doi/abs/10.2200/S00432ED1V01Y201207CSL005
3. Genesereth, M., Kao, E.J.Y.: Herbrand semantics. Tech. Rep. LG-2015-01, Logic Group, Computer Science Dept., Stanford University (2015). http://logic.stanford.edu/herbrand/herbrand.html
4. Goubault-Larrecq, J., Mackie, I.: Proof theory and automated deduction. Applied Logic Series, 1st edn. Springer, Netherlands (1997)
5. Keller, U.: Some remarks on the definability of transitive closure in first-order logic and datalog. Tech. rep, Digital Enterprise Research Institute (DERI) (2004)
6. Van Emden, M.H., Kowalski, R.A.: The semantics of predicate logic as a programming language. Journal of the ACM (JACM) **23**(4), 733–742 (1976)

---

[2] MOOC URL: http://online.stanford.edu/course/introduction-logic

Constraint Handling Rules - What Else?

Thom Frühwirth$^{(\boxtimes)}$

University of Ulm, Ulm, Germany
thom.fruehwirth@uni-ulm.de
http://www.constraint-handling-rules.org

Abstract. Constraint Handling Rules (CHR) is both an effective concurrent declarative constraint-based programming language and a versatile computational formalism. While conceptually simple, CHR is distinguished by a remarkable combination of desirable features:

- a semantic foundation in classical and linear logic,
- an effective and efficient sequential and parallel execution model
- guaranteed properties like the anytime online algorithm properties
- powerful analysis methods for deciding essential program properties.

This overview of some CHR-related research and applications is by no means meant to be complete. Essential introductory reading for CHR provide the survey article [122] and the books [55,62]. Up-to-date information on CHR can be found online at the CHR web-page www.constraint-handling-rules.org, including the slides of the keynote talk associated with this article. In addition, the CHR website dtai.cs.kuleuven.be/CHR/ offers everything you want to know about CHR, including online demo versions and free downloads of the language.

1 Executive Summary

Constraint Handling Rules (CHR) [55] tries to bridge the gap between theory and practice, between logical specification and executable program by abstraction through constraints and the concepts of computational logic. CHR has its *roots* in constraint logic programming and concurrent constraint programming, but also integrates ideas from multiset transformation and rewriting systems as well as automated reasoning and theorem proving. It seamlessly blends multi-headed rewriting and concurrent constraint logic programming into a compact user-friendly rule-based programming language. CHR consists of guarded reactive rules that transform multisets of relations called constraints until no more change occurs. By the notion of constraint, CHR does not need to distinguish between data and operations, and its rules are both descriptive and executable.

In CHR, one distinguishes two main kinds of rules: *Simplification rules* replace constraints by simpler constraints while preserving logical equivalence, e.g., $X \leq Y \wedge Y \leq X \Leftrightarrow X = Y$. *Propagation rules* add new constraints that are logically redundant but may cause further simplification, e.g., $X \leq Y \wedge Y \leq Z \Rightarrow X \leq Z$. Together with $X \leq X \Leftrightarrow$ true, these rules encode the axioms of a partial order relation. The rules compute its transitive closure and replace inequalities $\leq$ by equalities $=$ whenever possible. For example, $A \leq B \wedge B \leq C \wedge C \leq A$ becomes $A = B \wedge B = C$. More program examples can be found in Section 2. Semantics of CHR are discussed in Section 3.

© Springer International Publishing Switzerland 2015
N. Bassiliades et al. (Eds.): RuleML 2015, LNCS 9202, pp. 13–34, 2015.
DOI: 10.1007/978-3-319-21542-6_2

1.1   Powerful Program Analysis

One advantage of a declarative programming language is the ease of *program analysis*. CHR programs have a number of desirable properties guaranteed and can be analyzed for others. They will be discussed in Section 4.

Since CHR (and many of its fragments) are Turing-complete, *termination* is undecidable, but often a ranking in the form a a well-founded termination order can be found to prove termination. From the ranking, a crude upper bound for the time complexity can automatically be derived. More precise bounds on the complexity can also be found by inspecting the rules.

Confluence of a program guarantees that any computation starting from the same initial state results in the same final state no matter which of the applicable rules are applied. There is a decidable, sufficient and necessary condition for confluence of terminating programs.

Any terminating and confluent CHR program has a consistent logical reading. It will automatically implement a *concurrent any-time (approximation) and on-line (incremental) algorithm*, where constraints can arrive during the computation that can be stopped and restarted at any time. It ensures that rules can be applied in parallel to different parts of a state without any modification and without harming correctness. This property is called *declarative concurrency* or *logical parallelism*.

Surprisingly, there is also a decidable, sufficient and necessary syntactic condition for *operational equivalence* of terminating and confluent programs (we do not know of any other programming language in practical use with this property). So one can check if two programs behave in the same way and if a program has redundant parts.

1.2   Implementations and Applications

CHR is often used as a language extension to other programming languages, its syntax can be easily adapted to that of the *host language*. In the host language, CHR constraints can be posted and inspected; in the CHR rules, host language statements can be included. CHR libraries are now available in almost all Prolog implementations, but also in Haskell, Curry, Java and C as well as in hardware.

It has been proven that every algorithm can be implemented in CHR with *best known time and space complexity*, something that is not known to be possible in other pure declarative programming languages. The *efficiency* of the language is empirically demonstrated by optimizing CHR compilers that compete well with both academic and commercial rule-based systems and even classical programming languages. The fastest implementations of CHR, e.g. in C, allow to apply up to millions of rules per second.

Other rule- and logic-based approaches have been successfully and rather straightforwardly embedded in CHR. For this reason, CHR is considered a candidate for a *lingua franca* of such approaches with the potential for cross-fertilization of research in computational systems and languages. Implementations and embeddings are discussed in Section 5.

CHR has been used for such *diverse applications* as type system design for Haskell, time tabling, optimal sender placement, computational linguistics, spatio-temporal reasoning, verification, semantic web reasoning, data mining and computational linguistics. Successful *commercial application* include financial services, network design, mould design, robot vehicle control, enterprise applications and software verification. Applications of CHR and research using CHR are discussed in Section 6.

CHR is also available *online* for demos and experimentation at chrjs.net at an introductory level and as WebCHR at chr.informatik.uni-ulm.de/~webchr/ with more than 50 example programs. More than 200 academic and industrial projects worldwide use CHR, and about 200 scientific books and 2000 research papers reference it. The CHR community and other interested researchers and practitioners gather at the yearly CHR workshops and the biannual CHR summer schools.

2   A Taste of CHR Programs

The following programs can be run with little modification in the online versions of CHR just mentioned. Note that all programs have the anytime online algorithm properties. So they can be stopped at any time for intermediate results, constraints can be added while they already run (incrementality), and they can be directly executed in parallel. These program examples are explained more in [54] and discussed in detail in [55].

Some examples use a third kind of rule, a hybrid rule called simpagation rule. It has the form $H_1 \backslash H_2 \Leftrightarrow C|B$. Basically, if H_1 and H_2 match constraints and the guard C holds, then the constraints matching H_1 are kept, the constraints matching H_2 are removed and the body C is added. For logical conjunction $\wedge$ we will simply write a comma between constraints.

Multiset Transformation - One-Rule Algorithms

Compute minimum of a set of `min` candidates
`min(I) \ min(J) ⇔ J>I | true.`
Compare two numbers, keep smaller one.

Compute greatest common divisor of a set of numbers
`gcd(I) \ gcd(J) ⇔ J>=I | gcd(J mod I).`
Replace I and J by I and (J mod I) until all numbers are the same.

Compute primes, given `prime(2),...,prime(MaxN)`
`prime(I) \ prime(J) ⇔ J mod I = 0 | true.`
Keep removing multiples until only primes are left.

Sort array with elements `a(Index,Value)`
`a(I,V), a(J,W) ⇔ I>J, V<W | a(I,W), a(J,V).`
Keep swapping numbers that are out of order until sorted.

Merge Sort, given values as `next(start,Value)`
`next(A,B) \ next(A,C) ⇔ A<B,B<C | next(B,C).`
Turn common successors into direct successors until sorted chain results.

Newton's Method for Square Root Approximation for `N>1`
`eps(E) \ sqrt(X,R) ⇔ R*R/X-1>E | sqrt(X,(R+X/R)/2).`
Start with `sqrt(N,N)`. `E` is the required precision factor.

Fibonacci Variations - `M` is the `N`th Fibonacci number

Top-down Evaluation
`fib(0,M) ⇔ M=1.`
`fib(1,M) ⇔ M=1.`
`fib(N,M) ⇔ N>=2 | fib(N-1,M1), fib(N-2,M2), M=M1+M2.`
Matching is used on left hand sides of rules.

Top-down Evaluation with Memorization (in first rule)
`fib(N,M1) \ fib(N,M2) ⇔ M1=M2.`
`fib(0,M) ⇒ M=1.`
`fib(1,M) ⇒ M=1.`
`fib(N,M) ⇒ N>=2 | fib(N-1,M1), fib(N-2,M2), M=M1+M2.`
Turned simplification into propagation rules.

Bottom-up Evaluation without Termination
`fibstart ⇔ fib(0,1), fib(1,1).`
`fib(N1,M1), fib(N2,M2) ⇒ N2=N1+1 | fib(N2+1,M1+M2).`
Basically, original simplification rules have been reversed.

Bottom-up Evaluation with Termination at `Max`
`fib(Max) ⇒ fib(0,1), fib(1,1).`
`fib(Max), fib(N1,M1), fib(N2,M2) ⇒ Max>N1, N1=N2+1 |`
                    `fib(N2+1,M1+M2).`
The auxiliary constraint `fib(Max)` is added. Computation stops when `Max=N1`.

All-Pair Shortest Paths

The distance from `X` to `Y` is `D`
`path(X,Y,D1) \ path(X,Y,D2) ⇔ D1=<D2 | true.`
`arc(X,Y,D) ⇒ path(X,Y,D).`
`arc(X,Y,D), path(Y,Z,Dn) ⇒ path(X,Z,D+Dn).`
Compute all paths with propagation rules, keep smaller ones.

Dynamic Programming - Bottom-up Parsing with CYK Algorithm

Grammar rules are in Chomsky normal form `A->T` or `A->B*C`.
A sequence of terminal symbols is encoded as a chain of arcs.
`parse(X,Y,A) \ parse(X,Y,A) ⇔ true.`

```
terminal @ A->T, arc(X,Y,T) ⇒ parse(X,Y,A).
non-term @ A->B*C, parse(X,Y,B), parse(Y,Z,C) ⇒ parse(X,Z,A).
```
Note the similarity with All-Pair Shortest Paths.

Boolean Conjunction as Constraint

The result of X∧Y is Z
```
and(X,Y,Z) ⇔ X=0 | Z=0.        and(X,Y,Z) ⇔ Y=0 | Z=0.
and(X,Y,Z) ⇔ X=1 | Z=Y.        and(X,Y,Z) ⇔ Y=1 | Z=X.
and(X,Y,Z) ⇔ X=Y | Y=Z.        and(X,Y,Z) ⇔ Z=1 | X=1,Y=1.
```
Also computes with unknown input values and backwards. Such rules can
be automatically generated from specifications [8].

3 CHR Semantics

In this section we give an overview of the main semantics for CHR. More detailed
overviews can be found in [19,62]. As a declarative programming language and
formalism, CHR features both operational semantics that describe the execution
of a program and declarative semantics that interpret a program as a logical
theory. These semantics exist at various levels of refinement. They are related
by soundness and completeness results, showing their correspondence.

3.1 CHR Rules and Their Declarative Semantics

To simplify the presentation, we use a generic notation for all three kinds of CHR
rules. *Built-in constraints* are host language statements that can be used as tests
in the guard or auxiliary computations in the body of a rule. A *generalized
simpagation rule* is of the form

$$H_1 \backslash H_2 \Leftrightarrow C | B$$

where in the rule head (left-hand-side), H_1 and H_2 are conjunctions of user-
defined constraints, the optional guard C is a conjunction of built-in constraints
from the host language and the body (right-hand-side) B is a conjunction of
arbitrary constraints. If H_1 and H_2 are non-empty, the rule corresponds to a
simpagation rule. If H_1 is empty, the rule corresponds to a simplification rule, if
H_2 is empty, the rule corresponds to a propagation rule.

The declarative semantics is based on first-order predicate logic, where
constraints are viewed as predicates and rules as logical implications and
equivalences. A generalized simpagation rule basically corresponds to a logical
equivalence

$$H_1 \wedge H_2 \wedge C \leftrightarrow H_1 \wedge C \wedge B.$$

An interesting refinement is the *linear-logic semantics* [19,20]. It is closer to the
operational semantics in that it captures the meaning of constraints as resources,
where multiplicities matter.

3.2   Operational Semantics for CHR

The execution of CHR can be described by structural operational semantics, which are given as state transition systems. Basically, states are conjunctions of constraints. These semantics exist in various formulations and at various levels of refinement, going from the abstract (analytical) to the concrete (pragmatic):

- The *very abstract semantics* [55] is close to modus ponens of predicate logic.
- The *abstract (or theoretical) semantics* [5] is often used for program analysis.
- The *refined semantics* [43] describes the behavior of CHR implementations.

Several alternative operational semantics for CHR have also been proposed, among them [21,66,78,106].

The essential aspect of the operational semantics is the application of a rule: Take a generalized simpagation rule from the program. If there are constraints in the current state that match the head of the rule and if the guard holds under this matching, then the constraints matching second part of the head H_2 (if any) are removed and the guard and body of the rule are added to the state.

There are alternative formulations for the above semantics. Chapter 8 in the book [62] and [19,101] develop an axiomatic notion of state equivalence. The equivalence relation $\equiv$ on states treats built-in constraints semantically and user-defined constraints syntactically. Basically, two states are equivalent if they are logically equivalent while taking into account that - forming multisets - multiplicities of user-defined constraints matter. For example, $X{=}{<}Y \wedge Y{=}{<}X \wedge c(X,Y) \equiv X{=}Y \wedge c(X,X)$ which is different to $X{=}Y \wedge c(X,X) \wedge c(X,X)$.

Using state equivalence, the presentation of the abstract semantics can be simplified. It basically boils down to

$$\frac{S \equiv (H_1 \wedge H_2 \wedge C \wedge G) \quad (H_1 \backslash H_2 \Leftrightarrow C | B) \quad (H_1 \wedge C \wedge B \wedge G) \equiv T}{S \longmapsto T}$$

where all upper-case letters stand for conjunctions of constraints. G is called the context of the rule application, G is not affected by it. Note that the transition $S \longmapsto T$ is only allowed if the built-in constraints in state S are consistent and if the rule has not been applied before to the same constraints under the same matching.

3.3   Operational Semantics for Parallel CHR

One of the main features of CHR is its inherent *concurrency*. Intuitively, in a parallel execution of CHR we can apply rules simultaneously to different parts of a state. But we can do more than that: We can also apply rules to overlapping parts of a state as long as the overlap is only removed by at most one rule. In Chapter 4 of [55], this parallelism in CHR is defined by an interleaving semantics as

$$\frac{A \wedge G \longmapsto C \wedge G \quad B \wedge G \longmapsto D \wedge G}{A \wedge B \wedge G \longmapsto C \wedge D \wedge G}$$

This inference rule is justified by the monotonicity property of CHR (explained below). If a program executed under the refined semantics makes use of the order of constraints in a state and the order of rules in a program, this kind of automatic parallelization may not work. Such programs are not *confluent*. On the other hand, confluent programs can be executed in parallel without modification. As we will see, we can check CHR programs for confluence, and we can even semi-automatically complete them to make them confluent. Thus, using completion, we can turn non-confluent programs into parallel programs. This method has been applied to the classical Union-Find algorithm which is very hard to parallelize [51] (with [128] showing the effectiveness of the resulting program) and to the Preflow-Push algorithm [92]. Alternative and more refined semantics for parallel CHR are e.g. [62,85,86,103,113].

4 Properties of CHR and Their Analysis

We first introduce three essential types of monotonicity and the anytime online algorithm properties that all come for free in CHR. We then discuss the analysis of termination and time complexity as well as of confluence, completion and operational equivalence of CHR programs.

4.1 CHR Monotonicity Properties

In the abstract operational semantics we can observe three essential types of monotonicity.

First, adding rules to a program cannot inhibit the applicability of any rules that were applicable. This aids incremental program development and rapid prototyping. Already a program with a few first rules is executable, and we can add rules to cover more and more cases, enabling more and more desired computations. The confluence test (see next Section) can be used to discover situations where old and new rules lead to different results.

Second, built-in constraints (that occur in the guard and body of a rule) can only be added to a state, they are never removed. Hence they accumulate monotonically. On the other hand, user-defined constraints are non-monotonic in that they can be added and removed from a state. This means that an applicable rule will remain applicable as long as the user-defined constraints it matches are present in the state and as long as the state is consistent.

Third, during a rule application, the context G stays unchanged. We can actually change it without influencing the rule application itself. So if a rule is applicable in a state, it is also applicable in any larger state where constraints have been added (as long as the state is consistent) [5]. This is an important *modularity property* of CHR, it is usually called CHR's *monotonicity property*. Clearly such context-independence does not hold in traditional programming languages, where the context may update as well, resulting in write conflicts.

On the other hand, if we have an empty context G, we get the *minimal transition* for to the given rule:

$$(H_1 \wedge H_2 \wedge C) \longmapsto (H_1 \wedge C \wedge B).$$

The state $(H_1 \wedge H_2 \wedge C)$ is called *minimal state* of the rule. Removing any constraint from it would make its rule inapplicable. Adding constraints to it cannot inhibit the applicability due to monotonicity. Since minimal states and transitions capture the essence of a rule application, they will come handy later when analyzing CHR programs for confluence and operational equivalence.

4.2   Anytime Online Algorithm Properties

Any algorithm expressed properly as a CHR program will enjoy several important properties: It will be an anytime algorithm and it will be an online algorithm and it can be run in parallel without modification.

The *anytime (approximation) algorithm property* means that we can interrupt the execution of a program at any time, observe the current state as an approximation to the result and restart from that intermediate result. This is obvious from the operational semantics and the notion of states and transitions used there.

The *online (incremental) algorithm property* means that we can add additional constraints while the program is running without the need to recompute from scratch. This is an immediate consequence of the monotonicity property of CHR. The program will behave as if the newly added constraints were present from the beginning but had been ignored so far. Therefore only a minimal amount of computation is performed to accommodate the new constraint. Incrementality is useful for interactive, reactive and control systems, in particular for agent and constraint programming.

In the refined semantics, the order of constraints in a state and the order of rules in a program can be made to matter, and this may weaken the above properties.

4.3   Termination and Time Complexity Analysis

One way to show termination is to prove that in each rule, if the guard holds, the rule head is strictly larger than the rule body using some well-founded termination order called a ranking. For CHR programs that mainly use simplification rules, simple rankings are often sufficient to prove termination [48,49]. More sophisticated methods are needed in the presence of propagation rules [56,96,97]. An approximation of CHR programs by constraint logic programs (CLP) has also been used to analyse the termination behavior of CHR [80].

The run-time of a CHR program not only depends on the number of rule applications (derivation lengths), but also on the number of rule application attempts. The meta-complexity theorem in [50] basically states that the complexity is bounded by the derivation length taken to the power of the number of heads in a rule. This only gives crude upper-bounds.

Actual CHR systems achieve much better complexity results since they implement the refined semantics and feature compiler optimizations such as indexing. For CHR with and without priorities, there is a more realistic sophisticated meta-complexity result derived from the Logical Algorithms (LA) formalism [33].

4.4   Confluence and Completion

Confluence means that it does not matter for the result which of the applicable rules are applied in which order in a computation. The resulting states will always be equivalent to each other. For terminating CHR programs, there is a decidable, sufficient and necessary condition for confluence [5]. These papers also have shown the many benefits of confluent programs:

- Confluent programs are always implement anytime online algorithms.
- Confluent programs can be run in parallel without modification.
- Confluence implies consistency of the logical reading of the program.
- Confluence improves the soundness and completeness results between the operational and declarative semantics. These theorems are stronger than those for other (concurrent) constraint programming languages.
- The least models of confluent CHR programs and its CLP approximation coincide [80].

The idea of the confluence test is to construct a finite number of so-called *critical states* by overlapping minimal states of rules in the program. An overlap equates some user-defined constraints and removes the resulting duplicate occurrences. If these constraints are to be removed by more than one rule, we have generated a conflict. One now checks if these conflicting rule applications on its own can be continued with computations that lead to equivalent states. If this holds for all critical states in the program, we have proven confluence.

In practice, this notion of confluence can be too strict. In [44] the notion of *observable confluence* is introduced, where the states considered must satisfy a user-defined invariant. Other related notions of confluence are considered in [31,79]. Confluence for non-terminating programs is in general undecidable, it is discussed in [104].

Completion is the process of adding rules to a non-confluent program until it becomes confluent [2]. These rules are generated between the successor states of critical states. In contrast to completion for term rewriting, in CHR we generally need more than one rule to make a critical pair joinable: a simplification rule and a propagation rule. Unfortunately, completion may not terminate. Completion can be also used for program specialisation [2,4].

4.5   Operational Equivalence

Operational equivalence means that given two programs, for any given state, its computations in both programs lead to the same final state. There is a decidable, sufficient and necessary condition for operational equivalence of terminating and confluent CHR programs [3]. We do not know of any other programming language in practical use that admits such a test.

The test is straightforward: The minimal states of the rules in both programs are each executed in both programs, and for each minimal state, the computations must reach equivalent states in both programs. This test can also be used to discover redundant rules in a program.

5   CHR Implementations and Embeddings in CHR

We discuss efficient implementations, variants and extensions of CHR and embeddings of other rule- and graph-based approaches in CHR.

5.1   CHR Implementations and Their Efficiency

The first wide-spread implementations of CHR were based on [82]. Most available CHR implementations today - be it in Prolog, Java or C - are based on the expertise of the CHR team at Katholieke Universiteit Leuven [129,133,136].

State-of-the-art CHR libraries with mode and type declarations in Prolog and C allow to implement any algorithm in a natural and high-level way, with time and space consumption that is typically within an order of magnitude from the best-known implementations in any other language [120,130]. Indeed, [120] has proven that *every algorithm can be implemented in CHR with the best known time and space complexity*. This has been exemplified by providing elegant implementations with optimal time-complexity of the classical union-find algorithm [111] and Fibonacci heaps [119]. CHR is the only known declarative language where this results holds, it is unlikely to hold for other declarative languages like Prolog or Haskell [120]. Actually, CHR cannot be embedded in pure Prolog [64]. The fastest CHR implementations in CCHR [136] and hProlog allow to up to apply millions of rules per second.

One reason for the effectiveness of CHR is that it uses a compiler and run-time system that is a significant advancement over existing algorithms (such as RETE, TREAT, LEAPS) for executing rule-based languages as has been impressively demonstrated in [130]. In addition to a superior rule-application mechanism, CHR compilers use sophisticated optimizations (besides indexing on constraint arguments taking into account mode and type information), such as memory reuse, late storage, guard optimization and join ordering optimization [62,83,130].

CLIPS (in C) and JESS (in Java)) are considered by many to be the most efficient rule-based systems available. The benchmarks of [130] show that his novel Java implementation of CHR as well as CHR in C (CCHR) [136] are faster than CLIPS and JESS, sometimes by several orders of magnitude. In benchmarks of [120], CHR with mode declarations achieves the optimal time and space complexity (as do imperative languages). Prolog and strict Haskell have a time complexity which is a polylogarithmic factor from optimal, and their space complexity is not optimal. Lazy Haskell quickly gets into memory problems.

As for concurrency, prototype *parallel CHR* implementations exist in software using Haskell [85] and in hardware using Nvidia CUDA by transforming a subset of CHR to C++ [137] and using FPGA's [128]. These papers feature experiments that show a potential for optimal linear speedup by parallelization of CHR programs (and super-linear speed-up e.g. in the case of the greatest-common-divisor program).

5.2   CHR Language Variants and Extensions

We start with a remark on fragments of CHR, indicating the adequacy of the overall language. We then discuss language extensions for CHR, program transformation and new programming languages based on CHR.

While there are many Turing-complete language subsets of CHR [65,91,115] (a single multi-headed simplification rule suffices), it has also been shown in [37, 64] that each of the following features of CHR can be considered essential, since they increase the expressive power of CHR: constraints with arguments, built-in constraints, function symbols to build complex terms, multi-headed rules, introduction of new variables in the body of a rule.

Since CHR libraries in Prolog naturally allow to use backtracking *search* by Prolog's disjunction, most operational semantics can be extended to the resulting language $CHR^{\vee}$ [10]. In [34] the authors extend the refined operational semantics of CHR to support the implementation of different search strategies.

In *adaptive* CHR, constraints can be declaratively removed together with the consequences they produced by getting involved in rule applications. This means that any properly written algorithm becomes adaptive. An adaptive semantics is defined in [135]. Adaptive CHR is used for realizing intelligent search strategies in [134,135].

In [35] the authors extend CHR with user-defined rule *priorities* that can be static or dynamic. This language extension reduces the level of non-determinism that is inherent to the abstract operational semantics of CHR, and gives a more high-level form of execution control compared to the refined operational semantics. Priorities make CHR more expressive.

Other notable *extensions* of CHR include non-monotonic negation-as-absence [132], aggregates such as sum, count, findall, and min [121], rules with probabilities [29,60,118], Except for search, all above CHR extensions have been implemented by simple effective *source-to-source program transformation* in CHR itself, also see Chapter 6 in [55] and the online transformation tool at http://pmx.informatik.uni-ulm.de/chr/stssemantics/. Program transformation in itself has been studied in [1,61]. Partial evaluation is covered by [52], discussing specialisation of CHR rules, and by [67], which is concerned with unfolding of CHR rules. Confluence completion can be used to great effect for program specialisation [2,4].

Notable *new programming languages* that are based on CHR are:

- HYPROLOG [30] as an extension of Prolog with assumptions and abduction.
- DatalogLB adds features of CHR to Datalog [77].
- CHRiSM is CHR with probabilistic reasoning and statistical learning [118].
- CADMIUM is an implementation of ACD Term Rewriting, a generalization of CHR and Term Rewriting (TRS) [42].
- SMCHR is an implementation of Satisfiability Modulo Theories (SMT) [39], where the theory part can be implemented in CHR.
- Linear Meld (LM) is a linear logic language closely related to CHR [32].
- CoMingle is CHR for distributed logic programming (on Android) [87].

5.3   Embedding Other Formalisms and Languages in CHR

The expressiveness, effectiveness and efficiency of CHR enables the embedding of the characteristic features of other rule-based and graph-based formalisms, systems and languages in CHR by simple *source-to-source transformations*:

- Prolog and Constraint Logic Programming (CLP) programs are translated into CHR$^\vee$ in [10] using Clark's completion.
- Logical Algorithms (LA) are mapped into CHR with and without rule priorities in [84]. This are the only known implementations of LA. They achieve the tight time complexity required for the LA meta-complexity theorem.
- Term Rewriting Systems (TRS) are translated to rules with equational constraints in CHR in [102].
- Graph Transformation Systems (GTS) are encoded in CHR in [99]. Soundness and completeness of the encoding is proven. GTS joinability of critical pairs can be mapped onto joinability of specific critical pairs in CHR.
- Petri Nets are translated to CHR in [18]. It is proven that there is a one-to-one correspondence between Colored Petri Nets and positive ground range-restricted CHR simplification rules over finite domains.

Chapter 6 and 9.3 of [55] and the CHR web-page also describe these embeddings:

- Production Rules and Business Rules,
- Event-Condition-Action (ECA) Rules,
- Functional Programming,
- General Abstract Model for Multiset Manipulation (GAMMA),
- Deductive databases languages like DATALOG,
- Description logic (DL) with OWL- and SWRL-style rules,
- Concurrent Constraint Programming (CC) language framework.

The online tool http://pmx.informatik.uni-ulm.de/chr/translator supports the basic translation for some of these embeddings: term rewriting systems, functional programming, multiset transformation, production rules with negation-as-absence.

The embeddings are quite useful for comparing and for cross-fertilization between different approaches. For example, in the CHR embedding, the close relationship between colored Petri Nets and the GAMMA chemical abstract machine (CHAM) can be immediately seen. On the other hand, it seems difficult to come up with an embedding of full CHR in one of the afore-mentioned formalisms. Basically, other approaches either lack the notion of constraints and logical variables or they lack multi-headed rules and propagation rules. Given these embeddings and its power in general, CHR can be considered a candidate for a *lingua franca* for computational systems with the potential for cross-fertilization of research.

6   CHR in Research and Applications

Typical research applications of CHR can be found in areas of computational linguistics, constraint solving, cognitive systems, spatio-temporal reasoning, agent-based systems, bio-informatics, semantic web, type systems, verification and testing and many more.

Commercial applications include financial services in stockbroking (SecuritEase, New Zealand), vehicle control by robotic brains (Cognitive Systems, Spain), injection mould design (Cornerstone Intelligent Software Corp, Canada), optical network design (Mitre, USA), enterprise applications (LogicBlox, USA), and software verification (BSSE, Germany). See Section 7 in [122] for details.

6.1   Language Design and Algorithm Design

One of the most successful research applications of CHR is in the design, prototyping and analysis of advanced type systems for the functional programming language Haskell [40,124,125]. Type reconstruction with CHR is performed for functional and logic programs in [109]. A flow-based approach for a variant of parametric polymorphism in Java is based on CHR in [27].

The union-find algorithm can be seen as solving simple equations between variables or constants. By choosing the appropriate equational relations, one can derive fast incremental algorithms for solving certain propositional logic (SAT) problems and polynomial equations in two variables [53]. Almost-linear tree equation solving algorithms are reconstructed with CHR in [93]. Parallelizing classical algorithms is discussed for Union-Find using confluence analysis [51] and for Preflow-Push [92].

6.2   Software Verification and Testing

The authors of [73,74] present a new method for automatic test data generation (ATDG) applying to semantically annotated control-flow graphs (CFGs), covering both ATDG based on source code and assembly or virtual machine code. The method supports a generic set of test coverage criteria, including all structural coverage criteria currently in use in industrial software test for safety critical software. The work [11] gives test cases a denotational semantics by viewing them as specification predicates. The authors develop a testing theory and implementation for fault-based mutation testing.

Other applications of CHR in testing include [36,76,98,107]. An an effective methodology for verifying properties of imperative programs is their transformation to constraint-based programs [12,41,95]. Somewhat related is lightweight string reasoning for OCL [25].

6.3   Constraints Solving and Reasoning

CHR was originally designed to write or even automatically generate constraint solvers [7,8,100,123]. Solvers written in CHR and applications of CHR in constraint reasoning can be found in [58] and further references in [47,62,122]. For example, CHR-based spatio-temporal reasoning is applied to robot path planning in [45, 89]. In the soft constraints framework [22–24], constraints and partial assignments are given preference or importance levels, and constraints are combined according to combinators which express the desired optimization criteria.

The goal of argumentation-based *legal reasoning* [117] is to determine the chance of winning a court case, given the probabilities of the judge accepting certain claimed facts and legal rules. In *computer linguistics*, CHR Grammars (CHRG) [28] execute as robust bottom-up parsers with an inherent treatment of ambiguity. *Computational Cognitive Modeling* is a research field at the interface of computer science and psychology. It enables researchers to build detailed cognitive models using a cognitive architecture. A popular cognitive architecture, ACT-R, has been implemented in CHR and given a proper formal semantics for the first time [68, 69].

6.4 Multi-agent Systems and Abduction

The agent-based system FLUX is implemented in CHR [126, 127]. Its application FLUXPLAYER [108] won the General Game Playing competition at the AAAI conference in 2006. SCIFF is a framework to specify and verify interaction in open agent societies [13, 15]. The SCIFF language is equipped with a semantics based on abductive logic programming. Other applications in multi-agent systems and abductive reasoning are for example [14, 71, 94, 114]. HYPROLOG [30] extends Prolog with CHR rules for assumptions, abduction and integrity constraints. Probabilistic Abductive Logic Programs (PALPs) are introduced and and implemented in CHR for solving abductive problems providing minimal explanations together with their probabilities [29].

6.5 Semantic Web

In Chapter 9.3. of [55] a straightforward and effective implementation of description logic with OWL- and SWRL-style rules in CHR is given. For the Semantic Web, the integration and combination of data from different information sources is an important issue that can be handled with CHR [16, 138]. In [17] a composition and verification framework for Semantic Web Services specified using WSSL is proposed, a novel service specification language based on the fluent calculus, that addresses issues related to the frame, ramification and qualification problems. An earlier paper on web service composition using fluent calculus is [105]. The paper [26] proposes a service modeling approach consisting of service contracts and a process model. Service contracts are used as service advertisement and service request in this approach. The Cuypers Multimedia Transformation Engine [75] supports the automatic generation of Web-based presentations adapted to the user's needs.

6.6 The Diversity of CHR Applications

Scheduling and timetabling are popular constraint-based applications, and this also holds for CHR implementation of course scheduling and room planning for the University of Munich [6,9], which has become an often-cited standard work in the area.

The tool Popular [59] uses a path-loss model to describe radio-wave transmission and constraint-based programming to optimize the placement of base stations (transmitters) for local wireless communication at company sites.

The Munich Rent Advisor [57] allows the calculation of the estimated fair rent for a flat based on statistical data using an online form. Simply by translating the calculation scheme into CHR-based arithmetic interval constraints, the functionality is significantly extended: The user need not answer all questions, and so an interval range for the possible rent is returned.

The papers [72,116] present a new system for automatic music generation, in which music is modeled using very high level probabilistic rules in CHRISM [118]. The probabilistic parameters can be learned from examples, resulting in a system for personalized music generation.

The authors of [88] present an algorithm for long-term routing of autonomous sailboats. It is based on the A*-algorithm and incorporates changing weather conditions by dynamically adapting the underlying routing graph. The software also takes individual parameters of the sailboat into account, and proved to be faster than commercial systems. The system was successfully put to test during an attempt to break the world record in long-distance robot sailing with the ASV RoBoat of INNOC (Vienna).

7 Conclusions

Constraint Handling Rules - what else?

References

1. Fakhry, G., Sharaf, N., Abdennadher, S.: Towards the implementation of a source-to-source transformation tool for CHR operational semantics. In: Gupta, G., Peña, R. (eds.) LOPSTR 2013, LNCS 8901. LNCS, vol. 8901, pp. 145–163. Springer, Heidelberg (2014)
2. Abdennadher, S., Frühwirth, T.: On completion of constraint handling rules. In: Maher, M.J., Puget, J.-F. (eds.) CP 1998. LNCS, vol. 1520, pp. 25–39. Springer, Heidelberg (1998)
3. Abdennadher, S., Frühwirth, T.: Operational equivalence of CHR programs and constraints. In: Jaffar, J. (ed.) CP 1999. LNCS, vol. 1713, pp. 43–57. Springer, Heidelberg (1999)
4. Abdennadher, S., Frühwirth, T.: Integration and optimization of rule-based constraint solvers. In: Bruynooghe, M. (ed.) LOPSTR 2004. LNCS, vol. 3018, pp. 198–213. Springer, Heidelberg (2004)
5. Abdennadher, S., Frühwirth, T., Meuss, H.: Confluence and Semantics of Constraint Simplification Rules. Constraints 4(2), 133–165 (1999)
6. Abdennadher, S., Marte, M.: University course timetabling using constraint handling rules. In: Holzbaur, C., Frühwirth, T. (eds.) Special Issue on Constraint Handling Rules, vol. 14(4), pp. 311–325. Taylor & Francis, London (2000). Journal of Applied Artificial Intelligence

7. Abdennadher, S., Rigotti, C.: Automatic generation of rule-based constraint solvers over finite domains. ACM TOCL **5**(2), 177–205 (2004)

8. Abdennadher, S., Rigotti, C.: Automatic generation of chr constraint solvers. Theory Pract. Log. Program. **5**(4–5), 403–418 (2005)

9. Abdennadher, S., Saft, M., Will, S.: Classroom assignment using constraint logic programming. In: Proc. 2nd Intl. Conf. and Exhibition on Practical Application of Constraint Technologies and Logic Programming, PACLP 2000, April 2000

10. Abdennadher, S., Schütz, H.: CHR $^\vee$: a flexible query language. In: Andreasen, T., Christiansen, H., Larsen, H.L. (eds.) FQAS 1998. LNCS (LNAI), vol. 1495, pp. 1–14. Springer, Heidelberg (1998)

11. Aichernig, B.K.: A systematic introduction to mutation testing in unifying theories of programming. In: Borba, P., Cavalcanti, A., Sampaio, A., Woodcook, J. (eds.) PSSE 2007. LNCS, vol. 6153, pp. 243–287. Springer, Heidelberg (2010)

12. Albert, E., García de la Banda, M.J., Gómez-Zamalloa, M., Rojas, J.M., Stuckey, P.J.: A CLP heap solver for test case generation. TPLP **13**(4–5), 721–735 (2013). Cambridge University Press

13. Alberti, M., Chesani, F., Gavanelli, M., Lamma, E., Mello, P., Torroni, P.: Verifiable agent interaction in abductive logic programming: the sciff framework. ACM Transactions on Computational Logic (TOCL) **9**(4), 29 (2008)

14. Alberti, M., Daolio, D., Torroni, P., Gavanelli, M., Lamma, E., Mello, P.: Specification and verification of agent interaction protocols in a logic-based system. In: 2004 ACM Symposium on Applied Computing, pp. 72–78. ACM (2004)

15. Alberti, M., Gavanelli, M., Lamma, E.: The CHR-based implementation of the sciff abductive system. Fundamenta Informaticae **124**(4), 365–381 (2013)

16. Badea, L., Tilivea, D., Hotaran, A.: Semantic web reasoning for ontology-based integration of resources. In: Ohlbach, H.J., Schaffert, S. (eds.) PPSWR 2004. LNCS, vol. 3208, pp. 61–75. Springer, Heidelberg (2004)

17. Baryannis, G., Plexousakis, D.: Fluent calculus-based semantic web service composition and verification using WSSL. In: Lomuscio, A.R., Nepal, S., Patrizi, F., Benatallah, B., Brandić, I. (eds.) ICSOC 2013. LNCS, vol. 8377, pp. 256–270. Springer, Heidelberg (2014)

18. Betz, H.: Relating coloured petri nets to constraint handling rules. In: Fourth Workshop on Constraint Handling Rules, pp. 32–46 (2007)

19. Betz, H.: A Unified Analytical Foundation for Constraint Handling Rules. BoD-Books on Demand (2014)

20. Betz, H., Frühwirth, T.: Linear-logic based analysis of Constraint Handling Rules with disjunction. ACM Transactions on Computational Logic (TOCL) **14**(1), 1 (2013)

21. Betz, H., Raiser, F., Frühwirth, T.: A complete and terminating execution model for constraint handling rules. In: Hermenegildo and Schaub [81], pp. 597–610

22. Bistarelli, S., Frühwirth, T., Marte, M., Rossi, F.: Soft constraint propagation and solving in Constraint Handling Rules. Computational Intelligence: Special Issue on Preferences in AI and CP **20**(2), 287–307 (2004)

23. Bistarelli, S., Martinelli, F., Santini, F.: A formal framework for trust policy negotiation in autonomic systems: abduction with soft constraints. In: Xie, B., Branke, J., Sadjadi, S.M., Zhang, D., Zhou, X. (eds.) ATC 2010. LNCS, vol. 6407, pp. 268–282. Springer, Heidelberg (2010)

24. Bistarelli, S., Martinelli, F., Santini, F.: A semiring-based framework for the deduction/abduction reasoning in access control with weighted credentials. Computers & Mathematics with Applications **64**(4), 447–462 (2012)

25. Büttner, F., Cabot, J.: Lightweight string reasoning for OCL. In: Vallecillo, A., Tolvanen, J.-P., Kindler, E., Störrle, H., Kolovos, D. (eds.) ECMFA 2012. LNCS, vol. 7349, pp. 244–258. Springer, Heidelberg (2012)
26. Chen, R., Liao, L., Fang, Z.: Contracting of web services with constraint handling rules. In: 2012 IEEE Eighth World Congress on Services (SERVICES), pp. 211–218 (2012)
27. Chin, W.-N., Craciun, F., Khoo, S.-C., Popeea, C.: A flow-based approach for variant parametric types. In: 21st annual ACM SIGPLAN Conference on Object-Oriented Programming Systems, Languages, and Applications, pp. 273–290. ACM (2006)
28. Christiansen, H.: Chr grammars. Theory and Practice of Logic Programming 5(4–5), 467–501 (2005)
29. Christiansen, H.: Implementing probabilistic abductive logic programming with constraint handling rules. In: Schrijvers, T., Frühwirth, T. (eds.) Constraint Handling Rules. LNCS, vol. 5388, pp. 85–118. Springer, Heidelberg (2008)
30. Christiansen, H., Dahl, V.: HYPROLOG: a new logic programming language with assumptions andabduction. In: Gabbrielli and Gupta [63], pp. 159–173
31. Christiansen, H., Kirkeby, M.H.: Confluence modulo equivalence in Constraint Handling Rules. [90]
32. Cruz, F., Rocha, R.: On compiling linear logic programs with comprehensions, aggregates and rule priorities. In: Pontelli, E., Son, T.C. (eds.) PADL 2015. LNCS, vol. 9131, pp. 34–49. Springer, Heidelberg (2015)
33. De Koninck, L.: Logical Algorithms meets CHR: A meta-complexity result for Constraint Handling Rules with rule priorities. TPLP 9(2), 165–212 (2009)
34. De Koninck, L., Schrijvers, T., Demoen, B.: Search strategies in CHR(Prolog). In: Schrijvers and Frühwirth [110], pp. 109–124
35. De Koninck, L., Schrijvers, T., Demoen, B.: Chr^{rp}: Constraint Handling Rules with rule priorties. Technical Report CW 479, K.U.Leuven, Dept. Comp. Sc., Leuven, Belgium, March 2007
36. Degrave, F., Schrijvers, T., Vanhoof, W.: Automatic generation of test inputs for mercury. In: Hanus, M. (ed.) LOPSTR 2008. LNCS, vol. 5438, pp. 71–86. Springer, Heidelberg (2009)
37. Di Giusto, C., Gabbrielli, M., Meo, M.C.: Expressiveness of multiple heads in CHR. In: Nielsen, M., Kučera, A., Miltersen, P.B., Palamidessi, C., Tůma, P., Valencia, F. (eds.) SOFSEM 2009. LNCS, vol. 5404, pp. 205–216. Springer, Heidelberg (2009)
38. Djelloul, K., Duck, G.J., Sulzmann, M. (eds.) Proc. 4th Workshop on Constraint Handling Rules, CHR 2007, September 2007
39. Duck, G.J.: SMCHR: Satisfiability modulo Constraint Handling Rules. CoRR, abs/1210.5307 (2012)
40. Duck, G.J., Haemmerlé, R., Sulzmann, M.: On termination, confluence and consistent CHR-based type inference. TPLP 14(4–5), 619–632 (2014)
41. Duck, G.J., Jaffar, J., Koh, N.C.H.: Constraint-based program reasoning with heaps and separation. In: Schulte, C. (ed.) CP 2013. LNCS, vol. 8124, pp. 282–298. Springer, Heidelberg (2013)
42. Duck, G.J., Koninck, L.D., Stuckey, P.J.: Cadmium: an implementation of ACD term rewriting. In: García de la Banda and Pontelli [70], pp. 531–545
43. Duck, G.J., Stuckey, P.J., García de la Banda, M., Holzbaur, C.: The refined operational semantics of constraint handling rules. In: Demoen, B., Lifschitz, V. (eds.) ICLP 2004. LNCS, vol. 3132, pp. 90–104. Springer, Heidelberg (2004)

44. Duck, G.J., Stuckey, P.J., Sulzmann, M.: Observable confluence for constraint handling rules. In: Dahl, V., Niemelä, I. (eds.) ICLP 2007. LNCS, vol. 4670, pp. 224–239. Springer, Heidelberg (2007)
45. Escrig, M., Toledo, F.: Qualitative Spatial Reasoning: Theory and Practice. IOS Press (1998)
46. Fink, M., Tompits, H., Woltran, S. (eds.) Proc. 20th Workshop on Logic Programming, WLP 2006, T.U.Wien, Austria, INFSYS Research report 1843–06-02, February 2006
47. Frühwirth, T.: Theory and practice of Constraint Handling Rules. J. Logic Programming, Special Issue on Constraint Logic Programming **37**(1–3), 95–138 (1998)
48. Frühwirth, T.: Proving termination of constraint solver programs. In: Apt, K.R., Kakas, A.C., Monfroy, E., Rossi, F. (eds.) Compulog Net WS 1999. LNCS (LNAI), vol. 1865, pp. 298–317. Springer, Heidelberg (2000)
49. Frühwirth, T.: As time goes by: automatic complexity analysis of simplification rules. In: Eighth International Conference on Principles of Knowledge Representation and Reasoning, San Francisco, CA, USA. Morgan Kaufmann (2002)
50. Frühwirth, T.: As Time Goes By II: More Automatic Complexity Analysis of Concurrent Rule Programs. ENTCS **59**(3), 185–206 (2002)
51. Frühwirth, T.: Parallelizing union-find in constraint handling rules using confluence. In: Gabbrielli and Gupta [63], pp. 113–127
52. Frühwirth, T.: Specialization of concurrent guarded multi-set transformation rules. In: Etalle, S. (ed.) LOPSTR 2004. LNCS, vol. 3573, pp. 133–148. Springer, Heidelberg (2005)
53. Frühwirth, T.: Quasi-linear-time algorithms by generalisation of union-find in CHR. In: Fages, F., Rossi, F., Soliman, S. (eds.) CSCLP 2007. LNCS (LNAI), vol. 5129, pp. 91–108. Springer, Heidelberg (2008)
54. Frühwirth, T.: Welcome to constraint handling rules. In: Schrijvers and Frühwirth [112], pp. 1–15
55. Frühwirth, T.: Constraint Handling Rules. Cambridge University Press (2009)
56. Frühwirth, T.: A devil's advocate against termination of direct recursion. In: 17th International Symposium on Principles and Practice of Declarative Programming, PPDP 2015, Siena, Italy, 2015. ACM (2015)
57. Frühwirth, T., Abdennadher, S.: The Munich rent advisor: A success for logic programming on the internet. TPLP **1**(3), 303–319 (2001)
58. Frühwirth, T., Abdennadher, S.: Essentials of Constraint Programming. Springer (2003)
59. Frühwirth, T., Brisset, P.: Placing base stations in wireless indoor communication networks. IEEE Intelligent Systems and Their Applications **15**(1), 49–53 (2000)
60. Frühwirth, T., di Pierro, A., Wiklicky, H.: Probabilistic constraint handlingrules. In: 11th International Workshop on Functional and (Constraint) Logic Programming. ENTCS, vol. 76, pp. 115–130 (2002)
61. Frühwirth, T., Holzbaur, C.: Source-to-source transformation for a class of expressive rules. In: Buccafurri, F. (ed.) Joint Conf. Declarative Programming APPIA-GULP-PRODE, AGP 2003, pp. 386–397, September 2003
62. Frühwirth, T., Raiser, F. (eds.) Constraint Handling Rules: Compilation, Execution, and Analysis. BOD (2011)
63. Gabbrielli, M., Gupta, G. (eds.): ICLP 2005. LNCS, vol. 3668. Springer, Heidelberg (2005)
64. Gabbrielli, M., Mauro, J., Meo, M.C.: The expressive power of CHR with priorities. Inf. Comput. **228**, 62–82 (2013)

65. Gabbrielli, M., Mauro, J., Meo, M.C., Sneyers, J.: Decidability properties for fragments of CHR. In: Hermenegildo and Schaub [81], pp. 611–626
66. Gabbrielli, M., Meo, M.C.: A compositional semantics for CHR. ACM TOCL 10(2), 1–36 (2009)
67. Gabbrielli, M., Meo, M.C., Tacchella, P., Wiklicky, H.: Unfolding for CHR programs. Theory and Practice of Logic Programming, 1–48 (2013)
68. Gall, D., Frühwirth, T.: A formal semantics for the cognitive architecture ACT-R. [90]
69. Gall, D., Frühwirth, T.: A refined operational semantics for ACT-R. In: 17th International Symposium on Principles and Practice of Declarative Programming, PPDP 2015, Siena, Italy, 2015. ACM (2015)
70. Garcia de la Banda, M., Pontelli, E. (eds.): ICLP 2008. LNCS, vol. 5366. Springer, Heidelberg (2008)
71. Gavanelli, M., Alberti, M., Lamma, E.: Integrating abduction and constraint optimization in constraint handling rules. In: 18th European Conf. on Artif. Intell., ECAI 2008, pp. 903–904. IOS press, July 2008
72. Geiselhart, F., Raiser, F., Sneyers, J., Frühwirth, T.: MTSeq - multi-touch-enabled music generation and manipulation based on CHR. In: Van Weert and De Koninck [131]
73. Gerlich, R.: Generic and extensible automatic test data generation for safety critical software with CHR. In: Van Weert and De Koninck [131]
74. Gerlich, R.: Automatic test data generation and model checking with CHR. arXiv preprint arXiv:1406.2122 (2014)
75. Geurts, J., Ossenbruggen, J.V., Hardman, L.: Application-specific constraints for multimedia presentation generation. In: 8th International Conference on Multimedia Modeling, pp. 247–266 (2001)
76. Gouraud, S.-D., Gotlieb, A.: Using CHRs to generate functional test cases for the Java card virtual machine. In: Van Hentenryck, P. (ed.) PADL 2006. LNCS, vol. 3819, pp. 1–15. Springer, Heidelberg (2005)
77. Green, T.J., Aref, M., Karvounarakis, G.: LogicBlox, platform and language: a tutorial. In: Barceló, P., Pichler, R. (eds.) Datalog 2.0 2012. LNCS, vol. 7494, pp. 1–8. Springer, Heidelberg (2012)
78. Haemmerlé, R.: (Co-)Inductive semantics for Constraint Handling Rules. TPLP 11(4–5), 593–609 (2011). Cambridge University Press
79. Haemmerlé, R.: Diagrammatic confluence for Constraint Handling Rules. Theory Pract. Log. Program. 12(4–5), 737–753 (2012)
80. Haemmerlé, R., Lopez-Garcia, P., Hermenegildo, M.: CLP projection for constraint handling rules. In: Hanus, M. (ed.), PPDP 2011, pp. 137–148. ACM Press, July 2011
81. Hermenegildo, M., Schaub, T. (eds.) Proc. 26th Intl. Conf. Logic Programming, ICLP 2010. TPLP, vol. 10(4–6). Cambridge University Press, July 2010
82. Holzbaur, C., Frühwirth, T.: A Prolog Constraint Handling Rules compiler and runtime system. Journal of Applied Artificial Intelligence 14(4), 369–388 (2000). Taylor & Francis
83. Holzbaur, C., García de la Banda, M., Stuckey, P.J., Duck, G.J.: Optimizing compilation of Constraint Handling Rules in HAL. Theory and Practice of Logic Programming 5(4–5), 503–531 (2005). Cambridge University Press
84. De Koninck, L., Schrijvers, T., Demoen, B.: The correspondence between the logical algorithms language and CHR. In: Dahl, V., Niemelä, I. (eds.) ICLP 2007. LNCS, vol. 4670, pp. 209–223. Springer, Heidelberg (2007)

85. Lam, E., Sulzmann, M.: Parallel execution of multi-set constraint rewrite rules. In: Tenth International ACM SIGPLAN Symposium on Principles and Practice of Declarative Programming. ACM (2008)
86. Lam, E.S., Sulzmann, M.: Concurrent goal-based execution of Constraint Handling Rules. TPLP **11**, 841–879 (2009)
87. Lam, E.S.L., Cervesato, I., Fatima, N.: Comingle: distributed logic programming for decentralized mobile ensembles. In: Holvoet, T., Viroli, M. (eds.) COORDINATION 2015. LNCS, vol. 9037, pp. 51–66. Springer, Heidelberg (2015)
88. Langbein, J., Stelzer, R., Frühwirth, T.: A rule-based approach to long-term routing for autonomous sailboats. In: Schlaefer, A., Blaurock, O. (eds.) Robotic Sailing. Non-series, vol. 79, pp. 195–204. Springer, Heidelberg (2011)
89. Martınez-Martın, E., Escrig, M.T., del Pobil, A.P.: A general qualitative spatio-temporal model based on intervals. Journal of Universal Computer Science **18**(10), 1343–1378 (2012)
90. Proietti, M., Seki, H. (eds.): LOPSTR 2014. LNCS, vol. 8981. Springer, Heidelberg (2015)
91. Mauro, J.: Constraints Meet Concurrency. Springer (2014)
92. Meister, M.: Fine-grained parallel implementation of the preflow-push algorithm in CHR. In: Fink et al. [46], pp. 172–181
93. Meister, M., Frühwirth, T.: Reconstructing almost-linear tree equation solving algorithms in CHR. In: Proceedings of CSCLP 2007: Annual ERCIM Workshop on Constraint Solving and Constraint Logic Programming, p. 123 (2007)
94. Montali, M., Torroni, P., Chesani, F., Mello, P., Alberti, M., Lamma, E.: Abductive logic programming as an effective technology for the static verification of declarative business processes. Fundamenta Informaticae **102**(3), 325–361 (2010)
95. Pettorossi, A., Fioravanti, F., Proietti, M., De Angelis, E.: Program verification using constraint handling rules and array constraint generalizations. In: Second International Workshop on Verification and Program Transformation, VPT 2014, July 17–18, 2014, Vienna, Austria, vol. 28, pp. 3–18. EasyChair (2014)
96. Pilozzi, P., De Schreye, D.: Automating termination proofs for CHR. In: Hill, P.M., Warren, D.S. (eds.) ICLP 2009. LNCS, vol. 5649, pp. 504–508. Springer, Heidelberg (2009)
97. Pilozzi, P., De Schreye, D.: Improved termination analysis of CHR using self-sustainability analysis. In: Vidal, G. (ed.) LOPSTR 2011. LNCS, vol. 7225, pp. 189–204. Springer, Heidelberg (2012)
98. Pretschner, A., Lötzbeyer, H., Philipps, J.: Model based testing in incremental system development. Journal of Systems and Software **70**(3), 315–329 (2004)
99. Raiser, F.: Graph transformation systems in CHR. In: Dahl, V., Niemelä, I. (eds.) ICLP 2007. LNCS, vol. 4670, pp. 240–254. Springer, Heidelberg (2007)
100. Raiser, F.: Semi-automatic generation of CHR solvers for global constraints. In: Stuckey, P.J. (ed.) CP 2008. LNCS, vol. 5202, pp. 588–592. Springer, Heidelberg (2008)
101. Raiser, F., Betz, H., Frühwirth, T.: Equivalence of CHR states revisited. In: Raiser, F., Sneyers, J. (eds.), CHR 2009, pp. 33–48. K.U.Leuven, Dept. Comp. Sc., Technical report CW 555, July 2009
102. Raiser, F., Frühwirth, T.: Towards term rewriting systems in constraint handling rules. In: Schrijvers, T., Raiser, F., Frühwirth, T. (eds.) CHR 2008, pp. 19–34. RISC Report Series 08–10, University of Linz, Austria (2008)
103. Raiser, F., Frühwirth, T.: Exhaustive parallel rewriting with multiple removals. In: Abdennadher, S. (ed.) WLP 2010, September 2010

104. Raiser, F., Tacchella, P.: On confluence of non-terminating CHR programs. In: Djelloul et al. [38], pp. 63–76
105. Salomie, I., Chifu, V., Harsa, I., Gherga, M.: Web service composition using fluent calculus. International Journal of Metadata, Semantics and Ontologies **5**(3), 238–250 (2010)
106. Sarna-Starosta, B., Ramakrishnan, C.R.: Compiling constraint handling rules for efficient tabled evaluation. In: Hanus, M. (ed.) PADL 2007. LNCS, vol. 4354, pp. 170–184. Springer, Heidelberg (2007)
107. Sarna-Starosta, B., Stirewalt, R.E.K., Dillon, L.K.: A model-based design-for-verification approach to checking for deadlock in multi-threaded applications. Intl. Journal of Softw. Engin. and Knowl. Engin. **17**(2), 207–230 (2007)
108. Schiffel, S., Thielscher, M.: Fluxplayer: a successful general game player. In: 22nd Conference on Artificial Intelligence, pp. 1191–1196. AAAI Press (2007)
109. Schrijvers, T., Bruynooghe, M.: Polymorphic algebraic data type reconstruction. In: Eighth ACM SIGPLAN International Conference on Principles and Practice of Declarative Programming, pp. 85–96. ACM (2006)
110. Schrijvers, T., Frühwirth, T. (eds.) Proc. 3rd Workshop on Constraint Handling Rules, CHR 2006. K.U.Leuven, Dept. Comp. Sc., Technical report CW 452, July 2006
111. Schrijvers, T., Frühwirth, T.: Optimal union-find in Constraint Handling Rules. TPLP **6**(1–2), 213–224 (2006)
112. Schrijvers, T., Frühwirth, T. (eds.): Constraint Handling Rules. LNCS, vol. 5388. Springer, Heidelberg (2008)
113. Schrijvers, T., Sulzmann, M.: Transactions in constraint handling rules. In: García de la Banda and Pontelli [70], pp. 516–530
114. Seitz, C., Bauer, B., Berger, M.: Multi agent systems using constraint handling rules for problem solving. In: International Conference on Artificial Intelligence, pp. 295–301. CSREA Press (2002)
115. Sneyers, J.: Turing-complete subclasses of CHR. In: García de la Banda and Pontelli [70], pp. 759–763
116. Sneyers, J., De Schreye, D.: APOPCALEAPS: automatic music generation with CHRiSM. In: Danoy, G. et al., (eds.) 22nd Benelux Conference on Artificial Intelligence (BNAIC 2010), Luxembourg, October 2010
117. Sneyers, J., De Schreye, D., Frühwirth, T.: Probabilistic legal reasoning in CHRiSM. Theory and Practice of Logic Programming **13**(4–5), 769–781 (2013)
118. Sneyers, J., Meert, W., Vennekens, J., Kameya, Y., Sato, T.: Chr (PRISM)-based probabilistic logic learning. Theory and Practice of Logic Programming **10**(4–6), 433–447 (2010)
119. Sneyers, J., Schrijvers, T., Demoen, B.: Dijkstra's algorithm with Fibonacci heaps: an executable description in CHR. In: Fink et al. [46], pp. 182–191
120. Sneyers, J., Schrijvers, T., Demoen, B.: The computational power and complexity of Constraint Handling Rules. ACM TOPLAS **31**(2), February 2009
121. Sneyers, J., Van Weert, P., Schrijvers, T.: Aggregates for constraint handling rules. In: Djelloul et al. [38], pp. 91–105
122. Sneyers, J., Van Weert, P., Schrijvers, T., De Koninck, L.: As time goes by: Constraint Handling Rules - A survey of CHR research between 1998 and 2007. TPLP **10**(1), 1–47 (2010)
123. Sobhi, I., Abdennadher, S., Betz, H.: Constructing rule-based solvers for intentionally-defined constraints. In: Schrijvers and Frühwirth [112], pp. 70–84
124. Stuckey, P.J., Sulzmann, M.: A Theory of Overloading. ACM Transactions on Programming Languages and Systems **27**(6), 1216–1269 (2005)

125. Sulzmann, M., Duck, G.J., Peyton-Jones, S., Stuckey, P.J.: Understanding functional dependencies via Constraint Handling Rules. J. Functional Prog. **17**(1), 83–129 (2007)
126. Thielscher, M.: FLUX: A Logic Programming Method for Reasoning Agents. Theory and Practice of Logic Programming **5**, 533–565 (2005)
127. Thielscher, M.: Reasoning robots: the art and science of programming robotic agents, vol. 33. Springer Science & Business Media (2006)
128. Triossi, A., Orlando, S., Raffaetà, A., Frühwirth, T.: Compiling chr to parallel hardware. In: Proceedings of the 14th symposium on Principles and practice of declarative programming, pp. 173–184. ACM (2012)
129. Van Weert, P.: Compiling Constraint Handling Rules to Java: A reconstruction. Technical Report CW 521, K.U.Leuven, Dept. Comp. Sc., Leuven, Belgium, August 2008
130. Van Weert, P.: Efficient lazy evaluation of rule-based programs. IEEE Transactions on Knowledge and Data Engineering **22**(11), 1521–1534 (2010)
131. Van Weert, P., De Koninck, L. (eds.) Proc. 7th Workshop on Constraint Handling Rules, CHR 2010. K.U.Leuven, Dept. Comp. Sc., Technical report CW 588, July 2010
132. Van Weert, P., Sneyers, J., Schrijvers, T., Demoen, B.: Extending CHR with negation as absence. In: Schrijvers and Frühwirth [110], pp. 125–140
133. Van Weert, P., Wuille, P., Schrijvers, T., Demoen, B.: CHR for imperative host languages. In: Schrijvers and Frühwirth [112], pp. 161–212
134. Wolf, A.: Intelligent search strategies based on adaptive Constraint Handling Rules. Theory and Practice of Logic Programming **5**(4–5), 567–594 (2005)
135. Wolf, A., Robin, J., Vitorino, J.: Adaptive CHR meets CHR$^\vee$: an extended refined operational semantics for CHR$^\vee$ based on justifications. In: Schrijvers and Frühwirth [112], pp. 48–69
136. Wuille, P., Schrijvers, T., Demoen, B.: CCHR: the fastest CHR implementation. In: Djelloul, C. et al. [38], pp. 123–137
137. Zaki, A., Frühwirth, T., Geller, I.: Parallel execution of constraint handling rules on a graphical processing unit. In: Sneyers, J., Frühwirth, T. (eds.) CHR 2012, pp. 82–90. K.U.Leuven, Dept. Comp. Sc., Technical report CW 624, September 2012
138. Zhu, H., Madnick, S.E., Siegel, M.D.: Enabling global price comparison through semantic integration of web data. IJEB **6**(4), 319–341 (2008)

Consistency Checking of Re-engineered UML Class Diagrams via Datalog+/-

Georg Gottlob[1], Giorgio Orsi[1], and Andreas Pieris[2]([⊠])

[1] Department of Computer Science, University of Oxford, Oxford, UK
{georg.gottlob,giorgio.orsi}@cs.ox.ac.uk
[2] Institute of Information Systems, Vienna University of Technology, Vienna, Austria
pieris@dbai.tuwien.ac.at

Abstract. UML class diagrams (UCDs) are a widely adopted formalism for modeling the intensional structure of a software system. Although UCDs are typically guiding the implementation of a system, it is common in practice that developers need to recover the class diagram from an implemented system. This process is known as reverse engineering. A fundamental property of reverse engineered (or simply re-engineered) UCDs is consistency, showing that the system is realizable in practice. In this work, we investigate the consistency of re-engineered UCDs, and we show is PSPACE-complete. The upper bound is obtained by exploiting algorithmic techniques developed for conjunctive query answering under guarded Datalog+/-, that is, a key member of the Datalog+/- family of KR languages, while the lower bound is obtained by simulating the behavior of a polynomial space Turing machine.

1 Introduction

Models play a central role in computer science by providing two fundamentally different representational functions: they can be used to capture interesting aspects of the real world, and they can also be employed to represent axioms of abstract theories. System designers use models for representing the requirements and the architecture of software systems. The urge for model construction, maintenance and manipulation becomes evident as soon as systems and data grow in size and complexity.

1.1 UML Class Diagrams

UML class diagrams (UCDs) are a widely adopted formalism for modeling the intensional structure of a software system, and are commonly employed in CASE tools for system design, maintenance and analysis. In fact, UCDs are used to represent classes (entities) of a domain of interest with their attributes (fields) and operations (methods). Classes can be related to each other by means of associations representing relationships among their instances. Due to their simplicity, UCDs are frequently used also for data modeling, de-facto replacing traditional

© Springer International Publishing Switzerland 2015
N. Bassiliades et al. (Eds.): RuleML 2015, LNCS 9202, pp. 35–53, 2015.
DOI: 10.1007/978-3-319-21542-6_3

formalisms like the ER model. Although the usual procedure is to go from a class diagram to a system, it is common that developers need to follow the opposite route, i.e., to recover the class diagram from an implemented system. This process is known as *reverse engineering* [14].

Apart from guiding the implementation of a software system, class diagrams can be used to verify relevant properties so as to assess the quality of a specification to objective criteria. The typical property of interest is *consistency*, proving that the system is realizable in practice, namely its classes can be populated without violating any of the imposed constraints.

1.2 Research Challenges

It is apparent that consistency checking is a key algorithmic task that is relevant for re-engineered class diagrams. UCDs for complex systems usually become very large, and the various constraints may interact in an arbitrary way. This makes the study of the above task urgent, and at the same time very challenging. While consistency checking has been heavily investigated in the past in different scenarios (see, e.g., [3,4,8,12]), nothing is known in the case of re-engineered class diagrams. It is the precise aim of this work to pinpoint the computational complexity of this problem under re-engineered class diagrams.

Towards this direction, we first need to answer the following key question: which fragment of UCDs can be recovered by existing reverse engineering tools? To answer this question, we set up a simple experiment to determine which constructs appear in re-engineered class diagrams. We observed that the constructs that can be recovered are: (1) classes with attributes and operations, where different classes may have attributes/operations with the same name; (2) generalization hierarchies but without completeness assertions; and (3) associations with mandatory or functional participation of classes. This led us to the formalization of the syntax and the semantics of the fragment of UCDs, dubbed RevEng, which can be re-engineered.

After formalizing RevEng diagrams, we proceed with the investigation of the computational complexity of our problem. One may claim that the desired complexity results can be immediately inherited from existing results on UML class diagrams, for instance in [4] which shows that consistency of UCDs is EXPTIME-complete, or results on knowledge representation formalisms such as, e.g., DL-Lite [9], $\mathcal{EL}$ [2] and Horn-$\mathcal{FL}^-$ [13]. This is not true since always the candidate formalism is either not expressive enough to capture RevEng class diagrams, or gives an upper bound which is not optimal. Therefore, RevEng class diagrams form a totally novel formalism w.r.t. complexity, and novel decision procedures beyond the state of the art must be developed.

We exploit algorithmic techniques developed for conjunctive query answering under guarded Datalog$^\pm$, that is, a key member of the Datalog$^\pm$ family of KR languages [5,6]. Given a RevEng class diagram $\mathcal{C}$, the problem of deciding whether $\mathcal{C}$ is consistent can be naturally reduced to conjunctive query answering under a fragment of guarded Datalog$^\pm$. In particular, we construct the following three components: a database D, which stores a witness atom for each class of $\mathcal{C}$; a set of guarded Datalog$^\pm$ rules Σ, which represents $\mathcal{C}$; and a union of conjunctive queries Q that encodes the disjointness assertions among classes, which form the only source of inconsistency occurring in $\mathcal{C}$. The consistency problem of a diagram is then tantamount to the problem of deciding whether D and Σ do not entail the query Q, which in turn implies that there are no inconsistencies. The latter is tackled by exploiting a classical algorithmic tool from the database literature, in particular the *chase algorithm* (see, e.g., [11]), and a novel chase-like decision procedure is proposed.

1.3   Summary of Contributions

Our contribution can be summarized as follows:

1. We set up a simple experiment in Section 2 with the aim of understanding which UML constructs can be recovered by existing reverse engineering algorithms. In particular, we collect a number of Java open-source software packages, mostly taken from the literature on the benchmarking of UML reverse engineering tools. We then consider several prominent CASE tools for software engineering, and we reverse engineer the packages in the benchmark into UCDs. We observe that the UML constructs that can be recovered are: classes with attributes and operations; generalization hierarchies but without completeness assertions; and associations with multiplicities 0..1, 1..1, 0..∞ and 1..∞. Based on the above observation, we then provide a formalization of the syntax and the semantics of the fragment of UCDs, called RevEng, which can be recovered.

2. We consider the problem of deciding the consistency of RevEng diagrams in Section 3. We reduce our problem to query answering under a fragment of guarded Datalog$^\pm$, which in turn is shown to be PSPACE-complete. The upper bound is obtained via a novel nondeterministic chase-like algorithm, while the lower bound is shown by simulating the behavior of a polynomial space Turing machine by means of a RevEng diagram.

2   Reverse Engineering

We set up a simple experiment to determine which fragment of UCDs, called RevEng, can be recovered via reverse engineering, and then we provide a formalization of the syntax and the semantics of RevEng.

2.1   Our Experiment

We collected a number of Java open-source software packages, listed in Figure 1, mostly taken from the DaCapo benchmark[1] and the web. We then considered a list of prominent CASE tools with reverse engineering capabilities, given in

---

[1] http://www.dacapobench.org/

Software	Version	CASE Tool	Version	Vendor
antlr	3.5.1	ARGOUML	0.34	Tigris
eje	3.2	ASTAH	6.7	Astah
fop	0.93	BOUML	6.4.7	Bouml
hsqldb	2.31	ENTREPRISE ARCHITECT	10	Sparx Systems
jamaleon	3.3	ESS MODEL	2.2	ESSModel
jolden	N/A	MAGICDRAW	17.0.2	LTR NoMagic
junit	4.11	METAMILL	6.1	Metamill Software
pcj	1.2	POSEIDON UML	6.0.2	Gentleware
pmd	5.05	UMODEL	2014 SP1	Altova
Vuze	5.2	VISUALPARADIGM	11	VisualParadigm

Fig. 1. Software packages and CASE tools

Figure 1. We re-engineered the packages in the benchmark into class diagrams in XMI format for automated processing. Whenever multiple options for reverse engineering were available, e.g., for fields, we used the option that would result in the more general diagram. We observed, in fact, that interpreting fields as attributes leads to simpler diagrams. We noticed that every single re-engineered class diagram consists of the following: (1) Classes with attributes and operations, where different classes may have attributes/operations with the same name; (2) Generalization hierarchies (is-a) but without completeness assertions; and (3) Associations with multiplicities with one of the following forms: 0..1, 1..1, 0..∞ and 1..∞.

Interestingly, when recovering fields as associations, the tools are often unable to recover the exact multiplicity of the association. A possible explanation for this unexpected behavior is that tools tend not to constrain the upper multiplicity when collections and arrays are involved. This seems not to affect fields referencing another class, where a simple check on the assignment of these fields in either the class constructor or in the field declaration provides enough information to determine the correct multiplicity. Another interesting observation is on the lower bounds of the associations that are often recovered as 1 despite having no evidence of that happening from the code.

2.2 Formalizing Reverse Engineered UCDs

Based on the above observations, we proceed to formalize the syntax of UCDs, called RevEng, that can be obtained by reverse engineering, and also give their formal semantics in terms of first-order logic.

Syntax. A *class*, possibly with *attributes* and *operations*, represents a set of objects with common features, and is graphically represented as shown in Figure 2(a); notice that both the middle and the bottom part are optional.

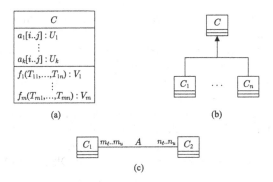

Fig. 2. RevEng UML class diagram constructs

An attribute assertion of the form $a[i..j] : T$, where $i \in \{0,1\}$ and $j \in \{1,\infty\}$, states that the class C has an attribute a of *type*[2] T, where the optional multiplicity $[i..j]$ specifies that a associates to each instance of C at least i and at most j instances of T. Notice that attributes are unique within a class. However, different classes may have attributes with the same name, possibly with different types. An operation of a class C is a function from the instances of C (and possibly additional parameters) to objects and values. An operation assertion of the form $f(T_1, \ldots, T_n) : V$ asserts that the class C has an operation f with $n \geqslant 0$ parameters, where its i-th parameter is of type T_i and its result is of type V. Let us clarify that the class diagram represents only the *signature*, that is, the name of the functions, the number and the types of their parameters, and the type of their result. Notice that operations are unique within a class. However, different classes may have operations with the same name, possibly with different signature but the same number of parameters. One can use *class generalization* to assert that each instance of a child class is also an instance of the parent class. Several generalizations can be grouped together to form a class hierarchy, as shown in Figure 2(b).

An *association* is a relation between the instances of two classes, that are said to *participate* in the association. Names of associations are unique in the diagram. An association A between two classes C_1 and C_2 is graphically represented as in Figure 2(c). The multiplicity $n_\ell..n_u$, where $n_\ell \in \{0,1\}$ and $n_u \in \{1,\infty\}$, specifies that each instance of class C_1 can participate at least n_ℓ times and at most n_u times to A; analogously we have $m_\ell..m_u$ for C_2.

Sometimes, in UML class diagrams, it is assumed that all classes not in the same hierarchy are *disjoint*. In this work, we do not enforce this assumption, and we allow two classes to have common instances. When needed, disjointness can be enforced by means of assertions of the form $\{C_1, \ldots, C_n\}$, stating that the classes $C_1, \ldots, C_n$ do not have a common instance. Another standard assumption in UML class diagrams is the *most specific class* assumption, stating that objects in a hierarchy must belong to a single most specific class. We do not enforce this

---

[2] For simplicity, data types, i.e., collections of values such as integers, are considered as classes, i.e., as collections of objects.

assumption, and two classes in a hierarchy may have common instances, even though they may not have a common subclass. When needed, the existence of the most specific class can be enforced by means of disjointness assertions and most specific class assertions of the form $(\{C_1, \ldots, C_n\}, C_{n+1})$ stating that, if $C_1, \ldots, C_n$ have a common instance c, then c is also an instance of C_{n+1}, i.e., C_{n+1} is a most specific class for $C_1, \ldots, C_n$.

Let $class(\mathcal{C})$ be the set of classes occurring in the diagram $\mathcal{C}$. A RevEng *specification* is a triple $(\mathcal{C}, \mathsf{DISJ}, \mathsf{MSC})$, where $\mathcal{C}$ is a RevEng UML class diagram, $\mathsf{DISJ} \subseteq 2^{class(\mathcal{C})}$ is a set of disjointness assertions, and $\mathsf{MSC} \subseteq 2^{class(\mathcal{C})} \times class(\mathcal{C})$ is a set of most specific class assertions. Notice that DISJ and MSC can be seen as sets of constraints expressed using the *object constraint language (OCL)*[3]. OCL is an expressive language that allows us to impose additional constraints which are not diagrammatically expressible in a UCD. Although OCL has its own syntax, for brevity, we consider the simpler syntax presented above.

Semantics. The formal semantics of RevEng specifications is given in terms of first-order logic (FOL). Given a RevEng specification $\mathcal{S} = (\mathcal{C}, \mathsf{DISJ}, \mathsf{MSC})$, we first define the translation τ of $\mathcal{S}$ into FOL. The semantics of $\mathcal{S}$ is defined as certain models of the first-order theory $\tau(\mathcal{S})$. The formalization adopted here is based on the one presented in [4,12]. For brevity, let $[n] = \{1, \ldots, n\}$, for $n > 0$.

A class C occurring in $\mathcal{C}$ is represented by a unary predicate C, while an attribute a for class C corresponds to a binary predicate a. The attribute assertion $a[i..j] : T$ is translated into:

$$\forall X \forall Y \, (C(X) \wedge a(X, Y) \to T(Y)),$$
$$\forall X \, (C(X) \to \exists Y \, a(X, Y)), \text{ if } i = 1,$$
$$\forall X \forall Y \forall Z \, (C(X) \wedge a(X, Y) \wedge a(X, Z) \to Y = Z), \text{ if } j = 1.$$

The first one asserts that for each instance c of C, an object c' related to c by the attribute a is an instance of T. The second and the third assertions state that for each instance c of C, there exist at least one and at most one different objects, respectively, related to c by a. An operation f, with $m \geqslant 0$ parameters, for class C corresponds to an $(m+2)$-ary predicate f, and the operation assertion $f(T_1, \ldots, T_m) : T$ is translated into:

$$\forall X \forall Y_1 \ldots \forall Y_m \forall Z \, (C(X) \wedge f(X, Y_1, \ldots, Y_m, Z) \to T_i(Y_i)), \text{ for each } i \in [m],$$
$$\forall X \forall Y_1 \ldots \forall Y_m \forall Z \, (C(X) \wedge f(X, Y_1, \ldots, Y_m, Z) \to T(Z)),$$
$$\forall X \forall Y_1 \ldots \forall Y_m \forall Z \forall W \, (C(X) \wedge f(X, Y_1, \ldots, Y_m, Z)$$
$$\wedge f(X, Y_1, \ldots, Y_m, W) \to Z = W).$$

The first two impose the correct typing for the parameters and the result, and the third one asserts that the operation f is a function from the instances of C and the parameters to the result. A class hierarchy, as the one in Figure 2(b), is translated into:

$$\forall X \, (C_i(X) \to C(X)), \text{ for each } i \in [n],$$

---

[3] http://www.omg.org/spec/OCL/

which assert that each instance of C_i is an instance of C. An association A occurring in $\mathcal{C}$ corresponds to a binary predicate A. If A is among classes C_1 and C_2 with multiplicities $m_\ell..m_u$ and $n_\ell..n_u$, then we have the FOL assertions:

$$\forall X \forall Y \, (A(X, Y) \to C_1(X)),$$
$$\forall X \forall Y \, (A(X, Y) \to C_2(Y)),$$
$$\forall X \, (C_1(X) \to \exists Y \, A(X, Y)), \text{ if } n_\ell = 1,$$
$$\forall X \forall Y \forall Z \, (C_1(X) \wedge A(X, Y) \wedge A(X, Z) \to Y = Z), \text{ if } n_u = 1,$$
$$\forall X \, (C_2(X) \to \exists Y \, A(Y, X)), \text{ if } m_\ell = 1,$$
$$\forall X \forall Y \forall Z \, (C_2(X) \wedge A(Y, X) \wedge A(Z, X) \to Y = Z), \text{ if } m_u = 1.$$

An assertion $\{C_1, \ldots, C_n\} \in \mathsf{DISJ}$ is translated into

$$\forall X \, (C_1(X) \wedge \ldots \wedge C_n(X) \to \bot),$$

where $\bot$ denotes the truth constant *false*, while an assertion $(\{C_1, \ldots, C_n\}, C_{n+1}) \in \mathsf{MSC}$ is translated into

$$\forall X \, (C_1(X) \wedge \ldots \wedge C_n(X) \to C_{n+1}(X)).$$

We are now ready to define the semantics of RevEng specifications via FOL. We consider the following pairwise disjoint sets of symbols: a set $\mathbf{C}$ of *constants* and a set $\mathbf{N}$ of *labeled nulls* (used as placeholders for unknown values, and thus can be also seen as globally existentially quantified variables). Different constants represent different values (*unique name assumption*), while different nulls may represent the same value. An *interpretation* $\mathcal{I} = (\Delta, \mu)$ consists of a non-empty *interpretation domain* $\Delta \subseteq \mathbf{C} \cup \mathbf{N}$, and an *interpretation function* μ for a first-order language. Let $\mathcal{S} = (\mathcal{C}, \mathsf{DISJ}, \mathsf{MSC})$ be a RevEng specification. A *UML-model* of $\mathcal{S}$ is an interpretation $\mathcal{I} = (\Delta, \mu)$ such that *(i)* $\mathcal{I}$ satisfies the first-order theory $\tau(\mathcal{S})$, written $\mathcal{I} \models \tau(\mathcal{S})$; and *(ii)* for each $C \in class(\mathcal{C})$, $\mu(C) \neq \varnothing$. The first condition above implies that $\mathcal{I}$ is a *first-order model* (or simply *FO-model*) of the theory $\tau(\mathcal{S})$, while the second condition indicates that each class in $\mathcal{I}$ is non-empty, i.e., an instance of each class exists without violating any of the requirements imposed by the specification.

3   Consistency Check of Diagrams

The fact that RevEng specifications can be translated into FOL allows one to formally check relevant properties so as to assess the quality of a specification to objective quality criteria. The typical property of interest is consistency: a RevEng specification $\mathcal{S}$ is *consistent* if there exists at least one UML-model of $\mathcal{S}$. We proceed to pinpoint the exact complexity of the problem of deciding whether a RevEng specification is consistent.

Fix a RevEng specification $\mathcal{S} = (\mathcal{C}, \mathsf{DISJ}, \mathsf{MSC})$. To check the consistency of $\mathcal{S}$ it suffices to add to the first-order theory $\tau(\mathcal{S})$ a witness for each class of *class*($\mathcal{C}$), and then check whether the obtained theory has at least one FO-model, i.e., is satisfiable. In other words, we can reduce our problem to the satisfiability problem of a first-order theory. Assuming that *class*($\mathcal{C}$) = $\{C_1, \ldots, C_n\}$, let $\mathcal{W_S}$ be the conjunction of atomic formulas $(C_1(c_1) \wedge \ldots \wedge C_n(c_n))$, where $c_1, \ldots, c_n$ are arbitrary constants of **C**, and let $\Phi_\mathcal{S}$ be the sentence $(\mathcal{W_S} \wedge \tau(\mathcal{S}))$. It is not difficult to show that:

Lemma 1. *$\mathcal{S}$ is consistent iff $\Phi_\mathcal{S}$ is satisfiable.*

In the following, we investigate the satisfiability of $\Phi_\mathcal{S}$. Observe that, if $\Phi_\mathcal{S}$ is satisfiable, then it has an FO-model $\mathcal{I} = (\Delta, \mu)$ where $\mu(f) = \varnothing$, for each operation f in $\mathcal{S}$, since the absence of an operation atom cannot lead to a violation of $\Phi_\mathcal{S}$. This implies that the conjuncts that appear in $\tau(\mathcal{S})$ because of an operation assertion are irrelevant for satisfiability purposes and can be safely ignored; in the rest of this section, we exclude from $\tau(\mathcal{S})$ those formulas. By definition, $\tau(\mathcal{S})$ can be equivalently rewritten (by simply reordering its conjuncts) as the conjunction $(\mathcal{X_S} \wedge \mathcal{E_S} \wedge \mathcal{F_S})$, where:

- $\mathcal{X_S}$ is a conjunction of formulas of the form $\forall \mathbf{X} \, (\varphi(\mathbf{X}) \to \exists Y \alpha(\mathbf{X}, Y))$ (possibly without existentially quantified variables);
- $\mathcal{E_S}$ is a conjunction of formulas of the form $\forall \mathbf{X} \, (\varphi(\mathbf{X}) \to X_i = X_j)$; and
- $\mathcal{F_S}$ is a conjunction of formulas of the form $\forall \mathbf{X} \, (\varphi(\mathbf{X}) \to \bot)$.

The following technical result follows immediately:

Lemma 2. *$\Phi_\mathcal{S}$ is satisfiable iff the following hold:*

1. *$(\mathcal{W_S} \wedge \mathcal{X_S} \wedge \mathcal{E_S})$ is satisfiable; and*
2. *there exists an FO-model $\mathcal{I}$ of $(\mathcal{W_S} \wedge \mathcal{X_S} \wedge \mathcal{E_S})$ such that $\mathcal{I} \models \mathcal{F_S}$.*

3.1   A Database-Theoretic Approach

Interestingly, the two decision problems stated in Lemma 2 can be tackled following a database-theoretic approach:

- The conjunction $\mathcal{W_S} = (\alpha_1 \wedge \ldots \wedge \alpha_n)$ can be seen as the relational database $D_\mathcal{S} = \{\alpha_1, \ldots, \alpha_n\}$;
- The conjunction $\mathcal{X_S} = (\sigma_1 \wedge \ldots \wedge \sigma_m)$ can be conceived as the set $T_\mathcal{S} = \{\sigma_1, \ldots, \sigma_m\}$ of *tuple-generating dependencies (TGDs)*;
- The conjunction $\mathcal{E_S} = (\eta_1 \wedge \ldots \wedge \eta_k)$ can be seen as the set $E_\mathcal{S} = \{\eta_1, \ldots, \eta_k\}$ of *equality-generating dependencies (EGDs)*; and
- The conjunction $\mathcal{F_S} = (\nu_1 \wedge \ldots \wedge \nu_\ell)$ can be conceived as the *union of conjunctive queries (UCQs)* $Q_\mathcal{S} = (q_{\nu_1} \vee \ldots \vee q_{\nu_\ell})$, where, assuming that ν is of the form $\forall \mathbf{X} \, (\varphi(\mathbf{X}) \to \bot)$, q_ν is the conjunctive query $\exists \mathbf{X} \, (\varphi(\mathbf{X}))$.

Tuple- and equality-generating dependencies are well-known in the database world as a unifying framework for classical database dependencies such as inclusion and functional dependencies [1], and form the basis of the Datalog$^\pm$ family of KR languages [7]. Conjunctive queries correspond to the select-project-join fragment of relational algebra, and form one of the most natural and commonly used languages for querying relational databases [1].

An FO-model of $(\mathcal{W}_\mathcal{S} \wedge \mathcal{X}_\mathcal{S} \wedge \mathcal{E}_\mathcal{S})$ can be equivalently defined as a relational instance I, called a *model* of $D_\mathcal{S}$ w.r.t. $T_\mathcal{S} \cup E_\mathcal{S}$, such that $I \supseteq D_\mathcal{S}$ and I satisfies $T_\mathcal{S} \cup E_\mathcal{S}$ (written as $I \models T_\mathcal{S} \cup E_\mathcal{S}$); I satisfies $\forall \mathbf{X} (\varphi(\mathbf{X}) \rightarrow \exists Y \alpha(\mathbf{X}, Y))$ if, whenever there exists a homomorphism h such that $h(\varphi(\mathbf{X})) \subseteq I$, then there exists an extension h' of h such that $h(\alpha(\mathbf{X}, Y)) \subseteq I$, while I satisfies $\forall \mathbf{X} (\varphi(\mathbf{X}) \rightarrow X_i = X_j)$ if the existence of h such that $h(\varphi(\mathbf{X})) \subseteq I$ implies $h(X_i) = h(X_j)$. Let $mods(D_\mathcal{S}, T_\mathcal{S} \cup E_\mathcal{S})$ be the set of models of $D_\mathcal{S}$ w.r.t. $T_\mathcal{S} \cup E_\mathcal{S}$. It is clear that $(\mathcal{W}_\mathcal{S} \wedge \mathcal{X}_\mathcal{S} \wedge \mathcal{E}_\mathcal{S})$ is satisfiable iff $mods(D_\mathcal{S}, T_\mathcal{S} \cup E_\mathcal{S}) \neq \varnothing$. A conjunctive query $\exists \mathbf{X} (\varphi(\mathbf{X}))$ is entailed by an instance I if there exists a homomorphism h such that $h(\varphi(\mathbf{X})) \subseteq I$. $Q_\mathcal{S}$ is entailed by I, written $I \models Q_\mathcal{S}$, if at least one of its disjuncts is entailed by I. It is easy to show that there exists an FO-model of $(\mathcal{W}_\mathcal{S} \wedge \mathcal{X}_\mathcal{S} \wedge \mathcal{E}_\mathcal{S})$ that satisfies $\mathcal{F}_\mathcal{S}$ iff the following *does not* hold: for every $I \in mods(D_\mathcal{S}, T_\mathcal{S} \cup E_\mathcal{S})$, $I \models Q_\mathcal{S}$.

In general, $mods(D_\mathcal{S}, T_\mathcal{S} \cup E_\mathcal{S})$ is infinite, and thus not explicitly computable. To overcome this difficulty, we employ a classical algorithmic tool from the database literature called the *chase procedure*, which repairs $D_\mathcal{S}$ w.r.t. $T_\mathcal{S} \cup E_\mathcal{S}$ so that the result, denoted $chase(D_\mathcal{S}, T_\mathcal{S} \cup E_\mathcal{S})$, satisfies $T_\mathcal{S} \cup E_\mathcal{S}$. It works on $D_\mathcal{S}$ through the $\exists$-*chase step*, which aims at satisfying TGDs by adding atoms, and the $=$-*chase step*, which aims at satisfying EGDs by unifying terms; if constants of $\mathbf{C}$ must be unified, then we have a *hard violation* of an EGD and the chase *fails*; for details, see, e.g., [6]. It is implicit in [10] that $mods(D_\mathcal{S}, T_\mathcal{S} \cup E_\mathcal{S}) \neq \varnothing$ iff $chase(D_\mathcal{S}, T_\mathcal{S} \cup E_\mathcal{S})$ does not fail. Moreover, if $chase(D_\mathcal{S}, T_\mathcal{S} \cup E_\mathcal{S})$ does not fail, then $chase(D_\mathcal{S}, T_\mathcal{S} \cup E_\mathcal{S})$ is a *universal model* of $D_\mathcal{S}$ w.r.t. $T_\mathcal{S} \cup E_\mathcal{S}$, i.e., for each $I \in mods(D_\mathcal{S}, T_\mathcal{S} \cup E_\mathcal{S})$, there exists a homomorphism h such that $h(chase(D_\mathcal{S}, T_\mathcal{S} \cup E_\mathcal{S})) \subseteq I$. The next technical result can be established.

Lemma 3. *It holds that:*

1. $(\mathcal{W}_\mathcal{S} \wedge \mathcal{X}_\mathcal{S} \wedge \mathcal{E}_\mathcal{S})$ *is satisfiable iff* $chase(D_\mathcal{S}, T_\mathcal{S} \cup E_\mathcal{S})$ *does not fail; and*
2. *there exists an FO-model* $\mathcal{I}$ *of* $(\mathcal{W}_\mathcal{S} \wedge \mathcal{X}_\mathcal{S} \wedge \mathcal{E}_\mathcal{S})$ *such that* $\mathcal{I} \models \mathcal{F}_\mathcal{S}$ *iff* $chase(D_\mathcal{S}, T_\mathcal{S} \cup E_\mathcal{S}) \not\models Q_\mathcal{S}$.

Thus, the above lemma, combined with Lemmas 1 and 2, suggests the following:

Corollary 1. $\mathcal{S}$ *is consistent iff the following hold:*

1. $chase(D_\mathcal{S}, T_\mathcal{S} \cup E_\mathcal{S})$ *does not fail; and*
2. $chase(D_\mathcal{S}, T_\mathcal{S} \cup E_\mathcal{S}) \not\models Q_\mathcal{S}$.

3.2 Chase Failure

It can be shown that $E_\mathcal{S}$ can be safely ignored and proceed only with $T_\mathcal{S}$. In particular, we can show that the initial segment of $chase(D_\mathcal{S}, T_\mathcal{S})$ obtained starting from D_S and applying the $\exists$-chase step i times, satisfies E_S, for each $i \geqslant 0$; this can be established by induction on i. Therefore, during the construction of $chase(D_S, T_S \cup E_S)$ the $=$-chase step is not applied, and the next lemma follows:

Lemma 4. $chase(D_S, T_S \cup E_S) = chase(D_S, T_S)$.

As an immediate consequence we get that:

Proposition 1. $chase(D_S, T_S \cup E_S)$ does not fail.

3.3 Query Entailment

Although the problem of deciding whether the chase fails is trivial, the problem of deciding whether $chase(D_S, T_S \cup E_S) \not\models Q_S$ is rather challenging. By Lemma 4, we can focus on the problem of deciding whether $chase(D_S, T_S) \not\models Q_S$. It turned out that it is more convenient to study the complement of the problem under consideration. We present a novel nondeterministic algorithm which decides whether $chase(D_S, T_S) \models Q_S$. Before we proceed further, let us give some auxiliary terminology. We denote by $I\langle\sigma, h\rangle I'$ a single $\exists$-chase step, which means that during the chase we apply the TGD σ of the form $\forall \mathbf{X}\, (\varphi(\mathbf{X}) \rightarrow \exists Y\, \alpha(\mathbf{X}, Y))$ due to the existence of a homomorphism h such that $h(\varphi(\mathbf{X})) \subseteq I$, and $I' = I \cup h'(\alpha(\mathbf{X}, Y))$, where h' is an extension of h, and $h'(Y)$ is a "fresh" null of $\mathbf{N}$. Interestingly, the TGDs of T_S enjoy a crucial syntactic property: for each $\sigma \in T_S$, the left-hand side of σ, denoted $body(\sigma)$, has a *guard* atom, denoted $guard(\sigma)$, that contains all the universally quantified variables of σ; such TGDs are known as *guarded* TGDs [6]. The guarded chase forest is a tree-like representation of the instance constructed by the chase; the formal definition follows:

Definition 1. *The* guarded chase forest *of D_S and T_S, denoted* $\mathsf{gcf}(D_S, T_S)$, *is a labeled directed forest (N, E, λ), where $\lambda : N \rightarrow chase(D_S, T_S)$, defined as follows: (i) for each $\alpha \in D_S$, there exists exactly one $v \in N$ with $\lambda_1(v) = \alpha$; (ii) for each step $I\langle\sigma, h\rangle I'$ applied during the construction of $chase(D_S, T_S)$: for every atom $\alpha \in \{h(guard(\sigma))\} \cup (I' \setminus I)$, there exists exactly one node $v \in N$ such that $\lambda(v) = \alpha$, and for every $\alpha \in I' \setminus I$, there exists an edge $(v, u) \in E$, where $\lambda(v) = h(guard(\sigma))$ and $\lambda(u) = \alpha$; and (iii) no other nodes and edges occur in N and E, respectively. Let $\mathsf{gcf}^k(D_S, T_S)$ be the initial part of $\mathsf{gcf}(D_S, T_S)$ up to depth $k \geqslant 0$.* □

Based on $\mathsf{gcf}(D_S, T_S)$ we define the notion of the guarded chase of D_S and T_S up to a certain depth:

Definition 2. *The* guarded chase *of D_S and T_S of depth up to $k \geqslant 0$ is the instance* $gchase^k(D_S, T_S) = \{\lambda(v)\}_{v \in N^k}$ *assuming that* $\mathsf{gcf}^k(D_S, T_S) = (N^k, E, \lambda)$. □

Interestingly, for our purposes, we can focus on an initial part of the guarded chase; the following is implicit in [6]:

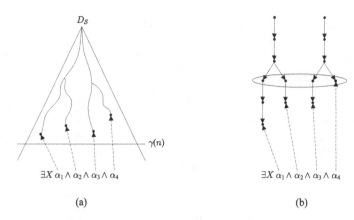

Fig. 3. Proof of a disjunct of Q_S

Lemma 5. *There exists $\gamma(n) \in \mathcal{O}(2^n)$, where n is the number of predicates in T_S, such that $chase(D_S, T_S) \models Q_S$ iff $gchase^{\gamma(n)}(D_S, T_S) \models Q_S$.*

Therefore, one can simply build $gchase^{\gamma(n)}(D_S, T_S)$, and then check whether there exists a homomorphism that maps at least one disjunct of Q_S to it. This naive approach shows that our problem is in 2EXPTIME. However, this upper bound is not optimal. A more clever procedure, which needs only polynomial space, can be designed. Let us first give an informal description of this procedure.

An Informal Description. Assume that Q_S is entailed by $chase(D_S, T_S)$. By Lemma 5, there exists a disjunct q of Q_S that can be mapped via a homomorphism h to $gchase^{\gamma(n)}(D_S, T_S)$. Let P be the subforest of $gcf^{\gamma(n)}(D_S, T_S)$ that is obtained by keeping only the paths from the root nodes to the nodes which are labeled by the atoms of $h(q)$; in other words, P is the proof of q w.r.t. D_S and T_S. Observe that, for each $0 \leqslant i \leqslant \gamma(n)$, the number of nodes occurring at the i-th level of P is at most $|q|$, i.e., the number of conjuncts in q. An abstract example is depicted in Figure 3 — the general shape of the subforest P is given in (a), while its actual structure is shown in (b). It is clear that at each level of P, at most $|q|$ atoms may appear; e.g., in the third level (see shaded nodes) there are exactly $|q|$ atoms. The key idea underlying our algorithm is to nondeterministically construct, in a *level-by-level* fashion, the atoms of each level of P until we reach $h(q)$. In other words, our intention is to generate, by applying some $\exists$-chase steps, the $(i+1)$-th level of P from the i-th level of P, and thus we do not need to store more than $2 \cdot |q|$ atoms at each step. A crucial notion, necessary for this construction, is the type of an atom which is defined as follows:

Definition 3. *The* type *of an atom $\alpha \in chase(D_S, T_S)$, denoted $type(\alpha, D_S, T_S)$ (or simply $type(\alpha)$), is the set of atoms of the form $C(t)$, where $C \in class(S)$[4], occurring in $chase(D_S, T_S)$ such that t appears in α.* □

---

[4] By abuse of notation, we refer to the set of classes occurring in the UCD of the specification S by $class(S)$.

Let us explain the importance of the notion of type. Consider a node v occurring at the i-th level of P which is labeled by the atom α. Assume now that there exists a TGD $\sigma \in T_S$ such that $guard(\sigma)$ is mapped via a homomorphism μ to α, and also μ maps the rest of the body of σ, denoted φ_σ, to $chase(D_S, T_S)$. This implies that v has a child node u at the $(i+1)$-th level of P which is labeled by the atom obtained after applying σ. Since the TGD σ is guarded, all the variables occurring in $guard(\sigma)$ appear also in φ_σ, and thus μ necessarily maps φ_σ to $type(\alpha)$. From the above informal discussion, we conclude that the level-by-level construction proposed above is feasible, providing that we are also able to construct the type of the generated atoms. Notice that, at each step of the procedure, apart from the $2 \cdot |q|$ atoms, we also need to store their types. However, the size of the type of an atom is at most the cardinality of $class(S)$, and thus overall we need only polynomial space. In what follows, we discuss in depth how the type of an atom can be effectively computed, and we formalize the level-by-level construction sketched above.

Computing the Type of an Atom. In general, the problem of computing the type of an atom is not easier than the problem of query entailment itself. However, in our case, it is possible to construct the type of an atom $\alpha \in chase(D_S, T_S)$ by exploiting α and the type of its parent in the guarded chase forest. Let us first formally define what we mean by saying the type of the parent of an atom in the guarded chase forest. To this end, we need the notion of the parent-type function defined as follows:

Definition 4. *The* parent-type function pt *from* $chase(D_S, T_S)$ *to* $2^{chase(D_S, T_S)}$ *is defined as follows:*

$$pt(\alpha) = \begin{cases} \varnothing, & \alpha \in D_S, \\ type(h(guard(\sigma))), & I\langle \sigma, h\rangle(I \cup \{\alpha\}). \end{cases}$$

Let also $pt^+(\alpha) = \{\alpha\} \cup pt(\alpha)$. □

We also need the notion of the distinguished term of an atom $\alpha \in chase(D_S, T_S)$, which is crucial for the computation of $type(\alpha)$. In fact, to compute $type(\alpha)$, it suffices to add to the common part between the type of α and the type of its parent the atoms of $chase(D_S, T_S)$ which contain only the distinguished term of α.

Definition 5. *The* distinguished term *of an atom* $\alpha \in chase(D_S, T_S)$, *denoted* $d(\alpha)$, *is defined as follows: if* $\alpha = C(t)$, *where* $C \in class(S)$, *then* $d(\alpha) = t$; *otherwise*, $d(\alpha)$ *is the null of* $\mathbf{N}$ *invented in* α. □

Finally, we define the so-called projection set of T_S, which will allows us to complete the common part between the type of α and the type of its parent, and thus computing $type(\alpha)$, by starting from $pt^+(\alpha)$. Let $A[i]$, where $i \in \{1, 2\}$, be an auxiliary predicate which is used to store the projection to the i-th argument of the predicate A.

Input: An atom α, an instance I, a term t, a specification $\mathcal{S}$.
Output: A finite instance.

1. $J := \varnothing$.
2. $K := chase((\{\alpha\} \cup I)_\downarrow, T_{\mathcal{S}}^\pi)$.
3. For each $C \in class(\mathcal{S})$: if $C(t)_\downarrow \in K$, then $J := J \cup \{C(t)\}$.
4. If $\alpha = C(t)$, where $C \in class(\mathcal{S})$, then return J; otherwise, return $(I_{|t'} \cup J)$, where $t' \neq t$ and t' occurs in α.

Fig. 4. The Procedure Type

Definition 6. *Consider a TGD $\sigma \in T_{\mathcal{S}}$ of the form $\varphi \to \alpha$, and an atom β occurring in σ. If $\beta = A(X,Y)$, where A is an association class, and the variable X (resp., Y) occurs in both φ and α, then $\tau_\pi(\beta,\sigma) = A[1](X)$ (resp., $A[2](Y)$); otherwise, $\tau_\pi(\beta,\sigma) = \beta$. The projection set of $T_{\mathcal{S}}$, denoted $T_{\mathcal{S}}^\pi$, is obtained as follows: for each $\sigma \in T_{\mathcal{S}}$ of the form $\varphi \to \alpha$ where the predicate of α is either a class or an association, and for each atom β in σ, replace β by $\tau_\pi(\beta,\sigma)$.* $\square$

An example of a projection set follows:

Example 1. Let $\mathcal{S} = (\mathcal{C}, \varnothing, \varnothing)$, where $\mathcal{C}$ is the diagram in Figure 2(c) with $n_\ell..n_u = m_\ell..m_u = 1..\infty$, expressing that there is an association A between the classes C_1 and C_2, and each instance of C_1 and C_2 participates at least once in A. $T_{\mathcal{S}}^\pi$ is as follows:

$$\forall X \ (C_1(X) \to \exists Y \ \tau_\pi(A(X,Y))) = \forall X \ (C_1(X) \to A[1](X)),$$
$$\forall X \ (C_2(X) \to \exists Y \ \tau_\pi(A(Y,X))) = \forall X \ (C_2(X) \to A[2](X)),$$
$$\forall X \forall Y \ (\tau_\pi(A(X,Y)) \to C_1(X)) = \forall X \ (A[1](X) \to C_1(X)),$$
$$\forall X \forall Y \ (\tau_\pi(A(X,Y)) \to C_2(Y)) = \forall Y \ (A[2](Y) \to C_2(Y)).$$

For brevity, the second parameter of τ_π is omitted. $\square$

We are now ready to give our key technical lemma. Henceforth, given an atom α, we denote by $\alpha_\downarrow$ the atom obtained by *freezing* α, i.e., replacing each null $z \in \mathbf{N}$ occurring in α with a new constant $c_z \in \mathbf{C}$; this notation naturally extends to sets of atoms.

Lemma 6. *For each atom $\alpha \in chase(D_{\mathcal{S}}, T_{\mathcal{S}})$, and for each class $C \in class(\mathcal{S})$, $C(d(\alpha)) \in chase(D_{\mathcal{S}}, T_{\mathcal{S}})$ iff $C(d(\alpha))_\downarrow \in chase(pt^+(\alpha)_\downarrow, T_{\mathcal{S}}^\pi)$.*

The crucial observation in the proof of the above lemma is that in a chase derivation from an atom $\alpha \in chase(D_{\mathcal{S}}, T_{\mathcal{S}})$ to an atom $C(d(\alpha)) \in chase(D_{\mathcal{S}}, T_{\mathcal{S}})$, it is not possible to lose and reintroduce the term $d(\alpha)$; this is because of the fact that the TGDs of $T_{\mathcal{S}}$ are guarded. Therefore, the TGDs that are involved in such a chase derivation are neither of the form $\forall X \ (C'(X) \to \exists Y \ a(X,Y))$ nor of the form $\forall X \forall Y \ (C'(X) \wedge a(X,Y) \to T(Y))$; otherwise, we immediately get a contradiction. Moreover, these TGDs are contributing in such a chase derivation only by projecting out the term $d(\alpha)$; this justifies the definition of $T_{\mathcal{S}}^{\pi}$. Based on Lemma 6, we design the procedure Type, depicted in Figure 4, which computes the type of an atom α by adding to the part of $pt(\alpha)$ that contains only the non-distinguished term t' of α, denoted as $pt(\alpha)_{|t'}$, the set of atoms $J = \{C(d(\alpha)) \mid C \in class(\mathcal{S}) \text{ and } C(d(\alpha)) \in chase(D_{\mathcal{S}}, T_{\mathcal{S}})\}$; clearly, $(pt_{|t'} \cup J) = type(\alpha)$. Since each TGD of $T_{\mathcal{S}}^{\pi}$ does not contain an existentially quantified variable, and also its size is fixed, $chase(pt^+(\alpha)_{\downarrow}, T_{\mathcal{S}}^{\pi})$ is finite and can be constructed in polynomial time in the size of $pt^+(\alpha)_{\downarrow}$. The instance $pt^+(\alpha)_{\downarrow}$ is of polynomial size, and thus $chase(pt^+(\alpha)_{\downarrow}, T_{\mathcal{S}}^{\pi})$ can be constructed in polynomial time; hence, the second step of Type terminates after polynomially steps.

Proposition 2. *For each atom* $\alpha \in chase(D_{\mathcal{S}}, T_{\mathcal{S}})$,

1. $\mathsf{Type}(\alpha, pt(\alpha), d(\alpha), \mathcal{S}) = type(\alpha)$; *and*
2. $\mathsf{Type}(\alpha, pt(\alpha), d(\alpha), \mathcal{S})$ *terminates after polynomially many steps.*

The Level-by-level Construction. We have now all the necessary ingredients in order to proceed with our novel algorithm for deciding whether $chase(D_{\mathcal{S}}, T_{\mathcal{S}}) \models Q_{\mathcal{S}}$. The main idea, as sketchily described above, is to nondeterministically construct, in a level-by-level fashion, a segment of $gchase^{\gamma(n)}(D_{\mathcal{S}}, T_{\mathcal{S}})$, which contains at most as many atoms as the biggest disjunct q of $Q_{\mathcal{S}}$, and then check whether there exists a homomorphism that maps q to it. During this procedure, we can compute the children of a node v by exploiting the instance $type(\alpha)$, where α is the label of v, and then forget v and its type. Moreover, the type of an atom α can be constructed by exploiting $pt^+(\alpha)$ and the procedure Type. The formal algorithm, called Ent (which stands for entailment), is depicted in Figure 5. Note that D and D' are vectors that hold integer numbers and are used to store the depth of the generated atoms, while P and P' are vectors that hold sets of atoms and are to store the types of the generated atoms. Moreover, $\gamma(n)$ is the bound on the depth of $gcf(D_{\mathcal{S}}, T_{\mathcal{S}})$ provided by Lemma 5. A simple example of the execution of Ent follows:

Example 2. Let $S = (\mathcal{C}, \{T_1, T_3\}, \varnothing)$, where $\mathcal{C}$ is the RevEng UCD in Figure 6. The forest $gcf(D_{\mathcal{S}}, T_{\mathcal{S}})$ is depicted in Figure 6 (for brevity, the atoms $T_1(c_4), T_2(c_5)$ and $T_2(c_6)$ are not shown). A possible execution of $\mathsf{Ent}(\mathcal{S})$, which explores in a level-by-level fashion the shaded nodes of $gcf(D_{\mathcal{S}}, T_{\mathcal{S}})$, is as follows:

- We choose $(S_1, \prec_1)$ to be $(\{C_3(c_3)\}, \varnothing)$, and the type of $C_3(c_3)$ is stored in P_1;
- We construct $(S_2, \prec_2) = (\{a(c_3, z_3)\}, \varnothing)$ from $C_3(c_3)$ by applying $\forall X (C_3(X) \to \exists Y\, a(X, Y))$, and the type of $a(c_3, z_3)$ is stored in P'_1;
- We assign $(S_2, \prec_2)$ to $(S_1, \prec_1)$ and P'_1 to P_1 — this means that we forget the atom $C_3(c_3)$ and its type;
- We construct $(S_2, \prec_2) = (\{T_1(z_3), T_3(z_3)\}, T_1(z_3) \prec_2 T_3(z_3))$ from the atom $a(c_3, z_3)$ by applying the TGDs $\forall X \forall Y (C_1(X) \wedge a(X, Y) \to T_1(Y))$ and $\forall X \forall Y (C_3(X) \wedge a(X, Y) \to T_3(Y))$ (notice that the crucial atoms $C_1(c_3)$

Input: A RevEng specification $\mathcal{S}$.
Output: yes if $chase(D_{\mathcal{S}}, T_{\mathcal{S}}) \models Q_{\mathcal{S}}$; otherwise, no.

1. Guess a disjunct q of $Q_{\mathcal{S}}$.
2. $Image := \varnothing$ and $L := \{z_1, \ldots, z_k\} \subset \mathbf{N}$, where $k = 2 \cdot |q|$.
3. Guess a totally ordered set $(S_1, \prec_1)$, where $S_1 \subseteq D_{\mathcal{S}}$ and $|S_1| \in \{1, \ldots, |q|\}$; assume that
   $\alpha_1 \prec_1 \ldots \prec_1 \alpha_m$.
4. For each $i \in [|S_1|]$: $D[i] := 0$ and $P[i] := \mathsf{Type}(\alpha_i, \varnothing, c, \mathcal{S})$, where c is the constant in α_i.
5. Guess a set of atoms $I \subseteq S_1$; $Image := Image \cup I$.
6. If $|Image| = |q|$, then goto 15.
7. Guess to proceed with the next step or goto 15.
8. Construct a totally ordered set $(S_2, \prec_2)$ as follows:
   a. $(S_2, \prec_2) := (\varnothing, \varnothing)$ and $ctr := 1$.
   b. Guess $\sigma = (\varphi \rightarrow \exists Y \alpha) \in T_{\mathcal{S}}$ for which there exists $i \in [|S_1|]$ and a homomorphism h
      such that
      – $h(guard(\sigma)) = \alpha_i$,
      – $D[i] < \gamma(n)$, and
      – $h(body(\sigma) \setminus \{guard(\sigma)\}) \subseteq P_i$;
      if there is no such σ, then $\sigma := \epsilon$.
   c. If $\sigma \neq \epsilon$, then do the following:
      – $\beta_{ctr} := h'(\alpha)$, where $h' := h \cup \{Y \rightarrow t \mid t \in L$ and t does not occur in $S_1 \cup S_2\}$.
      – $S_2 := S_2 \cup \{\beta_{ctr}\}$.
      – If $ctr > 1$, then $\beta_{ctr-1} \prec_2 \beta_{ctr}$.
      – $D'[ctr] := D[i] + 1$.
      – $P'[ctr] := \mathsf{Type}(\beta_{ctr}, P[i], h'(Y), \mathcal{S})$.
      – $ctr := ctr + 1$.
   d. If $|S_2| = |q|$ or $\sigma = \epsilon$, then goto 9.
   e. Guess to proceed to the next step or goto 8b.
9. Guess a set $I \subseteq S_2$; $Image := Image \cup I$.
10. If $|Image| = |q|$, then goto 15.
11. Guess to proceed to the next step or goto 15.
12. $(S_1, \prec_1) := (S_2, \prec_2)$; assume that $\alpha_1 \prec_1 \ldots \prec_1 \alpha_m$.
13. $D := D'$ and $P := P'$.
14. Goto 8.
15. If there exists h such that $h(q) \subseteq Image$, then return yes; otherwise, return no.

Fig. 5. The Nondeterministic Algorithm Ent

and $C_3(c_3)$ occur in $type(a(c_3, z_3)))$, and the type of $T_1(z_3)$ and $T_3(z_3)$ are
stored in P_1' and P_2', respectively; and
– Finally, we choose to assign $\{T_1(z_3), T_3(z_3)\}$ to $Image$, and then check
  whether there exists a homomorphism that maps $Q_{\mathcal{S}}$ to $Image$.

Clearly, since such a homomorphism exists, the algorithm returns yes, which in
turn implies that $chase(D_{\mathcal{S}}, T_{\mathcal{S}}) \models Q_{\mathcal{S}}$. $\qquad\square$

By construction, $\mathsf{Ent}(\mathcal{S}) = yes$ iff $gchase^{\gamma(n)}(D_{\mathcal{S}}, T_{\mathcal{S}}) \models Q_{\mathcal{S}}$, where $\gamma(n)$ is
the bound provided by Lemma 5, which in turn is equivalent to $chase(D_{\mathcal{S}}, T_{\mathcal{S}}) \models Q_{\mathcal{S}}$. Let us now analyze the space complexity of our algorithm. During the
execution of $\mathsf{Ent}(\mathcal{S})$ we need to maintain the following:

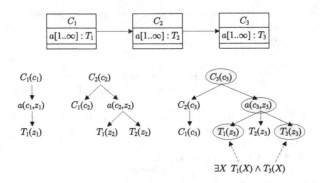

Fig. 6. Execution of the Algorithm Ent

1. The totally ordered sets $(S_1, \prec_1)$ and $(S_2, \prec_2)$;
2. The vectors D, D', P and P'; and
3. The set of atoms *Image*.

It is possible to show that the above structures need $\mathcal{O}(m^3 \cdot \log m)$ space, where $m = |class(\mathcal{S})|$. By Proposition 2, the computation of the types at steps 4 and 8 is feasible in polynomial time, and thus in polynomial space. Finally, since the problem of deciding whether there exists a homomorphism from a query to an instance is feasible in NP (and thus a fortiori in PSPACE), we get that step 15 is feasible in polynomial space. The next result follows:

Proposition 3. *It holds that,*

1. Ent$(\mathcal{S}) = yes$ *iff* $chase(D_{\mathcal{S}}, T_{\mathcal{S}}) \models Q_{\mathcal{S}}$; *and*
2. *Each step of the computation of* Ent$(\mathcal{S})$ *uses polynomial space.*

3.4   Pinpointing the Complexity

By using the results established in the previous section, we can now pinpoint the computational complexity of the problem of deciding whether $\mathcal{S}$ is consistent.

Upper Bound. By Corollary 1 and Proposition 1, we conclude that $\mathcal{S}$ is consistent iff $chase(D_{\mathcal{S}}, T_{\mathcal{S}}) \not\models Q_{\mathcal{S}}$. Since Ent describes a nondeterministic algorithm, Proposition 3 implies that the problem of deciding whether $chase(D_{\mathcal{S}}, T_{\mathcal{S}}) \models Q_{\mathcal{S}}$, that is, the complement of the problem under consideration, is in NPSPACE, and thus in PSPACE since NPSPACE = PSPACE. But PSPACE = coPSPACE, and therefore:

Theorem 1. *The problem of deciding whether* $\mathcal{S}$ *is consistent is in* PSPACE.

Lower Bound. We show that the upper bound established above is tight. This is done by simulating a polynomial space Turing machine (TM) by means of a RevEng specification. Consider a TM $M = (S, \Lambda, \delta, s_0, F)$, where S is the set of states, Λ is the tape alphabet, $\delta : S \setminus F \times \Lambda \to S \times \Lambda \times \{-1, 0, 1\}$ is the transition

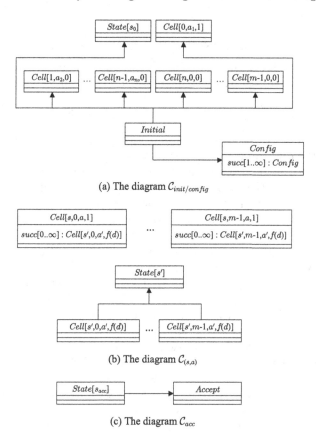

(a) The diagram $\mathcal{C}_{init/config}$

(b) The diagram $\mathcal{C}_{(s,a)}$

(c) The diagram $\mathcal{C}_{acc}$

Fig. 7. Simulating a polynomial space TM

function, s_0 is the initial state, and $F \subseteq S$ is the set of final or accepting states. We assume w.l.o.g. that M has exactly one accepting state, denoted as s_{acc}. We also assume that $\Lambda = \{0, 1\}$, and that each input string has an 1 as the rightmost bit. Consider the computation of M on an input string $I = a_1 a_2 \ldots a_n$, and suppose that it halts using $m = n^k$ cells, where $k > 0$. We shall construct a RevEng specification $\mathcal{S} = (\mathcal{C}, \mathsf{DISJ}, \mathsf{MSC})$ such that M accepts I iff $\mathcal{S}$ is not consistent; this shows that the complement of our problem is PSPACE-hard, and thus also our problem is PSPACE-hard.

The initial configuration of M is reflected by the class diagram $\mathcal{C}_{init/config}$ in Figure 7(a). Roughly, $Initial(c)$ states that c is the initial configuration, $State[s](c)$ asserts that the state of the configuration c is s, and $Cell[i, x, y](c)$ says that in the configuration c the i-th cell contains x, and the cursor is on the i-th cell iff $y = 1$.

The auxiliary classes $Cell[s, i, x, y]$, where $(s, i, x, y) \in S \times \{0, \ldots, m - 1\} \times \{0, 1\} \times \{0, 1\}$, are needed in order to describe the configuration transition via a RevEng class diagram. Roughly,

$$Cell[i, x, y](c) \land State[s](c) \rightarrow Cell[s, i, x, y](c),$$

which is formally defined using the set MSC_{state} of most specific class assertions consisting of: for each $(s, i, x, y) \in S \times \{0, \ldots, m-1\} \times \{0, 1\} \times \{0, 1\}$,

$$(\{Cell[i, x, y], State[s]\}, Cell[s, i, x, y]).$$

The fact that each configuration has a valid configuration as a successor is captured by the diagram $\mathcal{C}_{init/config}$, shown in Figure 7(a); $Config(c)$ expresses that c is a valid configuration, while $succ(c, c')$ states that c' is derived from c.

We now show how the configuration transition can be simulated. Consider an arbitrary pair $(s, a) \in S \setminus F \times \{0, 1\}$, and assume that $\delta((s, a)) = (s', a', d')$. The state transition, as well as the updating of the tape, is reflected by the diagram $\mathcal{C}_{(s,a)}$, shown in Figure 7(b); notice that $f(0) = 1$ and $f(-1) = f(1) = 0$. Eventually, the configuration transition is achieved by the diagram $\mathcal{C}_{trans}$, which is obtained by merging the diagrams $\{\mathcal{C}_{(s,a)}\}_{(s,a) \in S \setminus F \times \{0,1\}}$. It should not be forgotten that those cells which are not changed during the transition keep their old values. This can be ensured by a RevEng UCD, and a set of most specific class constraints. Finally, with the diagram $\mathcal{C}_{acc}$, shown in Figure 7(c), we say that M accepts if it reaches the accepting state.

We define $\mathcal{S}$ to be the specification $(\mathcal{C}, \mathsf{DISJ}, \mathsf{MSC})$, where $\mathcal{C}$ is the UCD obtained by merging the diagrams introduced above, DISJ consists of the single assertion $\{Initial, Accept\}$, and MSC consists of the most specific class assertions introduced above. It is easy to verify that $\mathcal{S}$ is a RevEng specification, and that can be constructed in polynomial time. By providing an inductive argument, we can show that M accepts I iff $chase(D_\mathcal{S}, T_\mathcal{S}) \models Q_\mathcal{S}$ iff $\mathcal{S}$ is inconsistent, and the next result follows:

Theorem 2. *The problem of deciding whether $\mathcal{S}$ is consistent is* PSPACE*-hard*[5].

The following complexity characterization follows from Theorems 1 and 2:

Corollary 2. *The problem of deciding whether $\mathcal{S}$ is consistent is* PSPACE-*complete.*

4   Conclusions

In this work, we focus on the fragment of UML class diagrams that can be recovered from an implemented system. We study the problem of consistency of such diagrams, and we show that is PSPACE-complete. Interestingly, the upper bound is obtained by exploiting algorithmic techniques developed for conjunctive

---

[5] An alternative way to establish this result is by adapting the construction in the proof of an analogous result for the description logic Horn-$\mathcal{FL}^-$ [13]. However, the resulting diagram is counterintuitive, and does not give any insights about the inherent difficulty of RevEng UCDs. For this reason, and also for self-containedness, we provide a new proof from first principles.

query answering under guarded Datalog$^\pm$, that is, a key member of the Datalog$^\pm$ family of KR languages. Although the proposed consistency algorithm is theoretically interesting, and allows us to establish a worst-case optimal upper bound for the problem under investigation, it is not very well-suited for a practical implementation. It is unlikely that it will lead to procedures that guarantee the required level of scalability, especially in the presence of very large diagrams. The designing of a more practical consistency algorithm, which will exploit existing database technology, will be the subject of future research.

Acknowledgements. This research has received funding from the EPSRC Programme Grant EP/M025268/ "VADA".

References

1. Abiteboul, S., Hull, R., Vianu, V.: Foundations of Databases. Addison-Wesley (1995)
2. Baader, F., Brandt, S., Lutz, C.: Pushing the $\mathcal{EL}$ envelope. In: Proc. of IJCAI, pp. 364–369 (2005)
3. Balaban, M., Maraee, A.: Finite satisfiability of UML class diagrams with constrained class hierarchy. ACM Trans. Softw. Eng. Methodol. **22**(3) (2013)
4. Berardi, D., Calvanese, D., De Giacomo, G.: Reasoning on UML class diagrams. Artif. Intell. **168**(1–2), 70–118 (2005)
5. Calì, A., Gottlob, G., Kifer, M.: Taming the infinite chase: Query answering under expressive relational constraints. J. Artif. Intell. Res. **48**, 115–174 (2013)
6. Calì, A., Gottlob, G., Lukasiewicz, T.: A general Datalog-based framework for tractable query answering over ontologies. J. Web Sem. **14**, 57–83 (2012)
7. Calì, A., Gottlob, G., Lukasiewicz, T., Marnette, B., Pieris, A.: Datalog+/-: a family of logical knowledge representation and query languages for new applications. In: Proc. of LICS, pp. 228–242 (2010)
8. Calì, A., Gottlob, G., Orsi, G., Pieris, A.: Querying UML class diagrams. In: Birkedal, L. (ed.) FOSSACS 2012. LNCS, vol. 7213, pp. 1–25. Springer, Heidelberg (2012)
9. Calvanese, D., De Giacomo, G., Lembo, D., Lenzerini, M., Rosati, R.: Tractable reasoning and efficient query answering in description logics: The DL-Lite family. J. Autom. Reasoning **39**(3), 385–429 (2007)
10. Fagin, R., Kolaitis, P.G., Miller, R.J., Popa, L.: Data exchange: Semantics and query answering. Theor. Comput. Sci. **336**(1), 89–124 (2005)
11. Johnson, D.S., Klug, A.C.: Testing containment of conjunctive queries under functional and inclusion dependencies. J. Comput. Syst. Sci. **28**(1), 167–189 (1984)
12. Kaneiwa, K., Satoh, K.: On the complexities of consistency checking for restricted UML class diagrams. Theor. Comput. Sci. **411**(2), 301–323 (2010)
13. Krötzsch, M., Rudolph, S., Hitzler, P.: Complexities of horn description logics. ACM Trans. Comput. Log. **14**(1), 2 (2013)
14. Müller, H.A., Jahnke, J.H., Smith, D.B., Storey, M., Tilley, S.R., Wong, K.: Reverse engineering: a roadmap. In: Proc. of ICSE, pp. 47–60 (2000)

A Brief Overview of Rule Learning

Johannes Fürnkranz[1] and Tomáš Kliegr[2]([✉])

[1] Department of Computer Science, TU Darmstadt, Hochschulstraße 10,
64289 Darmstadt, Germany
juffi@ke.informatik.tu-darmstadt.de

[2] Department of Information and Knowledge Engineering, University of Economics,
Prague, nám. Winstona Churchilla 4, 13067 Prague, Czech Republic
tomas.kliegr@vse.cz

Abstract. In this paper, we provide a brief summary of elementary research in rule learning. The two main research directions are descriptive rule learning, with the goal of discovering regularities that hold in parts of the given dataset, and predictive rule learning, which aims at generalizing the given dataset so that predictions on new data can be made. We briefly review key learning tasks such as association rule learning, subgroup discovery, and the covering learning algorithm, along with their most important prototypes. The paper also highlights recent work in rule learning on the Semantic Web and Linked Data as an important application area.

1 Introduction

Rule-based methods are a popular class of techniques in machine learning and data mining [19]. They share the goal of finding regularities in data that can be expressed in the form of an IF-THEN rule. Depending on the type of rule that should be found, we can discriminate between *descriptive rule discovery*, which aims at describing significant patterns in the given dataset in terms of rules, and *predictive rule learning*. In the latter case, one is often also interesting in learning a collection of the rules that collectively cover the instance space in the sense that they can make a prediction for every possible instance. In the following, we will briefly introduce both tasks and point out some key works in this area.

While in some application areas rule learning algorithms are superseded by statistical approaches such as Support Vector Machines (SVMs). An emerging use case for rule learning is the Semantic Web, whose representation is built on rule-based formalisms. We give a brief overview of recent papers in this domain, focusing on algorithms for completing large linked open data knowledge bases, such as DBpedia or YAGO.

This paper is organized as follows. Section 2 covers descriptive rule discovery algorithms, with emphasis on subgroup discovery and association rule mining. Section 3 discusses predictive rule discovery. This section includes the topic of classification by association rules, providing a connection to descriptive rule learning. The seminal algorithms of the rule learning field, including RIPPER

© Springer International Publishing Switzerland 2015
N. Bassiliades et al. (Eds.): RuleML 2015, LNCS 9202, pp. 54–69, 2015.
DOI: 10.1007/978-3-319-21542-6_4

and CN2, are presented in Section 4. Section 5 focuses on recent work in rule learning on the Semantic Web and Linked Data. The conclusion highlights some advantages of rule learning compared to its arguably biggest rival – decision tree learning, and points at emerging research in the linked data domain.

2 Descriptive Rule Discovery

In descriptive rule discovery, the key emphasis lies on finding rules that describe patterns and regularities that can be observed in a given dataset. In contrast to predictive rule learning (Section 3), the focus lies on finding individual rules. Consequently, evaluation does typically not focus on predictive performance, but on the statistical validity of the found rules. Predominant in the literature are two main tasks, namely subgroup discovery, where a given property of interest is analyzed (supervised learning), and association rule discovery, where arbitrary dependencies between attributes can be considered (unsupervised learning).

2.1 Subgroup Discovery

The task of subgroup discovery was defined by Klösgen [29] and Wrobel [59] as follows: *Given a population of individuals and a property of those individuals that we are interested in, find population subgroups that are statistically 'most interesting', e.g., are as large as possible and have the most unusual statistical (distributional) characteristics with respect to the property of interest.*

Thus, a subgroup may be considered as an IF-THEN rule that relates a set of independent variables to a target variable of interest. The condition of the rule (the *rule body* or *antecedent*) typically consists of a conjunction of Boolean terms, so-called *features*, each one constituting a constraint that needs to be satisfied by an example. If all constraints are satisfied, the rule is said to *fire*, and the example is said to be *covered* by the rule. The *rule head* (also called the *consequent* or *conclusion*) consists of a single class value, which is predicted in case the rule fires. In the simplest case, this is a binary target class c, and we want to find one or more rules that are predictive for this class.

In the literature, one can also find several closely related tasks, where the head of the rule does not only consist of a single binary attribute. Examples include mining for subgroup discovery, contrast sets [4], correlated pattern mining [40], mining for emerging patterns [11], exceptional model mining, and others. For more information, we refer to Kralj Novak et al. [30] and Zimmermann and De Raedt [64], who present unifying frameworks for these approaches.

The rule bodies typically consist of features that test for the presence of a particular attribute value or, in the case of numerical attributes, of an inequality that requires that the observed value is above or below a threshold. More expressive constraints include *set-valued attributes* (several values of the same attribute can be observed in the training examples), *internal disjunctions* (only one of several values of the same attribute needs to be present), *hierarchical attributes* (certain values of the attributes subsume other values), etc. Conjunctive combinations of features may be viewed as statements in propositional logic

---

function FINDPREDICTIVERULE (Examples)

Input: *Examples*, a set of positive and negative examples for a class c.

```
//initialize the rule body
rb ← ∅
// repeatedly find the best refinement
repeat
        build refinements R ← {rb' | rb' = rb ∧ f,  for some feature f}
        evaluate all rb' ∈ R according to some quality criterion
        rb = the best refinement in R
until rb satisfies a stopping criterion
     or covers no examples
```

Output: rule ($c \leftarrow R$)

Fig. 1. Greedy search for a predictive rule

(propositional rules). If relations between features can be considered (i.e., if propositions can be formulated in first-order logic), we speak of first-order rules.

Top-Down Hill-Climbing Algorithm. Figure 1 shows a simple greedy hill-climbing algorithm for finding a single predictive rule. It starts with an empty rule body and successively adds new conditions. For adding a condition, it tries all possible additions and evaluates them with a heuristic quality criterion, which typically depends on the number of covered and uncovered examples that belong to the class c (positive examples) or do not belong to c (negative examples). A few important ones are (assume that p out of P positive examples and n out of N negative examples are covered by the rule):

Laplace estimate (Lap $= \frac{p+1}{p+n+2}$) computes the fraction of positive examples in all covered examples, where each class is initialized with 1 virtual example in order to penalize rules with low coverage.

m-**estimate** (m $= \frac{p+m \cdot P/(P+N)}{p+n+m}$) is a generalization of the Laplace estimate which uses m examples for initialization, which are distributed according to the class distribution in the training set [7].

information gain (ig $= p \cdot (\log_2 \frac{p}{p+n} - \log_2 \frac{p'}{p'+n'})$, where p' and n' are the number of positive and negative examples covered by the rule's predecessor) is Quinlan's (1990) adaptation of the information gain heuristic used for decision tree learning. The main difference is that this only focuses on a single branch (a rule), whereas the decision tree version tries to optimize all branches simultaneously.

correlation and χ^2 (corr $= \frac{p(N-n)-(P-p)n}{\sqrt{PN(p+n)(P-p+N-n)}}$) computes the four-field correlation of covered/uncovered positive/negative examples. It is equivalent to a χ^2 statistic ($\chi^2 = (P+N)\,\text{corr}^2$).

An exhaustive overview and theoretical comparison of various search heuristics in coverage space, a variant of ROC space, can be found in [18].

In the simplest case, conditions are added until the rule covers no more negative examples. In practical applications, we may want to stop earlier in order to avoid overfitting. In this case, a separate *stopping criterion* may be used in order to stop the refinement process when a certain quality threshold for the learned rule is satisfied, or the rule set may be optimized on an independent pruning set [16].

A greedy hill-climbing search is quite likely to get stuck in a local optimum. However, it is fairly straight-forward to generalize this algorithm so that different search strategies can be employed (e.g., beam search [9] or best-first search) or that not only one but multiple rules are returned (typically the top-k rules for some value of k).

2.2 Association Rule Discovery

An association rule is a rule where certain properties of the data in the body of the rule are related to other properties in the head of the rule.

A typical application example for association rules are product associations. For example, the rule

$$\texttt{bread, butter} \rightarrow \texttt{milk, cheese}$$

specifies that people who buy bread and butter also tend to buy milk and cheese.

The importance of an association rule is often characterized with two measures:

Support measures the fraction of all rows in the database that satisfy both, body and head of the rule. Rules with higher support are more important.

Confidence measures the fraction of the rows that satisfy the body of the rule, which also satisfy the head of the rule. Rules with high confidence have a higher correlation between the properties described in the head and the properties described in the body.

If the above rule has a support of 10% and a confidence of 80%, this means that 10% of all people buy bread, butter, milk, and cheese together, and that 80% of all people who buy bread and butter also buy milk and cheese.

Apriori Algorithm. The discovery of association rules typically happens in two phases, which were pioneered in the APRIORI algorithm [2]. First, all *frequent itemsets* (i.e., conditions that cover a certain minimum number of examples) are found. In a second pass, these are then converted into association rules.

For finding all frequent itemsets, APRIORI generates all rules with a certain minimum frequency in parallel with a so-called *level-wise search*, as shown in

---

function FREQSET (Examples)

Input: *Examples*, described with a set of binary features, so-called *Items*.

// the first iteration consists of all single items $k = 1$
$C_1 = Items$

//loop until no nor candidate items left **while** $C_k \neq \emptyset$ **do**
       // remove all infrequent items from C_k
       // (requires check on database of *Examples*)
       $S_k = C_k \setminus \{$ all infrequent itemsets in $C_k\}$

       // generate new candidates
       $C_{k+1} = \{$ all sets with $k + 1$ elements that
                               can be formed by uniting two itemsets in $S_k\}$

       $C_{k+1} = C_{k+1} \setminus \{$ all itemsets for which not all subsets of size k
                                 are contained in $S_k\}$
     $S = S \cup S_k$
     $k = k + 1$
endwhile

Output: S, the set of all frequent itemsets

Fig. 2. Find all Frequent Itemsets

Figure 2. The level-wise search first generates all frequent itemsets of size one, then all frequent itemsets of size two, and so on, thereby performing a breadth-first search. However, from each iteration to the next, a large number of possible extensions can be pruned because of the *anti-monotonicity* of the frequency of the itemsets (their *support*). This essentially means that if a conjunction of conditions is extended with a new condition, the resulting rule body will only cover a subset of the examples covered by the original rule body. Thus, when computing C_{k+1}, the set of candidate itemsets of size $k + 1$, we only need to consider itemsets that result as a combination of two itemsets of size k which overlap in $k - 1$ items. For example, if the two itemsets $\{A, B, C\}$ and $\{B, C, D\}$ are in S_3, the itemset $\{A, B, C, D\}$ will be in C_4. It may be later removed if either one of its subsets of size 3 is not frequent (if, e.g., $\{A, C, D\}$ is not contained in S_3), or if the subsequent check on the dataset shows that it is itself not frequent.

The resulting frequent itemsets are then used for constructing rules in a post-processing phase. The key idea here is to try all possible ways of using an implication sign to separate a frequent itemset into items that are used in the rule body and items that are used in the rule head, and keeping only those where the resulting association rule has a certain minimum strength (confidence). This can, again, be sped up considerably using a similar idea to the anti-monotonicity of the support.

Apriori Successors. While the second phase of APRIORI remains almost unchanged, a number of alternative algorithms, such as ECLAT [62] or FP-GROWTH [25], have been proposed for the frequent itemset discovery phase. Mining for *closed* frequent itemsets proposed by Pasquier et al. [46] is another optimization. A frequent itemset P is closed if P is included in no other itemset that has the same support as P.

In recent years there was a growing interest in approaches that support parallel execution of frequent itemset mining in order to harness modern multi-core architectures. PLCM [45] and MT-Closed [38] are parallel implementations of two fastest algorithms LCMv2 [56] and DCI CLOSED [37] according to the FIMI'04 workshop[1], which provided a benchmark of submitted frequent itemset mining implementations [44]. The recently proposed PARAMINER [44] algorithm yields comparable execution times to PLCM and MT-CLOSED, while it allows to mine not only for closed frequent itemsets, but also for additional types of patterns such as connected relational graphs and gradual itemsets.

For surveys of frequent set mining and association rule discovery we refer the reader to [22,63]. A freely accessible implementations of multiple frequent itemset mining implementations can be found at http://borgelt.net/fpm.html, PARAMINER is also made available by the authors under an open license.

Connections to Mathematical Logic and Statistics. The notion of association rules was introduced already in mid 1960's by Petr Hájek in the frame of development of the GUHA method (abbrev. of General Unary Hypothesis Automaton) [23]. The purpose was to automatically generate large number of (statistical) hypotheses which had the form of association rules. These hypotheses are automatically verified using a number of criteria, including Chi-square and Fisher statistical tests and what is now known as support and confidence. The hypotheses that pass the criteria are represented as (true) logical formulas of *observational calculi*, a theoretical framework for exploratory data analysis combining logic and mathematical statistics. Example of such a formula is:

$$\texttt{bread(brown)} \wedge \texttt{butter(yes)} \implies_{B,p} \texttt{milk(skimmed)} \wedge \texttt{cheese(french)}$$

This example features the *founded implication* quantifier $\implies_{B,p}$, which asserts that the support of the rule is at least B instances and the confidence is at least p. Observational calculi are further studied by Rauch [54]. One practical result is the introduction of deduction rules, which allow to identify redundant hypotheses a to deal with domain knowledge.

A maintained implementation of GUHA method is LISp-Miner, which is freely available from lispminer.vse.cz. This software supports the distinct GUHA features such as negated literals, e.g. ¬bread(brown), and disjunctions, e.g. bread(brown) ∨ butter(yes), or cheese(french ∨ dutch). The higher expressiveness leads to a considerable increase in computational cost [28]. Kliegr et al. [28] suggested that GUHA may find use in business rule learning, where a lower number of more expressive rules can be desirable.

---

[1] http://fimi.ua.ac.be/fimi04/

3   Predictive Rule Learning

Whereas descriptive rule discovery aims at finding individual rules that capture some regularities and patterns of the input data, the task of predictive rule learning is to generalize the training data so that predictions for new examples are possible. As individual rules will typically only cover part of the training data, we will need to enforce completeness by learning an unordered rule set or a decision list.

An *unordered rule set* is a collection of individual rules that collectively form a classifier. In contrast to a decision list, the rules in the set do not have an inherent order, and all rules in the set have to be tried for deriving a prediction for an example. This may cause two types of problems that have to be resolved with additional algorithms:

Multiple rules fire: More than one rule can fire on a single example, and these rules can make contradicting predictions. This type of conflict is typically resolved by preferring rules that cover a higher fraction of training examples of their class (typically estimated with Laplace correction). This is equivalent to converting the rule set into a decision list that is ordered according to this evaluation heuristic. More elaborate tie breaking schemes, such as using the *Naive Bayes* algorithm, or inducing a separate rule set for handling these conflicts (*double induction* [32]) have also been tried.

No rules fire: It may also occur that no rule fires for a given example. Such cases are typically handled via a so-called *default rule*, which typically predicts the majority class. Again, more complex algorithms, such as FURIA [26] trying to find the closest rule (*rule stretching* [13]) have been proposed.

A rule set in which all rules predict the same class needs to be complemented with an (implicit) default rule that predicts the other class in case none of the previous rules fires (very much like the closed world semantics in PROLOG). If all rules are conjunctive, such rule sets may be interpreted as a definition in *disjunctive normal form* for this class.

In contrast to an unordered rule set, a *decision list* has an inherent order, which makes classification quite straightforward. For classifying a new instance, the rules are tried in order, and the class of the first rule that covers the instance is predicted. If no induced rule fires, a *default rule* is invoked, which typically predicts the majority class of the uncovered training examples. Decision lists are particularly popular in *inductive logic programming* [10,12], because PROLOG programs may be considered to be simple decision lists, where all rules predict the same concept.

Both decision trees and rule sets are often learned with the same or very similar strategies. The two most popular strategies for learning rule sets may be viewed as extensions of the association rule and subgroup discovery algorithms discussed in the previous section, and are discussed in the following.

3.1 Classification by Association

A prototypical instantiation of this framework is *associative classification*, as exemplified by the CBA rule learning algorithm [35,36]. This type of algorithm typically uses a conventional association rule discovery algorithm, such as APRIORI [2], to discover a large number of patterns. From these, all patterns that have the target class in the head are selected, and only those are subsequently used for inducing a rule set. This is formed by sorting the patterns according to some heuristic function and adding the best to the rule set.

A variety of successor systems have been proposed that follow the same principal architecture [e.g., 5,27,31,43,60]. Sulzmann and Fürnkranz [55] compare various approaches for combining association rules into a rule-based theory. Azevedo and Jorge [3] propose to generate an ensemble of rule sets instead of a single rule set.

CBA and its direct successors such as CMAR are restricted to nominal attributes. If the dataset contains numeric (quantitative) attributes, these attributes need to be discretized e.g. using the minimum description length principle [14]. This is a severe limitation compared to many other learning algorithms which natively handle numerical attributes.

As in association rule discovery, there are approaches to associative classification that employ fuzzy logic to alleviate this problem. A recent example of such an approach is the FARC-HD algorithm [1]. Alcala-Fdez et al. [1] also provide a benchmark comparing their algorithm against the C4.5 decision tree learner as well as against multiple association rule classification algorithms including CBA, CBA2, CPAR and CMAR. The results show that FARC-HD provides a slight improvement in average accuracy across the basket of 25 datasets but at a several orders of magnitude higher computational cost. The benchmark also reveals large differences in the size of the rule set among classifiers. While CBA achieves slightly smaller accuracy than its successor algorithms CPAR and CMAR, it produces a notably smaller number of rules.

Free implementations of CBA, CMAR and CPAR are available at http://cgi.csc.liv.ac.uk/~frans/KDD/Software/. A good survey of associative classification and related algorithms can be found in [6].

3.2 Covering Algorithm

An alternative approach, the so-called *covering* or *separate-and-conquer* algorithm, relies on repeatedly learning a single rule (e.g., with a subgroup discovery algorithm). After a new rule has been learned, all examples that are covered by this rule are removed. This is repeated until all examples are covered or a given stopping criterion fires. A simple version of this so-called *covering* algorithm is shown in Figure 3, a survey of this family of algorithms can be found in [17]. The members of this family differ mostly in the way the FINDPREDICTIVERULE method is implemented.

---

procedure COVERING (Examples,Classifier)

Input: *Examples*, a set of positive and negative examples for a class c.

// initialize the rule set
$R = \emptyset$

//loop until no more positive examples are covered
while not all positive examples are covered **do**
 // find the best rule for the current examples
 $r = $ FINDPREDICTIVERULE (Examples)

 // check if we need more rules
 if $R \cup r$ is good enough
 then break while

 // remove covered examples and add rule to rule set
 Examples = Examples \ { examples covered by r}
 $R = R \cup r$
endwhile

Output: the learned rule set R

Fig. 3. The covering algorithm for finding a rule set

4   Well-Known Rule Learning Algorithms

AQ can be considered as the original covering algorithm. Its original version was conceived by Ryszard Michalski in the sixties [39], and numerous versions and variants of the algorithm appeared subsequently in the literature. AQ uses a top-down beam search for finding the best rule. It does not search all possible specializations of a rule, but only considers refinements that cover a particular example, the so-called *seed example*. This idea is basically the same as the use of a bottom clause in inductive logic programming [10, 41, 42].

CN2 [8, 9] employs a beam search guided by the Laplace or m-estimates, and the above-mentioned likelihood ratio significance test to fight overfitting. It can operate in two modes, one for learning rule sets (by modeling each class independently), and one for learning decision lists.

FOIL [51] was the first relational learning algorithm that received attention beyond the field of inductive logic programming. It learns a concept with the covering loop and learns individual concepts with a top-down refinement operator, guided by information gain. The main difference to previous systems is that FOIL allowed the use of first-order background knowledge. Instead of only being able to use tests on single attributes, FOIL could employ tests that compute relations between multiple attributes, and could also introduce new variables in the body of a rule.

RIPPER was the first rule learning system that effectively countered the over-fitting problem via *incremental reduced error pruning* [16]. It also added a post-processing phase for optimizing a rule set in the context of other rules. The key idea is to remove one rule out of a previously learned rule set and try to re-learn it not only in the context of previous rules (as would be the case in the regular covering rule), but also in the context of subsequent rules. RIPPER is still state-of-the-art in inductive rule learning. A freely accessible re-implementation can be found in the WEKA machine learning library [58] under the name of JRIP.

OPUS [57] was the first rule learning algorithm to demonstrate the feasibility of a full exhaustive search through all possible rule bodies for finding a rule that maximizes a given quality criterion (or heuristic function). The key idea is the use of *ordered search* that prevents that a rule is generated multiple times. This means that even though there are $l!$ different orders of the conditions of a rule of length l, only one of them can be taken by the learner for finding this rule. In addition, OPUS uses several techniques that prune significant parts of the search space, so that this search method becomes feasible. Follow-up work has shown that this technique is also an efficient alternative for association rule discovery, provided that the database to mine fits into the memory of the learning system.

5 Applications in Linked Data and Semantic Web

While research in machine learning currently tends to move away from learn-ing logical concept representations towards statistical learning algorithms, rules are still used in many application areas. A particularly important case is the Semantic Web, whose representation is built on rule-based formalisms. As it is difficult to manually write a complete set of rules for representing knowledge, rule learning algorithms have great potential in supporting automation of this process.

Inductive logic programming algorithms are one obvious candidate for this purpose, because they allow to operate in more expressive, relational logical frameworks such as RDF[2] or OWL[3], which form the backbone of the Seman-tic Web [33,34]. However, their expressiveness has to be paid for with a high computational complexity. Compared to approaches based on inductive logic programming (ILP), APRIORI and its successors are not only much more effi-cient, but also they do not require counter examples [20], on which most ILP approaches rely. This is important because semantic knowledge bases such as DBpedia (http://dbpedia.org) do not contain negative statements. Additionally, since they are built under the *open world assumption*[4], the negative statements cannot be directly inferred. It was observed that semantic reasoners may not provide meaningful results on real open world knowledge bases yet for another reason: these crowd-sourced resources contain errors. A single erroneous fact can cause the RDFS reasoner to infer an incorrect statement [49].

---

[2] http://www.w3.org/TR/rdf-primer/

[3] http://www.w3.org/TR/owl2-primer/

[4] A statement which is not present in the knowledge base is not necessarily false.

A current use case demonstrating advantages of association rule learning in the linked data domain is the completion of the large DBpedia knowledge base. Association rules were applied to infer missing types for entities in [48] and to perform schema induction (infer new classes) in [61]. These approaches for DBpedia completion directly use the APRIORI algorithm, which implies limitations stemming from the inherently relational setting of linked data. AMIE [20] is a state-of-the-art algorithm that extends the association rule learning principles allowing to mine Horn clauses such as

$$\texttt{hasAdvisor(x, y)} \land \texttt{graduateFrom(x, z)} \implies \texttt{worksAt(y, z)}$$

AMIE is reported to be highly computationally efficient, it processes entire DBpedia in less than 3 minutes and the larger YAGO2 ontology (www.mpi-inf. mpg.de/yago/) in 4 minutes. In contrast, the authors report that in their benchmark state-of-the-art ILP approaches did not finish within days.

Rule learning may not only support the construction of Semantic Web resources, but, conversely, the Semantic Web may also serve as a source for background knowledge in many data mining tasks. For example, Paulheim and Fürnkranz [50] have shown that unsupervised feature generation from various knowledge sources in the Linked Open Data (LOD) cloud may yield interesting and useful features. One can even go as far as trying to mine databases that have no inherent background knowledge. For example, Paulheim [47] used LOD knowledge for trying to find explanation for common statistics such as the quality-of-living index of cities.

This short survey shows that rule learning algorithms can be with success directly applied to large linked datasets available on the "Semantic Web". Apart from the inference of new facts or identification of errors in semantic knowledge bases, it was recently suggested that association rule learning can serve e.g. for schema alignment between ontologies [21]. There is an ongoing research into specialized approaches tailored for RDF datasets which opens new opportunities as well as challenges.

6   Conclusion

This paper provided a brief introduction to rule learning, mainly focusing on the best-known algorithms for descriptive and predictive rule learning. Whereas the main goal of association rule and subgroup discovery is to discover single rules that capture patterns in parts of the data, the main task of classification by association and the covering strategy for learning predictive rule sets and decision lists is to be able to generalize the training data so that predictions on new data can be made. In comparison with other popular classification algorithms such as Support Vector Machines, predictive rule learning together with decision trees has the advantage of easy interpretability. The individual rules that comprise the classifier can be explained to a human expert.

Obviously, this brief survey is far from complete. Other techniques for generating rule sets are possible. For example, rules can be generated from induced decision trees. Standard algorithms for learning decision trees (such as C4.5 [53]) are quite similar to the covering algorithm for learning decision lists in that the aim of extending a decision tree with another split is to reduce the class impurity in the leaves (usually measured by entropy or the Gini index). However, whereas a decision tree split is chosen to optimize all successor branches simultaneously, a rule learning heuristic only focuses on a single rule. As a result, rule sets are often more compact than decision trees. Consequently, a rule set can be considerably simplified during the conversion of a decision tree to a set of rules [52,53]. For example, Frank and Witten [15] suggested the PART algorithm, which tries to integrate this simplification into the tree induction process by focusing only on a single branch of a tree.

The APRIORI algorithm [2], which provides means to discover association rules in large datasets, is considered as one of the major advancements in data mining technology in the seminal book of Hastie et al. [24]. Its recent successors, such as the LCM group of algorithms provide further improvements in terms of computational efficiency. Other algorithms, such as PARAMINER provide generic framework allowing to discover not only frequent itemsets but also other types of patterns. The performance of parallel implementations of association rule learning stimulates novel applications on large datasets that are becoming freely available as part of the linked open data initiative. Examples of such efforts include completion of semantic knowledge bases with new facts.

Acknowledgment. Tomáš Kliegr was partly supported by the Faculty of Informatics and Statistics, University of Economics, Prague within "long term institutional support for research activities" scheme and grant IGA 20/2013.

References

1. Alcala-Fdez, J., Alcala, R., Herrera, F.: A fuzzy association rule-based classification model for high-dimensional problems with genetic rule selection and lateral tuning. IEEE Transactions on Fuzzy Systems **19**(5), 857–872 (2011)
2. Agrawal, R., Imielinski, T., Swami, A.N.: Mining association rules between sets of items in large databases. In: Buneman, P., Jajodia, S. (eds.) Proceedings of the ACM International Conference on Management of Data (SIGMOD 1993), Washington, D.C., pp. 207–216 (1993)
3. Azevedo, P.J., Jorge, A.J.: Ensembles of jittered association rule classifiers. Data Mining and Knowledge Discovery **21**(1), 91–129 (2010). Special Issue on Global Modeling using Local Patterns
4. Bay, S.D., Pazzani, M.J.: Detecting group differences: Mining contrast sets. Data Mining and Knowledge Discovery **5**(3), 213–246 (2001)
5. Bayardo Jr., R.J.: Brute-force mining of high-confidence classification rules. In: Proceedings of the 3rd International Conference on Knowledge Discovery and Data Mining (KDD 1997), pp. 123–126 (1997)
6. Bringmann, B., Nijssen, S., Zimmermann, A.: Pattern-based classification: a unifying perspective. In: Knobbe, A., Fürnkranz, J. (eds.) Proceedings of the ECML/PKDD 1909 Workshop From Local Patterns to Global Models (LeGo 1909), Bled, Slovenia, pp. 36–50 (2009)

7. Cestnik, B.: Estimating probabilities: a crucial task in Machine Learning. In: Aiello, L. (ed.) Proceedings of the 9th European Conference on Artificial Intelligence (ECAI 1990), Pitman, Stockholm, Sweden, pp. 147–150 (1990)

8. Clark, P., Boswell, R.: Rule induction with CN2: Some recent improvements. In: Kodratoff, Y. (ed.) Machine Learning – EWSL-91. LNCS, vol. 482, pp. 151–163. Springer, Heidelberg (1991)

9. Clark, P., Niblett, T.: The CN2 induction algorithm. Machine Learning **3**(4), 261–283 (1989)

10. De Raedt, L.: Logical and Relational Learning. Springer-Verlag (2008)

11. Dong, G., Li, J.: Efficient mining of emerging patterns: discovering trends and differences. In: Proceedings of the 5th ACM SIGKDD International Conference on Knowledge Discovery and Data Mining (KDD 1999), San Diego, CA, pp. 43–52 (1999)

12. Džeroski, S., Lavrač, N. (eds.): Relational Data Mining: Inductive Logic Programming for Knowledge Discovery in Databases. Springer-Verlag (2001)

13. Eineborg, M., Boström, H.: Classifying uncovered examples by rule stretching. In: Rouveirol, C., Sebag, M. (eds.) ILP 2001. LNCS (LNAI), vol. 2157, pp. 41–50. Springer, Heidelberg (2001)

14. Fayyad, U.M., Irani, K.B.: Multi-interval discretization of continuous-valued attributes for classification learning. In: Proceedings of the 13th International Joint Conference on Artificial Intelligence (IJCAI 1993), pp. 1022–1029 (1993)

15. Frank, E., Witten, I.H.: Generating accurate rule sets without global optimization. In: Shavlik, J. (ed.) Proceedings of the 15th International Conference on Machine Learning (ICML 1998), pp. 144–151. Morgan Kaufmann, Madison (1998)

16. Fürnkranz, J.: Pruning algorithms for rule learning. Machine Learning **27**(2), 139–171 (1997)

17. Fürnkranz, J.: Separate-and-conquer rule learning. Artificial Intelligence Review **13**(1), 3–54 (1999)

18. Fürnkranz, J., Flach, P.A.: ROC 'n' rule learning - Towards a better understanding of covering algorithms. Machine Learning **58**(1), 39–77 (2005)

19. Fürnkranz, J., Gamberger, D., Lavrač, N.: Foundations of Rule Learning. Springer-Verlag (2012)

20. Galárraga, L.A., Teflioudi, C., Hose, K., Suchanek, F.: AMIE: association rule mining under incomplete evidence in ontological knowledge bases. In: Proceedings of the 22nd International Conference on World Wide Web (WWW 2013), Switzerland, pp. 413–422 (2013)

21. Galárraga, L.A., Preda, N., Suchanek, F.M.: Mining rules to align knowledge bases. In: Proceedings of the 2013 Workshop on Automated Knowledge Base Construction (AKBC 2013), pp. 43–48. ACM, New York (2013)

22. Goethals, B.: Frequent set mining. In: Maimon, O., Rokach, L. (eds.) The Data Mining and Knowledge Discovery Handbook, 2nd edn., pp. 321–338. Springer-Verlag (2010)

23. Hájek, P., Holena, M., Rauch, J.: The GUHA method and its meaning for data mining. Journal of Computer and System Sciences **76**(1), 34–48 (2010). Special Issue on Intelligent Data Analysis

24. Hastie, T., Tibshirani, R., Friedman, J.: The Elements of Statistical Learning. Springer Series in Statistics. Springer, New York (2001)

25. Han, J., Pei, J., Yin, Y., Mao, R.: Mining frequent patterns without candidate generation: A frequent-pattern tree approach. Data Mining and Knowledge Discovery **8**(1), 53–87 (2004)

26. Hhn, J., Hllermeier, E.: Furia: an algorithm for unordered fuzzy rule induction. Data Mining and Knowledge Discovery **19**(3), 293–319 (2009)
27. Jovanoski, V., Lavrač, N.: Classification rule learning with APRIORI-C. In: Brazdil, P.B., Jorge, A.M. (eds.) EPIA 2001. LNCS (LNAI), vol. 2258, pp. 44–51. Springer, Heidelberg (2001)
28. Kliegr, T., Kuchař, J., Sottara, D., Vojíř, S.: Learning business rules with association rule classifiers. In: Bikakis, A., Fodor, P., Roman, D. (eds.) RuleML 2014. LNCS, vol. 8620, pp. 236–250. Springer, Heidelberg (2014)
29. Klösgen, W.: Explora: a multipattern and multistrategy discovery assistant. In: Fayyad, U.M., Piatetsky-Shapiro, G., Smyth, P., Uthurusamy, R. (eds.) Advances in Knowledge Discovery and Data Mining, chap. 10, pp. 249–271. AAAI Press (1996)
30. Kralj Novak, P., Lavrač, N., Webb, G.I.: Supervised descriptive rule discovery: A unifying survey of contrast set, emerging pattern and subgroup mining. Journal of Machine Learning Research **10**, 377–403 (2009)
31. Li, W., Han, J., Pei, J.: CMAR: accurate and efficient classification based on multiple class-association rules. In: Proceedings of the IEEE Conference on Data Mining (ICDM 2001), pp. 369–376 (2001)
32. Lindgren, T., Boström, H.: Resolving rule conflicts with double induction. Intelligent Data Analysis **8**(5), 457–468 (2004)
33. Lisi, F.: Building Rules on Top of Ontologies for the Semantic Web with Inductive Logic Programming. Theory and Practice of Logic Programming **8**(3), 271–300 (2008)
34. Lisi, F., Esposito, F.: An ilp perspective on the semantic web. In: Bouquet, P., Tummarello, G. (eds.) Semantic Web Applications and Perspectives - Proceedings of the 2nd Italian Semantic Web Workshop (SWAP-05), pp. 14–16. University of Trento, Trento (2005)
35. Liu, B., Hsu, W., Ma, Y.: Integrating classification and association rule mining. In: Agrawal, R., Stolorz, P., Piatetsky-Shapiro, G. (eds.) Proceedings of the 4th International Conference on Knowledge Discovery and Data Mining (KDD 1998), pp. 80–86 (1998)
36. Liu, B., Ma, Y., Wong, C.K.: Improving an association rule based classifier. In: Zighed, D.A., Komorowski, J., Żytkow, J.M. (eds.) PKDD 2000. LNCS (LNAI), vol. 1910, pp. 504–509. Springer, Heidelberg (2000)
37. Lucchese, C.: DCI closed: a fast and memory efficient algorithm to mine frequent closed itemsets. In: Proceedings of the IEEE ICDM 2004 Workshop on Frequent Itemset Mining Implementations (FIMI 2004) (2004)
38. Lucchese, C., Orlando, S., Perego, R.: Parallel mining of frequent closed patterns: harnessing modern computer architectures. In: Proceedings of the 7th IEEE International Conference on Data Mining (ICDM 2007), pp. 242–251 (2007)
39. Michalski, R.S.: On the quasi-minimal solution of the covering problem. In: Proceedings of the 5th International Symposium on Information Processing (FCIP-69) (Switching Circuits), vol. A3, Bled, Yugoslavia, pp. 125–128 (1969)
40. Morishita, S., Sese, J.: Traversing itemset lattice with statistical metric pruning. In: Proceedings of the 19th ACM SIGMOD-SIGACT-SIGART Symposium on Principles of Database Systems (PODS 2000), pp. 226–236. ACM (2000)
41. Muggleton, S.H.: Inverse entailment and Progol. New Generation Computing **13**(3,4), 245–286 (1995). Special Issue on Inductive Logic Programming
42. Muggleton, S.H., De Raedt, L.: Inductive Logic Programming: Theory and methods. Journal of Logic Programming **19–20**, 629–679 (1994)

43. Mutter, S., Hall, M., Frank, E.: Using classification to evaluate the output of confidence-based association rule mining. In: Webb, G.I., Yu, X. (eds.) AI 2004. LNCS (LNAI), vol. 3339, pp. 538–549. Springer, Heidelberg (2004)

44. Negrevergne, B., Termier, A., Rousset, M.C., Mhaut, J.F.: Para miner: a generic pattern mining algorithm for multi-core architectures. Data Mining and Knowledge Discovery 28(3), 593–633 (2014)

45. Negrevergne, B., Termier, A., Rousset, M.C., Mhaut, J.F., Uno, T.: Discovering closed frequent itemsets on multicore: parallelizing computations and optimizing memory accesses. In: Proceedings of the International Conference on High Performance Computing and Simulation (HPCS 2010), pp. 521–528 (2010)

46. Pasquier, N., Bastide, Y., Taouil, R., Lakhal, L.: Discovering frequent closed itemsets for association rules. In: Beeri, C., Bruneman, P. (eds.) ICDT 1999. LNCS, vol. 1540, pp. 398–416. Springer, Heidelberg (1998)

47. Paulheim, H.: Generating possible interpretations for statistics from linked open data. In: Simperl, E., Cimiano, P., Polleres, A., Corcho, O., Presutti, V. (eds.) ESWC 2012. LNCS, vol. 7295, pp. 560–574. Springer, Heidelberg (2012)

48. Paulheim, H., Browsing linked open data with auto complete. In: Proceedings of the Semantic Web Challenge co-located with ISWC 2012. Univ., Mannheim, Boston (2012)

49. Paulheim, H., Bizer, C.: Type inference on noisy rdf data. In: Alani, H., Kagal, L., Fokoue, A., Groth, P., Biemann, C., Parreira, J.X., Aroyo, L., Noy, N., Welty, C., Janowicz, K. (eds.) ISWC 2013, Part I. LNCS, vol. 8218, pp. 510–525. Springer, Heidelberg (2013)

50. Paulheim, H., Fürnkranz, J.: Unsupervised feature construction from linked open data. In: Proceedings of the ACM International Conference Web Intelligence, Mining, and Semantics (WIMS 2012) (2012)

51. Quinlan, J.R.: Learning logical definitions from relations. Machine Learning 5, 239–266 (1990)

52. Quinlan, J.R.: Generating production rules from decision trees. In: Proceedings of the 10th International Joint Conference on Artificial Intelligence (IJCAI 1987), pp. 304–307. Morgan Kaufmann (1987)

53. Quinlan, J.R.: C4.5: Programs for Machine Learning. Morgan Kaufmann, San Mateo (1993)

54. Rauch, J.: Observational Calculi and Association Rules, Studies in Computational Intelligence, vol. 469. Springer (2013)

55. Sulzmann, J.N., Fürnkranz, J.: A comparison of techniques for selecting and combining class association rules. In: Knobbe, A.J. (ed.) Proceedings of the ECML/PKDD 2008 Workshop From Local Patterns to Global Models (LeGo 2008), Antwerp, Belgium, pp. 154–168 (2008)

56. Uno, T., Kiyomi, M., Arimura, H.: LCM ver. 2: efficient mining algorithms for frequent/closed/maximal itemsets. In: Proceedings of the IEEE ICDM 2004 Workshop on Frequent Itemset Mining Implementations (FIMI 2004) (2004)

57. Webb, G.I.: OPUS: An efficient admissible algorithm for unordered search. Journal of Artificial Intelligence Research 5, 431–465 (1995)

58. Witten, I.H., Frank, E.: Data Mining - Practical Machine Learning Tools and Techniques with Java Implementations, 2nd edn. Morgan Kaufmann Publishers (2005)

59. Wrobel, S.: An algorithm for multi-relational discovery of subgroups. In: Komorowski, J., Żytkow, J.M. (eds.) PKDD 1997. LNCS, vol. 1263, pp. 78–87. Springer, Heidelberg (1997)

60. Yin, X., Han, J.: CPAR: classification based on predictive association rules. In: Proceedings SIAM Conference on Data Mining (SDM 2003) (2003)
61. Völker, J., Niepert, M.: Statistical schema induction. In: Antoniou, G., Grobelnik, M., Simperl, E., Parsia, B., Plexousakis, D., De Leenheer, P., Pan, J. (eds.) ESWC 2011, Part I. LNCS, vol. 6643, pp. 124–138. Springer, Heidelberg (2011)
62. Zaki, M.J., Parthasarathy, S., Ogihara, M., Li, W.: New algorithms for fast discovery of association rules. In: Proceedings of the 3rd International Conference on Knowledge Discovery and Data Mining (KDD 1997), Newport, CA, pp. 283–286 (1997)
63. Zhang, C., Zhang, S.: Association Rule Mining –Models and Algorithms. Springer (2002)
64. Zimmermann, A., De Raedt, L.: Cluster grouping: From subgroup discovery to clustering. Machine Learning **77**(1), 125–159 (2009)

Distribution and Uncertainty in Complex Event Recognition

Alexander Artikis[1,2] and Matthias Weidlich[3(✉)]

[1] Department of Maritime Studies, University of Piraeus, Piraeus, Greece
a.artikis@unipi.gr
[2] Institute of Informatics and Telecommunications, NCSR "Demokritos",
Athens, Greece
[3] Department of Computer Science, Humboldt-Universität zu Berlin,
Berlin, Germany
weidlima@informatik.hu-berlin.de

Abstract. Complex event recognition proved to be a valuable tool for a wide range of applications, reaching from logistics over finance to healthcare. In this paper, we reflect on some of these application areas to outline open research problems in event recognition. In particular, we focus on the questions of (1) how to distribute event recognition and (2) how to deal with the inherent uncertainty observed in many event recognition scenarios. For both questions, we provide a brief overview of the state-of-the-art and point out research gaps.

1 Introduction

Event processing has been established as a generic computational paradigm in a wide range of applications, spanning data processing in Web environments, over logistics and networking, to finance and the health sector [9]. Events, in general, report on state changes of a system and its environment, thereby enabling reactive and pro-active computing. At the very core of event processing systems is an event recognition mechanism (also known as event pattern matching [21]). It is the ability of a system to detect events that are considered relevant for processing and, as such, is the basis of realizing situation awareness in a system.

Event recognition systems are a key technology in the 'intelligent economy' that, based on the omnipresent availability of data that characterizes the information economy, provides means to analyze and act upon information. Detecting and understanding situations in computational as well as cyber-physical systems creates competitive advantage in commercial transactions, enables sustainable management of urban communities, and promotes appropriate distribution of social, healthcare and educational services [38]. By detecting relevant events also in the presence of extremely large scale data that is spread over geographical locations, event recognition systems help to extract actionable knowledge from Big Data.

The aim of this paper is to provide a brief overview of two open research questions related to event recognition. Based on a reflection of applications, we

N. Bassiliades et al. (Eds.): RuleML 2015, LNCS 9202, pp. 70–80, 2015.
DOI: 10.1007/978-3-319-21542-6_5

argue that distribution and uncertainty handling are of utmost importance for effective and efficient use of event recognition. By briefly reviewing the state-of-the-art with respect to these two aspects, we carve out directions for future research in event recognition.

The rest of this paper is structured as follows. Section 2 illustrates the concept of event recognition using real-world applications. Section 3 gives details on the identified research challenges of event recognition related to distribution and uncertainty handling. Finally, Section 4 summarizes the paper.

2 Applications

Credit card fraud management is one of the applications in which complex event recognition plays a key role[1]. The goal is to detect fraud within 25 milliseconds, and even forecast it, in order to prevent the financial loss. Example fraud types include:

- 'cloned card' — a credit card is being used simultaneously in different countries;
- 'brute force attack' — multiple attempts to use a credit card per second;
- 'spike usage' — the 24-hour running sum is higher than the monthly average of the last 6 months;
- 'new high use' — the card is being frequently used in merchants or countries never used before;
- 'potential batch fraud' — many transactions from multiple cards are being used in the same point-of-sale terminal in high amounts.

The event patterns expressing fraudulent activity are highly complex involving hundreds of rules and performance indicators. They are also very diverse: fraud patterns heavily depend on the country, merchant, amount and customer. Fraud is continuously evolving — new fraud patterns appear on almost a weekly basis. Moreover, fraud detection is a needle in the haystack problem as fraudulent transactions constitute at most 0.1% of the total number of transactions. Perfect recall (finding all fraud cases) and perfect precision (never raise a false alarm) are out of reach — the state-of-practice recall and precision rates are about 60% and 10% respectively. At the same time, raising false alarms, that is, unnecessarily calling customers or blocking cards, is very costly in time and customer relationships. Missing true alarms is also very costly in terms of lost money.

Credit card fraud recognition and forecasting requires the analysis of large data streams storming from all over the world, as well as large amounts of historical data. For example, the SPEEDD project[2] will recognize fraud using up to 10,000 transactions/sec streaming from all over the world, and about 700 million events representing a 6 month history. Data streams are highly noisy: several of the data fields of credit card transactions could be left empty or contain incorrect

---

[1] https://www.feedzai.com/
[2] http://speedd-project.eu/

information due to terminal misconfiguration. Examples include incorrect times-tamps and timezone information, incorrect merchant group codes, and missing or incorrect location information.

Traffic management is another application in which complex event recognition plays a crucial role. The goal here is to detect and forecast traffic congestions, and make decisions in order to attenuate them. For example, the SPEEDD project will forecast traffic congestions 5-20 minutes before they happen, and make decisions within 30 seconds of the forecast about the adjustment of traffic light settings and speed limits. Traffic management may be realized as follows:

- *Detect* traffic flow and density patterns as well as traffic incidents and safety violations.
- *Forecast* flow, density and travel duration for different temporal horizons. The carbon print and energy consumption can also be forecast.
- *Decide* which are the optimal variable speed limits and duty cycles for the ramp metering lights.
- *Act* by automatically changing the values of the variable speed limit panels and the operation of lights on the ramp metering course.

Traffic management requires the analysis of very large noisy data streams storm-ing from various sensors, including fixed sensors installed in highways and city streets measuring traffic flow and density, mobile sensors such as smartphones and public transport vehicles reporting on traffic conditions [4], as well as large amounts of historical data. Sensors are frequently out of order, not calibrated appropriately and inaccurate. Data is often delayed and even completely lost during transmission. The data volume is expected to grow significantly in the following years as fixed sensors are installed on an increasing number of road segments. Moreover, there is a high penetration of mobile sensors such as GPS and accelerometers mounted on public transport vehicles, and smartphones used by drivers and pedestrians.

Maritime surveillance has been attracting attention both for economic and environmental reasons [26]. As an example, preventing accidents at sea by moni-toring vessel activity results in substantial financial savings for shipping compa-nies and averts maritime ecosystem damages. Complex event recognition allows for the fusion of various streaming data expressing, among others, vessel activity, with static geographical information, for the detection of suspicious or potentially dangerous situations that may have a serious impact on the environment and on safe navigation at sea.

Maritime navigation technology can automatically provide real-time infor-mation from sailing vessels. For instance, the Automatic Identification System (AIS)[3] is a tracking system for identifying and locating vessels at sea through data exchange. AIS information is continuously emitted from over 400,000 ships worldwide[4]. AIS-equipped vessels report their position in different time scales

---

[3] http://www.imo.org/OurWork/Safety/Navigation/Pages/AIS.aspx
[4] http://www.marinetraffic.com

(the frequency of AIS messages depends, for example, on the proximity to base stations and the vessel type). Moreover, AIS messages are often noisy, offering contradicting information. This data source alone then creates a Big Data problem for event recognition. For effective vessel identification and tracking, additional data sources should be taken into consideration, such as weather reports and frequently updated satellite images of the surveillance areas. Furthermore, streaming data must be continuously correlated with static geographical data for detecting, among others, violations of protected areas and shipping in unsafe areas.

3 Research Challenges

To perform complex event recognition in applications such as those mentioned above, one has to deal with a series of challenges [5]. For instance, complex events may evolve over multiple scales of time and space [37]. The variety of the event stream may be reflected by sources that report events ranging from (milli-)seconds to days. Moreover, historical data spanning over long periods of time need to be taken into consideration. Taking up the credit card fraud management application from above, for instance, transaction events for a credit card may be observed within milliseconds, but to detect fraud, their occurrence needs to be related to common usage patterns ranging over weeks or even months. To cope with multiple scales of time and space a recognition system should be adaptable, computing dynamically the appropriate lengths of multi-granular windows of varying levels of detail, being able to recognize complex events from lower-level events of varying spatio-temporal granularity, without compromising efficiency [20,22,25].

In what follows, we focus on two challenges of complex event recognition: (1) how to distribute event recognition (Section 3.1) and (2) how to deal with the inherent uncertainty observed in many event recognition scenarios (Section 3.2). An answer to the first question is a prerequisite for coping with the continuously growing volume and velocity of event streams. Computation as well as communication resources need to be used efficiently in order to allow for large-scale event recognition. The second question is motivated by the different types of uncertainty exhibited by event recognition applications. On the one hand, event streams used as input may be incomplete, include inaccurate or even erroneous information. On the other hand, the notion of an event that shall be recognized may be imprecise, which renders any event recognition probabilistic. As such, comprehensive handling of these types of uncertainty is a prerequisite for effective event recognition.

3.1 Distributed Event Recognition

Distributed deployment of event recognition enables scalability and allows for reaching the throughput that is required by contemporary applications, such as credit card fraud detection. Systems that exploit distribution and realise event recognition by independent processors, may be classified as *clustered* or *networked* [9]. In a clustered system, the processors realising event recognition are strongly connected (e.g. part of the same local area network), meaning that the link between them is faster than the link between the system and the event sources. In the case of credit card fraud detection, for instance, processing may be shared in a large cluster of machines, connected by high-speed network connections, that receives the input event streams from remote sources. Examples for clustered recognition systems include Borealis [1], NextCEP [30], or commercial offerings such as IBM System S [41]. Networked systems, in turn, try to push computation to the sources in order to reduce communication costs [3], e.g., based on publish-subscribe middleware [19,27]. The advent of scalable infrastructures for distributed event processing, such as Storm [35] or Spark Streaming [42] further provides opportunities for scalable event recognition. That is, the detection logic for a composite event may be encoded directly as a processor or instances of wrapped engines for centralised event recognition can be used as processors in these infrastructures.

Distribution strategies determine how the event recognition task is split up among different processors, may they be clustered or networked. Many of these techniques are *query-driven*, i.e., they apply distribution schemes that leverage the syntax and semantics of the composite event that shall be recognised. Examples includes the row/column scaling and pipelining, see [8], to distribute the execution of automata expressing queries in the Cayuga event language [7]. Semantic dependencies between composite events can be used to identify strata of independent queries, which are then executed on different nodes of a distributed system [18]. Other work showed how event recognition can be distributed to nodes while reusing operators that are part of the detection of multiple composite events [30]. Yet, distribution strategies may be even more fine-granular. That is, *instance-driven* techniques are not guided by the definition of the composite event, but focus on its partial materialisations (i.e., partial matches). For instance, input events that belong to individual run instances of the finite state machine of a composite event may be distributed to different nodes [6], thereby providing fine-grained partitioned data parallelism [13].

Distribution strategies for networked systems particularly aim at reducing the volume of data sent between the processors realising event recognition. Such strategies are particular valuable in sensor networks, such as those mentioned earlier in the context of traffic management. Methods proposed in this space decompose the event recognition task into a set of local constraints that can be verified at the event sources that generate the input data. The definition of these constraints typically relates to the absence of a composite event, i.e., as long as the local constraints are satisfied, it can be concluded that the composite event of interest has not occurred. As such, the constraints avoid unnecessary communication between the processor in situations where the composite event cannot be detected. Existing techniques following this idea have been tailored for events that are defined as a function over aggregate values derived at the event sources. In traffic management, for instance, such an approach enables to check whether the aggregated traffic flow in a certain neighbourhood stays above a threshold, even though, most of the time, the sensed values are only locally checked at each sensor. Specific methods to realise this approach include sketching [24] and geometric reasoning [12,15,31].

Open Issues. Despite much work on the distribution of event recognition, there are notable research gaps:

Distribution of probabilistic event recognition. As will be detailed below, event recognition is inherently uncertain, e.g., because of manual data input (credit card transactions) or noisy sensor data (traffic management, maritime surveillance). One way of handling this uncertainty is to rely on probabilistic instead of deterministic techniques. However, this renders the vast majority of existing distribution techniques inapplicable and calls for new deployment models and distribution strategies that are geared towards probabilistic methods.

Networked distribution of complex composite events. Techniques that aim at minimisation of communication in networked event recognition have focussed on composite events that are defined as functions over aggregate values. Yet, composite events that correlate events based on logical, temporal, and spatial conditions cannot be addressed with existing methods. Broadening the set of types of composite events that can be considered in the minimisation of communication between event recognition processors is an important direction for future research. For the above mentioned example of monitoring traffic flow, for instance, it may be relevant to not only detect that a threshold is exceeded, but to identify a sequence of spatially related violations of such a threshold.

Semantic distribution. Most distribution approaches are guided by the definition of the composite event (query-driven) or its partial materialisations (instance-driven). However, in many event processing scenarios, the input event streams also exhibit characteristics that enable effective distribution of event recognition tasks. Recently, it was shown how regularities in the occurrences of events can be leveraged to rewrite composite event patterns, see [10,40]. For instance, the knowledge that events of one type may only be followed, but never preceded, by events of another type enables rewriting of a conjunction pattern over these types into a sequence pattern. Similarly, such knowledge about stream characteristics may be exploited to spread the event recognition task among the nodes of a distributed system.

3.2   Event Recognition under Uncertainty

Event recognition applications exhibit various types of uncertainty. Sensor networks introduce uncertainty due to reasons that range from inaccurate measurements through local network failures to unexpected interference of mediators. As mentioned earlier, for example, several of the data fields of credit card transactions could be left empty or contain incorrect information due to terminal misconfiguration. Similarly, Automatic Identification System (AIS) messages in the maritime domain are often noisy with contradicting information. For all of these reasons, input event streams lack veracity. Furthermore, in many application domains, we only have imprecise knowledge about the pattern/definition of a complex event, or the available events and context information are insufficient for expressing a complex event.

Noisy input streams are handled, to various extents, by several approaches. For instance, the Lahar system [28], which is based on Cayuga, has an inference mechanism for answering queries over probabilistic data streams, that is, streams whose events are tagged with a probability value. In [32], each input event is defined as a set of alternatives, each with its occurrence probability, with all alternatives summing to a probability value of 1, or less than 1 if non-occurrence is possible. Tran and Davis [36] assume a computer vision setting where input events are detected by visual information processing algorithms with some degree of belief. This degree is propagated to a Markov Logic Network [11] expressing the complex event patterns using weighted utility formulas. Syntactically, each formula F_i in Markov logic is represented in first-order logic and it is associated with a weight w_i. The higher the value of the weight, the stronger the constraint represented by F_i. Semantically, a set of Markov logic formulas (F_i, w_i) represents a probability distribution over possible worlds. A world violating formulas becomes less probable, but not impossible as in first-order logic. Skarlatidis et al. [33] represent and reason over probabilistic data streams using the ProbLog logic programming framework [16]. ProbLog allows for assigning probabilities to events and can compute the 'success' probability of a query by summing the probabilities of all the subprograms that entail it.

Imperfect event patterns are naturally handled by techniques based on probabilistic graphical models. Morariu and Davis [23] use Markov Logic Networks in combination with Allen's interval algebra [2] to determine the most consistent sequence of complex events, based on the observations of low-level classifiers. Sadilek and Kautz [29] propose a method based on hybrid-Markov Logic Networks [39] in order to recognize (un)successful human interactions using noisy GPS streams. Other work relies on a hierarchy of Markov Logic Networks where mid-level networks process the output of low-level computer vision algorithms, and high-level networks fuse the output of mid-level networks to recognize complex events [14]. An attempt for generic event recognition in Markov Logic Networks is presented in [34]. In this setting, a dialect of the Event Calculus [17] is combined with probabilistic domain-dependent rules. Consequently, the approach supports probabilistic inertia. In other words, in the absence of relevant information the probability of a complex event may increase or decrease over time. The inertia behaviour of a complex event may be customized by appropriately adjusting the weight values of the corresponding rules.

Open Issues. Probabilistic event recognition has been recently attracting attention. However, there are still open issues — below we discuss two of them.

Real-time event recognition under uncertainty. Although there is considerable work on optimising probabilistic reasoning techniques, the imposed overhead does not allow for real-time performance in a wide range of applications. To deal with Big Data, the focus has to shift to *distributed* and *parallelised* probabilistic reasoning. While we mentioned the challenge of distributing probabilistic techniques in the previous section, this challenge also refers to the creation of new reasoning models and algorithms that offer greater potential for distribution than existing methods and which can exploit the full potential of infrastructures for highly-parallel execution.

Machine learning. Estimating manually the confidence values of the complex event patterns is a tedious and error-prone process. Using machine learning techniques, it is possible, in Markov Logic Networks for instance, to estimate the weights of the rules expressing a complex event pattern, given a set of training data. Weight learning in Markov Logic Networks is performed by optimising a likelihood function, which is a statistical measure of how well the probabilistic model fits the training data. In addition to weight learning, the structure of a Markov Logic Network, that is, the rules expressing complex events, can be learned from training data. Currently, the structure of a complex event is constructed first, and then weight learning is performed. However, separating the two learning tasks in this way may lead to suboptimal results, as the first optimisation step needs to make assumptions about the weight values, which have not been optimized yet. Better results can be obtained by combining structure learning with weight learning in a single stage.

4 Summary

In this paper, we took three applications for event recognition—credit card fraud management, traffic management, and maritime surveillance—as a starting point to motivate two research challenges: the distribution of event recognition and uncertainty handling. For both challenges, we gave a brief overview of the state-of-the-art and then identified research gaps. Those relate in particular to the distribution of probabilistic event recognition, networked distribution of composite events, semantic distribution, real-time event recognition under uncertainty, and machine learning in event recognition.

Acknowledgements. The authors have received financial support from the EU FP7 project SPEEDD (619435), the project *"AMINESS: Analysis of Marine INformation for Environmentally Safe Shipping"* which is co-financed by the European Fund for Regional Development and from Greek National funds through the operational programs "Competitiveness and Entrepreneurship" and "Regions in Transition" of the National Strategic Reference Framework - Action: "COOPERATION 2011 – Partnerships of Production and Research Institutions in Focused Research and Technology Sectors", and the German Research Foundation (DFG) in the Emmy Noether Programme (4891).

References

1. Abadi, D.J., Ahmad, Y., Balazinska, M., Çetintemel, U., Cherniack, M., Hwang, J., Lindner, W., Maskey, A., Rasin, A., Ryvkina, E., Tatbul, N., Xing, Y., Zdonik, S.B.: The design of the borealis stream processing engine. In: CIDR, pp. 277–289 (2005). http://www.cidrdb.org/cidr2005/papers/P23.pdf
2. Allen, J.: Maintaining knowledge about temporal intervals. Communications of the ACM **26**(11), 832–843 (1983)
3. Artikis, A., Baber, C., Bizarro, P., de Wit, C.C., Etzion, O., Fournier, F., Goulart, P., Howes, A., Lygeros, J., Paliouras, G., Schuster, A., Sharfman, I.: Scalable proactive event-driven decision-making. IEEE Technology and Society Magazine **33**(3), 35–41 (2014)
4. Artikis, A., Weidlich, M., Schnitzler, F., Boutsis, I., Liebig, T., Piatkowski, N., Bockermann, C., Morik, K., Kalogeraki, V., Marecek, J., Gal, A., Mannor, S., Gunopulos, D., Kinane, D.: Heterogeneous stream processing and crowdsourcing for urban traffic management. In: International Conference on Extending Database Technology (EDBT), pp. 712–723 (2014)
5. Artikis, A., Gal, A., Kalogeraki, V., Weidlich, M.: Event recognition challenges and techniques: Guest editors' introduction. ACM Trans. Internet Techn. **14**(1), 1 (2014). http://doi.acm.org/10.1145/2632220
6. Balkesen, C., Dindar, N., Wetter, M., Tatbul, N.: Rip: run-based intra-query parallelism for scalable complex event processing. In: DEBS, pp. 3–14 (2013)
7. Brenna, L., Demers, A.J., Gehrke, J., Hong, M., Ossher, J., Panda, B., Riedewald, M., Thatte, M., White, W.M.: Cayuga: a high-performance event processing engine. In: SIGMOD Conference, pp. 1100–1102 (2007)
8. Brenna, L., Gehrke, J., Hong, M., Johansen, D.: Distributed event stream processing with non-deterministic finite automata. In: DEBS (2009)
9. Cugola, G., Margara, A.: Processing flows of information: From data stream to complex event processing. ACM Computing Surveys **44**(3), 15 (2012)
10. Ding, L., Works, K., Rundensteiner, E.A.: Semantic stream query optimization exploiting dynamic metadata. In: Abiteboul, S., Böhm, K., Koch, C., Tan, K. (eds.) Proceedings of the 27th International Conference on Data Engineering, ICDE 2011, April 11–16, 2011, Hannover, Germany, pp. 111–122. IEEE Computer Society (2011). http://dx.doi.org/10.1109/ICDE.2011.5767840
11. Domingos, P., Lowd, D.: Markov Logic: An Interface Layer for Artificial Intelligence. Morgan & Claypool Publishers (2009)
12. Giatrakos, N., Deligiannakis, A., Garofalakis, M., Sharfman, I., Schuster, A.: Distributed geometric query monitoring using prediction models. ACM TODS (2014)
13. Hirzel, M.: Partition and compose: parallel complex event processing. In: DEBS, pp. 191–200 (2012)
14. Kanaujia, A., Choe, T.E., Deng, H.: Complex events recognition under uncertainty in a sensor network. arXiv:1411.0085 [cs] (Nov 2014), arXiv:1411.0085
15. Keren, D., Sagy, G., Abboud, A., Ben-David, D., Schuster, A., Sharfman, I., Deligiannakis, A.: Geometric monitoring of heterogeneous streams. IEEE TKDE (2014)
16. Kimmig, A., Demoen, B., Raedt, L.D., Costa, V.S., Rocha, R.: On the implementation of the probabilistic logic programming language ProbLog. Theory and Practice of Logic Programming **11**, 235–262 (2011)
17. Kowalski, R., Sergot, M.: A logic-based calculus of events. New Generation Computing **4**(1), 67–96 (1986)

18. Lakshmanan, G.T., Rabinovich, Y.G., Etzion, O.: A stratified approach for supporting high throughput event processing applications. In: Gokhale, A.S., Schmidt, D.C. (eds.) DEBS. ACM (2009)
19. Li, G., Jacobsen, H.-A.: Composite subscriptions in content-based publish/subscribe systems. In: Alonso, G. (ed.) Middleware 2005. LNCS, vol. 3790, pp. 249–269. Springer, Heidelberg (2005)
20. Lijffijt, J., Papapetrou, P., Puolamäki, K.: Size matters: finding the most informative set of window lengths. In: Flach, P.A., De Bie, T., Cristianini, N. (eds.) ECML PKDD 2012, Part II. LNCS, vol. 7524, pp. 451–466. Springer, Heidelberg (2012)
21. Luckham, D.: The Power of Events: An Introduction to Complex EventProcessing in Distributed Enterprise Systems. Addison-Wesley (2002)
22. Maier, D., Grossniklaus, M., Moorthy, S., Tufte, K.: Capturing episodes: may the frame be with you. In: DEBS, pp. 1–11 (2012)
23. Morariu, V.I., Davis, L.S.: Multi-agent event recognition in structured scenarios. In: CVPR, pp. 3289–3296 (2011)
24. Papapetrou, O., Garofalakis, M.N., Deligiannakis, A.: Sketch-based querying of distributed sliding-window data streams. PVLDB 5(10), 992–1003 (2012)
25. Patroumpas, K.: Multi-scale window specification over streaming trajectories. J. Spatial Information Science 7(1), 45–75 (2013)
26. Patroumpas, K., Artikis, A., Katzouris, N., Vodas, M., Theodoridis, Y., Pelekis, N.: Event recognition for maritime surveillance. In: Alonso, G., Geerts, F., Popa, L., Barceló, P., Teubner, J., Ugarte, M., den Bussche, J.V., Paredaens, J. (eds.) Proceedings of the 18th International Conference on Extending Database Technology, EDBT 2015, Brussels, Belgium, March 23–27, 2015, pp. 629–640. OpenProceedings.org (2015). http://dx.doi.org/10.5441/002/edbt.2015.63
27. Pietzuch, P.R., Bacon, J.: Peer-to-peer overlay broker networks in an event-based middleware. In: Jacobsen, H. (ed.) Proceedings of the 2nd International Workshop on Distributed Event-Based Systems, DEBS 2003, Sunday, June 8th, 2003, San Diego, California, USA (in conjunction with SIGMOD/PODS). ACM (2003). http://doi.acm.org/10.1145/966618.966628
28. Ré, C., Letchner, J., Balazinksa, M., Suciu, D.: Event queries on correlated probabilistic streams. In: Proceedings of the 2008 ACM SIGMOD International Conference on Management of Data, pp. 715–728. SIGMOD 2008, ACM, New York (2008). http://doi.acm.org/10.1145/1376616.1376688
29. Sadilek, A., Kautz, H.A.: Location-based reasoning about complex multi-agent behavior. J. Artif. Intell. Res. (JAIR) 43, 87–133 (2012)
30. Schultz-Møller, N.P., Migliavacca, M., Pietzuch, P.R.: Distributed complex event processing with query rewriting. In: DEBS (2009)
31. Sharfman, I., Schuster, A., Keren, D.: A geometric approach to monitoring threshold functions over distributed data streams. In: SIGMOD Conference, pp. 301–312 (2006)
32. Shen, Z., Kawashima, H., Kitagawa, H.: Probabilistic event stream processing with lineage. In: Proc. of Data Engineering Workshop (2008)
33. Skarlatidis, A., Artikis, A., Filippou, J., Paliouras, G.: A probabilistic logic programming event calculus. Theory and Practice of Logic Programming 15(2), 213–245 (2015)
34. Skarlatidis, A., Paliouras, G., Artikis, A., Vouros, G.: Probabilistic event calculus for event recognition. ACM Transactions on Computational Logic 16(2), 11:1–11:37 (2015)

35. Toshniwal, A., Taneja, S., Shukla, A., Ramasamy, K., Patel, J.M., Kulkarni, S., Jackson, J., Gade, K., Fu, M., Donham, J., Bhagat, N., Mittal, S., Ryaboy, D.V.: Storm@twitter. In: Dyreson, C.E., Li, F., Özsu, M.T. (eds.) International Conference on Management of Data, SIGMOD 2014, Snowbird, UT, USA, June 22–27, 2014, pp. 147–156. ACM (2014). http://doi.acm.org/10.1145/2588555.2595641
36. Tran, S.D., Davis, L.S.: Event modeling and recognition using markov logic networks. In: Forsyth, D., Torr, P., Zisserman, A. (eds.) ECCV 2008, Part II. LNCS, vol. 5303, pp. 610–623. Springer, Heidelberg (2008)
37. Vespier, U., Nijssen, S., Knobbe, A.J.: Mining characteristic multi-scale motifs in sensor-based time series. In: He, Q., Iyengar, A., Nejdl, W., Pei, J., Rastogi, R. (eds.) 22nd ACM International Conference on Information and Knowledge Management, CIKM 2013, San Francisco, CA, USA, October 27 - November 1, 2013, pp. 2393–2398. ACM (2013). http://doi.acm.org/10.1145/2505515.2505620
38. Vesset, D., Flemming, M., Shirer, M.: Worldwide decision management software 2010–2014 forecast: A fast-growing opportunity to drive the intelligent economy. IDC report 226244 (2011)
39. Wang, J., Domingos, P.: Hybrid markov logic networks. In: AAAI, pp. 1106–1111 (2008)
40. Weidlich, M., Ziekow, H., Gal, A., Mendling, J., Weske, M.: Optimizing event pattern matching using business process models. IEEE Trans. Knowl. Data Eng. **26**(11), 2759–2773 (2014). http://doi.ieeecomputersociety.org/10.1109/TKDE.2014.2302306
41. Wu, K., Yu, P.S., Gedik, B., Hildrum, K., Aggarwal, C.C., Bouillet, E., Fan, W., George, D., Gu, X., Luo, G., Wang, H.: Challenges and experience in prototyping a multi-modal stream analytic and monitoring application on system S. In: Koch, C., Gehrke, J., Garofalakis, M.N., Srivastava, D., Aberer, K., Deshpande, A., Florescu, D., Chan, C.Y., Ganti, V., Kanne, C., Klas, W., Neuhold, E.J. (eds.) Proceedings of the 33rd International Conference on Very Large Data Bases, University of Vienna, Austria, September 23–27, 2007, pp. 1185–1196. ACM (2007). http://www.vldb.org/conf/2007/papers/industrial/p1185-wu.pdf
42. Zaharia, M., Das, T., Li, H., Hunter, T., Shenker, S., Stoica, I.: Discretized streams: fault-tolerant streaming computation at scale. In: Kaminsky, M., Dahlin, M. (eds.) ACM SIGOPS 24th Symposium on Operating Systems Principles, SOSP 2013, Farmington, PA, USA, November 3–6, 2013, pp. 423–438. ACM (2013). http://doi.acm.org/10.1145/2517349.2522737

General RuleML Track

Compact Representation of Conditional Probability for Rule-Based Mobile Context-Aware Systems

Szymon Bobek$^{(\boxtimes)}$ and Grzegorz J. Nalepa

AGH University of Science and Technology, al. Mickiewicza 30,
30-059 Krakow, Poland
{szymon.bobek,gjn}@agh.edu.pl

Abstract. Context-aware systems gained huge popularity in recent years due to rapid evolution of personal mobile devices. Equipped with variety of sensors, such devices are sources of a lot of valuable information that allows the system to act in an intelligent way. However, the certainty and presence of this information may depend on many factors like measurement accuracy or sensor availability. Such a dynamic nature of information may cause the system not to work properly or not to work at all. To allow for robustness of the context-aware system an uncertainty handling mechanism should be provided with it. Several approaches were developed to solve uncertainty in context knowledge bases, including probabilistic reasoning, fuzzy logic, or certainty factors. In this paper, we present a representation method that combines strengths of rules based on the attributive logic and Bayesian networks. Such a combination allows efficiently encode conditional probability distribution of random variables into a reasoning structure called XTT2. This provides a method for building hybrid context-aware systems that allows for robust inference in uncertain knowledge bases.

Keywords: Context-awareness · Mobile devices · Knowledge management · Uncertainty · Probabilistic rules

1 Introduction

Context-aware systems make use of contextual information to adapt their functionality to current environment state, or user needs and habits [3,26]. The variety of sensors available on mobile devices allows for building more advanced reliable context-aware systems. However, in many cases these systems are based on the assumption that the information they require is always available and certain. In mobile environments this assumption almost never holds.

Contextual data can be delivered to the mobile context-aware system in many different ways: directly from the device sensors [13], from other devices' sensors,

This work was funded by the National Science Centre, Poland as a part of the KnowMe project (registration number 2014/13/N/ST6/01786).

over peer-to-peer communication channels [2,10], from external data sources like contextual servers [6], from reasoning engines [22]. In each of this cases, the information may be temporarily unavailable, corrupted, or inaccurate. This may cause the system to work improperly unless an appropriate uncertainty handling mechanism is implemented to cope with such situations. The choice of the mechanisms for modelling and resolving uncertainty is highly correlated with a choice of the model of the system. As we have shown in our previous work presented in [4], one of the most expressive ways of modelling knowledge in user centric systems are rules. They provide high support for intelligibility, which is understood as an ability of the system to being understood. It is one of the most important features in the systems which aim at direct communication with the user. It was proven that providing appropriate level of intelligibility increases user trust in the system in environments characterised by high uncertainty of data [18]. Choosing rules as a main knowledge modelling formalism also has consequences on the choice of the uncertainty modelling method. Several approaches were developed to solve uncertainty in context knowledge bases, including probabilistic reasoning, fuzzy logic, or certainty factors [4].

In [4] we provided a comparison of these methods with respect to the type of uncertainty they handle and an implementation effort required to integrate them with the system. Based on that comparison, we chose the XTT2 rule representation method together with modified certainty factors algebra for uncertainty handling in mobile context-aware systems. In this paper, we present a continuation of this research with primary objective of providing a probabilistic interpretation of the XTT2 tables. This allows for compact encoding of conditional probability using a human-readable rule format. Additionally, such an interpretation gives the opportunity for building hybrid models that combines efficiency of rule-based reasoning with uncertainty and learning capabilities of Bayesian networks.

The rest of the paper is organised as follows. Section 2 presents the current state of the art in the area of uncertainty handling in mobile context-aware systems. It discusses the main drawbacks of the available solutions and presents the motivation for our work. The XTT2 rule-based knowledge representation is presented in Section 3. Probabilistic interpretation of the XTT2 models is sketched in Section 4. This section also describes a hybrid algorithm for reasoning in the XTT2 based probabilistic models. Summary and future work was presented in Section 5.

2   Related Work and Motivation

Among many proposals of uncertainty handling mechanisms [25] like Hartley Theory, Shannon Theory, Dempster-Shafer Theory, the following have been found the most successful in the area of context-awareness:

- Probabilistic approaches, mostly based on Bayes theorem, that allows for describing uncertainty caused by the lack of machine precision and lack of knowledge [5,11].

- Fuzzy logic, that provides mechanism for handling uncertainty caused by the lack of human precision [8,30]. It ignores law of excluded middle allowing for imprecise, ambiguous and vague descriptions of knowledge.
- Certainty factors (CF), that describe both uncertainties caused by the lack of knowledge and lack of precision [1,9]. They are mostly used in expert systems that rely on the rule-based knowledge representation.
- Machine learning approaches, that use data driven rather than model driven approaches for reasoning [15]. They allow for handling both uncertainties due to lack of knowledge and lack of precision.

Majority of modern context-aware systems use probabilistic methods for modeling uncertainty, as they provide a very effective way of modelling and reasoning on dynamic and incomplete information. However, the exact inference in complex probabilistic models is an NP-hard task and is not always tractable. Intractability of the system inference, on the other hand, violates intelligibility feature, which is one of the fundamental requirements for the user-centric systems [19]. Intelligibility is defined as the capability of the system for being understood. This feature is crucial in systems that require interaction with the user, like mobile context-aware systems [22]. The ability to explain system decisions to the user makes it possible to collect user feedback about system and hence improve system adaptability capabilities. Therefore, to provide both intelligibility and effective uncertainty handling mechanism, rules have to be combined with robust probabilistic approach.

There are several attempts made to bind rules and probabilistic reasoning. Problog is a probabilistic extension of Prolog programming language [29]. A ProbLog program defines a distribution over logic programs by specifying for each logic clause the probability that it belongs to a randomly sampled program. The semantics of ProbLog is then defined by the success probability of a query, which corresponds to the probability that the query succeeds in a randomly sampled program.

Simillar approach was implemented in AILog2 [28] (formerly CILog). It is an open-source purely declarative representation and reasoning system, that includes pure Prolog (including negation as failure) and allows for probabilistic reasoning. The probability is based on the Independent Choice Logic [27] which can represent Bayesian networks, Markov decision processes and complex mixes of logic and probability.

Probabilistic inference as a continuous optimization task was proposed in probabilistic soft logic (PSL) [12]. PSL is a framework for collective, probabilistic reasoning in relational domains. PSL uses first order logic rules as a template language for graphical models over random variables with soft truth values from the interval $[0; 1]$.

2.1   Motivation

Although the idea of incorporating probability into rules is not new, all of the aforementioned approaches use unstructured knowledge model, and assumes that the reasoning will be done in a pure probabilistic manner. We do not make any assumption on that.

In our previous research, we used modified certainty factors algebra and the XTT2 rule representation to handle uncertainty in mobile context-aware systems [4]. The certainty factors for rules were assigned by an expert or were discovered with data mining approaches (like associations rules mining algorithms). One of the biggest problems of this approach was lack of proper handling for uncertainty caused by unavailable context providers. In a case when the value of an attribute from the conditional part of the rule was unknown, the certainty of the entire rule was defined as zero. In such case every rule within a table was considered as completely uncertain and no further reasoning was possible. This was caused by the fact that certainty factors algebra do not take into consideration historical data while evaluating. In contrary, probabilistic approaches are strictly based on statistical analysis of historical data. The idea of exploiting this strength, for the purpose of providing an efficient uncertainty handling mechanism in rule based mobile context-aware systems, was the primary motivation for the research presented in this paper.

The XTT2 decision tables allows to build structured probabilistic models in a human-readable way. What is more, the idea of dividing rules into separate tables allows building hybrid rule-based models, that uses probabilistic reasoning only when needed. And finally, the XTT2 knowledge representation is used by the HEARTDROID inference engine which allows to implement the solutions on a mobile platform easily.

3   XTT2 Knowledge Representation

The XTT2 representation is based on the Attribute Logic with Set Values over Finite Domains [17,24] (ALSV(FD) for short). The basic elements of the language of ALSV(FD) are attributes names and attributes values. There are two attribute types: *simple* which allows the attribute to take a single value at a time, and *generalized* that allows the attribute to take set values. The values that every attribute can take are limited by their domains. For the purpose of further discussion let's assume that: A_i represents some arbitrarily chosen attribute, D_i is a domain of this attribute, and V_i represents a subset of values from domain D_i, where $d_i \in V_i$. Therefore we can define a valid ALSV(FD) formula as $A_i \propto d_i$ for simple attributes, where $\propto$ is one of the operators from the set $=, \neq, \in, \notin$ and $A_i \propto V_i$ for generalized attributes, where $\propto$ is one of the operators from the set $=, \neq, \sim, \not\sim, \subset, \supset$. ALSV(FD) formulae are basic parts of the XTT2 rule, which can be represented as:

$$(A_i \propto d_i) \wedge (A_j \propto d_j) \wedge \ldots (A_n \propto d_n) \longrightarrow (A_k = d_k) \wedge \ldots \wedge (A_z = d_z)$$

Attributes from the conditional part of the rules and attributes from the rules decision forms schemas. A schema is a tuple of the form $(\text{COND}_i, \text{DEC}_i)$, where COND_i is a set of attributes from the conditional part of the $i\text{-}th$ rule, and

Table id: tab_4 - Actions

	(?) location	(?) daytime	(?) today	(->) action
1	= home	= morning	= workday	:= leaving_home
2	= outside	= morning	= workday	:= travelling_work
3	= work	= daytime	= workday	:= working
4	= work	= afternoon	= workday	:= leaving_work
5	= outside	= afternoon	= workday	:= travelling_home
6	= home	= evening	= any	:= resting
7	= home	= night	= any	:= sleeping
8	= home	= any	= weekend	:= resting
9	= outside	= evening	= any	:= entertaining
10	= outside	= night	= any	:= travelling_home

Table id: tab_5 - Applications

	(?) action	(?) transportation	(->) {application}
1	= leaving_home	= idle	:= {news,weather}
2	∈ {leaving_work,leaving_home}	∈ {walking,running}	:= {clock,navigation}
3	∈ {travelling_home,travelling_work}	∈ {driving,cycling}	:= navigation
4	∈ {travelling_home,travelling_work}	∈ {bus,train}	:= {news,clock}
5	∈ {resting,entertaining}	∈ {running,cycling}	:= {sport_tracker,weather}
6	= working	= any	:= {calendar,mall}
7	= sleeping	= idle	:= clock
8	∈ {resting,entertaining}	∈ {driving,bus,train}	:= trip_advisor

Table id: tab_6 - Profile

	(?) action	(->) profile
1	∈ {travelling_home,travelling_work,leaving_home,leaving_work}	:= loud
2	∈ {working,resting,entertaining}	:= vibrations
3	= sleeping	:= offline

Fig. 1. Fragment of an XTT2 model for context-aware application recommendation system

DEC_i is a set of attributes that values are set in the decision part of the i-th rule. Rules that have the same schema are grouped within separated XTT2 tables, and the system is split into such tables linked by arrows representing the inference control strategy [20]. An example of the XTT2 table is presented in Figure 1. It describes a fragment of a mobile context-aware recommendation system, that based on the user activity, location and time, suggests applications for the user and switches profiles in the user mobile phone.

The inference in the XTT2 knowledge bases is performed by the HEART-DROID engine. HEARTDROID is a rule-based inference engine for Android mobile devices, that is based on HeaRT inference engine[1]. The HEARTDROID inference engine consists of three main components depicted in the Figure 2. These components are: *XTT2 Model Manager*, responsible for switching between XTT2 models; *Reasoning mechanism*, that performs inference based on one of four inference modes [20], and *Working Memory* component – a common memory for all the models, where current and historical states are stored. The state of the system is defined as a set of all attributes and its values captured at some point in time.

HEARTDROID uses HMR notation which is a textual, human-readable representation of the visual XTT2 models. The example of the rule written in HMR notation is presented below. It corresponds to the first rule in the XTT2 table *Actions* from Figure 1.

```
xrule 'Actions'/1:
    [location eq home,
     daytime eq morning,
     today eq workday]
    ==>
    [action set leaving_home]
```

The rule above should be read as: *If a user is at home, it is morning, and today is a workday, then the user will be leaving home soon.* Rules covering different user locations, days and times are located in the same XTT2 table, as they share the

---

[1] See https://bitbucket.org/sbobek/heartdroid for details.

same schema. Different tables that represent different schemas are linked together defining an inference control. The inference control determine sequence in which the XTT2 tables should be processed. For instance, if the context-aware system wants to know which applications should be suggested to the user, the inference engine will have to process the table *Actions* at the first place, and later the table *Applications*, as it depends on the output from the former.

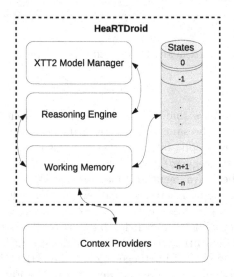

Fig. 2. Architecture of XTT2 inference engine

In case when all of the data is available and certain, such a reasoning is done with traditional forward-chaining approach. Alternatively, when there is data available but uncertain, the inference based on certainty factors (CF) algebra is performed [4]. However, certainty factors algebra does not handle situations when some of the information from the conditional parts of the rules are missing. For instance if the GPS sensor was turned off, and the location of the user could not be established, the rule from the example above will not be fired, and therefore no valid output for the context-aware system could be provided. It is because in CF algebra the certainty of the rule is determined by the smallest certainty of its conditions. Therefore, in case when some of the attributes values from conditional parts are unknown the certainty of the entire rule equals zero. In such a situation all the rules in the table will be equally uncertain and it will not be possible to make a decision which rule choose to fire. However, such a decision can be made with a probabilistic approach, which uses historical data to estimate the most likely value of a random variable (or attribute in this case). In the HEARTDROID inference engine the Working Memory component is responsible for logging all the system states, providing a valuable learning data for probabilistic models. The next section discusses the probabilistic interpretation of XTT2 models in details.

4   Probabilistic Interpretation of XTT2 Models

In Section 3 the XTT2 knowledge representation was described. Although the representation is based on rules, the structure of the XTT2 formalism allows for its probabilistic interpretation. In such interpretation every attribute can be considered a random variable, and every XTT2 table a deterministic conditional distribution table. The connections between XTT2 tables can be further interpreted as dependencies between random variables, and the XTT2 model can be easily transformed to a Bayesian network. Figure 3 represents a Bayesian interpretation of the XTT2 model presented in Figure 1.

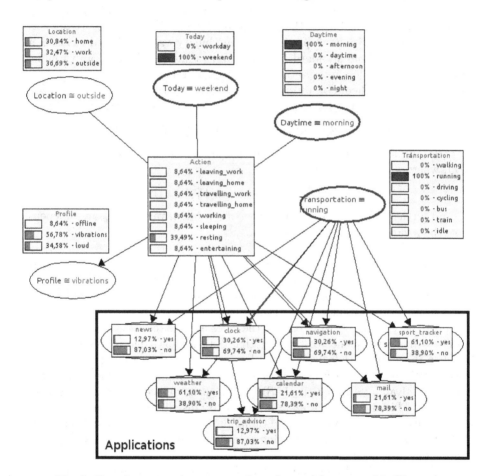

Fig. 3. Bayesian network representation of a model presented in Figure 1

In such an interpretation, every schema $(\mathbb{COND}, \mathbb{DEC})$ can be represented as a conditional probability of a form:

$$P(\mathbb{DEC} \mid \mathbb{COND}) \tag{1}$$

Therefore, in the probabilistic interpretation of schema $(\mathbb{COND}, \mathbb{DEC})$, every rule is represented by a pair $\langle r, p \rangle$, where r is an XTT2 rule defined in Section 3 and $p \in [0; 1]$ is the conditional probability assigned to it. The probability p defines a certainty of a rule given its preconditions. We will refer to p as to certainty, not the probability in the further discussion. Therefore, in case where all the attributes from the $\mathbb{COND}$ part of the rule are known, the conditional probability distribution (CPD) is deterministic and traditional rule-based reasoning can be performed. In case when some of the attributes values from the conditional part are unknown, the probabilistic reasoning is triggered.

The XTT2 representation allows generalized attributes to be present in both $\mathbb{COND}$ and $\mathbb{DEC}$. This may lead to serious problems in probabilistic interpretation of the XTT2 rules, as the generalized attributes have to be treated as random variables with multiple independent binary values allowed. This is a serious departure from standard Bayesian understanding of a random variable. Therefore, the following interpretation was proposed. Let assume that the XTT2 model contains a schema of a form $(\{A_i, A_j\}, \{A_g\})$, where A_g is a generalized attributes. The rule that falls into this schema is given as follows:

$$r : (A_i \propto d_i) \wedge (A_j \propto d_j) \longrightarrow A_g = \{v_1, v_2, \ldots v_n\}$$

Following the equation (1), the rule from above formula can be represented $\langle r, p \rangle$, where p is defined as follows:

$$p : P\left(A_g = \{v_1, v_2, \ldots v_n\} \mid A_i, A_j\right)$$

And further, assuming that the values of a random variable A_g are independent, the p can be rewritten as:

$$
\begin{aligned}
P(A_g = \{v_1, v_2, \ldots v_n\} \mid A_i, A_j) = \\
P(v_1 \mid A_i, A_j) \cdot P(v_2 \mid A_i, A_j) \cdot \ldots \cdot P(v_n \mid A_i, A_j)
\end{aligned}
\tag{2}
$$

The interpretation of the generalized attributes as a set of independent random variables are extremely important in the inference process in special cases when attributes from decision part of the rules are treated as evidences.

The other consequence of the fact that XTT2 knowledge representation is based on the attributive logic, is that it has some advantages over the traditional table distribution approaches in terms of notation compactness. One of the most important advantages is that the ALSV(FD) logic introduces operators like $=, \neq,$ $\sim, \not\sim, \subset, \supset$. This allows to represent a probability distribution in a more efficient way. For instance to encode the conditional probability distribution presented in table *Applications* from Figure 1 using traditional conditional probability tables (CPT), one will need 50 rows to cover all the combinations of attributes values presented in the *Applications* table. The complexity of the representation is highly dependant on the nature of the problem, and in worst case even for XTT2 it can be the same as for the standard CPT representation. However, in most cases there will be an advantage of usage of the XTT2 notation over the standard CPT as it presents probability distributions in human readable rule-based form. What is more, the XTT2 representation allows explaining probabilistic reasoning by exploiting rule-based system capabilities of intelligibility.

4.1 Learning Probability Distribution in XTT2 Models

Probabilistic interpretation of the XTT2 models presented in this paper assumes that the XTT2 tables and rules are given. They can be provided by an expert, or mined with data mining algorithms. Although learning structure of the model and automatic discovery of rules is a very important task in terms of adaptability of the system, it is beyond the scope of this work. In this paper, we focus on learning distribution of the random variables (attributes) for a given set of rules and XTT2 schemas.

HEARTDROID inference engine consists of a working memory component that logs all the system states in a given time window. The state is defined as a set of attributes and their values at a given point in time. Therefore, all the states within a specified time window can be considered as a training set for the probabilistic XTT2 tables. Below the sample of such a training set is presented. This training set was used to learn distribution of random variables in the Bayesian network presented in Figure 3.

```
Action,[Applications],Daytime,Location,Profile,Today,Transportation
sleeping,[no,no,no,no,yes,no,no,no],night,home,offline,workday,idle
sleeping,[no,no,no,no,yes,no,no,no],night,home,offline,workday,idle
working,[no,yes,yes,no,no,no,no,no],daytime,work,vibrations,workday,cycling
working,[no,yes,yes,no,no,no,no,no],daytime,work,vibrations,workday,bus
working,[no,yes,yes,no,no,no,no,no],daytime,work,vibrations,workday,idle
....
```

One of the biggest challenges in learning probabilistic XTT2 models is to wisely choose time windows from which the training set will be generated. The window cannot be too small, as the states logged within a short period of time will not cover all the cases. It cannot be too large, as storing and processing large amount of data may be an overload for a mobile device. The size of the time window has to be adjusted experimentally for a specific model.

Because the learning of Bayesian network is not an incremental process, and therefore it may be necessary to relearn the model. The relearning is very important as the user habits may change over time and therefore affect the probabilities of certain rules.

4.2 Inference in the Probabilistic XTT2 Models

There are three possibilities of performing reasoning in the probabilistic XTT2 models:

1. purely deterministic inference – in such an inference only tables that have all values of attributes from their conditional parts known can be processed. This may therefore end up in interrupted inference when some values are missing;
2. purely probabilistic inference – in such an inference the XTT2 model is queried as if it was Bayesian network. No deterministic reasoning is performed;

3. hybrid inference – in such an inference tables that can be processed in a deterministic way are processed according to such paradigm, and the probabilistic reasoning is triggered only in the other cases.

To exploit fast and efficient reassigning provided by the rule-based approach, with probabilistic uncertainty handling, a hybrid inference model was proposed. The procedure for processing the XTT2 tables in such an approach was presented in Algorithm 1.

Algorithm 1. Algorithm for probabilistic inference in XTT2 models

---

   Data: E – the set of all known attributes values

        A – the set of attributes which values are to be found

   Result: V – values for attributes from the set A

1 Create a stack of tables T that needs to be processed to obtain V;

2 **while** *not empty* T **do**

3     $t = pop(T)$;

4   Identify schema $(\mathbb{COND}, \mathbb{DEC})$ of table t;

5   **if** $\forall c \in \mathbb{COND},\ Val(c) \in E$ **then**

6   Execute table t;

7        $\forall a \in \mathbb{DEC} \cap A$: add $Val(a)$ to E and V;

8   **else**

9   Run probabilistic reasoning to obtain $P(a) \forall a \in \mathbb{DEC}$;

10   Select rule $\langle r_{max}, p_{max} \rangle$ such that: $\forall \langle r, p \rangle \in t : p \leq p_{max}$;

11   **if** $p_{max} \leq \epsilon$ **then**

12   execute rule r;

13        $\forall a \in \mathbb{DEC} \cap A$: add $Val(a)$ to E and V;

14   **else**

15        $\forall a \in \mathbb{DEC} \cap A$: add $P(a)$ to E and V;

16   **end**

17 **end**

18 **end**

19 **return** V;

The first step of the algorithm is the identification of a list of the XTT2 tables T that have to be processed to obtain values of a given set of attributes A. This is done according to one of the inference modes available [20]. For every table $t \in T$ popped from the list, a deterministic inference is performed if possible, and the values of the attributes from the conclusion part of the executed rule are added to evidence set E. When it is impossible to run deterministic inference (e.g. some values of the attributes are missing), the probabilistic inference is triggered. It uses all the evidences E to calculate probability of the attributes values from the current schema. After that, a rule with the highest certainty (or probability in this case) is selected and triggered, and the reasoning returns to be deterministic. In cases when the probability of a rule is very low, say less than some value ϵ, no rule is executed. However, if the conclusion part of the schema for currently processing table contains an attribute that belongs to a set A, the most probable estimation of this attribute value is added to the result.

The evidences for the evidences set E are obtain from two types of sources:

- from the Working Memory component of the inference engine that stores all the attributes values (see Figure 2), and
- from the reasoning process, when new values are inferred.

The XTT2 notation allows three types of attributes: *comm, in,* and *out.* Attributes that are marked as *out* cannot be treated as evidences, even though their value is known. For example if the value of the attribute *Profile* from the model presented in Figure 3 was known, and marked as *in* or *comm,* it will be included as evidence in the reasoning process. In other cases it will not be used in the inference process. This is very important for the probabilistic reasoning strategy, where every evidence can have an impact on the reasoning results.

4.3 Use Case Scenario

The inference procedure presented in Algorithm 1 can be shown in practice on the model from Figure 1 and its probabilistic interpretation depicted in Figure 3. It is a model for a mobile context-aware application that based on the user context, suggests applications to be launched, and sets appropriate mobile phone profile. The context in this model is defined as an information about values of the attributes: *today, daytime, location, action, transportation, application* and *profile.*

Let us assume that the values of the attributes *today, daytime* and *transportation* are given and are equal respectively to: *weekend, morning* and *running.* In the contrary, the information about the user position is unknown (i.e. the GPS module is turned off or user is underground). Because the value of the attribute *action* is derived partially from the user location, this attribute value remains unknown as well. In traditional reasoning mode, at this point the inference will not continue, and no further conclusion could be made. However, in the hybrid mode presented in this work, such an inference is possible. During the processing of the table *Actions,* once the algorithm notices that there is a value of the user location missing, the probabilistic inference is triggered. For this purpose the Bayesian network presented in Figure 3 is used. The algorithm uses values of known attributes as evidences, and queries the probabilistic model for unknown values. In this example, evidence attributes are *today, daytime* and *transportation.* In a case when the value of the attribute *profile* was known, and this attribute was marked as *comm* in XTT2 model, it will also be used as evidence, despite the fact that it is not delivered by any of the context providers, but inferred by the system. Filling the probabilistic model with evidences, it can be calculated that the most probable value of the *action* attribute is *resting.* This value is produced by two rules: by the rule number 6 and 8 from the *Action* table. In a hybrid reasoning, if the certainty of a rule is greater than the ϵ, the rule is fired and inference is continued in a deterministic way. If the ϵ is grater than the certainty of a rule, the algorithm moves to another table and process it in a probabilistic way. For the purpose of this example, let assume, that the ϵ from the Algorithm 1 equals 0.3. Such an assumption means that during a probabilistic reasoning, rule with assigned certainty greater than 0.3 will be fired. In the example that we discuss there are two rules which certainty greater than epsilon. Hence, the conflict set resolution mechanism has to be used to select the rule to fire [16]. For the sake of simplicity we can use order-based conflict set resolution and pick the rule which appears first in the XTT2 table. Therefore, the rule number 6 from the table *Actions* will be fired and the value of the attribute *action* will be set to *resting*, as if it was certain. After that, the inference will be continued in a deterministic way, which will finally lead to execution of the rule number 5 from the table *Applications* and the rule number 2 from the table *Profile*.

5   Summary and Future Work

In this paper, we presented a new approach for modelling context-aware systems with the usage of a compact representation of conditional probability which is based on the XTT2 knowledge representation formalism. Such an approach allows to encode conditional probability in a compact, structured and human-readable format. It also allows for hybrid reasoning that exploits fast and efficient reassigning provided by the rule-based approach, with probabilistic uncertainty handling. The XTT2 knowledge representation is used by the HEARTDROID inference engine, which is a rule engine dedicated for mobile devices. This allows to use the probabilistic XTT2 representation in modelling mobile context-aware systems.

Future work will include practical implementation of the method presented in the paper and their evaluation on real use-cases. Especially a comparison to purely probabilistic and purely deterministic inference is planned, both in terms of computational efficiency and the correctness of inference. another aspect of the future plans is automation of the rule generation. At this point, the rule based model has to be provided by an expert. In the future, it is planned to use data mining techniques to learn the models automatically from the data, or to generate the models based on the pre-prepared data [14]. The method presented in this paper could also be extended by the mediation techniques [7]. It will allow to collect feedback from users in an interactive way, and modify the XTT2 rules, so they can better fit user preferences. Furthermore, to provide integrity of such on-the-fly modified knowledge, the HALVA verification tool [21] can be used. Finally, although the approach presented in this paper was dedicated to mobile context-aware systems, it can be easily integrated with other, non-mobile systems that are based on rules [23].

References

1. Almeida, A., Lopez-de Ipina, D.: Assessing ambiguity of context data in intelligent environments: Towards a more reliable context managing systems. Sensors 12(4), 4934–4951 (2012). http://www.mdpi.com/1424-8220/12/4/4934
2. Benerecetti, M., Bouquet, P., Bonifacio, M., Italia, A.A.: Distributed context-aware systems (2001)
3. Bobek, S., Nalepa, G.J., Ligęza, A., Adrian, W.T., Kaczor, K.: Mobile context-based framework for threat monitoring in urban environment with social threat monitor. Multimedia Tools and Applications (2014). http://dx.doi.org/10.1007/s11042-014-2060-9
4. Bobek, S., Nalepa, G.J.: Incomplete and uncertain data handling in context-aware rule-based systems with modified certainty factors algebra. In: Bikakis, A., Fodor, P., Roman, D. (eds.) RuleML 2014. LNCS, vol. 8620, pp. 157–167. Springer, Heidelberg (2014). http://dx.doi.org/10.1007/978-3-319-09870-8_11
5. Bui, H.H., Venkatesh, S., West, G.: Tracking and surveillance in wide-area spatial environments using the abstract hidden markov model. Intl. J. of Pattern Rec. and AI 15 (2001)
6. Chen, H., Finin, T.W., Joshi, A.: Semantic web in the context broker architecture. In: PerCom, pp. 277–286. IEEE Computer Society (2004)
7. Dey, A.K., Mankoff, J.: Designing mediation for context-aware applications. ACM Trans. Comput.-Hum. Interact. 12(1), 53–80 (2005). http://doi.acm.org/10.1145/1057237.1057241
8. Fenza, G., Furno, D., Loia, V.: Hybrid approach for context-aware service discovery in healthcare domain. J. Comput. Syst. Sci. 78(4), 1232–1247 (2012)
9. Hao, Q., Lu, T.: Context modeling and reasoning based on certainty factor. In: Asia-Pacific Conference on Computational Intelligence and Industrial Applications. PACIIA 2009, vol. 2, pp. 38–41, November 2009
10. Hu, H.: ContextTorrent: A Context Provisioning Framewrok for Pervasive Applications. University of Hong Kong (2011)
11. van Kasteren, T., Kröse, B.: Bayesian activity recognition in residence for elders. In: 3rd IET International Conference on Intelligent Environments. IE 2007, pp. 209–212 (2007)
12. Kimmig, A., Bach, S.H., Broecheler, M., Huang, B., Getoor, L.: A short introduction to probabilistic soft logic. In: NIPS Workshop on Probabilistic Programming: Foundations and Applications (2012)
13. Kjaer, K.E.: A survey of context-aware middleware. In: Proceedings of the 25th conference on IASTED International Multi-Conference: Software Engineering. SE 2007, pp. 148–155. ACTA Press (2007)
14. Kluza, K., Nalepa, G.J.: Towards rule-oriented business process model generation. In: Ganzha, M., Maciaszek, L.A., Paprzycki, M. (eds.) Proceedings of the Federated Conference on Computer Science and Information Systems - FedCSIS 2013, Krakow, Poland, September 8–11, 2013, pp. 959–966. IEEE (2013)
15. Krause, A., Smailagic, A., Siewiorek, D.P.: Context-aware mobile computing: Learning context-dependent personal preferences from a wearable sensor array. IEEE Transactions on Mobile Computing 5(2), 113–127 (2006)
16. Ligęza, A.: Logical Foundations for Rule-Based Systems. Springer-Verlag, Heidelberg (2006)
17. Ligęza, A., Nalepa, G.J.: A study of methodological issues in design and development of rule-based systems: proposal of a new approach. Wiley Interdisciplinary Reviews: Data Mining and Knowledge Discovery 1(2), 117–137 (2011)

18. Lim, B.Y., Dey, A.K.: Investigating intelligibility for uncertain context-aware applications. In: Proceedings of the 13th International Conference on Ubiquitous Computing. UbiComp 2011, pp. 415–424. ACM, New York (2011). http://doi.acm.org/10.1145/2030112.2030168

19. Lim, B.Y., Dey, A.K., Avrahami, D.: Why and why not explanations improve the intelligibility of context-aware intelligent systems. In: Proceedings of the SIGCHI Conference on Human Factors in Computing Systems. CHI 2009, pp. 2119–2128. ACM, New York (2009). http://doi.acm.org/10.1145/1518701.1519023

20. Nalepa, G.J., Bobek, S., Ligęza, A., Kaczor, K.: Algorithms for rule inference in modularized rule bases. In: Bassiliades, N., Governatori, G., Paschke, A. (eds.) RuleML 2011 - Europe. LNCS, vol. 6826, pp. 305–312. Springer, Heidelberg (2011)

21. Nalepa, G.J., Bobek, S., Ligęza, A., Kaczor, K.: HalVA - rule analysis framework for XTT2 rules. In: Bassiliades, N., Governatori, G., Paschke, A. (eds.) RuleML 2011 - Europe. LNCS, vol. 6826, pp. 337–344. Springer, Heidelberg (2011). http://www.springerlink.com/content/c276374nh9682jm6/

22. Nalepa, G.J., Bobek, S.: Rule-based solution for context-aware reasoning on mobile devices. Computer Science and Information Systems 11(1), 171–193 (2014)

23. Nalepa, G.J., Kluza, K., Kaczor, K.: Proposal of an inference engine architecture for business rules and processes. In: Rutkowski, L., Korytkowski, M., Scherer, R., Tadeusiewicz, R., Zadeh, L.A., Zurada, J.M. (eds.) ICAISC 2013, Part II. LNCS, vol. 7895, pp. 453–464. Springer, Heidelberg (2013). http://www.springer.com/computer/ai/book/978-3-642-38609-1

24. Nalepa, G.J., Ligęza, A., Kaczor, K.: Formalization and modeling of rules using the XTT2 method. International Journal on Artificial Intelligence Tools 20(6), 1107–1125 (2011)

25. Parsons, S., Hunter, A.: A review of uncertainty handling formalisms. In: Hunter, A., Parsons, S. (eds.) Applications of Uncertainty Formalisms. LNCS (LNAI), vol. 1455, pp. 8–37. Springer, Heidelberg (1998). http://dx.doi.org/10.1007/3-540-49426-X_2

26. Pascalau, E., Nalepa, G.J., Kluza, K.: Towards a better understanding of the concept of context-aware business applications. In: Ganzha, M., Maciaszek, L.A., Paprzycki, M. (eds.) Proceedings of the Federated Conference on Computer Science and Information Systems - FedCSIS 2013, Krakow, Poland, September 8–11, 2013, pp. 959–966. IEEE (2013)

27. Poole, D.: The independent choice logic and beyond. In: De Raedt, L., Frasconi, P., Kersting, K., Muggleton, S.H. (eds.) Probabilistic Inductive Logic Programming. LNCS (LNAI), vol. 4911, pp. 222–243. Springer, Heidelberg (2008). http://dblp.uni-trier.de/db/conf/ilp/lncs4911.html#Poole08

28. Poole, D., Mackworth, A.K.: Artificial Intelligence - Foundations of Computational Agents. Cambridge University Press (2010). http://www.cambridge.org/uk/catalogue/catalogue.asp?isbn=9780521519007

29. Raedt, L.D., Kimmig, A., Toivonen, H.: Problog: A probabilistic prolog and its application in link discovery. In: Veloso, M.M. (ed.) IJCAI, pp. 2462–2467 (2007). http://dblp.uni-trier.de/db/conf/ijcai/ijcai2007.html#RaedtKT07

30. Yuan, B., Herbert, J.: Fuzzy cara - a fuzzy-based context reasoning system for pervasive healthcare. Procedia CS 10, 357–365 (2012)

FOWLA, A Federated Architecture for Ontologies

Tarcisio M. Farias[1]([✉]), Ana Roxin[2], and Christophe Nicolle[2]

[1] Active3D, Dijon, France
`t.mendesdefarias@active3D.net`
[2] Checksem, Laboratory LE2I (UMR CNRS 6306), University of Burgundy, Dijon, France
`{ana-maria.roxin,cnicolle}@u-bourgogne.fr`

Abstract. The progress of information and communication technologies has greatly increased the quantity of data to process. Thus, managing data heterogeneity is a problem nowadays. In the 1980s, the concept of a Federated Database Architecture (FDBA) was introduced as a collection of components to unite loosely coupled federation. Semantic web technologies mitigate the data heterogeneity problem, however due to the data structure heterogeneity the integration of several ontologies is still a complex task. For tackling this problem, we propose a loosely coupled federated ontology architecture (FOWLA). Our approach allows the coexistence of various ontologies sharing common data dynamically at query execution through logical rules. We have illustrated the advantages of adopting our approach through several examples and benchmarks. We also compare our approach with other existing initiatives.

Keywords: SWRL · Horn-like rules · Federated ontology architecture · OWL · SPARQL · Backward-chaining reasoning · Semantic interoperability

1 Introduction

With advances of the information and communication technologies the amount of data to process and share has exponentially increased. Consequently, there is a growing demand for information interoperability. Indeed, with the advent of the personal computer in the 1980s, data interoperability first became an issue, then with the advent of the Internet has risen the need for more principled mechanisms for interoperability. When considering enterprise information systems, three layers of interoperability exist. Physical interoperability (first level) concerns the lower levels of the ISO/OSI network hierarchy and has been solved through network protocols such as Ethernet and TCP/IP. The second level concerns syntactic interoperability, namely the form of the messages exchanged in the information system. This issue has been solved through syntactic standards such as the Extensible Markup Language (XML) [6]. Finally, the third level of interoperability addresses the meaning of the exchanged messages and is called semantic interoperability. When implemented, semantic interoperability allows automatic machine-processing of data. These advances are really important in the context of enterprise information integration (EII) [1], building information models [2] and more in general in semantic web. Ontologies defined using

© Springer International Publishing Switzerland 2015
N. Bassiliades et al. (Eds.): RuleML 2015, LNCS 9202, pp. 97–111, 2015.
DOI: 10.1007/978-3-319-21542-6_7

standard ontology languages such as Web Ontology Language (OWL) [3] represent the building bricks for achieving such semantic interoperability. Indeed, interoperability at the data model level has been pointed out as a solution to information integration [4], and the usage of ontologies allows having data exchanges respecting the same original schema meaning (i.e. semantics).

Nevertheless, semantic heterogeneity remains a problem when integrating data from various ontologies which model the same information in different ways. Indeed, even if an ontology is defined as an "explicit and shared specification of a conceptualization of a given knowledge domain" [5] different ontologists (i.e. ontology designers) can produce different ontologies for a same knowledge domain. Thus, just adopting ontologies, like just using XML [6], does not eliminate heterogeneity for good: it elevates heterogeneity problems at a higher level. As noted by Alon Y. Halevy in [4], semantic heterogeneity exists whenever there is more than one way to structure a body of data (i.e. schema).

Therefore, in order to address the problem of semantic interoperability by means of ontologies, we propose a loosely coupled federated architecture for OWL ontologies. This architecture is based on ontology alignments, logical rules and inference mechanisms. The article at hand is structured as follows: Section 2 gives the scientific background for our work; Section 3 presents most important related work in the considered domain. Section 4 details our approach, notably the components and underlying processes of the FOWLA architecture. Numerical results in terms of query time execution improvement are illustrated in Section 5. Finally, we conclude this article by identifying additional works that could be undertaken.

2   Background

Semantic Web technologies constitute one of the most promising trends for the future Web, notably as they come with the potential of making existing data machine-understandable. The architecture of Semantic Web comprises several layers and components. The Resource Description Framework (RDF) [7] data model is the reference component. On top of it, three components exist [8]:

- Components for ontologies: several standard languages for specifying ontologies exist, from the most basic (RDF Schema [9]) to the most expressive OWL [3] and its inheritor OWL 2 [10]. Ontology languages rely on Description Logics (DL) formalisms. A knowledge base comprises a terminological model (i.e. TBox) and an assertional model (i.e. ABox). In this work, we use the term ontology or knowledge base for referring to the whole TBox and ABox. Such knowledge box is stored using triple store repositories.
- Components for queries: the equivalent of SQL for databases is the SPARQL [11] language. SPARQL allows querying RDF graphs and OWL ontologies, along with several possibilities for results processing (e.g. limit, order, offset). A SPARQL query comes in the form of a triple pattern *<Subject, Predicate, Object>*.
- Components for reasoning: with the Open World Assumption, queries over the data present in a knowledge base are often incompletely answered. Moreover,

when applying reasoning over such data, conclusions cannot be drawn. The Close World Assumption states that knowledge that cannot be derived from existing data is considered to be false. With this assumption, and by means of logical rules (expressed using rule languages), one can perform rule inference on top of ontology-based knowledge specifications. Rules are expressed with terms defined in ontologies. Rule languages have been developed since 2000, with the RuleML initiative [12], which is based on the Logic Programming paradigm and implements a RDF syntax. The Semantic Web Rule Language (SWRL) [13] is based on Logic Programming as well, but combines OWL and RuleML. SWRL allows defining conjunctive rules over the concepts and relationships present in an OWL ontology.

Besides the above considerations and for a better understanding of the work presented in this paper, we provide the following terms definition:

Definition 1. (*Ontology matching*) When determining if two ontologies have the same meaning (addressing the issue of semantic interoperability), an ontology matching process has to be implemented. Matching is the process of identifying correspondences between entities of different ontologies [14].

Definition 2. (*Ontology alignment*) An alignment is a set of correspondences between one or more ontologies. The alignment is the output of the process of ontology matching [14]. In this paper, we consider that such alignment is expressed by means of Horn rules (rule axioms).

Definition 3. (*Rule or rule axiom*) A rule is composed of a rule head (also called *consequent*) and a body (also called *antecedent*). If the body of a rule is true, then its head is derived as a new assertion [23].

Definition 4. (*Target and source ontology*) The target ontology is the ontology that we want to interoperate with. The source ontology is the ontology that contains the data (ontology's ABox) to be made interoperable.

3   Related Work

Many efforts were done since the 1980s to interoperate different database schemas, for instance, Sheth and Larson in [15] classify the multi-database systems into two types: non-federated and federated. An example of a non-federated database is a centralized database which means a single integrated database schema. The expression Federated Database Architecture (FDBA) was first introduced by Heimbigner and McLeod in 1985 as a "collection of components to unite loosely coupled federation in order to share and exchange information" using "an organization model based on equal, autonomous databases, with sharing controlled by explicit interfaces." [16]. Despite of our work being inspired on such definition of federated architecture; we define FOWLA as an architecture based on autonomous ontologies (including TBox and ABox) with sharing described as a rule-based format controlled by inference mechanisms (e.g. SWRL engine associated to OWL reasoner).

[17] presents a SPARQL query rewriting approach in the context of implementing interoperability over various ontologies stored in federated RDF datasets. Queries are

addressed to different SPARQL endpoints and are rewritten based on the alignments defined among the ontologies. Alignments implement a specific alignment format, as specified by the authors. Still, [17] authors do not clearly justify the need of this alignment format. Their approach is further detailed in [18], notably by defining several functions for graph pattern rewriting.

In [19], Correndo et al. present a similar approach. They perform query rewriting for retrieving data from several different SPARQL endpoints. However, their algorithm takes into account only information specified as a graph pattern. For example, it ignores constructs such as constraints expressed within the SPARQL reserved word FILTER.

When comparing both methods, [17] has the advantage of relying on Description Logic, and consequently supporting different query types (SELECT, CONSTRUCT, etc.) along with different SPARQL solution modifiers (LIMIT, ORDER BY, etc.). In this approach, the query rewriting process does not modify graph pattern operators. Still, both methods ignore the cases where several source and target ontologies can be involved. Correndo et al. [19] provide an explanation for SPARQL query rewriting implementation for ontology interoperation by stating that ontology alignments defined on top of the logical layer imply reasoning over a considerable amount of data thus compromising query execution time. Approaches presented in [17] [19] represent successful optimizations of query execution times. Still, their main drawbacks concern addressing the possibility for writing queries using terms from different ontologies, along with offering extended inference capabilities (e.g. through reasoners and rule engines).

Despite the extensive studies, to the best of our knowledge, there is no work proposing a federated architecture in the context of semantic interoperability of OWL ontologies.

4   A Federated Architecture for Ontologies   (FOWLA)

For addressing the issue of ontology interoperability, we have developed an approach based on a federated architecture for ontologies, FOWLA. This architecture contains two main components: the Federal Descriptor (FD) and the Federal Controller (FC). The FD component is responsible for describing ontology alignments. The FC module is executed at query time and allows exchanging data among ontologies according to FD generated alignment. It is also at query time that we check the data access policy for federated ontologies. The FOWLA architecture is illustrated in Fig. 1.

In order to describe ontology federation, we can rely on any alignment format present in the literature [14]. However, as the FC is a rule-based controller, it is preferable to use alignment formats based on rule syntax, as, for instance, SWRL rules. This avoids converting alignment formats later in the process.

As illustrated in Fig. 1, the FD module contains two sub-modules: Federal Logical Schema (FLS) and Federal Concept Instantiation (FCI). The first sub-module is an ensemble of logical rules describing the correspondences between ontologies. These mappings are expressed as logical rules, such as SWRL. Nevertheless, such logical rules are not capable of creating new concept instances. This is due to undecidability problems when integrating OWL and SWRL. Therefore, DL-safe rules are implemented for regaining decidability [20]. To overcome the drawback of new instances' inference, we propose including the FCI sub-module in our architecture.

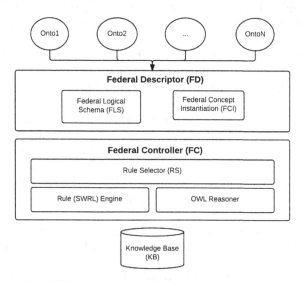

Fig. 1. FOWLA, Federated Architecture for Ontologies

Indeed, data can be modelled in various ways [4]. This implies semantic heterogeneity, and consequently, increases the difficulty for establishing ontology interoperability. A first step in mitigating this issue is to use only ontologies specified with one formal language, such as OWL. Still, the same data can be encapsulated through several concepts from different and independent OWL ontologies. To illustrate this, let us suppose we want to achieve interoperability over two OWL ontologies (*Onto1* and *Onto2*), for which we define an alignment through SWRL rules. For the sake of simplicity, we consider that the URI's (Uniform Resource Identifier) namespace identifying a predicate specifies the ontology containing the predicate's definition. In other words, *onto1:q1(?x,?y)* means that predicate *q1* is defined in the ontology *Onto1*. We consider the alignment between *Onto1* and *Onto2* is defined using the SWRL rules listed in 4.1.

$swrl_1$: *onto1:D(?x)* → *onto2:C(?x)*

$swrl_2$: *onto2:C(?x)* → *onto1:D(?x)*

$swrl_3$: *onto1:D(?x)* ∧ *onto1:q1(?x, ?y)* ∧ *onto1:A(?y)* ∧ *onto1:q2(?y, ?z)*   (4.1)
→ *onto2:p2(?x, ?z)*

$swrl_4$: *onto2:C(?x)* ∧ *onto2:p2(?x,?z)* ∧ *onto1:A(?y)* ∧ *onto1:q1(?x, ?y)*
→ *onto1:q2(?y,?z)*

where *onto1:q1* is an OWL object property; *onto1:q2* and *onto2:p2* are OWL datatype properties. $swrl_1$ and $swrl_2$ state that *onto1:D* is equivalent to *onto2:C*.

In OWL, *owl:equivalentClass* is the predicate that allows specifying class equivalence. Still, in our approach, we define SWRL rules for asserting such class equivalence in order to separate ontology alignments from ontology schemas. By doing so, we preserve the ontology schema definition. *swrl₃* exemplifies a complex alignment that maps a graph pattern from *Onto1* to a datatype property from *Onto2*(i.e. *p2*). *swrl₄* is another complex alignment mapping a graph pattern from *Onto1* and *Onto2* to a datatype property from *Onto1* (i.e. *q2*).

In our approach, these rules are part of the FLS sub-module. When considering *swrl₄*, sharing the data values of *onto2:p2* to *Onto1* implies creating the necessary instances for concept *onto1:A*. This is the case because these data values are represented (i.e. encapsulated) in a different way by *Onto1*. Nevertheless, defining an alignment rule such as *"onto2:C(?x) ∧ onto2:p2(?x,?z) → onto1:q1(?x, ?y) ∧ createInstances(?y, onto1:A) ∧ onto1:q2(?y,?z)"* is not possible due to undecidability issues. This is because DL-safe rules can only consider instances that are explicitly defined in the knowledge base.

To tackle this limitation, the FCI sub-module previously creates instances of necessary concepts from the target ontology (*Onto1*) to encapsulate the data shared by the source ontology (*Onto2*). In other words, the FCI sub-module creates a graph pattern in the Knowledge Base (KB) by means of class instantiation and property assertion. Doing so, the data values for *onto2:p2* are represented with vocabulary terms from *Onto1* based on previously defined alignment rules.

For the rules listed in 4.1, the FCI sub-module only considers class instantiation and property assertion for predicates in *swrl₄*'s body. Therefore, for each instance C_i of type *onto2:C* (which becomes also an instance of type *onto1:D* when applying *swrl₂*), one *onto1:q1* property is asserted to C_i having as value one newly created instance A_i of type *onto1:A*. Once this assertion performed, the SWRL rule engine is capable of inferring the value of *onto1:q2* for C_i by applying *swrl₄*. In addition to what has been said, the value of *onto2:p2* is not materialized for *onto1:q2* by the FCI sub-module. This, however, is inferred by the rule engine. Fig. 2 illustrates the process of class instantiation (in bold) and property assertion (underlined), as implemented when sharing the value "data" of *onto2:p2* to ontology *Onto1*, based on rule *swrl₄*.

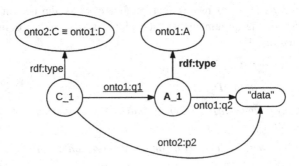

Fig. 2. Class instantiation (in bold) and property assertion (underlined)

The FC module performs the bulk of necessary inferences to satisfy a data request from a system based on one or more federated ontologies. To do so, FC contains the following sub-modules: a Rule Selector (RS) and a Rule Engine associated to an OWL reasoner. These components are responsible to control the interoperation among the considered ontologies based on an ensemble of rules (contained in the FLS sub-module) and some description logic formalism (e.g.: OWL).

The Rule Selector (RS) sub-module is responsible for improving backward-chaining reasoning. Indeed, when considering the context of executing queries over complex and numerous alignments, the number of SWRL rules highly impacts query execution time. The RS module attempts to select the necessary and sufficient ensemble of rules to answer a given query. This avoids the reasoner to perform unnecessary inferences which would considerably slow down query processing. Further details of the functioning of the RS sub-module are presented in section 4.2.

We motivate our choice of a backward-chaining (or hybrid) reasoner for the FC module by the fact that interoperating several ontologies with forward-chaining reasoner requires storing a considerable amount of materialized data. Besides, any ontology modification can imply a re-computation of all inferred data.

Our implementation of the FOWLA architecture comprises two phases (see Fig. 3): a pre-processing phase and a query execution phase.

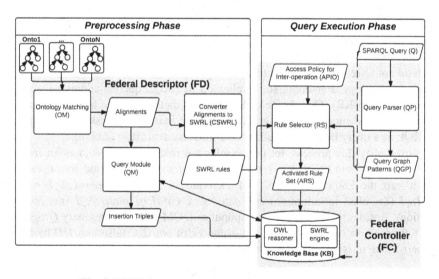

Fig. 3. FOWLA: pre-processing and query execution phases

The pre-processing phase is responsible for creating the FD. The query execution phase relies on the FC module for retrieving data from the federated ontologies. These two phases are detailed in sections 4.1 and 4.2, respectively.

4.1   Pre-processing Phase

For a full ontology interoperation, several complex alignments can be necessary. The ontology matching process is a fastidious and time consuming task. Because of this, we recommend the use of automatic ontology matching tools such as ASMOV [21] to support the alignments' conception (i.e. matching results). Nevertheless, these automatic matching solutions depend on the level of user involvement when verifying and validating the output alignments. Moreover, such solutions are not able to output complex alignments, such as the one listed in 4.2, where a sub-graph of *Onto2* is mapped to a sole *Onto1* property. Therefore, the user involvement in the ontology matching process is crucial as it was also noticed by Shvaiko and Euzenat in [21].

$$onto2{:}C_{21}(\textit{?x1}) \land \quad onto2{:}C_{22}(\textit{?x6}) \land onto2{:}C_{23}(\textit{?x3}) \land \quad onto2{:}C_{23}(\textit{?x7}) \land$$
$$onto2{:}C_{24}(\textit{?x5}) \quad onto2{:}C_{25}(\textit{?x4}) \land onto2{:}C_{26}(\textit{?x2}) \land onto2{:}p_{21}(\textit{?x4, ?x5})$$
$$\land onto2{:}p_{22}(\textit{?x5, ?x6}) \land \quad onto2{:}p_{23}(\textit{?x2, ?x4}) \land onto2{:}p_{24}(\textit{?x2, ?x1}) \land$$
$$onto2{:}p_{25}(\textit{?x2, ?x3}) \land \quad onto2{:}p_{28}(\textit{?x7, ?x8}) \land onto2{:}p_{26}(\textit{?x5, ?x7}) \land \qquad (4.2)$$
$$onto2{:}p_{27}(\textit{?x6; "Category"}) \land onto2{:}p_{28}(\textit{?x3; "ProductResource"}) \rightarrow$$
$$onto1{:}p_{11}(\textit{?x1; ?x8})$$

Once we defined the rules forming ontology alignments, if the alignment format is not a rule-based format such as SWRL, a conversion process is executed (as illustrated in Fig. 3). The resulting alignments in SWRL rules format are included in the FLS sub-module. Afterwards, the Query Module (QM) identifies each alignment presenting schema heterogeneity, and therefore needing class instantiations and property assertions for modelling data from other ontologies. The QM retrieves instances which do not have property assertions for mapping the data from a source ontology to one target ontology. For doing so, it relies on SPARQL queries addressed over the knowledge base (KB). Our choice of SPARQL is dictated by the triple store chosen for the implementation (see section 5). Indeed, the Stardog triple store only supports SPARQL as a query language (see http://docs.stardog.com/).

To exemplify this process, let us consider the rule $swrl_4$ (see 4.1) as an input to QM. If a triple *onto2:C_1 onto2:p2 "data"^^xsd:string* is inserted by an external system into the knowledge base, QM materializes the triples *onto1:A_1 rdf:type onto1:q1* (i.e. class instantiation) and *onto2:C_1 onto1:q1 onto1:A_1* (i.e. property assertion). Besides, if *Onto2* is already populated, QM executes the query Q (see 4.3) over KB based on $swrl_4$ to retrieve the instances of *onto2:C* (also *onto1:D* by applying $swrl_2$) with missing property assertions.

SPARQL Query : Q : SELECT ?x WHERE { ?x rdf:type onto2:C.
executed   FILTER NOT EXISTS {?x onto1:q1 ?y} }   (4.3)

These properties block the data mapping between *Onto2* and *Onto1* created when applying $swrl_4$. Finally, the absent properties are materialized along with new instances for each one (i.e. object property value).

The pre-processing phase materializes some property assertions if and only if necessary due to schema heterogeneity. This materialized data is deleted when the contents of the FLS sub-module changes. Besides, if ontology alignments are modified, the QM is re-executed. The pre-processing phase outputs an ensemble of SWRL rules for the query execution phase that is described in the following section.

4.2   Query Execution Phase

Once federal description is accomplished, we select the specific rules necessary to answer a given query addressed over the federated ontologies. For addressing this task, we have developed a SPARQL Query Parser (QP). As shown in Fig. 3, the SPARQL query is passed to the QP module which parses it and isolates the concepts and properties it contains. Based on elements such as domain/range restrictions for properties involved in the query, the RS sub-module selects SWRL rules that have to be taken into account for answering the query. The first action performed by the RS module is to filter rules in FLS sub-module selecting only those rules that can infer data for the properties and/or concepts in the query (i.e. query graph patterns QGP as illustrated in Fig. 3). Secondly, for further rule filtering, the RS sub-module identifies the rules which have the same property in their head and selects only those respecting the domain/range restriction defined in the query. To exemplify this, let us suppose the query Q' (see 4.4) and the same FLS described in (4.1).

Federal Logical Schema	$swrl_1: onto1:D(?x) \rightarrow onto2:C(?x)$
	$swrl_2: onto2:C(?x) \rightarrow onto1:D(?x)$
	$swrl_3: onto1:D(?x) \land onto1:q1(?x, ?y) \land$ $onto1:A(?y) \land onto1:q2(?y, ?z) \rightarrow onto2:p2(?x, ?z)$
	$swrl_4: onto2:C(?x) \land onto2:p2(?x,?z) \land$ $onto1:A(?y) \land onto1:q1(?x, ?y) \rightarrow$
SPARQL Query executed	$onto1:q2(?y,?z)$
	$Q' : SELECT\ ?x\ ?y\ WHERE\{\ ?x\ rdf:type\ onto2:C.$ $?x\ onto2:p2\ ?y\ \}$

$$(4.4)$$

Considering query Q', the RS sub-module selects only the rules $swrl_1$ and $swrl_3$ because they are the only ones capable of inferring data for $onto2:C$ and for $onto2:p2$, respectively. Besides, $swrl_3$ is chosen because it satisfies the domain restriction defined in the query Q' (i.e. $onto2:C$). These rules represent the necessary and sufficient subset of FLS for answering Q'. Moreover, access policy for interoperation (APIO) is also used as an input for the RS sub-module (see Fig. 3). This input identifies which rules are allowed to be considered by the FC module, with respect to data access rights. For example, if we consider the case where one system is based uniquely on *Onto1*, such system could choose not to share the data from $onto1:q2$. In this case, and if query Q' is addressed by another system uniquely based on *Onto2*, RS does not select $swrl_3$. This is justified by the fact that the system addressing query Q' is not allowed to have access to $onto1:q2$ data values. Finally, our system outputs the eligible set of rules for interoperate the federated ontologies. This is called the Activated Rule Set (ARS). We therefore execute the initial query over the data contained in the KB and considering only the rules present in the ARS set.

Therefore, the data present in the KB, for the considered ontologies, is automatically restructured according to the rules in the ARS set. The SWRL engine associated with the OWL reasoner processes these rules (see Fig. 3). This mechanism allows us to handle different schemas, thus addressing schema interoperability issue.

5   Results and Discussion

The implementation of the FOWLA architecture comes with several advantages for interoperating numerous ontologies: (1) it allows inferring new ontology alignments; (2) it allows avoiding data redundancy; (3) it allows modularizing the maintainability, through preserving the autonomy among ontology-based systems; (4) it allows querying with vocabulary terms issued from different ontologies and (5) it allows improving query execution time.

For demonstrating advantage (1), let us suppose four ontologies (*A*, *B*, *C* and *D*) and the alignments described as *FD(A, B)*, *FD(B, C)*, *FD(C, D)*, *FD(A, D)* and illustrated in Fig. 4. *FD(X, Y)* represents the contents of the Federal Descriptor module between ontologies *X* and *Y*. For each of the considered ontologies, we define an Interoperable Schema (IS) as the sub-graph of this ontology that contains all schemas necessary for exchanging data with another ontology. The IS sub-graph is composed of correspondent classes and properties between the two considered ontologies. We note *IS(X,Y)* the interoperable schema of ontology *X* for ontology *Y*. Allowing the inference of data from one ontology to others (i.e. rule-based interoperability) reduces the number of alignments (i.e. rules) that we need to conceive and, in some cases, the conception of the whole *FD(X,Y)* component between two ontologies.

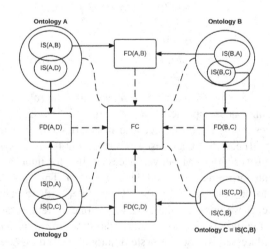

Fig. 4. Case study of four ontologies implementing FOWLA

For example, let us consider that ontology *C* is already populated and *IS(C,B)* is equivalent to the whole ontology *C*. Therefore, with the complete *FD(B,C)* component defined, all data of *C* is accessible by querying ontology B. Moreover, the definition of *FD(A,B)* allows retrieving data from the so populated ontology *C* by querying *A* (more precisely the data modelled using *IS(B,A)* ∩ *IS(B,C)*). In this case, we do not need to define *FD(C,A)* because *A* and *C* are indirectly aligned and totally integrated by the FC using *FD(A,B)* and *FD(B,C)*. For further explanation, let us suppose that *FD(A,B)* and *FD(B,C)* respectively contain $swrl_5$ and $swrl_6$.

SWRL rules	$swrl_5 : ontoA{:}Aa(?x) \rightarrow ontoB{:}Bb(?x)$	(5.1)
	$swrl_6 : ontoB{:}Bb(?x) \rightarrow ontoC{:}Cc(?x)$	

SPARQL Query executed	$Q'' : SELECT\ ?x\ WHERE\ \{\ ?x\ rdf{:}type$ $ontoC{:}Cc.\ \}$	(5.2)

Inferred fact(s)	$ontoA{:}Aa(?x) \rightarrow ontoC{:}Cc(?x)$	(5.3)

Considering a rule engine for interpreting those rules and the SPARQL query *Q''* (5.2), the rule engine infers the transitive relation: $ontoA{:}Aa(?x) \rightarrow ontoC{:}Cc(?x)$ (5.3). Then, the query *Q''* retrieves all instances which belong to *ontoA:Aa*, *ontoB:Bb* and *ontoC:Cc* classes. Therefore, we do not need to define the alignment (5.3) in *FD(A,C)*, because it is inferred by the FC at query execution time.

The advantage (2) is justified with the use of backward-chaining techniques [22] by the Federal Controller. They allow the federated ontologies to not replicate interoperable data. This is because rule inference is performed at query (i.e. goal) execution and doesn't need materializing the same data. Consequently, the data modelled with one ontology is available (inferred) for the other ontologies by applying rule-based alignments through backward reasoning (i.e. backward from the goal). Moreover, once data changes in the source ontology, the FC infers the newly modified data to the target ontologies at next query execution.

For exemplifying the advantage (3), let us suppose a modification in the ontology schema *A*, more precisely in the sub-graph *IS(A,D)* – *{ IS(A,B)* ∩ *IS(A,D) }* from our previous case study represented in Fig. 4. In this case, the sole components which have to evolve are *FD(A,D)* and *IS(D,A)*. Doing so, we preserve the full interoperability among *A*, *D* and the other ontologies. The other FDs and ontology schemas remain unchanged. Note that only the system based on ontology *A* has to evolve which is not the case for systems based on ontologies *B*, *C* and *D*. This is explained by the fact that the underlying schemas for ontologies *B*, *C* and *D* have not been modified. Therefore, besides implementing ontology interoperability, we also preserve each systems' autonomy.

For evaluating FOWLA and justifying the advantage (4) and (5), we consider two OWL ontologies (*Onto1* and *Onto2*), for which we define the *FD(Onto1,Onto2)*. Table 1 lists some characteristics of these ontologies. The FLS (i.e. alignments) between these two ontologies comprises 474 SWRL rules which were manually created (most of them are complex alignments, involving numerous predicates). The number of rules necessary for aligning *Onto1* and *Onto2* is justified by the fact that *IS(Onto1,Onto2)* is almost equivalent to *Onto1*. Thus, it means that practically all data described by using terms from *Onto1* can be also described using terms from *Onto2*.

For our experiments, we have used a 2.2.1 Stardog triple store (see `http://docs.stardog.com/`) which played the role of the server and was encapsulated in a virtual machine with the following configuration: one microprocessor Intel Xeon CPU E5-2430 at 2.2GHz with 2 cores out of 6, 8GB of DDR3 RAM memory and the "Java Heap" size for the Java Virtual Machine set to 6GB.

Table 1. Characteristics of *Onto1* and *Onto2*

OWL entities	Onto1	Onto2
Classes	30	802
Object properties	32	1292
Data properties	125	247
Inverse properties	7	115
Triples in the TBox	2212	9978
DL expressivity	$ALCHIF^{(D)}$	$ALUIF^{(D)}$

We chose Stardog because it provides an OWL reasoner associated to a SWRL engine and it is based on backward-chaining reasoning [22]. Indeed, our RS sub-module only aims at hybrid or backward-chaining reasoning approaches (as in forward-chaining reasoning [22] are materialized all facts entailed before query execution). So, Stardog's reasoner and the RS sub-module constitute the Federal Controller (FC) module. The considered triple store contains 4 repositories. Each repository stores the *Onto1* and *Onto2* knowledge base (*Onto1*'s TBox and ABox and *Onto2*'s TBox and ABox). We name those repositories KB1, KB2, KB3 and KB4. For the considered example, each repository's ABox contains 1,146,294 triples. For testing purposes and for each repository, we have implemented sets of rules for interoperability with different cardinalities. Table 2 lists the considered set of rules along with their characteristics.

Table 2. Rules implemented for each knowledge base (KB)

	Number of rules	Characteristics
KB1	474	All the rules contained in the FLS (all the rules forming the alignment between *Onto1* and *Onto2*)
KB2	266	All subsumption rules along with all the rules that have elements from *Onto1* in their head
KB3	178	All rules from KB2 minus some of the rules that have elements from *Onto1* in their head (we aimed at reducing the data inferred)
KB4	variable	All the rules contained in the Activated Rule Set (ARS) conceived by the RS.

The client machine has the following configuration: one microprocessor Intel Core CPU I7-4790 at 3.6GHz with 4 cores, 8GB of DDR3 RAM memory at 1600MHz and the "Java Heap" size set to 1GB. The Rule Selector is executed on the client machine.

Table 3 shows the queries used in our experiments. For the sake of simplicity, we note *Cij* the class *Cj* in ontology *Ontoi*, respectively p_{kl} the p_l property in ontology

Ontok, where $i, j, k, l \in \mathbb{N}^*$. Each one was executed 30 times over the knowledge bases KB1, KB2, KB3 and KB4. Table 4 shows the results we obtained. The capability of retrieving results for query Q2 and Q3 demonstrate that our approach allows querying federated ontologies, considering them as one unique ontology. This is justified by the fact that we can write queries using, at same time, terms from *Onto1* and *Onto2*. So, this justifies the advantage (4).

Table 3. List of queries addressed over the considered knowledge bases

Query name	SPARQL Query
Q1	SELECT ?x ?y WHERE { ?x onto1:p_{11} ?y . }
Q2	SELECT ?x ?y WHERE { ?x a onto2:C_{21} . ?x onto1:p_{11} ?y . }
Q3	SELECT ?x ?u WHERE { ?x a onto1:C_{11} . ?y a onto2:C_{22} . ?x onto1:p_{12} ?y . ?y onto1:p_{11} ?x . }

In Table 4, the "**#RuleSet**" column displays the number of rules as implemented over the considered KB, at query execution time. The "**#Results**" column shows the number of tuples that were retrieved as a result for the considered query (e.g. (?x,?y) for Q1). In Table 4, "-" means that no results were retrieved for the considered query after more than one minute waiting time. The reason relies in the fact that the memory heap size (6GB) for the Java Virtual Machine is exceeded.

Table 4. Query Performance Evaluation

Query	Knowledge base	Mean execution time (in seconds)	Standard Deviation (σ)	#RuleSet	#Results
Q1	KB1	-	-	474	0
	KB2	-	-	266	0
	KB3	9.25	12.21	178	1683
	KB4	**2.23**	**1.78**	**16**	**38318**
Q2	KB1	-	-	474	0
	KB2	-	-	266	0
	KB3	32.99	0.75	178	74
	KB4	**0.16**	**0.04**	**2**	**74**
Q3	KB1	-	-	474	0
	KB2	-	-	266	0
	KB3	71.62	0.95	178	0
	KB4	**0.88**	**0.43**	**5**	**9**

When analyzing results, we can see that, for answering query Q1, our methodology has selected 16 rules from the initial set of 474 rules (i.e. the FLS). The results also indicate that without our approach no result is retrieved as long as the entire FLS is considered, due to memory overload and after about 3 minutes of query execution over KB1. When executed over KB2, Q1 evidences that reducing the cardinality of the initial rule set to 266 does not prevent memory overload. When executing Q1 over KB3 (which implements less than 40% of FLS rules), Q1 returns less than 5% of all expected results. This is explained by the fact that several of the relevant rules for Q1 were removed when conceiving our test knowledge bases. Moreover, when compared to Q1 over KB4, Q1 over KB3 has a duration 4 times greater and retrieves 22 times less results. Indeed, KB4 implements the only rules contained in the ARS, so the results of Q1 executed over KB4 represent the gain (in terms of query execution time and results retrieved) achieved by implementing our approach. When applied to Q2, the RS sub-module takes into account the domain restriction defined within Q2 (e.g. $?x\ a\ onto2{:}C_{21}$). It then creates an ARS set containing only 2 rules instead of 16, as it was previously the case for Q1 (which did not had any domain information for the property $onto1{:}p_{11}$). For the above considered tests, the mean query execution times have been considerably reduced. The standard deviation for the query response time is much lower using our RS sub-module, meaning the query response time is more centralized onto the mean.

6   Conclusion and Future Work

In this paper, we have presented an approach for federating ontologies in order to address the problem of semantic interoperability. When comparing our approach to existing ones (i.e. [17] or [19]), we identify the following advantages:

- It allows composing queries using terms from different ontologies (be it source or target);
- It takes advantage of existing inference mechanisms for deducing new knowledge. This is useful as it allows writing less alignment rules when performing ontology matching.

The FOWLA architecture is proven, through the above presented benchmarks, as allowing reducing execution time for queries addressed over rule-based alignments between the considered ontologies. Future work will concern defining the strategies for ordering ontologies to be aligned in order to best exploit the existing inference mechanisms. Another improvement may concern the integration of SWRL built-ins (e.g. *swrlb* vocabulary [13]) at the level of the FLS sub-module. Furthermore, we wish to investigate the use of query languages other than SPARQL for implementing our approach.

Acknowledgements. This work has been financed by the French company ACTIVe3D (see http://www.active3d.net/fr/) and supported by the Burgundy Regional Council (see http://www.region-bourgogne.fr/).

References

1. Halevy, A.Y., Ashish, N., Bitton, D., Carey, M., Draper, D., Pollock, J., Rosenthal, A., Sikka, V.: Enterprise information integration: successes, challenges and controversies. In: Proceedings of the 2005 ACM SIGMOD international conference on Management of data, pp. 778–787 . ACM, New York, NY, USA (2005)

2. de Farias, T.M., Roxin, A., Nicolle, C.: A Rule based system for semantical enrichment of building information exchange. In: CEUR Proceedings of RuleML (4th Doctoral Consortium), Prague, Czech Republic. Vol. 1211, p. 2 (2014)
3. Dean, M., Schreiber, G. (Eds): OWL Web Ontology Language Reference, W3C Recommendation (2004). www.w3.org/TR/2004/REC-owl-ref-20040210
4. Halevy, A.: Why Your Data Won't Mix. Queue 3(8), 50–58 (2005)
5. Borst, P.: Construction of Engineering Ontologies for Knowledge Sharing and Reuse. Ph.D. Dissertation, Tweente University (1997)
6. The World Wide Web Consortium (W3C). XML Technology, www.w3.org/standards/xml
7. Beckett, D. (Ed.): RDF/XML syntax specification (Revised), W3C Recommendation (2004). www.w3.org/TR/REC-rdf-syntax/
8. Data Management and Query Processing in Semantic Web Databases, Sven Groppe, Institute of Information Systems, University of Lübeck,, Springer-Verlag Berlin Heidelberg (2011). ISBN 978-3-642-19356-9
9. Brickley, D., Guha, D.V.: RDF vocabulary description language 1.0: RDF Schema, W3C Recommendation (2004). www.w3.org/TR/rdf-schema/
10. Motik, B., Patel-Schneider, P.F., Parsia, B.: OWL 2 Web ontology language structural specification and functional-style syntax (Second Edition). W3C Recommendation (2012). www.w3.org/TR/owl2-syntax/
11. Clark, K.G., Feigenbaum, L., Torres, E. (ed): SPARQL protocol for RDF, W3C Recommendation (2008). www.w3.org/TR/rdf-sparql-protocol/
12. RuleML, www.ruleml.org
13. The World Wide Web Consortium (W3C). SWRL: A Semantic Web Rule Language Combining OWL and RuleML (2004). www.w3.org/Submission/SWRL/
14. Euzenat, J., Shvaiko, P.: Ontology Matching, 2nd edn. Springer-Verlag, Berlin Heidelberg, Germany (2013)
15. Sheth, A.P., Larson, J.A.: Federated Database Systems for Managing Distributed, Heterogeneous, and Autonomous Databases. ACM Computing Surveys 22(3) (1990)
16. Heimbigner, D., McLeod, D.: A Federated Architecture for Information Management. ACM Trans. Off. Znf. Syst. 3(3), 253–278 (1985)
17. Makris, K., Gioldasis, N., Bikakis, N., Christodoulakis, S.: Ontology Mapping and SPARQL Rewriting for Querying Federated RDF Data Sources. In: Meersman, R., Dillon, T., Herrero, P. (eds.) OTM 2010. LNCS, vol. 6427, pp. 1108–1117. Springer, Heidelberg (2010)
18. Makris, K., Gioldasis, N., Bikakis, N., Christodoulakis, S.: SPARQL Rewriting for Query Mediation over Mapped Ontologies (2010). http://www.music.tuc.gr/reports/SPARQLRE WRITING.PDF
19. Correndo, G., Salvadores, M., Millard, I., Glaser, H., Shadbolt, N.: Sparql query rewriting for implementing data integration over linked data. In: Proceedings of the 2010 EDBT/ICDT Workshops, pp. 4:1–4:11, New York, NY, USA. ACM (2010)
20. Motik, B., Sattler, U., Studer, R.: Query Answering for OWL-DL with Rules. Journal of Web Semantics 3(1), 41–60 (2005)
21. Shvaiko Pavel and Jerome Euzenat: Ontology matching: State of the art and future challenges. IEEE Trans. on Knowl. and Data Eng. 25(1), 158–176 (2013)
22. Russell, S.J., Norvig, P.: Artificial Intelligence: A Modern Approach, 3rd edn (2009)
23. Horrocks, I., Patel-Schneider, P.F., Bechhofer, S., Tsarkov, D.: OWL rules: A proposal and prototype implementation. Journal of Web Semantics 3(1), 23–40 (2005)

User Extensible System to Identify Problems in OWL Ontologies and SWRL Rules

João Paulo Orlando[1]([✉]), Mark A. Musen[2], and Dilvan A. Moreira[1]

[1] SCC-ICMC University of São Paulo, São Paulo, Brazil
{orlando,dilvan}@icmc.usp.br
[2] BMIR - Stanford University, Stanford, USA
musen@stanford.edu

Abstract. The Semantic Web uses ontologies to associate meaning to Web content so machines can process it. One inherent problem to this approach is that, as its popularity increases, there is an ever growing number of ontologies available to be used, leading to difficulties in choosing appropriate ones. With that in mind, we created a system that allows users to evaluate ontologies/rules. It is composed by the Metadata description For Ontologies/Rules (MetaFOR), an ontology in OWL, and a tool to convert any OWL ontology to MetaFOR. With the MetaFOR version of an ontology, it is possible to use SWRL rules to identify anomalies in it. These can be problems already documented in the literature or user defined ones. SWRL is familiar to users, so it is easier to define new project specific anomalies. We present a case study where the system detects 9 problems, from the literature, and two user defined ones.

Keywords: Semantic web · Swrl rules · Detect problems · Detect anomalies · Evaluate ontologies

1 Introduction

The Semantic Web is a technology that explores the association of meaning to content present on the Web, so it can be processed by machines. To enable such processing, it is necessary to have a structured collection of information (ontologies) and an inference rule set [2]. In addition, for the development of practical semantic applications, ontologies may use rules to facilitate the definition of logical deductions [1]. The Semantic Web has renewed and increased the interest in rule-based systems and their development [14].

In order to define and instantiate ontologies on the Web, the W3C recommended the OWL (Web Ontology Language). The OWL expressiveness may not be sufficient to model all kinds of problems, as several problems need rules in the Horn-like (IF-THEN) format. To represent this type of rules, in 2004 the Semantic Web Rule Language (SWRL) was proposed to the W3C as a recommendation. SWRL complements OWL because it includes a high-level abstract syntax for Horn-like rules [9]. SWRL rules can be added to an OWL file as valid

© Springer International Publishing Switzerland 2015
N. Bassiliades et al. (Eds.): RuleML 2015, LNCS 9202, pp. 112–126, 2015.
DOI: 10.1007/978-3-319-21542-6_8

OWL. Even if SWRL is not a W3C recommendation (standard), it is a popular language with support in many tools, such as Protégé, Pellet and Hermit[1].

As the Semantic Web popularity increases there is an ever-growing number of ontologies available to be used, leading to difficulties in choosing appropriate ones [12]. In addition, other problems (circularity, redundancy, etc.) may occur when the integration of these different ontologies is needed [1]. To help solve these problems, inherent to the Semantic Web structure, techniques that help users to analyze and evaluate ontologies and its rules are needed.

With that in mind, we created a system that helps in this evaluation scenario. This system includes an OWL ontology, the METAdata description For Ontologies/Rules (MetaFOR), and a tool to convert any OWL ontology to MetaFOR. It aims to help OWL/SWRL users in the process of analyzing and evaluating any OWL ontology. In order to do so, the system converts ontologies to MetaFOR and applies rules to the resulting metadata to find problems. The system provides default rules to detect a set of problems, known in the literature, but users can also write their own rules using SWRL. These user rules can detect new or unusual problems or enforce project-wide specific conventions in an ontology (or ontologies).

This system offers two main advantages. The first one is to use rules in OWL and SWRL to identify patterns/problems/anomalies in ontologies. These languages are well known among users, so that they will find no difficulties in using them. The second advantage is that users can choose the patterns/problems/ anomalies that they wish to identify. With the ontology converted to MetaFOR, users can create their own rules to identify the patterns/problems they are interested in. Moreover, one can also use other tools and libraries, already available for OWL ontologies, to extract more information from the MetaFOR format.

For the examples used in this paper, we are going to use the Family Relationships Ontology (FRO)[2] as the ontology being converted to MetaFOR.

2   Related Work

Before developing this system, the authors have conducted a survey in the literature for works describing systems that identify problems/patterns on OWL ontologies with/without SWRL rules. This survey showed that such systems have very limited functionality.

In the first system, the authors focus on the detection of anomalies that occur when rules and ontological definitions are combined [1]. For instance, an anomaly detected is the Circularity Between Rules and Taxonomy: it occurs when a head atom implies some body atom of the same rule. This anomaly occurs because a consequent predicate is subclass of antecedent predicate. Anomaly identification is done using a language called DATALOG* with a system called DisLog Developers' Kit. One drawback of this approach is that semantic web users must learn the DATALOG* language, and the system that runs it. In addition, in our work,

---

[1] http://clarkparsia.com/pellethttp://hermit-reasoner.com

[2] http://protegewiki.stanford.edu/wiki/Protege_Ontology_Library

metadata is extracted from the ontology and then used by the rules detecting anomalies that simplify the work of writing them.

Some systems use metrics, in the form of frameworks and guidelines [4,6,11], to evaluate ontologies. These metrics have to be verified in the ontologies. They allow the creation of more consistent ontologies. However, users still have the need to perform extensive manual verification. On the other hand, our system converts the target ontology to MetaFOR and then checks it automatically. It even checks some of the guidelines in Gomez-Perez [6].

In Hassanpour et al. [7] and Orlando et al. [10], two different methods to visualize SWRL rules are presented. Hassanpour et al. [7] shows a visualization technique that creates a rule dependency graph. This method groups graph nodes into layers, based on their dependencies, clustering nodes within a layer if they have similar dependencies. Users can then examine patterns of logical relationships in a rule set. In the other work, Orlando et al. [10] visualize rules by their similarities (patterns). They use decision trees to group rule atoms in nodes of the trees. Two methods to cluster SWRL rules are presented in Orlando et al. [10] and Hassanpour et al. [8]. In the first one, the clustering is based on the occurrence of common atoms [10]. In the second, the clustering is based on syntactic structure techniques in which two rules are in the same group if they have common features, such as having the same number of classes, object properties, data properties, etc [8]. A limitation, of these visualization and clustering techniques, is that they only use pre-defined similarity patterns; users cannot add new patterns. In our work, users can build their own rule sets to find patterns in OWL ontologies (and SWRL rules).

Some kinds of redundancy (a problem type in ontologies) may be detected by the use of some specific tools [1,13]. But each tool detects only one kind of problem and the detection is limited to pre-defined problems/patterns. Some contradiction problems in ontologies can also be detect by a reasoner, but only if the ontology has individuals instantiated. That is not always the case. Most reasoners will also not work with big ontologies.

After analyzing these systems, we concluded that each has one or more of this three deficiencies: (i) work only with a limited set of predefined patterns, (not allowing users to create new ones), (ii) ontology evaluation is done manually and (iii) use languages that are not familiar to most users in the semantic web community. To solve these deficiencies, our system converts the target ontology to the MetaFOR ontology (section 3) and then applies rules, written in SWRL, to find problems/patterns in the ontology. Users can also extend these SWRL rules with their own. To test this approach, a case study (section 4) was created and analyzed.

3   The MetaFOR Ontology

The first step so that users can identify problems in an OWL ontology is to perform the ontology conversion to the MetaFOR ontology. In this ontology, all elements (from converted ontologies) considered important for analyses are represented. These elements will be discussed in the next sections. We believe that the current MetaFOR format represents sufficient elements, from OWL ontologies, to be used to identify the most useful patterns in them. At the same time, it is simple enough to produce ontology representations that are simple to use when writing pattern detection rules. That has been the case in our tests writing rules to detect problems, documented in the literature or created by us.

The MetaFOR ontology separates the OWL ontology elements in three types: entities, entity relationships and data relationships.

3.1 Entities

Entities represent the ontology entities (classes, properties, datatypes and named individuals) minus individuals that do not represent SWRL rules, annotation properties and datatypes. Entities of the ontology being processed are converted to MetaFOR individuals of the following classes:

- Class: class entities.
- ObjectProperty: object property entities. This class has tree subclasses:
  - TransitiveObjectProperty: transitive property entities;
  - SymmetricObjectProperty: symmetric property entities;
  - FunctionalObjectProperty: functional property entities;
- Rule: rule instance entities.
- Atom: atom instance entities.
- Argument: argument instance entities.
- Cardinality: cardinality instance entities.
  - MaxCardinality: cardinality instance entities of Maximum type.
  - MinCardinality: cardinality instance entities of Minimum type.
  - ExactCardinality: cardinality instance entities of Exact type.
  - SomeValuesFromCardinality: cardinality instance entities of Some Values From type.
  - AllValuesFromCardinality: cardinality instance entities of All Values From type.

For example, an object property entity (from FRO), called *hasParent*, that represents the relation between a child and his father in an ontology becomes an individual of the class ObjectProperty in the MetaFOR. If in this same ontology there is also a *hasAncestor* property (maybe a parent property of *hasParent*), it becomes an individual of TransitiveObjectProperty.

3.2 Entity Relationships

Entity relationships represents the possible relations between entities in an ontology, such as disjoint, equivalent, inverse, etc. They are converted to object properties in MetaFOR.

For instance, if the *hasParent* property entity (from last example) has a cardinality limiting the number of parents to a maximum of two, the MetaFOR individual representing it will have a hasCardinality property connecting it to an anonymous individual of type MaxCardinality. This anonymous individual will also have a hasCardinalityNumber data property of value 2. The object properties in MetaFOR represent:

- hasCardinality: cardinality restrictions.
- isDisjoint: disjointness with another class or property.
- hasDomain: the relationship between a property and a domain class.
- hasRange: the relationship between a property and a range class.
- isEquivalent: equivalence with another class or property.
- hasInverse: the relationship between inverse properties.
- hasSuper: the relationship between a subclass and each of its parents, immediate ones or on the hierarchy above.
- hasDirectSuper: the relationship between a subclass and each of its direct parents.
- hasSub: the inverse of hasSuper.
- hasDirectSub: the inverse of hasDirectSuper.

There are also object properties to represent just relationships between rule elements:

- hasAntecedentAtom, hasConsequentAtom: the relationship between a rule and one of its atoms.
- hasPredicate: relationship between an atom and one of its predicates.
- hasArgument, hasFirstArgument, hasSecondArgument: relationship between an atom and one of its arguments. hasFirstArgument and hasSecondArgument are hasArgument sub properties. For example, in the atom *hasParent(?X, ?Y)*, X is the first argument and Y is the second.
- sameAntecedent, sameConsequent: relationship between two rules stating that they have, respectively, the same antecedents or consequents. It means that each atom, in one rule antecedent (or consequent), is equal or equivalent to another atom in the other rule antecedent (or consequent).
- subsumes: relationship between two rules where the antecedent of the first subsumes the antecedent of the second. If rule A subsumes rule B, it means that all atoms in B's antecedent exist in A's antecedent but A's antecedent has atoms not contained in B's. The system also checks if they are used as built-ins as greaterThanOrEqual, lessThanOrEqual, among others.

It is possible to implement the last three relationships as SWRL built-ins and leave them to be defined as part of the rules detecting specific problems. However, many reasoners (including Hermit) and rule engines do not work with built-ins, so it was decided to define them as part of the ontology and as a relationship that a converter program must generate.

3.3 Data Relationships

Data relationships are just MetaFOR data properties used to save some key information about the ontology being converted. For instance, in the previous example, the anonymous individual (representing *hasParent* cardinality) had a hasCardinalityNumber data property of value 2.

These data properties are added to individuals of the MetaFOR ontology to inform:

- hasCardinalityNumber: numerical values of the cardinality (to Cardinality individuals).
- hasInstancesNumber: the number of individuals belonging to a class;
- isLeaf: that the represented entity does not have a sub entity (boolean). For example, if a class has no subclasses;
- usedInRestrictions: that the represented entity is used in any restriction in the ontology (boolean);
- usedInRules: that the represented entity is used in at least one rule (boolean);

3.4 Converter

The first step to identify problems in OWL ontologies (and/or SWRL rules) is to perform the conversion of the ontology to MetaFOR format (sections 3.1, 3.2 and 3.3). We have created a program, in Java, for this conversion.

To show an example of conversion, the FRO ontology was converted to MetaFOR. Figure 1 shows some individuals of the resulting conversion, using the Protégé tool [5]. In it, the instance URI1_Child, which represents the class *Child* of the original ontology, is selected. It is an instance of class Class. The URI of URI1_Child is generated by the converter that has to manage name spaces to avoid name collisions. Ontologies can use many base URIs (specially when multiple ontologies are integrated).

Figure 1 also shows the object properties of URI1_Child. This instance has hasSuper relations with the instances URI1_Person, URI1_Relative and URI0_owl_Thing (representing classes *Person*, *Relative* and *owl:Thing*), but a *hasDirectSuper* relation only with URI1_Relative. The figure also shows the data properties of the instance: they inform that the class *Child*, represented by this instance, is not used in any rule or restriction, does not have any instances and is not a leaf class.

In order to create the converter, we used the OWL API[3] and Java. The Protégé ontology editor[4] is used to view the converted ontologies. After an ontology is converted to MetaFOR, sets of rules can be used to find problems with it. In the next section, we show a case study where rule sets are used to find ontology problems.

---

[3] The OWL API: http://owlapi.sourceforge.net/
[4] Protégé: http://protege.stanford.edu/

Fig. 1. Result of conversion

4   Case Study

In this section, we show a case study where we were able to detect 9 problems, described in the literature [4,6,11], and two user defined ones in modified versions of the FRO ontology. Each subsection presents a problem (using the FRO), a rule (or rules) to find it and an explanation of the rule action. Normally, these types of problems may occur during the integration of different ontologies. However, to make the examples easy to understand, only the FRO ontology is used and problematic axioms/rules are inserted into it. It is important to highlight that some of the problems shown may seem straightforward (when using a simple ontology, such as the FRO), but one has to keep in mind that they may occur in a big ontology, where it is difficult to keep track of the many entities on it, or involve problematic classes or properties distant in the hierarchy.

To identify the problems, SWRL rules are going to be used. But other rule languages could have been used like, for instance, SPARQL 1.1. We preferred SWRL because its syntax is more compact. To execute the SWRL rules, we used Protégé 4.3 and the Hermit 1.3.8 and Pellet reasoners available in it.

This case study is divided in three problem types: circularity, contradictory knowledge and redundant knowledge.

4.1   Circularity Problems

Circular problems occur when a class is defined as a specialization or generalization of itself [1,6]. Circular problems have a severe impact in reasoner performance [1]. In this subsection, one circularity problem is presented, it occurs between properties.

Problems in Properties. The circular properties problem occurs in ontologies in which there are two inverse properties that have the same or equivalent domain and the same or equivalent range [1]. In order to identify this problem, we have created the following SWRL rule:

```
hasInverse(?p1, ?p2), hasDomain(?p1, ?d1), hasDomain(?p2, ?d2),
isEquivalent(?d1, ?d2), hasRange(?p1, ?r1), hasRange(?p2, ?r2),
                isEquivalent(?r1, ?r2) ->
     Circular_Properties(?p1), Circular_Properties(?p2)
```

With this rule two properties were found in FRO: *hasChild* and *hasParent*, represented by the URI1_hasChild and URI1_hasParent individuals (classified as instances of the Circular_Properties class). The properties have the range equal to domain (*Person*) and this ontology does not have more specific classes that could represent the domain and range. In this knowledge domain, these properties do not represent a problem, but in other ontologies that could be a problem. Users will have to decide if this is a problem or not. If a user wants to check only the properties that have different ranges and domains, it is necessary to add *DifferentFrom(?d1, ?r1)* to the rule antecedent. This is an important advantage of this system; users can reconfigure its rules to identify what they need.

4.2   Problems with Contradictory Knowledge

Contradictory knowledge is another important type of problem regarding ontologies [1]. These kinds of problems can occur of two ways: the first situation creates inconsistent assertions in the ontology and in the second, the assertions will never be created because of the contradiction. In this subsection, five Contradictory Knowledge problems are presented.

Contradicting Rules. Contradicting Rules problems occur when two rules have the same or equivalent antecedent atoms and a two of their consequent atoms (one in each rule) are disjoint. To test this case, we added this rule to FRO: *Person(?x), Woman(?y), hasChild(?x, ?y) -> hasSon(?x, ?y)*. It generates a contradiction with the rule: *Person(?x), Woman(?y), hasChild(?x, ?y) -> hasDaughter(?x, ?y)*. During the FRO conversion to MetaFOR, sameAntecedent relations were created when appropriate. With this in mind, it is possible to create a rule that identifies this problem, which is defined as follows.

```
sameAntecedents(?r1, ?r2), hasConsequentAtom(?r1, ?c1),
hasConsequentAtom(?r2, ?c2), hasPredicate(?c1, ?p1),
   hasPredicate(?c2, ?p2), isDisjoint(?p1, ?p2) ->
             Contradicting_Rules(?r1)
```

After this rule fires, the instances URI0_Rule_2 and URI0_Rule_7, which represent the rules we added to FRO, are asserted as being instances of class Contradicting_Rules (subclass of Problems), as show in figure 2.

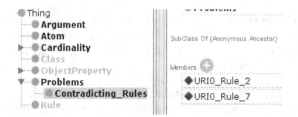

Fig. 2. Contradicting rules problem detected in the two rules

Figure 3 shows the structure of the URIO_Rule_2 instance. The instance has four atoms, three in the antecedent and one in the consequent. One of this atoms, URIO_Rule_2_Person_~x, represents the atom *Person(?x)*. To generate this unique URI (to avoid name conflicts): The first part is the rule name URIO_Rule_2, the second part is the predicate Person and the last part the argument ~x (the three parts are separated by underscore). The URI of the others three atoms are generated in the same way.

Fig. 3. Rule structure in MetaFOR

Figure 4 shows the structure of the URIO_Rule_2_hasChild_~x~y individual. It has a predicate URI1_hasChild and two argument ~x and ~y. The predicate URI1_hasChild is an instance of ObjectProperty and represents the *hasChild* object property (from FRO).

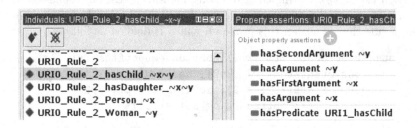

Fig. 4. Atom structure in MetaFOR

Partition Error in Taxonomy. The Partition Error in Taxonomy occurs when an incorrect combination of disjoint and derives relations happens. For instance, when two disjoint classes have the same subclass. If the subclasses are direct ones, the inconsistence is easier, but, if they happen to be down on the hierarchy, it can be far more difficult to find. To create such an error on the FRO, a *FatherMother* class was added to it as a subclass of *Father* and *Mother* (which are disjoint). To identify this problem, we create the following SWRL rule:

```
isDisjoint(?c1, ?c2), hasSub(?c1, ?cf), hasSub(?c2, ?cf) ->
              Partition_Error_in_Taxonomy(?cf)
```

It is important to point out that DL reasoners can find this kind of error, but, if the ontology is big, they do not work or take a long time to finish [3].

Incompatible Rule Antecedent. The Incompatible Rule Antecedent error happens when there is an incompatibility among antecedent atoms [1]. A disjoint in two predicate atoms that are from the same rule antecedent can be detected as the cause for this problem, as long as the atoms use the same variables. To test this kind of error, we added to FRO a rule with *hasChild(?a, ?b)* and *hasParent(?a, ?b)* in the antecedent which is a disjoint combination (the two properties have been declared disjoint). Therefore this rule will never fire, as it is impossible to an individual to have a parent and a child corresponding to the same instance. This is a very hard to find error as it may not affect the final interference result. But this condition should be identified because nobody defines rules with the intent that they never fire. In order to identify this problem, it was necessary to create two different rules. The first one treats disjoint classes and the second disjoint properties:

```
hasAntecedentAtom(?r, ?a1), hasAntecedentAtom(?r, ?a2),
      hasPredicate(?a1, ?p1), hasPredicate(?a2, ?p2),
          isDisjoint(?p1, ?p2), Class(?p1),
hasFirstArgument(?a1, ?var), hasFirstArgument(?a2, ?var) ->
          Incompatible_Rule_Antecedent(?r)


    hasAntecedentAtom(?r, ?a1), hasAntecedentAtom(?r, ?a2),
          hasPredicate(?a1, ?p1), hasPredicate(?a2, ?p2),
                  isDisjoint(?p1, ?p2),
hasFirstArgument(?a1, ?var1), hasFirstArgument(?a2, ?var1),
hasSecondArgument(?a1, ?var2), hasSecondArgument(?a2, ?var2) ->
          Incompatible_Rule_Antecedent(?r)
```

Self-Contradicting Rule. Similar to the last problem, in the Self-Contradicting Rule problem there are is a disjointness incompatibility between two atoms, but this time one is in the antecedent and the other in the consequent. Differently from the previous one, this problem can generate inconsistent results if not fixed. To test this kind of error, we added to FRO a rule with *hasChild(?a, ?b)* and *hasParent(?a, ?b)*, one in the antecedent and the other in the consequent, which forms a disjoint combination (the two properties have been declared disjoint). The rules, created to identify this problem, are also similar to the previous section. The only difference being that hasAntecedentAtom(?r, ?a2) was replaced to hasConsequentAtom(?r, ?a2):

```
hasAntecedentAtom(?r, ?a1), hasConsequentAtom(?r, ?a2),
      hasPredicate(?a1, ?p1), hasPredicate(?a2, ?p2),
            isDisjoint(?p1, ?p2), Class(?p1),
  hasFirstArgument(?a1, ?var), hasFirstArgument(?a2, ?var) ->
              Self_Contradicting_Rule(?r)


hasAntecedentAtom(?r, ?a1), hasConsequentAtom(?r, ?a2),
      hasPredicate(?a1, ?p1), hasPredicate(?a2, ?p2),
                 isDisjoint(?p1, ?p2),
hasFirstArgument(?a1, ?var1), hasFirstArgument(?a2, ?var1),
hasSecondArgument(?a1, ?var2), hasSecondArgument(?a2, ?var2) ->
              Self_Contradicting_Rule(?r)
```

Multiple Functional Properties. Multiple Functional Properties problems happens because functional properties can only have one value for each instance [1], but it is possible, for a user, to define a minimum or a maximum cardinality restriction that is greater than 1. That generates contradictory knowledge. In this case study, a functional object property was added to FRO called hasMaritalStatus with maximum cardinality restriction equal 2, in order to demonstrate this problem. To perform the identification of this problem, the following SWRL rule was created:

```
FunctionalObjectProperty(?x), hasCardinality(?x, ?c),
  MaxCardinality(?c), hasCardinalityNumber(?c, 2) ->
          Multiple_Functional_Properties(?x)
```

This rule identifies only functional object properties with maximum cardinality restriction equal to 2. If users want to make the rule more generic, they can replace hasCardinalityNumber(?c, 2) for hasCardinalityNumber(?c, ?cn), greaterThan (?cn, 2). We have run this this example using a reasoner that supports SWRL built-ins (Pellet).

4.3 Redundant Knowledge

Redundant Knowledge is generated when adding an assertion that is already defined or that can be inferred by another assertion. It is a problem hard to find because it does not affect the firing of the rules. However, it does point out to flaws in the knowledge base design that can become real problems as the base changes over time. In this subsection, three redundant knowledge problems are presented:

Redundant Implication of Transitivity. When a transitive property P is defined, P(x, y) and P(y, z) are sufficient for a reasoner to infer P(x, z). A Redundant Implication of Transitivity happens when a rule has at least three properties, nominated here as P1, P2 and P3, that are equivalent and transitive and it uses P1 and P2 to assert P3: *P1(?x, ?y), P2(?y, ?z), ... -> P3(?x, ?z)*. Although not incorrect, this rule is not necessary because the reasoner can already infer P3.

In this case study, as *hasSibling* was already defined as transitive in FRO and we just added to it the rule: *hasSibling(?x, ?y), hasSibling(?y, ?z), DifferentFrom (?x, ?z) -> hasSibling(?x, ?z)*. The SWRL rule to identify this problem is the following:

```
hasAntecedentAtom(?r, ?a1), hasAntecedentAtom(?r, ?a2),
    hasConsequentAtom(?r, ?c), hasPredicate(?a1, ?p1),
    hasPredicate(?a2, ?p2), hasPredicate(?c, ?p3),
    hasEquivalent(?p1, ?p2), hasEquivalent(?p1, ?p3),
hasFirstArgument(?a1, ?arg1), hasSecondArgument(?a1, ?arg2),
hasFirstArgument(?a2, ?arg2), hasSecondArgument(?a2, ?arg3),
hasFirstArgument(?c, ?arg1), hasSecondArgument(?c, ?arg3),
        TransitiveObjectProperty(?p1)->
    Redundant_Implication_of_Transitivity(?r)
```

We assume that all MetaFOR entities are equivalents to themselves. In other words, all entities X have hasEquivalent(X, X).

Redundant Implication of Symmetry. A symmetry property P defines that if there is P(x, y), the reasoner can infer P(y, x). A Redundant Implication of Symmetry occurs when a rule uses two properties P1 and P2, which are equivalent and symmetric, to assert: *P1(?x, ?y), ... -> P2(?y, ?x)*. The reasoner can already infer this consequent. To demonstrate this kind of problem, we add a rule, to FRO, with *hasSibling(?x, ?y)* in the antecedent and *hasSibling(?y, ?x)* in the consequent. To identify the problem, we create the SWRL rule:

```
hasAntecedentAtom(?r, ?a), hasConsequentAtom(?r, ?c),
    hasPredicate(?a, ?p1), hasPredicate(?c, ?p2),
            isEquivalent(?p1, ?p2),
hasFirstArgument(?a, ?arg2), hasSecondArgument(?a, ?arg1),
hasFirstArgument(?c, ?arg1), hasSecondArgument(?c, ?arg2),
        SymmetricObjectProperty(?p1) ->
    Redundant_Implication_of_Symmetry(?r)
```

Rule Subsumption. This problem occurs when a rule antecedent can be fully mapped to another rule antecedent and their consequents are the same. To demonstrate this, the following two rules were added to FRO:

- *Person(?p), hasAge(?p, ?a), greaterThan(?a, 18) -> isAdult(?p, true)*
- *Person(?p), hasAge(?p, ?a), greaterThan(?a, 21) -> isAdult(?p, true)*

To identify this problem, we create the following SWRL rule:

```
subsumes(?r1, ?r2), sameAntecedents(?r1, ?r2) ->
    Rule_Subsumption(?r1), Rule_Subsumption(?r2)
```

4.4 Two Possible User Scenarios

Besides the 9 problems, documented in the literature, that we showed this technique could detect, we also include two anomalies that could have been added by users. This class of anomalies does not have to be real errors or problems, but constructs that users, for some reason, do not want in their ontology. For instance, a project may have an agreed upon format to represent knowledge that users want to enforce in the whole ontology.

As examples of use, we present two different scenarios that can be of interest to users, along with the rules that can be applied in each case (in a way similar to what was described in previous sections).

Useless Inheritance Scenario. In this scenario, a user found an ontology for a domain he is interested. He evaluated this ontology, added all instances he needed and created rules to classify its instances. After that, the user decides to analyze the ontology and the inferences made. He wants to find classes or properties that are not used in instances or in restriction and that are in a subclass or sub property cascade. He wants to find these classes or properties because he wants to analyze them and delete the ones that are not really useful for his application.

In order to do that, this user converts the ontology to MetaFOR and writes a rule that identifies this pattern. He decides to try using three classes/properties in cascade and creates the rule:

```
hasDirectSuper(?a, ?b), hasDirectSuper(?b, ?c),
hasInstancesNumber(?b, 0), usedInRestrictions(?b, false) ->
                ClassToEliminate(?b)
```

He then finds the entities he is looking for. The user should not have problems writing those rules if he understands how to use SWRL and how the MetaFOR map is done, for this reason we kept it simple.

Class with Low Use. In this scenario, a user built and evaluated his own ontology, adding instances and creating rules to classify instances in different classes. Afterwards, he wants to analyze the inference results. In this scenario, the user wants to know which classes have less than 7 instances or more than 100 instances. He wants to have an idea of class usage so he can refine its model. The classes the user is interested in are subclasses of *Classifications*. So, he converts his ontology to MetaFOR and writes two rules that will identify this pattern:

```
     hasDirectSuper(?x, URI1_Classifications),
hasInstancesNumber(?x, ?xn), lessThan(?xn, 7) ->
              ClassToAnalyze(?x)

     hasDirectSuper(?x, URI1_Classifications),
hasInstancesNumber(?x, ?xn), greaterThan(?xn, 100) ->
              ClassToAnalyze(?x)
```

After running the rules, he can use a tool, such as Protégé, and find all detected classes classified as instances of ClassToAnalize. By converting his ontology to MetaFOR and writing two simple rules, the process of pattern identification is greatly facilitated.

The methodology being proposed here provides users with the possibility to focus more their efforts on the understanding of the generated results, rather than having to search manually the ontology.

5   Conclusions

This paper presents a technique to find problems that occur in ontologies and rules. This technique relies in an ontology that represents information (metadata) about OWL ontologies, called MetaFOR, to convert an ontology to instances of MetaFOR using an automatic converter. Once an ontology is in this new format, rules can be applied to it to find problems or usage patterns.

We demonstrated that using this technique it is possible to develop a prototype and rules capable to detect 9 problems (documented in the literature) related to ontologies and rules. We also showed two scenarios in which users could write their own rules, in SWRL, to expand the system to work with new problems unique to their particular domain needs. Most ontology errors, of course, are going to be problems in domain modeling that a set of domain-independent rules are not going to detect. It is one of the main goals of this project that users be able to write their own rule sets to identify patterns/problems in their specific ontology domains.

As a limitation of this case study, we inserted the problems the system detected. It would be more convincing to detect problems in real ontologies, but it would be more difficult to explain them. As a future work, we are going to test this system using a set of real world ontologies, such as the ones available at Bioportal[5]

The two major advantages of this technique are (i) the use of OWL and SWRL, two popular languages among ontologists, to identify patterns/problems in ontologies, and (ii) the fact that users can expand the system themselves creating new rules to identify patterns they are interested in. Also, SWRL is not the only language that can be used. Once an ontology is converted to MetaFOR, any rule language that works with OWL can be used, including SPARQL 1.1. It means that even very big ontology, not supported by reasoners today, can be

---

[5] http://bioportal.bioontology.org.

loaded in triple stores and tested. That will be tested in future research. Another important direction will be to provide visualization, for the reported problems/patterns, so users can more easily find solutions to them.

Acknowledgments. This work has been funded by grants from the Coordination for the Improvement of Higher Education Personnel - CAPES, a Brazilian research agency.

References

1. Baumeister, J., Seipel, D.: Anomalies in ontologies with rules. Web Semantics: Science, Services and Agents on the World Wide Web **8**(1), 55–68 (2010)
2. Berners-Lee, T., Hendler, J., Lassila, O.: The Semantic Web, pp. 29–37. Scientific American, May 2001
3. Dentler, K., Cornet, R., ten Teije, A., de Keizer, N.: Comparison of Reasoners for Large Ontologies in the OWL 2 EL Profile. Semant. Web **2**(2), 71–87 (2011)
4. Fahad, M., Qadir, M.A.: A Framework for Ontology Evaluation. ICCS Supplement **354**, 149–158 (2008)
5. Gennari, J.H., Musen, M.A., Fergerson, R.W., Grosso, W.E., Crubezy, M., Eriksson, H., Noy, N.F., Tu, S.W.: The evolution of Protege: an environment for knowledge-based systems development. International Journal of Human-Computer Studies **58**(1), 89–123 (2003)
6. Gomez-Perez, A.: Evaluation of ontologies. International Journal of Intelligent Systems **16**(3), 391–409 (2001)
7. Hassanpour, S., O'Connor, M.J., Das, A.K.: Visualizing logical dependencies in SWRL rule bases. In: Dean, M., Hall, J., Rotolo, A., Tabet, S. (eds.) RuleML 2010. LNCS, vol. 6403, pp. 259–272. Springer, Heidelberg (2010)
8. Hassanpour, S., O'Connor, M.J., Das, A.K.: Clustering Rule Bases Using Ontology-based Similarity Measures. Web Semantics: Science, Services and Agents on the World Wide Web **25**, June 2014
9. Horrocks, I., Patel-Schneider, P.F., Boley, H., Tabet, S., Grosof, B., Dean, M.: SWRL: A Semantic Web Rule Language Combining OWL and RuleML (May 2004). http://www.w3.org/Submission/SWRL/
10. Orlando, J.P., Rivolli, A., Hassanpour, S., O'Connor, M.J., Das, A., Moreira, D.A.: SWRL Rule Editor - A Web Application as Rich as Desktop Business Rule Editors, pp. 258–263. SciTePress - Science and and Technology Publications (2012)
11. Pak, J., Zhou, L.: A framework for ontology evaluation. In: Sharman, R., Rao, H.R., Raghu, T.S. (eds.) WEB 2009. LNBIP, vol. 52, pp. 10–18. Springer, Heidelberg (2010)
12. Sugumaran, V., Gulla, J.A. (eds.): Applied Semantic Web Technologies, 1st edn. Auerbach Publications, Boca Raton, August 2011
13. Sun, Y., Zhang, J., Bie, R., Wang, H.: Managing Rules in Semantic Web: Redundancy Elimination and Consistency Check **5**(2), 191–200, February 2011
14. Zacharias, V.: Development and verification of rule based systems — a survey of developers. In: Bassiliades, N., Governatori, G., Paschke, A. (eds.) RuleML 2008. LNCS, vol. 5321, pp. 6–16. Springer, Heidelberg (2008)

Semantics of Notation3 Logic: A Solution for Implicit Quantification

Dörthe Arndt[1]([⊠]), Ruben Verborgh[1], Jos De Roo[2], Hong Sun[2], Erik Mannens[1], and Rik Van De Walle[1]

[1] Ghent University – iMinds – Multimedia Lab, Gaston Crommenlaan 8 bus 201, 9050 Ledeberg-Ghent, Belgium
{dorthe.arndt,ruben.verborgh,erik.mannens,vandewalle}@ugent.be
[2] Agfa Healthcare, Moutstraat 100, 9000 Ghent, Belgium
hong.sun@agfa.com

Abstract. Since the development of Notation3 Logic, several years have passed in which the theory has been refined and used in practice by different reasoning engines such as cwm, FuXi or EYE. Nevertheless, a clear model-theoretic definition of its semantics is still missing. This leaves room for individual interpretations and renders it difficult to make clear statements about its relation to other logics such as DL or FOL or even about such basic concepts as correctness. In this paper we address one of the main open challenges: the formalization of implicit quantification. We point out how the interpretation of implicit quantifiers differs in two of the above mentioned reasoning engines and how the specification, proposed in the W3C team submission, could be formalized. Our formalization is then put into context by integrating it into a model-theoretic definition of the whole language. We finish our contribution by arguing why universal quantification should be handled differently than currently prescribed.

Keywords: Notation3 · Formal semantics · Quantification · Logic · Semantic web

1 Introduction

With the invention of Notation3 (N3) [7], about one decade ago, a new easily understandable way of representing and interpreting logical data in the Semantic Web was provided. Driven by the idea of defining one common language to represent both data and logic the developers of N3 offered a new human-readable serialization of Resource Description Framework (RDF) [9] models but they also extended RDF by logical symbols and created a new Semantic Web logic, Notation3 Logic (N3Logic). While the syntactical innovation on RDF is already established—it resulted in a W3C-recommendation of its subset Turtle [2]—the full description of N3Logic is still lagging behind: although it is used by different semantic web reasoners such as cwm [3], FuXi [1] or EYE [10], there is no common standard which fully defines the model-theoretic semantics of N3Logic. This has

© Springer International Publishing Switzerland 2015
N. Bassiliades et al. (Eds.): RuleML 2015, LNCS 9202, pp. 127–143, 2015.
DOI: 10.1007/978-3-319-21542-6_9

consequences for the theoretical examination—the relation to first-order-logic or description logic is not clear yet, the correctness of reasoning cannot be proven— but in practice as well: developers of reasoning engines have to come up with their own solutions when it comes to the interpretation of certain constructs. This increases the risk that the results of different reasoning engines differ and are not exchangeable. Especially given the background that N3Logic is designed for the Semantic Web whose goal is interoperability—logical rules are expected to be written and used by different independent parties—these uncertainties form a barrier.

This paper focuses on one of the most important constructs mentioned above: implicit quantification. In Notation3 it is possible to use quantified variables without explicit quantifiers. The definition of the scope of those variables varies in different reasoning engines. We will show how cwm and EYE solve this problem and how we understand the current state of the W3C team submission [6]. We give a formal definition of the latter and embed it into a semantic definition of the logic. We especially focus on the difficulties we encounter. Our contribution is concluded by a critical discussion of whether the current specification offers the best option to interpret implicit quantification, which is, in our opinion, not the case. We identify the development of an alternative solution as one of the main goals for future work.

The structure of this paper is as follows: we start by discussing related work (Section 2) and continue by introducing the syntax of N3 (Section 3). After that we analyze different interpretations of implicit quantification in N3Logic (Section 4). We then transfer our observations into a formal definition (Section 5) which we afterwards put into the context of the logic (Section 6). Further on we briefly discuss the elements of N3 not included in our formalization (Section 7). We conclude our contribution and give an outlook to future work in Section 8.

2   Related Work

Our related work section is divided in three parts; we start by explaining relevant material available about N3Logic, followed by an introduction to N3-reasoners and finally a part explaining other logics supporting implicit quantification.

N3Logic was introduced in 2008 [7]. In their paper, Tim Berners-Lee et al. explain the "informal semantics" of Notation3 by illustrating the ideas of special properties such as quoting, rules or implicit quantification with examples. Being a good introduction into the main concepts of N3, the paper leaves the model-theoretic definition of the logic open[1]. Further on, the definitions were clarified on the corresponding web pages, the W3C team submission [6], and a design issues web page [4]. While certain details such as the dominance of universal quantifiers over existentials are elucidated, the main model-theoretic definition, and thereby also a formalization of implicit quantification, is skipped with the remark that N3 is a superset of RDF plus the specific predicates and features

---

[1] "As such, developing a formal model theory for N3Logic is quite challenging, and is the focus of current work." [7, p. 17].

defined. The definition of RDF-semantics was updated in 2014 [12] and includes a model theory which solves, inter alia, the problem that for RDF, in opposition to classical first order logic, predicates and constants are not clearly separated. But as RDF is just a subset of N3, the theory is not able to cover universal quantification, quoting or implication.

The reasoning engines which support N3Logic such as FuXi, cwm or EYE do not give a model-theoretic definition of the semantics, but as they implement such a definition, they provide an important input when it comes to the question of how uncertainties in the current informal definition can be resolved. FuXi [1] is a forward-chaining production system for Notation3 whose reasoning is based on the RETE algorithm. To ensure decidability, FuXi only supports a subset of Notation3, N3-Datalog. The forward-chaining cwm [3] reasoner is a general-purpose data processing tool which can be used for querying, checking, transforming and filtering information. As the first of its kind, this N3 reasoner was used to test the implementation of most of the language's concepts. The reasoner therefore supports a major part of the logic. EYE [10] is a high performance reasoner enhanced with Euler path detection. It supports both backward and forward reasoning. In its coverage of N3 it is comparable to cwm, but it also supports additional concepts not mentioned in the language's specification, such as the option to use boolean variables as the consequence of a rule. As this last aspect, the covered extent of the language—especially regarding implicit quantification—is most important for this paper, we use the last two reasoners mentioned for our observations.

Implicit quantification, in particular on universal variables, can also be found in other contexts: in Prolog [8] variables are understood to be universally quantified. The scope of this quantification is the clause in which the variable occurs. But Prolog is only partly comparable to N3Logic, as it does not allow the construction of nested rules, which are very challenging constructs for the determination of scoping in N3. SPARQL [15] does allow nesting of graph patterns containing universal variables. The scope of a universal variable occurring in such a pattern depends on the keyword, if existing, via which this pattern is connected to other graph patterns as described by its formal semantics [14]. This makes the evaluation of nested patterns in SPARQL easier than in N3Logic.

3   Syntax

Before coming to the main topic of this paper, implicit quantification, we start by defining the general syntax of N3Logic. We exclude built-ins and explicit quantification (for more information see section 7). The syntax-definition below is oriented on the context-free grammar as provided at the team submission web page [6].

Definition 1 (Basic N3 vocabulary). *An N3 alphabet A consists of the following disjoint classes of symbols:*

- *A set U of URI symbols.*
- *A set $V = V_E \,\dot\cup\, V_U$ of (quantified) variables, with V_E being the set of existential variables and V_U the set of universal variables.*
- *A set L of literals.*
- *Brackets {, }, (,)*
- *Logical implication =>*
- *Period .*

We define the elements of U as in the corresponding specification [11]. As for example in Turtle [2], N3 allows to abbreviate URLs by using prefixes. Literals are strings beginning and ending with quotation marks '"'; existentials start with '_:', universals with '?'. Unlike first order logic, N3 does not distinguish between predicates and constants—a single URI symbol can stand for both at the same time—so the first-order-concept of a *term* has a slightly different counterpart in N3: an *expression*. Since the definition of expressions (Definition 2) is closely related to the concept of a formula (Definition 3), the two following definitions should be considered together.

Definition 2 (Expressions). *Let A be an N3 alphabet. The set of expressions $E \subset A^*$ is defined as follows:*

1. *Each URI is an expression.*
2. *Each variable is an expression.*
3. *Each literal is an expression.*
4. *If $e_1, \ldots, e_n$ are expressions, $(e_1 \ldots e_n)$ is an expression.*
5. *If $f \in F$ is a formula, then $\{f\}$ is an expression.*

The expression defined by 4 is called a list. We call the expressions defined by 5 formula expressions and denote the set of all formula expressions by FE.

Note that point 5 of the definition above makes use of formulas, defined below:

Definition 3 (N3 Formulas). *The set F of N3 formulas over an alphabet A is recursively defined as follows:*

1. *If e_1, e_2, e_3 are expressions, $e_1\ e_2\ e_3$. is a formula, an atomic formula.*
2. *If t_1, t_2 are formula expressions, t_1=> t_2. is a formula, an implication.*
3. *If f_1 and f_2 are formulas, $f_1 f_2$ is a formula, a conjunction.*

We will refer to a formula without any variables as a *ground formula*. Analogously, we call such kind of expressions *ground expressions*. We denote the corresponding sets by F_g respectively E_g.

The definition explicitly allows all expressions in all positions of atomic formulas. Literals or even formula expressions can be subjects, objects or predicates. In the examples in the remainder of this paper, we will use the common RDF shortcuts:

Remark 1 (Syntactic variants).

- A formula consisting of two triple subformulas starting with the same element `<d> <p> <e>. <d> <q> <f>.` can be abbreviated using a semicolon: `<d> <p> <e>; <q> <f>.`
- Two triple formulas sharing the first two elements `<d> <p> <e>. <d> <p> <f>.` can be abbreviated using a comma: `<d> <p> <e>, <f>.`
- An expression of the form `[<p> <o>]` is a shortcut for a new existential variable `_:x`, which is subject to the statement `_:x <p> <o>`. So `<s> <p> [<q> <o>].` stands for `<s> <p> _:x. _:x <q> <o>.`

To emphasize the difference between brackets which form part of the N3 vocabulary, i.e. "(", ")", "{", and "}", and the brackets occurring in mathematical language, we will underline the N3 brackets in all definitions where both kinds of brackets occur.

4 Implicit Quantification

As in RDF, atomic formulas are triples consisting of subject, predicate and object. They can be intuitively understood as first order formulas like *predicate(subject, object)*. It is also easy to get an idea of the meaning of conjunctions or implications if no variables are involved. Including implicit quantification is more difficult. Definition 1 distinguishes between two kinds of variables: universal and existential variables. As the names indicate, these variables are meant to be implicitly quantified. But how do we have to understand this "implicit" quantification? Some cases are quite simple. If we have the formulas

$$\_:x \ :knows \ :Kurt. \quad \text{and} \quad ?x \ :knows \ :Kurt.$$

It is rather straight forward to understand them as "someone knows Kurt." and "everyone knows Kurt." In first order logic:

$$\exists x : \mathrm{knows}(x, \mathrm{Kurt}) \quad \text{and} \quad \forall x : \mathrm{knows}(x, \mathrm{Kurt}).$$

But the above grammar also enables us to construct more complicate statements. Does the construct

$$?x \ :loves \ \_:y. \tag{1}$$

mean "everybody loves someone" or "there is someone who is loved by everyone", in first order formulas:

$$\forall x \exists y : \mathrm{loves}(x, y) \quad \text{vs.} \quad \exists y \forall x : \mathrm{loves}(x, y) \tag{1a, b}$$

In this case we know the answer, the team submission [6] clearly chooses (1a):

> "If both universal and existential quantification are specified for the same formula, then the scope of the universal quantification is outside the scope of the existentials". (I)

```
1  @prefix : <http://example.org/test#>.
2
3  _:x_1 :says {_:x_2 :knows :Albert.}.
```

Listing 1. Reasoning result of EYE for formula (3)

```
1  @prefix : <http://example.org/test#>.
2
3  [ :says { [ :knows :Albert ]. } ].
```

Listing 2. Reasoning result of cwm for formula (3)

And also the reasoners we tested, EYE and cwm, have implemented the first interpretation (1a).

Such clarity is lacking when it comes to nested formulas or co-occurring formula expressions which contain variables. We will treat this in the following sections, first for existential variables, then for universals.

4.1 Existentials

To test how both cwm and EYE understand existential quantification, we confronted them with some examples. Both reasoners offer the option to output all knowledge they are aware of, this includes all derived formulas and rules as well as the input. In most cases, different variables sharing the same name are renamed to be distinguishable. Therefore we can use the derived output of such a reasoning process with a simple rule as input as indication of how the formula is interpreted. As a first example we invoked both reasoners with a formula containing nested existentials:

$$\_:x \ :says \ \{\_:x \ :knows \ :Albert.\}. \tag{3}$$

Is there someone who says about himself that he knows Albert, or does this someone just state that someone exists who knows Albert? In (enhanced) first order logic

$$\exists x : \text{says}(x, \text{knows}(x, \text{Albert})) \quad or \quad \exists x_1 : \text{says}(x_1, (\exists x_2 : \text{knows}(x_2, \text{Albert})))$$
$$\tag{3a,b}$$

Listing 1 shows the output of EYE given formula (3) as only input, Listing 2 the output of cwm. We clearly see[2] that both reasoners favor option (3b).

We observe similar behavior using the same existential quantifier in two co-occurring graphs. In an example formula such as

$$\{ \_:x \ :knows \ :Albert.\} \Rightarrow \{ \_:x \ :knows \ :Kurt.\}. \tag{4}$$

---

[2] To see this evidence for cwm, recall that every new bracket "[...]" corresponds with a *new* existential variable, see also Remark 1 or [2] for further information.

The two _:x are interpreted as different variables by both reasoners. In first order logic this would be:

$$(\exists x_1 : \text{knows}(x_1, \text{Albert})) \rightarrow (\exists x_2 : \text{knows}(x_2, \text{Kurt}))$$

This interpretation is also in line with the official team submission [6]:

> *"When formulae are nested, _: blank nodes syntax [is] used to only identify blank node in the formula it occurs directly in. It is an arbitrary temporary name for a symbol which is existentially quantified within the current formula (not the whole file). They can only be used within a single formula, and not within nested formulae."*   (II)

This means, the scope of an existential quantifier is always only the formula-expression "{...}" it occurs in, but not its nested dependency.

4.2   Universals

When it comes to the definition of the scope, universal quantifiers are more complicated. To illustrate that, we consider the following example:

$$\{\{?x \; :p \; :a.\} \; \Rightarrow \; \{?x \; :q \; :b.\}.\} \; \Rightarrow \; \{\{?x \; :r \; :c.\} \; \Rightarrow \; \{?x \; :s \; :d.\}.\}. \quad (5)$$

Are all ?x the same? If not, which ones do we have to understand as equal? Two options seem to be most probable:

$$(\forall x_1 : p(x_1, a) \rightarrow q(x_1, b)) \rightarrow (\forall x_2 : r(x_2, c) \rightarrow s(x_2, d)) \quad (5a)$$

or

$$\forall x : ((p(x, a) \rightarrow q(x, b)) \rightarrow (r(x, c) \rightarrow s(x, d))) \quad (5b)$$

As above, we gave formula (5) as input for both reasoners, cwm and EYE. Lines 1-9 of Listing 3 show the result of EYE which seems to imply[3] that EYE supports the second interpretation (5b), but as it does not differ from the input, we ran another test to verify that and added the formula

$$\{:e \; :p \; :a.\} \; \Rightarrow \; \{:e \; :q \; :b.\}. \quad (6)$$

to the reasoning input in order to see whether the reasoner outputs

$$\{:e \; :r \; :c.\} \; \Rightarrow \; \{:e \; :s \; :d.\}. \quad (7)$$

as it would be the case with interpretation (5b) but not with interpretation (5a). The reasoning output of EYE shown in Listing 3 (all lines) verifies that EYE

---

[3] Where applicable, EYE employs the "standardization apart" mechanism of its programming language Prolog.

```
 1  @prefix : <http://example.org/test#>.
 2
 3  {
 4    {?U0 :p :a.} => {?U0 :q :b.}.
 5  }
 6  =>
 7  {
 8    {?U0 :r :c.} => {?U0 :s :d.}.
 9  }.
10  {:e :p :a.} => {:e :q :b.}.
11  {:e :r :c.} => {:e :s :d.}.
```

Listing 3. Output of EYE for formula (5) and formula (6)

interprets all variables with the same name which occur in one single implication equally regardless of how deeply nested they occur.

In contrast to this, Listing 4 shows the result cwm gives. Here, the keyword "@forAll" can be understood as its first order counterpart "∀" (see Section 7). Cwm understands formula (5) as stated in interpretation (5a). We see a clear difference between the two reasoners.

After examining universals in co-ordinated expressions such as in the above implication, we are also interested in how those variables are handled in subordinated formula expressions, similar to those in formula (3). We consider the following formula:

$$\{?x :p :o.\} => \{?x :pp \{?x :ppp :ooo.\}.\}. \tag{8}$$

To learn how the reasoners interpret this formula, we give the simple formula

$$:s :p :o. \tag{9}$$

as additional input. Listings 5 and 6 show the reasoning results of EYE respectively cwm. We clearly see that the two reasoners agree in their interpretation and that this interpretation of formula (8) differs from the interpretation of the existential counterpart formula (3).

Having considered the contrary behavior of the reasoners in the interpretation of formula (5), the obvious question is: how is this interpretation meant to be according to the official sources? The team submission [6] states the following:

> *"Apart from the set of statements, a formula also has a set of URIs of symbols which are universally quantified, and a set of URIs of symbols which are existentially quanitified. Variables are then in general symbols which have been quantified. There is a also a shorthand syntax ?x which is the same as :x except that it implies that x is universally quantified not in the formula but in its parent formula."* (III)

This quote strengthens the position of cwm but makes the formalization and implementation of Notation3 challenging, especially considering it together with

```
1  @prefix : <http://example.org/test#>.
2  @prefix ex: <#> .
3
4  {
5    @forAll ex:x. {ex:x :p :a.} => {ex:x :q :b.}.
6  }
7  =>
8  {
9    @forAll ex:x. {ex:x :r :c.} => {ex:x :s :d.}.
10 }.
```

Listing 4. Output of cwm for formula (5)

```
1  @prefix : <http://example.org/test#>.
2
3  :s :p :o.
4  :s :pp {:s :ppp :ooo}.
5  {?U0 :p :o} => {?U0 :pp {?U0 :ppp :ooo}}.
```

Listing 5. Output of EYE for formulas (8) and (9)

our observation on equations (8) and (9): If a universal variable occurs in a deeply nested formula, the scope of this particular variable can either be its direct parent, the parent of any predecessor containing a variable with the same name or even the direct parent of a predecessor's sibling containing the same variable on highest level. Consider for example the formula

$$\{?x\ :p\ :o.\} => \{\ \{\{?x\ :p2\ ?y.\} => \{?x\ :p3\ ?y.\}.\}$$
$$=>\{\{?x\ :p4\ ?y.\} => \{?x\ :p5\ ?y.\}.\}.\}. \quad (10)$$

Which, according to (III), has to be interpreted as the first order formula

$$\forall x : p(x,o) \rightarrow ((\forall y_1 : p_2(x, y_1) \rightarrow p_3(x, y_1)) \rightarrow (\forall y_2 : p_4(x, y_2) \rightarrow p_5(x, y_2)))$$

Note that in this example, there are two different scopes for ?y, but only one for ?x. One can easily think of more complicated cases.

5 Formalization of Quantification

After having discussed the characteristics of implicit quantification in Notation3 in the last section, we now formalize our observations. Where possible, we will follow the team submission [6] as this is the most official source indicating how the language is meant to be understood.

To enable us to distinguish between variables occurring directly in a formula and variables only occurring in formula expressions which are dependent on a formula—as it is necessary to interpret for example formula (3)—we give the following definition:

```
1  @prefix : <http://example.org/test#>.
2  @prefix ex: <#> .
3
4  @forAll ex:x .
5  :s  :p  :o;
6      :pp {:s :ppp :ooo .}.
7  { ex:x :p :o .} => {ex:x :pp {ex:x :ppp :ooo.}.}.
```

Listing 6. Output of cwm for formulas (8) and (9)

Definition 4 (Components of a formula). *Let $f \in F$ be a formula and $c : E \to 2^E$ a function such that:*

$$c(e) = \begin{cases} c(e_1) \cup \ldots \cup c(e_n) & \text{if } e = \underline{(e_1 \ldots e_n)} \text{ is a list,} \\ \{e\} & \text{otherwise.} \end{cases}$$

We define the set $comp(f) \subset E$ of components of f as follows:

- *If f is an atomic formula of the form $e_1\ e_2\ e_3.$, $comp(f) = c(e_1) \cup c(e_2) \cup c(e_3)$.*
- *If f is an implication of the form t_1`=>` $t_2.$, then $comp(f) = \{t_1, t_2\}$.*
- *If f is a conjunction of the form $f_1 f_2$, then $comp(f) = comp(f_1) \cup comp(f_2)$.*

Likewise, for $n \in \mathbb{N}_{>0}$, we define the components of level n as:

$$comp^n(f) := \{e \in E | \exists f_1, \ldots, f_{n-1} \in F : e \in comp(f_1) \wedge \underline{\{f_1\}} \in comp(f_2) \wedge \ldots \\ \wedge \underline{\{f_{n-1}\}} \in comp(f)\}$$

The definition allows us to distinguish between direct components and nested components. As an example take the following N3 formula:

$$\text{:John :says \{:Kurt :knows :Albert.\}.} \tag{11}$$

Direct components are `:John`, `:says` and `{:Kurt :knows :Albert.}` while `:Kurt`, `:knows` and `:Albert` are nested components of level two.

For variables, we can now clarify the depth of a nesting:

Definition 5 (Nesting level). *Let $f \in F$ be an N3 formula and $v \in V$ a variable. The nesting level $n_f(v)$ of v in f is defined as follows:*

$$n_f(v) := \begin{cases} \min\{n \in \mathbb{N} | v \in comp^n(f)\} & \text{if } v \in comp^n(f) \text{ for some } n. \\ 0 & \text{otherwise.} \end{cases}$$

As an illustration of the definition, consider the following formula:

$$f = \text{ \_:x :says \{\_:y :says \{\_:x :knows ?z.\}.\}.}$$

Here we have $n_f(\text{\_:x}) = 1$, $n_f(\text{\_:y}) = 2$, $n_f(?z) = 3$ and $n_f(?v) = 0$, as the latter does not occur in the formula.

At first glance this definition might seem counter-intuitive as we count the nesting level starting from the top of the formula and not, as one might expect, from the bottom. The reason for our definition is the intended use: we want to employ it to easily find the scope of a universal quantifier. Here, nesting level two is of special importance. Starting from above, i.e. with the formula as a whole, and then exploring subformulas, the scope of a universal quantified variable ?x is always the first (sub-)formula where ?x occurs on a nesting level less or equal than two. We illustrate this on example (5):

$$f = (\{\{?x \ :p \ :a.\} \ => \ \{?x \ :q \ :b.\}.\} \ => \ \{\{?x \ :r \ :c.\} \ => \ \{?x \ :s \ :d.\}.\}.)$$

Using the definition above, we get $n_f(?x) = 3$. Our first order translation (5a) contains no universal quantifier for the formula as a whole. Now, consider the subformulas on the next level:

$$f_1 = (\{\{?x \ :p \ :a.\}=>\{?x \ :q \ :b.\}.) \text{ and } f_2 = (\{\{?x \ :r \ :c.\}=>\{?x \ :s \ :d.\}.\}.)$$

We get $n_{f_1}(?x) = 2$ and $n_{f_2}(?x) = 2$. If we, again, go back to the first order translation of the formula (5a), we see that those two formulas are carrying quantifiers for ?x:

$$\{ \underbrace{\{?x \ :p \ :a.\} \ => \ \{?x \ :q \ :b.\}.\}}_{(\forall x_1 : (p(x_1, a) \to q(x_1, b)))} \ => \ \{ \underbrace{\{?x \ :r \ :c.\} \ => \ \{?x \ :s \ :d.\}.\}}_{(\forall x_2 : (r(x_2, c) \to s(x_2, d)))} $$

Motivated by this observation, we define the set of accessible variables in a formula:

Definition 6 (Accessible Variables). *Let $f \in F$ be an N3 formula over an alphabet A. We define the sets of accessible universals $AC_U(f)$ and the set of accessible existentials $AC_E(f)$ of f as follows:*

$$AC_U(f) := \{u \in V_U | 0 < n_f(u) \leq 2\} \quad and \quad AC_E(f) := \{v \in V_E | n_f(v) = 1\}$$

The set of all accessible variables of f as defined as $AC(f) := AC_E(f) \cup AC_U(f)$.

For any formula, accessible variables are those variables which are quantified on its top level. For universal variables this definition becomes clear considering the above example, formula (5): we get $AC_U(f) = \emptyset$, $AC_U(f_1) = \{?x\}$ and $AC_U(f_2) = \{?x\}$. To understand the definition of accessible existentials, remember our previous study on formulas (3) and (4): the scope of an existential variable is always the formula it occurs in as a component, i.e. on nesting level one.

Because of our observation on formulas (4) and (8) that universal quantification effects subformulas while existential does not, we need to define two ways to apply a substitution:

Definition 7 (Substitution). *Let A be an N3 alphabet and $f \in F$ an N3 formula over A.*

- A substitution *is a finite set of pairs of expressions* $\{v_1/e_1, \ldots, v_n/e_n\}$ *where each e_i is an expression and each v_i a variable such that $v_i \neq e_i$ and $v_i \neq v_j$, if $i \neq j$.*
- *For a formula f and a substitution* $\sigma = \{v_1/e_1, \ldots, v_n/e_n\}$, *we obtain the* component application *of σ to f, $f\sigma^c$, by simultaneously replacing each v_i which occurs as a* direct *component in f by the corresponding expression e_i.*
- *For a formula f and a substitution* $\sigma = \{v_1/e_1, \ldots, v_n/e_n\}$, *we obtain the* total application *of σ to f, $f\sigma^t$, by simultaneously replacing each v_i which occurs as a* direct *or* nested *component in f by the corresponding expression e_i.*

As the definition states, component application of a substitution only changes the direct components of a formula. For a substitution $\sigma = \{?\text{x}/:\text{Kurt}\}$ we obtain:

$$(?\text{x :says } \{?\text{x :knows :Albert.}\}.)\sigma^c =$$
$$(\text{ :Kurt :says } \{?\text{x :knows :Albert.}\}.)$$

A total application, in contrast, replaces each *occurrence* of a variable in a formula:

$$(?\text{x :says } \{?\text{x :knows :Albert.}\}.)\sigma^t =$$
$$(:\text{Kurt :says } \{:\text{Kurt :knows :Albert.}\}.)$$

The ingredients defined in this section, accessible variables, and component-wise and total substitution, enable us to define the semantics of N3. Before doing this in the next chapter (Definition 10), we consider one more example:

$$f = (\{?\text{x :p \_:y}\} => \{:\text{s2 :p2 } \{?\text{x :p3 \_:y}\}.\}.) \tag{12}$$

Applied to the triple :s :p :o. the rule above leads to the result

$$:\text{s2 :p2 } \{:\text{x :p3 \_:y}\}. \tag{13}$$

How do we get there? First, we consider the whole formula f and identify its accessible variables $AC(f) = \{?\text{x}\}$. Thus, the variable ?x is universally quantified on the formula level. This means that the formula $f\sigma^t$ is valid for all substitutions $\sigma : \{?\text{x}\} \rightarrow E_g$. We totally apply $\sigma = \{?\text{x}/:\text{s}\}$ and get:

$$f\sigma^t = (\{:\text{s :p \_:y}\} => \{:\text{s2 :p2 } \{:\text{s :p3 \_:y}\}.\}.)$$

Now, we consider the antecedence $f_1 = (:\text{s :p \_:y})$ of the implication. Accessible variables are $AC(f_1) = \{\_:\text{y}\}$. As $\_:\text{y}$ is an existential variable, it is existentially quantified on the level of function f_1. We know that the condition of the antecedent of the rule is fulfilled as the triple :s :p :o. is true and there exists a substitution $\mu = \{\_:\text{y}/:\text{o}\}$ such that $f_1\mu^c = (:\text{s :p :o.})$. Thus, we can derive (13).

6   Semantics of Notation3

In this section we are going to embed our concept for the evaluation of implicit quantified variables into a definition for the semantics of Notation3. To do so, we still have to overcome one obstacle: in this paper, and in N3 in general, the exact meaning of a context is not fully defined. We have to decide how to handle ground formula expressions such as {:Kurt :knows :Albert.} in example (11). We will understand them as one single constant. For formula expressions containing variables, this decision is more complicated: if we consider formula (3) and its first order like translation (3b)

$$\exists x_1 : \text{says}(x_1, (\exists x_2 : \text{knows}(x_2, \text{Albert})))$$

we have a clear understanding what the existential quantifier for x_1 means, but we do not know how to interpret the second existential quantifier for x_2 nor whether the expression $(\exists x_2 : \text{knows}(x_2, \text{Albert}))$ in combination with the predicate *says* refers to one or several elements in the domain of discourse. For our definition, we will assume the former for all unknown predicates. Furthermore, we expect that the sets of universal and existential variable names are infinite and exchangeable within a formula, i.e. that :s :p _:y. has the same meaning as :s :p _:x.

We encounter the problem explained above for every formula expression whose formula contains an existential on any nesting level. For universals, the situation is slightly more complicated. A universal as a direct component of an expression's formula is quantified outside, the same holds for universals also occurring in a predecessor formula as a component (see for example the different scopes in formula (10)). To identify this kind of ungrounded formula expressions, we make the following definition:

Definition 8 (Formula expressions with unaccessible variables). *Let A be an N3 alphabet. For a formula $g \in F$ over A we define the set of formula expressions which contain for g unaccessible universals as follows:*

$$FE_U(g) := \{\{\underline{f}\} \in FE | \forall v \in V_U : n_f(v) \neq 1 \text{ and if } n_f(v) > 1 \text{ then } n_g(v) = 0\}$$

By $FE_U := \bigcup_{g \in F} FE_U(g)$ we denote the union of all formula expressions of that kind. The set of formula expressions with unaccessible existentials is defined as:

$$FE_E = \{\{\underline{f}\} \in FE | \exists n \in \mathbb{N} : comp^n(f) \cap U_E \neq \emptyset\}$$

By $FE_X := FE_U \cup FE_E$ we denote the set of all formula expressions containing unaccessible variables, by $FE_X(g) := FE_U(g) \cup FE_E$ the corresponding set for the formula g.

Definition 9 (Interpretation). *An interpretation $\mathfrak{I}$ of an alphabet A consists of:*

1. *A set $\mathcal{D}$ called the domain of $\mathfrak{I}$.*
2. *A function $\mathfrak{a} : E_g \cup FE_X \to \mathcal{D}$ called the object function.*
3. *A function $\mathfrak{p} : \mathcal{D} \to 2^{\mathcal{D} \times \mathcal{D}}$ called the predicate function.*

Note that in contrast to the classical definition of RDF-semantics [9] our domain does not distinguish between properties (IP) and resources (IR). The definitions are nevertheless compatible, as we assume $\mathfrak{p}(p) = \emptyset \in 2^{\mathcal{D} \times \mathcal{D}}$ for all resources p which are not properties (i.e. $p \in$ IR $\setminus$ IP in the RDF-sense). By extending given RDF ground interpretation functions to Notation 3 interpretation functions, the meaning of all valid RDF triples can be kept in Notation3 Logic. The main necessary extension would be a function which assigns domain values to formula expressions.

The following definition combines this definition with the techniques explained in the last section:

Definition 10 (Semantics of N3). *Let $\mathfrak{I} = (\mathcal{D}, \mathfrak{a}, \mathfrak{p})$ be an interpretation of A. Let f be a formula over A. Then the following holds:*

1. *If $AC(f) \neq \emptyset$ then $\mathfrak{I} \models f$ iff for all substitutions $\sigma : AC_U(f) \to E_g \cup FE_X(f)$ there exist a substitution $\mu : AC_E(f) \to E_g \cup FE_X(f)$ such that: $\mathfrak{I} \models f\sigma^t \mu^c$*
2. *If $AC(f) = \emptyset$:*
   (a) *If f is an atomic formula $c_1 \, p \, c_2$, then $\mathfrak{I} \models c_1 \, p \, c_2$. iff $(\mathfrak{a}(c_1), \mathfrak{a}(c_2)) \in \mathfrak{p}(\mathfrak{a}(p))$.*
   (b) *If f is a conjunction $f_1 f_2$, then $\mathfrak{I} \models f_1 f_2$ iff $\mathfrak{I} \models f_1$ and $\mathfrak{I} \models f_2$.*
   (c) *If f is an implication $\{f_1\}\texttt{=>}\{f_2\}$, then $\mathfrak{I} \models \{f_1\}\texttt{=>}\{f_2\}$ iff $\mathfrak{I} \models f_2$ if $\mathfrak{I} \models f_1$.*

Number 1 of the definition respects the constraint explained at the beginning of section 4 and illustrated by example (1). Note that in contrast to first order logic or RDF, we make use of a substitution function which maps into the set ground- and ungroundable expressions instead of a classical valuation function mapping directly into the domain of discourse. We do this due to the rather unusual nature of the implicit universal quantifier. If the object function is surjective, both approaches are similar.

We finally define a model:

Definition 11 (Model). *Let Φ be a set of N3 formulas. We call an interpretation $\mathfrak{I} = (\mathcal{D}, \mathfrak{a}, \mathfrak{p})$ a model of Φ iff $\mathfrak{I} \models f$ for every formula $f \in \Phi$.*

7   Towards full N3Logic

For this paper we excluded explicit quantification and built-in predicates. After having seen in the last sections that the formalization of implicit quantification is rather difficult, one might wonder: why did we make this choice if full N3Logic even provides explicit quantification? Notation3 offers in fact the opportunity of using @forAll as a universal and @forSome as an existential quantifier. We chose not to include them here because we consider their formalization even more difficult. This has two main reasons:

Firstly, quote (I) is not limited to implicit quantification. Also for explicit quantification the scope of universal quantification has always to be outside the scope of the existential quantification. As a consequence the following formulas

```
@forAll <#x>. @forSome <#y>. <#x> <#loves> <#y> .
```

and   `@forSome <#y>. @forAll <#x>.   <#x> <#loves> <#y> .`

mean exactly the same, namely: $\forall x \exists y : loves(x, y)$. It is not difficult to imagine that such kind of restriction can cause problems.

Secondly, the set of variables is not explicitly separated from the set of constants. There is nothing which prevents us from using the same URI :x as quantified variable and as constant at the same time. This can already cause confusion on its own, combined with our first reason, the interpretation of formulas becomes complicated. What does for example the formula

```
@forSome :y. :x :p :y. @forAll :x. :x :q :o.
```

mean? Is the first :x a variable or a constant?

Another interesting topic for formalization are built-in predicates. In the first publication about Notation3 Logic [7] the most complex of those predicates were, among others, `log:includes`, `log:notIncludes` and `log:semantics`. We consider a careful examination of those predicates important.

The definition of different possibilities to apply substitutions in Section 5 of this paper can also be used to formalize the semantics of explicit quantification. The model theory in Section 6 will be helpful to specify the meaning of the built-ins. We see this paper as the starting point to address those and other topics.

8   Conclusion and Future Work

In this paper we described how implicit quantification is understood by the reasoning engines EYE and cwm. While there seems to be a consensus on the interpretation of implicit existential quantifiers, the reasoners disagree on the scope of implicitly quantified universal variables.

Cwm follows the W3C team submission. The scope of an implicitly quantified universal is always the parent of the least deeply nested formula the variable occurs in. The main argument for this definition of scoping in N3Logic is the analogy to SPARQL [15], as for example expressed on the cwm mailing list [5]. If the SPARQL keyword UNION is used between two graph patterns, the substitutions applied to interpret those two patterns can be different, such as in our example case (5). There we had different substitutions for the same variable, because this variable occurred on nesting level 3 in two separated formula expressions (graphs). But there are also differences between this special SPARQL construct and N3's way of scoping universals: in SPARQL the scoping does not depend on the nesting; a UNION can be found and interpreted directly and it separates all variables at the same time. Cases as presented in formula (10) where some variables sharing the same name (?y in the example) have different scopes while others, occurring next to them as a component in the same formula expression (?x in the example), are interpreted equally, cannot occur in SPARQL. This makes the connection between SPARQL and N3Logic rather loose. To the best of our knowledge, there is also no other logic behaving similarly to N3 regarding implicit universal quantification. Looking back on the cumbersome steps which lead to Definition 10, it can be difficult to compare or translate N3Logic to other logics.

EYE is oriented on classical logic programming [13]. The scope of a nested variable is the outermost implication rule it occurs in, similar to the clause in logic programming. This interpretation has practical advantages: it is easy to implement and also easy to formalize as the nesting level of a variable has not to be taken into account. Unaccessible universals as introduced by Definition 8 cannot be expressed using EYE's implicit quantification. Although we would lose expressivity by following the semantics of EYE, we consider this loss minimal, as we expect the cases where an interpretation such as (5a) is needed to barely occur in practice.

We see all these as reasons to propose a change in the specification: the scope of a universally quantified variable should be the whole formula it occurs in and not just a nested sub-formula. The formalization of the semantics for this interpretation is therefore the next goal we are planning to achieve in future work. By providing a solid formalization of our proposal we aim to raise a new discussion about the topic and to improve the logic. We thereby will provide one step further towards the full understanding of Notation3 Logic.

References

1. FuXi 1.4: A Python-based, bi-directional logical reasoning system for the semantic web. http://code.google.com/p/fuxi/
2. Beckett, D., Berners-Lee, T., Prud'hommeaux, E., Carothers, G.: Turtle - Terse RDF Triple Language. W3C Recommendation, February 2014. http://www.w3.org/TR/turtle/
3. Berners-Lee, T.: cwm (2000–2009). http://www.w3.org/2000/10/swap/doc/cwm.html
4. Berners-Lee, T.: Notation 3 logic (2005). http://www.w3.org/DesignIssues/N3Logic
5. Berners Lee, T.: Re: Implicit quantification in n3. Public-cwm-talk (2015). http://lists.w3.org/Archives/Public/public-cwm-talk/2015JanMar/0001.html
6. Berners-Lee, T., Connolly, D.: Notation3 (N3): A readable RDF syntax. W3C Team Submission, March 2011. http://www.w3.org/TeamSubmission/n3/
7. Berners-Lee, T., Connolly, D., Kagal, L., Scharf, Y., Hendler, J.: nthreelogic: A logical framework for the World Wide Web. Theory and Practice of Logic Programming 8(3), 249–269 (2008)
8. Clocksin, W.F., Mellish, C.S.: Programming in PROLOG. Springer (1994)

9. Cyganiak, R., Wood, D., Lanthaler, M.: RDF 1.1: Concepts and Abstract Syntax. W3C Recommendation, February 2014. http://www.w3.org/TR/2014/REC-rdf11-concepts-20140225/

10. De Roo, J.: Euler yet another proof engine, (1999–2014). http://eulersharp.sourceforge.net/

11. Duerst, M., Suignard, M.: Internationalized Resource Identifiers (IRIs), January 2005. http://www.ietf.org/rfc/rfc3987.txt

12. Hayes, P.J., Patel-Schneider, P.F.: RDF 1.1 Semantics. W3C Recommendation, February 2014. http://www.w3.org/TR/2014/REC-rdf11-mt-20140225/

13. Lloyd, J.W.: Foundations of Logic Programming, 2nd edn. Springer-Verlag New York Inc., Secaucus (1987)

14. Pérez, J., Arenas, M., Gutierrez, C.: Semantics and complexity of SPARQL. ACM Trans. Database Syst. **34**(3), 16:1–16:45 (2009). http://doi.acm.org/10.1145/1567274.1567278

15. Prud'hommeaux, E., Seaborne, A.: SPARQL Query Language for RDF. W3C Recommendation, January 2008. http://www.w3.org/TR/rdf-sparql-query/

API4KP Metamodel: A Meta-API for Heterogeneous Knowledge Platforms

Tara Athan[1], Roy Bell[2], Elisa Kendall[3], Adrian Paschke[4]($\boxtimes$),
and Davide Sottara[5]

[1] Athan Services (athant.com), West Lafayette, IN, USA
taraathan@gmail.com
[2] Raytheon, Fort Wayne, IN, USA
Roy_M_Bell@raytheon.com
[3] Thematix Partners LLC, New York, NY, USA
ekendall@thematix.com
[4] AG Corporate Semantic Web, Freie Universitaet Berlin, Berlin, Germany
paschke@inf.fu-berlin.de
[5] Department of Biomedical Informatics, Arizona State University, Tempe, USA
davide.sottara@asu.edu

Abstract. API4KP (API for Knowledge Platforms) is a standard development effort that targets the basic administration services as well as the retrieval, modification and processing of expressions in machine-readable languages, including but not limited to knowledge representation and reasoning (KRR) languages, within heterogeneous (multi-language, multi-nature) knowledge platforms. KRR languages of concern in this paper include but are not limited to RDF(S), OWL, RuleML and Common Logic, and the knowledge platforms may support one or several of these. Additional languages are integrated using mappings into KRR languages. A general notion of structure for knowledge sources is developed using monads. The presented API4KP metamodel, in the form of an OWL ontology, provides the foundation of an abstract syntax for communications about knowledge sources and environments, including a classification of knowledge source by mutability, structure, and an abstraction hierarchy as well as the use of performatives (inform, query, ...), languages, logics, dialects, formats and lineage. Finally, the metamodel provides a classification of operations on knowledge sources and environments which may be used for requests (message-passing).

1 Introduction

The inherent complexity of many application domains - including but not limited to finance, healthcare, law, telecom and enviromental protection - paired with the fast pace of innovation, requires increasingly robust, scalable and maintainable software solutions. Design patterns have shifted from monolithic applications towards distribution and service-orientation. Standards have been published to improve interoperability. Model driven architectures (MDA) have been adopted to support declarative, platform-independent specifications of an application's

© Springer International Publishing Switzerland 2015
N. Bassiliades et al. (Eds.): RuleML 2015, LNCS 9202, pp. 144–160, 2015.
DOI: 10.1007/978-3-319-21542-6_10

business logic [7]. A special type of MDA, Knowledge Driven Architectures (KDA) [13], rely on models such as ontologies that are not only standard, but also have a formal grounding in KRR. KDA, while not yet ubiquitous, have a variety of applications. We consider as a running example a scenario from the healthcare domain.

A connected patient system gathers input from biomedical devices, part of a publish-subscribe architecture, which post observations including physical quantities, spatio-temporal coordinates and other context information. The data can be represented in a device-specific format (e.g. using XMPP[1]) or as streams of RDF graphs over time. The vocabularies referenced in the streams include units of measure, time, geospatial and biomedical ontologies, expressed in RDF(S), OWL or Common Logic (CL). Healthcare providers will submit SPARQL queries and receive incremental streams as new data becomes available. A Clinical Decision Support System (CDS), implemented using event-condition-action (ECA) rules, will also react to events simple (e.g. a vital parameter exceeding a threshold) and complex (e.g. a decreasing trend in the average daily physical activity) and intervene with alerts and reminders. If an alert is not addressed in a timely fashion, it will escalate to another designated recipient. Some patients will qualify for clinical pathways and the system will maintain a stateful representation of their cases, allowing clinicians to check for compliance with the planned orders (e.g. drug administrations, tests, procedures, . . .). This representation will include an ontology-mediated abstraction of the patient's electronic medical record, extracted from the hospital's database. As medical guidelines evolve, the logic of the pathway may need revision: queries to the patient's history should be contextualized to whatever logic was valid at the time orders were placed.

From a systems-oriented perspective communicating entities in distributed systems are processes (or simple nodes in primitive environments without further abstractions) and from a programming perspective they are objects, components or services/agents. They may be single-sorted or many-sorted, with sorts being characterized by the kind of communications that may be initiated, forwarded or received, and by the kind of entity that may be received or forwarded from or sent to. Communication channels may in general be many-to-many and uni- or bidirectional. Each communication has a unique source; multi-source communications are not modelled directly, but are emulated by knowledge sources that publish streams that may be merged to give the appearance of multiple sources. We will allow for failure, either in communication or in execution, but do not specify any particular failure recovery strategy. Various types of communication paradigms are supported from strongly-coupled communication via low-level inter-process communication with ad-hoc network programming, loosely coupled remote invocation in a two-way exchange via interfaces (RPC/RMI/Component/Agent) between communicating entities, to decoupled indirect communication, where sender and receiver are time and space uncoupled via an intermediary such as a publish-subscribe and event processing middleware. The communication entities fulfill different roles and responsibilities

---

[1] http://xmpp.org/rfcs/rfc3920.html

(client, server, peer, agent) in typical architectural styles such as client-server, peer-to-peer and multi-agent systems. Their placement (mapping) on the physical distributed infrastructure allows many variations (partitioning, replication, caching and proxing, mobile) such as deployment on multiple servers and caches to increase performance and resilience, use of low cost computer resources with limited hardware resources or adding/removing mobile computers/devices.

Given this variety of architectural requirements, an abstraction is required to facilitate the interchange, deployment, revision and ultimately consumption of formal, declarative pieces of knowledge within a knowledge-driven application. In 2010 the Object Management Group (OMG) published the first formalized set of KDA requirements in an RFP titled "the API for Knowledge Bases (API4KB)". In 2014 the OMG published a second RFP titled "Ontology, Model, and Specification Integration and Interoperability (OntoIOp)"[9]. This second RFP contains the requirements for a substantial part of the API4KB, and a submission, called DOL[1] is near completion. To address the remaining aspects of the RFP, a working group is creating a standard meta-API, called API4KP, for interaction with the Knowledge Platforms at the core of KDAs.

To provide a semantic foundation for the API4KP operations and their arguments, we have created a metamodel of knowledge sources and expressed it as an OWL ontology[2]. The primary concepts of the API4KP metamodel are described in Sec. 2, with details for structured knowledge resources and their relationship to nested functor structures in Sec. 3. In Sec. 4 we provide an application of the metamodel to the healthcare scenario. Related work is discussed in Sec. 5, with conclusions and future work described in Sec. 6.

2   Upper-Level Concepts and Basic Knowledge Resources

The current API4KP metamodel focuses on the notion of knowledge resources, the environment where the resources are to be deployed and their related concepts. The metamodel is hierarchical, with a few under-specified concepts at the upper levels, and more precisely defined concepts as subclasses. These upper-level concepts indicate, at a coarse level, the kinds of things that are in the scope of API4KP. The main upper-level concepts in the API4KP metamodel are

Knowledge Source: source of machine-readable information with semantics. Examples: a stream of RDF graphs providing data from biomedical devices, a stateful representation of a patient's history with OWL snapshots, or a database with a mapping to an ontology.

Environment: mathematical structure of mappings and members, where the domain and codomains of the mappings are members of the environment. Example: a KRR language environment containing semantics-preserving translations from RDF and OWL into CL, assisting in the integrated interpretation of a stream of RDF graphs and OWL ontologies.

---

[2] https://github.com/API4KBs/api4kbs

Knowledge Operation: function (possibly with side-effects. i.e. effects beyond the output value returned) having a knowledge source, environment or operation type in its signature. Examples: publishing or subscribing to a stream of RDF graphs; submitting a SPARQL query; initiating an ECA Rulebase; checking for compliance with plans; revising an ontology of guidelines.

Knowledge Event: successful evaluation or execution of a knowledge operation by a particular application at a particular time[3] Examples: when a nurse activates a biomedical device, a stream of RDF graphs is "published" describing a patient's vital signs; a specialist, like a cardiologist, taps the heartrate symbol on a touchscreen that results in the submission of a SPARQL query about a semantically-defined subset of a patient's vital signs.

These definitions are intentionally vague so as to be adaptable to a variety of implementation paradigms. We have developed a hierarchy of *knowledge source level* of abstraction that is a generalization of the FRBR [3] Work-Expression-Manifestation-Item (WEMI) hierarchy of abstraction tailored for machine-readable KRR languages. The fundamental building blocks of knowledge sources are *basic knowledge resources*, which are immutable knowledge sources without structure. Subclasses of basic knowledge resources are defined according to their knowledge source level.

Basic Knowledge Expression: well-formed formula in the abstract syntax of a machine-readable language.[4] Example KE1: the instance of the OWL 2 DL abstract syntax for the latest version of a biomedical ontology from an ontology series KA1 defining observable entities, such as the 2015 international version of the SNOMED-CT knowledge base[5] (see also the definition of Basic Knowledge Asset below). This ontology differs from other versions of the series only in the natural language definitions.

Basic Knowledge Manifestation: character-based embodiment of a basic knowledge expression in a concrete dialect. Example KM1: the OWL/RDF XML Document Object Model (DOM) document instance of example KE1.

Basic Knowledge Item: single exemplar of a basic knowledge manifestation in a particular location. Example KI1: a file on a network server embodying example KM1.

Basic Knowledge Asset: equivalence class of basic expressions determined by the equivalence relation of an asset environment (see Sec. 2.2.) Example KA1: an OWL2 DL series for a biomedical ontology, viewed as an equivalence class of basic knowledge expressions, including example KE1, according to a semantics-preserving environment for the OWL2 DL language where the

---

[3] Some Knowledge Operations can be used as transition functions for a mutable knowledge source, where their evaluation describes an event in the sense of [14], as a state transition of a dynamic entity; we generalize this concept of events because not all API4KP Knowledge Events correspond to state transitions.

[4] The use of "basic" in API4KP differs from its usage in DOL - a DOL basic OMS (ontologies, models and specifications) is a set, and corresponds to a Set-structured knowledge asset in API4KP.

[5] http://browser.ihtsdotools.org/

mapping to the focus language strips the natural language definitions from the axioms.

API4KP lifting/lowering operations (see 2.4) provide transformations from one level to another complying with the following relations:

exemplify: to instantiate (a knowledge manifestation) in particular format(s) and at particular location(s) (address in some virtual address space). Example: KI1 exemplifies KM1, KM1 prototypes KI1. Inverse: *prototype*

embody: to represent (a knowledge expression) in concrete syntax(es) (dialects) of particular KRR language(s). Example: KM1 embodies KE1, KE1 parses KM1. Inverse: *parse*

express: to represent (a knowledge asset) in abstract syntax(es) of particular KRR language(s). Example: KE1 expresses KA1, KA1 conceptualizes KE1. Inverse: *conceptualize*

2.1   Mutability

Following RDF concepts[6], knowledge sources are characterized as mutable or immutable. Immutable knowledge sources are called *knowledge resources*. In this context, immutable does not necessarily mean static; a stream of knowledge, e.g. a feed from a biomedical device, may be considered an *observable* knowledge resource that is revealed over time, as described further in Sec. 3. A *mutable knowledge source* is a container that has, at any point in time, an explicit state that is fully represented by a knowledge resource, e.g. the snapshot of a patient's current condition (with timestamp). The language, structure and content of a mutable knowledge source may change over time, but the abstraction level is unchanging. We distinguish between the *implicit* state that a mutable knowledge source holds indirectly when operators such as actions, complex event patterns or aggregations are computed, and the explicit state that evolves with time and that can be managed explicitly by an additional state transformer component responsible for *explicit* state management, concurrency control, reasoning (specifically, inference of state deltas), and state updates. There are various ways to manage explicit state, e.g. embedded inside the processors of the knowledge source in global variables or state-accumulating variables or tuples that are available either locally to an individual operator or across the operators as a shared storage, or with explicit state and concurrency control which lies outside of knowledge resource processors, e.g. by threading the variables holding state through a functional state transformer and by using State monads (see 3), which exist within the context of another computation or transformation, thus allowing to attach state information to any kind of functional expression.

2.2   Environments

In DOL, a concept of heterogeneous logical environment is defined as "environment for the expression of homogeneous and heterogeneous OMS, comprising a

---

[6] http://www.w3.org/TR/rdf11-concepts/

logic graph, an OMS language graph and a supports relation". In API4KP, we generalize this concept of environment as follows.

Categorical Environment: environment with an associative composition operation for mappings, that is closed under composition and contains an identity mapping for every member

Language Environment: environment whose members are languages

Focused Environment: nonempty environment which has a member F (called the focus or focus member) such that for every other member A, there is a mapping in the environment from A to F

Preserving Environment: environment where every mapping preserves a specified property

Asset Environment: focused, categorical, preserving language environment where the focus is a KRR language

The special case where all languages in an asset environment are KRR languages supporting model-theoretic semantics without side-effects (logics), and the preserving property is characterized by a logical graph reduces to a heterogeneous logical environment as defined in DOL.

The Knowledge Query and Manipulation Language[2] introduced the concept of *performatives*, which was later extended by FIPA-ACL[7]. The KRR Languages covered by API4KP include ontology languages (e.g. OWL), query languages (e.g. SPARQL), languages that describe the results of queries, events and actions (e.g KR RuleML), and declarative executable languages (e.g. Prolog, ECA RuleML). In the latter case, the languages typically includes syntactic constructs for performatives, e.g. *inform*, *query*, and the description of a knowledge resource may include a list of the performatives that are used within it. Performatives will be modelled as *operations* as defined in Sec. 2.4.

2.3 Descriptions

As stated above, we do not make assumptions regarding the drivers for communications, e.g. an implementation may be message-driven, event-driven, or a combination of both. However, our metamodel takes a message-centric perspective, with the message body typically being a description of a knowledge source or a knowledge operation.

A *knowledge source description* is a knowledge resource whose subject matter is another knowledge source, which may be expressed, e.g., as an OWL ontology of individuals or an RDF graph. The properties and classes in the API4KP namespace that may be employed in knowledge source descriptions are listed in the following tables and formalized in the API4KP OWL ontologies. Further, IRIs in other namespaces may be used to express metadata within a knowledge source description. A description about the description itself may be referenced through an IRI, or included within the description explicitly through the :hasDescription property, OWL annotations, or as an RDF dataset.

---

[7] http://www.fipa.org/repository/aclspecs.html

Table 1. Legend

Key	Value
Y	exactly 1
Yor	1 or more
Y?	0 or 1
Y*	0 or more
N	exactly 0
I[or?*]	indirect

Table 2. Prefix Mappings

Prefix	Expansion
:	http://www.omg.org/spec/API4KP/API4KPTerminology/
ks:	:KnowledgeSource/
kr:	:KnowledgeResource/
ka:	kr:Asset/
ke:	kr:Expression/
km:	kr:Manifestation/
ki:	kr:Item/
lang:	:Language/
map:	:Mapping/
xsd:	http://www.w3.org/2001/XMLSchema#

Table 3. Knowledge Resource Metamodel

Property	Range	ka:	ke:	km:	ki:
:hasIdentifier	:Identifier	Y?	Y?	Y?	Y?
:level	ks:Level	Y	Y	Y	Y
:usesPerformative	:Operation	I*	Y*	I*	I*
:hasLocator	:Address	Y?	Y?	Y?	Y
:usesLanguage	:Language	I*	Y*	I*	I*
:usesDialect	km:Dialect	N	N	Y*	I*
:usesConfiguration	ki:Configuration	N	N	N	Y*
:accordingTo	lang:Environment	Y	N	N	N
:isBasic	xsd:boolean	Y	Y	Y	Y
:isOutputOf	ev:	Y?	Y?	Y?	Y?
:hasMetaData	:KnowledgeResource	Y*	Y*	Y*	Y*
:hasDescription	:KnowledgeResource	Y*	Y*	Y*	Y*

2.4   Operations and Events

In the API4KP metamodel, the building blocks for all knowledge operations are *actions* – unary functions, possibly with side-effects and possibly of higher-order. Actions are defined in terms of their possible events. To maintain a separation of concerns, side-effectful actions are assumed to be void, with no significant return value. Particular kinds of actions include:

Lifting Action: side-effect-free action whose output is at a higher knowledge source level than the input

Lowering Action: side-effect-free action whose output is at a lower knowledge source level than the input

Horizontal Action: side-effect-free action whose output is at the same knowledge source level as the input

Idempotent Action: side-effect free action that is equal to its composition with itself (A = A o A)

Higher-Order Action: side-effect-free action whose input or output (or both) is an action

Table **4.** Knowledge Resource Elevation Properties

Property	Domain	Range	Inverse
:exemplify (?)	ki:	km:	:prototype (*)
:embody (?)	km:	ke:	:parse (*)
:express (*)	ke:	ka:	:conceptualize (*)

Table **5.** Knowledge Resource Configuration Metamodel

Property	Range	ke:Language	km:Dialect	ki:Configuration
:hasIdentifier	:Identifer	Y	Y	Y
:hasLocator	:Address	N	N	Y?
:supports	:Logic	Y	I	I
:usesLanguage	ke:Language	N	Y	I
:usesDialect	km:Dialect	N	N	Y
:usesFormat	ki:Format	N	N	Y
:location	:Address	N	N	Y

Lifting and lowering are utility actions for changing the knowledge source level, e.g. parsing and IO. Horizontal actions are useful e.g. for constructing structured knowledge sources, while higher-order actions are needed to specify more complex operations e.g. querying.

In the metamodel, we define two void actions that have side-effects on the state of mutable knowledge resources:

Put: void action whose input is a mutable knowledge source and has the side-effect of setting the mutable knowledge source to a particular specified state

Update: void action whose input is a mutable knowledge source and has the side-effect of setting the mutable knowledge to a new state that is the result of applying a side-effect-free action to the current state

A side-effectful operation can be considered idempotent if its successful execution multiple times (synchronously) leads to no additional detectable side-effects beyond that of the first execution. Note that this is a different, but related, concept of idempotence than that for side-effect-free actions. An Update action based on an idempotent side-effect-free action is idempotent in this sense, an important factor in failure recovery.

3   Structured Knowledge Resources

We generalize the DOL concept for structured OMS to define a concept of structured knowledge resource for each level of abstraction. In DOL, a structured OMS "results from other basic and structured OMS by import, union, combination, ... or other structuring operations". In API4KP, A *structured knowledge resource* is a collection whose components are knowledge resources of the same level of abstraction; structuring knowledge operations are described in Sec. 2.4.

Table 6. Generic Environment Metamodel. The generic prefix T: specifies the member type. Specific environments include lang:Environment (a system of mappings between the abstract syntax of languages) .

Property	Range	T:Environment
:hasIdentifier	:Identifier	Y?
:mapping	T:Mapping	Y*
:focus	T:	Y?
:preserves	T:EquivalenceRelation	Y*
:isOutputOf	ev:	Y?

Table 7. Generic Mapping Metamodel

Property	Range	T:Mapping
:hasIdentifier	:Identifier	Y?
:location	:Address	Y?
:start	T:	Y
:end	T:	Y
:preserves	:EquivalenceRelation	Y*
:usesLanguage	map:Language	Y*
:isBasic	xsd:boolean	Y
:components	T:MappingList	Y?

Structured Knowledge Expression: collection of knowledge expressions (either structured or basic), which are not necessarily in the same language and may themselves have structure. Example KE2: a heterogeneous collection of streaming data and RDF graphs, together with static OWL ontologies and CL texts, and ECA rules describing actions of a CDS. Example KE3: the OWL 2 DL ontology series KA1, viewed as a collection of expressions rather than an equivalence class.

Structured Knowledge Manifestation: collection of knowledge manifestations (either structured or basic), which are not necessarily in the same language or dialect and may themselves have structure. Example KM2: a heterogeneous structure of RDF Turtle, OWL Manchester as sequences of string tokens, and XMPP, OWL/XML, ECA RuleML and CL XCL2 (the XML-based dialect of Common Logic Edition 2) as XML DOM documents embodying example KE2.

Structured Knowledge Item: collection of knowledge items (either structured or basic), which are not necessarily in the same language, dialect, format or location, and may themselves have structure. Example KI2: a heterogeneous structure of an RDF triple store, network connections to binary input streams cached in a MySQL database, RuleML XML files on a local hard drive and CL XCL2 files on a network server in a content management system, exemplifying example KM2.

Table 8. Knowledge Resource Operation and Event Properties

Property	Domain	Range	Inverse
:hasEvent (*)	op:	ev:	:isEventOf (1)
:executes (*)	:Application	ev:	:isExecutedBy (1)
:input (?)	ev:ActionEvent	:	:isInputOf (*)
:output (?)	ev:	:	:isOutputOf (?)
:atTime (1)	ev:	xsd:dateTime	

Structured Knowledge Asset: collection of knowledge assets (either structured or basic), which are not necessarily according to the same environment, but where there is a unique language that is the focus of the environment of each component. Example KA2: a heterogeneous structure of assets conceptualized from the RDF, OWL and CL expressions of example KE2 according to an environment that provides translations from RDF or OWL into CL, and an ontology-based data access (OBDA) source schema providing a mapping from XMPP schemas to OWL.

To assist in defining operations on structured knowledge sources while still maintaining generality, the collection structure of a structured knowledge resource is required to arise from a monadic functor (monad). Collection structures that satisfy these requirement include sets, bags and sequences, but other useful structures also meet these requirements.

3.1 Monads

In seminal work that established a theoretical foundation for proving the equivalence of programs, Moggi[8] applied the notion of monad from category theory[5] to computation. As defined in category theory, a monad is an endofunctor on a category C (a kind of mapping from C into itself) which additionally satisfies some requirements (the monad laws). In functional programming, monads on the category with types as objects and programs as arrows are employed. For example, the List[_] typeclass is a monad, e.g. List[Int], a list of integers, is a type that is a member of the List[_] monad.

Each monad M has functor M and two natural transformations as follows (exemplified for the List monad where lists are denoted with angle brackets)

- unit: A $\Rightarrow$ M[A] lifts the input into the monad (e.g. unit(2) = $\langle 2 \rangle$)
- join: M[M[A]] $\Rightarrow$ M[A] collapses recursive monad instances by one level (e.g. join($\langle\langle 1, 2 \rangle, \langle 3, 4 \rangle\rangle$) = $\langle 1, 2, 3, 4 \rangle$)
- M: (A $\Rightarrow$ B) $\Rightarrow$ (M[A] $\Rightarrow$ M[B]) takes a function between two generic types and returns a function relating the corresponding monadic types (e.g. $List$(s $\Rightarrow$ 2*s)($\langle 1, 2 \rangle$) = $\langle 2, 4 \rangle$)

Note that we choose the category-theory-oriented unit and join transformations [16] as fundamental in this development of the monad laws because it is useful for later discussion on structured expressions, whereas the functional-programming-oriented treatment based on unit and bind $:\equiv$ join o M (aka flatmp), is more concise. Monads of relevance to API4KP include, but are not limited to

Try: handles exceptions, has subclasses Success, which wraps a knowledge resource, and Failure, which wraps a (non-fatal) exception

IO: handles IO side-effects, wraps a knowledge resource and an *item configuration*

Task: handles general side-effects, wraps a knowledge resource and a description of a side-effectful task

Stream: a.k.a. Observable handles concurrent streams, wraps a sequence of knowledge resources that become available over time

State: handles state, wraps a knowledge resource (the state) and implements state transitions

These monad functors may be composed; for example, given a basic knowledge expression type E, the type (State o Try o List) [E] $:\equiv$ State[Try[List[E]]] may be defined. In general, the composition of monads is not necessarily a monad.

3.2   Nested Monadic Structures

In DOL, the concept of structured expression using sets is introduced. For example, let B be the category of (basic) CL text expressions, and OptionallyNested-Set[B] $:\equiv$ B + NestedSet[B], where NestedSet[B] $:\equiv$ Set[OptionallyNestedSet[B]] $\equiv$ Set[B + NestedSet[B]] is the recursive type definition of set-structured CL expressions. An instance of type NestedSet[B] is a Set whose members are either basic leaves (of type B) or structured branches (of type NestedSet[B]).

The Set monad is appropriate for defining structured expressions in monotonic logics, like CL, because the order and multiplicity of expressions in a collection has no effect on semantics. The semantics of CL is provided by the CL interpretation structure that assigns a truth-value to each basic CL text expression. The truth-value of a set of CL text expressions is true in an interpretation J if each member of the set maps to true in J. The truth value $J(y)$ of a NestedSet-structured CL expression y is defined to be $J(\text{flatten}(y))$, where flatten(y) is the set of leaves of y.

We generalize this approach for defining the semantics of structured expressions to an arbitrary language L with basic expressions E and NestedM structured expressions. We assume that

- M is a monad on the category of types,
- model-theoretic semantics is supplied through an interpretation structure J defined for basic expressions in E and simply-structured expressions M[E + **0**], where **0** is the empty type.
- a post-condition contract for side-effects is specified by a truth-valued function P(F, y) for all supported void knowledge actions F and all y in E + M[E + **0**].

Let $N[\_]$ be the NestedM monad corresponding to the minimal (finite) fixed point of $N[E] :\equiv M[E + N[E]]$, where $A + B$ is the coproduct[8] of types A and B. We name the NestedM monad by prepending "Nested" to the name of the underlying monad; thus, $\mathrm{NestedSet}[E] :\equiv \mathrm{Set}[E + \mathrm{NestedSet}[E]]$.

If E is a type of basic knowledge resources, then the monad OptionallyNestedM$[E] :\equiv E + \mathrm{NestedM}[E] \equiv E + M[\mathrm{OptionallyNestedM}[E]]$ is the corresponding type of knowledge resources that are either basic or structured. We note that OptionallyNestedM$[E]$ is a free monad[9] of M; this property holds for a large class of functors and does not depend on M being a monad.

NestedM is also a monad under an appropriate join transformation; this property does depend on M being a monad. Further, we take advantage of the monadic properties of M in order to "flatten" the nested structure for purposes of interpretation and pragmatics. The unit, map and join functions for NestedM are defined in terms of the unit, join, and map functions for monad M, and the constructors, recursor and bimap function of the coproduct. The details and proof[10] that NestedM structures satisfy the monad laws depends on the use of the coproduct to handle the union of types, so that the left or right intention is indicated even in the case when the types are not disjoint.

For all $y \in Q[E] :\equiv \mathrm{OptionallyNestedM}[E]$, we define a flatten transformation flatten(y). Let I be the identity transformation, $N[E] :\equiv \mathrm{NestedM}[E]$, joinN be the join natural transformation of monad N, $Q_1 :\equiv E + M[E + \mathbf{0}]$, and

joinN: $N[N[E]] \Rightarrow N[E] \ni \mathrm{joinN} :\equiv \mathrm{joinM} \circ M(\ I + \mathrm{unitM} \circ \mathrm{inr} \circ \mathrm{joinN})$
level: $Q[E] \Rightarrow N[E] \ni \mathrm{level} :\equiv \mathrm{unitM} \circ \mathrm{inl} + I$
flatten: $Q[E] \Rightarrow Q_1[E] \ni \mathrm{flatten}(y) = y$ if $y \in Q_1[E]$,
    $\mathrm{flatten}(y) = \mathrm{flatten}(\ \mathrm{joinN} \circ M(\mathrm{inl} \circ \mathrm{level})(y))$ otherwise

Then for all $y \in Q[E]$, we may define the interpretation $J(y) :\equiv J(\mathrm{flatten}(y))$, with entailments defined accordingly. Implementations that honor the semantics must satisfy $P(F)(y) = P(F)(\mathrm{flatten}(y))$, where $P(F)$ is a function representing the post-conditions after execution of side-effectful knowledge operation F on the knowledge resource y.

The monad laws and the flatten transformation have been verified experimentally for NestedSet and NestedList monads by implementation in Java8 together with the Functional Java[11] libraries, with the source available on Github[12]. Informal tests confirm that the map and join operations are linear in the size of the collection, as expected.

---

[8] The coproduct, a.k.a. disjoint union, $A + B$ can be treated as the type (False x A) | (True x B), with the first (Boolean) argument of the pair providing the intention of left or right injection (inl and inr). The operation $f + g$ on functions f and g means $(f+g)(\mathrm{inl}(a)) :\equiv f(a)$ and $(f+g)(\mathrm{inr}(b)) :\equiv g(b)$.
[9] http://ncatlab.org/nlab/show/free+monad
[10] https://github.com/API4KBs/api4kbs/blob/currying/Monad_Trees.pdf
[11] http://www.functionaljava.org/
[12] https://github.com/ag-csw/Java4CL

3.3   Heterogeneous Structures

Suppose A and B are expression types of two languages where an environment provides a semantics-preserving transformation T from B to A. Further suppose that an interpretation mapping is defined on A + M[A + 0]. The coproduct E := A + B defines the basic knowledge expressions in this environment, while structured expressions are N[E] := NestedM[E], and the coproduct Q[E] := E + N[E] is the type for all expressions in this environment, basic or structured.

Using the transformation T from the environment, we may define the interpretation J_+ of structured expressions of type NestedM[A+B] in terms of the interpretations J of basic expressions in A and structuring operations. In particular,

$$J_+(\mathbf{x}) := J(\text{ NestedM}(T + I)(\text{flatten(x)})) \equiv J(\text{flatten(NestedM}(T + I)(\text{x})))$$

Notice that the expressions of type B are not required to be in a knowledge representation language. They could be in a domain-specific data model based on, e.g., XML, JSON or SQL. The semantics of expressions of type B are derived from the transformation to type A, the focus knowledge representation language of the environment. API4KP employs this feature to model OBDA and rule-based data access (RBDA).

Structured expressions can always be constructed in a monad that has more structure than necessary for compatibility with the semantics of a given language. For example, List and Stream monads can be used for monotonic, effect-free languages even though the Set monad has sufficient structure for these languages; a forgetful functor is used to define the semantics in the monad with greater structure in terms of the monad of lesser structure. A heterogeneous structure of languages containing some languages with effects and others without effects (e.g. an ECA rulebase supported by ontologies) could thus make primary use of an NestedM monad that preserves order, such as NestedList or NestedStream, while permitting some members of the collection to have a NestedSet structure.

While an immutable knowledge source (i.e. a knowledge resource) has a specific structure, as discussed above, a mutable knowledge source has structure only indirectly through the structure of its state. In general, the structure of a mutable knowledge source's state changes arbitrarily over time, but could be restricted in order to emulate common dynamic patterns. Simple examples include state as a basic knowledge resource (linear history without caching), a key-value map with values that are basic knowledge resources (branching history without caching), or a sequence of basic knowledge resources (linear cached history).

4   Metamodel Appplied to the Scenario

In the connected patient scenario, an RDF stream from a biomedical device can be modelled using a Stream monad. A query registered against this RDF Stream will generate another Stream, with each Stream item containing additions (if any) to the query results due to the assertion of the newly-arrived graph. Because RDF has monotonic semantics, the accumulated query results will always be equivalent to the result of the query applied to the accumulated graphs of the stream. Cumulative queries and other cumulative operations on Streams may be implemented through *fold* operations, while windowing and filtering are implemented through map. The connected-patient system uses a heterogeneous language environment to map input XMPP data from biomedical devices into a KRR language, e.g. RDF, employing terms from a vocabulary defined in a common ontology. Thus streaming data may be transformed into streaming knowledge which is queryable as discussed in the previous item. The structure of this system may be modelled as a NestedSet of Streams, since each device streams its output asynchronously. State, Task and IO monads are appropriate to the use case of an active knowledge base where evaluation of an operation leads to side-effects; the choice of monad depends on the nature of the side-effects and the implementation. Equivalence of such knowledge resources requires not only the same entailments, but also side-effects that are equivalent. The CDS monitoring our connected patient may be modelled using a State monad, where the sending of a message is a side-effect. The connected patient's case history may be modelled as a mutable knowledge asset because of the possibility of correction of the history without a change of case identifier. The modular nature of medical records is amenable to NestedSet (a set of laboratory test results) or NestedList (a procedure performed) structures. Although some aspects, such as the addition of new medical orders, would fit with the Stream structure, queries of the case history are not expected to produce streaming results, and so the mutable asset model is a better fit than a Stream-based model. Failure recovery in the CDS alert system may be modelled using the Try monad, so that results can be reported as Success or Failure. A Success response is a wrapper around a result from the successful execution of a request. A Failure response includes information about the nature of the failure (e.g. timeout exception) so that the system can recover appropriately, e.g. by escalating to another recipient. A possible extension of the CDS which allows a streaming model in combination with explicit state management and concurrency follows an implementation[4] that was demonstrated for sports competitions using the Prova rule engine[13].

5   Related Work

While various APIs and interface languages for different knowledge platforms and representation languages exist[14], API4KP provides a unified abstract API metamodel. Also, various ontologies and semantic extensions for Semantic Web Service interfaces [15] as well as REST interfaces [16] exist. None of them is specific

---

[13] https://prova.ws/

[14] e.g., OWL API , JSR-94 , Linked Data Platform , RuleML Rule Responder IDL , OntoMaven and RuleMaven , FIPA ACL , CTS-2

[15] e.g., OWL-S, WSDL-S, SAWSDL, SWWS / WSMF, WSMO / WSML, Meteor-S, SWSI

[16] Semantic URLs, RSDL, SA-Rest, Odata

to APIs for knowledge platforms and services in general. Some works present operations on structured knowledge bases (e.g.[15]), but are not exposed using APIs. General top-level ontologies and general model-driven architecture and software engineering metamodels have certain overlaps with the concepts used in API4KP, but fulfill a different purpose. They can be used for the representational analysis of API4KP. [10]. From a conceptual point of view reference models and reference architectures [17] for knowledge platforms are related and API4KB can be used in such reference architectures for the description of functional interfaces and component APIs.

So, DOL is the most closely related endeavor. The API4KP metamodel introduces the following generalizations of DOL concepts:

- Knowledge sources can have different levels of abstraction. DOL's OMS concept correspond to knowledge expressions, while we consider also the levels of asset, manifestation and item.
- Knowledge sources can be mutable or immutable. DOL's OMS correspond to immutable knowledge expressions.
- Each API4KP knowledge asset is conceptualized according to a customizable environment, instead of assuming a single logical environment in which all OMS are interpreted.
- Environment members can be any language with an abstract syntax, instead of requiring each member to have a specific semantics. Only the focus of the environment is required to have its own semantics.
- Semantics is generalized to include side-effects as well as logical entailment.
- Structured knowledge resources may have structures other than nested sets.

The variety of monad structures necessary to model the diversity of usecases demonstrates that a high level of abstraction is needed to define operations for modifying knowledge resources - adding, subtracting or modifying. Category theory provides the tools for these abstractions, through applicative functors (a generalization of monads having a binary operator allowing a structure of functions to be applied to another structure), catamorphisms (generalization of aggregation over a list to other monads) and anamorphisms (e.g. generation of a list from a seed and recursion formula)[6].

6   Conclusion and Future Work

The primary contributions of this paper are two-fold: (i) a metamodel of heterogeneous knowledge sources, environments, operations and events, providing an abstract syntax for interaction with the Knowledge Platforms at the core of KDAs and (ii) a structure of nested monads, as the conceptual basis of structured knowledge resources in the metamodel, supporting modularity, state management, concurrency and exception handling. We have used a scenario from

---

[17] e.g., the EPTS Event-Processing Reference Architecture [11] and the EPTS/RuleML Event Processing Standards Reference Model [12]

healthcare to show the kinds of complexities that will be needed and that our metamodel in combination with monads will meet this challenge. The healthcare scenario brought up things such as input RDF streams, heterogeneous language environments, and mutable persistent storage, and we have shown how they will be accomplished. Future work on API4KP may include a generalization of the approach to include structures based on applicative functors, and operations in terms of catamorphisms and anamorphisms, as well as the population of the ontology with specifications of additional operations, especially querying and life-cycle management.

References

1. The distributed ontology, model, and specication language (dol). https://github.com/tillmo/DOL/blob/master/Standard/ebnf-OMG_OntoIOp_current.pdf
2. Finin, T., Fritzson, R., McKay, D., McEntire, R.: KQML as an agent communication language. In: Proceedings of the Third International Conference on Information and Knowledge Management, CIKM 1994, pp. 456–463. ACM, New York (1994). http://doi.acm.org/10.1145/191246.191322
3. IFLA Study Group on the Functional Requirements for Bibliographic Records: Functional requirements for bibliographic records : final report (1998). http://www.ifla.org/publications/functional-requirements-for-bibliographic-records (accessed: 2007-12-26)
4. Kozlenkov, A., Jeffery, D., Paschke, A.: State management and concurrency in event processing. In: Proceedings of the Third ACM International Conference on Distributed Event-Based Systems, DEBS 2009, Nashville, Tennessee, USA, July 6–9, 2009. http://doi.acm.org/10.1145/1619258.1619289
5. Mac Lane, S.: Categories for the Working Mathematician (Graduate Texts in Mathematics). Springer (1998)
6. Meijer, E., Fokkinga, M., Paterson, R.: Functional Programming with Bananas, Lenses, Envelopes and Barbed Wire, pp. 124–144. Springer-Verlag (1991)
7. Mellor, S.J., Kendall, S., Uhl, A., Weise, D.: MDA Distilled. Addison Wesley Longman Publishing Co. Inc., Redwood City (2004)
8. Moggi, E.: Notions of computation and monads. Selections from 1989 IEEE Symposium on Logic in Computer Science 93(1), 55–92 (1991). http://www.sciencedirect.com/science/article/pii/0890540191900524
9. Object Management Group (OMG): OntoIOp request for proposal. http://www.omg.org/cgi-bin/doc?ad/2013-12-02
10. Paschke, A., Athan, T., Sottara, D., Kendall, E., Bell, R.: A representational analysis of the API4KB metamodel. In: Proceedings of the 7th Workshop on Formal Ontologies meet Industry (FOMI 2015). Springer-Verlag (2015)
11. Paschke, A., Vincent, P., Alves, A., Moxey, C.: Tutorial on advanced design patterns in event processing. In: Proceedings of the Sixth ACM International Conference on Distributed Event-Based Systems, DEBS 2012, Berlin, Germany, July 16–20, 2012, pp. 324–334 (2012)
12. Paschke, A., Vincent, P., Springer, F.: Standards for Complex Event Processing and Reaction Rules. In: Palmirani, M. (ed.) RuleML - America 2011. LNCS, vol. 7018, pp. 128–139. Springer, Heidelberg (2011)

13. Rector, A.: Knowledge driven software and "fractal tailoring": ontologies in development environments for clinical systems. In: Proceedings of the 2010 Conference on Formal Ontology in Information Systems: Proceedings of the Sixth International Conference (FOIS 2010), pp. 17–28. IOS Press, Amsterdam (2010)
14. Rosemann, M., Green, P.: Developing a Meta Model for the Bunge-Wand-Weber Ontological Constructs. Inf. Syst. **27**(2), 75–91 (2002). doi:10.1016/S0306-4379(01)00048-5
15. Slota, M., Leite, J., Swift, T.: Splitting and updating hybrid knowledge bases. Theory and Practice of Logic Programming **11**(4–5), 801–819 (2011). 27th Int'l. Conference on Logic Programming (ICLP 2011) Special Issue
16. Wadler, P.: Comprehending monads. In: Mathematical Structures in Computer Science, pp. 61–78 (1992)

Rule-Based Exploration of Structured Data in the Browser

Sudhir Agarwal[1][(✉)], Abhijeet Mohapatra[1], Michael Genesereth[1],
and Harold Boley[2]

[1] Logic Group, Computer Science Department, Stanford University, Stanford, USA
{sudhir,abhijeet,genesereth}@cs.stanford.edu
[2] Faculty of Computer Science, University of New Brunswick, Fredericton, Canada
harold.boley@unb.ca

Abstract. We present Dexter, a browser-based, domain-independent structured-data explorer for users. Dexter enables users to explore data from multiple local and Web-accessible heterogeneous data sources such as files, Web pages, APIs and databases in the form of tables. Dexter's users can also compute tables from existing ones as well as validate the tables (base or computed) through declarative rules. Dexter enables users to perform ad hoc queries over their tables with higher expressivity than that is supported by the underlying data sources. Dexter evaluates a user's query on the client side while evaluating sub-queries on remote sources whenever possible. Dexter also allows users to visualize and share tables, and export (e.g., in JSON, plain XML, and RuleML) tables along with their computation rules. Dexter has been tested for a variety of data sets from domains such as government and apparel manufacturing. Dexter is available online at http://dexter.stanford.edu.

1 Introduction

Data is the fuel of innovation and decision support. Structured data is available to users through different sources. Examples include local files, Web pages, APIs and databases. Oftentimes, users need to quickly integrate and explore the data in an *ad hoc* manner from multiple such sources to perform planning tasks, make data-driven decisions, verify or falsify hypotheses, or gain entirely new insights.

Unfortunately, it can be very cumbersome, tedious or time consuming for users to explore data in an ad hoc manner using the current state of the art tools. This is because the current state of the art tools (a) provide limited or no querying support over the underlying data (e.g. domain-specific Web applications, public sources), (b) cannot compile information from multiple sources (e.g. search engines), or (c) require users' private data to be shipped to a remote server.

For example, consider the Govtrack website (https://www.govtrack.us) which has information (e.g. age, role, gender) about members of the U.S. Congress. Suppose, a user wishes to know "Which U.S. senators are 40 years old?" or "Which senate committees are chaired by a woman?". Even though

© Springer International Publishing Switzerland 2015
N. Bassiliades et al. (Eds.): RuleML 2015, LNCS 9202, pp. 161–175, 2015.
DOI: 10.1007/978-3-319-21542-6_11

Govtrack has the requisite data, it is very tedious to find answers to such elementary questions. This is because Govtrack's UI and APIs present limited querying capabilities to a user. It is even harder to query across data from multiple sources e.g. "Which members of U.S. Congress were the Head of DARPA".

To address these problems, we have developed Dexter, a *domain-indepedent, browser-based* structured data explorer for users. Dexter enables users to create and connect multiple Web-accessible structured data (e.g. from Web pages, databases, APIs) as tables, and to explore these tables through Dexlog [14] rules with higher expressivity than is supported by the underlying data sources. Dexlog is a variant of Datalog [9] that is extended using negation and aggregation [15], and supports an extensive list of built-in arithmetic, string, as well as tuple- and set-manipulation operators.

The fundamental novelty of Dexter is its *client side evaluation* of user queries. To reduce query processing times, Dexter leverages two techniques. First, Dexter follows a hybrid-shipping strategy [13] and fetches query answers, instead of base data, from sources that offer support for queries. We note that, in such cases, a user's private data (e.g. locally stored data) is *never* shipped to a remote source. Second, to overcome browsers' memory limitations and to efficiently evaluate a user's query, Dexter horizontally partitions the tables and executes queries over the partitions in parallel, subsequently compiling the answers in a manner similar to the MapReduce [8] programming paradigm.

To enable users to effectively and conveniently explore structured data, Dexter presents users with two interfaces: (a) an intuitive table editor to work with data and (b) the *Dexlog Rule Editor* that is equipped with syntax highlighting and auto-completion. In addition, Dexter allows users to *visualize* their tables as charts and *export* their table along with their associated Dexlog rules in various formats including RuleML [4,7]. Moreover, Dexter also allows users to *share* their tables with other users through a publicly accessible server.

The rest of the paper is organized as follows. In Section 2, we present an overview of the Dexlog language, which serves as the foundation of Dexter's data exploration capabilities. Then, in Section 3, we describe Dexter's features that enable users to *plug-in* structured data as tables and *play* with these tables (e.g. explore, visualize, export and share). In Section 4, we describe how Dexter efficiently evaluates a user's queries on the client side. Dexter has been tested for a variety of ad hoc queries over data sets from multiple domains. In Section 5, we present some scenarios involving ad hoc exploration of data about the U.S. government, apparel manufacturing, and restaurants. We compare and contrast Dexter to related tools and technologies in Section 6.

2   Dexlog

Dexter presents to its users a unified notion of tables that transcends the traditional separation between base tables and views. In Dexter, a table can contain tuples that are manually entered, computed using Dexlog rules, or both. We note that manual entry of a tuple in a table can be emulated through a trivial

Dexlog rule where the tuple appears in the head and the body is a *valid* Dexlog formula i.e. it evaluates to true in all possible interpretations. In this regard, Dexlog rules serve as the foundation for data exploration in Dexter. Dexlog is a variant of standard Datalog that is extended using negation (as failure), aggregation, and built-in operators over numbers, strings, tuples and sets. In this section, we present an overview of Dexlog, highlighting its distinguishing features with respect to standard Datalog and refer the reader to [15] for details regarding the syntax and semantics of Dexlog.

The vocabulary of Dexlog consists of *basic constants, relation constants, variables, tuples, sets*, and reserved keywords (such as `illegal`, which are discussed shortly). Basic constants are strings that are enclosed within double quotes e.g. `"1.23"` and `"Dexter"`. Relation constants and variables are strings of alphanumeric characters and underscore. However, relation constants must begin with a lower-case letter, e.g. `person`, `q_12`, while variables must begin with an upper-case letter, e.g. `X1`, `Y_`.

A key difference between standard Datalog and Dexlog is the introduction of tuples and sets as *first-class* citizens. A tuple is a non-empty, ordered collection of basic constants, variables, sets or other tuples which are separated using commas and enclosed within square brackets, e.g. `["John", "2"]`. Sets can be specified in Dexlog as *set constants*, each being a possibly empty unordered collection of basic constants, tuples or additional sets enclosed within braces, e.g. `{}` and `{{"1", "2"},{"3"}}`. In addition, Dexlog supports a special operator, called `setof`, for constructing sets.

Suppose that $\bar{X}$ and $\bar{Y}$ are two collections of Dexlog terms (i.e. constants and variables) and suppose that $\phi(\bar{X}, \bar{Y})$ is a conjunction of Dexlog literals. The `setof` atom `setof(`$\bar{X}$`, `$\phi(\bar{X}, \bar{Y})$`, S)` computes a set $S_{\bar{Y}} = \{\bar{X} \mid \phi(\bar{X}, \bar{Y})\}$ for every binding of values in $\bar{Y}$.

Consider two relations: a unary relation `continent` and a binary relation called `located`, and their respective instances[1] as shown below.

continent
Asia
Africa
North America

located	
India	Asia
USA	North America
Canada	North America

Assuming that the `located(X,Y)` indicates that country `X` is geographically located in continent `Y`, the following Dexlog rule computes the set of countries for each continent.

```
v(X, S) :- continent(X) & setof(Y, located(Y, X), S)
```

The above Dexlog rule computes a set $S_X = \{Y \mid \texttt{located(Y,X)}\}$ for every binding of `X` such that `continent(X)` is true. Evaluation of the above rule on the instances of the tables `continent` and `located` results in the following tuples.

---

[1] For the sake of better readability, we omit quotes when a table cell is a basic constant.

	v
Asia	{"India"}
Africa	{}
North America	{"USA","Canada"}

Safe Dexlog Rules: To ensure the *safety* of Dexlog rules, all variables that occur in a negated atom in a rule's body must also occur in a positive atom. In addition, all the variables that occur in the body of a `setof` atom (but not as an aggregated argument) must be bound in some positive atom outside the `setof` atom. For example, the following rule is *unsafe* because there are infinitely many possible bindings of X such that q(X, {}) evaluates to true.

$$q(X, S) :- setof(Y, located(Y, X), S)$$

Constraints in Dexlog: In addition to the rules for computing new facts from existing facts, Dexlog also allows users to validate a table's base or computed data by defining *constraints* over the table. Constraints have the general form `illegal :- ` ϕ, where `illegal` indicates constraint violation [10] and ϕ is a Dexlog formula. Suppose that we wish to specify a constraint over the table `located` such that the second argument of every tuple in the `located` table must be contained in the `continent` table as well. We note that this constraint is an example of a *foreign-key constraint* [9] which can be specified using the following Dexlog rule involving negation.

$$illegal :- located(Y, X) \ \& \sim continent(X)$$

Dexlog also supports an extensive list of built-in operators. Such operators include arithmetic operators (e.g. `gt`, `plus`, `mod`), string-manipulation operators (e.g. `length`, `substr`, `concat`), set-based operators (e.g. `sumOf`, `unionOf`) and tuple-based operators (e.g. `attr`). The complete listing of the built-in operators, their arity, binding patterns and description, is provided in [14].

3   Dexter: Interface and Features

In this section, we walk the reader through Dexter's interface and describe some of its main features and their role in enabling ad hoc exploration of structured data.

Dexter introduces a unified notion of tables that transcends the traditional separation between base tables and computed tables. In Dexter, a table can have manually entered data as well as rules that compute further data and constraints. To accommodate this unified notion of a table, Dexter presents its users with two interfaces to interact with tables. The first interface is a table editor that allows a user to manually enter data into a table or to update the data and the schema of a table. In addition, the user is also presented with an interface, called the Dexlog Rule Editor, for computing and validating a table's data through Dexlog rules.

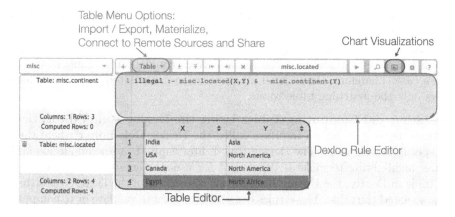

Fig. 1. Screenshot of Dexter's User Interface

A screenshot of Dexter's user interface depicting its different components is shown in Figure 1. On the left hand side, a list of tables is shown with the currently selected table highlighted with yellow background.

Creating and Managing Tables Through the Table Editor: When a user creates a table or views a previously created table by selecting it in the list of tables through Dexter's UI, he/she is presented with a table editor as shown in lower right area of Figure 1.

The simplest way to populate a table in Dexter is to manually fill in values into the cells of the table editor. Dexter also allows a user to import data from CSV, JSON, or XML files that are located in the user's file system or accessible through a URL by interacting with the *Table* menu in Dexter's UI. Furthermore, a user can also extract structured data from a Web page into a table in Dexter by copying the relevant HTML DOM fragment and pasting it on to the table. Dexter uses the extraction algorithm that is proposed in [2] to convert a copied HTML DOM fragment into a table.

In addition to above methods, Dexter also allows users to create *remote tables* by connecting to MySQL databases (by specifying the MySQL server's address, the database name and the authentication details) as well as to Web APIs that support responses in JSON format. In contrast to Web applications that typically hard-code the set of underlying sources, Dexter is based on a generic source model that characterizes (a) the querying capability of a source, (b) accessibility of the source from the client side (e.g. whether the source is directly accessible or requires a proxy), and (c) the conversion of the data sent from the source to a table in Dexter. We note that, unlike tables that are created by manual data entry, importing files or extracting HTML DOM fragments, the data in a remote table cannot be directly updated. Instead, users may duplicate and edit a copy of a remote table in Dexter.

Users can manage the data and the schema of their tables through Dexter's table editor by updating the values in the table's cells, by inserting or deleting rows or columns of a table respectively, or changing the column names. Users can *sort* a table by choosing an appropriate column through the table editor. Sometimes a user wishes to quickly see only a selected part of a large table. Defining a query for selecting the relevant rows could be too cumbersome in such a case. Therefore, Dexter's UI allows users to define filters on columns and shows only the matching table rows.

Validating and Computing Tables Using the Dexlog Rule Editor: Dexter presents to its users an interface called the Dexlog Rule Editor where they can specify Dexlog rules. The Dexlog Rule Editor supports auto-completion and syntax highlighting to make it convenient for users to enter Dexlog rules. For any table in Dexter, the Dexlog Rule Editor records *all* of the Dexlog rules that are associated the table. These rules can either be used to validate or to compute the tuples of the table.

Consider our example from Section 2 of a Dexlog constraint over the `located` table.

$$\texttt{illegal :- located(X, Y) \& } \sim \texttt{continent(Y)}$$

As shown in Figure 1, a user can associate such a constraint with the `located` table in Dexter by entering the constraint into the Dexlog Rule Editor. Traditional database systems [9] enforce constraints on a table by preventing violations. Since rejection of violating rows is only one of multiple possibilities for resolving a violation, Dexter allows constraint violations to occur and employs visual feedback to pinpoint violations to a user. Specifically, the rows of a table that contribute to a constraint violation are *colored red* when the table's data is validated against the constraints. An example of such a violation pinpointing is shown in Figure 1. Since the tuple `"North Africa"` is not present in the `continent` table, the tuple (`"Egypt"`, `"North Africa"`) violates the constraint on the `located` table and is, therefore, colored red.

Similar to specifying Dexlog constraints and validating tables, a user can also use the Dexlog rule editor to specify Dexlog rules and evaluate these rules to compute a table's data. When a user evaluates a computed table, the answers are streamed into Dexter's table editor as *read-only* rows. We discuss the process of evaluating Dexlog Rules in Section 4.

Materializing Tables: Dexter allows users to *materialize* computed tables in their browser's local storage. Materializing a computed table can significantly reduce the time taken to evaluate Dexlog rules over the table by using the materialization of the computed table instead of re-computing the table. We note that, currently, Dexter does not automatically update the materialization of computed tables when the data in the underlying sources is changed. Rather, Dexter relies on users to re-evaluate and re-materialize the computed tables any time they wish to do so.

Visualizing Tables: Charts are a great way to comprehend, analyze, and effectively interact with a table's data. In addition to allowing users to explore tables through Dexlog rules, Dexter enables users to visualize their table's data (including computed tuples) as charts. In order to create a chart based on the data in the currently selected table in Dexter's UI, a user opens the chart creation window by clicking on the "Chart Visualization" button (see Figure 1). A user can then select the columns to be plotted and the type of the chart and inspect the chart. Dexter supports popular chart types such as line chart, area chart, bar chart, column chart, scatter plot and pie chart. Dexter allows users to export their charts as images in popular image formats.

Exporting and Sharing Tables: Dexter stores user's tables locally inside their respective browsers. Tables that are accessible through Dexter in one browser are not accessible through a different browser (even within the same machine). In order to support inter-application exchange of user's data, Dexter allows its users to *export* their tables in two different ways. First, users can export their table's *data* as CSV, XML or JSON files. Users can also export a table's data along with the associated *validation* and *computation rules* in Dexter's native file format, which uses the extension .dxt and in Naf Datalog RuleML / XML[2], which uses the extension ruleml.

Dexter makes it possible for users to share their data with other users and use data shared by other users. With Dexter's UI users can easily publish their tables to Dexter's sharing server to make their tables accessible through different browsers or to other users. The shared tables are accessible to all Dexter users by selecting the folder "shared" in the upper left corner in Dexter's UI.

4 Efficient Evaluation of Dexlog Rules

Dexter allows users to query their tables by specifying Dexlog rules over the (relational) schemas of the involved sources. These queries are evaluated by Dexter on the client side by employing a Hybrid-Shipping strategy [13]. Our query evaluation strategy ensures acceptable query answering performance without requiring users to compromise on their privacy or overloading the client machines. We note that the naive approach of fetching all the required data to the client machine and subsequently, evaluating the query answers, also referred to as Data-Shipping [13], is not practical mainly because the client machines are usually not high-performance machines.

Dexter evaluates a user's query in the following steps. First, an input query is *decomposed* into partial queries, such that each partial query can be answered independently at a source. Next, the resulting sub-queries are filtered to remove rules that would never be fired while evaluating the user's query. After, *removing irrelevant rules*, the resulting partial queries are *fragmented* by horizontally partitioning the data of the underlying sources. Finally, the fragmented queries are executed in parallel and the resulting answers are compiled to construct the answers to the input query.

---

[2] http://wiki.ruleml.org/index.php/Dexter_and_RuleML

4.1   Query Decomposition

A query over the internal schema is decomposed into partial queries and rules that assemble the answers to the partial queries. The hybrid-shipping strategy [13] for query decomposition in Dexter depends on the sources that are required to evaluate a query and on the querying capability of a source.

Suppose that `senator(Name, Party, State)` and `party(Id, PartyName)` are two tables in Dexter that are created by connecting to Govtrack's relational database. Furthermore, suppose that the table `tweet(U, Tweet)`, which represents the Twitter posts of a user `U`, is created by connected to the Twitter API. Since databases support filtering of table on its attribute values, the query `q(T):-senator(U,P,S) & tweet(U,T) & party(P,"Rep")` will be decomposed into partial queries q1 and q2 as follows.

$$q(T) :- q1(U) \& q2(U, T)$$
$$q1(U) :- senator(U, P, S) \& party(P,"Rep")$$
$$q2(U, T) :- tweet(U, T)$$

In order to evaluate the query q, the partial queries `q1(U)` and `q2(U,T)` are sent to Govtrack's database and the Twitter API respectively.

However, if Govtrack does not allow the `senator` table to be filtered by the attribute `Party`, then the whole table is shipped to the client side where the filters are, subsequently, applied. In addition, if it is not known whether a certain operation (say, join or negation) can be performed at a source, then the relevant operation is performed on the client side after shipping the data from the source. We note that, in Dexter, the queries over local data (such as CSV, XML or JSON files) are *always* evaluated on the client side and never shipped to a source. Thus, the privacy of a user's local data is always preserved.

4.2   Removal of Irrelevant Rules

The collection of partial queries that results from the decomposition step is filtered to remove any irrelevant rules from it. The irrelevant rules are filtered using a simple procedure that, for a given input predicate, iterates through the rules and recursively selects all the rules that the input predicate depends on. Using this procedure for the query predicate as input gives us all the relevant rules filtering out any irrelevant rules.

We note that Dexter supports stratified evaluation of queries with negation or `setof`. In order to evaluate such queries, the strata of the predicates involved in the query are computed using the technique presented in [1]. The evaluation of the query starts by evaluating the predicates at strata 0.

4.3   Query Fragmentation

The straightforward evaluation of the partial queries resulting from the previous steps can become a double bottleneck due to (a) the complexity of the query, and (b) the size of the answers, especially when the size of the data shipped from a source is too big to handle for a user's browser. To resolve these bottlenecks, partial queries are fragmented horizontally into chunks based on the the size of the browser's local store and the maximum number of answers to a query that can be returned from a source. For example, suppose that the Twitter API allows a maximum of 500 tweets to be returned per call. If the number of senators, number of parties and the total number of tweets are, say, 500, 100 and 10000, respectively, then the query q(T) is fragmented into 20 fragments (assuming the chunk size to be 500). In order to be able to execute the fragments in parallel, the corresponding offsets and limits are appended to the relation names in the rules of a fragment. For our example, the rules for the first fragment will be as follows (and analogous for the other 19 fragments):

```
q(T) :- q1(U) & q2(U,T)
q1(U) :- senator_0_500(U,P,S) & party_0_100(P,"Rep")
q2(U,T) :- tweet_0_500(U,T)
```

4.4 Parallel Evaluation of Queries

In general, the number of partitions obtained from the previous step can be so large that it may not be feasible for a user's machine to evaluate all of them at the same time in parallel. Dexter allows users to set the maximum number of parallel threads they want Dexter to use while evaluating queries. Dexter schedules the execution of partitions such that at any time the number of query fragments executed in parallel does not exceed this limit.

Source Invocation and Building the Cache. A partition first builds the fact base required for answering the query. For this purpose, its rules are processed and appropriate source-specific queries are constructed. The construction of source-specific queries takes into consideration the source-connection information as well as the information about offset and limit appended to the relation names in the previous steps. Then, the source-specific queries are sent to the sources and results are converted to relations by using the appropriate wrappers, which could be located either on the client (e.g. local files, servers that support JSONP requests) or on the server (e.g. Twitter API, databases such as MySQL). To increase efficiency and relieve the sources, Dexter caches the data of a source invocation as long as doing so does not exceed the maximum cache size. Dexter's cache can be used by all partitions. In our example, since party_0_100(P,"Rep") is present in every partition, not caching source responses would lead to 20 Govtrack API invocations for the same data.

Answer Construction. In the answer construction stage, the answers of the partial query fragments are assembled to compute the answer to the user's input query. Although one query fragment does not return one answer multiple times, the same tuple could be returned by different query fragments. Therefore, the final answer is computed by taking the set-union of the answers of all query fragments.

5   Demonstration Scenarios

In this section, we present some example scenarios for which Dexter has been successfully evaluated. Note that Dexter is a *domain-independent* data browser and the number of scenarios for which it can be used is potentially infinite. The purpose of the scenarios described in this section is merely to demonstrate Dexter's features.

Table 1. Data Sources used in the Demonstration Scenarios

Nr.	Format	URL and Description
1	CSV	http://www.fec.gov/data/AdminFine.do Data about administrative fines
2	API	https://www.govtrack.us/developers/api Data about current U.S. senators and committees / sub-committees.
3	API	http://www.yelp.com/developers/documentation/search_api Data about pizzerias in Downtown, Washington D.C.
4	CSV	http://www.opendatadc.org/dataset/restaurant-inspection-data Health inspection data in Washington D.C restaurants
5	Webpage	https://www.eecs.mit.edu/people/faculty-advisors Data about MIT faculty
6	JSON	http://manufacturingmap.nikeinc.com/maps/export_json Data about manufacturers of Nike collegiate products.

S1: *Which U.S. senator or representative has incurred the maximum administrative fine? What is the distribution of administrative fines across the U.S. states?*

For this scenario, a user imports the CSV file (Line 1 of Table 1) into a table called fines, and sorts the table by column containing fines amounts (Finamo) in descending order. The user, then, creates e.g. a chart such as the one shown in Figure 2 with Dexter's interactive interface for visualizing the distribution of administrative fines across U.S. states.

S2: *Which of the current U.S. senators have been fined by the Federal Election Commission (FEC)? Do any of them chair a committee or a sub-committee?*

For this scenario, a user creates two tables persons and committees in Dexter and connects the tables to the Govtrack API (Line 2 in Table 1) to obtain the data about members of the U.S. congress and the congressional committees, respectively. Then, the user joins the persons table with the fines table (from Scenario **S1**) to find the senators who have been fined by the FEC. By joining

Distribution of Administrative Fines across U.S. States

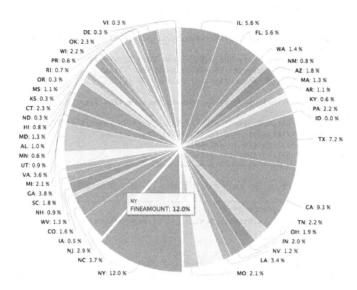

Fig. 2. Distribution of administrative fines across U.S. states

the result of the previous query with the `committees` table, the user can find the current U.S. senators, who chair a committee or a sub-committee and have been fined by the FEC.

S3: *Which pizzerias in Downtown, Washington D.C. have health code violations?*

For this scenario, a user creates a table called `dcPizzerias` and connects the table to the Yelp API (see Line 3 in Table 1) to obtain the data about pizzerias in Downtown, Washington D.C. Then, the user imports the data about health code violations (see Line 4 in Table 1) into a table called `healthViolation`. By evaluating a join over the two tables, the user can obtain the list of pizzerias in Washington D.C. that violate the health code regulations.

S4: *Which MIT CS faculty have not listed their contact details (phone number, office)?*

For this scenario, a user opens the MIT CS faculty Web page (Line 5 in Table 1) in his/her browser, selects the fragment of the Web page that contains the information on MIT CS faculty members, and pastes it in a table, say `mitCSFaculty` in Dexter. Dexter converts the pasted Web page fragment automatically into a table (for more details see [2]). Then, the user specifies the

```
<?xml version="1.0" encoding="UTF-8"?>
<?xml-model href="http://deliberation.ruleml.org/1.01/xsd/nafdatalog.xsd"?>
<RuleML xmlns="http://ruleml.org/spec">
  <Assert>
    <Forall>
      <Var>Name</Var><Var>Pos</Var><Var>Email</Var><Var>Off</Var><Var>Inst</Var>
      <Implies>
        <Atom><Rel>mitCSFaculty</Rel><Var>Name</Var><Var>Pos</Var><Var>Email</Var>
          <Data></Data><Var>Off</Var><Var>Inst</Var></Atom>
        <Atom><Rel>illegal</Rel></Atom></Implies></Forall>
      <Forall>
        <Var>Name</Var><Var>Pos</Var><Var>Email</Var><Var>Ph</Var><Var>Inst</Var>
        <Implies>
          <Atom><Rel>mitCSFaculty</Rel><Var>Name</Var><Var>Pos</Var><Var>Email</Var>
            <Var>Ph</Var><Data></Data><Var>Inst</Var></Atom>
          <Atom><Rel>illegal</Rel></Atom>
        </Implies></Forall></Assert></RuleML>
```

Fig. 3. Validation Rules (Constraints)

```
<?xml version="1.0" encoding="UTF-8"?>
<?xml-model href="http://deliberation.ruleml.org/1.01/xsd/nafdatalog.xsd"?>
<RuleML xmlns="http://ruleml.org/spec">
  <Assert>
    <Forall>
      <Var>A</Var><Var>B</Var><Var>C</Var><Var>D</Var><Var>E</Var><Var>F</Var><Var>I</Var>
      <Implies>
        <And>
          <Atom><Rel>mitCSFaculty</Rel><Var>A</Var><Var>B</Var><Var>C</Var>
              <Var>D</Var><Var>E</Var><Var>F</Var></Atom>
          <Atom><Rel>indexOf</Rel><Var>F</Var><Data>CSAIL</Data><Var>I</Var></Atom>
          <Atom><Rel>gt</Rel><Var>I</Var><Data>-1</Data></Atom>
        </And>
        <Atom><Rel>mitCSAIL</Rel><Var>A</Var><Var>B</Var><Var>C</Var>
            <Var>D</Var><Var>E</Var><Var>F</Var>
        </Atom>
      </Implies></Forall></Assert></RuleML>
```

Fig. 4. Computation Rule

following constraints on the `mitCSFaculty` table.

$$illegal :- mitCSFaculty(Name,Pos,Email,"",Off,Inst)$$
$$illegal :- mitCSFaculty(Name,Pos,Email,Ph,"",Inst)$$
$$illegal :- mitCSFaculty(Name,Pos,Email,"","",Inst)$$

When the above constraints are evaluated, the rows corresponding to MIT CS faculty members who have not listed a phone number or their office details are *colored red* in Dexter's UI to indicate a constraint violation.

Figure 3 shows the Naf Datalog RuleML/XML generated with Dexter for the above two constraints. Dexter can also export computation rules in Naf Datalog RuleML/XML syntax. Suppose, we have the following computation rule to compute only those MIT CS faculty members that are members of CSAIL.

```
mitCSAIL(A,B,C,D,E,F)   :-
    mitCSFaculty(A,B,C,D,E,F) & indexOf(F,"CSAIL",I) & gt(I,"-1")
```

Figure 4 shows the Naf Datalog RuleML/XML generated with Dexter for the above computation rule.

S5: *For every Nike product type, what is the total number of immigrant workers in the factories that supply the product?*

For this scenario, a user imports the file containing data about manufacturers of Nike collegiate products (see Line 6 in Table 1) into a table called `nikeFactories`. By evaluating the following rules, the user obtains the total number of migrant workers per product type. Note that in the second rule we use '*' only for the sake of readability of the paper.

```
s5(PType,NumMigWrkrs)  :- aux(PType,IdTemp,MwTemp) &
    setof([Id,Mw],aux(PType,Id,Mw),MwSet) & sumOf(MwSet,2,NumMigWrkrs)

aux(PType,Id,MigWrkrs) :- nikeFactories(Id,*,Wrkrs,*,MwP,*,PType,*) &
    replace(MwP,"%","",MwPer) & times(MwPer,.01,Wrkrs,MigWrkrs)
```

Table 2. Features of Dexter covered by the Demonstration Scenarios S1–S5

Feature\Scenario	S1	S2	S3	S4	S5
Import	✓	✓	✓		✓
Export				✓	
Web Extraction				✓	
API/Database		✓	✓		
Sorting	✓				
Constraints				✓	
Queries (Select / Project)	✓	✓		✓	✓
Queries (Join / Aggregates)		✓	✓		✓
Data Visualization	✓				
Table Editing	✓	✓	✓		✓

We note that the scenarios described above cover *most* of the features of Dexter. The features that are not covered in the demonstration scenarios S1–S5 are the exporting and sharing of tables. Table 2 summarizes the coverage of Dexter's features in the demonstration scenarios S1–S5.

6 Related Work and Concluding Remarks

We presented Dexter, a tool that empowers users to explore structured data from various Web-accessible sources such as databases, local files (e.g. CSV, XML and JSON), Web pages and Web-APIs expressively and in ad hoc fashion. To the best of our knowledge, Dexter is the first system to provide such functionality to users. Popular search engines do not support *compilation of information from multiple documents*, a prerequisite to satisfy the overall information need of a user. Semantic Web [5] and Linked Data [6] rely on existence of semantic annotations for websites or directly accessible semantic data respectively. Dexter takes a bottom-up approach by supporting multiple widely used types of data sources and data formats instead of only RDF.

Dexter stores user's data locally inside his/her browser as opposed to typical server-side systems that store user's data on the server. This feature of Dexter ensures that users can combine their private and confidential data with public data without compromising on their privacy. Although popular spreadsheet software such as Microsoft Excel support local storage and ad hoc analysis of user's data, they lack data capability of querying across multiple remote sources such as *joins across multiple sources*. Google's Fusion Tables [11] supports more expressive queries than traditional spreadsheets. However, Google's Fusion Tables is a purely server-side system and requires all the data to be on the server.

DataWrangler is a browser-based interactive data cleaning and transformation tool [12]. While DataWrangler can suggest edits based on user's interactions and Dexter does not, Dexter supports complex validation rules incl. conditions involving multiple tables whereas DataWrangler can check only for missing values. In addition to research prototypes, there is an ever increasing number of commercial systems such as Trifacta, Microsoft Azure, Tamr, MindTagger, Informatica, and Tableaux. While each of them has its own strengths and weaknesses, they all are targeted primarily toward making organization-internal data easily consumable for the employees of an organization. In contrast, Dexter is primarily targeted toward making publicly available data easily consumable for users.

Apart from the lack of support for privacy, server-side systems targeted toward users such as Wikidata [16] and Socrata (http://www.socrata.com/) typically do not support expressive queries; scalability being one of the many reasons for this choice. Dexter addresses the scalability problem with a novel architecture combined with the hybrid shipping strategy [13], in which queries are evaluated on the client side while exploiting the querying capabilities of remote sources. Dexter-Client communicates directly with data sources when possible, and through Dexter-Server (proxy) otherwise. Dexter query evaluation technique respects a user's privacy as it never ships a user's local data to a remote server. By enabling users to pose highly expressive queries over a source, across sources (including local data), Dexter bridges the gap between the querying capability of sources and the information need of a user. For detailed analysis of the above mentioned and more Dexter-related tools and technologies we refer to [3].

References

1. Abiteboul, S., Hull, R., Vianu, V.: Foundations of Databases. Addison-Wesley (1995). http://www-cse.ucsd.edu/users/vianu/book.html
2. Agarwal, S., Genesereth, M.R.: Extraction and integration of web data by end-users. In: He, Q., Iyengar, A., Nejdl, W., Pei, J., Rastogi, R. (eds.) CIKM, pp. 2405–2410. ACM (2013)

3. Agarwal, S., Mohapatra, A., Genesereth, M.: Survey of dexter related tools and techonologies (2014). http://dexter.stanford.edu/semcities/TR-DexterRelated Work.pdf
4. Athan, T., Boley, H.: The MYNG 1.01 Suite for Deliberation RuleML 1.01: Taming the language lattice. In: Patkos, T., Wyner, A., Giurca, A. (eds.) Proceedings of the RuleML 2014 Challenge, at the 8th International Web Rule Symposium, CEUR, vol. 1211, August 2014
5. Berners-Lee, T., Hendler, J., Lassila, O.: The Semantic Web: a new form of Web content that is meaningful to computers will unleash a revolution of new possibilities. Scientific American 5(284), 34–43 (2001)
6. Bizer, C., Heath, T., Berners-Lee, T.: Linked data - the story so far. International Journal on Semantic Web and Information Systems 5(3), 1–22 (2009)
7. Boley, H., Paschke, A., Shafiq, O.: RuleML 1.0: the overarching specification of web rules. In: Dean, M., Hall, J., Rotolo, A., Tabet, S. (eds.) RuleML 2010. LNCS, vol. 6403, pp. 162–178. Springer, Heidelberg (2010)
8. Dean, J., Ghemawat, S.: Mapreduce: Simplified data processing on large clusters. Commun. ACM 51(1), 107–113 (2008)
9. Garcia-Molina, H., Ullman, J.D., Widom, J.: Database systems - the complete book (2. ed.). Pearson Education (2009)
10. Genesereth, M.R.: Data Integration: The Relational Logic Approach. Synthesis Lectures on Artificial Intelligence and Machine Learning. Morgan & Claypool Publishers (2010)
11. Gonzalez, H., Halevy, A.Y., Jensen, C.S., Langen, A., Madhavan, J., Shapley, R., Shen, W.: Google fusion tables: data management, integration and collaboration in the cloud. In: Hellerstein, J.M., Chaudhuri, S., Rosenblum, M. (eds.) Proceedings of the 1st ACM Symposium on Cloud Computing, SoCC 2010, Indianapolis, Indiana, USA, June 10–11, 2010. pp. 175–180. ACM (2010)
12. Kandel, S., Paepcke, A., Hellerstein, J., Heer, J.: Wrangler: interactive visual specification of data transformation scripts. In: Tan, D.S., Amershi, S., Begole, B., Kellogg, W.A., Tungare, M. (eds.) Proceedings of the International Conference on Human Factors in Computing Systems, CHI 2011, Vancouver, BC, Canada, May 7–12, 2011, pp. 3363–3372. ACM (2011)
13. Kossmann, D.: The state of the art in distributed query processing. ACM Comput. Surv. 32(4), 422–469 (2000)
14. Mohapatra, A., Agarwal, S., Genesereth, M.: Dexlog: An overview (2014). http://dexter.stanford.edu/main/dexlog.html
15. Mohapatra, A., Genesereth, M.R.: Reformulating aggregate queries using views. In: Frisch, A.M., Gregory, P. (eds.) SARA. AAAI (2013)
16. Vrandecic, D., Krötzsch, M.: Wikidata: a free collaborative knowledgebase. Commun. ACM 57(10), 78–85 (2014)

PSOA2Prolog: Object-Relational Rule Interoperation and Implementation by Translation from PSOA RuleML to ISO Prolog

Gen Zou[(✉)] and Harold Boley

Faculty of Computer Science, University of New Brunswick, Fredericton, NB, Canada
{gen.zou,harold.boley}@unb.ca

Abstract. PSOA2Prolog consists of a multi-step source-to-source normalizer followed by a mapper to a pure (Horn) subset of ISO Prolog. We show the semantics preservation of the steps. Composing PSOA2Prolog and XSB Prolog, a fast Prolog engine, we achieved a novel instantiation of our PSOATransRun framework. We evaluated this interoperation and implementation technique with a suite of 30 test cases using 90 queries, and found a considerable speed-up compared to our earlier instantiation.

1 Introduction

In the Semantic Web and AI, the relational and object-centered modeling paradigms have been widely used for representing knowledge. The relational paradigm (e.g., classical logic and relational databases) models entity relationships using predicates applied to positional arguments, while the object-centered paradigm (e.g., RDF and N3) uses *frames* to model each entity using a globally unique Object IDentifier (OID) typed by a class and described by an unordered collection of slotted (attribute-value) arguments. To facilitate interoperation between the two paradigms, e.g. for expressing the mapping between frames and relational database schemas in rule-based data access, combined object-relational paradigms have been studied. F-logic [1,2] and RIF-BLD [3] employ a heterogeneous approach which allows the mixed use of both relations and frames. In contrast, the Web rule language PSOA RuleML [4] employs a homogeneous approach by generalizing relations and frames into **p**ositional-slotted **o**bject-applicative terms, which permit a relation application to have an OID – typed by the relation – and, orthogonally, to have positional or slotted arguments.

In order to reuse knowledge bases (KBs) and implementations of different rule languages, translators among them have been developed, including one from an F-logic-based language to Prolog [5,6], and one from the object-centered language KM into answer set programs [7]. To create a major interoperation path for the homogeneous object-relational PSOA RuleML, we developed a translator PSOA2Prolog from PSOA RuleML to a subset of the relational ISO Prolog [8,9], a logic programming standard with subsets supported by many fast engines. The translator supports KBs and queries employing all major PSOA features but restricting the use of equality to external-function evaluation. PSOA2Prolog

N. Bassiliades et al. (Eds.): RuleML 2015, LNCS 9202, pp. 176–192, 2015.
DOI: 10.1007/978-3-319-21542-6_12

is composed of a source-to-source normalizer followed by a mapper to a pure (Horn) subset of ISO Prolog. The normalizer is composed of five transformation layers, namely objectification, Skolemization, slotribution/tupribution, flattening, as well as rule splitting. Each layer is a self-contained component that can be reused for processing PSOA KBs in other applications. The mapper performs a recursive transformation from the normalization result to Prolog clauses.

By composing PSOA2Prolog and XSB Prolog, a fast Prolog engine for an ISO Prolog superset, we realized the PSOATransRun[PSOA2Prolog,XSBProlog][1] instantiation of our PSOATransRun framework. The implementation performs query answering in PSOA RuleML by translating a user-provided PSOA presentation syntax (PSOA/PS) KB and queries into Prolog, executing the queries in the Prolog engine, and translating the results back to PSOA/PS. Within its realm of Horn logic, the new instantiation supports more PSOA features than our earlier instantiation PSOATransRun[PSOA2TPTP,VampirePrime] [10], and our empirical evaluation shows a considerable speed-up on large test cases.

The rest of the paper is organized as follows. Section 2 reviews the basics of PSOA RuleML and ISO Prolog. Sections 3 and 4 explain the techniques employed by the normalizer and the mapper components of PSOA2Prolog. Section 5 explains the realization of PSOATransRun[PSOA2Prolog,XSBProlog], and compares it with PSOATransRun[PSOA2TPTP,VampirePrime] through test cases. Section 6 concludes the paper and discusses future work.

2 Background on the Source and Target Languages

In this section we introduce the basics of the source language PSOA RuleML and the target language ISO Prolog, of the PSOA2Prolog translator.

2.1 PSOA RuleML

PSOA RuleML [4] is an object-relational Web rule language that integrates relations and frames into positional-slotted, object-applicative (psoa)[2] terms, which have the general form

$$o \# f([t_{1,1} \ldots t_{1,n_1}] \ldots [t_{m,1} \ldots t_{m,n_m}] \ p_1 \text{->} v_1 \ldots p_k \text{->} v_k)$$

Here, an object is identified by an Object IDentifier (OID) o and described by (1) a class membership $o \# f$, (2) a set of tupled arguments $[t_{i,1} \ldots t_{i,n_i}]$, $i = 1, \ldots, m$, each being a sequence of terms, and (3) a set of slotted arguments $p_j \text{->} v_j$, $j = 1, \ldots, k$ representing attribute-value pairs. The OID as well as tuples and, orthogonally, slots in a psoa term are all optional. A psoa term can express untyped objects by treating them as being typed by the root class $f = \text{Top}$. For an *anonymous psoa term*, without a 'user' OID, *objectification* will introduce a 'system' OID as explained in Section 3.1. For the most often used special case

---

[1] http://psoa.ruleml.org/transrun/
[2] We use the upper-cased "PSOA" as a qualifier for the language and the lower-cased "psoa" for its terms.

of single-tuple psoa terms (m=1), the square brackets enclosing the tuple can be omitted.

PSOA RuleML constants have the form `"literal"^^symspace`, where `literal` is a sequence of Unicode characters and `symspace` is a symbol space identifier. Six kinds of shortcuts for constants are defined in [11], including numbers, strings, Internationalized Resource Identifiers (IRIs), and '_'-prefixed *local constants* (e.g., _a) whose `symspace` is specialized to `rif:local`. Top is a shortcut for the root class. PSOA RuleML variables are '?'-prefixed sequences.

A *base term* can be a constant, a variable, an anonymous psoa term, or an external term of the form `External(t)`, where t is an anonymous psoa term. An atomic formula is a psoa term with or without an OID, a subclass term c1 ## c2, an equality term t1=t2, or an external term. Complex formulas are constructed using the Horn-like subset of first-order logic (FOL), e.g. conjunctions and rule implications.

The semantics of PSOA RuleML is defined through semantic structures [4]. A semantic structure $\mathcal{I}$ is a tuple $<TV, DTS, D, D_{ind}, D_{func}, I_C, I_V, I_{psoa}, I_{sub}, I_{=}, I_{external}, I_{truth}>$. Here D is a non-empty set called the domain of $\mathcal{I}$. D_{ind} and D_{func} are subsets of D for interpreting individuals and functions, respectively. I_C, I_V, I_{psoa} interpret constants, variables, and psoa terms. $I_{sub}, I_{=}, I_{external}$ interpret subclass, equality and external terms. $TV = \{t, f\}$ is the set of truth values. I_{truth} maps domain elements to TV, allowing HiLog-like generality. Truth evaluation for well-formed formulas is determined by an evaluation function $TVal_{\mathcal{I}}$. A semantic structure $\mathcal{I}$ is called a *model* of a KB ϕ if $TVal_{\mathcal{I}}(\phi) = t$, denoted by $\mathcal{I} \models \phi$. A PSOA KB ϕ is said to *entail* a formula ψ, denoted by $\phi \models \psi$, if for every model $\mathcal{I}$ of ϕ, $\mathcal{I} \models \psi$ holds.

A more detailed introduction, with many examples leading to the semantics, can be found in [12].

Startup Example. The KB in Fig. 1 demonstrates key features of PSOA RuleML via a startup company scenario, serving as the paper's running example.

The example contains four facts, a rule, and a subclass (' ## ') formula. The rule derives an anonymous psoa term (in [12] called a "relpairship") with class _startup from: (1) a _cofounders relationship between the CEO and the CTO; (2) a _hire relationship between the CEO and an employee; (3) two _equity relationships describing the equity shares of the CEO and the CTO; (4) external calls ensuring that the sum of the equity percentages of the CEO and the CTO is not greater than 100. The _startup term has one tuple for the _ceo and the _cto, as well as one slot for one or more _employees (PSOA slots can be multi-valued). The ' ## ' formula states that _startup is a subclass of _company.

Leaving the topic of normalization to Section 3, the rule can be applied to the four facts, deriving the anonymous psoa term _startup(_Ernie _Tony _employee->_Kate). Combined with the subclass formula, a _company psoa term _company(_Ernie _Tony _employee->_Kate) with the same tuple and slot can be derived. This entails all psoa terms omitting the tuple or the slot, namely _company(_employee->_Kate) and _company(_Ernie _Tony).

```
Document (
  Group (
    Forall ?X ?Y ?Z ?EX ?EY (
      _startup(?X ?Y _employee->?Z) :-
        And(_cofounders(?X ?Y) _hire(?X ?Z)
            _equity(?X ?EX) _equity(?Y ?EY)
            External(
              pred:numeric-less-than-or-equal(
                External(func:numeric-add(?EX ?EY)) 100)))
    )

    _cofounders(_Ernie _Tony)  _hire(_Ernie _Kate)
    _equity(_Ernie 50)         _equity(_Tony 30)
    _startup##_company
  )
)
```

Fig. 1. KB using psoa-term rule with implicit OID typed as startup company

Amongst the many possible queries over the KB in Fig. 1, our running query will be

```
_company(?X ?Y)
```

It asks for the positional arguments ?X and ?Y of the _company psoa term, omitting the _employee slot. The desired answer is ?X=_Ernie ?Y=_Tony.

2.2 ISO Prolog

Prolog is a widely used logic programming language. ISO Prolog [8] is the international standard of Prolog. In this paper we focus on the Horn subset of ISO Prolog, which excludes procedural features like negation-as-failure. The syntax of ISO Prolog is built on top of *terms*: A term can be a *variable*, a *number*, an *atosym* (atomic symbol)[3], or a *compound term* of the form $p(t_1, \ldots, t_n)$, where p is an atosym and $t_1, \ldots, t_n$ are terms. A variable is basically a sequence of letters or digits starting with an upper-case letter, e.g. X1. An atosym, for a predicate or a function (including a nullary function, i.e. an individual), starts with a lower-case letter, e.g. a1, or is a single-quoted sequence of arbitrary characters, e.g. 'http://abc'. An ISO Prolog *predication* is an atosym (for a nullary predicate) or a compound term. A *clause* is either a *fact* in the form of a predication or a *rule* of the form Head :- Body. The Head is a predication, while the Body can be a predication, a conjunction of bodies (Body , ... , Body), or a disjunction or bodies (Body ; ... ; Body). All variables in a clause are considered to be in the scope of universal quantifiers preceding the entire clause. A *logic program* consists of a set of clauses.

---

[3] To avoid confusion with logical atoms, we use "atosym" to refer to symbols that ISO Prolog calls "atoms".

3   Normalization of the PSOA Source in Five Steps

The first translation phase is to transform the input PSOA *KB* and *queries* into a normalized form such that all clauses are objectified, existential-free, and contain only elementary formulas which cannot be split into equivalent subformulas. For PSOA KBs, there are five steps applied in sequential order: (1) Objectification; (2) Skolemization; (3) slotribution and tupribution; (4) flattening of external function applications; (5) splitting of rules with conjunctive heads. For PSOA queries, only steps (1), (3), and (4) are needed. The semantics preservation of the normalization steps will be indicated in English for the easier steps (1), (3), and (4), while detailed correctness proofs will be given for the more involved steps (2) and (5).

3.1   Objectification

In PSOA RuleML, an atomic psoa formula without an OID is regarded as having an implicit OID, which can be made explicit through *objectification*. We employ a modified version of the objectification technique introduced in [4]. For an OID-less psoa formula `p(...)` in a KB clause, we define three cases:

- If it is a ground fact, it is objectified into `_i#p(...)`, where `_i` is a newly generated local constant name in the KB.
- If it is a non-ground fact or an atomic formula in a rule conclusion, it is objectified into `Exists ?j (?j#p(...))`.
- If it is an atomic formula in a rule premise, it is objectified into `?j#p(...)`, where `?j` is a new variable in the universal scope of the enclosing rule. In [4], an anonymous variable '?' is used as the OID in this case. However, the next Skolemization step, which will be explained in Section 3.2, requires all universally quantified variables in an existential rule to be named, since they will become arguments of Skolem functions. Thus, we further parse the stand-alone '?'s into explicitly named variables `?j` quantified in the top-level universal scope in our objectification step.

We define the objectification of an OID-less psoa formula in a (conjunctive) query as `Exists ?j (?j#p(...))`. Here, the new variable `?j` is not a free query variable but encapsulated in an existential scope, so that the bindings of `?j` will not be returned in contrast to those of user-provided free query variables.

3.2   Skolemization

After objectification, existentially quantified formulas may occur in rule conclusions. Since such conclusion existentials are not allowed in logic programming languages such as Prolog, we employ a specialized FOL Skolemization [13] to eliminate them. Our approach is adapted for PSOA RuleML clauses, whose universals are already in prenex form and whose existentials are confined to (conjunctive) conclusions, hence does not require preprocessing of formulas. We replace each formula `Exists ?X` (σ) in a clause (specifically, in a rule conclusion or a fact) with $\sigma[?X/\_\text{skolem}k(?v_1 \ldots ?v_m)]$, where each occurrence of `?X` in σ becomes a Skolem function _skolem$k$ applied to all universally quantified variables ?v_1 ... ?v_m from the clause's quantifier prefix. For each existentially quantified variable in the KB, a fresh Skolem function name _skolem$k$ is chosen from the first name in the sequence _skolem1, _skolem2, ... that has not yet been used.

Skolemization Example. The following PSOA rule

```
Forall ?v ( Exists ?1 (?1#_c1(?v)) :- _o#_c2(?v) )
```

has an existentially quantified formula in the rule conclusion. Skolemization removes the existential quantifier and replaces the variable ?1 with _skolem1(?v), which is a unary Skolem function _skolem1 applied to the variable ?v in the clause's quantifier prefix, yielding

```
Forall ?v ( _skolem1(?v)#_c1(?v) :- _o#_c2(?v) )
```

Next we prove the correctness of our Skolemization. In the proof, we use $\mathcal{I}[?v_1 \ldots ?v_m]$ to denote the set of semantic structures that coincide with $\mathcal{I}$ on everything but the variables ?v_1 ... ?v_m, $t^{\mathcal{I}}$ to denote the interpretation of a base term t in $\mathcal{I}$, and $SK(\psi)$ to denote the Skolem form of a formula ψ.

Lemma 1. *Let ϕ be a formula and $\mathcal{I}, \mathcal{I}'$ be semantic structures. Then (1) if $\mathcal{I}' \models SK(\phi)$ then $\mathcal{I}' \models \phi$; (2) if $\mathcal{I} \models \phi$, there exists $\mathcal{I}'$ such that $\mathcal{I}' \models SK(\phi)$ and $\mathcal{I}'$ coincides with $\mathcal{I}$ on everything but the interpretation of Skolem functions.*

Proof. If ϕ does not have an existential (not necessarily proper) subformula then $SK(\phi) = \phi$ and the lemma holds trivially. Next we prove (1) and (2) by induction over every subformula σ of ϕ that contain an existential subformula. Proof for (1):

- $\sigma = \text{Exists } ?X \ (\sigma_1)$
  If $TVal_{\mathcal{I}'}(SK(\sigma)) = \mathbf{t}$, there exists a semantic structure $\mathcal{I}^*$ in $\mathcal{I}'[?X]$ which interprets ?X as _skolem$k$(?v_1 ... ?v_m)$^{\mathcal{I}'}$, and

$$TVal_{\mathcal{I}^*}(\sigma_1) = TVal_{\mathcal{I}'}(\sigma_1[?X/\text{_skolem}k(?v_1 \ldots ?v_m)]) = TVal_{\mathcal{I}'}(SK(\sigma)) = \mathbf{t}.$$

  Hence $TVal_{\mathcal{I}'}(\sigma) = \mathbf{t}$.
- $\sigma = \text{And}(\sigma_1 \ldots \sigma_n)$
  Since $SK(\sigma) = \text{And}(SK(\sigma_1) \ldots SK(\sigma_n))$, if $TVal_{\mathcal{I}'}(SK(\sigma)) = \mathbf{t}$, then $TVal_{\mathcal{I}'}(SK(\sigma_i)) = \mathbf{t}$, $i = 1, \ldots, n$. If σ_i has an existential subformula, then by induction hypothesis $TVal_{\mathcal{I}'}(\sigma_i) = \mathbf{t}$. Otherwise, $TVal_{\mathcal{I}'}(\sigma_i) = TVal_{\mathcal{I}'}(SK(\sigma_i)) = \mathbf{t}$. Thus, $TVal_{\mathcal{I}'}(\sigma_i) = \mathbf{t}, i = 1, \ldots, n$, and $TVal_{\mathcal{I}'}(\sigma) = \mathbf{t}$.
- $\sigma = \sigma_1 \ \text{:-} \ \sigma_2$
  Since existentials occur only in rule conclusions, $SK(\sigma) = SK(\sigma_1) \ \text{:-} \ \sigma_2$. So

$$TVal_{\mathcal{I}'}(SK(\sigma)) = \mathbf{t} \Rightarrow TVal_{\mathcal{I}'}(SK(\sigma_1)) = \mathbf{t} \text{ or } TVal_{\mathcal{I}'}(\sigma_2) = \mathbf{f}$$
$$\Rightarrow TVal_{\mathcal{I}'}(\sigma_1) = \mathbf{t} \text{ or } TVal_{\mathcal{I}'}(\sigma_2) = \mathbf{f}$$
$$\Rightarrow TVal_{\mathcal{I}'}(\sigma) = \mathbf{t}$$

- $\sigma = $ Forall $?v_1 \ldots ?v_m \ (\sigma_1)$

  Since $SK(\sigma) = $ Forall $?v_1 \ldots ?v_m \ (SK(\sigma_1))$, we have

$$TVal_{\mathcal{I}'}(SK(\sigma)) = \mathbf{t} \Rightarrow \text{for all } \mathcal{I}^* \in \mathcal{I}'[?v_1 \ldots ?v_m], TVal_{\mathcal{I}^*}(SK(\sigma_1)) = \mathbf{t}$$
$$\Rightarrow \text{for all } \mathcal{I}^* \in \mathcal{I}'[?v_1 \ldots ?v_m], TVal_{\mathcal{I}^*}(\sigma_1) = \mathbf{t}$$
$$\Rightarrow TVal_{\mathcal{I}'}(\sigma) = \mathbf{t}$$

- $\sigma = $ Group$(\sigma_1 \ldots \sigma_n)$

  The semantics of a group formula is the same as a conjunction. So the same proof can be applied.

Proof for (2): For each semantic structure $\mathcal{I}$, we construct $\mathcal{I}'$ by adding the interpretation for all Skolem functions in ϕ. Assume Exists $?X \ (\sigma_1)$ is a subformula of ϕ, and $?X$ is replaced with $\_skolemk(?v_1 \ldots ?v_m)$ during Skolemization. For elements $x_1, \ldots, x_n$ in the domain of $\mathcal{I}$, if there exists one $\mathcal{I}^*$ such that $TVal_{\mathcal{I}^*}(\sigma_1) = \mathbf{t}$ and $?v_i^{\mathcal{I}'} = x_i, i = 1, \ldots, n$, then we define $\_skolemk^{\mathcal{I}'}(x_1, \ldots, x_n)$ to be $?X^{\mathcal{I}^*}$. Next we prove if $TVal_{\mathcal{I}}(\sigma) = \mathbf{t}$, then $TVal_{\mathcal{I}'}(SK(\sigma)) = \mathbf{t}$ by induction over all σ that contain an existential subformula.

- $\sigma = $ Exists $?X \ (\sigma_1)$

  In this case $TVal_{\mathcal{I}'}(SK(\sigma)) = \mathbf{t}$ follows by the definition of $\mathcal{I}'$.
- $\sigma = $ And$(\sigma_1 \ldots \sigma_n)$

  If $TVal_{\mathcal{I}}(\sigma) = \mathbf{t}$, then $TVal_{\mathcal{I}}(\sigma_i) = \mathbf{t}$ for all $i = 1, \ldots, n$. If σ_i has an existential subformula, then by induction hypothesis $TVal_{\mathcal{I}'}(SK(\sigma_i)) = \mathbf{t}$. Otherwise $SK(\sigma_i) = \sigma_i$, and $TVal_{\mathcal{I}'}(SK(\sigma_i)) = TVal_{\mathcal{I}}(\sigma_i) = \mathbf{t}$. Hence $TVal_{\mathcal{I}'}(SK(\sigma_i)) = \mathbf{t}$ holds for all $i = 1, \ldots, n$, and $TVal_{\mathcal{I}'}(SK(\sigma)) = \mathbf{t}$.
- $\sigma = \sigma_1 \ \text{:-} \ \sigma_2$

$$TVal_{\mathcal{I}}(\sigma) = \mathbf{t} \Rightarrow TVal_{\mathcal{I}}(\sigma_1) = \mathbf{t} \text{ or } TVal_{\mathcal{I}}(\sigma_2) = \mathbf{f}$$
$$\Rightarrow TVal_{\mathcal{I}'}(SK(\sigma_1)) = \mathbf{t} \text{ or } TVal_{\mathcal{I}'}(\sigma_2) = \mathbf{f}$$
$$\Rightarrow TVal_{\mathcal{I}'}(SK(\sigma)) = \mathbf{t}$$

- $\sigma = $ Forall $?v_1 \ldots ?v_m \ (\sigma_1)$

$$TVal_{\mathcal{I}}(\sigma) = \mathbf{t} \Rightarrow \text{for all } \mathcal{J} \in \mathcal{I}[?v_1 \ldots ?v_m], TVal_{\mathcal{J}}(\sigma_1) = \mathbf{t}$$
$$\Rightarrow \text{for all } \mathcal{J}' \in \mathcal{I}'[?v_1 \ldots ?v_m], TVal_{\mathcal{J}'}(SK(\sigma_1)) = \mathbf{t}$$
$$\Rightarrow TVal_{\mathcal{I}'}(\sigma) = \mathbf{t}$$

- $\sigma = $ Group$(\psi_1 \ldots \psi_n)$

  The proof for conjunction formulas can be reused.

Theorem 1. *Let Γ be a PSOA KB, and τ be a clause that does not contain Skolem functions used in $SK(\Gamma)$. Then $\Gamma \models \tau$ if and only if $SK(\Gamma) \models \tau$.*

Proof. (Only if) If $\Gamma \models \tau$, then by part (1) of Lemma 1, for every model $\mathcal{I}'$ of $SK(\Gamma)$, $TVal_{\mathcal{I}'}(SK(\Gamma)) = TVal_{\mathcal{I}}(\Gamma) = TVal_{\mathcal{I}}(\tau) = \mathbf{t}$. So $SK(\Gamma) \models \tau$ holds.

(If) We prove the contrapositive statement, i.e. if $\Gamma \not\models \tau$ then $SK(\Gamma) \not\models \tau$. If $\Gamma \not\models \tau$, there exists a semantic structure $\mathcal{I}$ such that $TVal_{\mathcal{I}}(\Gamma) = \mathbf{t}$ and $TVal_{\mathcal{I}}(\tau) = \mathbf{f}$. By part (2) of Lemma 1, there exists $\mathcal{I}'$ such that $TVal_{\mathcal{I}'}(SK(\Gamma)) = \mathbf{t}$ and $\mathcal{I}'$ coincides with $\mathcal{I}'$ on everything but the Skolem functions, which do not occur in τ. Hence, $TVal_{\mathcal{I}'}(\tau) = TVal_{\mathcal{I}}(\tau) = \mathbf{f}$, making $\mathcal{I}'$ a counter-model of $SK(\Gamma) \models \tau$. Thus $SK(\Gamma) \not\models \tau$ and the statement holds.

3.3   Slotribution/Tupribution

The truth value of a psoa formula is defined via slotribution and tupribution [4]:

- $TVal_{\mathcal{I}}(\text{o\#f}([t_{1,1} \ldots t_{1,n_1}] \ldots [t_{m,1} \ldots t_{m,n_m}] \ p_1\text{->}v_1 \ldots p_k\text{->}v_k)) = \mathbf{t}$
  if and only if
  $TVal_{\mathcal{I}}(\text{o\#f}) =$
  $TVal_{\mathcal{I}}(\text{o\#Top}([t_{1,1} \ldots t_{1,n_1}])) = \ldots = TVal_{\mathcal{I}}(\text{o\#Top}([t_{m,1} \ldots t_{m,n_m}])) =$
  $TVal_{\mathcal{I}}(\text{o\#Top}(p_1\text{->}v_1)) = \ldots = TVal_{\mathcal{I}}(\text{o\#Top}(p_k\text{->}v_k)) = \mathbf{t}$.

According to the semantics of psoa formulas, we can rewrite each psoa formula $\text{o\#f}([t_{1,1} \ldots t_{1,n_1}] \ldots [t_{m,1} \ldots t_{m,n_m}] \ p_1\text{->}v_1 \ldots p_k\text{->}v_k)$, containing m tuples and k slots, into an equivalent conjunction of $1 + m + k$ subformulas, including 1 class membership formula, m single-tuple formulas and k single-slot formulas:

```
And(o#f
    o#Top(t_{1,1} ... t_{1,n_1}) ... o#Top(t_{m,1} ... t_{m,n_m})
    o#Top(p_1->v_1) ... o#Top(p_k->v_k))
```

For the special case where f=Top but $m + k > 0$, we omit the tautological Top-typed class membership of the form o # Top from the conjunction for efficiency.[4] The correctness of this step follows directly from the definition. This step is central to both PSOA2TPTP [14] and PSOA2Prolog.

3.4   Flattening Nested External Function Applications

A PSOA function application can use a constructor function with no definition, a user-defined function specified by equalities in the KB, or an externally defined function such as an arithmetic built-in. The latter two types of applications evaluate an 'interpreted' function to a returned value. Flattening is employed to create a conjunction extracting an embedded interpreted function application as a separate equality. This version of PSOA2Prolog supports only the use of equalities of the form ?X=External(f(...)), equating a variable and an external function application for the evaluation of a function call, in preparation of the mapping to the Prolog is-primitive in Section 4.2.

In the flattening step, each atomic formula φ (in a rule premise or a query) that embeds an external function application ψ, which is not on the top level of an equality, is replaced with And(?i=ψ $\varphi[\psi/?i]$), where ?i is the first variable in ?1, ?2, ... that does not occur in the enclosing rule. If ψ is in a KB rule, then the variable ?i becomes a universal variable of the rule; otherwise ?i is encapsulated

---

[4] For $m+k = 0$, the description-less o # Top does not undergo slotribution/tupribution.

in a top-level existential scope in a query. This step is repeated for every clause in the KB until there are no more nested function applications. The correctness of this step follows from back-substitution of the embedded application for the variable $?i$.

3.5 Splitting Rules with Conjunctive Conclusions

A rule with a conjunction in the conclusion

$$\texttt{Forall } ?v_1 \ \ldots \ ?v_m \ (\texttt{And}(\varphi_1 \ \ldots \ \varphi_n) \ \texttt{:-} \ \varphi')$$

can be split into n rules

$$\texttt{Forall } ?v_1 \ \ldots \ ?v_m \ (\varphi_1 \ \texttt{:-} \ \varphi'),$$

$$\ldots$$

$$\texttt{Forall } ?v_1 \ \ldots \ ?v_m \ (\varphi_n \ \texttt{:-} \ \varphi')$$

with each conjunct becoming the conclusion of one rule, and with the premise and the quantification copied unchanged.

Lemma 2. *Let ϕ be the given rule, $\phi_1, ..., \phi_n$ be the split rules, and $\mathcal{I}$ be a semantic structure, then $\mathcal{I} \models \phi$ if and only if $\mathcal{I} \models \phi_i, i = 1, \ldots, n$.*

Proof.   Let ϕ be of the form $\texttt{Forall } ?v_1 \ \ldots \ ?v_m \ (\texttt{And}(\varphi_1 \ \ldots \ \varphi_n) \ \texttt{:-} \ \varphi')$. If $\mathcal{I} \models \phi$, then for all $\mathcal{I}^* \in \mathcal{I}[?v_1 \ \ldots \ ?v_m]$, we have

$$TVal_{\mathcal{I}^*}(\texttt{And}(\varphi_1 \ \ldots \ \varphi_n) \ \texttt{:-} \ \varphi')) = \mathbf{t}$$
$$\Longleftrightarrow \quad TVal_{\mathcal{I}^*}(\texttt{And}(\varphi_1 \ \ldots \ \varphi_n)) = \mathbf{t} \text{ or } TVal_{\mathcal{I}^*}(\varphi') = \mathbf{f}$$
$$\Longleftrightarrow \quad (TVal_{\mathcal{I}^*}(\varphi_1) = \ldots = TVal_{\mathcal{I}^*}(\varphi_n) = \mathbf{t}) \text{ or } TVal_{\mathcal{I}^*}(\varphi') = \mathbf{f}$$
$$\Longleftrightarrow \quad (TVal_{\mathcal{I}^*}(\varphi_1) = \mathbf{t} \text{ or } TVal_{\mathcal{I}^*}(\varphi') = \mathbf{f}) \text{ and } \ldots \text{ and}$$
$$(TVal_{\mathcal{I}^*}(\varphi_n) = \mathbf{t} \text{ or } TVal_{\mathcal{I}^*}(\varphi') = \mathbf{f})$$
$$\Longleftrightarrow \quad TVal_{\mathcal{I}^*}(\varphi_1 \ \texttt{:-} \ \varphi') = \ldots = TVal_{\mathcal{I}^*}(\varphi_n \ \texttt{:-} \ \varphi') = \mathbf{t}$$

Hence $\mathcal{I} \models \phi_i, i = 1, \ldots, n$.

Theorem 2. *If Γ is a PSOA KB and Γ' is the KB after performing rule splitting in Γ. Then for any formula τ, $\Gamma \models \tau$ if and only if $\Gamma' \models \tau$.*

Proof.   By extending Lemma 2 for KBs, we have $TVal_{\mathcal{I}}(\Gamma) = TVal_{\mathcal{I}}(\Gamma')$. If $\Gamma' \models \tau$, then for all $\mathcal{I}$ such that $\mathcal{I} \models \Gamma$, $TVal_{\mathcal{I}}(\Gamma') = TVal_{\mathcal{I}}(\tau) = \mathbf{t}$, so $\Gamma \models \tau$. The "only if" part can be proved similarly.

3.6 Normalizing the Startup Example

In this subsection we demonstrate the normalization steps with the Startup Example given in Section 2.1.

The objectification step introduces OIDs $\_1, \ldots, \_4$ for the ground facts. It also introduces an existentially quantified variable $?1$ for the anonymous psoa term in the rule conclusion while introducing four universally quantified variables $?2, \ldots, ?5$ for the OID-less relations in the rule premise. Moreover, the query is objectified using a variable $?1$, which is encapsulated in an existential scope to avoid being treated as a free query variable.

Objectified KB:

```
Document (
  Group (
    Forall ?X ?Y ?Z ?EX ?EY ?2 ?3 ?4 ?5 (
      Exists ?1 (
        ?1#_startup(?X ?Y _employee->?Z)) :-
          And(?2#_cofounders(?X ?Y) ?3#_hire(?X ?Z)
              ?4#_equity(?X ?EX) ?5#_equity(?Y ?EY)
              External(
                pred:numeric-less-than-or-equal(
                  External(func:numeric-add(?EX ?EY)) 100)))
    )
    _1#_cofounders(_Ernie _Tony)   _2#_hire(_Ernie _Kate)
    _3#_equity(_Ernie 50)          _4#_equity(_Tony 30)
    _startup##_company
  )
)
```

Objectified Query:

```
Exists ?1 (?1#_company(?X ?Y))
```

After objectification, the Skolemization step eliminates the existential in the rule conclusion and replaces the variable `?1` with a Skolem function application, giving `_skolem1(?X ?Y ?Z ?EX ?EY ?2 ?3 ?4 ?5)#_startup(?X ?Y _employee->?Z)`.[5]

Next, slotribution and tupribution transform each psoa formula into a conjunction (possibly merged into a surrounding `Group/And`). The result, which is shown on the next page, contains a rule with a conjunctive conclusion.

The application of the external predicate `pred:numeric-less-than-or-equal` is then flattened with the argument `External(func:numeric-add(...))` being replaced by a fresh universal variable `?6`, obtaining the conjunction

```
And(?6=External(func:numeric-add(?EX ?EY))
    External(pred:numeric-less-than-or-equal(?6 100))
```

Finally, the conjunction in the rule conclusion is split to obtain the normalized KB as shown on the next page. The four output rules have the same premise and the same argument list for the Skolem function. The normalized query after rule splitting is the same as the slotributed/tupributed version shown above.

The example can be easily refined, e.g. with additional conclusion slots such as `_founderEquity`, which would store the already computed sum of the equities held by the CEO and the CTO.

---

[5] Objectification generates an existential OID for each derived `_startup`. Skolemization then replaces that OID by a system function application dependent on all universal variables, including `?Z`, thus denoting different OIDs for startups with the same CEO/CTO pair and different employees. If a user wants all startups with the same CEO and CTO to have the same OID, he/she can specify the OID of the original rule conclusion explicitly via an application, `_startupid(?X ?Y)`, of a fresh function name, `_startupid`, to the CEO, `?X`, and the CTO, `?Y`, denoting the OID dependent on them but not on any employee, `?Z`.

Slotributed/Tupributed KB:

```
Document(
  Group (
    Forall ?X ?Y ?Z ?EX ?EY ?2 ?3 ?4 ?5 (
        And(_skolem1(?X ?Y ?Z ?EX ?EY ?2 ?3 ?4 ?5)#_startup
            _skolem1(...)#Top(?X ?Y)
            _skolem1(...)#Top(_employee->?Z)) :-
        And(?2#_cofounders ?2#Top(?X ?Y)  ?3#_hire ?3#Top(?X ?Z)
            ?4#_equity  ?4#Top(?X ?EX) ?5#_equity ?5#Top(?Y ?EY)
            External(
              pred:numeric-less-than-or-equal(
                External(func:numeric-add(?EX ?EY)) 100)))
    )

    _1#_cofounders _1#Top(_Ernie _Tony) _2#_hire   _2#Top(_Ernie _Kate)
    _3#_equity     _3#Top(_Ernie 50)    _4#_equity _4#Top(_Tony 30)
    _startup##_company
  )
)
```

Slotributed/Tupributed Query:

```
Exists ?1 (And(?1#_company ?1#Top(?X ?Y)))
```

Rule-split KB:

```
Document(
  Group (
    Forall ?X ?Y ?Z ?EX ?EY ?2 ?3 ?4 ?5 ?6 (
      _skolem1(?X ?Y ?Z ?EX ?EY ?2 ?3 ?4 ?5)#_startup :-
        And(?2#_cofounders ?2#Top(?X ?Y)  ?3#_hire ?3#Top(?X ?Z)
            ?4#_equity  ?4#Top(?X ?EX) ?5#_equity ?5#Top(?Y ?EY)
            And(?6=External(func:numeric-add(?EX ?EY))
                External(pred:numeric-less-than-or-equal(?6 100)))
    )

    Forall ?X ?Y ?Z ?EX ?EY ?2 ?3 ?4 ?5 ?6 (
      _skolem1(...)#Top(?X ?Y) :- And(...)
    )

    Forall ?X ?Y ?Z ?EX ?EY ?2 ?3 ?4 ?5 ?6 (
      _skolem1(...)#Top(_employee->?Z) :- And(...)
    )

    _1#_cofounders _1#Top(_Ernie _Tony) _2#_hire   _2#Top(_Ernie _Kate)
    _3#_equity     _3#Top(_Ernie 50)    _4#_equity _4#Top(_Tony 30)
    _startup##_company
  )
)
```

4 Mapping the Normalized PSOA Source to Prolog

In this section, we explain the mapping from normalized PSOA constructs to Prolog constructs. The mapping function is denoted by ρ_{psoa}, which is applied recursively in a top-down manner. The translation introduces three distinguished predicates shown in Table 2, `memterm`, `sloterm`, and `tupterm`, defined by Prolog clauses, to represent the three central constructs: membership terms, slot terms, and tuple terms from PSOA RuleML. Section 4.1 discusses the translation of constants and variables and Section 4.2 discusses the translation of central PSOA constructs.

4.1 Constants and Variables

The translation $\rho_{psoa}(c)$ of a constant c is determined as follows:

- If c is a number, $\rho_{psoa}(c)$ is the corresponding Prolog number.
- If c is an arithmetic built-in adopted from RIF [11], $\rho_{psoa}(c)$ is the corresponding Prolog built-in, as listed in Table 1.

Table 1. Mapping of PSOA built-ins to Prolog

PSOA/PS Built-in	Prolog Built-in
func:numeric-add	'+'
func:numeric-subtract	'-'
func:numeric-multiply	'*'
func:numeric-divide	'/'
func:numeric-integer-divide	'//'
func:numeric-mod	mod
pred:numeric-equal	'=:='
pred:numeric-less-than	'<'
pred:numeric-less-than-or-equal	'=<'
pred:numeric-greater-than	'>'
pred:numeric-greater-than-or-equal	'>='
pred:numeric-not-equal	'=\='

- Otherwise, $\rho_{psoa}(c)$ is the single-quoted version of c.

The translation $\rho_{psoa}(v)$ of a '?'-prefixed variable v replaces '?' with the upper-case letter 'Q' (Question mark) to make it a valid Prolog variable. For example, a PSOA variable ?x is mapped to a Prolog variable Qx.

4.2 Central PSOA Constructs

Table 2 gives mappings of all central PSOA constructs. The translation of tuple terms of the form o # Top($t_1 \ldots t_k$) and slot terms of the form o # Top(p -> v) is adopted from PSOA2TPTP [14], using distinguished predicates `tupterm` and `sloterm` respectively.

Table 2. Mapping from PSOA/PS constructs to Prolog constructs

PSOA/PS Constructs	Prolog Constructs
o#Top(t$_1$...t$_k$)	tupterm(ρ_{psoa}(o), ρ_{psoa}(t$_1$) ... ρ_{psoa}(t$_k$))
o#Top(p->v)	sloterm(ρ_{psoa}(o), ρ_{psoa}(p), ρ_{psoa}(v))
o#c()	memterm(ρ_{psoa}(o), ρ_{psoa}(c))
f(t$_1$...t$_k$)	ρ_{psoa}(f)(ρ_{psoa}(t$_1$), ... ,ρ_{psoa}(t$_k$))
And(f$_1$ ... f$_n$)	(ρ_{psoa}(f$_1$) , ... , ρ_{psoa}(f$_n$))
Or(f$_1$ ... f$_n$)	(ρ_{psoa}(f$_1$) ; ... ; ρ_{psoa}(f$_n$))
Exists ?v$_1$ ... ?v$_m$ (φ)	ρ_{psoa}(φ)
Forall ?v$_1$ ... ?v$_m$ (φ)	ρ_{psoa}(φ)
φ :- ψ	ρ_{psoa}(φ) :- ρ_{psoa}(ψ).
?v=External(f(t$_1$...t$_k$))	is(ρ_{psoa}(?v), ρ_{psoa}(f)(ρ_{psoa}(t$_1$), ... , ρ_{psoa}(t$_k$)))
c1##c2	memterm(X,ρ_{psoa}(c2)) :- memterm(X,ρ_{psoa}(c1)).

The translation of a membership term o#c() is a binary term using the predicate memterm.[6]

The translation of a constructor function application f(t$_1$...t$_k$) results from recursively mapping the function name and all arguments into Prolog. The translation of a conjunction And(...) is a parenthesized comma-separated Prolog formula, which can be nested inside an outer formula. Similarly, the translation of a disjunction Or(...) is a semicolon-separated Prolog formula.

The translation of an existential quantification, which can only occur in queries after the normalization phase, is the translation of the quantified formula. In the translation of queries, all existentially quantified variables become free Prolog variables in the translated query, and the bindings for them are discarded in the post-processing of query answers from the Prolog engine.

The translation of an universal quantification, which can only occur in KBs, is the translation of the quantified formula, since all free variables in a Prolog clause are treated as implicitly universally quantified.

The translation of an equality formula ?V=External(f(t$_1$...t$_k$)) that equates a variable and an external function application, which evaluates the function application, results in a binary is-primitive invocation in Prolog. The first argument of is is the translated variable, which will be bound to the evaluation result of the second argument, the translated external function application in Prolog syntax, omitting the keyword External. The mapping of PSOA built-ins to Prolog built-ins is listed in Table 1.

The translation of a subclass formula c1##c2 is the same as the translation of the equivalent PSOA rule Forall ?X (?X#c2 :- ?X#c1), resulting in memterm(X,ρ_{psoa}(c2)) :- memterm(X,ρ_{psoa}(c1)).

For each Prolog clause in the translated KB, a period '.' is added to its end.

---

[6] In our earlier translation from PSOA to the first-order TPTP, the predicate name member was used. We changed the name in both PSOA2Prolog and PSOA2TPTP, because member is a built-in predicate in some Prolog engines such as SWI Prolog.

4.3   Mapping the Startup Example

The Prolog KB and query mapped from the normalized Startup Example in Section 3.6, as well as the query answer are shown in the following. The first four rules share the same premise so we only expand the premise for the first rule due to space limitation.

Translated KB:

```
memterm('_skolem1'(QX,QY,QZ,QEX,QEY,Q2,Q3,Q4,Q5),'_startup') :-
 (((memterm(Q2,'_cofounders'),tupterm(Q2,QX,QY)),
   (memterm(Q3,'_hire'),tupterm(Q3,QX,QZ)),
   (memterm(Q4,'_equity'),tupterm(Q4,QX,QEX)),
   (memterm(Q5,'_equity'),tupterm(Q5,QY,QEY)),
   (is(Q0,'+'(QEX,QEY)),'=<'(Q0,100)))).
tupterm('_skolem1'(...),QX,QY) :- (...).
sloterm('_skolem1'(...),'_employee',QX) :- (...).
memterm('_1','_cofounders').    tupterm('_1','_Ernie','_Tony').
memterm('_2','_hire').          tupterm('_2','_Ernie','_Kate').
memterm('_3','_equity').        tupterm('_3','_Ernie',50).
memterm('_4','_equity').        tupterm('_4','_Tony',30).
memterm(X,'_company') :- memterm(X,'_startup').
```

Translated Query:

```
(memterm(Q1,'_company'),tupterm(Q1,QX,QY)).
```

Query Answer in Prolog:

```
Q1='_skolem1'(...), QX='_Ernie', QY='_Tony'
```

Since the variable ?1 is existentially quantified in the normalized query, the binding for its Prolog translation Q1 will be discarded, and the bindings for QX and QY are translated back to PSOA, resulting ?X=_Ernie ?Y=_Tony.

5   Realization and Evaluation

We realized the PSOA2Prolog translator in Java,[7] based on the ANTLR v3 software.[8] It is composed of a lexer, a parser, and multiple tree walkers, generated from ANTLR using the grammars we developed. The lexer and parser read the input PSOA/PS KB or query and constructs an ANTLR abstract syntax tree (AST), which is a condensed and structured internal representation of the input. The AST is then processed by six tree walkers. Five of them implement the five normalization steps explained in Section 3 by rewriting the AST. The other one implements the mapping step in Section 4 by traversing the normalized AST and generating the translated Prolog KB/query.

---

[7] We chose Java for better reusability of components of the implementation in other applications.

[8] A language framework for constructing recognizers, interpreters, compilers and translators from grammatical descriptions. http://www.antlr3.org/

Composing PSOA2Prolog and XSB Prolog,[9] a fast Prolog engine for an ISO Prolog superset, we achieved the instantiation PSOATransRun[PSOA2Prolog, XSBProlog][10] of our PSOATransRun framework [10]. XSB Prolog does tabling of subgoals and their answers, which ensures termination and optimal efficiency for queries to a large class of programs. This new PSOATransRun instantiation provides query answering in PSOA RuleML by translating the input PSOA KB and query into Prolog, executing them in XSB Prolog and obtaining all answers, discarding bindings of existentially quantified variables in the original query, and translating the results back to PSOA/PS. In our implementation, the InterProlog Java API[11] is employed for accessing XSB Prolog from Java.

We evaluated this Prolog instantiation of PSOATransRun by a comparison to our previous TPTP instantiation PSOATransRun[PSOA2TPTP,VampirePrime]. The experiments were executed on a virtual machine with Intel Core i5-2410M 2.30GHz CPU and 4GB memory running Ubuntu 11. The first evaluation was performed on a test suite[12] of 30 test cases and 90 queries, which covers all PSOA features that we have implemented. Each test case consists of one KB, multiple queries and one user-provided answer to each query. The Prolog instantiation passed all 30 test cases, while the TPTP instantiation failed on 10 test cases which contain features that it currently does not support: external functions, subclass formulas, and IRI constants. For the 20 test cases on which both instantiations succeeded, the Prolog instantiation takes 78.6ms on average for each query while the TPTP instantiation takes 12.6ms. Here, the Prolog instantiation is slower largely due to the communication overhead between the Inter-Prolog API and the engine, which takes constant time.

To compare the performance of the two instantiations on larger KBs, we started developing size-parameterized test-case generators including chain(k) in Python. Each call of chain(k) generates a KB consisting of one fact _r0(_a1 _a2 _a3) and k rules of the form

Forall ?X ?Y ?Z (_ri(?X ?Y ?Z) :- _ri'(?X ?Y ?Z)), $i = 1, \ldots, k, i' = i - 1$.

The query is _rk(?X ?Y ?Z), which has one answer ?X=_a1 ?Y=_a2 ?Z=_a3. We measured the average query execution time of the two instantiations on ten test cases, starting with $k = 20$ and increasing in steps of 20 rules until reaching $k = 200$. The results are shown in Fig. 2.

As seen in the chart, the Prolog instantiation is slower than the TPTP instantiation when $k = 20$ and $k = 40$, due to communication overhead, breaks even at $k = 60$, and becomes faster as k further increases. At $k = 200$, the Prolog instantiation takes 38% of time used by the TPTP instantiation.

Besides being more efficient on larger test cases, the Prolog instantiation is also more efficient when similar queries are posed to the engine, because XSB Prolog can reuse the tabled solutions to subgoals of a query for future queries

---

[9] http://xsb.sourceforge.net/

[10] http://psoa.ruleml.org/transrun/0.8/local/

[11] http://interprolog.com/

[12] http://psoa2tptp.googlecode.com/svn/trunk/PSOATransRun/test/

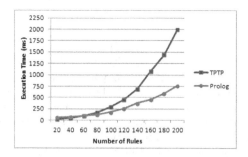

Fig. 2. Performance of PSOATransRun instantiations on `chain(k)` test cases

that use the same subgoals. We tested a special case on the `chain(200)` KB by posing the same query repeatedly. The initial query takes around 760ms while later ones take only around 70ms, which comprise mostly communication overhead.

6   Conclusions and Future Work

In this paper, we discussed the realization of PSOA2Prolog, a Java- and ANTLR-based translator from a subset of the homogeneous object-relational Web rule language PSOA RuleML (with restricted use of equality) to the relational ISO Prolog, for the interoperation and implementation of PSOA rules. PSOA2Prolog is composed of a multi-step source-to-source normalizer followed by a mapper to a pure (Horn) subset of ISO Prolog. The normalizer transforms the KB in five steps: Objectification, Skolemization, slotribution and tupribution, flattening, and rule splitting. We showed the semantics preservation of the steps. The subsequent mapper transforms the normalized PSOA KB into Prolog syntax. The PSOATransRun[PSOA2Prolog, XSBProlog] composition provides efficient query answering for PSOA RuleML. It outperforms our earlier PSOATransRun instantiation targeting TPTP on large test cases. The new interoperation and implementation platform also supports more PSOA features than the TPTP instantiation.

Future work includes versions of PSOA2Prolog that implement equality for user-defined functions and translate to an expanded set of built-ins. Further, detailed comparisons regarding the functionality and performance of comparable subsets of PSOA RuleML and (1) 'native' (not mapped) ISO Prolog and (2) F-logic, whose Flora-2 compiler also maps to XSB Prolog. Moreover, (1) exploring further relational translation targets besides TPTP and Prolog; (2) realizing translations between PSOA RuleML and object-centered languages such as N3; (3) studying subsets with interesting properties, e.g. function-free PSOA RuleML, and its connection to Datalog$^{\pm}$ [15].

References

1. Kifer, M., Lausen, G., Wu, J.: Logical foundations of object-oriented and frame-based languages. Journal of the ACM **42**(4), 741–843 (1995)
2. Yang, G., Kifer, M.: Reasoning about anonymous resources and meta statements on the semantic web. In: Spaccapietra, S., March, S., Aberer, K. (eds.) Journal on Data Semantics I. LNCS, vol. 2800, pp. 69–97. Springer, Heidelberg (2003)
3. Boley, H., Kifer, M.: RIF Basic Logic Dialect, 2nd edn (February 2013). W3C Recommendation. http://www.w3.org/TR/rif-bld
4. Boley, H.: A RIF-style semantics for RuleML-integrated positional-slotted, object-applicative rules. In: Bassiliades, N., Governatori, G., Paschke, A. (eds.) RuleML 2011 - Europe. LNCS, vol. 6826, pp. 194–211. Springer, Heidelberg (2011)
5. Yang, G., Kifer, M.: FLORA: implementing an efficient DOOD system using a tabling logic engine. In: Palamidessi, C., Moniz Pereira, L., Lloyd, J.W., Dahl, V., Furbach, U., Kerber, M., Lau, K.-K., Sagiv, Y., Stuckey, P.J. (eds.) CL 2000. LNCS (LNAI), vol. 1861, pp. 1078–1093. Springer, Heidelberg (2000)
6. Kifer, M., Yang, G., Wan, H., Zhao, C.: Flora-2: User Manual. http://flora.sourceforge.net/
7. Baral, C., Liang, S.: From knowledge represented in frame-based languages to declarative representation and reasoning via ASP. In: Brewka, G., Eiter, T., McIlraith, S.A. (eds.) KR, AAAI Press (2012)
8. ISO/IEC 13211-1: Prolog - part 1: General core (1995)
9. Deransart, P., Ed-Dbali, A., Cervoni, L.: Prolog: The Standard. Springer (1996)
10. Zou, G., Peter-Paul, R., Boley, H., Riazanov, A.: PSOATransRun: Translating and Running PSOA RuleML via the TPTP Interchange Language for Theorem Provers. In: Ait-Kaci, H., Hu, Y.J., Nalepa, G.J., Palmirani, M., Roman, D. (eds.) Proceedings of the RuleML2012@ECAI Challenge, at the 6th International Symposium on Rules, CEUR-874, August 2012
11. Polleres, A., Boley, H., Kifer, M.: RIF Datatypes and Built-ins 1.0, 2nd edn (February 2013). W3C Recommendation. http://www.w3.org/TR/2013/REC-rif-dtb-20130205/
12. Boley, H.: PSOA RuleML: integrated object-relational data and rules. In: Reasoning Web. Springer (2015)
13. Chang, C.L., Lee, R.C.T.: Symbolic Logic and mechanical Theorem Proving. Academic Press (1973)
14. Zou, G., Peter-Paul, R., Boley, H., Riazanov, A.: PSOA2TPTP: a reference translator for interoperating PSOA RuleML with TPTP reasoners. In: Bikakis, A., Giurca, A. (eds.) RuleML 2012. LNCS, vol. 7438, pp. 264–279. Springer, Heidelberg (2012)
15. Calì, A., Gottlob, G., Lukasiewicz, T.: A general Datalog-based framework for tractable query answering over ontologies. Journal of Web Semantics **14**, 57–83 (2012)

Similarity-Based Strict Equality in a Fully Integrated Fuzzy Logic Language

Pascual Julián-Iranzo[1]([✉]), Ginés Moreno[2], and Carlos Vázquez[2]

[1] Department of Technologies and Information Systems,
Castilla-La Mancha University, 13071 Ciudad Real, Spain
Pascual.Julian@uclm.es
[2] Department of Computing Systems,
Castilla-La Mancha University,
02071 Albacete, Spain
{**Gines.Moreno,Carlos.Vazquez**}**@uclm.es**

Abstract. The extension of a given similarity relation $\mathcal{R}$ between pairs of symbols of a particular alphabet to terms built with such symbols can be implemented at a very high abstract level by a set of fuzzy program rules defining a predicate called **sse**. This predicate is defined for incorporating "Similarity-based Strict Equality" into the new fuzzy logic language FASILL (acronym of "Fuzzy Aggregators and Similarity Into a Logic Language") that we have recently developed in our research group. FASILL aims to cope with implicit/explicit truth degree annotations, a great variety of connectives and unification by similarity. In this paper we show the benefits of using this sophisticated notion of equality which is somehow inspired by the so-called "Strict Equality" of functional and functional-logic languages with lazy semantics (e.g.: HASKELL and CURRY respectively) and the "Similarity-based Equality" of fuzzy logic languages using weak unification (Bousi∼Prolog, LIKELOG), a notion beyond classic syntactic unification.

Keywords: Fuzzy logic programming · Similarity relations · Equality

1 Introduction

Thanks to the high expressive power and the rule-based nature of declarative languages, their influences are growing in the design of intelligent systems and techniques related with artificial/computational intelligence, expert systems, soft-computing and so on. In particular, *Logic Programming* (LP) [12] has been widely used for problem solving and knowledge representation in the past. Nevertheless, traditional logic programming languages are not able to deal with partial truth. *Fuzzy Logic Programming* is an interesting and still growing research area that agglutinates the efforts for introducing Fuzzy Logic into Logic Programming, in order to provide these traditional languages with techniques or constructs (coming up from the mathematical background of fuzzy logic [21]) to deal with uncertainty in a natural way.

Work Supported by the EU (FEDER), and the Spanish MINECO Ministry (*Ministerio de Economía y Competitividad*) under grant TIN2013-45732-C4-2-P.

N. Bassiliades et al. (Eds.): RuleML 2015, LNCS 9202, pp. 193–207, 2015.
DOI: 10.1007/978-3-319-21542-6_13

In the last two decades, several fuzzy logic programming languages have been developed where, in essence, the classical SLD resolution principle of PROLOG [12] (based on syntactic unification) has been replaced by a fuzzy variant of itself, with the aim of dealing with partial truth and reasoning with uncertainty in a natural way. *Fuzzy logic languages* can be classified (among other criteria) regarding the emphasis they assign when fuzzifying the original unification/resolution mechanisms of PROLOG. So, whereas some approaches are able to cope with similarity/proximity relations at unification time [1,3,22,23], others extend their operational principles (maintaining syntactic unification) for managing a wide variety of fuzzy connectives and truth degrees on rules/goals beyond the simpler case of *true* or *false* [11,13,20].

Our research group has been involved both in the development of similarity-based logic programming systems and those that extend the resolution principle, as reveals the design of the Bousi~Prolog language[1] [9,10,22], where clauses cohabit with similarity/proximity equations, and the development of the FLOPER system[2], which manages fuzzy programs composed by rules richer than clauses [14–16,18]. In [6] we describe the embedding into FLOPER of the *weak unification* algorithm of Bousi~Prolog that brings to life the new fuzzy logic language FASILL. Our unifying approach is somehow inspired by [2], but in our framework we admit a wider set of connectives inside the body of program rules.

On the other hand, during the last three decades of investigation in the field of the integration of declarative programming paradigms (functional, fuzzy and logic), the scientific community of the area has produced important and advanced contributions related to both theoretical and practical aspects. However, whereas the functional and logic programming styles have been successfully integrated in the past and, as said before, more recently fuzzy logic has also been introduced into the logic programming paradigm, there is not precedent for a total integration of all these frameworks, apart from our preliminary approach presented in [17], where we proposed method combining different equality models traditionally supported by each one of these declarative paradigms. It is important to take into account that an appropriate notion of equality has a crucial importance when designing the repertoire of expressive resources for a particular declarative language. In general, when we use the term "equality" in declarative programming, there are several different meanings depending on the concrete paradigm being considered. A representative (not exhaustive) list of some cases could be:

- **Syntactic equality.** It is the simplest equality model used in the context of classical pure logic programming (as occurs with PROLOG, but also in the fuzzy logic language MALP) which is simply concerned with syntactic identity. In this sense, two element are considered "equal" if they have exactly the same syntax.

---

[1] Two different programming environments for Bousi~Prolog are available at http://dectau.uclm.es/bousi/.

[2] The tool is freely accessible from the Web site http://dectau.uclm.es/floper/.

- **Strict equality.** When considering lazy languages, both pure functional (HASKELL [4]) and integrated functional-logic (CURRY [5]) languages, this new equality notion is the only applicable in a lazy setting, mainly due to the possible presence of non terminating functions. For instance, if the evaluation of $f(a)$ does not finish then we can not say that $f(a)$ is strictly equal to itself. And, on the contrary, two terms with different syntax, such as $g(b)$ and $h(c)$, could be proved equal if they produce the same final value (for example 0) after being evaluated by rewriting or narrowing.
- **Similarity-based equality.** This model emerges as a direct consequence of several attempts for fuzzifying the original notion of syntactic equality, which are appreciable in the design of fuzzy logic languages such as LIKELOG, and Bousi~Prolog or akin (non fuzzy logic) languages like SQLP. In this case, the idea is to allow the presence of a set of what we called "similarity/proximity equations" between symbols of the alphabet generated by a given program. So, if we had a program with the equations $a \sim b = 0.5$ and $f \sim g = 0.3$, which respectively state that a is similar to b with approximation degree 0.5 and f is similar to g with approximation degree 0.3, then it would be checked that the expressions $f(a)$ and $g(b)$ are similar with a concrete truth degree (for instance 0.15, the product of their approximation degrees).

Here, we recall from [17] our original definition of SSE (*Similarity-based Strict Equality*) introduced to integrate fuzziness into a functional-logic programming language. SSE was initially modeled by means of a set of rewriting rules which fuses the last two equality versions above. The crucial idea of our method is to simply add to a given functional-logic program (written in CURRY, for instance) a set of rewriting rules defining the new symbol $\approx:\approx$ which captures similarities and thus, is implemented at a very low cost by simply performing a syntactic pre-process of programs.

In [19] we adapted such definition to the MALP framework, proving too some interesting formal properties for it. In Section 4 we will see that SSE admits a much more natural formulation by means of a set of MALP rules instead of using rewriting rules. Moreover, although this fuzzy programming style is based on pure syntactic unification, our method introduces a similarity-based equality model without altering its core, which is useful not only for testing if two ground data terms are comparable (as occurs with more complex languages -LIKELOG, Bousi~Prolog- with extended unification algorithms), but also for producing complete lists of similar terms, not achievable by LIKELOG or Bousi~Prolog. This last effect is inherited by the FASILL language, which in essence shares the syntax of MALP but uses weak unification instead of simple syntactic unification which, among other benefits, allows to cope with similarities between predicates (being this last feature forbidden in MALP even when using SSE).

The structure of this paper is as follows. Firstly, in Sections 2 and 3 we formally define and illustrate both the syntax and operational/declarative semantics of the FASILL language, initially presented in [6,8]. Next, in Section 4 we study how to define the sse fuzzy predicate by means of FASILL rules as well as the advantages of using it for producing complete lists of similar terms (instead of just a unique representative of such families) for a given goal. Finally, in Section 5 we present our conclusions and future research lines.

2   The FASILL Language

FASILL is a first order language built upon a signature Σ, that contains the elements of a countably infinite set of variables $\mathcal{V}$, function symbols and predicate symbols with an associated arity –usually expressed as pairs f/n or p/n where n represents its arity–, the implication symbol ($\leftarrow$) and a wide set of other connectives. The language combines the elements of Σ as terms, atoms, rules and formulas. A *constant* c is a function symbol with arity zero. A *term* is a variable, a constant or a function symbol f/n applied to n terms $t_1, \ldots, t_n$, and is denoted as $f(t_1, \ldots, t_n)$. We allow values of a lattice L as part of the signature Σ. Therefore, a well-formed formula can be either:

- r, if $r \in L$
- $p(t_1, \ldots, t_n)$, if $t_1, \ldots, t_n$ are terms and p/n is an n-ary predicate. This formula is called *atom*. Particularly, atoms containing no variables are called *ground atoms*, and atoms built from nullary predicates are called *propositional variables*
- $\varsigma(\mathcal{F}_1, \ldots, \mathcal{F}_n)$, if $\mathcal{F}_1, \ldots, \mathcal{F}_n$ are well-formed formulas and ς is an n-ary connective with truth function $\dot{\varsigma} : L^n \to L$

Definition 1 (Complete lattice). *A complete lattice is a partially ordered set* $(L, \leq)$ *such that every subset S of L has infimum and supremum elements. Then, it is a bounded lattice, i.e., it has bottom and top elements, denoted by $\perp$ and $\top$, respectively. L is said to be the carrier set of the lattice, and $\leq$ its ordering relation.*

The language is equipped with a set of *connectives*[3] interpreted on the lattice, including

- aggregators denoted by @, whose truth functions $\dot{@}$ fulfill the boundary condition: $\dot{@}(\top, \top) = \top$, $\dot{@}(\perp, \perp) = \perp$, and monotonicity: $(x_1, y_1) \leq (x_2, y_2) \Rightarrow \dot{@}(x_1, y_1) \leq \dot{@}(x_2, y_2)$.
- t-norms and t-conorms [21] (also named conjunctions and disjunctions, that we denote by & and |, respectively) whose truth functions fulfill the following properties:
  - Commutative: $\dot{\&}(x, y) = \dot{\&}(y, x)$ $\dot{|}(x, y) = \dot{|}(y, x)$
  - Associative: $\dot{\&}(x, \dot{\&}(y, z)) = \dot{\&}(\dot{\&}(x, y), z)$ $\dot{|}(x, \dot{|}(y, z)) = \dot{|}(\dot{|}(x, y), z)$
  - Identity element: $\dot{\&}(x, \top) = x$ $\dot{|}(x, \perp) = x$
  - Monotonicity in each argument:

$$z \leq t \Rightarrow \begin{cases} \dot{\&}(z, y) \leq \dot{\&}(t, y) & \dot{\&}(x, z) \leq \dot{\&}(x, t) \\ \dot{|}(z, y) \leq \dot{|}(t, y) & \dot{|}(x, z) \leq \dot{|}(x, t) \end{cases}$$

---

[3] Here, the connectives are binary operations but we usually generalize them with an arbitrary number of arguments.

$$\dot{\&}_P(x,y) \triangleq x * y \qquad\qquad \dot{|}_P(x,y) \triangleq x + y - xy \qquad Product$$

$$\dot{\&}_G(x,y) \triangleq \min(x,y) \qquad\qquad \dot{|}_G(x,y) \triangleq max(x,y) \qquad G\ddot{o}del$$

$$\dot{\&}_L(x,y) \triangleq \max(0, x + y - 1) \quad \dot{|}_L(x,y) \triangleq \min(x + y, 1) \quad \text{\L}ukasiewicz$$

Fig. 1. Conjunctions and disjunctions in $[0,1]$ for *Product*, *Łukasiewicz*, and *Gödel* fuzzy logics

Example 1. In this paper we use the lattice $([0,1], \leq)$, where $\leq$ is the usual ordering relation on real numbers, and three sets of connectives corresponding to the fuzzy logics of Gödel, Łukasiewicz and Product, defined in Figure 1, where labels L, G and P mean respectively *Łukasiewicz logic*, *Gödel logic* and *product logic* (with different capabilities for modeling *pessimistic*, *optimistic* and *realistic* scenarios).

It is possible to include also other connectives. For instance, the arithmetical average, defined by connective $@_{aver}$ (with truth function $\dot{@}_{aver}(x, y) \triangleq \frac{x+y}{2}$), that is a stated, easy to understand connective that does not belong to a known logic. Connectives with arities different from 2 can also be used, like the $@_{very}$ aggregation, defined by $\dot{@}_{very}(x) \triangleq x^2$, that is a unary connective.

Definition 2 (Similarity relation). *Given a domain $\mathcal{U}$ and a lattice L with a fixed t-norm $\wedge$, a similarity relation $\mathcal{R}$ is a fuzzy binary relation on $\mathcal{U}$, that is a fuzzy subset on $\mathcal{U} \times \mathcal{U}$ (namely, a mapping $\mathcal{R} : \mathcal{U} \times \mathcal{U} \to L$), such that fulfils the following properties[4]:*

- *Reflexive: $\mathcal{R}(x, x) = \top, \forall x \in \mathcal{U}$*
- *Symmetric: $\mathcal{R}(x, y) = \mathcal{R}(y, x), \forall x, y \in \mathcal{U}$*
- *Transitive: $\mathcal{R}(x, z) \geq \mathcal{R}(x, y) \wedge \mathcal{R}(y, z), \forall x, y, z \in \mathcal{U}$*

Certainly, we are interested in fuzzy binary relations on a syntactic domain. We primarily define similarities on the symbols of a signature, Σ, of a first order language. This makes possible to treat as indistinguishable two syntactic symbols which are related by a similarity relation $\mathcal{R}$. Moreover, a similarity relation $\mathcal{R}$ on the alphabet of a first order language can be extended to terms by structural induction in the usual way [23]. That is, the extension, $\hat{\mathcal{R}}$, of a similarity relation $\mathcal{R}$ is defined as:

1. let x be a variable, $\hat{\mathcal{R}}(x, x) = \mathcal{R}(x, x) = 1$,
2. let f and g be two n-ary function symbols and let $t_1, \ldots, t_n, s_1, \ldots, s_n$ be terms,

$$\hat{\mathcal{R}}(f(t_1, \ldots, t_n), g(s_1, \ldots, s_n)) = \mathcal{R}(f, g) \wedge (\bigwedge_{i=1}^{n} \hat{\mathcal{R}}(t_i, s_i))$$

---

[4] For convenience, $\mathcal{R}(x, y)$, also denoted $x\mathcal{R}y$, refers to both the syntactic expression (that symbolizes that the elements $x, y \in \mathcal{U}$ are related by $\mathcal{R}$) and the membership degree $\mu_{\mathcal{R}}(x, y)$, i.e., the affinity degree of the pair $(x, y) \in \mathcal{U} \times \mathcal{U}$ with the verbal predicate $\mathcal{R}$.

3. otherwise, the approximation degree of two terms is zero.

Analogously for atomic formulas. In this work conditional formulas of the form $C \equiv A \leftarrow B$, where A is an atom, have a special relevance (see below). For this kind of formulas we use a different and more restrictive notion of similarity than the one defined in [23]. The idea is that a conditional formula C is similar to another conditional formula C' if their heads are similar but maintain the same body. Hence, given $C \equiv A \leftarrow B$ and $C' \equiv A' \leftarrow B'$, $\hat{R}(C, C') = \hat{R}(A, A')$ if $B \equiv B'$; Otherwise $\hat{R}(C, C') = 0$.

Note that, in the sequel, we shall not make a notational distintion between the relation R and its extension $\hat{R}$.

Example 2. A similarity relation R on $U = \{vanguardist, elegant, metro, taxi, bus\}$ is defined by the following matrix:

R	vanguardist	elegant	metro	taxi	bus
vanguardist	1	0.6	0	0	0
elegant	0.6	1	0	0	0
metro	0	0	1	0.4	0.5
taxi	0	0	0.4	1	0.4
bus	0	0	0.5	0.4	1

It is easy to check that R fulfills the reflexive, symmetric and transitive properties. Particularly, using the *Gödel* conjunction as the t-norm $\wedge$, we have that: $R(taxi, metro) \geq R(metro, bus) \wedge R(bus, taxi) = 0.5 \wedge 0.4$.

Furthermore, the extension $\hat{R}$ of R determines that the terms $elegant(taxi)$ and $vanguardist(metro)$ are similar, since: $\hat{R}(elegant(taxi), vanguardist(metro)) = R(elegant, vanguardist) \wedge \hat{R}(taxi, metro) = 0.6 \wedge R(taxi, metro) = 0.6 \wedge 0.4 = 0.4$.

Definition 3 (Rule). *A rule has the form $A \leftarrow B$, where A is an atomic formula called head and B, called body, is a well-formed formula (ultimately built from atomic formulas $B_1, \ldots, B_n$, truth values of L and connectives). In particular, when the body of a rule is $r \in L$ (an element of lattice L), this rule is called fact and can be written as $A \leftarrow r$ (or simply A if $r = \top$).*

Definition 4 (Program). *A FASILL program (or simply program) is a tuple $\langle \Pi, R, L \rangle$ where Π is a set of rules, R is a similarity relation between the elements of Σ, and L is a complete lattice.*

Example 3. The set of rules Π given below, the similarity relation R of Example 2 and lattice $L = ([0, 1], \leq)$ of Example 1, form a program $P = \langle \Pi, R, L \rangle$.

$$\Pi = \begin{cases} R_1 : vanguardist(hydropolis) & \leftarrow 0.9 \\ R_2 : elegant(ritz) & \leftarrow 0.8 \\ R_3 : close(hydropolis, taxi) & \leftarrow 0.7 \\ R_4 : good\_hotel(x) & \leftarrow @_{aver}(elegant(x), @_{very}(close(x, metro))) \end{cases}$$

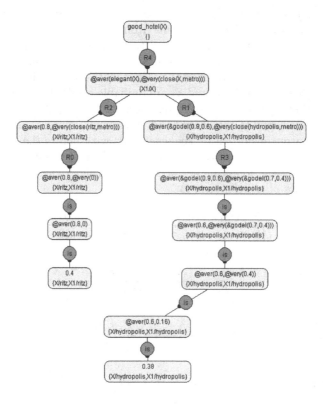

Fig. 2. An execution tree as shown by the FLOPER system

3   Operational Semantics of FASILL

Rules in a FASILL program have the same role as clauses in PROLOG (or MALP [7,13]) programs, that is, stating that a certain predicate relates some terms (the *head*) if some conditions (the *body*) hold.

As a logic language, FASILL inherits the concepts of substitution, unifier and most general unifier (mgu). Some of them are extended to cope with similarities. Concretely, following the line of Bousi~Prolog [9], the most general unifier is replaced by the concept of *weak most general unifier* (w.m.g.u.) and a weak unification algorithm is introduced to compute it. Roughly speaking, the *weak unification algorithm* states that two *expressions* (i.e, terms or atomic formulas) $f(t_1, \ldots, t_n)$ and $g(s_1, \ldots, s_n)$ weakly unify if the root symbols f and g are close with a certain degree (i.e. $\mathcal{R}(f, g) = r > \bot$) and each of their arguments t_i and s_i weakly unify. Therefore, there is a weak unifier for two expressions even if the symbols at their roots are not syntactically equal ($f \not\equiv g$).

More technically, the weak unification algorithm we are using is a reformulation/extension of the one which appears in [23] for arbitrary complete lattices. We formalize it as a transition system supported by a similarity-based unification relation "$\Rightarrow$". The unification of the expressions $\mathcal{E}_1$ and $\mathcal{E}_2$ is obtained by a state transformation sequence starting from an initial state $\langle G \equiv \{\mathcal{E}_1 \approx \mathcal{E}_2\}, id, \alpha_0 \rangle$, where id is the identity substitution and $\alpha_0 = \top$ is the supreme of $(L, \leq)$: $\langle G, id, \alpha_0 \rangle \Rightarrow \langle G_1, \theta_1, \alpha_1 \rangle \Rightarrow \cdots \Rightarrow \langle G_n, \theta_n, \alpha_n \rangle$. When the final state $\langle G_n, \theta_n, \alpha_n \rangle$, with $G_n = \emptyset$, is reached (i.e., the equations in the initial state have been solved), the expressions $\mathcal{E}_1$ and $\mathcal{E}_2$ are unifiable by similarity with w.m.g.u. θ_n and *unification degree* α_n. Therefore, the final state $\langle \emptyset, \theta_n, \alpha_n \rangle$ signals out the unification success. On the other hand, when expressions $\mathcal{E}_1$ and $\mathcal{E}_2$ are not unifiable, the state transformation sequence ends with failure (i.e., $G_n = Fail$).

The *similarity-based unification relation*, "$\Rightarrow$", is defined as the smallest relation derived by the following set of transition rules (where $Var(t)$ denotes the set of variables of a given term t)

$$\frac{\langle \{f(t_1,\ldots,t_n) \approx g(s_1,\ldots,s_n)\} \cup E, \theta, r_1 \rangle \qquad \mathcal{R}(f,g) = r_2 > \bot}{\langle \{t_1 \approx s_1, \ldots, t_n \approx s_n\} \cup E, \theta, r_1 \wedge r_2 \rangle} \; 1$$

$$\frac{\langle \{X \approx X\} \cup E, \theta, r_1 \rangle}{\langle E, \theta, r_1 \rangle} \; 2 \qquad \frac{\langle \{X \approx t\} \cup E, \theta, r_1 \rangle \qquad X \notin Var(t)}{\langle (E)\{X/t\}, \theta\{X/t\}, r_1 \rangle} \; 3$$

$$\frac{\langle \{t \approx X\} \cup E, \theta, r_1 \rangle}{\langle \{X \approx t\} \cup E, \theta, r_1 \rangle} \; 4 \qquad \frac{\langle \{X \approx t\} \cup E, \theta, r_1 \rangle \qquad X \in Var(t)}{\langle Fail, \theta, r_1 \rangle} \; 5$$

$$\frac{\langle \{f(t_1,\ldots,t_n) \approx g(s_1,\ldots,s_n)\} \cup E, \theta, r_1 \rangle \qquad \mathcal{R}(f,g) = \bot}{\langle Fail, \theta, r_1 \rangle} \; 6$$

Rule 1 decomposes two expressions and annotates the relation between the function (or predicate) symbols at their root. The second rule eliminates spurious information and the fourth rule interchanges the position of the symbols to be handled by other rules. The third and fifth rules perform an occur check of variable X in a term t. In case of success, it generates a substitution $\{X/t\}$; otherwise the algorithm ends with failure. It can also end with failure if the relation between function (or predicate) symbols in $\mathcal{R}$ is $\bot$, as stated by Rule 6.

Usually, given two expressions $\mathcal{E}_1$ and $\mathcal{E}_2$, if there is a successful transition sequence, $\langle \{\mathcal{E}_1 \approx \mathcal{E}_2\}, id, \top \rangle \Rightarrow^\star \langle \emptyset, \theta, r \rangle$, then we write that $wmgu(\mathcal{E}_1, \mathcal{E}_2) = \langle \theta, r \rangle$, being θ the *weak most general unifier* of $\mathcal{E}_1$ and $\mathcal{E}_2$, and r is their *unification degree*.

Finally note that, in general, a w.m.g.u. of two expressions $\mathcal{E}_1$ and $\mathcal{E}_2$ is not unique [23]. Certainly, the weak unification algorithm only computes a representative of a w.m.g.u. class, in the sense that, if $\theta = \{x_1/t_1, \ldots, x_n/t_n\}$ is a w.m.g.u., with degree β, then, by definition, any substitution $\theta' = \{x_1/s_1, \ldots, x_n/s_n\}$, satisfying $\mathcal{R}(s_i, t_i) > \bot$, for any $1 \leq i \leq n$, is also a w.m.g.u. with approximation degree $\beta' = \beta \wedge (\bigwedge_1^n \mathcal{R}(s_i, t_i))$, where "$\wedge$" is a selected t-norm. However, observe that, the w.m.g.u. representative computed by the weak unification algorithm is one with an approximation degree equal or greater than any other w.m.g.u. As in the case of the classical syntactic unification algorithm, our algorithm always terminates returning a success or a failure.

Next, we illustrate the weak unification process in the following example.

Example 4. Consider the lattice $L = ([0, 1], \leq)$ of Example 1 and the relation $\mathcal{R}$ of Example 2. Given terms $elegant(taxi)$ and $vanguardist(metro)$, it is possible the following weak unification process:

$$\langle\{elegant(taxi) \approx vanguardist(metro)\}, id, 1\rangle \overset{1}{\Rightarrow} \langle\{taxi \approx metro\}, id, 0.6\rangle \overset{1}{\Rightarrow}$$
$$\langle\{\}, id, 0.6 \wedge 0.4\rangle = \langle\{\}, id, 0.4\rangle$$

Also it is possible unify the terms $elegant(taxi)$ and $vanguardist(x)$, since:

$$\langle\{elegant(taxi) \approx vanguardist(x)\}, id, 1\rangle \overset{1}{\Rightarrow} \langle\{taxi \approx x\}, id, 0.6\rangle \overset{4}{\Rightarrow}$$
$$\langle\{x \approx taxi\}, id, 0.6\rangle \overset{3}{\Rightarrow} \langle\{\}, \{x/taxi\}, 0.6\rangle$$

and the substitution $\{x/taxi\}$ is their w.m.g.u. with unification degree 0.6.

In order to describe the procedural semantics of the FASILL language, in the following we denote by $\mathcal{C}[A]$ a formula where A is a sub-expression (usually an atom) which occurs in the –possibly empty– context $\mathcal{C}[]$ whereas $\mathcal{C}[A/A']$ means the replacement of A by A' in the context $\mathcal{C}[]$. Moreover, $Var(s)$ denotes the set of distinct variables occurring in the syntactic object s and $\theta[Var(s)]$ refers to the substitution obtained from θ by restricting its domain to $Var(s)$. In the next definition, we always consider that A is the selected atom in a goal $\mathcal{Q}$ and L is the complete lattice associated to Π.

Definition 5 (Computational Step). *Let $\mathcal{Q}$ be a goal and let σ be a substitution. The pair $\langle\mathcal{Q}; \sigma\rangle$ is a state. Given a program $\langle\Pi, \mathcal{R}, L\rangle$ and a t-norm $\wedge$ in L, a computation is formalized as a state transition system, whose transition relation $\leadsto$ is the smallest relation satisfying these rules:*

1) Successful step (denoted as $\overset{SS}{\leadsto}$):

$$\frac{\langle\mathcal{Q}[A], \sigma\rangle \qquad A' \leftarrow \mathcal{B} \in \Pi \qquad wmgu(A, A') = \langle\theta, r\rangle}{\langle\mathcal{Q}[A/\mathcal{B} \wedge r]\theta, \sigma\theta\rangle} \text{ SS}$$

2) Failure step (denoted as $\overset{FS}{\leadsto}$):

$$\frac{\langle\mathcal{Q}[A], \sigma\rangle \qquad \nexists A' \leftarrow \mathcal{B} \in \Pi : wmgu(A, A') = \langle\theta, r\rangle, r > \bot}{\langle\mathcal{Q}[A/\bot], \sigma\rangle} \text{ FS}$$

3) Interpretive step (denoted as $\overset{IS}{\leadsto}$):

$$\frac{\langle\mathcal{Q}[@(r_1, \ldots, r_n)]; \sigma\rangle \qquad \dot{@}(r_1, \ldots, r_n) = r_{n+1}}{\langle\mathcal{Q}[@(r_1, \ldots, r_n)/r_{n+1}]; \sigma\rangle} \text{ IS}$$

A *derivation* is a sequence of arbitrary length $\langle Q; id \rangle \rightsquigarrow^* \langle Q'; \sigma \rangle$. As usual, rules are renamed apart. When $Q' = r \in L$, the state $\langle r; \sigma \rangle$ is called a *fuzzy computed answer* (f.c.a.) for that derivation.

Example 5. Let $\mathcal{P} = \langle \Pi, \mathcal{R}, L \rangle$ be the program from Example 3. It is possible to perform this derivation with fuzzy computed answer $\langle 0, 4, \{x/ritz\} \rangle$ for $\mathcal{P}$ and goal $Q = good\_hotel(x)$:

$$D1 : \langle good\_hotel(x), id \rangle \qquad\qquad \overset{R4}{\underset{\sim}{SS}}$$

$$\langle @_{aver}(elegant(x), @_{very}(close(x, metro))), \{x_1/x\} \rangle \quad \overset{R2}{\underset{\sim}{SS}}$$

$$\langle @_{aver}(0.8, @_{very}(close(ritz, metro))), \{x_1/ritz, x/ritz\} \rangle \quad \underset{\sim}{FS}$$

$$\langle @_{aver}(0.8, @_{very}(0)), \{x_1/ritz, x/ritz\} \rangle \quad \underset{\sim}{IS}$$

$$\langle @_{aver}(0.8, 0), \{x_1/ritz, x/ritz\} \rangle \quad \underset{\sim}{IS}$$

$$\langle 0.4, \{x_1/ritz, x/ritz\} \rangle$$

This derivation corresponds to the leftmost branch in the tree of Figure 3 where we can also observe a second f.c.a. (that is, $\langle 0.38, \{x/hydropolis\} \rangle$) for the same goal in the rightmost branch of such tree.

	$\mathcal{I_P}$
vanguardist(hydropolis)	0.9
vanguardist(ritz)	0.6
elegant(hydropolis)	0.6
elegant(ritz)	0.8
close(hydropolis, taxi)	0.7
close(hydropolis, metro)	0.4
close(hydropolis, bus)	0.5
good_hotel(hydropolis)	0.38
good_hotel(ritz)	0.4

Moreover, as we explain in a detailed way in [8], the declarative semantics of the program in our running example is defined as the least fuzzy Herbrand model $\mathcal{I_P}$ given in the adjoint table (where the interpretations for all atoms not included on it are assumed to be 0).

In the previous example, we can see in the rightmost branch of the tree in Figure 3 that for obtaining the second solution $\langle 0.38, \{x/hydropolis\} \rangle$ it is necessary to exploit the similarities between predicates **vanguardist** and **elegant** as well as between constants **taxi** and **metro**. This effect is achieved by the weak unification technique used in FASILL computations, but in other frameworks based on syntactic unification, as occurs with the MALP language, some interesting results in this sense can even be achieved by using a sophisticated notion of equality as the one we are going to study in the next section.

4   Similarity-Based Strict Equality for MALP and FASILL

A classical, but even nowadays challenging research topic in declarative programming, consists in the design of powerful notions of "equality", as occurs with the flexible (fuzzy) and efficient (lazy) framework that we have initially proposed in [17] for hybrid declarative languages amalgamating fuzzy and functional-logic

$$\text{sse}(c,d) \leftarrow \mathcal{R}(c,d)$$
$$\text{sse}(f(x_1,..,x_n), g(y_1,..,y_n)) \leftarrow \mathcal{R}(f,g) \ \& \ \text{sse}(x_1, y_1) \ \& \ ... \& \ \text{sse}(x_n, y_n)$$

Fig. 3. Fuzzy Program Rules defining "Similarity-based Strict Equality"

features. The crucial idea is that, by extending at a very low cost the notion of "strict equality" typically used in lazy functional (HASKELL) and functional-logic (CURRY) languages, and by relaxing it to the more flexible one of similarity-based equality used in modern fuzzy-logic programming languages (such as LIKELOG and Bousi∼Prolog), similarity relations can be successfully treated while mathematical functions are lazily evaluated at execution time. The adaptation of this equality model to MALP was performed in [19], where we revisited our initial notion of SSE (*Similarity-based Strict Equality*) in order to re-model it at a very high abstraction level by means of a simple set of MALP rules. The resulting technique served as a preliminary attempt for coping with a given similarity relation $\mathcal{R}$ (in fact, the behavior of the new fuzzy predicate sse mirrors the extended similarity relation on terms $\hat{\mathcal{R}}$) even when the operational semantics of MALP relies on the purely syntactic unification method of PROLOG.

We start by recasting, from [19], our initial MALP-based model of SSE which is defined in Figure 3 for synthesizing a set of fuzzy program rules denoted by $\Pi^{\mathcal{R}}_{sse}$ from a given similarity relation $\mathcal{R}$. In the figure c and d are constants symbols (i.e., functions with arity 0) and f and g are function symbols with the same arity n. Note that the rules in Figure 3 are actually "rule schemes" and there is a rule for each pair of constants or functions symbols (with the same arity) related by the similarity relation $\mathcal{R}$ with an approximation degree greater than $\bot$. In order to illustrate our definition, we can consider again the similarity relation provided in our running example for generating the following nine rules (all they are simply facts since only constant symbols are compared) which conforms $\Pi^{\mathcal{R}}_{sse}$:

```
sse(taxi,taxi)<-1.      sse(taxi,bus)<-0.4.    sse(taxi,metro)<-0.4.
sse(bus,taxi)<-0.4.     sse(bus,bus)<- 1.      sse(bus,metro)<-0.5.
sse(metro,taxi)<- 0.4.  sse(metro,bus)<-0.5.   sse(metro,metro)<-1.
```

Observe that the second pattern of Figure 3 is not used in our case, since in particular, the following four rules:

```
sse(elegant(X),elegant(Y)) <- 1 & sse(X,Y).
sse(elegant(X),vanguardist(Y)) <- 0.6 & sse(X,Y).
sse(vanguardist(X),elegant(Y)) <- 0.6 & sse(X,Y).
sse(vanguardist(X),vanguardist(Y)) <- 1 & sse(X,Y).
```

does not belong to $\Pi^{\mathcal{R}}_{sse}$ due to the fact that elegant and vanguardist are not function symbols (useful for building data terms) but predicate symbols (used for generating atoms).

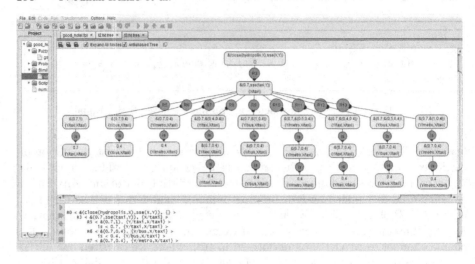

Fig. 4. The FLOPER system drawing a tree for a goal with *sse*

Now it is possible to execute with a MALP style (i.e., based on simple syntactic unification) the goal `sse(taxi,metro)` which produces the obvious fuzzy computed answer `<0.4,{}>`. Moreover, for goal `sse(taxi,X)` we obtain the three desired f.c.a.'s `<1,{X/taxi}>`, `<0.4,{X/bus}>` and `<0.4,{X/metro}>`, whereas for goal `sse(X,Y)` the system produces nine answers, each one of them associated to the use of a different rule in $\Pi^{\mathcal{R}}_{sse}$. This behavior is reflected by the following results, which establish a set of interesting properties enjoyed by our definition as formally proved in [19] (while the first claim reveals the ability of our technique for testing similar terms, the second and third ones confirm its capability for generating all pairs of similar ground terms).

Theorem 1. *Let t and t' be two ground terms, x and x' two variables, L a lattice of truth degrees, $\mathcal{R}$ a similarity relation and $\Pi^{\mathcal{R}}_{sse}$ the set of MALP rules defining predicate sse w.r.t. $\mathcal{R}$. Then, the following claims hold:*

1. *$\hat{\mathcal{R}}(t,t') = s$ iff $\langle s, id \rangle$ is a f.c.a. for goal $sse(t,t')$ w.r.t. $\Pi^{\mathcal{R}}_{sse}$.*
2. *$\hat{\mathcal{R}}(t,t') = s$ iff $\langle s, \{x/t'\} \rangle$ is a f.c.a. for goal $sse(t,x)$ w.r.t. $\Pi^{\mathcal{R}}_{sse}$.*
3. *$\hat{\mathcal{R}}(t,t') = s$ iff $\langle s, \{x/t, x'/t'\} \rangle$ is a f.c.a. for goal $sse(x,x')$ w.r.t. $\Pi^{\mathcal{R}}_{sse}$.*

Let us introduce the following notation that we use in the rest of this section. We will denote a MALP program by the tuple $\langle \Pi, L \rangle$, where Π is a set of program rules and L a lattice of truth degrees. Since, from a syntactic point of view, a FASILL program is a MALP program extended with a similarity relation $\mathcal{R}$, a FASILL program will be denoted by the tuple $\langle \Pi, \mathcal{R}, L \rangle$. Note that in a FASILL program the similarity relation $\mathcal{R}$ is used during the weak unification process (for computing weak most general unifiers), whereas MALP is simply based on syntactic unification, which does not require an underlying similarity relation. On the other hand, when we extend the set of rules of a program with the ones appearing in $\Pi_{sse}^{\mathcal{R}}$, we use $\langle \Pi \cup \Pi_{sse}^{\mathcal{R}}, L \rangle$ and $\langle \Pi \cup \Pi_{sse}^{\mathcal{R}}, \mathcal{R}, L \rangle$ for representing the corresponding MALP and FASILL programs.

Consider now the goal close(hydropolis,metro), whose execution (based on weak unification) w.r.t. the FASILL program $\langle \Pi, \mathcal{R}, L \rangle$ produces the desired result <0.4,{}>, using the third rule close(hydropolis,taxi)<- 0.7 together with the fact that the similarity relation has the entry $\mathcal{R}$(taxi,metro)= 0.4. However, this solution is not reached in the MALP program $\langle \Pi, L \rangle$ since this last similarity is not used by the syntactic unification algorithm of MALP. Fortunately, we can take profit of our set of rules $\Pi_{sse}^{\mathcal{R}}$ for executing the slightly modified goal close(hydropolis,X) & sse(X,Y) w.r.t. the augmented MALP program $\langle \Pi \cup \Pi_{sse}^{\mathcal{R}}, L \rangle$ which palliates our problem by answering the desired f.c.a. <0.4,{X/taxi,Y/metro}>. However, it is important to note that the use of $\Pi_{sse}^{\mathcal{R}}$ in MALP not always simulates the effects achieved by FASILL thanks to the use of weak unification, since those computations involving similarities between predicate symbols are avoided in MALP. As an example, goal vanguardist(ritz) is solved in the FASILL program $\langle \Pi, \mathcal{R}, L \rangle$ with f.c.a. <0.6,{}> (by exploiting at weak unification time the entry $\mathcal{R}$(vanguardist,elegant)= 0.6), but the same goal fails in our two MALP programs $\langle \Pi, L \rangle$ and $\langle \Pi \cup \Pi_{sse}^{\mathcal{R}}, L \rangle$.

Our last example is intended to illustrate that the use of $\Pi_{sse}^{\mathcal{R}}$ rules is useful not only in an augmented MALP program $\langle \Pi \cup \Pi_{sse}^{\mathcal{R}}, L \rangle$ but also in an augmented FASILL program $\langle \Pi \cup \Pi_{sse}^{\mathcal{R}}, \mathcal{R}, L \rangle$. So, let us consider now the goal close(hydropolis,X), for which MALP computes the single solution <0.7,X/taxi> w.r.t. $\langle \Pi, L \rangle$. In order to exploit the similarities between the three constants in our program, we can use $\Pi_{sse}^{\mathcal{R}}$ with goal close(hydropolis,X) & sse(X,Y) w.r.t. $\langle \Pi \cup \Pi_{sse}^{\mathcal{R}}, L \rangle$, for which we obtain the three desired answers <0.7,{X/taxi}>, <0.4,{X/bus}> and <0.4,{X/metro}>. These answers could not be achieved by the FASILL program $\langle \Pi, \mathcal{R}, L \rangle$ when executing the original goal close(hydropolis,X), since FASILL acts as MALP in this case, thus returning again the single solution <0.7,X/taxi>. Fortunately, we can run close(hydropolis,X) & sse(X,Y) w.r.t. the augmented FASILL program $\langle \Pi \cup \Pi_{sse}^{\mathcal{R}}, \mathcal{R}, L \rangle$ for obtaining the desired set of solutions, as shown in Figure 4, where some answers are redundant because they are repeated or subsumed by others (for instance, the f.c.a. <0.4,{Y/taxi,X/taxi}> occurs twice, and it is also subsumed by the better f.c.a. <0.7,{Y/taxi,X/taxi}>). We are nowadays improving the operational machinery of FASILL for introducing thresholding techniques devoted to prune redundant solutions or directly avoiding the generation of answers with degraded truth degrees below a given threshold.

5   Conclusions and Future Work

FASILL (acronym of "Fuzzy Aggregators and Similarity Into a Logic Language") is a fuzzy logic programming language with implicit/explicit truth degree annotations, a great variety of connectives and unification by similarity. In [6,8] we have recently provided the syntax, operational/declarative semantics and implementation issues[5] of this language which in essence integrates and extends features coming from MALP (*Multi-Adjoint Logic Programming*, a fuzzy logic language with explicitly annotated rules and based on syntactic unification) and Bousi~Prolog (which uses a weak unification algorithm and is well suited for flexible query answering). Hence, it properly manages similarity and truth degrees in a single framework combining the expressive benefits of both languages. In this work we have focused on the integration into FASILL of a notion of equality called SSE(*Similarity-based Strict Equality*) which is especially well-suited for the new language.

Since MALP and FASILL program rules share the same syntax, the set of rules defining the fuzzy predicate sse in both languages coincide, but the benefits achieved in each language are rather different, mainly due to the fact that the underlying unification algorithms used on their operational principles are different too. The main advantage of using sse in FASILL goals and bodies of program rules is that the system is able to produce a family of similar answers instead of just a representative of them as the weak unification algorithm usually do. In order to avoid the generation of redundant solutions that often occurs when evaluating some kind of goals containing variable symbols, we are nowadays implementing at a low level (directly on the core of the procedural mechanism of FASILL) different thresholding techniques for dynamically avoiding the generation of answers which are repeated, subsumed by others, or directly are useless because their associated truth degrees fall down below a cut value provided by users.

References

1. Arcelli, F.: Likelog for flexible query answering. Soft Computing **7**(2), 107–114 (2002)
2. Caballero, R., Rodríguez-Artalejo, M., Romero-Díaz, C.A.: A transformation-based implementation for clp with qualification and proximity. Theory and Practice of Logic Programming **14**(1), 1–63 (2014)
3. Formato, F., Gerla, G., Sess, M.I.: Similarity-based unification. Fundamenta Informaticae **41**(4), 393–414 (2000)
4. Hall, C.V., Hammond, K., Partain, W., Peyton Jones, S.L., Wadler, P.: The glasgow haskell compiler: a retrospective. In: Launchbury, J., Sansom, P.M. (Eds.) Functional Programming, Workshops in Computing, pp. 62–71. Springer (1992)
5. Hanus, M. (ed.): Curry: An Integrated Functional Logic Language (2003). http://www.informatik.uni-kiedl.de/~mh/curry/
6. Julián Iranzo, P., Moreno, G., Penabad, J., Vázquez, C.: A fuzzy logic programming environment for managing similarity and truth degrees. In: Escobar, S. (Eds.) Proc. of XIV Jornadas Sobre Programación y Lenguajes, PROLE 2015, vol. 173, pp. 71–86. EPTCS, Cádiz (2015)

---

[5] The last version of the FLOPER system which copes with similarity relations can be freely downloaded from http://dectau.uclm.es/floper/?q=sim and it can be tested on-line through http://dectau.uclm.es/floper/?q=sim/test.

7. Julián, P., Moreno, G., Penabad, J.: On the declarative semantics of multi-adjoint logic programs. In: Cabestany, J., Sandoval, F., Prieto, A., Corchado, J.M. (eds.) IWANN 2009, Part I. LNCS, vol. 5517, pp. 253–260. Springer, Heidelberg (2009)
8. Julián-Iranzo, P., Moreno, G., Penabad, J., Vázquez, C.: A declarative semantics for a fuzzy logic language managing similarities and truth degrees. In: Submitted to the 13th Int. Work-Conference on Artificial Neural Networks, IWANN 2015 (2015)
9. Julián-Iranzo, P., Rubio-Manzano, C.: A declarative semantics for Bousi~Prolog. In: Proc. of 11th Int. ACM SIGPLAN Conf. on Principles and Practice of Declarative Programming, PPDP 2009, Coimbra, Portugal, pp. 149–160. ACM (2009)
10. Julián-Iranzo, P., Rubio-Manzano, C.: An efficient fuzzy unification method and its implementation into the Bousi~Prolog system. In: Proc. of the 2010 IEEE Int. Conference on Fuzzy Systems, pp. 1–8 (2010)
11. Kifer, M., Subrahmanian, V.S.: Theory of generalized annotated logic programming and its applications. Journal of Logic Programming **12**, 335–367 (1992)
12. Lloyd, J.W.: Foundations of Logic Programming. Springer-Verlag, Heidelberg (1987)
13. Medina, J., Ojeda-Aciego, M., Vojtáš, P.: Similarity-based Unification: a multi-adjoint approach. Fuzzy Sets and Systems **146**, 43–62 (2004)
14. Morcillo, P.J., Moreno, G., Penabad, J., Vázquez, C.: A practical management of fuzzy truth-degrees using FLOPER. In: Dean, M., Hall, J., Rotolo, A., Tabet, S. (eds.) RuleML 2010. LNCS, vol. 6403, pp. 20–34. Springer, Heidelberg (2010)
15. Morcillo, P.J., Moreno, G.: Programming with fuzzy logic rules by using the FLOPER tool. In: Bassiliades, N., Governatori, G., Paschke, A. (eds.) RuleML 2008. LNCS, vol. 5321, pp. 119–126. Springer, Heidelberg (2008)
16. Morcillo, P.-J., Moreno, G., Penabad, J., Vázquez, C.: Declarative traces into fuzzy computed answers. In: Bassiliades, N., Governatori, G., Paschke, A. (eds.) RuleML 2011 - Europe. LNCS, vol. 6826, pp. 170–185. Springer, Heidelberg (2011)
17. Moreno, G.: Similarity-based equality with lazy evaluation. In: Hüllermeier, E., Kruse, R., Hoffmann, F. (eds.) IPMU 2010. CCIS, vol. 80, pp. 108–117. Springer, Heidelberg (2010)
18. Moreno, G., Vázquez, C.: Fuzzy logic programming in action with floper. Journal of Software Engineering and Applications **7**, 237–298 (2014)
19. Moreno, G., Penabad, J., Vázquez, C.: Fuzzy logic rules modeling similarity-based strict equality. In: Proc. of the 2014 Federated Conference on Computer Science and Information Systems, Warsaw, Poland, September 7–10, pp. 119–128 (2014)
20. Muñoz-Hernández, S., Ceruelo, V.P., Strass, H.: Rfuzzy: Syntax, semantics and implementation details of a simple and expressive fuzzy tool over prolog. Information Sciences **181**(10), 1951–1970 (2011)
21. Nguyen, H.T., Walker, E.A.: A First Course in Fuzzy Logic. Chapman & Hall/CRC, Boca Ratón (2000)
22. Rubio-Manzano, C., Julián-Iranzo, P.: A fuzzy linguistic prolog and its applications. Journal of Intelligent and Fuzzy Systems **26**(3), 1503–1516 (2014)
23. Sessa, M.I.: Approximate reasoning by similarity-based sld resolution. Theoretical Computer Science **275**(1–2), 389–426 (2002)

Building a Hybrid Reactive Rule Engine
for Relational and Graph Reasoning

Mario Fusco[1]([✉]), Davide Sottara[2]([✉]), István Ráth[3], and Mark Proctor[1,4]

[1] A Division of Red Hat Inc., JBoss, Milan, Italy
mfusco@redhat.com
http://www.jboss.org
[2] Department of Biomedical Informatics, Arizona State University, Tempe, AZ, USA
davide.sottara@asu.edu
[3] Department of Measurement and Information Systems,
Budapest University of Technology and Economics, Budapest, Hungary
rath@mit.bme.hu
[4] Department of Electrical and Electronic Engineering,
Imperial College London, London, UK
m.proctor13@imperial.ac.uk

Abstract. The relational syntax used by Rete rule engines is cumbersome when traversing paths compared to hierarchical or Object-Oriented languages like XPath or Java. Searching the join space for references has performance implications. This paper proposes reactive rule engine enhancements to support both relational and graph reasoning, with improvements at both the language and the engine level.

The language will contain both relational and graph constructs that can be used together, within the same rule. The implementation targets Drools, a Java open-source Rete based rule engine, but could be applied to any Rete engine and language of a similar class.

Examples are used to describe the language extensions and discuss their behaviour. Benchmarking is used to compare the performance of the two reasoning approaches in different scenarios and provide recommendations on how to optimize a rule base.

Keywords: Production rule systems · Rule engine · Rete · Relational · Graph · Reasoning · Xpath · Drools · Java

1 Introduction

Rete [6] based Production Rule Systems used to build reactive systems that provide a relational view over a changing data set. Rete does not require a full recomputation when any of that data changes, because it uses state saving techniques to process those changes incrementally. These systems use networks of joins for relational reasoning over the data. This requires a flat data model, like tables in a relational database. For Object-Oriented (OO) systems like Java, that rely on graph-like data structures, the model must be flattened before the rule engine is able to reason over it. Modern rule engines, like Drools' Rete-OO, are able to directly use Java objects as facts, filtering by polymorphic types, performing

© Springer International Publishing Switzerland 2015
N. Bassiliades et al. (Eds.): RuleML 2015, LNCS 9202, pp. 208–222, 2015.
DOI: 10.1007/978-3-319-21542-6_14

relational joins across properties and reacting to changes on properties. However, Drools can only access direct properties of an inserted object: it cannot traverse the object graph, nor can it react to nested property changes. Because of this limitation, developers must use a flat data model, insert all objects of the graph and use a relational syntax to search the candidate matches to navigate a reference. This work is redundant if the object graph maintains the references between edges (relationships) and nodes (objects) explicitly.

This paper addresses the gap between the relational and graph domains in three ways. Firstly, additional syntactical constructs are proposed that provide navigation and express constraints on the graph in a succinct way. The inspiration for this notation comes from XPath and has been introduced to simplify the dereferencing and navigation of one-to-many relationships. The syntax supports variable binding of path segments, for named back referencing as well as the normal XPath relative back referencing syntax. This allows the graph statements to be expressed in small chunks, where those chunks can be used inside of existing rule constructs such as negation and aggregation functions. The variable bindings can be used as arguments for existing query constructs, which already support unification, recursion and transitive closures.

Secondly, a new Rete node, a `From` node, is proposed and purposed to navigate references, iterate collections and propagate the results to the child Rete node(s). Thirdly, a mechanism is introduced which allows the rule engine to react to updates on any nested property that is accessed through this graph syntax. The relational and graph syntactical constructs can be used together in the same rule, creating a truly hybrid reasoning system for relational and graph reasoning.

The implementation has been done as an extension in Drools - at both the syntax and engine level. However it could be implemented in any Rete based engine of a similar class - which has support for negation, recursive queries with transitive closure support, aggregations and sub-networks. Benchmarks were created to assess the performance impact on rules executed against a graph-based business object model.

2 · Background

The Rete Algorithm was created by Charles Forgy (1979) to efficiently and incrementally match a set of rules against a set of facts. Rete eagerly materializes all relational joins and eventually the rule instantiations for all rules and then selects a rule instantiation for execution using a conflict resolution strategy. It has a simple recognize and react cycle that is driven by data insertions, updates or deletes. During the pattern matching stage data is inserted and propagated through a discrimination network as "tokens". The first part of the network contains single input, multiple output alpha nodes, which apply literal constraint filters. The second part of the network contains beta nodes, two input - multiple output nodes, that perform joins. The left input of a beta node is another beta node, the right input is an alpha node. When a token enters the right input from the alpha network, it is added to the nodes memory and then it attempts to join with each of the tokens in the right memory. For each successful join, a new token is formed by combining the left and right token, which is then propagated to the left input of each child beta node.

As the token enters each left input, it is added to the node's memory. It then attempts to join with each token stored in the right input memory. This produces a recursive descent evaluation model of the nodes and their tokens. During the execution phase, the engine will fire the first selected rule instantiation; if there are additional data inserts, updates or deletes, they will result in an another pattern matching cycle. Rules with the same constraints will share Rete nodes, collapsing the matching space - this is the reason why alpha and beta nodes may have more than one output.

3   Introducing OOPath

Due to the nature of the RETE algorithm, production rule languages are SQL-like in nature, exposing constructs derived from relational algebra. A simple example can be used to illustrate the issues of using such a language when working with a graph-oriented model. Assume a domain model consisting of a Student who has a Plan of study: a Plan can have zero or more Exams and an Exam zero or more Grades. To reason over this domain model, a relational language has to perform several joins on these properties. Consider the example rule in Listing 1.1, which applies only to grades obtained for exams belonging to the "Big Data" course[1].

Listing 1.1. Example Rule (relational)

```
rule R1 when
    $student : Student()
    $plan : Plan( owner == $student.name )
    $exam : Exam( plan == $plan.code, course == "Big Data" )
    $grade : Grade( exam == $exam.code )
then
    // RHS
end
```

In this example, to materialize the rule instantiations, all objects must be inserted and the engine must search the join space for each of the relations. To achieve this, N being the number of items in the working memory and P the number of patterns, the traditional Rete algorithm has to perform a number of relational joins that grows as N^P. Indexing, when supported, can help to improve the performances of the join operations, but requires additional memory occupation. If the model was not flattened and the graph representation retained, it would be possible to directly traverse the references, instead of searching the join space. This can be achieved by extending Rete with a new node, that is able to use the references in the domain model. The is called a From node. The node,

---

[1] Rules are written using Drools' technical language DRL.

in general, evaluates a given expression and the pattern iterates over and filters the returned results; here **From** means the pattern's data source is **From** a data source other than the working memory. Conceptually, a **From** node is a special type of **Beta** node whose left parent is determined by the preceding pattern, while its (virtual) right parent is the data source itself. The node embeds the "alpha" constraints to be applied to the values returned by the source as well as the usual "beta" constraints. The right source is evaluated, and its results joined, whenever a token propagates from the left parent. Each item in the iteration that is not blocked by the constraints in the node produces a new token that is propagated to the child node(s) for further processing. This definition of **From** is very general and can be used as an extension point for the engine. In this paper, however, we will focus on the use of **From** to navigate the relationships in an object graph, assuming the data source is a member of a previously matched object. Listing 1.2 updates the first example given in Listing 1.1 to use the **From** construct to traverse the reference between plan and exams, instead of searching for it in the join space.

Listing 1.2. Example Rule (**from** version)

```
rule R2 when
    $student: Student( $plan: plan )
    $exam: Exam( course == "Big Data" ) from $plan.exams
    $grade: Grade() from $exam.grades
then /* RHS */ end
```

This change also has the advantage that only the Student needs to be inserted into the working memory, while the **Plan**, **Exam** and **Grade** can remain outside of it and be reached by simply browsing the references among them. Notice also that the combination of bindings ($plan) and the using the expression ($plan.exams) allows for the elimination of the **Plan** pattern. However, the implementation of the **From** node is non-reactive: the engine will not respond to changes to **Plan**, **Exam** or **Grade** even if those objects are updated explicitly. In fact, the evaluation of the expression is driven by a left input propagation. Despite the reduction in the number of patterns, the rule in Listing 1.2 is still fairly verbose. By borrowing ideas from XPath, the syntax can be made even more succinct, as XPath has a compact notation for navigating through related elements while handling collections and filtering constraints. To this end, we propose a new construct, called OOPath, which is based on five key aspects.

1. When OOPath is used on the inside of patterns it must have a syntax that allows the parser to differentiate it from other constraints within the pattern.
2. When OOPath is used on the outside of patterns, it must use a syntax that allows the parser to differentiate it other rule constructs.
3. It must support both the iteration and the direct access to the collection property, when dealing with multiple cardinality relationships.
4. It must support inline constraints, allowing objects to be filtered in the traversed collections.
5. It must support named back referencing, in addition to an XPath-like relative back referencing.

Satisfying the first and fourth requirements is straightforward by following standard XPath conventions. An OOPath expression starts with a / and uses curly brackets (instead of the square ones used by XPath) to add constraints at any step (also referred to as a segment) of the dereferencing chain. Conversely, in OOPath notation square brackets are used to refer to the position of a specific item. The second requirement will need a ';' delimiter at the end - this use case must have a variable name in the first segment, acting as the root. The third requires an additional symbol, a ., that performs dereferencing instead of iteration. The fifth borrows from existing Drools syntax for binding of fields, where the field name is prefixed with a variable followed by a colon, 'var :'. That named variable can then be used in any constraints that come after, either in the same OOPath statement or in other rule constructs below. Shallow unification of variables is also supported by combining the colon with an equals ":=". Constraints can back referenced through these variables, or use the standard XPath double dot and slash notation for relative back reference '../../'. The relative back referencing only works within the same OOPath statement, where as named variables can work across other OOPath statements, as well as other standard rule constructs.

The OOPath syntax requires are summarised as:

1. It has to start with /.
2. It can dereference a property of an object with the . operator.
3. It can dereference a property of an object using the / operator. If a collection is returned, it will iterate over the values in the collection;
4. While traversing referenced objects it can filter away those not satisfying one or more constraints, expressed as predicate expressions between square brackets.
5. Items can also be accessed by their index

Formally, the core grammar of an OOpath expression can be defined in EBNF notation as Listing 1.3:

Listing 1.3. OOpath notation

```
OOPExpr = " / " OOPSegment { ( " / " | " . " ) OOPSegment } ;
OOPSegment = [ID ( " : " | " := " )] ID [ " [ " Number " ] " ] [ " { "
   Constraints " } " ];
```

The constraints follow the normal sub-grammar of the rule language such as DRL. Using this new notation, it is now possible to rewrite the Rule in Listing 1.2 in a more concise way, presented in Listing 1.4:

Listing 1.4. Rule v3

```
rule R3 when
    Student( $grade: /plan/exams{course == "Big Data"}/grades )
then
    // RHS...
end
```

The compilation of this OOPath expression uses a `From` node for each OOPath segment, effectively making the RETE networks for Listings 1.2 and 1.4 equivalent, as shown in Figure 1. The terms `shallow` facts and `deep` facts can now be used to differentiate between objects used for relational reasoning and graphs. A `deep` fact, in particular, is an object in the graph accessed through references further down than a "root", shallow object in the working memory.

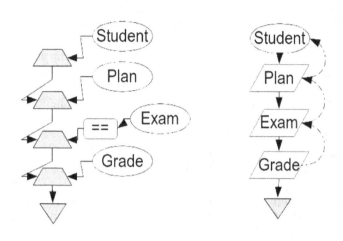

Fig. 1. RETE fragments for Listing 1.1 and Listing 1.2/1.4

OOPath syntax, like XPath, also supports indexed access. OOPath indexes are 0-based to adhere to Java convention, compared to XPath 1-based. The former pattern could be modified to only access the first `Exam` in each `Plan`, see Listing 1.5:

Listing 1.5. Accessing an item by index

```
Student( $grade: /plan/exams[0]{ course == "Big Data"}/grades )
```

Drools also supports polymorphic types with an inline match and cast construct using '`#`'. All collection access will infer types from Java generics, if they exist. For instance it will be possible to modify the pattern used in Listing 1.4 to accept only the `Exams` that are instances of the `PracticalExam` class and where its `lab` property is "hazard safe", see Listing 1.6. Note that the `lab` property is only available on the class `PracticalExam` and not on its superclass `Exam`. This allows Drools and OOPath to be both polymorphic and type safe at all times.

Listing 1.6. Filtering items of a given type

```
Student( $grade: /plan/exams{ this#PracticalExam.lab == "
   hazard safe",  course == "Material Explosions"}/grades )
```

3.1   Advanced Rule Constructs

Because OOPath is purely a syntactic feature, internally it is compiled into a (sequence of) Rete nodes that propagates tokens. So, it can be used with all of the existing constructs for more advanced rules. This section covers some of these constructs, along with examples of them being used with graphs and the OOPath graph notation. Note all of these constructs already exist in Drools, as part of its existing relational rule language.

Drools already features queries that support shallow unification[2], recursion and transitive closures. As the OOPath bindings are treated like normal variables, they can be used in queries. So, graph-oriented rules can also leverage unification, recursion and transitive closures. Drools patterns and queries support a syntax that provides functionality similar to that which is defined in RuleML "Position-Slotted Language" POSL [2]. Arguments can be named or positional. Positional arguments must come first and be delimited with a semi colon at the end. Positional arguments are always unified, compared to named arguments which can be bound ':' or unified ':='.

Negation in Drools creates a sub network [5] of nodes for the elements to be checked for negation. The token is split, one side goes into the sub network and the other into a negation node, called a not node in Drools. The sub network feeds into the right input of the not node. If a left input token has a match, then it's blocked as content exists, if there is no match it propagates. Negation will work with no additional changes when used with OOPath constructs, although it is not possible to express negation within an OOPath statement itself. This limitation is addressed by allowing OOPath statements outside of a pattern, which means OOPath statements can be split up into chunks that can be negated. The leaf segment must bound to a variable name, so that the variable name can be used as the root of the next OOPath statement.

Accumulate nodes are beta nodes providing aggregation functions over data flowing through sub-networks. Any type of function can be used, provided that it is wrapped by a class implementing the Drools Accumulate interface. Internally, accumulation nodes works like not nodes. Note that Accumulate in Drools is fully incremental and supports both removal and update of data.

A graph of Things can be used to demonstrate some of the above constructs. Each Thing has zero or more child Things, accessed by the children property. Listing 1.7 is a classical transitive closure example, it will recursively iterate a graph to check if $x is contained in $y. The $z is unbound and will always unify to produce all the children of $y, which drives the recursion. Note that Drools does not yet implement any cyclic recursion detection and control, so this must either be guarded against in the logic of the query or avoided in the data the query reasons over. As previously mentioned, the symbol ; is used to separate the positional and named (slotted) parts of a pattern, with positional to the left of the ;.

---

[2] Objects are considered ground terms and unify by equality.

Listing 1.7. A trasitive closure

```
query isContainedIn ( Thing $x, Thing $y )
    /$y/$x := children ;
    or
    /$y/$z := children ; and isContainedIn ($x, $z;) )
end
```

The query in Listing 1.7 can be used inside of other rule constructs. Listing 1.8 provides another query that negates the results of the nested query. In this example it will check if a Thing is not recursively contained in any other Thing:

Listing 1.8. Negation over a transitive closure

```
query isNotContainedIn ( Thing $x, Thing $y )
    not ( isContainedIn ( $x, $y; ) )
end
```

Accumulate rule constructs can be used to count the number of Things recursively contained inside a Thing, see Listing 1.9. Note in this example $x is unbound and will recursively unify and return all children which are applied to the count function.

Listing 1.9. Accumulation

```
query countItems ( Thing $y )
    acc ( isContainedIn ( $x, $y; ) ;
          count ( $x ) ; )
end
```

Structural constraints can be asserted by using index access on Lists. This can be combined with queries to recursively assert on the structure of a List. Listing 1.10 will check that the children are size ordered, where size is the number of children out edges.

Listing 1.10. Structural Control

```
query childrenOrderedByEdgeCount ( Parent $x, Child $c0, int
  index )
    /$x/$c1 : children [index] { children . size <= $c0. children .
    size } ;
    childrenOrderedByEdgeCount ( $x, $c1, index + 1; )
end
```

Drools supports the idea of reactive and non-reactive queries. By default all query, and nested query, invocations are incrementally reactive. Including all their recursive calls, which allows for incrementally reactive transitive closures. Reactive OOPath extensions are covered in section 4. If a query invocation is prefixed with '?' symbol then it will be evaluated just once and not left open for reactivity. This will be applied to all recursively called queries, as you cannot have a reactive query inside of a non-reactive one - although the opposite is possible. Internally non-reactive queries uses less references and also less memory.

The final example, in Listing 1.11, combines graph search with relational. In this example for a given Thing all the children will be recursively visited.

For each child it will unify and then relationally search the working memory to see if any other Things have the same number of children. Note that this requires any Thing that is to be relational searched against to be inserted into the working memory.

Listing 1.11. Combining graph search with relational

```
query findChildrenWithMatchingEdgeCounts( Parent $x, Child $c,
    int index )
    /$x/$c := children[index];
    // relational search
    exists( Thing( children.size == $c.children.size ) )
    findChildrenWithMatchingEdgeCounts( $x, $c1, index + 1; )
end
```

4 Reactive OOPath

At this stage, the proposed framework still has an important limitation. The engine will not be able to react to updates involving a deeply nested fact along an OOPath. For example, the rule in Listing 1.1 will be reevaluated when changes to Plan, Exam and Grade objects occur, but the rule in Listing 1.2 will not. A further extension is required to allow for reactive OOPath statements, that will track any visited objects during an OOPath evaluation. This tracking will allow the engine to react, even if the objects are not inserted into the working memory.

Internally, as the engine evaluates an OOPath expression, tokens propagate into the left input of the node for each segment. The expression is evaluated for each left input token and an object or collection is returned. The left input token is injected into the object or the collection. As each object or collection can be referenced from multiple OOPath statements it supports a list of left input parent tokens. In the case of a single object a single child token is created, for a collection a child per element is created. The child token references both parents. The node applies the constraint filters to the object and propagates the child token to the child node if they match. Or it applies the filter to each element in the collection, and propagates matching children. With this done reactivity is now possible. When an object or collection is updated it can use this token reference to notify the node to re-evaluate it's OOPath segment.

Consider Rule in Listing 1.4 again. If an exam is moved to a different course, the rule should be re-triggered and the list of grades matching the rule recomputed.

Listing 1.12. (Instrumented) Setter

```
public void setCourse(String course) {
    this.course = course;
    notifyModification(this);
}
```

For this to work, the classes in the users domain must be updated to support the described token injection and general notification handling. In our initial implementation, classes are expected to extend a provided abstract class, `AbstractReactiveObject`, that encapsulates all the logic necessary to support reactivity regardless of whether an object is inside or outside of the working memory. Moreover, setters (see Listing 1.12) and methods changing the state of an object need to trigger a method of `AbstractReactiveObject`. This method makes a call-back to the engine, which will iterate the injected token list and notify the node of changes. Collections must also extend or mix the (capabilities of) `AbstractReactiveObject` if reactivity is expected when elements are added or removed to a many-valued field.

Listing 1.13. Addition of a new item to a reactive list

```
public void add(Object obj) {
    // add the object to this data structure
    notifyModification(obj);
}
```

As a final note, all injected tokens are removed when OOPath statement that selected them is no longer selecting them, ensuring that there are no memory leaks. This is handled as part of the existing network delete propagation within the engine.

5   Benchmark

Two benchmarks have been used to evaluate the performance differences between a relational and graph reasoning. The first benchmark uses the examples from the earlier listings to demonstrate the performance for typical business rules using a Java class model. The second benchmark uses recursion over a large graph to demonstrate performance differences for the more extreme end between relational and graph based reasoning.

The first benchmark uses three rules for the same business logic on the same Java class model. The relational rule in Listing 1.1, the **From**-based rule in Listing 1.2 and the reactive OOPath rule in Listing 1.4. A data set was created consisting of 100,000 instances of **Student**, each having a **Plan** with 2 **Exams**. Of these **Exams**, one belongs to the Big Data course and has 2 **Grades**, the other belongs to the Artificial Intelligence one and has one **Grade**. The data set is first evaluated by the three rules, providing the batch execution time. The batch execution is non-reactive. After this, the incremental update execution time is found by moving the **Exam** belonging to the Artificial Intelligence course to the Big Data course and then re-evaluating the rules. This execution was repeated ten times, after a warm up phase consisting of three runs of the benchmark. The best and worst results were discarded with the remaining eight results averaged for the final result. These benchmarks have been executed on a i7-4600U CPU @ 2.10GHz Machine, running a 1.7 version of the Oracle JVM on top of Ubuntu 14.10. The average results, expressed in milliseconds, are reported in Table 1.

Table 1. Benchmark results with 100,000 items (ms.)

	Batch (ms)	Incremental (ms)	Total (ms)
Relational	1313	426	1739
From	613	697	1310
OOpath	752	328	1080

As expected the relational rule takes longer than the `From` or the OOPath rules for the batch execution part. This is due to the time required for the insertion of all the objects into the working memory. This insertion time consists of propagation through the literal and join parts of the network, as well as the indexing performed during this propagation.

Only the root object is inserted for both the `From` and the OOPath rules. The engine then leverages the accessors for faster navigation. These two rules have comparable performance times, with OOPath being slightly slower than `From`. This is due to the reactivity maintenance costs from injecting the left input tokens into the objects during evaluation of the OOPath expression.

Once the Relational model's objects are inserted and evaluated it is able to use the indexes (at the cost of a higher memory occupation) for better performance, with incremental evaluation only slightly slower than OOPath.

The `From` rule is unable to work incrementally, so all data must be reevaluated from the parent `Student` instances. The reason why it does not return the same value as the batch iteration is that both `Exam` instances satisfy the constraint, leading to more rule instantiations and thus more work.

When designing relational rule systems authors must take care to ensure that indexing can be applied when ever possible, these problems are not evident for graph reasoning. When non-indexed constraints are used in a rule the performance will degrade considerable for relational reasoning. Indexing was disable to demonstrate the differences between the two systems. Batch execution time took more than 68 minutes for the relational rule, the incremental execution time showed a similar performance degradation. OOPath does not rely on indexing and there was no performance loss when indexing was disabled..

To check how the 3 techniques compared in this paper scale with the dimension of the data set, the same benchmark has been also repeated with $200,000$ and $400,000$ instances of `Student` leaving all other conditions of the former experiment unchanged. The results of these further benchmarks are reported respectively in Tables 2 and 4.

Table 2. Benchmark results with 200,000 items (ms.)

	Batch (ms)	Incremental (ms)	Total (ms)
Relational	2769	897	3666
From	1285	1449	2734
OOpath	1610	705	2315

Table 3. Benchmark results with 400,000 items (ms.)

	Batch (ms)	Incremental (ms)	Total (ms)
Relational	5596	1844	7440
From	2698	2912	5610
OOpath	3373	1368	4741

These results do not show scaling issues for any of the 3 examined strategies. As each data set size is doubled the execution time has an almost linear increase, doubling each time between the ranges of 2.03 and 2.14. The slightly larger than linear increase is due to the bigger burden on the Java Virtual Machine garbage collector, due to the double of the created objects.

A second benchmark was developed, using large object graphs, to more strongly contrast the performance differences between relational and graph reasoning. It was executed on the same machine, using the same warm up and number of execution cycles.

The benchmark uses a tree consisting of Nodes connected by Edges. Each Node has a value. The query recursively iterates the Nodes in the tree, adding each Node with a specific value into a List. Listing 1.14 shows two versions of the same rule. One is relational the other is graph based using the From construct.

Listing 1.14. Visiting a tree with a relational strategy

```
query findNodesWithValue( int $id, int $value, List list )
    $n: Node( id == $id, $v : value )
    eval( $v != $value || ( $v == $value && list.add( $n ) ) )
    Edge( fromId == $id, $toId : toId )
    findNodesWithValue( $toId, $value, list; )
end
```

Listing 1.15. Visiting a tree with a object-oriented strategy

```
query findNodesWithValue( Node $from, int $value, List list )
    Edge( $n : to, $v : to.value ) from $from.outEdges
    eval( $v != $value || ( $v == $value && list.add( $n ) ) )
    findNodesWithValue( $n, $value, list; )
end
```

This version of the benchmark is executing in batch more only, there is no reactivity. The reactive version of this benchmark is delegated to future works. The queries were run against increasingly more nodes. The results are shown in table 4. As expected, when using graphs, the graph reasoning approach was far superior. Although the degree of difference was unexpected. The relational version did not scale linearly, while the the graph version did.

Table 4. Tree visit benchmark results (ms.)

	1K nodes	2K nodes	4K nodes	8K nodes	16K nodes
Relational	45	143	580	2380	27446
From	2	3	5	11	21

6   Related Works

The work of extending Rete for reactive graph reasoning was first done by a EMF-IncQuery [10]. EMF-IncQuery is a reactive query framework for a graph-based domain model. This framework allows for the definition of declarative queries over EMF models [4] using a graph pattern formalism as the query specification language. EMF-IncQuery supports negation, recursion, transitive closures and aggregate functions. This paper continues this work demonstrating how these graph language and engine constructs can be combine with relational ones, provide a reactive hybrid system.

The authors are not aware of any other system that, to date, can offer reactive, object-oriented hybrid relational and graph reasoning at the same time. However, aspects of the functionality can be found in some prominent pieces of work.

SPARQL [3] is a powerful query language specification from W3C, aimed at querying over RDF graphs. Its property path expression syntax shares several features with with OOPath. The main difference is that SPARQL has a syntax oriented towards RDF graphs whereas OOPath is object-oriented, so the distinction between a dereferencing ('.') and a navigation ('/') operator does not apply, nor does the notion of inner constraints. Further, SPARQL does not distinguish between reactive and non-reactive accessors.

Gremlin [9] is part of the Blueprints project and is a graph traversal language. It was investigated as it has many concepts that overlap with OOPath. The main difference in focus is that OOPath is defined at the level of the domain model and has fully typed classes, while Gremlin is a general purpose language that relies on (and exposes) the structure of the underlying graph. In fact, Gremlin works generically with Nodes and Edges and on un-typed properties, whereas OOPath works with domain classes and is type safe.

A language similar to OOPath has been implemented as part of the Apache Project JXPath [1]. JXPath, however, is more closely modeled on XPath. Its main purpose is navigation rather than the evaluation of logic expressions, so it would not support all the required operators. Neither Gremlin nor JXPath are able to work reactively.

7   Discussion

The proposed syntax and its underlying execution model can be discussed from several perspectives.

Being based on Java, Drools was already able to navigate single valued accessors within patterns using the canonical dot-notation. The decision to introduce the additional '/' symbol in section 3, which like the '.' symbol also traverses reference, was for two reasons. First, it provides a convenient way to navigate collection-valued relationships, iterating over the members, rather than just retrieving the collection as a whole. Second, the engine will consider paths expressed using '/' reactive, re-evaluating rules when deep facts are updated, while normal paths would not support such behavior.

The mechanism required to enable path reactivity is described in Section 4. The proposed implementation is one of several possible alternatives. The data structure of tokens can be externalized from the object using `PropertyChangeListeners` to trigger update propagations. The extension approach has been chosen as the initial implementation because it uses slightly less memory and is slightly faster due to tighter coupling, compared to Property-ChangeListeners. As a third option, the behavior can be built in if the domain model is generated using a model driven approach, e.g. using XJC on an XSD schema or using Drools' native "declare" feature, which allows to define a business object model directly within a rule base. Aspect-oriented programming techniques such as code weaving or class instrumentation could also be used.

The nature of the paths impacts the topology of the underlying RETE network. As shown in Figure 1, an OOPath rule is compiled into a chain of `From` nodes whose right data source is the object extracted by the previous node. Compared to a regular RETE, not requiring the join machinery affords for a simpler, linear structure, which reflects the improvement in performance. The need for a node for each OOPath segment is due to the reactivity requirement. As shown by JXPath, a path expression could be compiled into a series of nested loops and embedded in a single node. However, the individual nodes are needed to create adequate tokens chains, so that updates of deep facts can result in propagations which, starting at the most appropriate step, are correct and optimal at the same time.

Aside from the succinct syntax and potential performance gains, another major advantage to Java developers is the ability to work directly with their own domain models, without requiring mappings to a flattened version. This makes the solution an enticing option for java developers who want to keep their models, but use a rule engine. This aspect becomes even more important when object models are derived from more general models, such as OWL ontologies [7] or complex XSD schemas, which are deeply nested by nature.

8   Conclusions and Future Works

This paper has compared two different ways of querying a domain model, one based on the relational paradigm and the other on graph navigation, showing that the two are equivalent in terms of expressiveness, but quite different in terms of succinct syntax and execution performance. It was proven that using relational joins to navigate properties on a connected domain model can be much slow, especially when the constraints are not indexable. To address both these problems, an XPath-like syntax called OOPath was presented, combined with a new Rete From node, creating a truly hybrid system at both the language and engine level. This syntax was shown to express path constraints in much more succinct way and to be orthogonal in design. It can be used with existing rule constructs, allowing for more advanced logic than OOPath on its own. Further, it was shown that graph and relational constraints can be used in the same rule and interact with each other. OOPath statements are also incrementally reactive, provided a mechanism that allows objects, visited during a OOPath evaluation, to notify the engine when they are updated. This is true even when the objects are not inserted into the working memory.

Being an experimental feature, OOPath also needs further work in several areas. Currently there is additional work on the users, as they have to add logic to their domain models if they want reactive graphs. A number of the discussed alternatives will be implemented to alleviate this problem. With property reactivity [8] a pattern only reacts to properties it constrains on. This addresses both recursion issues and to a lesser extent performance. While this is supported for simple constraints, further work is required to ensure that OOPaths also support Property Reactivity. Finally, additional benchmarks and examples will be implemented to provide better recommendations on when to use the different syntax alternatives.

References

1. Apache commons jxpath. http://commons.apache.org/proper/commons-jxpath/
2. POSL: An integrated positional-slotted language for semantic web knowledge, draft 11. http://ruleml.org/submission/ruleml-shortation.html
3. Sparql 1.1 overview. http://www.w3.org/TR/sparql11-overview/
4. Eclipse modeling framework (emf) (2014). http://www.eclipse.org/modeling/emf/
5. Doorenbos, R.B.: Production Matching for Large Learning Systems. Ph.D. thesis, Pittsburgh, PA, USA (1995). uMI Order No. GAX95-22942
6. Forgy, C.L.: Expert systems. In: Rete: A Fast Algorithm for the Many Pattern/ Many Object Pattern Match Problem (chap), pp. 324–341. IEEE Computer Society Press, Los Alamitos (1990). http://dl.acm.org/citation.cfm?id=115710.115736
7. Meditskos, G., Bassiliades, N.: Clips-owl: A framework for providing object-oriented extensional ontology queries in a production rule engine. Data Knowl. Eng. **70**(7), 661–681 (2011)
8. Proctor, Mark, Fusco, Mario, Sottara, Davide: Extending an object-oriented rete network with fine-grained reactivity to property modifications. In: Morgenstern, Leora, Stefaneas, Petros, Lévy, François, Wyner, Adam, Paschke, Adrian (eds.) RuleML 2013. LNCS, vol. 8035, pp. 173–187. Springer, Heidelberg (2013)
9. Rodriguez, M.A., Mallette, S.: Gremlin - a graph traversal language (2014). https://github.com/tinkerpop/gremlin/wiki
10. Zoltán, U., Bergmann, G., Ábel, H., Horváth, A., Benedek, I., Ráth, I., Zoltán, S., Varró, D.: Emf-incquery: an integrated development environment for live model queries. In: Fifth issue of Experimental Software and Toolkits (EST): A Special Issue on Academics Modelling with Eclipse (ACME2012), pp. 80–99 (2014)

Complex Event Processing Track

Using PSL to Extend and Evaluate Event Ontologies

Megan Katsumi[✉] and Michael Grüninger

Department of Mechanical and Industrial Engineering,
University of Toronto, ON M5S 3G8, Canada
katsumi@mie.utoronto.ca

Abstract. The representation of events plays a key role in a wide range of Semantic Web applications, and several ontologies have been proposed to support this task. However, a review of existing event ontologies on the web reveals limited reasoning being done in their applications. To investigate this, we designed a set of reasoning problems (competency questions) aimed at providing a pragmatic assessment of the reasoning capabilities of three well-known Semantic Web event ontologies – SEM, The Event Ontology, and LODE. Using OWL and SWRL axiomatizations of the Process Specification Language (PSL) Ontology, we specify maximal extensions of the existing event ontologies. We then evaluate the resulting set of OWL and SWRL ontologies against our reasoning problems, using the results to both assess the abilities of existing Semantic Web event ontologies, and to explore the potential gains that may be achieved through additional axioms.

1 Introduction

The notion of events is pervasive, so it is natural to find that much existing work on the Semantic Web in some way addresses the challenge of representing and integrating event-related data. While integration is certainly a valuable application, more complex reasoning can and should be performed with the event information on the web. Given the strides that have been made for integration and basic information retrieval for event-related information, it is logical to now ask what can be done with this information. Many existing event ontologies tend to take a rather simplistic approach in order to better facilitate use with many diverse sources, resulting in a rather limited semantics. It is therefore unclear to what extent these theories can support the non-trivial reasoning problems that are required for applications such as complex event processing. The aim of this work is to address the following questions: What reasoning problems can be done with the status quo? What gains can we make by augmenting their axiomatizations? What kinds of queries require more substantial changes to the ontologies?

To investigate this, we identify a set of competency questions (CQs) in Section 3, motivated by several potential application domains related to complex event processing; these questions are representative of some of the more complex

© Springer International Publishing Switzerland 2015
N. Bassiliades et al. (Eds.): RuleML 2015, LNCS 9202, pp. 225–240, 2015.
DOI: 10.1007/978-3-319-21542-6_15

reasoning tasks of interest. Using three well-known event ontologies, we extend each one via the technique of *grafting* them with the Process Specification Language (PSL) ontology[1] in Section 4. The resulting set of event ontologies is then evaluated against the competency questions.

The outcomes of the evaluation, presented in Section 5 demonstrate many attainable opportunities to achieve substantial gains in the reasoning abilities of these Semantic Web ontologies. In Section 5.2 we consider our results and reflect on the possibilities for increased reasoning on the Semantic Web. In Section 6 we review some of the issues and insights that we identified and discuss some general directions for future work. We conclude with a summary of our contributions in Section 7.

2   Background

As mentioned in the previous section, there currently exist numerous efforts toward the development of ontologies for the representation of events on the Semantic Web. Although perhaps contrary to some of the underlying principles of ontologies (e.g. reuse), this is not entirely surprising given that the concept of an event plays an important role in such a wide variety of contexts. A review of existing event ontologies agrees with this observation as we have found the application areas for existing work to be quite diverse, including domains such as artefacts, historic events, and business processes. In the following sections we present a more detailed review of three of the more prominent generic event ontologies used for our investigation.

2.1   SEM

The Simple Event Model (SEM) ontology [8] was designed to represent event information on the web. Formalized in RDF, it stresses minimal semantic commitments, an approach that is intended to facilitate "maximal interoperability" with the variety of event information on the web. SEM contains four "core" classes: Event, Actor, Place, and Time, aimed at describing *what* occurred, *who* (or what) participated in the occurrence, *where* it occurred, and *when*.

Each of these core classes has an associated Type class (i.e. EventType, ActorType, etc) to allow for the specification of distinctions between the core classes. A Constraint class is also defined (with subclasses View, Temporary, and Role) to allow for some description of the properties of an event (e.g. to describe the nature of an actor's participation in an event).

Although there is some discussion of reasoning with the use of the SEM Prolog API, the demonstrated functionality is essentially limited to look-up queries; the application focus appears to be on event information integration.

---

[1] The axioms for all ontologies cited in this paper can be found online. First-order ontologies are specified using Common Logic, SROIQ ontologies are specified using OWL2, and rules are specified using SWRL.

2.2   LODE

The ontology for Linking Open Descriptions of Events (LODE) [7] also approaches the information integration problem – but in this case with the broader goal of creating an ontology that can also serve as an *interlingua* for existing event ontologies, thereby also (potentially) integrating their information. The view of the event domain taken here is focused more on the subject matter of journalists and historians – what might loosely be called world events.

Axiomatized in OWL, LODE aims to achieve this interoperability through a set of what they refer to as mapping axioms, (although we must note that the definition and use of such axioms differs from our perspective) between its concepts, and those of some existing event ontologies. In an effort to ensure interoperability, LODE focuses on representing what they refer to as the "factual" aspects of an event, core concepts which they believe are not subject to interpretation. LODE provides an Event class along with the properties: atPlace, atTime, circa, illustrate, inSpace, involved, and involvedAgent to describe an event.

2.3   The Event Ontology

The Event Ontology [2] evolved out of the Music Ontology project [5], which was developed to integrate music-related information from heterogeneous sources. Perhaps most notably, the Event Ontology is referenced in the development of the BBC Sports Ontology [3], which was implemented to facilitate automated curation of the BBC's world cup site.

Axiomatized in RDFS, the Event Ontology consists of the classes: Event, Factor, and Product; and the properties: agent, factor, literal_factor, place, product, sub_event, and time. Similar to LODE, (but without the explicit aim of facilitating interoperability) the Event Ontology also includes concepts from other ontologies, such as foaf [4] and the WGS84 Geo Positioning Ontology [5].

2.4   PSL

With its rich, rigorous axiomatization of such concepts, PSL was a natural choice for the task of grafting our chosen Semantic Web ontologies onto a more expressive ontology. PSL is an ontology designed to facilitate the correct and complete exchange of process information among manufacturing systems [1]. These applications include scheduling, process modelling, process planning, production planning, simulation, and project management. The PSL ontology T_{psl}[6] is organized into PSL-Core and a set of partially ordered extensions; the core ontology consists of four disjoint classes: *activities* can have zero or more occurrences,

---

[2] http://motools.sourceforge.net/event/event.html
[3] http://www.bbc.co.uk/ontologies/sport/2011-02-17.shtml
[4] http://www.foaf-project.org/
[5] http://www.w3.org/2003/01/geo/
[6] http://colore.oor.net/process_specification_language/psl_outercore.clif

activity occurrences begin and end at time points, *time points* constitute a linear ordered set with end points at infinity, and *objects* are elements that are not activities, occurrences, or time points [1]. There are five additional modules within the PSL Ontology – $T_{occtree}$ (which is closely related to situation calculus), $T_{subactivity}$ (which axiomatizes the composition relation on activities), T_{atomic} (which axiomatizes concurrent activities), $T_{complex}$ (which axiomatizes complex activities), and T_{actocc} (which axiomatizes the composition relation on occurrences of complex activities).

More recently, the PSL Ontology has been extended to capture the relations between activity occurrences, actors, locations, and time intervals. In particular, $T_{psl\_locations}$[7] merges T_{psl} with a multidimensional mereotopology that represents containment relations among spatial entities. The ontology T_{psl_actors}[8] specializes the *participates_in* relation from PSL-Core by introducing the relation *performed_in* between actors and the activity occurrences that they perform.

3 Generic Requirements

Up to this point, we have discussed the opportunities of reasoning about events at a high level. In this section, we aim to further motivate our work by identifying practical application domains where reasoning about events would offer significant value. The scenarios described below are quite diverse, yet the core of their reasoning problems is relatively general. Based on the commonly adopted scope of events as including the notion of participants and locations, we then elicit a set of competency questions that could provide useful support in the variety of the motivating scenarios described below.

3.1 Motivating Scenarios

We identify potential reasoning problems with applications for emergency response centres, city services management, and context awareness. Some of these scenarios are inspired by the application domains described by the various existing event ontologies. The following scenarios illustrate the different sorts of problems where reasoning about events could be valuable. Essentially, we are considering the following question – assuming that the existing ontologies have successfully integrated event information in their various application domains, what can we do with it? Although these scenarios are among many potential applications that include the notion of events, we speculate that certain patterns and types of questions are likely to arise repeatedly in many other, unrelated applications. The scenarios, described below, were used to motivate the set of general, event-oriented competency questions which are presented in Section 3.2.

---

[7] http://colore.oor.net/psl_locations/psl_locations.clif
[8] http://colore.oor.net/psl_actors/psl_actors.clif

Emergency Response Centre When responding to an incident report, any additional information could be valuable to prepare the dispatched units en route. Integrated event information could be leveraged to provide this additional information to the dispatch centre, by allowing the dispatchers to pose queries in order to identify information that might be relevant to a particular incident.

City Services Management Knowledge of planned events as well as the ability to reason and analyse past events could serve to better (and more easily) inform city workers in the planning of various projects, as well as to assist management in identifying potential issues or trends related to various aspects of city maintenance.

Context-awareness Consider the variety of opportunities for context-aware applications for personal use. Information about what events are occurring, or can occur in a city could be leveraged to better inform an individual how best to navigate to their destination, or complete a set of errands. Similar tools could also be applied to aid users in navigating or planning for recreational events (festivals, etc).

3.2   Informal Competency Questions

The CQs are first presented informally here, in natural language; followed by an overview of the test domain theory, necessary for the ontologies' evaluation with automated reasoners. For the subsequent evaluation, we opt to initially formalize the competency questions in the vocabulary of PSL, since it has the broadest scope of the event ontologies to be evaluated[9]. Further, since each of the Semantic Web event ontologies will be extended by PSL as part of our investigation, the translation of each of the CQs, (as well as the domain theory) will be straightforward from the identified mappings.

The following set of generic CQs are essentially patterns that we see as being applicable in any of the motivating scenarios described previously[10]:

CQ1 What actors may have participated in some activity occurrence?
CQ2 What can possibly occur next after an occurrence of some activity?
CQ3 Are occurrences of two activities possibly subactivity occurrences of the same complex activity occurrence?
CQ4 Are any other activities possibly taking place at the same place and the same time as a particular activity?
CQ5 Assuming that occurrences of two activities are part of the same overall activity occurrence, what activities possibly occurred between them?
CQ6 What activity could have occurred before an occurrence of some other observed activity?

---

[9] For the complete set of formalized CQs, the reader is referred to: http://stl.mie.utoronto.ca/ontologies/CQs.txt

[10] We have written these questions generically, but the reader should notice that they may easily be specialized to the motivating scenarios described previously. For example, CQ1 might become "What contractors may have performed road repairs?"

CQ7 Is there an activity that will definitely occur after an occurrence of some activity?

CQ8 What activities are scheduled to occur at a given time and location?

CQ9 During what time intervals are no events occurring at a given location?

CQ10 Do any occurrences of two activities overlap?

CQ11 What subactivities of some activity is a particular actor participating in?

CQ12 Is an actor of interest possibly participating in an activity?

CQ13 Given observed occurrences of two activities, what might an actor of interest participate in next?

4   Extensions of the Event Ontologies

One of the primary questions that we are addressing is whether existing event ontologies on the Web can better support reasoning about events (as specified by the competency questions) if they are extended by additional axioms. A key step in this endeavor is to determine the relationships between the PSL Ontology and the Semantic Web event ontologies. This will enable us to specify extensions of the event ontologies; further, it provides the opportunity for a model-theoretic evaluation of these ontologies, as well as the identification of any relationships among the different event ontologies themselves. In this section, we will discuss the axiomatization of subtheories of PSL which is definable in the description logic SROIQ and in the Semantic Web Rule Language (SWRL), which is equivalent to the extension of OWL with the Horn sublanguage of FOL. We then introduce the notion of ontology grafting, which is a generalization of definable interpretations of theories, and use this technique to specify maximal extensions of the event ontologies with respect to the SROIQ and SWRL axiomatizations of PSL. In the next section, these extensions will be evaluated with respect to the competency questions presented earlier.

We are facing two challenges – the relationship between the axiomatizations of different ontologies in the same logic, as well as the relationship between the axiomatizations of a given ontology in different logics. We therefore introduce the following notion:

Definition 1. *Let T_1 be a theory in a logic $\mathcal{L}_1$ and let T_2 be a theory in a logic $\mathcal{L}_2$.*

T_1 is language-equivalent to T_2 iff T_1 is logically equivalent to the translation of T_2 under the logic mapping from $\mathcal{L}_1$ to $\mathcal{L}_2$.

In this paper, we will use the logic mapping from SROIQ to FOL specified in [4] when specifying the language-equivalence of SROIQ and FOL theories.

4.1   Ontology Grafting

The basic relationship between theories T_A and T_B is the notion of interpretation [2], which is a mapping from the language of T_A to the language of T_B that preserves the theorems of T_A. The interpretation is faithful if the mapping also preserves the satisfiable sentences of T_A. If there is an interpretation of T_A in T_B, then there exists a set of sentences (referred to as translation definitions) in the language $L_A \cup L_B$ of the form

$$(\forall \overline{x}) \, p_i(\overline{x}) \equiv \varphi(\overline{x})$$

where $p_i(\overline{x})$ is a relation symbol in L_A and $\varphi(\overline{x})$ is a formula in L_B.

When applied with the Semantic Web event ontologies, we are faced with the additional problem that the translation definitions used to specify interpretations among theories are not definable either within SROIQ or SWRL. The approach of ontology mapping needs to be modified so that we can use the notion of faithful interpretation to first-order theories and then translate the resulting theories into SROIQ and SWRL. We therefore introduce the notion of ontology grafting, in which we extend one ontology via the translation definitions specified using the first-order translations of a set of other ontologies.

Definition 2. *An ontology T_3 is the grafting of the ontology T_2 onto the ontology T_1 iff there exists T_1', T_2', T_3' such that*

1. T_3' *is a nonconservative extension of T_2' such that both theories have the same signature;*
2. T_1' *faithfully interprets T_3';*
3. T_i *is language-equivalent to T_i'.*

In the rest of this section, we graft the event ontologies T_{sem}, T_{event}, and T_{lode} onto T_{psl}. In doing so, we specify maximal extensions of the event ontologies which are language-equivalent to subtheories of the PSL Ontology. In particular, we will be using T_{psl_dl}[11] which is language-equivalent to T_{psl}^{sroiq}[12], and T_{psl_swrl}[13] which is language-equivalent to T_{psl}^{swrl}[14].

4.2 OWL Extensions of the Ontologies

SEM. Let T_{sem}[15] be the first-order theory which is language-equivalent to the subtheory[16] of the SROIQ theory T_{sem}^{sroiq} that omits the axioms for the timestamp datatype properties[17].

---

[11] http://colore.oor.net/extended_psl/psl_dl.clif
[12] http://stl.mie.utoronto.ca/ontologies/process_specification_language/psl_loc_actors. owl
[13] http://colore.oor.net/extended_psl/psl_swrl.clif
[14] http://stl.mie.utoronto.ca/ontologies/process_specification_language/ psl_loc_actors_r.swrl
[15] http://colore.oor.net/simple_event_model/sem.clif
[16] stl.mie.utoronto.ca/ontologies/simple_event_model/sem.owl
[17] The Simple Event Model is the only one of the event ontologies that uses its own axiomatization of time, rather than reuse OWL-Time. The critique of the Simple Event Model's use of datatype properties rather than object properties for the relationships between timepoints and timeintervals is out of the scope of this paper.

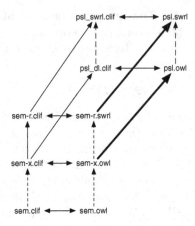

Fig. 1. Relationship between T_{psl} and extensions of the event ontologies. Dashed lines denote nonconservative extension, solid arrows denote faithful interpretation, double-headed arrows indicate language-equivalence, and thick lines show ontology grafting.

Lemma 1. T_{sem} *is interpreted by* T_{psl_dl}.

Proof. Let Δ_1 be the following set of translation definitions:

$$(\forall x) \text{ sem:EventType}(x) \equiv \text{activity}(x)$$

$$(\forall x) \text{ sem:Event}(x) \equiv \text{activity\_occurrence}(x)$$

$$(\forall x) \text{ sem:Time}(x) \equiv \text{timepoint}(x) \vee \text{timeinterval}(x)$$

$$(\forall x, y) \text{ sem:eventType}(x,y) \equiv \text{occurrence\_of}(x,y)$$

$$(\forall x, y) \text{ sem:hasSubEvent}(x,y) \equiv \text{subactivity\_occurrence}(y,x)$$

$$(\forall x, y) \text{ sem:hastime}(x,y) \equiv (\text{psl\_interval}(x,y) \vee \text{begins}(x,y) \vee \text{ends}(x,y))$$

$$(\forall x)\text{sem:Actor}(x) \equiv \text{actor}(x)$$

$$(\forall x)\text{sem:Place}(x) \equiv \text{location}(x)$$

$$(\forall x, y)\text{sem:hasPlace}(x,y) \equiv \text{occurred\_at}(x,y)$$

$$(\forall x, y)\text{sem:hasActor}(x,y) \equiv \text{performed\_in}(y,x)$$

We can use Prover9[18] to show that $T_{psl\_dl} \cup \Delta_1 \models T_{sem}$.

It is important to realize that this interpretation is not faithful because there are sentences in the signature of T_{sem} which are entailed by the interpretation but which are not entailed by T_{sem} itself. The key idea is that we can use the set of such sentences to extend T_{sem} until we find a theory which is faithfully interpreted by T_{psl_dl}. We will refer to this extension as T_{sem_x}[19] and the translation of the resulting theory to be T_{sem-x}^{sroiq} [20] Since $T_{psl\_dl} \cup \Delta_1$ is a conservative extension of T_{sem_x}, T_{sem_x} is faithfully interpreted by T_{psl_dl}.

---

[18] https://www.cs.unm.edu/~mccune/mace4/
[19] http://colore.oor.net/simple_event_model/sem_x.clif
[20] stl.mie.utoronto.ca/ontologies/simple_event_model/sem_x.owl

Theorem 1. $T_{sem\_x}^{sroiq}$ is the grafting of T_{sem}^{sroiq} onto T_{psl}^{sroiq}.

Thus, $T_{sem\_x}^{sroiq}$ is a maximal extension of T_{sem}^{sroiq} which has the same signature as T_{sem}^{sroiq} any stronger extension would require an expanded signature.

A summary of the results is shown in Figure 1.

Event Ontology. Let T_{event}[21] be the first-order theory which is language-equivalent to the SROIQ theory T_{event}^{sroiq}[22].

Lemma 2. T_{event} is interpreted by T_{psl_dl}.

We can extend T_{event} with the additional sentences which are entailed by $T_{psl\_dl} \cup \Delta_2$; we will refer to this nonconservative extension as T_{event_x}[23]. Each of these sentences can also be axiomatized in SROIQ, and we refer to the resulting theory as $T_{event-x}^{sroiq}$[24]. As we saw with the Simple Event Model, the ontology T_{event_x} is a maximal extension of T_{event} within its hierarchy.

Theorem 2. $T_{event\_x}^{sroiq}$ is the grafting of T_{event}^{sroiq} onto T_{psl}^{sroiq}.

In terms of the definition of ontology grafting, we can see that T_{event_x} is a nonconservative extension of T_{event_x} and that T_{psl_dl} faithfully interprets T_{event_x}.

LODE. Let T_{lode}[25] be the first-order theory which is language-equivalent to T_{lode}^{sroiq}[26].

Lemma 3. T_{lode} is interpreted by T_{psl_dl}.

As we saw with the other two event ontologies, we can extend T_{lode} with the additional sentences which are entailed by $T_{psl\_dl} \cup \Delta_3$, giving us T_{event_x}[27]. Each of these sentences can also be axiomatized in SROIQ, and the resulting ontology is $T_{lode\_x}^{sroiq}$[28]. As we saw with the other event ontologies, the extension of T_{lode} is conservative, so that $T_{lode\_x}^{sroiq}$ is faithfully interpreted by T_{psl_dl}. We therefore have

Theorem 3. $T_{lode\_x}^{sroiq}$ is the grafting of T_{lode}^{sroiq} onto T_{psl}^{sroiq}.

---

[21] http://colore.oor.net/event_ontology/event.clif
[22] stl.mie.utoronto.ca/ontologies/event_ontology/event.owl
[23] http://colore.oor.net/event_ontology/event_x.clif
[24] stl.mie.utoronto.ca/ontologies/event_ontology/event_x.owl
[25] http://colore.oor.net/lode/lode.clif
[26] stl.mie.utoronto.ca/ontologies/lode/lode.owl
[27] http://colore.oor.net/lode/lode_x.clif
[28] stl.mie.utoronto.ca/ontologies/lode/lode_x.owl

4.3 SWRL Extensions of the Ontologies

Looking at the axiomatizations of the event ontologies, it is clear that the restriction to OWL omits axioms that may be required to support the competency questions. We can now consider extensions of the event ontologies in which we exploit the additional expressiveness of SWRL.

Theorem 4. $T_{sem\_r}^{swrl}$ *is the grafting of* T_{sem}^{sroiq} *onto* T_{psl}^{swrl}.

Proof. Let $T_{sem\_r.swrl}$[29] be the first-order ontology which is language-equivalent to $T_{sem\_r}^{swrl}$[30]. Using the translation definitions from the proof of Theorem 1, we have

$T_{psl_swrl} \cup \Delta_1 \models T_{sem\_r.swrl}$.

Theorem 5. $T_{event\_r}^{swrl}$ *is the grafting of* T_{event}^{sroiq} *onto* T_{psl}^{swrl}.

Proof. Let $T_{event\_r.swrl}$[31] be the first-order ontology which is language-equivalent to $T_{event\_r}^{swrl}$[32]. Using the same translation definitions as in the proof of Lemma 2, we have

$$T_{psl_swrl} \cup \Delta_2 \models T_{event\_r.swrl}$$

Theorem 6. $T_{lode\_r}^{swrl}$ *is the grafting of* T_{lode}^{sroiq} *onto* T_{psl}^{swrl}.

Proof. Let $T_{lode\_r.swrl}$[33] be the first-order ontology which is language-equivalent to $T_{lode\_r}^{swrl}$[34]. Using the same translation definitions as in the proof of Lemma 3, we have

$$T_{psl_swrl} \cup \Delta_3 \models T_{lode\_r.swrl}$$

5   Evaluation

In order to demonstrate the evaluation of these competency questions, we need to specify a domain theory, i.e. a set of individuals of the classes of our ontology. Note that the evaluation of these competency questions is meant to demonstrate the scope (both in terms of lexicon and semantics) distinctions between the event ontologies; given that the size and complexity of the domain theory has no impact on the scope of the ontology, a toy scenario is sufficient for our purposes. The generic domain theory we employ consists of two complex activities, A_1, A_2, as well as five atomic activities $(A_{21}, A_{22}, A_3, A_4, A_5)$, each with varying possible occurrences and orderings. Additional information is also specified regarding times and locations of occurrences and participating actors, as well as

---

[29] http://colore.oor.net/simple_event_model/sem_r.clif
[30] stl.mie.utoronto.ca/ontologies/simple_event_model/sem_r.swrl
[31] http://colore.oor.net/event_ontology/event_r.clif
[32] stl.mie.utoronto.ca/ontologies/event_ontology/event_r.swrl
[33] http://colore.oor.net/lode/lode_r.clif
[34] stl.mie.utoronto.ca/ontologies/lode/lode_r.swrl

possible locations and participation for activities. The complete domain theory specifications for each theory to be evaluated may be found either embedded in the OWL ontologies, or in the related input files (in the case of first-order logic proofs).

In transitioning from the informal set of competency questions to a formal specification of queries, there are often a variety of subtle distinctions in the way the queries could be interpreted. For example, CQ1, when made more specific, can be interpreted in several ways:

CQ1-1 What actors participated in the occurrence, O_{21}?
CQ1-2 What actors perform A_2?
CQ1-3 What actors participated in some occurrences of A_2?

Each such interpretation may result in a distinct query when formalized, which may impact the ontologies' ability to represent or answer it. For example, notice that the first interpretation (CQ1-1) is expressible by all ontologies, whereas none of the Semantic Web event ontologies are able to express the second interpretation (CQ1-2). We have therefore opted to consider all such recognized alternate interpretations in our evaluation to avoid excluding any potentially interesting results.

CQ1-1 :
 – first-order logic: $(\exists a)(actor(a) \wedge performed\_in(a, O21))$
 – psl.owl: `Actor and performed_in value O21`
 – The Event Ontology: `Agent and agent value O21`
 – SEM:`Actor and inverse ('has Actor') value O21`
 – LODE:`Agent and 'involved agent' value O21`
CQ1-2 :
 – first-order logic:$(\exists a)(actor(a) \wedge performs(a, A_2))$
 – psl.owl:`Actor and performs value A2`
 – Query out of the scope of SEM, LODE, and the Event Ontology's lexicon.

5.1 Results

Using the HermiT 1.3.8 plug-in provided by Protege version 4.3 [35] we evaluated each of the original event ontologies, their extensions via ontology grafting onto T_{psl}^{sroiq} and T_{psl}^{swrl}, as well as T_{psl}^{sroiq} and T_{psl}^{swrl} against the formalized competency questions.

In the case of certain queries we found we were unable to specify a formalization in OWL. Here, we utilised the first-order logic translations of each of the OWL theories (available online, as referenced in the previous section), and attempted evaluation using the first-order automated theorem prover, Prover9. The idea behind this was that a positive result would demonstrate that the axioms specified in the ontology were in fact sufficient to answer the query; thus

---

[35] http://protege.stanford.edu/

we would avoid faulting the ontology for an issue of query language expressivity/tool support. Only in the case that a query was still not provable in the first-order translation would we infer that the axioms were too weak.

The results of each ontology against our reasoning problems are summarized in Table 1.

Table 1. A high-level summary of the evaluation results

CQ	Entailed By	Expressible By
1-1	psl.owl, psl_dl.clif, psl.swrl, psl_swrl.clif, sem_x.owl, sem_x.clif, sem_r.swrl, sem_r.clif, event_x.owl, event_x.clif, event_r.swrl, event_r.clif	psl.owl, psl_dl.clif, psl.swrl, psl_swrl.clif, sem.owl, sem.clif, sem_x.owl, sem_x.clif, sem_r.swrl, sem_r.clif, event.owl, event.clif, event_x.owl, event_x.clif, event_r.swrl, event_r.clif, lode.owl, lode.clif, lode_x.owl, lode_x.clif, lode_r.swrl, lode_r.clif
1-2	psl.owl, psl_dl.clif, psl.swrl, psl_swrl.clif	psl.owl, psl_dl.clif, psl.swrl, psl_swrl.clif
1-3	psl.owl, psl_dl.clif, psl.swrl, psl_swrl.clif, sem_x.owl, sem_x.clif, sem_r.swrl, sem_r.clif	psl.owl, psl_dl.clif, psl.swrl, psl_swrl.clif, sem.owl, sem.clif, sem_x.owl, sem_x.clif, sem_r.swrl, sem_r.clif
2	-	psl_dl.clif, psl_swrl.clif
3-1	psl.owl, psl_dl.clif, psl.swrl, psl_swrl.clif, sem_x.owl, sem_x.clif, sem_r.swrl, sem_r.clif	psl.owl, psl_dl.clif, psl.swrl, psl_swrl.clif, sem.owl, sem.clif, sem_x.owl, sem_x.clif, sem_r.swrl, sem_r.clif
3-2	psl.owl, psl_dl.clif, psl.swrl, psl_swrl.clif	psl.owl, psl_dl.clif, psl.swrl, psl_swrl.clif
4	-	psl.owl, psl_dl.clif, psl.swrl, psl_swrl.clif
5	-	psl_dl.clif, psl_swrl.clif
6	psl.owl, psl_dl.clif, psl.swrl, psl_swrl.clif	psl.owl, psl_dl.clif, psl.swrl, psl_swrl.clif
7	psl.owl, psl_dl.clif, psl.swrl, psl_swrl.clif	psl.owl, psl_dl.clif, psl.swrl, psl_swrl.clif
8	-	psl.owl, psl_dl.clif, psl.swrl, psl_swrl.clif
9	-	psl.owl, psl_dl.clif, psl.swrl, psl_swrl.clif, sem.owl, sem.clif, sem_x.owl, sem_x.clif, sem_r.swrl, sem_r.clif, event.owl, event.clif, event_x.owl, event_x.clif, event_r.swrl, event_r.clif, lode.owl, lode.clif, lode_x.owl, lode_x.clif, lode_r.swrl, lode_r.clif
10	-	psl_dl.clif, psl_swrl.clif
11	psl.owl, psl_dl.clif, psl.swrl, psl_swrl.clif	psl.owl, psl_dl.clif, psl.swrl, psl_swrl.clif
12-1	psl.owl, psl_dl.clif, psl.swrl, psl_swrl.clif	psl.owl, psl_dl.clif, psl.swrl, psl_swrl.clif
12-2	psl.owl, psl_dl.clif, psl.swrl, psl_swrl.clif, sem_x.owl, sem_x.clif, sem_r.swrl, sem_r.clif	psl.owl, psl_dl.clif, psl.swrl, psl_swrl.clif, sem.owl, sem.clif, sem_x.owl, sem_x.clif, sem_r.swrl, sem_r.clif
13	psl.owl, psl_dl.clif, psl.swrl, psl_swrl.clif	psl.owl, psl_dl.clif, psl.swrl, psl_swrl.clif

A detailed summary of the evaluation results is available online [36]. Note that although all ontologies were capable of formalizing CQ9, none were able to return a solution as the test domain theory did not include the use of closure axioms.

In OWL. Both the Event Ontology and LODE had major scope limitations which prevented all but a single competency question from being expressible in

---

[36] http://stl.mie.utoronto.ca/ontologies/results_summary_reformat.pdf

their lexicon (CQ1-1). Further, neither ontology was able to return the answer to this question as both lacked sufficient semantics to make the necessary inferences. SEM fared comparably better as its lexicon was able to formalize a total of four of the CQs (CQ1-1, CQ1-3, CQ3-1, and CQ12-2). However, similar to its counterparts, SEM also lacked the necessary axioms to answer any of the four CQs.

Not surprisingly, given its broad scope, the signature of T_{psl}^{sroiq} supported the specification of all but three of the CQs. In fact, the three CQs that were *not* expressible (CQ2, CQ5, and CQ10) were hindered not by the scope of the lexicon, but by the limitations of the OWL query language. In terms of reasoning abilities, T_{psl}^{sroiq} also fared better; the correct answer was returned for all of the expressible CQs, apart from CQ4 and CQ8.

When grafted to T_{psl}^{sroiq}, we achieved improvements in each of the resulting event ontology extensions, with the exception of $T_{lode\_x}^{sroiq}$; its were still insufficient to answer the query. We found that the Event Ontology extension was sufficient to return the answer to CQ1-1. Further, T_{sem}^{sroiq} was capable of correctly solving all four of the CQs that were in its scope.

In First-Order Logic. The queries CQ2, CQ5, and CQ10 were outside of the expressive capabilities of the DL query tool, and therefore attempted in Prover9[37]. We were unable to attempt any evaluation of the queries for LODE, the Event Ontology, or SEM (likewise with their extensions) as the necessary concepts were outside of the ontologies' lexicons. Using a translation of T_{psl}^{sroiq} (i.e., T_{psl_dl}, we were able to obtain a proof, yielding the correct answer to CQ2[38]. Neither a proof nor a counterexample was found by Prover9 for both CQ5 and CQ10, although a manual counterexample can be found in both cases, showing that the subtheory of the PSL Ontology which is definable in SROIQ is not strong enough to entail solutions to the competency questions.

Since SWRL is an extension of OWL, any competency question entailed by an OWL axiomatization is also entailed by the SWRL axiomatization. In evaluating the adequacy of the SWRL extensions of the Semantic Web event ontologies, we therefore only need to consider *lode_r.swrl* against CQ1-1, as all of the other competency questions not entailed by the Semantic Web event ontologies were not expressible. We found that the extension *lode_r.swrl* was still unable to infer the correct answer to CQ1-1; its scope is too restricted to allow for the necessary extension (specifically, the subactivity_occurrence relation).

5.2   Troubleshooting Ontology Expressivity

The results of our evaluation are generally quite encouraging for the goal of supporting more complex reasoning about events on the Semantic Web. We find that T_{psl}^{sroiq} serves as a particularly motivating example of the potential function-ality that can be achieved. Further, and specifically with respect to the gains

---

[37] http://stl.mie.utoronto.ca/ontologies/psl_dl.owl.in

[38] http://stl.mie.utoronto.ca/ontologies/psl_cq2.proof

illustrated with $T_{sem\_x}^{sroiq}$, our results indicate the effectiveness of ontology grafting. We should also note that the theories of actors and locations translated to create T_{psl}^{sroiq} were designed to be root theories in COLORE [2]. In other words they are intentionally weak and make minimal commitments; we speculate that there is further potential for increased reasoning abilities with the creation of even stronger theories.

Where reasoning is limited, the cause is lack of expressivity in one or multiple ways: insufficient scope of concepts (lexicon), insufficient axioms (semantics), or limitations of the language itself (logic). Our results indicate that a key factor in the reasoning limitations of existing ontologies is the scope of their lexicons. This observation could be a cause of the lack of reasoning about events on the Semantic Web, but it is more likely a symptom of the lack of focus on such applications. We speculate that this may be due to the fact that the integration and search-oriented applications represent more low-hanging fruit for ontology developers, or perhaps the fact that the widely adopted approach of using lightweight axiomatizations for integration is simply not conducive to creating ontologies capable of supporting more sophisticated reasoning. While we do certainly agree that it is logical for the task of information integration to be tackled prior to reasoning tasks, we feel strongly that to fully benefit from these previous efforts, the focus should now shift to potential reasoning applications.

In any case, analysis of our results highlights two commonly omitted concepts that we find to be primary causes of the event ontologies' inability to solve our reasoning problems: the activity/occurrence distinction, and the notion of an ordering over occurrences. It was SEM's inclusion of the notion of an activity ("event type") that provided the ability to represent multiple CQs, over and above its peers. Although this may seem like a PSL-specific distinction, we emphasize that it is one which is necessary to ask more interesting questions about events. When limited to occurrences, we are restricted to simply asking about particular instances. Without the activity/occurrence distinction we lose the ability to pose queries regarding occurrences of a particular kind. Returning to the motivating scenarios presented initially, this means that queries such as: *is there some sort of construction event occurring at a location?* are not possible.

None of the selected event ontologies provided a definition for ordering over occurrences. Instead, only some notion of time is associated with an event – likely intended to be instantiated with, or otherwise attached to some form of a timestamp. This over-reliance on datatype-oriented representations (in conjunction with the lack of an activity/occurrence distinction) precludes the reasoning about potential, future orderings of possible events. If we are relying on timestamps associated with particular occurrences, we are unable to ask questions such as – is it possible that flooding occurred prior to the reported power outage?

6   Looking Forward

While our results demonstrate the potential abilities that could be achieved with an ontology for events, we certainly make no claims regarding the suitability of

T_{psl}^{sroiq} as a definitive theory for such applications. However, we do claim that it demonstrates the feasibility of our goal of performing valuable reasoning tasks on the Semantic Web. Future work should extend this study of feasibility to consider additional ontologies such as DOLCE [3], Event Model-F [6], and the like. In contrast with the application-oriented ontologies included in this study, these ontologies have a more foundational-style and it would be interesting to examine how they fare against our reasoning problems with respect to both the necessary concept scope and depth of semantics. Further, this study has focused on illustrating the potential reasoning abilities, based on the semantic content. This would be well-complimented with an examination of scalability. In other words, can these abilities be preserved with larger datasets, or will the reasoning problems become too difficult? Future work with real-world data will serve to inform us of the necessary implementation paradigm.

The potential demonstrated here also encourages us to consider a broader variety of event-related reasoning applications. For example, the question of disagreement could be tackled by attempting queries to ascertain whether two instances are really describing the same event. The current issue of occurrence orderings and timestamps could be resolved with a robust dates and durations ontology; such concepts could also be used to account for things like hours of operation when reasoning about events. Further, the addition of concepts to describe betweenness and summation for locations would provide the ability to answer questions related to routes, e.g. is some event occurring (or, not occurring) on my route to some destination?

While two types of expressivity issues (lexicon and semantics) may be addressed by extension, the issue of logic expressivity re-enforces the fact that there is a limit to the types of reasoning that can be accomplished with conventional Semantic Web technologies. In general, we were unable to use OWL and SWRL to formalize and entail queries concerned with possible orderings of several activity occurrences. These are certainly potentially useful questions, and while we do acknowledge that there exist tools capable of formalizing such queries for Semantic Web ontologies, such languages and tools are not yet standardized or widely available. This is not to say that first-order logic ontologies are better suited for such questions, as our results have also highlighted the issues of intractability that may be encountered when working in a more expressive language. However, it does indicate a requirement for better tools or alternate approaches in order to elicit the full benefit from existing and future efforts on the Semantic Web.

7 Summary

Existing work with event ontologies has focused heavily on the task of representing event information for integration, leaving the task of automated reasoning relatively untouched. We motivated our goal of increased reasoning about events on the Semantic Web, and used this motivation as a source of pragmatic reasoning problems for our evaluation. Through our investigation, we have demonstrated some of the reasoning abilities that Semantic Web ontologies are capable of supporting. Further, we analysed our findings in order to offer explanations for the current lack of such reasoning.

The notion of ontology grafting may serve as the basis for the reuse of first-order logic ontologies to augment theories in less expressive languages. Although these ontologies often have relatively weak axiomatizations, other ontologies such as PSL have rich axiomatizations, albeit sometimes in a different language. Our approach outlines the technique of grafting more expressive ontologies to less-expressive, integration-oriented ontologies as a means of augmenting their axiomatizations and consequently their reasoning power. The formal nature of this approach also lays the groundwork for interoperability between the ontologies being extended. With the mappings created, we could potentially use the signature of PSL to query information represented by any of the three ontologies. There is also the potential to perform model-theoretic verification of these ontologies, as in [2]. We hope that this work may serve not only to motivate continued efforts towards reasoning on the Semantic Web, but also as a guide for those looking to reuse and reason with existing ontologies.

References

1. Grüninger, M.: Using the PSL ontology. In: Handbook on Ontologies, pp. 423–443. Springer (2009)
2. Grüninger, M., Hahmann, T., Hashemi, A., Ong, D., Özgövde, A.: Modular first-order ontologies via repositories. Applied Ontology 7(2), 169–209 (2012)
3. Masolo, C., Borgo, S., Gangemi, A., Guarino, N., Oltramari, A., Oltramari, R., Schneider, L., Istc-cnr, L.P., Horrocks, I.: Wonderweb deliverable d17. The wonderweb library of foundational ontologies and the dolce ontology (2002)
4. Mossakowski, T., Lange, C., Kutz, O.: Three semantics for the core of the distributed ontology language. In: Donnelly, M., Guizzardi, G. (eds) FOIS, volume 239 of Frontiers in Artificial Intelligence and Applications, pp. 337–352. IOS Press (2012)
5. Raimond, Y., Abdallah, S., Sandler, M., Giasson, F.: The music ontology. In: ISMIR 2007: 8th International Conference on Music Information Retrieval, Vienna, Austria, September 2007
6. Scherp, A., Franz, T., Saathoff, C., Staab, S.: F-a model of events based on the foundational ontology dolce+ dns ultralight. In: Proceedings of the Fifth International Conference on Knowledge Capture, pp. 137–144. ACM (2009)
7. Shaw, R., Troncy, R., Hardman, L.: LODE: linking open descriptions of events. In: Gómez-Pérez, A., Yu, Y., Ding, Y. (eds.) ASWC 2009. LNCS, vol. 5926, pp. 153–167. Springer, Heidelberg (2009)
8. van Hage, W.R., Malaisé, V., Segers, R., Hollink, L., Schreiber, G.: Design and use of the simple event model (SEM). Web Semantics: Science, Services and Agents on the World Wide Web 9(2), 128–136 (2011). Provenance in the Semantic Web

Probabilistic Event Pattern Discovery

Ahmad Hasan$^{(\boxtimes)}$, Kia Teymourian, and Adrian Paschke

Corporate Semantic Web Research Group, Institute for Computer Science,
Freie Universität Berlin, Berlin, Germany
{ahmadhasan,kia,paschke}@inf.fu-berlin.de
http://www.mi.fu-berlin.de/en/inf/groups/ag-csw/

Abstract. Detecting occurrences of complex events in an event stream requires designing queries that describe real-world situations. However, specifying complex event patterns is a challenging task that requires domain and system specific knowledge. Novel approaches are required that automatically identify patterns of potential interest in a heavy flow of events.

We present and evaluate a probability-based approach for discovering frequent and infrequent sequences of events in an event stream. The approach was tested on a real-world dataset as well as on synthetically generated data with the task being the identification of the most frequent event patterns of a given length. The results were evaluated by measuring the values of Recall and Precision. Our experiments show that the approach can be applied to efficiently retrieve patterns based on their estimated frequencies.

Keywords: Complex event processing · Information retrieval · Pattern detection · Pattern discovery · Conditional probability

1 Introduction

CEP engines are able to detect occurrences of complex events in a stream of primitive ones. Domain experts usually design queries that correspond to interesting patterns of events and feed those queries to a CEP engine whose task is to send a proper notification when a relevant complex event occurs.

However, a wide range of event patterns can not be devised even by domain experts. A domain expert can design a query that fires a notification when the temperature increases beyond a given threshold, but she can not always tell which series of user actions led to a system crash.

In such scenarios, the interest is focused on extreme cases, i.e., most frequent and most infrequent sequences of events. Frequent sequences describe interesting phenomena in the event source or specify a series of events that led to a specific situation, while infrequent sequences might be warnings for unusual situations.

Deciding which are the most frequent patterns requires collecting information about all patterns that occurred in the past. But in the context of event streams, where the flow of events never stops and where the history of the stream can

© Springer International Publishing Switzerland 2015
N. Bassiliades et al. (Eds.): RuleML 2015, LNCS 9202, pp. 241–257, 2015.
DOI: 10.1007/978-3-319-21542-6_16

not be entirely stored, remembering pattern history leads to a huge amount of data that grows rapidly with the number of event types we are interested in as well as the length of the sequences we want to trace. In other words, the longer the patterns we want to detect, the more memory and CPU power we have to provide, which makes detecting all occurring patterns with no restriction on pattern length challenging or even impossible.

On the other hand, detecting short patterns is straightforward, especially when considering only a handful of frequent event types. But such patterns do not contain enough information to make a decision about an observed phenomenon unless suitable heuristics were applied to extend them to longer patterns.

The probability-based approach for event pattern detection which we propose starts from a small set of previously detected short patterns (Section 4 and extends them based on stream properties to longer and more detailed patterns (Section 5). We evaluated the approach by applying it on a real-world dataset as well as on synthetic data. To quantitatively estimate the quality of the resulted patterns, we applied measures of information retrieval on the sets of most frequent and most infrequent event patterns (Section 6). We discuss relevant approaches to pattern mining in event streams and show how our approach relate to them (Section 7) and conclude with a discussion of the results.

2   Preliminaries

We start from a set E of primitive events. A primitive event is an event object that records a real-world event. A set of primitive events can be summarized, represented, or denoted by complex events [8]. Complex events can be expressed in terms of primitive and complex ones using event algebra operators like SEQ, AND and OR, defined for instance in [2]. In this paper, we will deal with the sequence operator that binds two events that occur after one another.

We consider only discrete event types. An event can occur or not occur at a specific point of time. Continuous events, like temperature readings, have to be converted into some discrete space. In such cases, our approach could be applied on a stream of events that summarize such raw events by inducing events. Instead of handling raw temperature readings, events of increase or decrease in temperature can be considered.

Moreover, we distinguish between an event type that provides a definition or a schema for a class of events and an event instance that refers to an actual occurrence of an event type at a specific point in time. The complex event type $(A; B)$ for example refers to the occurrences of an instance of the event type A followed by an instance of the event type B. Multiple occurrences of an event type are referred to collectively by a pattern. We use the notation $\{A; B\}^4$ to refer to a pattern of the former event type that occurred 4 times in the event source.

3   The Framework

Our probabilistic approach expects an initial set of event patterns with their
frequencies to be provided. The frequencies of longer patterns are then estimated
probabilistically. Figure 1 shows an example scenario in which our approach
could be applied.

On a stream of primitive events, a pattern *detection* algorithm (Section 4) is
first applied to determine the frequencies of patterns of a given initial length n_0.

The resulting patterns are extended by estimating the frequencies of longer
patterns as we will describe in the following sections. Each extension we apply
to the available set of event patterns adds one additional event to each pattern
extending its length by one. The extension procedure can be repeated multiple
times extending available patterns by one event each time until we reach n, the
desired length of patterns.

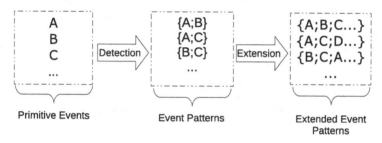

Fig. 1. An example context in which probabilistic event pattern discovery can be
applied

An abstract example is shown in Table 1 where the first column contains a
sample of the patterns directly detected from the stream with their frequencies.
We use the notation $\{P\}^f$ where P is an event pattern and f is its frequency.

Table 1. Example of input patterns of length 2 and the resulted patterns after extending them to length 3

Detected patterns $(n = 2)$	Extended patterns $(n = 3)$
$\{A;B\}^3$	
$\{B;C\}^5$	$\{A;B;C\}^1$
$\{B;D\}^{10}$	$\{A;B;D\}^2$

The second column of the table shows the resulting patterns generated by
applying conditional probability calculations on the frequencies of the shorter
patterns from the initial set of patterns.

The table shows for example how the frequency of the complex event
$\{A;B;C\}$ can be estimated if the frequencies of all subpatterns, i.e. the patterns $\{A;B\}$ and $\{B;C\}$, are provided. Frequencies of the initial set of patterns

of length 2 indicate that the event C occurs in one third of the times, i.e. $\frac{5}{5+10}$, in which the event B occurs. For all patterns that end with the event B, we expect the event C to follow in one third of the times which enables us to estimate the frequencies of such patterns.

4   Pattern Detection

For keeping track of pattern frequencies, we maintain a tree structure whose nodes represent sequential event patterns. Child nodes are events that occurred after their parents. Each path in the tree represents a pattern and each node on such path holds the frequency of the pattern that starts from the root of the tree and ends at this node.

In Figure 2 a pattern tree for two event types is partially depicted. The figure shows the branch of the tree that represent patterns that start with the event A. The A node on level holds the frequency of the short pattern consisting of a single event A, while the B node on level 2 under the A node holds the frequency of the pattern $\{A; B\}$.

We always remember the last $n - 1$ events by pointing to the corresponding pattern in the tree. The bold circles in the tree in Figure 2 marks the path of the current pattern. After reading $\{A; A\}$, we point to the corresponding path in the tree. When the event B occurs, we increment the frequency of the child node B on level n, i.e. of the pattern $\{A; A; B\}$, and point to the new pattern $\{A; B\}$.

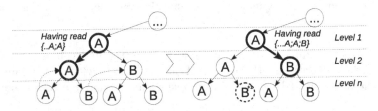

Fig. 2. A pattern tree with the current pointer pointing at the pattern $\{A; A\}$ (left) then $\{A; B\}$(*right*). The doted arrows show where the current pattern will be after reading the event referred to by the node.

Another feature of our pattern tree is that each leaf on level n refers to a node on level $n-1$ that corresponds to a postfix of its pattern which will be the future current pattern after an occurrence of the event referred to by the node. Those relations are depicted in Figure 2 as doted arrows. The node corresponding to the pattern $\{A; A; B\}$ for example, refers to the pattern $\{A; B\}$ which becomes the current pattern if the event B occurs after the pattern $\{A; A\}$.

Reporting a new event using this structure requires looking for the corresponding node under the children of the current node, which is an $O(|E|)$ operation, then looking for the node representing the new current path. Since each leaf already refers to the proper pattern to be the next, shifting the current pattern has a constant cost of $O(1)$.

5   Probabilistic Pattern Extension

Starting with patterns of length n_0 provided in the initial set, our aim is to estimate the frequencies of all patterns of length $n_0 + 1$. Equation 1 shows how such patterns can be split into two overlapping shorter pattern. The two subpatterns have the length n_0, i.e., they belong to the initial set with known frequencies.

$$
\begin{aligned}
P &= \{A_1; A_2; A_3; \ldots A_{n_0-1}; A_{n_0}; A_{n_0+1}\} \\
P_0 &= \{A_1; A_2; A_3; \ldots A_{n_0-1}; A_{n_0} \quad \} \\
\acute{P}_0 &= \{ \quad A_2; A_3; \ldots A_{n_0-1}; A_{n_0}; A_{n_0+1}\}
\end{aligned}
\tag{1}
$$

where:

- P: The target pattern whose probability is to be calculated.
- P_0: The known pattern of length n_0 detected in a previous phase.
- $\acute{P}_0$: The second part of P that overlaps with P_0 and contains the extension event. We do have the frequency of this pattern too.
- Primitive events $A_i \in E$.

We now want to estimate the frequency of P based on the frequencies of its sub-patterns. We know that this value is proportional to the frequency of P_0 and that it depends on the probability for A_{n_0+1} to occur after the P_0.

P will occur each time A_{n_0+1} occurs after P_0, so the frequency of P is calculated as follows:

$$
Fr(P) = Fr(P_0) \times Pr(A_{n_0+1} | P_0)
\tag{2}
$$

where:

- Fr: The frequency function that returns the frequency of a given pattern if already available.
- Pr: The probability function.
- P, P_0, $\acute{P}_0$ and A_i: as in Equation 1 above.

Since we do not have all the information required to calculate the exact frequency of P, we propose to estimate it as follows:

$$
Fr(P) \approx Fr(P_0) \times Pr(\acute{P}_0)
\tag{3}
$$

In other words, the probability for the new event A_{n_0+1} to follow P_0 approximately equals the probability for it to follow the longest postfix of P_0.

6   Evaluation

In order to evaluate the results of our approach, the patterns resulting from extension have to be compared to the real patterns in the event source. Those actual patterns make our *gold standard* that serves as a control set.

The quality of pattern retrieval can be estimated based on the values of *Precision* and *Recall* [13] by ordering the resulted patterns according to their estimated frequencies and comparing the most frequent among them to the most frequent patterns of the gold standard.

Measuring the quality of retrieval by examining the set of most frequent patterns, we are no longer concerned about the exact value of the pattern's frequency, but about its ranking among other patterns of the same length. However, we will evaluate the accuracy of the estimated frequencies before examining the quality of information retrieval.

6.1   Experimental Dataset

For experiments on real-world data, we used the dataset provided by a Dutch academic hospital [1]. The event log contains data of treatments received by cancer patients and was distributed in XES format with the history of each patient listed within a *trace*. Each of those traces contains *event* tags that correspond to treatments. Events are marked with timestamps that indicate the date on which a treatment was performed.

For the purpose of our evaluation, we are particularly interested in temporal relations between successive treatments received by each patient. A patient, as the data suggests, usually visits the hospital regularly and receives multiple treatments in one *session*. Sessions do not have dedicated structural elements in XES format, but they can be recognized by the timestamps of the treatments where a session consists of events that have the same timestamp and are logged within the same trace.

The dataset contains 675 different *activities* corresponding to various treatments, 134 of which were applied in more than 50 sessions. The total number of distinct patients is 1143 as the number of traces indicates. We could identify a total of 19.981 sessions, i.e. about 17 sessions per patient. In average, 7.5 treatments were performed per session. In some sessions, the same treatment is performed more than once.

6.2   Warm-Up Experiment

The first test is a simple one-step extension from binary patterns with two events to patterns of length 3. In order to reach meaningful results, we applied the procedure to the dataset of the Dutch academic hospital.

---

[1] Real-life log of a Dutch academic hospital, originally intended for use in the first Business Process Intelligence Contest (BPIC 2011) http://data.3tu.nl/repository/uuid:d9769f3d-0ab0-4fb8-803b-0d1120ffcf54 published by Eindhoven University of Technology.

Table 2 shows an excerpt of the results where the patterns of our gold standard are shown with their frequencies in addition to their estimated frequencies calculated by an implementation of our procedure.

As the first line of Table 2 shows, the treatment 370000 appeared in 6782 session. In 4800 of those sessions, a treatment of the type 40014 followed in the next session, which means 4800 occurrences of the pattern {370000;40014}. The frequency of 4357 for the pattern {370000;40014;40014} indicates that the treatment 40014 almost always follow the pattern {370000;40014}.

Lines in bold face correspond to extended patterns. The frequency of the pattern {370000;40014;40014} for example is estimated to be 4148 while its actual value is 4357, which means that the one-step-extension led to an error of 4%.

Table 2. A sample of the results of extending patterns from length 2 to 3

Pattern	Detected	Extended	Error Rate
{370000}	6782	-	-
{370000;40014}	4800	-	-
{370000;40014;40014}	**4357**	**4148**	**209(4%)**
{370000;40014;370000}	**2095**	**1921**	**174(8%)**
{370000;40014;379999}	**2095**	**1921**	**174(8%)**
{370000;40014;613000}	**4038**	**3807**	**231(5%)**
{370000;40014;614400}	**2695**	**2557**	**138(5%)**
{370000;370000}	3782	-	-
{370000;370000;40014}	**2488**	**2677**	**189(7%)**
{370000;370000;370000}	**2394**	**2110**	**284(12%)**
	. . .	. . .	. . .

Table 2 presented only a sample of the results to demonstrate the feasibility of the approach. More comprehensive evaluation will be presented in the following sections.

6.3 Execution Time: Deterministic vs. Probabilistic Discovery

To estimate the gain in execution time that can be achieved by applying our approach, we performed a test in which a detection algorithm was applied on the dataset of the Dutch academic hospital to detect sequential event patterns of lengths 1 to 10.

Each iteration i of the experiment consisted of two steps:

- Detection of i-long patterns by applying the detection algorithm described in Section 4.
- Detection patterns of length 2 and extending them to length i.

Since the goal of this test is to compare the execution time, we do not reuse any information from the first step. Instead, the second step repeats a part of the first step to guarantee having the same overhead.

Furthermore, both steps are performed on the same machine, hence the concrete resources are irrelevant for the comparison. However, we present here the results of a test performed on a machine with Intel Celeron Dual-core processor and 3 GB of memory.

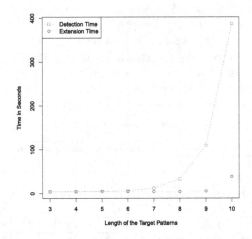

Fig. 3. Comparing execution time between deterministic (detection) and probabilistic (extension) discovery of event patterns.

As Figure 3 shows, the two approaches hardly differ for short patterns, but form a pattern length of 7, the probabilistic procedure begins to outperform the detection algorithm.

Although both methods have the same IO overhead because both have to read the entire content of the dataset for once, estimating frequencies instead of calculating them still has the crucial advantage of dealing a whole pattern, i.e. calculating the frequency for each pattern at once without having to report each single notification of an occurrence of the pattern and processing it as done by the detection algorithm we used and with any procedure that has to build the pattern structure gradually while receiving event notifications.

6.4   Frequency Error Rates

To compute error rates in the results, we need to examine the deviation of the estimated frequencies from the real frequencies of the gold standard.

Mean Absolute Percentage Error [11], or MAPE, is an error measure for evaluating the quality of prediction by comparing the predicted value to the actual one. Equation 5 gives the definition of MAPE:

$$MAPE = \frac{1}{N} \times \sum_{i=1}^{N} |\frac{R_i}{F_i}| \qquad (4)$$

- R_i is the difference between the predicted value and the actual one for item i.
- F_i is the actual frequency of the pattern i.
- N the total number of patterns.

We have already seen a part of this equation in Table 2 where the difference between estimated and actual frequencies was calculated and given in percent.

For calculating the error rate of single value rather than a set of values, we define the Absolute Percentage Error, or APE, as follows:

$$APE = |\frac{R_i}{F_i}| \qquad (5)$$

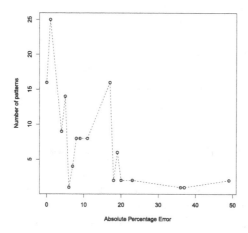

Fig. 4. Absolute percentage error values in frequencies of patterns extended from length 2 to 3. The resulted mean (MAPE) was 8.5% for the whole dataset.

Figure 4 shows the distribution of this part of MAPE in the results of the last experiment of one-step extension on patterns of length 2 of the 5 most frequent events in the dataset of the Dutch academic hospital reaching patterns of length 3.

The horizontal axis in Figure 4 represents values of absolute percentage error whereas the vertical values are the numbers of patterns whose estimation led to these error values. The figure shows that the frequencies of 16 patterns could be estimated correctly, i.e. with a zero error percentage, while the estimated frequencies of 25 patterns out of 125 deviate from the actual frequency by 1%.

We see that most of the patterns that resulted from a one step extension had an absolute error under 20%. Indeed, the value of MAPE for all the patterns in the dataset was 8.5%.

6.5 Accumulated MAPE

For a more comprehensive evaluation of the estimated frequencies, we measured the MAPE values under various configurations, each corresponding to a different combination of the length of the patterns in the start set and the target length.

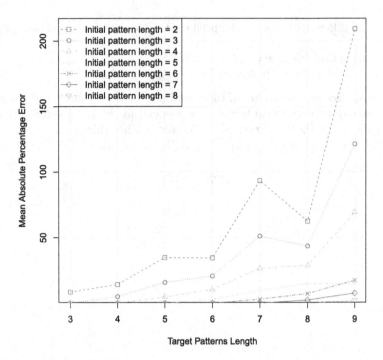

Fig. 5. MAPE values resulting from extension of patterns

In an iteration with a start length n_0 and a target length n, all patterns of length n_0 are detected directly from the dataset and used as an initial set for extension. The patterns of this set are then extended step by step and the MAPE value is calculated for the whole set of patterns whose frequencies have been estimated.

As the results in Figure 5 show, the error rate increases with each extension step. We reach the worst estimations when the initial set of patterns does not provide enough information about the patterns in the event source.

Indeed, the highest error rate results when we start with patterns of length 2. After extending such patterns 7 times to get patterns of length 9, the MAPE value even exceeds one hundred percent.

However, when we start with longer patterns, the MAPE error rate starts low and grows more slowly. When we are provided with the patterns of length 5 as initial set, we can even double the length of the given patterns with negligible error rates of less than 15%.

6.6 Discovery of Frequent and Infrequent Patterns

In this experiment, we apply information retrieval measures to evaluate the retrieval quality of our probability-based approach. We apply the same test strategy as in the previous section to study the effect of the pattern length in the initial set and the desired length of target patterns.

The patterns come again from the dataset of the Dutch academic hospital and are submitted to two experiments. In the first one, we evaluate the retrieval of frequent event patterns, then we repeat the same test for infrequent patterns.

To estimate the quality of discovery of the most frequent patterns, we take 10% of the most frequent patterns of the length in question and compare them to their parallels in the gold standard to calculate recall and precision.

Higher values of recall and precision are reached when the extended patterns get the same order as in the gold standard. While recall is sensitive to false negatives, i.e. to patterns that are incorrectly considered infrequent, precision is sensitive to false positives, i.e. patterns that were falsely considered frequent.

We notice that recall and precision have the same value when the sets of relevant and retrieved patterns have the same size, which is the case in our experiment. When the pattern tree is saturated and all of its branches exist, the number of patterns on each level of any given length reaches its maximum value on the tree of the gold standard as well as on the tree returned by our procedure. In this case, if we take 10% of the patterns from the same level on both trees, both of the resulting sets will have the same size leading to equal values for recall and precision.

Figure 6a shows the results of retrieving the top 10% of patterns of the eight most frequent event types in the dataset of the Dutch academic hospital.

As the figure shows, all results start with 100% when no estimation is performed. With each extension step, the recall/precision value drops about 5% percent representing an increasing error rate. This loss in retrieval quality seems to deaccelerate with each extension leading to less dramatic drop in recall and precision.

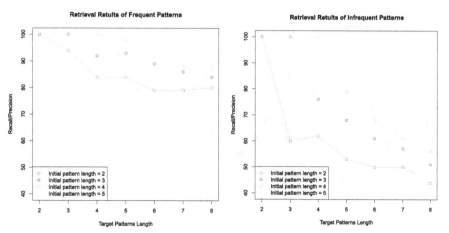

(a) Evaluation of discovery results of the **most** frequent patterns in the Dataset.

(b) Evaluation of discovery of the **least** frequent patterns in the Dataset.

Fig. 6. Retrieval results for frequent and infrequent event patterns

Again, the more information we provide as the basis for frequency estimation, the better the results that can be expected. The results of the tests that started with patterns of length 5, as Figure 6a suggests, have retrieved almost 90% of the most frequent patterns correctly.

We notice in the diagram that the retrieval quality sometimes gets better with a further extension step, as when extending from length 4 to length 5 starting from a pattern length of 3. We might intuitively expect that each extension leads to worse results and that the error rates of previous levels accumulate and always rise, which is true in most of the cases.

However, as we will see later, the quality of the results is determined by the entropy of the event source and this value can differ from one level on the pattern tree to another. Thus, if the entropy of the patterns on some level is lower than that of the parent level, i.e., we can tell with more confidence what events will follow the patterns of this level, the extension results will be better.

We can now take a look at the same results for infrequent patterns shown in Figure 6b. In this test we compared the least frequent 10% of the patterns from the gold standard with those retrieved based on the estimated frequencies.

As Figure 6b illustrates, the results in this category is less promising. Already after the first extension we lose about 20-30% of the correct patterns. Multiple extensions lead to unusable results where even less than 50% of the patterns could be retrieved.

By examining the data, we noticed that frequent patterns in our example dataset are more disperse than infrequent ones. Most of the patterns have low frequency, while patterns with high frequencies are rare and show larger differences in their frequencies. This phenomenon makes discovering infrequent patterns sensitive to small errors that can not be avoided in a probabilistic configuration.

6.7 Pattern Discovery under Controlled Entropy

For observing the behaviour of our method under various grades of entropy, we ran a test in which a synthetic event stream was generated using only two event types. The probability distribution of the two event types was manipulated leading to different values of entropy in the resulting stream that had a known entropy of twenty values ranging from 0 to 1 bit.

With each of those levels of entropy, a randomizer generates event instances for 30 seconds and sends them to a consumer. The later builds two pattern tree:

- *Gold standard Tree* containing patterns of length 12.
- *Initial Patterns Tree* with patterns of length 10 only.

When a generation burst is done, the consumer extends the patterns of the second tree to length 12. Recall and precision are then measured by comparing the 10% of the most frequent patterns from both trees.

Figure 7 shows how the recall and precision changed under various entropy values. The obvious trend confirms that the retrieval quality worsen when the entropy increases.

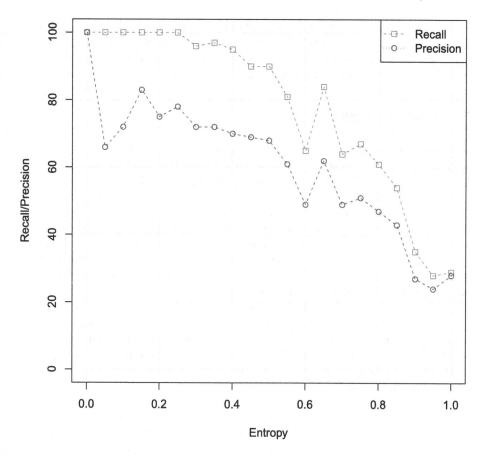

Fig. 7. Evaluation results of the discovery of the most frequent patterns extended from pattern length 10 to 12 under controlled stream entropy

When the entropy is zero, i.e. when there is only a single pattern occurring in the stream, our approach achieves perfect recall and precision of 100%. The greater the entropy, the worse the results become. Indeed, under a high entropy, the results are simply useless and seem to be produced by accident.

The entropy is a measurable property of the stream, though some interpretation might be necessary to calculate its value. The entropy of a stream might also change over time, which requires special consideration. However, having an estimation of the entropy would help make a realistic expectation about the quality of retrieval in a probabilistic configuration as with our approach.

High entropy indicates that there are no particularly frequent events or patterns to be discovered in the stream. Frequencies of patterns and events are so close that the question of frequent patterns has no meaning. With such negligible differences in frequency *frequent* patterns are only coincidentally frequent.

On the opposite, streams with low entropy have characteristic patterns whose importance is manifested in their frequencies. Under such conditions, as out experiment shows, the set of most frequent patterns can be identified with *acceptable* error rates, with the tolerance against error rates being application dependent.

7   Related Work

Since we want to support event streams in addition to bounded event sources, we can not apply methods that require accessing the history events of the whole source more than once, like it is done in algorithms for mining sequential databases, e.g. in [1,7,12,14,16]. But we can keep and analyze a limited portion of the event history (in CEP and event streaming often called a window).

The goal of related algorithms for data streaming, like Lossy Counting [9] or Moment [5], that handle streams and access the event source only once, keeping only a portion of its data, is to minimize both processing time and the amount of data that has to be kept for later analysis. None of those algorithms claims to be able to detect *all* the patterns of the source. Lossy Counting [9] and FPDM [15] take an approximate approach and accept an error margin, in order to keep the data structure that contains information about the past at its minimum. Moment concentrates on *closed* event patterns and maintains a compact data structure to which only necessary changes has to be made minimizing the processing time required when receiving event notifications. Enhancements of our work over these approaches can be summarized as follows:

- *Memory Size*: The amount of data we can, or we have to, keep from the past. Algorithms tend to keep only the necessary data either by restricting the set of target patterns to frequent or recent patterns, or by summarizing data of the past, like the approach of aggregation at multiple granularities taken in [6].
- *Realtime Processing*: The processing required when an event notification arrives. This depends particularly on the data structure being used, but we always want to minimize the processing required at this phase in order to stay realtime and keep our data up-to-date. The Moment [5] algorithm changes its data structure only on the boundaries between frequent and infrequent patterns.
- *Error Tolerance*: Because we know that we can not keep trace of all patterns in the stream, we accept a controlled margin of error, like in Lossy Counting [9], or we just accept less information about those patterns, like estDec [3] that concentrates on recent patterns.
- *Relevance*: Algorithms attempt to answer the question of relevance. Deciding which patterns are more important than the others is crucial since only a part of the patterns can be traced. Lossy Counting [9] and FPDM [15] target frequent patterns, while estDec [3] considers *recent* patterns to be relevant. Furthermore, $\lambda - HCount$ [4] and [6] merge both factors by regarding frequent *and* recent patterns.

In our work, we made a further step in the same direction and tested the potential of those possibilities.

Probabilistic Event Patterns Discovery:

- Maintains an incomplete set of complex event patterns.
- Uses a data structure already prepared for receiving new patterns so that the costs of reporting a new event stays minimal.
- Applies probability-based calculations to predict missing information.
- Depends on relative frequency to identify relevant patterns.

A further recent work that inspired our approach was the comprehensive framework for automated rule generation suggested by Margara et al. in [10]. The aim of the framework was to identify rules of causality between events in historical traces and a situation of interest. The method rely on Information Gain Retrieval, which makes use of event distribution and probabilities of the source events, which is the basis of our estimation of frequencies of event patterns.

Comparison to Association Rule Learning

When mining association rules, we are interested in quantitatively expressing the strength of association among different items. Association rule mining counts simultaneous occurrences of observed items and applies metrics like support and confidence to assess the detected associations.

An association rule within a set of items $\mathcal{I} = I_1 \ldots I_n$ has the following form:

$$X \Rightarrow I_j : X \subset \mathcal{I}, I_j \in \mathcal{I} \tag{6}$$

If we compare rules of this form to formulations of conditional probabilities, as in Equation 2, we find that the strength of an association rule depends on the probability of the event to follow a pattern.

In the context of association rules, we can interpret the probability $Pr(A_{n_0+1}|P_0)$ in Equation 2 for example as the confidence in the rule $P_0 \Rightarrow A_{n_0+1}$.

However, the essential difference between association rules and our probabilistic approach lies in the structure of information handled by each method. While association rules depend on the relatively open structure of sets, which suites the original problems addressed by this technique, we adopt a more strict patterns structure in which the order of elements also counts.

Our probabilistic approach can be regarded as a vertical interpretation of association rules. Instead of studying how items happen *simultaneously*, we are here interested in the temporal order of events and how they occur *successively* after one another.

Applying our approach for retrieving frequent patterns for basket analysis, the classical application of association rules, would mean examining those items appearing in successive purchases instead of those occurring together within the same purchase.

8   Conclusion

Probability-based discovery of complex event patterns is an efficient way to estimate the frequencies of long patterns that are otherwise uncomputable. The method saves processing time by computing the frequencies of whole patterns instead of processing single events.

The initial set of patterns that makes the basis for estimating frequencies of unknown patterns is crucial to the retrieval quality. The more information this set provides the better the results can be achieved in terms of recall and precision.

Estimation of frequencies can be applied multiple times to reach longer patterns. However, each iteration causes further errors to accumulate leading to lower recall and precision.

Finally, the resulting quality of the proposed approach depends on the entropy of the event source. The best results can be achieved under low entropy. The higher the entropy the worse the results get. However, measuring the entropy of the source helps estimate the reliability of the resulted ranking of patterns and decide whether the approach can be applied at all.

There is still much to be done to benefit from the approach proposed in this paper. The most urgent task would be to find more applications and to investigate the feasibility of the procedure in domains like stock market or traffic congestion detection. Including more event operators, like the AND and OR operators, is a challenging, yet interesting, task.

References

1. Agrawal, R., Srikant, R.: Mining sequential patterns. In: Proceedings of the Eleventh International Conference on Data Engineering, ICDE 1995, pp. 3–14. IEEE Computer Society, Washington, DC, USA (1995). http://dl.acm.org/citation.cfm?id=645480.655281

2. Chakravarthy, S., Krishnaprasad, V., Anwar, E., Kim, S.K.: Composite events for active databases: semantics, contexts and detection. In: VLDB 1994. pp. 606–617. Morgan Kaufmann Publishers Inc., San Francisco (1994). http://dl.acm.org/citation.cfm?id=645920.672994

3. Chang, J.H., Lee, W.S.: Finding recent frequent itemsets adaptively over online data streams. In: Proceedings of the Ninth ACM SIGKDD International Conference on Knowledge Discovery and Data Mining, KDD 2003, pp. 487–492. ACM, New York (2003). http://doi.acm.org/10.1145/956750.956807

4. Chen, L., Mei, Q.: Mining frequent items in data stream using time fading model. Information Sciences 257, 54–69 (2014). http://www.sciencedirect.com/science/article/pii/S0020025513006403

5. Chi, Y., Wang, H., Yu, P.S., Muntz, R.R.: Moment: maintaining closed frequent itemsets over a stream sliding window. In: In ICDM, pp. 59–66 (2004)

6. Giannella, C., Han, J., Pei, J., Yan, X., Yu, P.: Mining frequent patterns in data streams at multiple time granularities. Next Generation Data Mining 212, 191–212 (2003)

7. Gomariz, A., Campos, M., Marin, R., Goethals, B.: ClaSP: an efficient algorithm for mining frequent closed sequences. In: Pei, J., Tseng, V.S., Cao, L., Motoda, H., Xu, G. (eds.) PAKDD 2013, Part I. LNCS, vol. 7818, pp. 50–61. Springer, Heidelberg (2013)

8. Luckham, D., Schulte, W.R.: Event processing glossary – version 2.0 (2011)

9. Manku, G.S., Motwani, R.: Approximate frequency counts over data streams. In: Proceedings of VLDB 2002, pp. 346–357 (2002)

10. Margara, A., Cugola, G., Tamburrelli, G.: Learning from the past: automated rule generation for complex event processing. In: Proceedings of the 8th ACM International Conference on Distributed Event-Based Systems, DEBS 2014, pp. 47–58. ACM, New York (2014). http://doi.acm.org/10.1145/2611286.2611289

11. Mitsa, T.: Temporal Data Mining, 1st edn. Chapman & Hall/CRC (2010)

12. Pei, J., Han, J., Mortazavi-asl, B., Pinto, H., Chen, Q., Dayal, U., chun Hsu, M.: Prefixspan: mining sequential patterns efficiently by prefix-projected pattern growth. In: ICDE 2001, p. 215. IEEE Computer Society, Washington, DC (2001). http://dl.acm.org/citation.cfm?id=876881.879716

13. Rijsbergen, C.J.V.: Information Retrieval, 2nd edn. Butterworth-Heinemann, Newton (1979)

14. Yan, X., Han, J., Afshar, R.: Clospan: mining closed sequential patterns in large datasets. In. In SDM, pp. 166–177 (2003)

15. Yu, J.X., Chong, Z., Lu, H., Zhou, A.: False positive or false negative: mining frequent itemsets from high speed transactional data streams. In: VLDB 2004, pp. 204–215. VLDB Endowment (2004). http://dl.acm.org/citation.cfm?id=1316689.1316709

16. Zaki, M.J.: Spade: An efficient algorithm for mining frequent sequences. Mach. Learn. 42(1–2), 31–60 (2001). http://dx.doi.org/10.1023/A:1007652502315

How to Combine Event Stream Reasoning with Transactions for the Semantic Web

Ana Sofia Gomes$^{(\boxtimes)}$ and José Júlio Alferes

NOVA-LINCS - Department de Informática, Faculdade Ciências e Tecnologias,
Universidade NOVA de Lisboa, Lisbon, Portugal
sofia.gomes@campus.fct.unl.pt

Abstract. Semantic Sensor Web is a new trend of research integrating
Semantic Web technologies with sensor networks. It uses Semantic Web
standards to describe both the data produced by the sensors, but also
the sensors and their networks, which enables interoperability of sensor
networks, and provides a way to formally analyze and reason about these
networks. Since sensors produce data at a very high rate, they require
solutions to reason efficiently about what complex events occur based on
the data captured. In this paper we propose $\mathcal{TR}^{ev}$ as a solution to combine the detection of complex events with the execution of transactions
for these domains. $\mathcal{TR}^{ev}$ is an abstract logic to model and execute reactive transactions. The logic is parametric on a pair of oracles defining the
basic primitives of the domain, which makes it suitable for a wide range
of applications. In this paper we provide oracle instantiations combining RDF/OWL and relational database semantics for $\mathcal{TR}^{ev}$. Afterwards,
based on these oracles, we illustrate how $\mathcal{TR}^{ev}$ can be useful for these
domains.

1 Introduction and Motivation

The future of the Internet-of-Things is filled with sensors, and with it, sensor data
and sensor networks. Nodes in these sensor networks use the internet to interact
and communicate with each other, but also with other services and applications,
helping with the detection of changes in the environment, and making daily
decisions based on these changes. Today, sensor networks are successfully used
in detecting emergency situations, monitoring agriculture conditions and animal
farming, industrial control, home automation, patient health surveillance, etc.

With the popularity increase of the Internet-of-Things and the widespread of
sensor networks, one important problem is how to deploy sensors' data so it can
be accessible by a larger number of different applications and services. Sensors
produce data at an extremely high rate, with extremely heterogeneous schemas,
vocabularies and data formats, making it very hard to discover and reuse. Based
on the premise that it is a waste of resources to use sensors' data for just one single application, an important research effort has been made recently in Semantic

A.S. Gomes and J.J. Alferes—This work was supported by project ERRO
(PTDC/EIA-CCO/121823/2010).

N. Bassiliades et al. (Eds.): RuleML 2015, LNCS 9202, pp. 258–273, 2015.
DOI: 10.1007/978-3-319-21542-6_17

Sensor Web (SSW) [8,20] with the goal to enable interoperability between sensors, and reuse of sensors' data. By using Semantic Web technologies, SSW solves this problem by providing a way to semantically describe sensors capabilities, sensors measurements and observations, deployments, etc. With interoperability as one of the main flagships of the Semantic Web, Semantic Web technologies allow one to integrate and reason about knowledge published across different sources, by using RDF as a data model in combination with ontology languages like OWL [16], and to use this knowledge to execute actions in several application domains. In the this context, the Semantic Sensor Network Incubator Group[1] defines an ontology for sensors based on OWL and RDFS, and publishes sensors' data using RDF statements, enabling users to reuse and integrate data from multiple sensors, but also to reason about such data in a powerful way.

In scenarios like sensor networks, where the production of data is high, the fields of Event Processing (EP) and Stream Reasoning provide important solutions to efficiently handle large volumes of data, and to detect complex changes based on these. In these areas, an *event* is a first-class citizen, encoding some change that may be relevant to the system, like e.g. a new sensor's observation. Then, based on the occurrence of a set of events (also called as a *stream*), EP solutions handle the detection of meaningful event patterns (also known as complex events), based on expressive operators and temporal relationship of events. Stream Reasoning exceeds EP by combining streams with domain application knowledge, allowing one to use this knowledge to reason about the events that become true over time. While traditionally EP and Stream Reasoning solutions were designed mostly for databases, the increase of popularity of the Semantic Web and its technologies led to the development of several solutions that can successfully handle and reason about RDF statements and RDFS/OWL models [1,15,19]. However, and by design, EP solutions are incomplete, as they do not deal with the problem of acting upon the event patterns they detect. Detecting these patterns is only meaningful if we can act upon this knowledge, and thus, in general, we need more complete solutions that allow us to define what to do when an event occurs.

In another context, Event-Condition-Action (ECA) languages solve this by explicitly defining how should a system *react* whenever a given pattern is detected. These languages support rules of the form: *on* **event** *if* **condition** *do* **action**, where whenever an event occurs, the condition is checked to hold in the current state and, if that is the case, the action is executed. Today a number of ECA languages exist, providing a semantics for reactive systems in the context of the Semantic Web [3,6,18], multi-agent systems [9,13,17], conflict resolution [7], etc. However, even though ECA languages started in the database context, and many solutions exist with rich languages for defining complex actions, most ECA languages do not allow the action component to be defined as a transaction. Moreover, when they do, they either lack from a declarative semantics (e.g. [18]), or are only suitable for databases since they only detect atomic events defined as primitive insertions/deletes on the database (e.g. [14,21]).

---

[1] http://www.w3.org/2005/Incubator/ssn/

In this case we sustain that in many applications, and especially applications dependent on sensor networks, it is important to guarantee transactional properties, like consistency or atomicity, over the execution of a set of actions issued in response to events. As an application scenario, consider the case where the police wants to monitor and detect traffic violations based on a sensor network deployed in some road. A sensor in such a network can identify plates of vehicles and distinguish between types of vehicles. Then, based on the information that the sensor publishes in RDF, the application must reason about what vehicles are indulging in traffic violations and, in these cases, issue fines for these violations and notify the corresponding drivers. Clearly, some transactional behavior regarding these actions must be ensured, as it can never be the case that a fine is issued and the driver is not notified, or vice-versa.

$\mathcal{TR}$ [4] is a general purpose logic to model and reason about the executional behavior of transactions. It provides a general model theory that is parametric on a pair of oracles defining the semantics of states and updates of the knowledge base (KB) (e.g. relational databases, action languages, description logics, etc.). With it, one can reason about the sequence of states (also denoted as a *path*) where a transaction is executed, *independently* of the semantics of states and primitive actions of the KB. Additionally, $\mathcal{TR}$ also provides a proof-theory to execute a subclass of $\mathcal{TR}$ programs that can be formulated as the Horn-like clauses of logic programming. However, $\mathcal{TR}$ fails to deal simultaneously with complex events and transactions, and for that we have previously proposed $\mathcal{TR}^{ev}$ in [11]. $\mathcal{TR}^{ev}$ is an extension of $\mathcal{TR}$ that can reason about the execution of transactions, but also about the complex events that become true in this transaction execution. Just like in EP algebras, with $\mathcal{TR}^{ev}$ one is able to define complex events by combining atomic (or other complex) events with temporal operators. In $\mathcal{TR}^{ev}$, atomic events can either be external events, which are signalled to the KB, primitive updates in the KB (similarly e.g. to the events "on insert" in databases), or events that the oracle defines to occur in state transitions. Moreover, as in active databases, transactions in $\mathcal{TR}^{ev}$ are *constrained* by the events that occur during their execution: a transaction can only successfully commit when all events triggered during its execution are addressed. $\mathcal{TR}^{ev}$ is parameterized with a pair of oracles as in the original $\mathcal{TR}$, but also takes an additional *choice* function, which abstracts the semantics of a reactive language from its response policies decisions. Of course, to be put to work in specific domains, $\mathcal{TR}^{ev}$ (and $\mathcal{TR}$) require the instantiation of such oracle.

In this paper we propose $\mathcal{TR}^{ev}$ as a solution to combine heterogeneous event stream reasoning with the execution of transactions for sensor networks that use Semantic Web technologies. This is done by providing an appropriate oracle instantiation to reason about RDF/OWL semantics. With it, one can decide what events become true in a given path, based on the occurrence of atomic events and the knowledge inferred from the sensors' ontology. After defining such an oracle, we provide an elaborated example to illustrate what kind of event stream reasoning can be done using $\mathcal{TR}^{ev}$, and how to combine more than one oracle instantiation for a sensor based application that uses RDF/OWL to describe and reason about events together with a relational database to perform transactions.

2   Background: $\mathcal{TR}^{ev}$

Transaction Logic [4], $\mathcal{TR}$, is a logic to execute and reason about general changes in a KB, when these changes need to follow a transactional behavior. In a nutshell[2], $\mathcal{TR}$ syntax extends that of first order logic with the operators $\otimes$ and $\Diamond$, where $\phi \otimes \psi$ denotes the action composed by an execution of ϕ followed by an execution of ψ, and $\Diamond\phi$ denotes the hypothetical execution of ϕ, i.e. a test to see whether ϕ can be executed but leaving the current state unchanged. Moreover, $\phi \wedge \psi$ denotes the simultaneous execution of ϕ and ψ; $\phi \vee \psi$ the execution of ϕ or ψ; and $\neg\phi$ an execution where ϕ is not executed.

In $\mathcal{TR}$ all formulas are read as transactions which are evaluated over sequences of KB states known as *paths*, and satisfaction of formulas means execution. I.e., a formula (or transaction) ϕ is true over a path π iff the transaction successfully executes over that sequence of states. A key feature of $\mathcal{TR}$ is the separation of primitive operations from the logic of combining them. $\mathcal{TR}$'s theory is parametric on two different oracles allowing the incorporation of a wide variety of KB semantics, from classical to non-monotonic to various other nonstandard logics. These oracles abstract the representation of KB states and how to query them (by including the data oracle $\mathcal{O}^d$), and abstract the way states change (defined by the transition oracle $\mathcal{O}^t$). Consequently, the language of primitive queries and actions is not fixed, and neither is the definition of what is a state. To distinguish between states, $\mathcal{TR}$ works with a set of state identifiers to uniquely identify a state. With this, the *data oracle* $\mathcal{O}^d$ is a mapping from state identifiers to sets of formulas where, given a state identifier i, $\mathcal{O}^d(i)$ returns the set of formulas true in state i. The *state transition oracle* $\mathcal{O}^t(i_1, i_2)$ is a function that maps pairs of KB states into sets of ground atoms called elementary transitions, where given two state identifiers i_1 and i_2, $\mathcal{O}^t(i_1, i_2)$ returns the set of elementary transitions that are true when the KB changes from state i_1 into i_2.

The logic provides the concept of a *model* of a $\mathcal{TR}$ theory, which allows one to prove properties of transactions that hold for every possible path of execution; and the notion of executional entailment, in which a transaction ϕ is entailed by a theory given an initial state D_0, and written $P, D_0- \models \phi$, if there is a path $D_0, D_1, \ldots, D_n$, which starts in that state D_0, and on which the transaction, as a whole, succeeds. Given a transaction and an initial state, the executional entailment provides a means to determine what should be the evolution of states of the KB, to succeed the transaction in a atomic way. Non-deterministic transactions are possible, and in this case several successful paths exist. For a special class of $\mathcal{TR}$ theories (known as serial-Horn programs) there is a proof procedure and corresponding implementation [4,10].

---

[2] For lack of space, and since $\mathcal{TR}^{ev}$ is an extension of $\mathcal{TR}$ (cf. [11]) we do not make a thorough overview of $\mathcal{TR}$ here. For complete details see e.g. [4,11]

$\mathcal{TR}^{ev}$ extends $\mathcal{TR}$ in that, besides dealing with the execution of transaction, it is also able to raise and detect complex events. For that, $\mathcal{TR}^{ev}$ separates the evaluation of events from the evaluation of transactions. This is reflected in its syntax, and on the two different satisfaction relations – the event satisfaction $\models_{ev}$ and the transaction satisfaction $\models$. $\mathcal{TR}^{ev}$'s alphabet contains an infinite number of constants $\mathcal{C}$, function symbols $\mathcal{F}$, variables $\mathcal{V}$ and predicate symbols $\mathcal{P}$. Furthermore, predicates in $\mathcal{TR}^{ev}$ are partitioned into transaction names ($\mathcal{P}_t$), event names ($\mathcal{P}_e$), and oracle primitives ($\mathcal{P}_\mathcal{O}$). Importantly, to support event stream reasoning in the oracle side, for this paper, we also consider the case where oracles primitives are partitioned into oracle actions $\mathcal{P}_{\mathcal{O}_a}$ and oracle events $\mathcal{P}_{\mathcal{O}_e}$. Finally, formulas in $\mathcal{TR}^{ev}$ are partitioned into transaction formulas and event formulas, and are evaluated differently: event formulas are meant to be detected w.r.t. a path encoding the history of execution; while transaction formulas are meant to be executed. One of the goals of $\mathcal{TR}^{ev}$'s theory is to find the paths where a given *reactive* transaction formula ϕ successfully executes.

Event formulas, i.e. formulas that can be *detected*, are either an event occurrence, or an expression defined inductively as $\neg\phi$, $\phi \wedge \psi$, $\phi \vee \psi$, or $\phi \otimes \psi$, where ϕ and ψ are event formulas. We further assume $\phi; \psi$, which is syntactic sugar for $\phi \otimes \mathbf{path} \otimes \psi$ (where $\mathbf{path}$ is just any tautology, cf. [5]), with the meaning: "ϕ followed by ψ, but where arbitrary events may be true between ϕ and ψ". An *event occurrence* is of the form $\mathbf{o}(\varphi)$ s.t. $\varphi \in \mathcal{P}_e$ or $\varphi \in \mathcal{P}_\mathcal{O}$ (the latter are events signalling changes in the KB, needed to allow reactive rules similar to e.g. "on insert" triggers in databases). *Transaction formulas*, i.e. formulas that can be *executed*, as in $\mathcal{TR}$ are either a transaction atom, or an expression defined inductively as $\neg\phi$, $\Diamond\phi$, $\phi \wedge \psi$, $\phi \vee \psi$, or $\phi \otimes \psi$. In $\mathcal{TR}^{ev}$, a *transaction atom* is either a transaction name (in $\mathcal{P}_t$), an oracle defined primitive (in $\mathcal{P}_\mathcal{O}$), the response to an event (written $\mathbf{r}(\varphi)$ where $\varphi \in \mathcal{P}_\mathcal{O} \cup \mathcal{P}_e$), or an event name (in $\mathcal{P}_e$). The latter corresponds to the (trans)action of *explicitly* triggering an event directly in a transaction. Finally, rules have the form $\varphi \leftarrow \psi$ and can be transaction or (complex) event rules. In a transaction rule φ is a transaction atom and ψ a transaction formula; in an event rule φ is an event occurrence and ψ is an event formula. A *program* is a set of transaction and event rules.

Central to $\mathcal{TR}^{ev}$'s theory is the correspondence between $\mathbf{o}(\varphi)$ and $\mathbf{r}(\varphi)$. As a transactional system, the occurrence of an event constrains the satisfaction path of the transaction where the event occurs, and a transaction can only "commit" if all the occurring events are answered. More precisely, a transaction is only satisfied in a path, if all the events occurring in that path are responded to. This behavior is achieved by evaluating event occurrences and transactions differently, and by imposing $\mathbf{r}(\varphi)$ to be true in the paths where $\mathbf{o}(\varphi)$ holds. For dealing with cases where more than one occurrence holds simultaneously, $\mathcal{TR}^{ev}$ takes as parameter, besides $\mathcal{TR}$'s data and transition oracles, also a *choice* function defining what event should be selected for being responded at a given time, in case of conflict. This function abstracts the operational decisions from the logic, and allows $\mathcal{TR}^{ev}$ to be useful in a wide spectrum of applications.

As a reactive system, $\mathcal{TR}^{ev}$ receives a series (or a stream) of external events which may cause the execution of transactions in response. As in $\mathcal{TR}$, $\mathcal{TR}^{ev}$'s formulas are also evaluated over paths (sequence of states), and the theory allows us to reason about *how* does the KB evolve in a transactional way, based on an initial KB state. This is defined as $P, D_0- \models e_1 \otimes \ldots \otimes e_k$, where D_0 is the initial KB state and $e_1 \otimes \ldots \otimes e_k$ is the sequence of events that arrived. A path $D_0 \xrightarrow{O_1} \ldots \xrightarrow{O_n} D_n$ that make $P, D_0- \models e_1 \otimes \ldots \otimes e_k$ true, represents a KB evolution responding to $e_1 \otimes \ldots \otimes e_k$

As usual, satisfaction of formulas is based on interpretations which define what atoms are true over what paths, by mapping paths to sets of atoms. If a transaction (resp. event) atom ϕ belongs to $M(\pi)$ then ϕ is said to execute (resp. occur) over path π given interpretation M:

Definition 1 (Interpretation). *An interpretation M is a mapping assigning a set of atoms (or $\top^3$) to every possible path, with the restrictions (where $D_i s$ are states, and φ an atom):*

1. $\varphi \in M(\langle D \rangle)$ *if* $\varphi \in \mathcal{O}^d(D)$
2. $\{\varphi, \mathbf{o}(\varphi)\} \subseteq M(\langle D_1 \xrightarrow{\mathbf{o}(\varphi)} D_2 \rangle)$ *if* $\varphi \in \mathcal{O}^t(D_1, D_2) \wedge \varphi \in \mathcal{P}_{\mathcal{O}_a}$
3. $\mathbf{o}(\varphi) \in M(\langle D_1 \xrightarrow{\mathbf{o}(\varphi)} D_2 \rangle)$ *if* $\mathbf{o}(\varphi) \in \mathcal{O}^t(D_1, D_2) \wedge \mathbf{o}(\varphi) \in \mathcal{P}_{\mathcal{O}_e}$
4. $\mathbf{o}(e) \in M(\langle D \xrightarrow{\mathbf{o}(e)} D \rangle)$

Understanding this notion of interpretation, and its restrictions, is important for understanding $\mathcal{TR}^{ev}$'s semantics. The first three points above, force all interpretations to satisfy primitive formulas on the paths where the oracles satisfy them, i.e., only the mappings that comply with the specified oracles are considered as interpretations. The second point also states that, whenever a primitive action φ (e.g. the insertion of a fact in the KB) is made true by the oracle, the occurrence associated with the primitive action $\mathbf{o}(\varphi)$ (e.g. "on insert" of that fact) is also made true in every M, and in this case, the path is annotated with φ's occurrence. As such, this restriction guarantees compliance with the oracles, viz. whenever the oracle satisfies a primitive action in a transition, all Ms also satisfy both the primitive action, and the primitive occurrence in that same transition. Similarly, the third point makes the correspondence between the primitive events defined by the oracle, and the primitive events made true by Ms. This allows the oracle to define primitive events different from primitive actions, and make interpretations satisfy these events in these transitions.

Finally, the fourth point guarantees that, whenever an event is observed to occur in a transition, then all interpretations necessarily satisfy this occurrence. This point is an important technical detail to satisfy the action of explicitly triggering an event. By forcing M to satisfy $\mathbf{o}(e)$ whenever it appears explicitly in the history of the path, we impose compliance between the history of occurrences on a path and the set of formulas that interpretations make true on that same path. Note that making the occurrence of an event explicitly true does not change the KB state *per se* and thus, these transitions only take place on paths

---

[3] For not having to consider partial mappings, besides formulas, interpretations can also return the special symbol $\top$. The interested reader is referred to [4] for details.

where the current state does not evolve. However, as we shall see, $\mathcal{TR}^{ev}$ theory imposes that, whenever $\mathbf{o}(e)$ is true in some part of a path (or subpath), then for a transaction to be satisfied, $\mathbf{r}(e)$ must also be true. Thus naturally, some actions may need to be executed to satisfy $\mathbf{r}(e)$ as an implicit result of making this occurrence true, which in turn, may cause changes in the KB.

Satisfaction of formulas requires the definition of operations on paths. E.g., $\phi \otimes \psi$ is true on a path if ϕ is true up to some point in the path, and ψ is true from that point onwards.

Definition 2 (Path Splits, Subpaths and Prefixes). *Let π be a k-path, i.e. a path of length k of the form $\langle D_1 \xrightarrow{O_1} \dots \xrightarrow{O_{k-1}} D_k \rangle$. A split of π is any pair of subpaths, π_1 and π_2, s.t. $\pi_1 = \langle D_1 \xrightarrow{O_1} \dots \xrightarrow{O_{i-1}} D_i \rangle$ and $\pi_2 = \langle D_i \xrightarrow{O_i} \dots \xrightarrow{O_{k-1}} D_k \rangle$ for some i $(1 \leq i \leq k)$. In this case, we write $\pi = \pi_1 \circ \pi_2$.*
A subpath π' of π is any subset of states of π where the order of the states is preserved. A prefix π_1 of π is any subpath of π sharing the initial state.

As mentioned above, satisfaction of complex formulas is different for event formulas and transaction formulas. While the former concerns the *detection* of an event, the latter concerns the *execution* of actions in a transactional way. As such, when compared to the original $\mathcal{TR}$, transactions in $\mathcal{TR}^{ev}$ are further required to execute *all* the responses of the events occurring in the original execution path of that transaction. In other words, a transaction φ is satisfied over a path π, if φ is executed in a prefix π_1 of π (i.e. where $\pi = \pi_1 \circ \pi_2$), and all events occurring over π_1 are *responded to* in π_2. This requires a non-monotonic behavior of the satisfaction relation of transaction formulas, making them dependent on the satisfaction of events.

Definition 3 (Satisfaction of Event Formulas). *Let M be an interpretation, π a path and ϕ a formula. If $M(\pi) = \top$ then $M, \pi \models_{ev} \phi$; else:*

1. **Base Case:** $M, \pi \models_{ev} \phi$ *iff $\phi \in M(\pi)$ for every event occurrence ϕ*
2. **Negation:** $M, \pi \models_{ev} \neg\phi$ *iff it is not the case that $M, \pi \models_{ev} \phi$*
3. **Disjunction:** $M, \pi \models_{ev} \phi \vee \psi$ *iff $M, \pi \models_{ev} \phi$ or $M, \pi \models_{ev} \psi$.*
4. **Serial Conjunction:** $M, \pi \models_{ev} \phi \otimes \psi$ *iff there is a split $\pi_1 \circ \pi_2$ of π s.t. $M, \pi_1 \models_{ev} \phi$ and $M, \pi_2 \models_{ev} \psi$*
5. **Executional Possibility:** $M, \pi \models_{ev} \Diamond\phi$ *iff π is a 1-path of the form $\langle D \rangle$ for some state D and $M, \pi' \models_{ev} \phi$ for some path π' that begins at D.*

Definition 4 (Satisfaction of Transaction Formulas). *Let M be an interpretation, π a path, ϕ transaction formula. If $M(\pi) = \top$ then $M, \pi \models \phi$; else:*

1. **Base Case:** $M, \pi \models p$ *iff there is a prefix π' of π s.t. $p \in M(\pi')$ and π is an expansion of path π' w.r.t. M, for every transaction atom p s.t. $p \notin \mathcal{P}_e$.*
2. **Event Case:** $M, \pi \models e$ *iff $e \in \mathcal{P}_e$ and there is a prefix π' of π s.t. $M, \pi' \models_{ev}$ $\mathbf{o}(e)$ and π is an expansion of path π' w.r.t. M.*
3. **Negation:** $M, \pi \models \neg\phi$ *iff it is not the case that $M, \pi \models \phi$*
4. **Disjunction:** $M, \pi \models \phi \vee \psi$ *iff $M, \pi \models \phi$ or $M, \pi \models \psi$.*
5. **Serial Conjunction:** $M, \pi \models \phi \otimes \psi$ *iff there is a prefix π' of π and a split $\pi_1 \circ \pi_2$ of π' s.t. $M, \pi_1 \models \phi$ and $M, \pi_2 \models \psi$ and π is an expansion of path π' w.r.t. M.*

6. **Executional Possibility:** $M, \pi \models \Diamond \phi$ iff π is a 1-path of the form $\langle D \rangle$ for some state D and $M, \pi' \models \phi$ for some path π' that begins at D.

The latter definition depends on the notion of expansion of a path. An *expansion* of a path π_1 w.r.t. to an interpretation M is an operation that returns a new path π_2 where all events occurring over π_1 (and also over π_2) are completely answered. Formalizing this expansion requires the prior definition of what it means to answer an event:

Definition 5 (Path response). *For a path π_1 and an interpretation M we say that π is a response of π_1 iff* $choice(M, \pi_1) = e$ *and we can split π into $\pi_1 \circ \pi_2$ s.t.* $M, \pi_2 \models \mathbf{r}(e)$.

The *choice* function picks, at each moment, the next event unanswered event to respond to. First it has to decide what events are unanswered in a path π w.r.t. an interpretation M and, based on a given criteria, selects what event among them should be responded to first. Just like $\mathcal{TR}$ is parametric to a pair of oracles ($\mathcal{O}^d$ and $\mathcal{O}^t$), $\mathcal{TR}^{ev}$ takes the *choice* function as an additional parameter. Before defining this *choice* function, we first define what is an expansion of a path. Nevertheless, an important notion here is that, if all events that occur on a path π are answered on π w.r.t. M, then $choice(M, \pi) = \epsilon$.

Definition 6 (Expansion of a path). *A path π is completely answered w.r.t. to an interpretation M iff* $choice(M, \pi) = \epsilon$. *$\pi$ is an expansion of the path π_1 w.r.t. M iff π is completely answered w.r.t. M, and:*
- *either $\pi = \pi_1$;*
- *or there is a sequence of paths $\pi_1, \ldots, \pi$, starting in π_1 and ending in π, s.t. each π_i in the sequence is a response of π_{i-1} w.r.t. M.*

The latter definition specifies how to expand a path π_1 in order to obtain another path π, where all events satisfied over subpaths of π are also answered within π. This must perforce have some procedural nature: it must start by detecting which are the unanswered events; pick one of them, according to some criteria given by a *choice* function; and finally, expand the path with the response of the chosen event. Each path π_i of the sequence $\pi_1, \pi_2, \ldots, \pi$ is a prefix of the path π_{i+1}, and where at least one of the unanswered events on π_i is now answered on π'; otherwise, if all events occurring over π_i are answered, then $\pi_i = \pi$, and the expansion is complete. Note that, since complex events are possible, in general nothing prevents π_{i+1} to have more unanswered events than π_i. In fact, it may be impossible to address all events in a finite path, and in that case, such a sequence of paths does not exists. In fact, non-termination is a known issue of reactive rules, and is an undecidable problem in the general case [2].

These definitions leave open the *choice* function, that is taken as a further parameter of $\mathcal{TR}^{ev}$, and specifies how to choose the next unanswered event to respond to. For its instantiation one needs to decide: 1) in which order should events be responded and 2) how should an event be responded. The former defines the handling order of events in case of conflict, e.g. based on when events have occurred (temporal order), on a priority list, or any other criteria. The latter defines the response policy of an ECA-language, i.e. when is an event considered to be responded. E.g., if an event occurs more than once before the system can respond to it, this specifies if such response should be issued only once or equally to the amount of occurrences. Choosing the appropriate operational semantics depends on the application in mind. For this paper, we fix an instantiation of *choice* function, where events are responded in the (temporal) order in which they occurred, and events for which there was already a response are not responded to again:

Definition 7 (Temporal *choice*)**.** *Let M be an interpretation and π a path. The temporal function is $choice(M, \pi) = firstUnans(M, \pi, order(M, \pi))$ where:*

- *$order(M, \pi) = \langle e_1, \ldots, e_n \rangle$ iff $\forall e_i\ 1 \leq i \leq n$, $\exists \pi_i$ subpath of π where $M, \pi \models_{ev} \mathbf{o}(e_i)$ and $\forall e_j$ s.t. $i < j$ then e_j occurs after e_i*
- *e_2 occurs after e_1 w.r.t. π and M iff there exists π_1, π_2 subpaths of π such that $\pi_1 = \langle D_i\ {}^{O_i}{\rightarrow} \ldots {}^{O_{j-1}}{\hookrightarrow} D_j \rangle$, $\pi_2 = \langle D_n\ {}^{O_n}{\rightarrow} \ldots {}^{O_{m-1}}{\hookrightarrow} D_m \rangle$, $M, \pi_1 \models_{ev} \mathbf{o}(e_1)$, $M, \pi_2 \models_{ev} \mathbf{o}(e_2)$ and $D_j \leq D_m$ w.r.t. the ordering in π.*
- *$firstUnans(M, \pi, \langle e_1, \ldots, e_n \rangle) = e_i$ iff e_i is the first event in $\langle e_1, \ldots, e_n \rangle$ where given π' subpath of π and $M, \pi' \models_{ev} \mathbf{o}(e)$ then $\neg \exists \pi''$ s.t. π'' is also a subpath of π, π'' is after π' and $M, \pi'' \models \mathbf{r}(e)$.*

Afterwards, we define the notion of *model* of formulas and programs.

Definition 8 (Models and Minimal Models). *An interpretation M is a model of a transaction (resp. event) formula ϕ iff for every path π, $M, \pi \models \phi$ (resp. $M, \pi \models_{ev} \phi$). M is a model of a program P (denoted $M \models P$) iff it is a model of every rule in P.*
Let M_1, M_2 be interpretations, $M_1 \leq M_2$ if $\forall \pi$: $M_2(\pi) = \top \vee M_1(\pi) \subseteq M_2(\pi)$. Let ϕ be a formula, and P a program. M is a minimal model of ϕ (resp. P) if M is a model of ϕ (resp. P) and $M \leq M'$ for every model M' of ϕ (resp. P).

This notion of models can be used to reason about properties of transaction and event formulas that hold for *every* possible path of execution. However, to know whether a formula succeeds in a particular path, we need only to consider the event occurrences *supported* by that path, either because they appear as occurrences in the transition of states, or because they are a necessary consequence of the program's rules given that path. Because of this, executional entailment in $\mathcal{TR}^{ev}$ is defined w.r.t. minimal models.

Definition 9 ($\mathcal{TR}^{ev}$ Executional Entailment). *Let P be a program, ϕ a transaction formula and $D_1\ {}^{O_0}{\rightarrow} \ldots {}^{O_n}{\rightarrow} D_n$ a path. Then $P, (D_1\ {}^{O_0}{\rightarrow} \ldots {}^{O_n}{\rightarrow} D_n) \models \phi\ (\star)$ iff for every minimal model M of P, $M, \langle D_1\ {}^{O_0}{\rightarrow} \ldots {}^{O_n}{\rightarrow} D_n \rangle \models \phi$. $P, D_1{-} \models \phi$ is true, if there is a path $D_1\ {}^{O_0}{\rightarrow} \ldots {}^{O_n}{\rightarrow} D_n$ that makes $(\star)$ true.*

3   Oracles for Stream Reasoning

$\mathcal{TR}^{ev}$ provides a powerful theory to talk about executional properties of abstract reactive transactions. With it, one is able to say what properties (or fluents) hold for every possible path of execution, or express relations between transactions and events, e.g. to say "event ψ occurs whenever transaction ϕ succeeds". In addition, with $\mathcal{TR}^{ev}$'s proof theory, one can also talk about a particular execution path, and say exactly *how* an abstract reactive transaction succeeds.

Of course, to use $\mathcal{TR}^{ev}$ in applications one needs to instantiate the appropriate oracles $\mathcal{O}^d$ and $\mathcal{O}^t$, on which $\mathcal{TR}^{ev}$ is parametric, that describe the behavior of the KBs in the domain at hands. As illustration of how this can be done, consider the relational oracle proposed in [4]:

Definition 10 (Relational Oracle). *In a relational oracle, states can be represented by sets of ground atomic formulas. The data oracle simply returns all these formulas, i.e., $\mathcal{O}^d(D) = D$. Moreover, for each predicate symbol p in D, the transition oracle defines two new predicates, p.ins and p.del representing the insertion and deletion atoms, respectively. Formally, $p.ins \in \mathcal{O}^t(D_1, D_2)$ iff $D_2 = D_1 \cup \{p\}$ and, $p.del \in \mathcal{O}^t(D_1, D_2)$ iff $D_2 = D_1 \backslash \{p\}$.*

Example 1 (Financial Transactions - adapted from [4]). Consider a bank's KB defined by the relational database of Definition 10 and where the balance of a bank account is given by the relation balance(Acnt, Amt). Using just _.*ins* and _.*del* as primitive actions, we define the transactions: withdraw(Amt, Acnt) to withdraw an amount from an account; deposit(Amt, Acnt) to deposit an amount into an account; changeBalance(Acnt, Bal, Bal') to change an account's balance; and, finally, transfer(Amt, Acnt, Acnt') for transferring an amount from one account to another. In $\mathcal{TR}^{ev}$ (and also in $\mathcal{TR}$) these can be defined in a logic programming style by the following rules:

$$\text{transfer}(\text{Amt}, \text{Acnt}, \text{Acnt}') \leftarrow \text{withdraw}(\text{Amt}, \text{Acnt}) \otimes \text{deposit}(\text{Amt}, \text{Acnt}')$$
$$\text{withdraw}(\text{Amt}, \text{Acnt}) \leftarrow \text{balance}(\text{Acnt}, \text{B}) \otimes \text{changeBalance}(\text{Acnt}, \text{B}, \text{B} - \text{Amt})$$
$$\text{deposit}(\text{Amt}, \text{Acnt}) \leftarrow \text{balance}(\text{Acnt}, \text{B}) \otimes \text{changeBalance}(\text{Acnt}, \text{B}, \text{B} + \text{Amt})$$
$$\text{changeBalance}(\text{Acnt}, \text{B}, \text{B}') \leftarrow \text{balance}(\text{Acnt}, \text{B}).\text{del} \otimes \text{balance}(\text{Acnt}, \text{B}').\text{ins}$$

$P, \langle d_1, d_2, d_3, d_4, d_5 \rangle \models \text{transfer}(10, \text{ac1}, \text{ac2})$ holds, if d_1 is e.g. a state where balance(ac1, 20) and balance(ac2, 30) are true, d_2 is a state obtained from d_1 by deleting balance(ac1, 20); d_3 is d_2 plus balance(ac1, 10); d_4 is d_3 minus balance(ac2, 30); and finally d_5 is obtained from d_4 by adding balance(ac2, 40).

We can also define complex event rules and their associated responses. E.g., the following event o(balanceViolation(Acnt)) occurs the first time the account balance is updated into a negative value, and in that case, the bank charges 5€ to the customer for that violation. This is expressed in $\mathcal{TR}^{ev}$ as follows:

$$\text{o}(\text{balanceViolation}(\text{Acnt})) \leftarrow (\text{o}(\text{balance}(\text{Acnt}, \text{B}).\text{del}) \otimes \text{o}(\text{balance}(\text{Acnt}, \text{B}').\text{ins}))$$
$$\wedge (\text{B}' < 0 \leq \text{B})$$
$$\text{r}(\text{balanceViolation}(\text{Acnt})) \leftarrow \text{balance}(\text{Acnt}, \text{B}) \otimes \text{changeBalance}(\text{Acnt}, \text{B}, \text{B} - 5)$$

Now imagine that we start on a state d_1' where balance(ac1, 5) is true instead of balance(ac1, 20). Then, transfer(10, ac1, ac2) to succeed from d_1' needs an expanded path $\langle d_1', d_2', d_3', d_4', d_5', d_6', d_7' \rangle$, where d_6', d_7' satisfy the action changeBalance(ac1, −5, −10), changing the balance of the account a_1 into balance(ac1, −10). I.e., for the transaction to succeed, it needs to respond to the event o(balanceViolation(Acnt)) that becomes true during its execution.

The later example shows how one can use $\mathcal{TR}^{ev}$ to reason about what are the paths that make a transaction succeed, given a set of basic primitives (actions and queries) defined by a pair of relational oracles. Note that oracles have an important role in $\mathcal{TR}^{ev}$, as one can only write transactions combining these primitives after knowing exactly what oracle primitives are available. The logic then takes care of the semantics of complex (trans)actions, defining over what paths such a complex transaction can succeed.

Moreover, while the previous relational oracles are rather simple, nothing prevent us from using more powerful and expressive oracles, or to combine of several oracles into one, making $\mathcal{TR}^{ev}$ useful in more sophisticated applications. In the following, we provide a new oracle definition that, as we shall see, can be used with $\mathcal{TR}^{ev}$ to perform event stream reasoning. We start by defining a data oracle based on RDF with an ontology model defined in OWL:

Definition 11 (RDF data Oracle). *A state is an RDF graph G, i.e., a set of RDF triples of the form $(s\ p\ o)$ together with an OWL ontology. The data oracle $(\mathcal{O}^d)$ is defined such that $\mathcal{O}^d(G) \models (s\ p\ o)$ iff $(s\ p\ o) \in Closure(G)$, where $Closure(G)$ is the closure of the graph under the ontology.*

Just like a state in the relational database oracle is represented by the set of formulas that are in the database, a state in the latter oracle is simply a set of instances defined in RDF triples, together with the ontology. This oracle also assumes a function $Closure(G)$ that computes the whole model of the RDF instance graph under the ontology.

Based on this function, we now define the possible transitions for an RDF/OWL graph, where the primitive actions are insertions and deletions of graphs composed by RDF instances[4]. In this case, inserting (or deleting) an RDF instance graph means to add (or remove) every individual triple to the graph. Notice that insertion a triple is the special case where the graph is a set of just one element. Similarly to the relational oracle, we assume the primitives *graph.ins* and *graph.del* where *graph* is a set of RDF triples. Recall that the syntactic choice of *.ins* and *.del* has no particular meaning in $\mathcal{TR}^{ev}$, and we could have chosen any other representation as e.g., *insert(graph)* and *delete(graph)*.

Definition 12 (RDF transition Oracle). *Let g_1 be an RDF graph, i.e., a set of RDF triples of the form $(s\ p\ o)$.*
$\mathcal{O}^t(D_1, D_2) \models g_1.ins$ *iff both statements are true:*
- $D_2 = D_1 \cup \{(s\ p\ o) : (s\ p\ o) \in g_1\}$ *and;*
- $\mathcal{O}^t(D_1, D_2) = \{g_1.ins\} \cup \{\mathbf{o}((s\ \ \ p\ \ \ o).ins)\ :\ (s\ \ \ p\ \ \ o) \in Closure(D_2) \backslash Closure(D_1)\}$

$\mathcal{O}^t(D_1, D_2) \models g_1.del$ *iff both statements are true:*

---

[4] To simplify, and since in most SSW applications this is not needed, we do not consider the case of updating the OWL ontology.

- $D_2 = D_1 \cap \{(s\ p\ o) : (s\ p\ o) \in g_1\}$ *and;*
- $\mathcal{O}^t(D_1, D_2) = \{g_1.del\} \cup \{\mathbf{o}((s\quad p\quad o).del) : (s\quad p\quad o) \in Closure(D_1)\backslash Closure(D_2)\}$

Notice that in the latter definition, $\mathcal{O}^t$ explicitly defines a set of primitive events true in a transition of states. This definition of $\mathcal{O}^t$ allows one to distinguish between the primitive actions executed by $\mathcal{TR}^{ev}$, and the primitive events that occurred as a result of this action. Namely, while in the insertion of an instance graph g_1, $\mathcal{O}^t$ only makes $g_1.ins$ true, it also satisfies the occurrences of primitive actions executed as a consequence of $g_1.ins$. This allows us to reason about what action was really executed ($g_1.ins$) in the transition by $\mathcal{TR}^{ev}$, but also about what happened inside the oracle as a consequence of this action. As we shall see next, this allows us to use application's knowledge to reason about what events hold, not only inside $\mathcal{TR}^{ev}$'s rules, but also at the oracle level.

4   An Example Combining Event Stream Reasoning and Transaction Execution

After defining oracles to reason about RDF/OWL graphs, we can now show how to use these oracles for SSW domains. Moreover, in these domains, it is often useful to use more than one representation semantics of states and actions. In fact, this is the case in the application example described in the introduction, where we need to combine data produced by a sensor network (published in RDF/OWL), with the government's relational database comprising information about drivers, fines, addresses, etc.

Although formally we can only have one oracle defining the primitives to query ($\mathcal{O}^d$), and one oracle defining the primitives to execute actions ($\mathcal{O}^t$), nothing prevents these oracles from being instantiated with more than one semantics. This is easily done by partitioning the oracle primitives ($\mathcal{P}_\mathcal{O}$) into as many as needed and, based on this partition, use $\mathcal{O}^t$ and $\mathcal{O}^d$ as "meta-oracles" deciding in which semantics a formula should be evaluated. Next we illustrate how to do this, and how to perform stream reasoning using the previously defined oracles.

Example 2. Consider the situation from the introduction, where we have a government's application to detect and issue fines for traffic violations. To detect traffic violations, the government depends on a sensor network deployed on some road. To model this network, its sensors, and sensors' observations, we have a Semantic Sensor Network based on OWL ontology, that publishes observations data using RDF triples. Besides information about the sensors, this ontology also describes information about the vehicles observed by the sensors. Such an ontology can include e.g., that `lightVehicle` and `heavyVehicle` are subclasses of `motorVehicle`[5], and that `sensor1` and `sensor2` are instances of type `Sensor`:

---

[5] Although, for this example, we chose to express the properties and knowledge about vehicles in our local ontology, we could have alternatively used any other external ontology to describe vehicles like, e.g., the Vehicular Sales Ontology [12].

ov : vehicle	rdf : type	owl : Class .
ov : motorVehicle	rdfs : subClassOf	ov : vehicle .
ov : lightVehicle	rdfs : subClassOf	ov : motorVehicle .
ov : heavyVehicle	rdfs : subClassOf	ov : vehicle .
ov : sensor	rdf : type	owl : Class .
ov : sensor1	rdf : type	ov : sensor .
ov : sensor2	rdf : type	ov : sensor .

where as usual rdf,rdfs and owl are the default namespaces for RDF, RDFS and OWL, and ov is the application's namespace where the objects and properties of the vehicular ontology are defined, and which includes additional statements.

The information about drivers, fines and addresses is on a government's relational database, and actions are performed w.r.t. this database. E.g., the following $\mathcal{TR}^{ev}$ rules define that processing a given violation V of a vehicle with plate P at a date-time DT is done by identifying, in the government's relational database, the cost Cost of the violation and the driver D of the vehicle, to insert into the database that the fine was issued for that driver, and to notify the driver:

processViolation(P, DT, V) ← fineCost(V, Cost) ⊗ isDriver(P, D)⊗
   fineIssued(P, D, DT, Cost).ins ⊗ notifyFine(P, D, DT, Cost)
notifyFine(P, D, DT, Cost) ← hasAddress(D, Addr)⊗sendLetter(D, Addr, P, DT, Cost)

Then, we can write events of interest in $\mathcal{TR}^{ev}$. E.g., in the following (simplified) rules we define the event o(passingSpeedA$_1$(P, VType, S, DT)) which detects if a vehicle with plate P and type VType has passed in area a$_1$ at time DT with speed S; or o(passingWrongWay(P, DT)) detecting any vehicle plate P passing the road in the wrong way at time DT, as long as this vehicle has the type motorVehicle:

o(passingSpeedA$_1$(P, VType, S, DT$_2$, S$_2$)) ←
  ([o((Obs$_1$ ov:plateRead P).ins) ∧ o((Obs$_1$ ov:vehicleDetected VType).ins)
  ∧ o((Obs$_1$ ov:dateTime DT$_1$).ins) ∧ o((Obs$_1$ ov:readBy sensor1).ins)]
  ⊗ [o((Obs$_2$ ov:plateRead P).ins) ∧ o((Obs$_2$ ov:vehicleDetected VType).ins)
  ∧ o((Obs$_2$ ov:dateTime DT$_2$).ins)) ∧ o((Obs$_2$ ov:readBy sensor2).ins)])
  ∧ ((DT$_2$ > DT$_1$) ∧ S = (10/DT$_1$ − DT$_2$))
o(passingWrongWay(P, DT$_1$)) ←
  (o((Obs$_1$ ov:plateRead P).ins) ∧ o((Obs$_1$ ov:vehicleDetected motorVehicle).ins)
  ∧ o((Obs$_1$ ov:dateTime DT$_1$).ins) ∧ o((Obs$_1$ ov:readBy sensor2).ins))
  ⊗ (o((Obs$_2$ ov:plateRead P).ins) ∧ o((Obs$_2$ ov:vehicleDetected motorVehicle).ins)
  ∧ o((Obs$_2$ ov:dateTime DT$_2$).ins) ∧ o((Obs$_2$ ov:readBy sensor1).ins)) ∧ (DT$_1$ < DT$_2$)
o(passingSpeed(P, VType, S, DT$_2$, a1)) ← o(passingSpeedA$_1$(P, VType, S, DT$_2$))

r(passingSpeed(P, VType, S, DT, A)) ←
  maxSpeed(VType, A, MS) ⊗ (MS ≤ S) ⊗ processViolation(P, DT, speed)
r(passingSpeed(_, VType, S, _, A)) ← maxSpeed(VType, A, MS) ⊗ (MS > S)
r(passingWrongWay(P, DT)) ← processViolation(P, DT, wrongWay)

In the rules above we also define what is executed whenever these events occur. Namely, we say that processViolation is only executed for the event passingSpeed if the vehicle's detected speed exceeds the speed limit, and always executed if passingWrongWay is detected.

With these rules, our system can prove statements of the form: $P, S_1 \models obs_1.ins \otimes obs_2.ins \otimes \ldots \otimes obs_n.ins$ where, based on given starting state S_1, $\mathcal{TR}^{ev}$ computes the path $\langle S_1 \overset{O_1}{\to} \ldots \overset{O_{n-1}}{\to} S_n \rangle$ satisfying the sequence of observations obtained so far. I.e., it computes *how* the system should evolve in order to respond to these observations, in a transactional way, and according to a $\mathcal{TR}^{ev}$ program P containing the rules above. Note that, since we are considering two different KBs, each state S_i in the path is a composed state (G_i, D_i), where G_i is the RDF graph describing vehicles and sensors' observations, and D_i is a state of the government's relational database. With this setting, let's assume we want to prove $P, S_1 \models (\text{ov:obs}_1).\text{ins} \otimes (\text{ov:obs}_2).\text{ins}$ where:

ov : obs$_1$	rdf : type	ov : Observation ;
	ov : plateRead	"01-01-AA" ;
	ov : dateTime	1426325213000 ;
	ov : vehicleDetected	ov : heavyVehicle ;
	ov : readBy	ov : sensor1 .
ov : obs$_2$	rdf : type	ov : Observation ;
	ov : plateRead	"01-01-AA" ;
	ov : dateTime	1426325213516 ;
	ov : vehicleDetected	ov : heavyVehicle ;
	ov : readBy	ov : sensor2 .

Then, based on the ontology definition, we know that heavyVehicle $\sqsubseteq$ vehicle, and thus $\mathbf{o}((\text{ov:obs}_1 \text{ ov:vehicleDetected motorVehicle}).\text{ins})$ will hold at the same time (i.e., transition) as $\mathbf{o}((\text{ov:obs}_1).\text{ins})$. In a similar way, the event $\mathbf{o}((\text{ov:obs}_2 \text{ ov:vehicleDetected motorVehicle}).\text{ins})$ will hold at the same as $\mathbf{o}((\text{ov:obs}_1).\text{ins})$. From this, $\mathbf{o}(\text{passingWrongWay}("01-01-AA", 1426325213000)$ holds for the same transition as where the actions $(\text{ov:obs}_1).\text{ins} \otimes (\text{ov:obs}_2).\text{ins}$ occur, and thus the *transaction* $(\text{ov:obs}_1).\text{ins} \otimes (\text{ov:obs}_2).\text{ins}$ will only succeed in an expanded path where the driver of vehicle "01-01-AA" is fined and notified, for the infraction of passing the road in the wrong way.

5   Discussion and Final Remarks

In this paper we propose a set of oracle instantiations to make $\mathcal{TR}^{ev}$ useful for domains involving sensor networks and Semantic Web technologies. With it, one can use $\mathcal{TR}^{ev}$ to reason about what complex events occur, and what transactions need to be executed to respond to these events. Moreover, like in EP/Stream Reasoning solutions [1, 15, 19], $\mathcal{TR}^{ev}$ can use the domain's application knowledge to reason about what complex events occur. This reasoning can be done either inside the oracle, using the oracle's domain knowledge to trigger primitive events, but also inside $\mathcal{TR}^{ev}$ rules, where we use this knowledge to decide what should be the response of the system for a given event.

Since EP/Stream Reasoning only deal with detecting complex event patterns, and not with executing actions, our work can be better compared with ECA solutions. While several ECA languages exist for several domains like the

Semantic Web [3,6,18] they normally do not support the execution of transactions. Some exceptions exist, but are either only procedural like [18], or can only detect simple events based on database inserts and deletes [14,21].

This is, in fact, one thing that distinguishes $\mathcal{TR}^{ev}$ from most solutions: combining the ability to detect and reason about complex and sophisticated event patterns, with the execution of complex transactions, and to do this in a way that can be useful for a wide range of applications by plugging in different oracles. The example presented in Section 4 uses a concrete oracle parametrization combining RDF/OWL and relational database semantics, and which is interesting for SSW applications. With it, one can use the sensor network ontology to help reason about the events that occur in a given transition, while simultaneously combining the execution of (trans)actions in the relational database.

References

1. Anicic, D., Fodor, P., Rudolph, S., Stojanovic, N.: EP-SPARQL: a unified language for event processing and stream reasoning. WWW **2011**, 635–644 (2011)
2. Bailey, J., Dong, G., Ramamohanarao, K.: On the decidability of the termination problem of active database systems. Theor. Comput. Sci. **311**(1–3), 389–437 (2004)
3. Behrends, E., Fritzen, O., May, W., Schenk, F.: Embedding event algebras and process for eca rules for the semantic web. Fundam. Inform. **82**(3), 237–263 (2008)
4. Bonner, A.J., Kifer, M.: Transaction logic programming. In: ICLP, pp. 257–279 (1993)
5. Bonner, A.J., Kifer, M.: Results on reasoning about updates in transaction logic. In: Kifer, M., Voronkov, A., Freitag, B., Decker, H. (eds.) Dagstuhl Seminar 1997, DYNAMICS 1997, and ILPS-WS 1997. LNCS, vol. 1472, p. 166. Springer, Heidelberg (1998)
6. Bry, F., Eckert, M., Patranjan, P.-L.: Reactivity on the web: Paradigms and applications of the language xchange. J. Web Eng. **5**(1), 3–24 (2006)
7. Chomicki, J., Lobo, J., Naqvi, S.A.: Conflict resolution using logic programming. IEEE Trans. Knowl. Data Eng. **15**(1), 244–249 (2003)
8. Compton, M., Henson, C.A., Neuhaus, H., Lefort, L., Sheth, A.P.: A survey of the semantic specification of sensors. In: SSN09, pp. 17–32 (2009)
9. Costantini, S., Gasperis, G.D.: Complex reactivity with preferences in rule-based agents. In: RuleML, pp. 167–181 (2012)
10. Fodor, P., Kifer, M.: Tabling for transaction logic. In: ACMPPDP, pp. 199–208 (2010)
11. Gomes, A.S., Alferes, J.J.: Transaction Logic with (complex) events. Theory and Practice of Logic Programming, On-line Supplement (2014) (to appear)
12. Hepp, M.: Vehicle Sales Ontology, March 18, 2015. http://www.heppnetz.de/ontologies/vso/ns
13. Kowalski, R., Sadri, F.: A logic-based framework for reactive systems. In: Bikakis, A., Giurca, A. (eds.) RuleML 2012. LNCS, vol. 7438, pp. 1–15. Springer, Heidelberg (2012)
14. Lausen, G., Ludäscher, B., May, W.: On active deductive databases: the statelog approach. In: Kifer, M., Voronkov, A., Freitag, B., Decker, H. (eds.) Dagstuhl Seminar 1997, DYNAMICS 1997, and ILPS-WS 1997. LNCS, vol. 1472, p. 69. Springer, Heidelberg (1998)

15. Margara, A., Urbani, J., van Harmelen, F., Bal, H.E.: Streaming the web: Reasoning over dynamic data. J. Web Sem. **25**, 24–44 (2014)
16. McGuinness, D.L., Van Harmelen, F., et al.: OWL web ontology language overview. W3C recommendation **10**(2004–03), 10 (2004)
17. Müller, R., Greiner, U., Rahm, E.: AgentWork: a workflow system supporting rule-based workflow adaptation. Data Knowl. Eng. **51**(2), 223–256 (2004)
18. Papamarkos, G., Poulovassilis, A., Wood, P.T.: Event-condition-action rules on RDF metadata in P2P environments. Comp. Networks **50**(10), 1513–1532 (2006)
19. Ren, Y., Pan, J.Z.: Optimising ontology stream reasoning with truth maintenance system. In: ACM CIKM, pp. 831–836 (2011)
20. Sheth, A.P., Henson, C.A., Sahoo, S.S.: Semantic sensor web. IEEE Internet Computing **12**(4), 78–83 (2008)
21. Zaniolo, C.: Active database rules with transaction-conscious stable-model semantics. In: DOOD, pp. 55–72 (1995)

Existential Rules and Datalog+/- Track

Ontology-Based Multidimensional Contexts with Applications to Quality Data Specification and Extraction

Mostafa Milani[(✉)] and Leopoldo Bertossi[(✉)]

School of Computer Science, Carleton University, Ottawa, Canada
{mmilani,bertossi}@scs.carleton.ca

Abstract. Data quality assessment and data cleaning are context dependent activities. Starting from this observation, in previous work a context model for the assessment of the quality of a database was proposed. A context takes the form of a possibly virtual database or a data integration system into which the database under assessment is mapped, for additional analysis, processing, and quality data extraction. In this work, we extend contexts with dimensions, and by doing so, multidimensional data quality assessment becomes possible. At the core of multidimensional contexts we find ontologies written as Datalog$^\pm$ programs with provably good properties in terms of query answering. We use this language to represent dimension hierarchies, dimensional constraints, dimensional rules, and specifying quality data. Query answering relies on and triggers dimensional navigation, and becomes an important tool for the extraction of quality data.

1 Introduction

Data quality assessment and data cleaning are context-dependent activities. More precisely, the quality of data has to be assessed with some form of contextual knowledge, in particular, about the *production and the use* of data, among other possible dimensions of data quality. Data quality refers to the degree to which data fits or fulfills a form of usage [1,20]. As expected, context-based data quality assessment requires a formal model of context. Accordingly, we propose a model of context that addresses quality concerns that are related to the production and use of data.

Here we follow and extend the approach in [2] that provides a model of context for data quality assessment. In that work, the assessment of a database D is performed by *putting D in context*, more precisely, by mapping it into a context $\mathcal{C}$ (Fig. 1, left), which is represented as another database, or as a database schema with partial information, or, more generally, as a virtual data integration system [22]. The latter may have some materialized data and access to external data sources.

The quality of data in D is determined through additional processing, material or virtual, of the data within the context. These contextual data may be

© Springer International Publishing Switzerland 2015
N. Bassiliades et al. (Eds.): RuleML 2015, LNCS 9202, pp. 277–293, 2015.
DOI: 10.1007/978-3-319-21542-6_18

imported from D or may be already available at the context. The context may also contain application-dependent knowledge associated to data quality, in the form of rules or semantic constraints. Data processing in the context leads to possibly several quality versions of D, forming a class $\mathcal{D}^q$ of intended, clean versions of D (Fig. 1, right). The quality of D is measured in terms of how much D departs from (its quality versions in) $\mathcal{D}^q$: $dist(D, \mathcal{D}^q)$. Of course, different distance measures may be used for this purpose [2].

In some cases, we may want to assess the quality of answers to a query $\mathcal{Q}$ posed to instance D or to obtain "quality answers" from D. This can be done appealing to the class $\mathcal{D}^q$ of intended clean versions of D. For assessment, the set of query answers to $\mathcal{Q}$ from D can be compared with the *certain answers* for $\mathcal{Q}$, i.e. the intersection of the sets of answers to $\mathcal{Q}$ from each of the instances in $\mathcal{D}^q$ [19]. The certain answers become what we could call the *clean answers* to $\mathcal{Q}$ from D [2]. So, if we want the clean answers to $\mathcal{Q}$ from D, instead of computing the answers from D as usual, we compute the clean answers (cf. right-hand side of Fig. 1).

When computing clean query answers, instead of computing, materializing and querying all the instances in class $\mathcal{D}^q$, a form of *query rewriting* can be attempted: a new query $\mathcal{Q}^q$ is posed to D to obtain the clean answers for

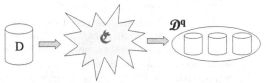

Fig. 1. Clean instances and query answers

$\mathcal{Q}$. Some cases of rewriting were investigated in [2]. In this work we continue adopting this approach to data quality assessment and clean query answering. However, as we will see, the contexts we consider in this work are more complex than those considered in [2], and for good reasons.

An important contextual element was not considered in [2]: *dimensions*. They were *not* considered as contextual elements for data quality analysis, but in practice, dimensions are naturally associated to contexts. Here, in order to capture general dimensional aspects of data for inclusion in contexts, we take advantage of and start from the Hurtado-Mendelzon (HM) multidimensional data model [18], whose inception was mainly motivated by data warehouses (DWH) and OLAP applications.

We extend the HM model by adding *categorical relations* associated to categories, at different levels of the dimension hierarchies, possibly to more than one dimension (think of generalized fact tables as found in data warehouses). It also includes *dimensional constraints* and *dimensional rules*, which could be treated both as *dimensional integrity constraints* on categorical relations that involve values from dimension categories. However, dimensional constraints are intended to be used as *denial constraints* that forbid certain combinations of values, whereas the dimensional rules are intended to be used for data completion, to generate data through their enforcement via *dimensional navigation*.

In this work we propose an ontological representation in Datalog$^\pm$ [6,7] of the extended HM model, and also mechanisms for data quality assessment based on query answering from the ontology via dimensional navigation. As already suggested, the idea is that a query to the ontology triggers dimensional navigation and the creation of missing data, in possible upward and downward directions, and on multiple dimensions. Datalog$^\pm$ supports data generation through the ontological rules. This is particularly useful, and also much in line with the way we understand and use contexts in everyday life: *Context allows us to extend or expand information that, otherwise, without this extension, would be impossible or difficult to understand or make sense of.* Furthermore, this ontological approach captures well our general philosophy according to which, *contexts should be represented as formal theories into which other objects, like database instances, are mapped*, for contextual analysis, assessment, interpretation, and additional processing [2].

Datalog$\pm$ is an extension of classical Datalog, mainly through the use of existentially quantified variables (a.k.a. value invention) in rule heads. It has been successfully applied to the logical representations of data models and ontologies [9,11]. Actually, a *multidimensional (MD) context* corresponding to the formalization of the extension of HM becomes a Datalog$\pm$ ontology, $\mathcal{M}$, that belongs to an interesting syntactic class of programs, for which some results are known. This allows us to give a semantics to our ontologies, and apply some established and new algorithms for query answering.

More precisely, the core MD ontology $\mathcal{M}$ is a weakly-sticky Datalog$^\pm$ program [10], for which (conjunctive) query answering has polynomial-time data complexity. In our case, weak-stickiness is due to the as we argue, natural assumptions that: (a) dimension navigation (as captured by data generation) happens through rules with body joins on *categorical attributes* (i.e. in categorical relations), whose values come from dimension categories; and (b) there is no value invention for categorical attributes. (We also discuss cases where these assumptions do not hold.)

MD ontologies are used to support quality data specification and extraction.[1] More precisely, and continuing with the above idea on this use of contexts, it amounts to: (a) defining application-dependent *quality predicates* (they can be seen as views capturing data quality concerns), (b) using them to define the *quality versions* of the original predicates (relations) in the database D under quality assessment, and (c) retrieving quality data by querying the (possibly virtual extensions of the) latter predicates [2]. These predicate definitions may be based on *data quality guidelines* that are captured as rules or semantic constraints, both of which may refer to categorical attributes of predicates in $\mathcal{M}$, without being part of $\mathcal{M}$. Rather, this "quality part" of the context comes on top of $\mathcal{M}$. We establish that under reasonable conditions on these extra definitions, the resulting extension of $\mathcal{M}$ still retains the tractability of query answering (even when weak-stickiness may be compromised).

---

[1] In this work we do not explicitly address the problem of assessing the quality of the original data through a numerical comparison with the quality data [2].

About related work, in [4] dimensions become the basis for *building* contexts, or more precisely database instances that are tailored according to certain dimensional elements. This is done through a process of selection of relevant dimensional elements: the dimension leaves a footprint on the data. As a result, the constructed database is implicitly dimensional, and the dimensions as such may be lost as first-class objects in the generated context.

In [23,24] the authors consider the generation of data at different levels of a category hierarchy, and at query answering time. This involves hierarchy navigation and an extension of relational algebra that computes data by appealing to data at other levels of the hierarchy. Actually, in our work we show how this process can be captured via our Datalog$^\pm$ MD ontologies.

DWHs have been represented in expressive description logics (DL) [14]. Preliminary research on extensions in DL of the HM model, also for data quality purposes, can be found in [21].

Summarizing, in this work we make the following contributions:[2]

1. We extend the HM data model and represent the extension as a Datalog$^\pm$ ontology that contains: (a) categorical relations, (b) tuple-generating-dependencies, *tgds* (a rule incarnation of referential constraints), to connect the original data to categorical relations, and the latter to dimensions; and (c) dimensional constraints.

2. We establish that the MD ontology is a *weakly-sticky* Datalog$^\pm$ program [10]. As a consequence, query answering can be done in polynomial time.

3. We analyze the effect of dimensional constraints on query answering, specifically the *separability condition* [10] between *tgds* and constraints that are equality-generating-dependencies, *egds*. We show that by restricting variables in equalities to appear categorical attributes, separability holds.

4. We propose a general approach for contextual data quality specification and extraction that is based on MD ontologies, emphasizing the dimensional navigation process that is triggered by queries about quality data. We illustrate the application of this approach by means of an extended example.

2   An Extended, Motivating Example

This section illustrates the intuition behind categorical relations, dimensional rules and constraints, and how they are used for data quality purposes. We assume, according to the HM model (cf. Section 3), that a dimension consists of a finite set of categories related to each other by a partial order.

Example 1. The relational table *Measurements* (Table 1) shows body temperatures of patients in an institution. A doctor wants to know *"The body temperatures of Tom Waits for September 5 taken around noon with a thermometer of brand B1"* (as he expected). Possibly a nurse, unaware of this requirement, used

---

[2] This work considerably extends [25], which contains basically the material of Section 2 here.

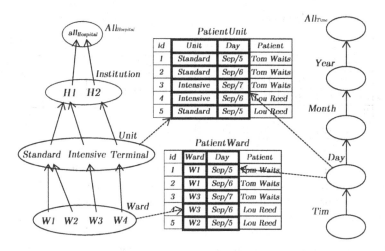

Fig. 2. An extended multidimensional model

a thermometer of brand *B2*, storing the data in *Measurements*. In this case, not all the measurements in the table are up to the expected quality. However, table *Measurements* alone does not discriminate between intended values (those taken with brand *B1*) and the others.

For assessing the quality of the data in *Measurements* according to the doctor's quality requirement, extra contextual information about the thermometers in use may help. In this case, the contextual information is in table *PatientWard*, linked to the *Ward* category (Fig. 2, middle, bottom). This *categorical relation* stores patient names for each ward of the institution.

Furthermore, the institution has a *guideline* prescribing that: *"Temperature measurement for patients in a standard care unit have to be taken with thermometers of Brand B1".* It can be used for data quality assessment when combined with categorical table *PatientUnit* (Fig. 2, middle, top), which is linked to the *Unit* category, and whose data are (at least partially) generated from *PatientWard* by upward-navigation through dimension Hospital (Fig. 2, left), from category *Ward* to category *Unit*.

According to the guideline, it is now possible to conclude that, on days when Tom Waits was in the standard care unit, his temperature

Table 1. *Measurements*

	Time	Patient	Value
1	Sep/5-12:10	Tom Waits	38.2
2	Sep/6-11:50	Tom Waits	37.1
3	Sep/7-12:15	Tom Waits	37.7
4	Sep/9-12:00	Tom Waits	37.0
5	Sep/6-11:05	Lou Reed	37.5
6	Sep/5-12:05	Lou Reed	38.0

Table 2. *Measurements^q*

	Time	Patient	Value
7	Sep/5-12:10	Tom Waits	38.2
8	Sep/6-11:50	Tom Waits	37.1

Table 3. *WorkingSchedules*

	Unit	Day	Nurse	Type
1	Intensive	Sep/5	Cathy	cert.
2	Standard	Sep/5	Helen	cert.
3	Standard	Sep/6	Helen	cert.
4	Terminal	Sep/5	Susan	non-c.
5	Standard	Sep/9	Mark	non-c.

Table 4. *Shifts*

	Ward	Day	Nurse	Shift
1	W4	Sep/5	Cathy	night
2	W1	Sep/6	Helen	morning
3	W4	Sep/5	Susan	evening

values were taken with the expected thermometer: for patients in wards *W1* or *W2* a thermometer of brand *B1* was used. These "clean data" in relation to the doctor's expectations appear in relation *Measurements^q* (Table 2).

Elaborating on this example, there could be a *dimensional constraint*: "*No patient in intensive care unit at any time during August 2005*". As stated, this constraint could be represented as a "static" constraint on the categorical relation *PatientUnit*. However, it could also be represented as one on the data generation process via upward-navigation from *PatientWard* to *PatientUnit*, preventing the use of the third tuple in table *PatientWard*. As such, this becomes a *navigational constraint* that also involves dimensions Hospital and Time (Fig. 2, right). A third alternative is handling the constraint as a "static" constraint on the join of *PatientWard* and *PatientUnit* via the patient name (*Tom Waits* could not be both in ward *W3* and intensive care on some dates). Our approach will allow to handle the constraint in any of these three forms.   ■

Categorical relations may be incomplete, and new data can be generated for them, which will be enabled through rules (*tgds*) of a Datalog± dimensional ontology. The previous example shows data generation via upward navigation. Our next example shows that *downward navigation* may also be useful. Our approach to MD contexts will support both.

Example 2. (ex. 1 cont.) Consider two additional categorical relations, *WorkingSchedules* (Table 3) and *Shifts* (Table 4), linked to categories *Unit* and *Ward*, resp. They store schedules of nurses in units and shifts of nurses in wards, resp. A query to *Shifts* asks for dates when *Mark* was working in ward *W2*, which has no answer with the data in Table 4. A new guideline states: "*If a nurse works in a unit on a specific day, he/she has shifts in every ward of that unit on the same day*". It can be captured as a dimensional rule connecting *WorkingSchedules* to *Shifts* via the dimension hierarchy. Downward data generation using this rule, tuple 5 in Table 3, and the dimensional connection of *Standard* to *W1*, *W2*, makes *Mark* have shifts in both *W1* and *W2* on *Sep/9*.   ■

3   Preliminaries

Contextual Data Quality: We first briefly review previous work in [2] on context-based data quality assessment. The starting point is that *data quality is context dependent*. A context provides *knowledge about the way data are interrelated, produced and used*, which allows us to make sense of the data. In our view, both the database under quality assessment and the context can be formalized as logical theories. The former is then *put in context* by mapping it into the latter, through logical mappings and possibly shared predicates.

In Fig. 3, D is a relational database (with schema $\mathcal{S}$) under quality assessment. It can be represented as a logical theory [28]. The context, $\mathfrak{C}$ in the middle, resembles a virtual data integration system, which can also be represented as a logical theory [22]. The context has a relational schema (or signature), $\mathcal{C}$, in particular pred-

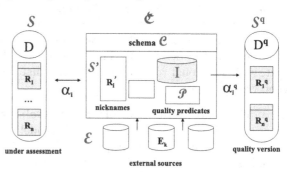

Fig. 3. A context for data quality assessment

icates with possibly partial extensions (incomplete relations). The mappings between $\mathcal{C}$ and D are of the kind used in data integration or data exchange [16], that can be expressed as logical formulas. In this paper, we are not concerned with how such a context is created [2].

A subschema of $\mathcal{C}$ may have an instance I, but $\mathcal{C}$ has nicknames (copies) R' for predicates R in $\mathcal{S}$. Nicknames are used to map (via α_i) the data in D into $\mathfrak{C}$, for further logical processing. So, schema $\mathcal{C}$ can be seen as an expansion of $\mathcal{S}$ through a subschema $\mathcal{S}'$. Some predicates in $\mathcal{C}$ are meant to be *quality predicates* (in $\mathcal{P}$), which are used to specify single quality requirements. There may be semantic constraints on schema $\mathcal{C}$, and also access (mappings) to external data sources, in $\mathcal{E}$, that could be used for data assessment or cleaning.

A clean version of D, obtained through the mapping into and processing within context $\mathfrak{C}$, is a possibly virtual instance D^q (or a collection thereof, as suggested in Fig. 1), for schema $\mathcal{S}^q$ (a "quality" copy of schema $\mathcal{S}$). The extension of every predicate in it, say R^q, is the "quality version" of relation R in D, and is defined as a view (via the α_i^q) in terms of the nickname predicates in $\mathcal{S}'$, those in $\mathcal{P}$, and other contextual predicates.

The quality of (the data in) instance D can be measured by comparing D with the instance D^q or the set, $\mathcal{D}^q$, of them. This latter set can also be used to define and possibly compute the *quality answers* to queries originally posed to D, as the *certain answers* w.r.t. $\mathcal{D}^q$. See [2] for more details, and different cases that may occur. In any case, the

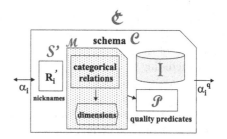

Fig. 4. A multidimensional context

main idea is that quality data can be extracted from D by querying the possibly virtual class $\mathcal{D}^q$.

In this paper, we extend the approach to data quality specification and extraction we just described, by adding dimensions to contexts, for multidimensional data quality specification and extraction. In this case, the context contains a generic MD ontology, the shaded $\mathcal{M}$ in Fig. 4, a.k.a. "core ontology" (and described in Section 4). This ontology can be extended, within the context, with additional rules and constraints that depend on specific data quality concerns (cf. Section 6).

The Hurtado-Mendelzon Data Model: According to the Hurtado-Mendelzon (HM) multidimensional data model [18], a *dimension schema*, $\mathcal{S} = \langle \mathcal{K}, \nearrow \rangle$, is a directed acyclic graph and lattice, with $\mathcal{K}$ a set of categories (represented as unary predicates), and $\nearrow$ the *parent-child relation* between categories. $\nearrow^*$ denotes the transitive and reflexive closure of $\nearrow$, and is a partial order with a *top category*, *All*, which is reachable from every other category. There is a unique *base category*, which does not have children. A *dimension instance* for schema $\mathcal{S}$ is a tuple $\mathcal{D} = \langle \mathcal{N}, <, \sigma \rangle$, with $\mathcal{N}$ a set of *elements*, $<$ is a *parent-child relation* between elements, and $\sigma : \mathcal{N} \rightarrow \mathcal{K}$, the *membership function*, is total and injective. A dimension instance is shown in Fig. 2, left. The partial order $<$ parallels (is consistent with) $\nearrow$: $a < b$ implies $\sigma(a) \nearrow \sigma(b)$. $\sigma(e) = k$ is also denoted as $e \in k$ or $k(e)$ (holds). $<^*$ is the transitive and reflexive closure of $<$, and is used to define the *roll-up* relations for any pair of categories k and k': $L_k^{k'}(\mathcal{D}) = \{(e, e') \mid e \in k, \ e' \in k' \text{ and } e <^* e'\}$.

Datalog$^\pm$: Datalog$^\pm$ [6,7] is a family of rule languages that properly extends plain Datalog with: (a) rules (*tgds*) may have existential quantifiers in the heads; (b) *equality-generating dependencies* (*egds*), i.e. rules with only equality in the head; and (c) *negative constraints* (NCs), that are rules with $\bot$, a false propositional atom, in the heads, indicating that the rule body cannot be true.

Example 3. This Datalog$^\pm$ program shows a *tgd*, an *egd*, and an *NC*, in this order: $\exists x Assist(d, x) \leftarrow Doctor(d); \quad x = x' \leftarrow Assist(d, x), Assist(d, x'); \quad \bot \leftarrow Specialist(d, x, n), Nurse(d, n).$ ∎

Datalog$^\pm$ has been used to represent ontological knowledge and conceptual data models [9,11]; and for *ontology-based data access* [13,15]. The underlying extensional, relational database (the facts) $\mathcal{I}$ for a program may be incomplete, and the *chase* is the standard procedure for completing the database, through the enforcement of the program rules. When a *tgd* is applied, new atoms are created, possibly including fresh nulls (for the existential variables), and the whole run of the chase may be non-terminating, leading to an infinite complete database. The enforcement of an *egd* equates nulls with nulls or nulls with constants or fails. For a set Σ of *tgds* and *egds*, $chase(\mathcal{I}, \Sigma)$ denotes the possibly infinite instance resulting from the non-failing chase of Σ on $\mathcal{I}$.

Even with an infinite $chase(\mathcal{I}, \Sigma)$ it is possible that *conjunctive query answering* (QA) is decidable (or computable). The $^-$ in Datalog$^\pm$ stands for syntactic restrictions on the interaction of *tgds* in Σ that ensure decidability of QA, and, in some cases, also tractability (in data). Datalog$^{\pm}$ is a family of languages with different degrees of expressivity and computational properties. Some of them are: *linear, guarded, weakly-guarded, sticky,* and *weakly-sticky* Datalog$^{\pm}$ [6–10]. In this work (cf. [27, appendixA]), we are particularly interested in *weakly-sticky* (WS) Datalog$^{\pm}$ [10], which extends *sticky* Datalog$^{\pm}$ [8].

4 Extending the HM Model with Datalog$^{\pm}$

We extend the HM model introducing *categorical relations*, each of them having a relational schema with a name, and attributes, some of which are *categorical* and the other, *non-categorical.* The former take values that are members of a dimension category. The latter take values from an arbitrary domain. Categorical relations have to be logically connected to dimensions. For this we use a Datalog$\pm$ ontology $\mathcal{M}$, which has a relational schema $\mathcal{S}_{\mathcal{M}}$, an instance $\mathcal{D}_{\mathcal{M}}$, and a set $\Sigma_{\mathcal{M}}$ of dimensional rules, and a set $\kappa_{\mathcal{M}}$ of constraints. Here, $\mathcal{S}_{\mathcal{M}} = \mathcal{K} \cup \mathcal{O} \cup \mathcal{R}$, with $\mathcal{K}$ a set of unary *category predicates*, $\mathcal{O}$ a set of *parent-child predicates*, capturing $<$-relationships for pairs of adjacent categories, and $\mathcal{R}$ a set of *categorical predicates*, say $R(C_1, \ldots ; N_1, \ldots)$, where, to highlight, categorical and non-categorical attributes (C_is vs. N_js) are separated by ";".

Example 4. Categorical relation *PatientWard(Ward,Day;Patient)* in Fig. 2 has categorical attributes *Ward* and *Day*, connected to the Hospital and Time dimensions, resp. *Patient* is non-categorical. $Ward(\cdot), Unit(\cdot) \in \mathcal{K}$; $\mathcal{O}$ contains, e.g. a binary predicate connecting *Ward* to *Unit*; and $\mathcal{R}$ contains, e.g. *PatientWard.* ∎

The (extensional) data, $\mathcal{D}_{\mathcal{M}}$, associated to the ontology $\mathcal{M}$'s schema are the complete extensions for categories in $\mathcal{K}$ and predicates in $\mathcal{O}$ that come from the dimension instances. The categorical relations (with predicates in $\mathcal{R}$) may contain partial data, i.e. they may be incomplete. They can belong to instance I in Fig. 4. Dimensional rules in $\Sigma_{\mathcal{M}}$ are those in (c) below; and constraints in $\kappa_{\mathcal{M}}$, those in (a) and (b).

(a) *Referential constraints* between categorical attributes and categories as negative constraint:[3]   ($R \in \mathcal{R}$, $K \in \mathcal{K}$; $\bar{e}, \bar{a}$ are categorical, non-categorical, resp.; $e \in \bar{e}$)

$$\bot \leftarrow R(\bar{e}; \bar{a}), \neg K(e). \tag{1}$$

Notice that K, to which negation is applied, is a closed, extensional predicate.

(b) Additional *dimensional constraints*, as egds or NCs: ($R_i \in \mathcal{R}$, $D_j \in \mathcal{O}$, and x, x' stand both for either categorical or non-categorical attributes in the body of (2))

$$x = x' \leftarrow R_1(\bar{e}_1; \bar{a}_1), ..., R_n(\bar{e}_n; \bar{a}_n), D_1(e_1, e'_1), ..., D_m(e_m, e'_m). \tag{2}$$

$$\bot \leftarrow R_1(\bar{e}_1; \bar{a}_1), ..., R_n(\bar{e}_n; \bar{a}_n), D_1(e_1, e'_1), ..., D_m(e_m, e'_m). \tag{3}$$

---

[3] An alternative and more problematic approach, may use *tgds* between categorical attributes and categories, making it possible to generate elements in categories or categorical attributes.

(c) *Dimensional rules* as Datalog$^\pm$ *tgds*:

$$\exists \bar{a}_z \ R_k(\bar{e}_k; \bar{a}_k) \leftarrow R_1(\bar{e}_1; \bar{a}_1), ..., R_n(\bar{e}_n; \bar{a}_n), D_1(e_1, e_1'), ..., D_m(e_m, e_m'). \quad (4)$$

Here, $\bar{a}_z \subseteq \bar{a}_k$, $\bar{e}_k \subseteq \bar{e}_1 \cup ... \cup \bar{e}_n \cup \{e_1, ..., e_m, e_1', ..., e_m'\}$, $\bar{a}_k \setminus \bar{a}_z \subseteq \bar{a}_1 \cup ... \cup \bar{a}_n$; and repeated variables in bodies are only in positions of categorical attributes (in the categorical relations $R_i(\bar{e}_i; \bar{a}_i)$), and attributes in parent-child predicates $D_j(e_j, e_j')^4$. Value invention is only on non-categorical attributes (we will consider relaxing this later on).

Some of the lists in the bodies of (2)-(4) may be empty, i.e. $n = 0$ or $m = 0$. This allows us to represent, in addition to properly "navigational" constraints, also classical constraints on categorical relations, e.g. keys or FDs.

Example 5. (ex. 1 and 4 cont.) In relation *PatientUnit*, the categorical attribute *Unit* takes values from the *Unit* category. We use a constraint of the form (1), namely: $\perp \leftarrow PatientUnit(u, d; p), \neg Unit(u)$. The constraint *"No patient in intensive care unit during August 2005"* becomes a dimensional (navigational) constraint of the form (3):

$$\perp \leftarrow [PatientWard(w, d; p), UnitWard(\texttt{Intensive}, w), \quad (5)$$

$$MonthDay(\texttt{August2005}, d)].$$

Alternatively, we could apply a constraint directly on *PatientUnit*, without explicit navigation in the Hospital dimension, but we still need to navigate in the Time dimension: $\perp \leftarrow PatientUnit(\texttt{Intensive}, d; p), MonthDay(\texttt{August2005}, d)$.

An *egd* of the form (2) says that *"All thermometers in a unit are of the same type"*:

$$t = t' \leftarrow Therm(w, t; n), Therm(w', t'; n'), UnitWard(u, w), UnitWard(u, w') \quad (6)$$

with *Therm(Ward, Thertype; Nurse)* a categorical relation, and *Ward, Thertype* categorical attributes (the latter for an Instrument dimension). This *egd* illustrates the flexibility of our approach. Even without having a categorical relation at the *Unit*, we could still impose a condition at that level.^{5}

The following *tgds* generate data from *PatientWard* to *PatientUnit*, and from *WorkingSchedules* to *Shifts*, resp. They are of the form (4).

$$PatientUnit(u, d; p) \leftarrow PatientWard(w, d; p), UnitWard(u, w). \quad (7)$$

$$\exists z \ Shifts(w, d; n, z) \leftarrow WorkingSchedules(u, d; n, t), UnitWard(u, w). \quad (8)$$

The existential variable in (8) makes up for the missing, non-categorical attribute in the "parent" relation *WorkingSchedules*. This is not needed in (7). ■

Remark 1. A general *tgd* of the form (4) enables *upward-* or *downward-navigation*, depending on the body joins. The direction is determined by the dimension levels of categorical attributes in the joins. For simplicity, assume that

---

^{4} This is a natural restriction since dimension navigation is captured by the joins only between variables of these attributes

^{5} If we have that relation, as in Example 1, then (6) could be replaced by a "static", non-navigational FD. This issue is further discussed in [27, appendixB].

there is a single $D_j \in \mathcal{O}$ in the body (as in (7) and (8)). If the join is between $R_i(\bar{e}_i; \bar{a}_i)$ and $D_j(e_j, e'_j)$ then: (a) (one-step) upward navigation is enabled, from e'_j to e_j, when $e'_j \in \bar{e}_i$ (i.e. e'_j appears in $R_i(\bar{e}_i; \bar{a}_i)$) and $e_j \in \bar{e}_k$, i.e in the head), (b) (one-step) downward navigation is enabled, from e_j to e'_j, when e_j occurs in R_i and e'_j occurs in R_k. Several occurrences of parent-child predicates in a body capture multi-step navigation. ∎

Example 6. (ex. 5 cont.) Rule (8) captures downward-navigation; and this is a general behavior with *tgds* of the form (4). That is, when drilling-down via (8), from a tuple, say $WorkingSchedules(u, d; n, t)$ via the category member u (for Unit), *for each* child w of u in the *Ward* category, a tuple for *Shifts* is generated, as specified in the body of (8). For example, chasing (8) with the last tuple in Table 3, generates the new tuple $\langle \mathtt{W1}, \mathtt{Sep/9}, \mathtt{Mark}, \perp \rangle$ in Table 4, with a fresh null for the shift (similarly for *W2*). This allows us to answer the query about the dates *Mark* works in *W1*: $\mathcal{Q}'(d)$: $\exists s Shifts(\mathtt{W1}, d, \mathtt{Mark}, s)$. We obtain *Sep/9*.

Instead, the join between *PatientWard* and *UnitWard* in (7) enables upward-dimension navigation; and generates only one tuple for *PatientUnit* from each tuple in *PatientWard*, because each *Ward* member has only one *Unit* parent. ∎

5 Properties of MD Datalog$^\pm$ Ontologies

Here, we first establish the membership of our MD ontologies, $\mathcal{M}$ (cf. Section 4) of a class of the Datalog$\pm$ family. Membership is determined by the set $\Sigma_\mathcal{M}$ of its *tgds*. Next, we analyze the role of the constraints in $\kappa_\mathcal{M}$, in particular, of the set $\epsilon_\mathcal{M}$ of *egds*.

Proposition 1. MD ontologies are weakly-sticky Datalog$\pm$ programs. ∎

The proof (as other proofs) and a review of *weakly-sticky* Datalog$\pm$ [10] can be found in the extended version [27, appendixA.]. A consequence of this result is that conjunctive query answering (QA) from $\Sigma_\mathcal{M}$ is in polynomial-time in data complexity [10]. The complexity stays the same if we add negative constraints, *NCs*, of the forms (1) and (3), because they can be checked through the conjunctive queries in their bodies [10]. However, combining the *egds* in $\epsilon_\mathcal{M}$ with $\Sigma_\mathcal{M}$ could change things, and, in principle, even lead to undecidability of QA [5].

Example 7. Consider $\mathcal{I} = \{Surgery(\mathtt{W1}, \mathtt{John})\}$ and a weakly-sticky set Σ_T of *tgds*: $\sigma_1 : \exists z\ Surgeon(w, z) \leftarrow Surgery(w, p)$; $\sigma_2 : \exists y\ Assist(w, y) \leftarrow Surgery(w, p)$; $\sigma_3 : \exists z\ Surgery(z, x) \leftarrow Assist(w, x), Surgeon(w', x)$. Here, $chase(\mathcal{I}, \Sigma_T) = \{Surgery$
$(\mathtt{W1}, \mathtt{John}), Assist(\mathtt{W1}, \perp_1), Surgeon(\mathtt{W1}, \perp_2)\}$.

Now, if we add the *egd* $\varepsilon : y = z \leftarrow Assist(w, z), Surgeon(w, y)$, the chase is infinite: $chase(\mathcal{I}, \Sigma_T \cup \{\varepsilon\}) = \{Surgery(\mathtt{W1}, \mathtt{John}), Assist(\mathtt{W1}, \perp_1), Surgeon(\mathtt{W1}, \perp_1), Surgery(\perp_2, \perp_1), Assist(\perp_2, \perp_3), Surgeon(\perp_2, \perp_3), Surgery(\perp_4, \perp_3), \ldots\}$.

These non-failing chases give different answers to the Boolean conjunctive query (BCQ) Q: $\exists wxw'(Assist(w; x) \wedge Surgeon(w'; x))$: $chase(\mathcal{I}, \Sigma_T \cup \{\varepsilon\}) \models Q$, but $chase(\mathcal{I}, \Sigma_T) \not\models Q$. ■

This example shows a harmful interaction between the *tgds* and an *egd*. They infinitely fire each other, making infinite an initially finite chase. The interaction also has an effect on QA. A *separability condition* on the combination of *egds* and *tgds* guarantees a harmless interaction w.r.t. QA.

Definition 1. [9,12] Let Σ be formed by a set Σ_T of *tgds* and a set Σ_E of *egds*. Σ_E and Σ_T are *separable* if, for every instance $\mathcal{I}$ for which the chase of Σ on $\mathcal{I}$ does not fail, and BCQ Q, $chase(\mathcal{I}, \Sigma) \models Q$ if and only if $chase(\mathcal{I}, \Sigma_T) \models Q$. ■

Example 7 shows a case of non-separability. Separability tells us that we can safely ignore Σ_E for QA. More precisely, if separability holds and QA is decidable under the *tgds*, then it is also decidable under the combination of *tgds* and *egds* : (a) (combined) chase failure can be decided by posing conjunctive queries associated to the bodies of the *egds* [12, theo.1]; (b) if it does not fail, QA can be done with the *tgds* alone. Even more, under separability, the complexity of QA on $\mathcal{I} \cup \Sigma$ is the same as for $\mathcal{I} \cup \Sigma_T$ [9,11,12].

Proposition 2. For an MD ontology $\mathcal{M}$ with a set $\Sigma_{\mathcal{M}}$ of *tgds* as in (4) and set $\epsilon_{\mathcal{M}}$ of *egds* as in (2), separability holds if, for every *egd* in $\epsilon_{\mathcal{M}}$, the variables in the equality (in the head) occur in categorical positions in the body. ■

In combination with Proposition 1, we obtain:

Corollary 1. Under the hypothesis of Proposition 2, QA from an MD ontology can be done in polynomial-time in data. ■

Under the hypothesis of Proposition 2, our MD ontologies are separable and enjoy the good properties we just mentioned. However, some good properties can still be preserved with non-separable MD ontologies. The next example motivates this result.

Example 8. (ex. 7 cont.) Let us modify our ontology. Now, $\Sigma'_T = \{\sigma_1, \sigma_2\}$, and the *egd* is still ε. Now, both chases are finite: $chase(\mathcal{I}, \Sigma'_T \cup \{\varepsilon\})$ = $\{Surgery(\texttt{W1}; \texttt{John}), Assist(\texttt{W1}; \bot_1), Surgeon(\texttt{W1}; \bot_1)\}$; and $chase(\mathcal{I}, \Sigma'_T)$ = $\{Surgery(\texttt{W1}; \texttt{John}), Assist (\texttt{W1}; \bot_1), Surgeon(\texttt{W1}; \bot_2)\}$. (As before, we use ";" to separate categorical from non-categorical attributes.) The *egd* is not separable from the *tgds*. Actually, for the same query Q of Example 7, and the non-failing chases, it holds: $chase(\mathcal{I}, \Sigma'_T \cup \{\varepsilon\}) \models Q$, but $chase(\mathcal{I}, \Sigma'_T) \not\models Q$. ■

In this example, despite the lack of separability, the application of *egds* does not trigger new *tgds* during the chase (as happens in Example 7). This is due (cf. Lemma 1 below) to the fact that $\Sigma'_T \cup \{\varepsilon\}$ respects a condition imposed on our MD ontologies: joins in *tgd* bodies only between categorical attributes. (The ontology in Example 7 had σ_3, which violates this condition.) Lemma 1 below tells us that with MD ontologies, applying *egd* chase steps does not increase the number of *tgd* chase steps.[6]

---

[6] We assume the chase, after the enforcement of a (ground) *tgd*, applies all the *egds*.

Lemma 1. For an MD ontology $\mathcal{M}$ with a set $\Sigma_{\mathcal{M}}$ of *tgds* as in (4) and a set $\epsilon_{\mathcal{M}}$ of *egds* as in (2), applying an *egd* chase step does not cause any new application of a ground *tgd*, i.e. a *tgd* body ground instantiation that did not appear without the *egds*. ∎

With weakly-sticky sets of *tgds* the chase may not terminate, due to an infinite number of *tgd* chase steps. This is in particular the case for the set of *tgds* in our MD ontologies. However, QA on weakly-sticky *tgds* can be done in polynomial-time by querying an initial portion of the chase that has a polynomial *depth* [10]. By Lemma 1, if we add *egds*, QA can still be done by querying an initial portion of the chase (including *egds* now) that has the same (polynomial) *depth* as that for *tgds* alone. So, although *egds* in our MD ontologies may have an effect on QA (the two initial portions can be different), the complexity does not change w.r.t. to having only the *tgds*.

Proposition 3. For an MD ontology, QA is in polynomial-time in data complexity. ∎

6   MD Contexts for Quality Data

We now show in general how to use a MD context, $\mathfrak{C}$, containing MD ontologies for quality data specification and extraction w.r.t. a database instance D for schema $\mathcal{S}$. We will at the same time, for illustration and fixing ideas, revisit the example in Section 2, putting it in terms of the MD context elements we presented in Section 4. Context $\mathfrak{C}$, as shown in Fig. 4, contains:

1. Nickname predicates $R' \in \mathcal{S}'$ for predicates R of original schema $\mathcal{S}$. In this case, the R' have the same extensions as in D, producing a material or virtual instance D' within $\mathfrak{C}$.

For example, *Measurements'* $\in \mathcal{S}'$ is a nickname predicate for *Measurements* $\in \mathcal{S}$, whose initial contents (in D) is under quality assessment.

2. The *core MD ontology*, $\mathcal{M}$, that includes a partial instance, $\mathcal{D}_{\mathcal{M}}$, containing dimensional, categorical data; and the Datalog± ontology with *tgds* $\Sigma_{\mathcal{M}}$, and constraints $\kappa_{\mathcal{M}}$, among them, the *egds* $\epsilon_{\mathcal{M}}$ of Section 4. We assume that application dependent guidelines and constraints are all represented as components of $\mathcal{M}$.

In our running example, *PatientUnit*, *PatientWard*, *WorkingSchedules* and *WorkingTimes* are categorical relations. *UnitWard*, *DayTime* are parent-child relations in the Hospital and Time dimensions, resp. The followings are dimensional rules (*tgds*) of $\Sigma_{\mathcal{M}}$:   (with (9) a new version of (7) allowing upward-navigation in two dimensions)[7]

$WorkingTimes(u, t; n, y) \leftarrow WorkingSchedules(u, d; n, y), DayTime(d, t).$

$PatientUnit(u, t; p) \leftarrow PatientWard(w, d; p), DayTime(d, t), UnitWard(u, w). \quad (9)$

---

[7] A *tgd* may support multidimensional navigation and in multiple directions.

3. The set of *quality predicates*, $\mathcal{P}$, with their definitions in, say non-recursive Datalog[8] (possibly with negation, *not*), in terms of categorical predicates in $\mathcal{R}$ and built-in predicates. They may have partial or full extensions in the contextual instance I (that includes $\mathcal{D}_\mathcal{M}$). A quality predicate reflects an application dependent specific quality concern.

Now, *TakenByNurse* and *TakenWithTherm* are quality predicates with definitions on top of $\mathcal{M}$, addressing quality concerns about the nurses and the thermometers:

$$TakenByNurse(t,p,n,y) \leftarrow WorkingTimes(u,t;n,y), PatientUnit(u,t;p). \quad (10)$$

$$TakenWithTherm(t,p,b) \leftarrow PatientUnit(u,t;p), u = \texttt{Standard}, b = \texttt{B1}. \quad (11)$$

Furthermore, and not strictly inside context $\mathfrak{C}$, there are predicates $R_1^q, ..., R_n^q \in \mathcal{S}^q$, the *quality versions* of $R_1, ..., R_n \in \mathcal{S}$. They are defined through *quality data extraction rules* written in non-recursive Datalog, in terms of nickname predicates (in $\mathcal{S}'$), categorical predicates (in $\mathcal{R}$), and the quality predicates (in $\mathcal{P}$), and built-in predicates. Their definitions (the α_i^q in Fig. 4) impose conditions corresponding to user's data quality profiles, and their extensions form the quality data (instance).

The quality version of *Measurements* is $Measurement^q \in \mathcal{S}^q$, with the following definition, which captures the intended, clean contents of the former:

$$Measurement^q(t,p,v) \leftarrow Measurement'(t,p,v), TakenByNurse(t,p,n,y), \quad (12)$$
$$TakenWithTherm(t,p,b), b = \texttt{B1}, y = \texttt{certified}.$$

Quality data can be obtained from the interaction between the original source D and the context $\mathfrak{C}$, in particular using the MD ontology $\mathcal{M}$. For that, queries have to be posed to the context, in terms of predicates $\mathcal{S}^q$, the quality versions of those of D. A query could be as direct as asking, e.g. about the contents of predicate $Measurement^q$ above, or a conjunctive query involving predicates $\mathcal{S}^q$.

A naive user —not familiar with the exact interaction with the context— who expects to obtain quality data from D will express a query $\mathcal{Q}$ in terms of the original schema $\mathcal{S}$. However, the information system will rewrite the query into $\mathcal{Q}^q$, in terms of the predicates in $\mathcal{S}^q$. Consequently, the *quality answers* to $\mathcal{Q}$, are defined as those that are *certain* through the context:

Definition 2. For D an instance for schema $\mathcal{S}$, $\mathfrak{C}$ the context containing MD ontology $\mathcal{M}$, and definitions $\Sigma^\mathcal{P}, \Sigma^q$ of quality and quality version predicates, resp., the set of *clean answers* to a conjunctive query $\mathcal{Q}(\bar{x})$ on schema $\mathcal{S}$ is:

$$QAns_D^{\mathfrak{C}}(\mathcal{Q}) = \{\bar{c} \mid D \cup \mathcal{M} \cup \Sigma^\mathcal{P} \cup \Sigma^q \models \mathcal{Q}^q[\bar{c}]\}. \qquad \blacksquare$$

For example, this is the initial query asking for (quality) values for Tom Waits' temperature: $\mathcal{Q}(t,v):$ $Measurements(t, \texttt{Tom Waits}, v) \wedge \texttt{Sep5-11:45} \leq t \leq \texttt{Sep5-12:15}$, which, in order to be answered, has to be first rewritten into: $\mathcal{Q}^q(t,v): Measurements^q(t, \texttt{Tom Waits}, v) \wedge \texttt{Sep5-11:45} \leq t \leq \texttt{Sep5-12:15}$.

---

[8] Actually, more general rules could be used if they do not increase the complexity of query answering with the MD ontology.

To answer this query, first (12) can be used, obtaining a contextual query:

$\mathcal{Q}^{\mathfrak{C}}(t,v)$: $Measurement'(t,p,v) \wedge TakenByNurse(t,p,n,\texttt{certified}) \wedge$

$Taken\,With\,Therm(t,p,\texttt{B1}) \wedge p = \texttt{Tom Waits} \wedge$

$\texttt{Sep/5-11:45} \leq t \leq \texttt{Sep/5-12:15}.$

This query will in turn, use the contents for $Measurement'$ coming from D, and the quality predicate definitions (10) and (11), eventually leading to a conjunctive query expressed in terms of $Measurement'$ and MD predicates only, namely:

$\mathcal{Q}^{\mathcal{M}}(t,v)$: $Measurement'(t,p,v) \wedge WorkingTimes(u,t;n,y) \wedge$

$PatientUnit(u,t;p) \wedge u = \texttt{Standard} \wedge y = \texttt{certified} \wedge$

$p = \texttt{Tom Waits} \wedge \texttt{Sep/5-11:45} \leq t \leq \texttt{Sep/5-12:15}.$

At this point, QA from a weakly-sticky ontology has to be performed. We know that this can be done in polynomial time in data. However, there is still a need for practical QA algorithms. Doing this goes beyond the scope of this paper. In [26] we describe some ideas on the development and optimization of such an algorithm.

7 Conclusions

Contexts, in particular, the multidimensional ones introduced in this work, allow us to specify data quality conditions, and to retrieve quality data. This is done by first mapping a data source, possibly with dirty data, into the context. The quality data can be materialized (possibly generating more than one intended clean instance) or be virtually defined. In both cases, it can be retrieved via queries. This latter idea of cleaning data on-the-fly is reminiscent of *consistent query answering* [3]. The main and important difference is that, instead of having (possibly violated) integrity constraints, with contexts we have a much more complex semantic framework for the definition of "repairs" (intended clean instances in our case) and consistent answers (the certain clean answers here).

There is still much to do in terms of development and optimization of practical query answering algorithms for weakly-sticky ontologies. Some first steps are reported in [26]. Implementation and experiments are matter of future work.

Several extensions of the current work have been or are being investigated. Those extensions can be found in the extended version of this paper [27]. Some of them are as follows:

1. Uncertain downward-navigation when *tgds* allow existentials on categorical attributes. A parent in a category may have multiple children in the next lower category. Under the assumption of complete categorical data, we know it is one of them, but not which one.

2. Our MD ontologies fully capture the taxonomy-based data model [23, 24] and its taxonomy relational algebra (TRA) for query answering. Our appraoch goes

beyond [24] in the sense that, first, our categorical relations, by having non-categorical attributes, generalize t-relations. Secondly, the dimensional rules in our MD ontologies capture the TRA, and offer existential variables for handling incomplete data. Finally, we also include and support ontological constraints, such as NCs and *egds* for restricting dimension navigation.

3. The negative constraints (and *egds*, mainly in the separable case) can and are checked on the result of the chase. We think a more natural and practical approach would be to integrate constraint checking with data generation, restricting the latter process. This would amount to compiling constraints into *tgds*, which might lead to the use of negation in *tgd* bodies [11,17].

4. We may relax the assumption on complete categorical data. This brings many new issues and problems that require investigation; from query answering to the maintenance of *structural semantic constraints*, such as strictness and homogeneity, on the HM model and our extension of it.

References

1. Batini, C., Scannapieco, M.: Data Quality: Concepts, Methodologies and Techniques. Springer (2006)
2. Bertossi, Leopoldo, Rizzolo, Flavio, Jiang, Lei: Data quality is context dependent. In: Löser, Alexander (ed.) BIRTE 2010. LNBIP, vol. 84, pp. 52–67. Springer, Heidelberg (2011)
3. Bertossi, L.: Database Repairing and Consistent Query Answering. Morgan & Claypool (2011)
4. Bolchini, C., Quintarelli, E., Tanca, L.: CARVE: Context-Aware Automatic View Definition over Relational Databases. Information Systems **38**, 45–67 (2013)
5. Cali, A., Lembo, D., Rosati, R.: On the decidability and complexity of query answering over inconsistent and incomplete databases. In: Proc. PODS, pp. 260–271 (2003)
6. Cali, A., Gottlob, G., Lukasiewicz, T.: Datalog$^{\pm}$: a unified approach to ontologies and integrity constraints. In: Proc. ICDT, pp. 14–30 (2009)
7. Cali, A., Gottlob, G., Lukasiewicz, T., Marnette, B., Pieris, A.: Datalog$^{\pm}$: a family of logical knowledge representation and query languages for new applications. In: Proc. LICS, pp. 228–242 (2010)
8. Cali, A., Gottlob, G., Pieris, A.: Query answering under non-guarded rules in datalog+/-. In: Proc. RR, pp. 1–17 (2010)
9. Cali, A., Gottlob, G., Pieris, A.: Ontological Query Answering under Expressive Entity-Relationship Schemata. Information Systems **37**(4), 320–335 (2012)
10. Cali, A., Gottlob, G., Pieris, A.: Towards More Expressive Ontology Languages: The Query Answering Problem. Artificial Intelligence **193**, 87–128 (2012)
11. Cali, A., Gottlob, G., Lukasiewicz, T.: A General Datalog-Based Framework for Tractable Query Answering over Ontologies. Journal of Web Semantics **14**, 57–83 (2012)
12. Cali, A., Console, M., Frosini, R.: On separability of ontological constraints. In: Proc. AMW, pp. 48–61 (2012)
13. Calvanese, D., De Giacomo, G., Lembo, D., Lenzerini, M., Poggi, A., Rodriguez-Muro, M., Rosati, R., Ruzzi, M., Savo, D.F.: The MASTRO System for Ontology-Based Data Access. Semantic Web **2**(1), 43–53 (2011)

14. Franconi, E., Sattler, U.: A data warehouse conceptual data model for multidimensional aggregation. In: Proc. DMDW, CEUR Proceedings, vol. 19 (1999)
15. Gottlob, G., Orsi, G., Pieris, A.: Query Rewriting and Optimization for Ontological Databases. ACM Trans. Database Syst. **39**(3), 25 (2014)
16. Fagin, R., Kolaitis, P.G., Miller, R.J., Popa, L.: Data Exchange: Semantics and Query Answering. Theoretical Computer Science **336**, 89–124 (2005)
17. Hernich, A., Kupke, C., Lukasiewicz, T., Gottlob, G.: Well-Founded semantics for extended datalog and ontological reasoning. In: Proc. PODS, pp. 225–236 (2013)
18. Hurtado, C., Mendelzon, A.: OLAP dimension constraints. In: Proc. PODS, pp. 169–179 (2002)
19. Imielinski, T., Lipski, W.: Incomplete Information in Relational Databases. Journal of the ACM **31**(4), 761–791 (1984)
20. Jiang, L., Borgida, A., Mylopoulos, J.: Towards a compositional semantic account of data quality attributes. In: Proc. ER, pp. 55–68 (2008)
21. Maleki, A., Bertossi, L., Rizzolo, F.: Multidimensional contexts for data quality assessment. In: Proc. AMW, 2012, CEUR Proceedings, vol. 866, pp. 196–209
22. Lenzerini, M.: Data integration: a theoretical perspective. In: Proc. PODS, pp. 233–246 (2002)
23. Martinenghi, D., Torlone, R.: Querying context-aware databases. In: Andreasen, T., Yager, R.R., Bulskov, H., Christiansen, H., Larsen, H.L. (eds.) FQAS 2009. LNCS, vol. 5822, pp. 76–87. Springer, Heidelberg (2009)
24. Martinenghi, D., Torlone, R.: Taxonomy-Based Relaxation of Query Answering in Relational Databases. The VLDB Journal **23**(5), 747–769 (2014)
25. Milani, M., Bertossi, L., Ariyan, S.: Extending contexts with ontologies for multidimensional data quality assessment. In: Proc. ICDEW (DESWeb), pp. 242–247 (2014)
26. Milani, M., Bertossi, L.: Tractable Query Answering and Optimization for Extensions of Weakly-Sticky Datalog± (2015). Submitted, under review
27. Milani, M., Bertossi, L.: Ontology-Based Multidimensional Contexts with Applications to Quality Data Specification and Extraction. Extended version of this paper. http://people.scs.carleton.ca/~bertossi/papers/obmcExt.pdf
28. Reiter, R.: Towards a logical reconstruction of relational database theory. In: Brodie, M.L., Mylopoulos, J., Schmidt, J.W. (eds.) On Conceptual Modelling, pp. 191–233. Springer (1984)

Existential Rules and Bayesian Networks for Probabilistic Ontological Data Exchange

Thomas Lukasiewicz[1], Maria Vanina Martinez[2],
Livia Predoiu[1(✉)], and Gerardo I. Simari[2]

[1] Department of Computer Science, University of Oxford, Oxford, UK
livia.predoiu@cs.ox.ac.uk
[2] Department of Computer Science and Engineering,
Universidad Nacional Del Sur and CONICET, Bahía Blanca, Argentina

Abstract. We investigate the problem of exchanging probabilistic data between ontology-based probabilistic databases. The probabilities of the probabilistic source databases are compactly and flexibly encoded via Bayesian networks, which are closely related to the management of provenance. For the ontologies and the ontology mappings, we consider existential rules from the Datalog+/– family. We analyze the computational complexity of the problem of deciding whether there exists a probabilistic (universal) solution for a given probabilistic source database relative to a (probabilistic) ontological data exchange problem. We provide a host of complexity results for this problem for different classes of existential rules. We also analyze the complexity of answering UCQs (unions of conjunctive queries) in this framework.

1 Introduction

Uncertainty is prevalent in many areas such as information extraction, RFID, scientific data management, data cleaning, web data integration, financial risk assessment, and weather forecasts. Such applications produce large volumes of uncertain data, which are best modeled, stored, and processed in probabilistic databases [24]. Enriching databases with terminological knowledge encoded in ontologies has recently gained increasing importance in the form of ontology-based data access (OBDA) [22]. A crucial problem in OBDA is to integrate and exchange knowledge.

Both in the context of OBDA and the Semantic Web in general, there are distributed ontologies that we may have to map and integrate in order to enable query answering over them. Apart from the uncertainty attached to source databases, the ontology mappings may also have associated uncertainty regarding the proper correspondence between items in the source ontology and items in the target ontology. This especially happens when the mappings are created automatically.

Data exchange [12] is an important theoretical framework used for studying data-interoperability tasks that require data to be transferred from existing databases to a target database that comes with its own (independently created) schema and schema constraints. The expressivity of the data exchange framework

© Springer International Publishing Switzerland 2015
N. Bassiliades et al. (Eds.): RuleML 2015, LNCS 9202, pp. 294–310, 2015.
DOI: 10.1007/978-3-319-21542-6_19

goes beyond the classical data integration framework [18]. Schema mappings are used for the translation, which are declarative specifications that describe the relationship between two database schemas. In classical data exchange, we have a source database, a target database, a deterministic mapping, and deterministic target dependencies. Recently, a framework for probabilistic data exchange was proposed in [11], where the classical data exchange framework based on weakly acyclic existential rules is extended to consider a probabilistic source database and a probabilistic source-to-target mapping.

In this paper, we propose and study a more expressive extension of the probabilistic data exchange framework of [11], in which the source and the target are ontological knowledge bases each consisting of a probabilistic database and a deterministic ontology describing terminological knowledge about the data stored in the database. The two ontologies and the mapping between them are expressed via existential rules. Our extension of the data exchange framework is strongly related to exchanging data between incomplete databases, as proposed in [3], which considers an incomplete deterministic source database in the data exchange problem. However, in that work, the databases are deterministic, and the mappings and the target database constraints are full existential rules only. In this paper, our complexity analysis considers a host of different classes of existential rules, including some subclasses of full existential rules. In addition, our source is a probabilistic database relative to an underlying ontology.

Our work in this paper is also related to the recently proposed knowledge base exchange framework [1,2], which allows knowledge to be exchanged between deterministic $DL\text{-}Lite_{RDFS}$ and $DL\text{-}Lite_{\mathcal{R}}$ ontologies. In this paper, besides considering probabilistic source databases, we are also using more expressive ontology languages, since already linear existential rules from the Datalog+/− family are strictly more expressive than the description logics (DLs) $DL\text{-}Lite_X$ of the $DL\text{-}Lite$ family [9] as well as their extensions with n-ary relations $DLR\text{-}Lite_X$. Guarded existential rules are sufficiently expressive to model the tractable DL $\mathcal{EL}$ [4,5] (and $\mathcal{ELI}^f$ [17]). Note that existential rules are also known as tuple-generating dependencies (TGDs) and Datalog+/− rules [7].

The main contributions of this paper are summarized as follows.

- We introduce deterministic and probabilistic ontological data exchange problems, where probabilistic knowledge is exchanged between two Bayesian network-based probabilistic databases relative to their underlying deterministic ontologies, and the deterministic and probabilistic mapping between the two ontologies is defined via deterministic and probabilistic existential mapping rules, respectively.
- We provide an in-depth analysis of the data and combined complexity of deciding the existence of probabilistic (universal) solutions and obtain a (fairly) complete picture of the data complexity, general combined complexity, bounded-arity combined (*ba*-combined), and fixed-program combined (*fp*-combined) complexity for the main sublanguages of the Datalog+/− family. We also delineate some tractable special cases, and we provide some complexity results for exact UCQ (union of conjunctive queries) answering.

- For the complexity analysis, we consider a compact encoding of probabilistic source databases and mappings, which is used in the area of both incomplete and probabilistic databases, and also known as data provenance or data lineage [13–15,24]. Here, we consider data provenance for probabilistic data that is structured according to an underlying Bayesian network.

The rest of this paper is organized as follows. In Section 2, we recall the basics of Datalog+/–. Sections 3.1 and 3.2 introduce the framework of ontological data exchange for deterministic and probabilistic existential mapping rules, respectively. In Sections 3.3 and 3.4, we define a compact encoding of the probabilistic source databases and the probabilistic mappings as well as the main computational tasks in deterministic and probabilistic ontological data exchange, respectively. Section 4 discusses the ontology and mapping languages used, and presents our complexity results for deterministic and probabilistic ontological data exchange for a host of Datalog+/– sublanguages. In Section 5, we summarize the main results and give an outlook on future research.

2   Preliminaries

We assume infinite sets of *constants* $\mathbf{C}$, *(labeled) nulls* $\mathbf{N}$, and regular *variables* $\mathbf{V}$. A *term* t is a constant, null, or variable. An *atom* has the form $p(t_1, \ldots, t_n)$, where p is an n-ary predicate, and $t_1, \ldots, t_n$ are terms. Conjunctions of atoms are often identified with the sets of their atoms. An *instance* I is a (possibly infinite) set of atoms $p(\mathbf{t})$, where $\mathbf{t}$ is a tuple of constants and nulls. A *database* D is a finite instance that contains only constants. A *homomorphism* is a substitution $h : \mathbf{C} \cup \mathbf{N} \cup \mathbf{V} \to \mathbf{C} \cup \mathbf{N} \cup \mathbf{V}$ that is the identity on $\mathbf{C}$. We assume familiarity with *conjunctive queries (CQs)*. The answer to a CQ q over an instance I is denoted $q(I)$. A Boolean CQ (BCQ) q evaluates to *true* over I, denoted $I \models q$, if $q(I) \neq \varnothing$.

A *tuple-generating dependency (TGD)* σ is a first-order formula $\forall \mathbf{X}\, \varphi(\mathbf{X}) \to \exists \mathbf{Y}\, p(\mathbf{X}, \mathbf{Y})$, where $\mathbf{X} \cup \mathbf{Y} \subseteq \mathbf{V}$, $\varphi(\mathbf{X})$ is a conjunction of atoms, and $p(\mathbf{X}, \mathbf{Y})$ is an atom. We call $\varphi(\mathbf{X})$ the *body* of σ, denoted $body(\sigma)$, and $p(\mathbf{X}, \mathbf{Y})$ the *head* of σ, denoted $head(\sigma)$. We consider only TGDs with a single atom in the head, but our results can be extended to TGDs with a conjunction of atoms in the head. An instance I *satisfies* σ, written $I \models \sigma$, if the following holds: whenever there exists a homomorphism h such that $h(\varphi(\mathbf{X})) \subseteq I$, then there exists $h' \supseteq h|_{\mathbf{X}}$, where $h|_{\mathbf{X}}$ is the restriction of h to $\mathbf{X}$, such that $h'(p(\mathbf{X}, \mathbf{Y})) \in I$. A *negative constraint (NC)* ν is a first-order formula $\forall \mathbf{X}\, \varphi(\mathbf{X}) \to \bot$, where $\mathbf{X} \subseteq \mathbf{V}$, $\varphi(\mathbf{X})$ is a conjunction of atoms, called the *body* of ν, denoted $body(\nu)$, and $\bot$ denotes the truth constant *false*. An instance I *satisfies* ν, denoted $I \models \nu$, if there is no homomorphism h such that $h(\varphi(\mathbf{X})) \subseteq I$. Given a set Σ of TGDs and NCs, I *satisfies* Σ, denoted $I \models \Sigma$, if I satisfies each TGD and NC of Σ. For brevity, we omit the universal quantifiers in front of TGDs and NCs.

Given a database D and a set Σ of TGDs and NCs, the answers we consider are those that are true in *all* models of D and Σ. Formally, the *models* of D and Σ, denoted $mods(D, \Sigma)$, is the set of instances $\{I \mid I \supseteq D$ and $I \models \Sigma\}$.

The *answer* to a CQ q relative to D and Σ is defined as the set of tuples $ans(q, D, \Sigma) = \bigcap_{I \in mods(D,\Sigma)} \{t \mid t \in q(I)\}$. The answer to a BCQ q is *true*, denoted $D \cup \Sigma \models q$, if $ans(q, D, \Sigma) \neq \varnothing$. The problem of *CQ answering* is defined as follows: given a database D, a set Σ of TGDs and NCs, a CQ q, and a tuple of constants t, decide whether $t \in ans(q, D, \Sigma)$. Following Vardi's taxonomy [25], the *combined complexity* of BCQ answering is calculated by considering all the components, i.e., the database, the set of dependencies, and the query, as part of the input. The *bounded-arity combined complexity* (or simply *ba-combined complexity*) is calculated by assuming that the arity of the underlying schema is bounded by an integer constant. Notice that in the context of description logics (DLs), whenever we refer to the combined complexity in fact we refer to the *ba*-combined complexity since, by definition, the arity of the underlying schema is at most two. The *fixed-program combined complexity* (or simply *fp-combined complexity*) is calculated by considering the set of TGDs and NCs as fixed.

3   Ontological Data Exchange

The source (resp., target) of the ontological data exchange problem that we consider in this paper is a probabilistic database (resp., probabilistic instance), each relative to a deterministic ontology. For clarity, in the following, we consider only one source database, but note that all our results carry over to the case where several source databases are at once mapped to a target instance. Note that in the source database, as usual in databases, there are no nulls (but all our results can be easily extended to source databases with nulls), while in the target instance, we may also have nulls.

Definition 1 (Probabilistic Databases and Instances). A *probabilistic database* (resp., *probabilistic instance*) over a schema **S** is a probability space $Pr = (\mathcal{I}, \mu)$ such that $\mathcal{I}$ is the set of all (possibly infinitely many) databases (resp., instances) over **S**, and $\mu \colon \mathcal{I} \to [0, 1]$ is a function that satisfies $\sum_{I \in \mathcal{I}} \mu(I) = 1$.

In Section 3.1, we introduce the *deterministic ontological data exchange* problem with deterministic mappings, while in Section 3.2, we present the *probabilistic ontological data exchange* problem with probabilistic mappings. In Section 3.3, we then introduce an encoding of both the probabilistic source databases and the probabilistic mappings. In this encoding, a common way to represent probabilistic databases with probabilistic conditions or provenance [13,14,24] is combined with a more flexible probabilistic model based on Bayesian networks, which does not necessarily assume probabilistic independence between all probabilistic events.

3.1   Deterministic Ontological Data Exchange

The deterministic ontological data exchange setting generalizes the classical logical framework of data exchange and integration [12] and its probabilistic extension [11]. It is tailored as data exchange from a probabilistic source database Pr_s

relative to a source ontology Σ_s (consisting of TGDs and NCs) over a schema $\mathbf{S}$ to a probabilistic target instance Pr_t relative to a target ontology Σ_t (consisting of a set of TGDs and NCs) over a schema $\mathbf{T}$ via a (source-to-target) mapping (also consisting of a set of TGDs and NCs). Formally, *ontological data exchange (ODE) problems* are defined as follows.

Definition 2 (Ontological Data Exchange (ODE)). An *ontological data exchange (ODE) problem* $\mathcal{M} = (\mathbf{S}, \mathbf{T}, \Sigma_s, \Sigma_t, \Sigma_{st})$ consists of (i) a source schema $\mathbf{S}$, (ii) a target schema $\mathbf{T}$ disjoint from $\mathbf{S}$, (iii) a finite set Σ_s of TGDs and NCs over $\mathbf{S}$ (called *source ontology*), (iv) a finite set Σ_t of TGDs and NCs over $\mathbf{T}$ (called *target ontology*), and (v) a finite set Σ_{st} of TGDs and NCs σ over $\mathbf{S} \cup \mathbf{T}$ (called *(source-to-target) mapping*) such that $body(\sigma)$ and $head(\sigma)$ are defined over $\mathbf{S} \cup \mathbf{T}$ and $\mathbf{T}$, respectively.

The semantics of ODE problems is defined by relating probabilistic source databases $Pr_s = (\mathcal{I}, \mu_s)$ and probabilistic target instances $Pr_t = (\mathcal{J}, \mu_t)$ in a meaningful way. We first describe the relationship in the deterministic case. A deterministic target instance J over $\mathbf{T}$ is a *solution* for a deterministic source database I over $\mathbf{S}$ relative to an ODE problem $\mathcal{M} = (\mathbf{S}, \mathbf{T}, \Sigma_s, \Sigma_t, \Sigma_{st})$ iff $(I \cup J) \models \Sigma_s \cup \Sigma_t \cup \Sigma_{st}$. We denote by $Sol_{\mathcal{M}}$ the set of all such pairs (I, J). Among the possible deterministic solutions J to a deterministic source database I relative to $\mathcal{M}$ in $Sol_{\mathcal{M}}$, we prefer the most general ones carrying only the necessary information for data exchange, i.e., those that transfer only the source database along with the relevant implicit derivations via Σ_s to the target ontology. Such solutions are called *universal* solutions. A universal solution can be homomorphically mapped to all other solutions leaving the constants unchanged. Hence, a deterministic target instance J over $\mathbf{T}$ is a *universal solution* for a deterministic source database I over $\mathbf{S}$ relative to a schema mapping $\mathcal{M}$ iff (i) J is a solution, and (ii) for each solution J' for I relative to $\mathcal{M}$, there is a homomorphism $h \colon J \to J'$. We denote by $USol_{\mathcal{M}}$ ($\subseteq Sol_{\mathcal{M}}$) the set of all pairs (I, J) of deterministic source databases I and target instances J such that J is a universal solution for I relative to $\mathcal{M}$.

In the probabilistic case, a joint probability space Pr over the solution relation $Sol_{\mathcal{M}}$ and the universal solution relation $USol_{\mathcal{M}}$ must exist. To this end, we define a joint probability space over the (universal) solution relation(s) as follows.

Definition 3 (Probabilistic (Universal) Solution). A probabilistic target instance $Pr_t = (\mathcal{J}, \mu_t)$ is a *probabilistic solution* (resp., *probabilistic universal solution*) for a probabilistic source database $Pr_s = (\mathcal{I}, \mu_s)$ relative to an ODE problem $\mathcal{M} = (\mathbf{S}, \mathbf{T}, \Sigma_s, \Sigma_t, \Sigma_{st})$ iff there exists a probability space $Pr = (\mathcal{I} \times \mathcal{J}, \mu)$ such that:

1. The left and right marginals of Pr are Pr_s and Pr_t, respectively. That is,
   (a) $\sum_{J \in \mathcal{J}} (\mu(I, J)) = \mu_s(I)$ for all $I \in \mathcal{I}$ and
   (b) $\sum_{I \in \mathcal{I}} (\mu(I, J)) = \mu_t(J)$ for all $J \in \mathcal{J}$;
2. $\mu(I, J) = 0$ for all $(I, J) \notin Sol_{\mathcal{M}}$ (resp., $(I, J) \notin USol_{\mathcal{M}}$).

Possible source database facts	
r_a	Researcher(Alice, UoO)
r_p	Researcher(Paul, UoO)
p_{aml}	Publication(Alice, ML, JMLR)
p_{adb}	Publication(Alice, DB, TODS)
p_{pdb}	Publication(Paul, DB, TODS)
p_{pai}	Publication(Paul, AI, AIJ)

Derived source database facts	
a_{aml}	ResearchArea(Alice, ML)
a_{adb}	ResearchArea(Alice, DB)
a_{pdb}	ResearchArea(Paul, DB)
a_{pai}	ResearchArea(Paul, AI)

Probabilistic source database $Pr_s = (I, \mu_s)$

$I_1 = \{r_a, r_p, p_{aml}, a_{aml}, p_{pdb}, a_{pdb}\}$	0.3
$I_2 = \{r_a, r_p, p_{aml}, a_{aml}, p_{pai}, a_{pai}\}$	0.3
$I_3 = \{r_a, r_p, p_{adb}, a_{adb}, p_{pai}, a_{pai}\}$	0.2
$I_4 = \{r_a, r_p, p_{adb}, a_{adb}, p_{pdb}, a_{pdb}\}$	0.1
$I_5 = \{r_a, p_{adb}, a_{adb}\}$	0.1

Possible target instance facts	
u_{ml}	UResearchArea(UoO, N_1, ML)
u_{ai}	UResearchArea(UoO, N_2, AI)
u_{db}	UResearchArea(UoO, N_3, DB)
l_{ml}	Lecture(ML, N_4)
l_{ai}	Lecture(AI, N_5)
l_{db}	Lecture(DB, N_6)

Probabilistic target instance $Pr_{ta} = (\mathcal{J}_a, \mu_{ta})$

$J_1 = \{u_{db}, l_{db}, u_{ml}, l_{ml}\}$	0.3
$J_2 = \{u_{ai}, l_{ai}, u_{ml}, l_{ml}\}$	0.3
$J_3 = \{u_{ai}, l_{ai}, u_{db}, l_{db}\}$	0.2
$J_4 = \{u_{db}, l_{db}\}$	0.2

Probabilistic target instance $Pr_{tb} = (\mathcal{J}_b, \mu_{tb})$

$J_5 = \{u_{db}, l_{db}, u_{ml}, l_{ml}\}$	0.35
$J_6 = \{u_{ai}, l_{ai}, u_{db}, l_{db}, u_{ml}, l_{ml}\}$	0.45
$J_7 = \{u_{ai}, l_{ai}, u_{ml}, l_{ml}\}$	0.2

Fig. 1. Probabilistic source database and two probabilistic target instances for Example 1 ($N_1, \ldots, N_6$ are nulls), which are both probabilistic solutions, but only Pr_{ta} is universal

The above condition (2) intuitively says that all non-solutions (I, J) have probability zero. Note that the existence of a solution does not exclude that some source databases with probability zero have no corresponding target instance.

Example 1. An ontological data exchange (ODE) problem $\mathcal{M} = (\mathbf{S}, \mathbf{T}, \Sigma_s, \Sigma_t, \Sigma_{st})$ is given by the source schema $\mathbf{S} = \{Researcher(name, univ), ResearchArea(name, topic), Publication(auth\_name, topic, jour\_name)\}$, the target schema $\mathbf{T} = \{UResearchArea(univ, dept, topic), Lecture(topic, term)\}$, the source ontology $\Sigma_s = \{\sigma_s, \nu_s\}$, the target ontology $\Sigma_t = \{\sigma_t, \nu_t\}$, and the mapping $\Sigma_{st} = \{\sigma_{st}, \nu_m\}$, where:

$\sigma_s : Publication(X, Y, Z) \rightarrow ResearchArea(X, Y),$

$\nu_s : Researcher(X, Y) \wedge ResearchArea(X, Y) \rightarrow \bot,$

$\sigma_t : UResearchArea(U, D, T) \rightarrow \exists Z \, Lecture(T, Z),$

$\nu_t : Lecture(X, Y) \wedge Lecture(Y, X) \rightarrow \bot,$

$\sigma_{st} : ResearchArea(N, T) \wedge Researcher(N, U) \rightarrow \exists D \, UResearchArea(U, D, T),$

$\nu_m : ResearchArea(N, T) \wedge UResearchArea(U, T, N) \rightarrow \bot.$

Given the probabilistic source database in Fig. 1, two possible probabilistic solution instances $Pr_{ta} = (\mathcal{J}_a, \mu_{ta})$ and $Pr_{tb} = (\mathcal{J}_b, \mu_{tb})$ are shown in Fig. 1: Pr_{ta} involves the following probability space over $Sol_{\mathcal{M}}$: $Pr_a = \{(I_1, J_1), 0.3), ((I_2, J_2), 0.3), ((I_3, J_3), 0.2), ((I_4, J_4), 0.1), ((I_5, J_4), 0.1)\}$, while Pr_{tb} involves the following probability space over $Sol_{\mathcal{M}}$: $Pr_b = \{(I_1, J_5), 0.3), ((I_2, J_6), 0.1), ((I_2, J_7), 0.2), ((I_3, J_6), 0.45), ((I_4, J_5), 0.05), ((I_4, J_6), 0.05), ((I_5, J_6), 0.1)\}$. Note that while both Pr_{ta} and Pr_{tb} are probabilistic solutions, only Pr_{ta} is also a probabilistic universal solution.   ∎

For a deterministic source database D relative to an ODE problem $\mathcal{M} = (\mathbf{S}, \mathbf{T}, \Sigma_s, \Sigma_t, \Sigma_{st})$ and a CQ $q(\mathbf{X}) = \exists \mathbf{Y} \, \Phi(\mathbf{X}, \mathbf{Y}, \mathbf{C})$ over $\mathbf{T}$, the set of answers for q to D relative to $\mathcal{M}$ is defined as $ans(q, D, \Sigma_s \cup \Sigma_t \cup \Sigma_{st})$. We now generalize this to probabilistic source databases relative to ODE problems and unions of CQs (UCQs).

Definition 4 (UCQs). A *union of conjunctive queries* (or *UCQ*) has the form $q(\mathbf{X}) = \bigvee_{i=1}^{k} \exists \mathbf{Y}_i \; \Phi_i(\mathbf{X}, \mathbf{Y}_i, \mathbf{C}_i)$, where each $\exists \mathbf{Y}_i \Phi_i(\mathbf{X}, \mathbf{Y}_i, \mathbf{C}_i)$ with $i \in \{1, \ldots, k\}$ is a CQ with exactly the variables $\mathbf{X}$ and $\mathbf{Y}_i$, and the constants $\mathbf{C}_i$. Given an ODE problem $\mathcal{M} = (\mathbf{S}, \mathbf{T}, \Sigma_s, \Sigma_t, \Sigma_{st})$, probabilistic source database $Pr_s = (\mathcal{I}, \mu_s)$, UCQ $q(\mathbf{X}) = \bigvee_{i=1}^{k} \exists \mathbf{Y}_i \Phi_i(\mathbf{X}, \mathbf{Y}_i, \mathbf{C}_i)$, and tuple $\mathbf{t}$ (a ground instance of $\mathbf{X}$ in q) over $\mathbf{C}$, the *confidence* of $\mathbf{t}$ relative to q, denoted $conf_q(\mathbf{t})$, in Pr_s relative to $\mathcal{M}$ is the infimum of $Pr_t(q(\mathbf{t}))$ subject to all probabilistic solutions Pr_t for Pr_s relative to $\mathcal{M}$. Here, $Pr_t(q(\mathbf{t}))$ for $Pr_t = (\mathcal{J}, \mu_t)$ is the sum of all $\mu_t(J)$ such that $q(\mathbf{t})$ evaluates to true in the instance $J \in \mathcal{J}$ (i.e., some BCQ $\exists \mathbf{Y}_i \Phi_i(\mathbf{t}, \mathbf{Y}_i, \mathbf{C}_i)$ with $i \in \{1, \ldots, k\}$ evaluates to true in J).

Example 2. Consider again the setting of Example 1, and let q be a UCQ of a student who wants to know whether she can study both machine learning and databases at the University of Oxford: $q() = \exists X, Y(\exists Z(Lecture(DB, X) \wedge UResearchArea(UoO, Z, DB)) \vee \exists Z(Lecture(ML, Y) \wedge UResearchArea(UoO, Z, ML)))$. Then, q yields the probabilities 0.65 and 0.8 on Pr_{ta} and Pr_{tb}, respectively. ∎

3.2   Probabilistic Ontological Data Exchange

Probabilistic ontological data exchange extends deterministic ontological data exchange by turning the deterministic source-to-target mapping into a probabilistic source-to-target mapping, i.e., we now have a probability distribution over the set of all subsets of Σ_{st}, which is formally expressed as follows.

Definition 5 (Probabilistic Ontological Data Exchange (PODE)).
A *probabilistic ontological data exchange (PODE) problem* $\mathcal{M} = (\mathbf{S}, \mathbf{T}, \Sigma_s, \Sigma_t, \Sigma_{st}, \mu_{st})$ consists of (i) a source schema $\mathbf{S}$, (ii) a target schema $\mathbf{T}$ disjoint from $\mathbf{S}$, (iii) a finite set Σ_s of TGDs and NCs over $\mathbf{S}$ (called *source ontology*), (iv) a finite set Σ_t of TGDs and NCs over $\mathbf{T}$ (called *target ontology*), (v) a finite set Σ_{st} of TGDs and NCs σ over $\mathbf{S} \cup \mathbf{T}$, and (vi) a function $\mu_{st}: 2^{\Sigma_{st}} \to [0, 1]$ such that $\sum_{\Sigma' \subseteq \Sigma_{st}} \mu_{st}(\Sigma') = 1$ (called *probabilistic (source-to-target) mapping*).

The following definition lifts also the notion of probabilistic (universal) solution from probabilistic source databases relative to deterministic ODE problems to probabilistic source databases relative to PODE problems.

Definition 6 (Probabilistic (Universal) Solution). A probabilistic target instance $Pr_t = (\mathcal{J}, \mu_t)$ is a *probabilistic solution* (resp., *probabilistic universal solution*) for a probabilistic source database $Pr_s = (\mathcal{I}, \mu_s)$ relative to a PODE problem $\mathcal{M} = (\mathbf{S}, \mathbf{T}, \Sigma_s, \Sigma_t, \Sigma_{st}, \mu_{st})$ iff there exists a probability space $Pr = (\mathcal{I} \times \mathcal{J} \times 2^{\Sigma_{st}}, \mu)$ such that:

1. The three marginals of μ are μ_s, μ_t, and μ_{st}, such that:
   (a) $\sum_{J \in \mathcal{J}, \, \Sigma' \subseteq \Sigma_{st}} \mu(I, J, \Sigma') = \mu_s(I)$ for all $I \in \mathcal{I}$,

(b) $\sum_{I \in \mathcal{I}, \Sigma' \subseteq \Sigma_{st}} \mu(I, J, \Sigma') = \mu_t(J)$ for all $J \in \mathcal{J}$, and
(c) $\sum_{I \in \mathcal{I}, J \in \mathcal{J}} \mu(I, J, \Sigma') = \mu_{st}(\Sigma')$ for all $\Sigma' \subseteq \Sigma_{st}$;

2. $\mu(I, J, \Sigma') = 0$ for all $(I, J, \Sigma') \in \mathcal{I} \times \mathcal{J} \times 2^{\Sigma_{st}}$ such that $(I, J) \notin Sol_{(\mathbf{S}, \mathbf{T}, \Sigma')}$ (resp., $(I, J) \notin USol_{(\mathbf{S}, \mathbf{T}, \Sigma')}$).

Using probabilistic (universal) solutions for probabilistic source databases relative to PODE problems, the semantics of UCQs is lifted to PODE problems as follows.

Definition 7 (UCQs). Given a PODE problem $\mathcal{M} = (\mathbf{S}, \mathbf{T}, \Sigma_s, \Sigma_t, \Sigma_{st}, \mu_{st})$, a probabilistic source database $Pr_s = (\mathcal{I}, \mu_s)$, a UCQ $q(\mathbf{X}) = \bigvee_{i=1}^{k} \exists \mathbf{Y}_i \; \Phi_i(\mathbf{X}, \mathbf{Y}_i, \mathbf{C}_i)$, and a tuple $\mathbf{t}$ (a ground instance of $\mathbf{X}$ in q) over $\mathbf{C}$, the *confidence* of $\mathbf{t}$ relative to q, denoted $conf_q(\mathbf{t})$, in Pr_s relative to $\mathcal{M}$ is the infimum of $Pr_t(q(\mathbf{t}))$ subject to all probabilistic solutions Pr_t for Pr_s relative to $\mathcal{M}$. Here, $Pr_t(q(\mathbf{t}))$ for $Pr_t = (\mathcal{J}, \mu_t)$ is the sum of all $\mu_t(J)$ such that $q(\mathbf{t})$ evaluates to true in the instance $J \in \mathcal{J}$.

3.3 Compact Encoding

We use a compact encoding of both probabilistic databases and probabilistic mappings, which is based on annotating facts, TGDs, and NCs by probabilistic events in a Bayesian network, rather than explicitly specifying the whole probability space. We first define annotations and annotated atoms.

Definition 8 (Annotations and Annotated Atoms). Let $e_1, \ldots, e_n$ be $n \geq 1$ *elementary events*. A *world* w is a conjunction $\ell_1 \wedge \cdots \wedge \ell_n$, where each ℓ_i, $i \in \{1, \ldots, n\}$, is either the elementary event e_i or its negation $\neg e_i$. An *annotation* λ is any Boolean combination of elementary events (i.e., all elementary events are annotations, and if λ_1 and λ_2 are annotations, then also $\neg \lambda_1$ and $\lambda_1 \wedge \lambda_2$). An *annotated atom* has the form $a \colon \lambda$, where a is an atom, and λ is an annotation.

The compact encoding of probabilistic databases is then defined as follows; note that this encoding also underlies our complexity analysis in Section 4.

Definition 9 (Compact Encoding of Probabilistic Databases). A set $\mathbf{A}$ of annotated atoms along with a probability $\mu(w) \in [0, 1]$ for every world w *compactly encodes* a probabilistic database $Pr = (\mathcal{I}, \mu)$ whenever:

1. the probability μ of every annotation λ is the sum of the probabilities of all worlds in which λ is true, and
2. the probability μ of every subset-maximal database $\{a_1, \ldots, a_m\} \in \mathcal{I}$ [1] such that $\{a_1 \colon \lambda_1, \ldots, a_m \colon \lambda_m\} \subseteq \mathbf{A}$ for some annotations $\lambda_1, \ldots, \lambda_m$ is the probability μ of $\lambda_1 \wedge \cdots \wedge \lambda_m$ (and the probability μ of every other database in $\mathcal{I}$ is 0).

---

[1] That is, we do not consider subsets of the databases here.

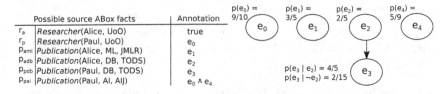

Fig. 2. Annotation-based encoding of the probabilistic source database in Fig. 1 (left), along with a Bayesian network defining the probabilities of the events (right)

We assume that the probability distributions for the underlying events are given by a Bayesian network, which is a well-known tool for compactly specifying a joint probability space, encoding also a certain causal structure between the variables. Note that Bayesian networks also provide a convenient relationship to provenance, as provenance is often used for explaining query results and outcomes, exploit results of prior reasoning, and establish trust in data, which is related to causal reasoning [20]. The following example illustrates the compact encoding of probabilistic source databases via Boolean annotations relative to an underlying Bayesian network.

Example 3. Fig. 2 shows an annotation-based encoding of the probabilistic source database in Fig. 1, where four elementary events are involved, and a Bayesian network defines the probabilities of the events and their underlying worlds.   ∎

If the mapping is probabilistic as well, then we use two disjoint sets of elementary events, one for encoding the probabilistic source database and the other one for the mapping. In this way, the probabilistic source database is independent from the probabilistic mapping. We now define the compact encoding of probabilistic mappings.

Definition 10 (Compact Encoding of Probabilistic Mappings). An *annotated* TGD (resp., NC) has the form $\sigma\colon \lambda$, where σ is a TGD (resp., NC), and λ is an annotation. A set Σ of annotated TGDs and NCs $\sigma\colon \lambda$ with $\sigma \in \Sigma_{st}$ along with a probability $\mu(w) \in [0,1]$ for every world w *compactly encodes a probabilistic mapping* $\mu_{st}\colon 2^{\Sigma_{st}} \to [0,1]$ whenever:

1. the probability μ of every annotation λ is the sum of the probabilities of all worlds in which λ is true, and
2. the probability μ_{st} of every subset-maximal $\{\sigma_1, \ldots, \sigma_k\} \subseteq \Sigma_{st}$ such that $\{\sigma_1\colon \lambda_1, \ldots, \sigma_k\colon \lambda_k\} \subseteq \Sigma$ for some annotations $\lambda_1, \ldots, \lambda_k$ is the probability μ of $\lambda_1 \wedge \cdots \wedge \lambda_k$ (and the probability μ_{st} of every other subset of Σ_{st} is 0).

3.4 Computational Problems

We consider the following computational problems:

Existence of a solution (resp., universal solution): Given an ODE or a PODE problem $\mathcal{M}$ and a probabilistic source database Pr_s, decide whether there exists a probabilistic (resp., probabilistic universal) solution for Pr_s relative to $\mathcal{M}$.

Answering UCQs: Given an ODE or a PODE problem $\mathcal{M}$, a probabilistic source database Pr_s, a UCQ $q(\mathbf{X})$, and a tuple $\mathbf{t}$ over $\mathbf{C}$, compute $conf_Q(\mathbf{t})$ in Pr_s w.r.t. $\mathcal{M}$.

4 Computational Complexity

We now analyze the computational complexity of deciding the existence of a (universal) probabilistic solution for deterministic and probabilistic ontological data exchange problems. We also delineate some tractable special cases, and we provide some complexity results for exact UCQ answering for ODE and PODE problems.

We assume some elementary background in complexity theory [16,21], but briefly recall the complexity classes that we encounter in our complexity results. The complexity classes PSPACE (resp., P, EXP, 2EXP) contain all decision problems that can be solved in polynomial space (resp., polynomial, exponential, double exponential time) on a deterministic Turing machine, while the complexity classes NP and NEXP contain all decision problems that can be solved in polynomial and exponential time on a nondeterministic Turing machine, respectively; CONP and CONEXP are their complementary classes, where "Yes" and "No" instances are interchanged. The complexity class AC^0 is the class of all languages that are decidable by uniform families of Boolean circuits of polynomial size and constant depth. The inclusion relationships among the above (decision) complexity classes (all currently believed to be strict) are as follows:

$$AC^0 \subseteq P \subseteq NP, CONP \subseteq PSPACE \subseteq EXP \subseteq NEXP, CONEXP \subseteq 2EXP$$

The (function) complexity class #P is the set of all functions that are computable by a polynomial-time nondeterministic Turing machine whose output for a given input string I is the number of accepting computations for I.

4.1 Decidability Paradigms

The main (syntactic) conditions on TGDs that guarantee the decidability of CQ answering are guardedness [6], stickiness [8], and acyclicity. Each one of these conditions has its "weak" counterpart: weak guardedness [6], weak stickiness [8], and weak acyclicity [12], respectively.

A TGD σ is *guarded* if there exists an atom in its body that contains (or "guards") all the body variables of σ. The class of guarded TGDs, denoted G, is defined as the family of all possible sets of guarded TGDs. A key subclass of guarded TGDs are the so-called linear TGDs with just one body atom (which is automatically a guard), and the corresponding class is denoted L. *Weakly guarded* TGDs extend guarded TGDs by requiring only "harmful" body variables to appear in the guard, and the associated class is denoted WG. It is easy to verify that $L \subset G \subset WG$.

Stickiness is inherently different from guardedness, and its central property can be described as follows: variables that appear more than once in a body (i.e., join variables) are always propagated (or "stick") to the inferred atoms. A set of TGDs that enjoys the above property is called *sticky*, and the corresponding class is denoted S. Weak stickiness is a relaxation of stickiness where only "harmful" variables are taken into account. A set of TGDs which enjoys weak stickiness is *weakly sticky*, and the associated class is denoted WS. Observe that $S \subset WS$.

A set Σ of TGDs is *acyclic* if its predicate graph is acyclic, and the underlying class is denoted A. In fact, an acyclic set of TGDs can be seen as a nonrecursive set of TGDs. We say Σ is *weakly acyclic* if its dependency graph enjoys a certain acyclicity condition, which actually guarantees the existence of a finite canonical model; the associated class is denoted WA. Clearly, $A \subset WA$.

Another key fragment of TGDs, which deserves our attention, are the so-called *full* TGDs, i.e., TGDs without existentially quantified variables, and the corresponding class is denoted F. If we further assume that full TGDs enjoy linearity, guardedness, stickiness, or acyclicity, then we obtain the classes LF, GF, SF, and AF, respectively.

4.2   Overview of Complexity Results

Our complexity results for deciding the existence of a probabilistic (universal) solution for both ODE and PODE problems with annotations over events relative to an underlying Bayesian network are summarized in Fig. 4 for all classes of existential rules discussed above in the data, combined, *ba*-combined, and *fp*-combined complexity (all entries are completeness results). For L, LF, AF, S, SF, and A in the data complexity, we obtain tractability when the underlying Bayesian network is a polytree. For all other cases, hardness holds even when the underlying Bayesian network is a polytree. Finally, for all classes of existential rules discussed above except for WG, answering UCQs for both ODE and PODE problems is in #P in the data complexity.

4.3   Deterministic Ontological Data Exchange

The first result shows that deciding whether there exists a probabilistic (or probabilistic universal) solution for a probabilistic source database relative to an ODE problem is complete for $\mathcal{C}$ (resp., co$\mathcal{C}$), if BCQ answering for the involved sets of TGDs and NCs is complete for a deterministic (resp., nondeterministic) complexity class $\mathcal{C} \supseteq$ PSPACE (resp., $\mathcal{C} \supseteq$ NP), and hardness holds even for ground atomic BCQs. As a corollary, by the complexity of BCQ answering with TGDs and NCs in Figure 3 [19], we immediately obtain the complexity results shown in Figure 4

	Data	Comb.	ba-comb.	fp-comb.
L, LF, AF	in AC^0	PSPACE	NP	NP
G	P	2EXP	EXP	NP
WG	EXP	2EXP	EXP	EXP
S, SF	in AC^0	EXP	NP	NP
F, GF	P	EXP	NP	NP
A	in AC^0	NEXP	NEXP	NP
WS, WA	P	2EXP	2EXP	NP

	Data	Comb.	ba-comb.	fp-comb.
L, LF, AF	CONP	PSPACE	CONP	CONP
G	CONP	2EXP	EXP	CONP
WG	EXP	2EXP	EXP	EXP
S, SF	CONP	EXP	CONP	CONP
F, GF	CONP	EXP	CONP	CONP
A	CONP	CONEXP	CONEXP	CONP
WS, WA	CONP	2EXP	2EXP	CONP

Fig. 3. Complexity of BCQ answering [19]. All entries except for "in AC^0" are completeness ones, where hardness in all cases holds even for ground atomic BCQs.

Fig. 4. Complexity of existence of a probabilistic (universal) solution (for both deterministic and probabilistic ODE). All entries are completeness results.

for deciding the existence of a probabilistic (universal) solution (in deterministic ontological data exchange) in the combined, ba-combined, and fp-combined complexity, and for the class WG of TGDs and NCs in the data complexity. The hardness results hold even when the underlying Bayesian network is a polytree.

Theorem 1. *Given a probabilistic source database Pr_s relative to a source ontology Σ_s and an ODE problem $\mathcal{M} = (\boldsymbol{S}, \boldsymbol{T}, \Sigma_s, \Sigma_t, \Sigma_{st})$ such that $\Sigma_s \cup \Sigma_t \cup \Sigma_{st}$ belongs to a class of TGDs and NCs for which BCQ answering is complete for a deterministic (resp., nondeterministic) complexity class $\mathcal{C} \supseteq$ PSPACE (resp., $\mathcal{C} \supseteq$ NP), and hardness holds even for ground atomic BCQs, deciding the existence of a probabilistic (universal) solution for Pr_s relative to Σ_s and $\mathcal{M}$ is complete for $\mathcal{C}$ (resp., co$\mathcal{C}$). Hardness holds even when the underlying Bayesian network is a polytree.*

Proof (sketch). It is not difficult to see that there exists a probabilistic universal solution relative to a probabilistic source database iff there exists a probabilistic solution. The latter is in turn equivalent to the existence of a deterministic solution relative to every world's deterministic database. For membership, we thus decide the complementary problem by guessing a world, which is in NP, and checking that there exists no deterministic solution relative to its database, which is in $\mathcal{C}$. Overall, the complementary problem is thus in $\mathcal{C}$; so, the problem itself is in co$\mathcal{C} = \mathcal{C}$ (resp., co$\mathcal{C}$).

Hardness for co$\mathcal{C} = \mathcal{C}$ (resp., co$\mathcal{C}$) holds by a reduction from the complement of the $\mathcal{C}$-hard problem of answering ground atomic BCQs q from a database D and a set Σ of TGDs and NCs. The probabilistic source database is defined relative to Σ as ontology and contains all atoms in D with probability 1. The mapping renames each predicate in Σ by a fresh predicate, and the target ontology consists of the single NC $q' \rightarrow \bot$, obtained via the same renaming from q. Then, $D \cup \Sigma \not\models q$ iff the defined deterministic ontological data exchange problem has a solution. Since this reduction is independent from the underlying Bayesian network G, hardness holds even when G is a polytree. $\square$

The following result shows that deciding whether there exists a probabilistic (universal) solution for a probabilistic source database relative to an ODE problem is complete for coNP in the data complexity, for all classes of sets of TGDs and NCs considered in this paper, except for WG. Hardness for coNP for the classes G, F, GF, WS, and WA holds even when the underlying Bayesian network is a polytree.

Theorem 2. *Given a probabilistic source database Pr_s relative to a source ontology Σ_s and an ODE problem $\mathcal{M} = (S, T, \Sigma_s, \Sigma_t, \Sigma_{st})$ such that $\Sigma_s \cup \Sigma_t \cup \Sigma_{st}$ belongs to a class among L, LF, AF, G, S, SF, F, GF, A, WS, and WA, deciding whether there exists a probabilistic (or probabilistic universal) solution for Pr_s relative to Σ_s and $\mathcal{M}$ is coNP-complete in the data complexity. Hardness for coNP for the classes G, F, GF, WS, and WA holds even when the underlying Bayesian network is a polytree.*

Proof (sketch). As argued in the proof of Theorem 1, there is a probabilistic universal solution relative to a probabilistic source database iff there is a probabilistic solution. The latter is in turn equivalent to the existence of a deterministic solution relative to every world's deterministic database. For membership, we thus decide the complementary problem by guessing a world, which is in NP, and checking that there exists no deterministic solution relative to its database, which is in P. Overall, the complementary problem is thus in NP; thus, the problem itself is in coNP.

Hardness of the complementary problem for NP follows from a reduction from the problem of deciding whether the probability $Pr(X_i = x_i)$ of a variable assignment $X_i = x_i$ in a Bayesian network G is greater than zero, which is complete for NP [10]. The ontological data exchange problem $\mathcal{M} = (S, T, \Sigma_s, \Sigma_t, \Sigma_{st})$ consists of the source schema $S = \{p\}$, the target schema $T = \{q\}$, the source ontology $\Sigma_s = \varnothing$, the source-to-target mapping $\Sigma_{st} = \{p() \rightarrow q()\}$, and the target ontology $\Sigma_t = \{q() \rightarrow \bot\}$. The source database is given by $\{p(): X_i = x_i\}$ and G. Then, $Pr(X_i = x_i) > 0$ in G iff the ontological data exchange problem $\mathcal{M}$ has no probabilistic solution.

Hardness for coNP for the classes G, F, GF, WS, and WA when the underlying Bayesian network is a polytree holds because of a polynomial reduction from the coNP-complete problem of deciding whether a CNF formula $\phi = c_1 \wedge \cdots \wedge c_n$ is unsatisfiable. Here, every c_i is a disjunction of literals over m propositional variables $x_1, \ldots, x_m$. We construct a fixed schema mapping and a source database depending on ϕ, with $x_1, \ldots, x_m$ as elementary events. The source database has a binary predicate E_S and a unary predicate P_S, and it consists of the atoms $E_S(i - 1, i)$ for all $i \in \{1, \ldots, n\}$, annotated with c_i, and the atom $P_S(0)$, annotated with the true event $\top$, while the probabilities of the variables x_i are defined as 0.5. Similarly to the source schema, the target schema T consists of a binary predicate E_T and a unary predicate P_T. We then define the set $\Sigma_{st} \cup \Sigma_t$ in the deterministic mapping as $m_1 : E_S(X, Y) \rightarrow E_T(X, Y)$, $m_2 : P_S(X) \rightarrow P_T(X)$, $m_3 : P_T(n) \rightarrow \bot$, and $m_4 : P_T(X) \wedge E_T(X, Y) \rightarrow P_T(Y)$. Note that $\Sigma_{st} \cup \Sigma_t$ is in G, F, GF, WS, and WA. It is then not difficult to see that the above probabilistic database and ODE problem have a probabilistic solution iff ϕ is unsatisfiable. □

The following result shows that deciding whether there exists a probabilistic (or probabilistic universal) solution for a probabilistic source database relative to an ODE problem is in P in the data complexity, if BCQ answering for the involved sets of TGDs and NCs is first-order rewritable as a Boolean UCQ, and the underlying Bayesian network is a polytree. As a corollary, by the complexity of BCQ answering with TGDs and NCs, deciding the existence of a solution is in P for the classes L, LF, AF, S, SF, and A in the data complexity, if the underlying Bayesian network is a polytree.

Theorem 3. *Given a probabilistic source database Pr_s relative to a source ontology Σ_s, with a polytree as Bayesian network, and an ODE problem $\mathcal{M}=(\boldsymbol{S}, \boldsymbol{T}, \Sigma_s, \Sigma_t, \Sigma_{st})$ such that $\Sigma_s \cup \Sigma_t \cup \Sigma_{st}$ belongs to a class of TGDs and NCs for which BCQ answering is first-order rewritable as a Boolean UCQ, deciding whether there exists a probabilistic (universal) solution for Pr_s relative to Σ_s and $\mathcal{M}$ is in P in the data complexity.*

Proof (sketch). Since NCs are the only source of inconsistency, we can decide inconsistency by evaluating BCQs, exactly one for each NC. Since BCQ answering is first-order rewritable as a Boolean UCQ, we can thus decide inconsistency by evaluating a Boolean UCQ directly on the database. Since this Boolean UCQ has a fixed size, independent from the database, we can thus identify a polynomial number of conjunctions of database atoms that lead to inconsistencies. The annotations associated with such conjunctions must either have probability 0 or be inconsistent in order to yield a (probabilistic (universal)) solution. We first check whether the probability of the annotation ϕ_i of an inconsistency is 0. If ϕ_i's probability is not 0, then we check whether ϕ_i is inconsistent. To check ϕ_i, we first create ϕ_i as the conjunction of the single annotations $\lambda_1, \ldots, \lambda_k$. Note that the annotations of the source database atoms are in DNF format, and we thus have a conjunction of formulas in DNF. When we transform this conjunction ϕ_i of formulas in DNF into a formula ϕ_i' in DNF, we obtain a disjunction of n^k conjuncts with n being the maximum number of conjuncts in the annotations of the k atoms of the current inconsistency. Hence, this transformation is in polynomial time in the length of the annotations. We then check for each ϕ_i' whether its probability is 0, i.e., whether the probability of each of the conjuncts is 0. This can be done in polynomial time in polytrees. If the probability of a ϕ_i' is not 0, we then check whether ϕ_i' is inconsistent which can be done in linear time (in the length of the formula) as well because it is represented in DNF format and, hence, we just have to check whether each conjunct contains e and $\neg e$, with e being an arbitrary event (possibly a different e in each conjunct). All these checks are clearly in P. Overall, since all ϕ_i' have either probability 0 or are consistent iff there exists a solution (and thus also a probabilistic (universal) solution), this shows membership in P. $\qquad\square$

Finally, the following theorem shows that answering UCQs for probabilistic source databases relative to an ODE problem is complete for #P in the data complexity for all above classes of existential rules except for WG.

Theorem 4. *Given (i) an ODE problem $\mathcal{M} = (S, T, \Sigma_t, \Sigma_s, \Sigma_{st})$ such that $\Sigma_s \cup \Sigma_{st} \cup \Sigma_t$ belongs to a class among* L, LF, AF, G, S, SF, F, GF, A, WS, *and* WA, *and (ii) a probabilistic source database Pr_s relative to Σ_s such that there exists a solution for Pr_s relative to $\mathcal{M}$, (iii) a UCQ $Q = q(X)$ over T, and (iv) a tuple $\mathbf{a}$, computing $conf_Q(\mathbf{a})$ is #P-complete in the data complexity.*

Proof. For membership in #P, w.l.o.g., for every variable X in the Bayesian network, the rational numbers in all conditional probability distributions for X have the same denominator d_X. Let $d = \Pi_X d_X$. Then, each world w_i has a probability n_i/d. If $n_i/d > 0$, we simply add $n_i - 1$ many copies and assign w_i and each of its copies the probability $1/d$. Then, we can guess in which worlds the tuple $\mathbf{a}$ is true and count these worlds, which is in #P. The probability of $\mathbf{a}$ follows by dividing this number by d.

Hardness for #P follows from a similar reduction as the one in the proof of Theorem 1, this time from the problem of computing the probability $Pr(X_i = x_i)$ of a variable assignment $X_i = x_i$ in a Bayesian network, which is #P-complete [23]. The ontology mapping consists only of the TGD $p() \rightarrow q()$ and the source database is given by $\{p(): X_i = x_i\}$. Then, $Pr(X_i = x_i) = conf_Q()$, where $Q = q()$. □

4.4 Probabilistic Ontological Data Exchange

All the results of Section 4.3 in Theorems 1 and 4 carry over to the case of probabilistic ontological data exchange. Clearly, the hardness results carry over immediately, since deterministic ontological data exchange is a special case of probabilistic ontological data exchange. As for the membership results, we additionally consider the worlds for the probabilistic mapping, which are iterated through in the data complexity and guessed in the combined, the ba-combined, and the fp-combined complexity.

5 Summary and Outlook

We have defined deterministic and probabilistic ontological data exchange problems, where probabilistic knowledge is exchanged between two ontologies. The ontologies and the mapping between them are defined via existential rules, where the rules for the mapping are deterministic and probabilistic, respectively. We have given a precise analysis of the computational complexity of deciding the existence of a probabilistic (universal) solution for different classes of existential rules in both deterministic and probabilistic ontological data exchange. We also have delineated some tractable special cases, and we have provided some complexity results for exact UCQ answering.

An interesting topic for future research is to further explore the tractable cases of probabilistic solution existence and whether they can be extended, e.g., by generalizing the type of the mapping rules. Another issue for future work is to further analyze the complexity of answering UCQs for different classes of existential rules in deterministic and probabilistic ontological data exchange.

Acknowledgments. This work was supported by an EU (FP7/2007-2013) Marie-Curie Intra-European Fellowship ("PRODIMA"), the UK EPSRC grant EP/J008346/1 ("ProQAW"), the ERC grant 246858 ("DIADEM"), a Yahoo! Research Fellowship, and funds provided by CONICET and Universidad Nacional del Sur.

References

1. Arenas, M., Botoeva, E., Calvanese, D., Ryzhikov, V.: Exchanging OWL2 QL knowledge bases. In: Proc. IJCAI, pp. 703–710 (2013)
2. Arenas, M., Botoeva, E., Calvanese, D., Ryzhikov, V., Sherkhonov, E.: Exchanging description logic knowledge bases. In: Proc. KR, pp. 563–567 (2012)
3. Arenas, M., Pérez, J., Reutter, J.L.: Data exchange beyond complete data. J. ACM **60**(4), 28:1–28:59 (2013)
4. Baader, F.: Least common subsumers and most specific concepts in a description logic with existential restrictions and terminological cycles. In: Proc. IJCAI, pp. 364–369 (2003)
5. Baader, F., Brandt, S., Lutz, C.: Pushing the $\mathcal{EL}$ envelope. In: Proc. IJCAI, pp. 364–369 (2005)
6. Calì, A., Gottlob, G., Kifer, M.: Taming the infinite chase: Query answering under expressive relational constraints. J. Artif. Intell. Res. **48**, 115–174 (2013)
7. Cali, A., Gottlob, G., Lukasiewicz, T., Marnette, B., Pieris, A.: Datalog+/-: a family of logical knowledge representation and query languages for new applications. In: Proc. LICS, pp. 228–242 (2010)
8. Calì, A., Gottlob, G., Pieris, A.: Towards more expressive ontology languages: The query answering problem. Artif. Intell. **193**, 87–128 (2012)
9. Calvanese, D., De Giacomo, G., Lembo, D., Lenzerini, M., Rosati, R.: Tractable reasoning and efficient query answering in description logics: The DL-Lite family. J. Autom. Reasoning **39**(3), 385–429 (2007)
10. Cooper, G.F.: The computational complexity of probabilistic inference using Bayesian belief networks. Artif. Intell. **42**(2–3) (1990)
11. Fagin, R., Kimelfeld, B., Kolaitis, P.G.: Probabilistic data exchange. J. ACM **58**(4), 15:1–15:55 (2011)
12. Fagin, R., Kolaitis, P.G., Miller, R.J., Popa, L.: Data exchange: Semantics and query answering. Theor. Comput. Sci. **336**(1), 89–124 (2005)
13. Fuhr, N., Rölleke, T.: A probabilistic relational algebra for the integration of information retrieval and database systems. ACM Trans. Inf. Sys. **15**(1), 32–66 (1997)
14. Green, T.J., Karvounarakis, G., Tannen, V.: Provenance semirings. In: Proc. PODS, pp. 31–40 (2007)
15. Imielinski, T.: Witold Lipski, J.: Incomplete information in relational databases. J. ACM **31**(4), 761–791 (1984)
16. Johnson, D.S.: A catalog of complexity classes. In: van Leeuwen, J. (ed.) Handbook of Theoretical Computer Science, vol. A, chap. 2, pp. 67–161. MIT Press (1990)
17. Krisnadhi, A., Lutz, C.: Data complexity in the $\mathcal{EL}$ family of description logics. In: Dershowitz, N., Voronkov, A. (eds.) LPAR 2007. LNCS (LNAI), vol. 4790, pp. 333–347. Springer, Heidelberg (2007)
18. Lenzerini, M.: Data integration: a theoretical perspective. In: Proc. PODS, pp. 233–246 (2002)

19. Lukasiewicz, T., Martinez, M.V., Pieris, A., Simari, G.I.: From classical to consistent query answering under existential rules. In: Proc. AAAI, pp. 1546–1552 (2015)
20. Meliou, A., Gatterbauer, W., Suciu, D.: Bringing provenance to its full potential using causal reasoning. In: Proc. TAPP (2011)
21. Papadimitriou, C.H.: Computational Complexity. Addison-Wesley (1994)
22. Poggi, A., Lembo, D., Calvanese, D., De Giacomo, G., Lenzerini, M., Rosati, R.: Linking data to ontologies. J. Data Sem. **10**, 133–173 (2008)
23. Roth, D.: On the hardness of approximate reasoning. Artif. Intell. **82**, 273–302 (1996)
24. Suciu, D., Olteanu, D., Ré, C., Koch, C.: Probabilistic Databases. M & C (2011)
25. Vardi, M.Y.: The complexity of relational query languages (extended abstract). In: Proc. STOC, pp. 137–146 (1982)

Binary Frontier-Guarded ASP
with Function Symbols

Mantas Šimkus[✉]

Institute of Information Systems, TU Wien, Vienna, Austria
simkus@dbai.tuwien.ac.at

Abstract. It has been acknowledged that emerging Web applications require features that are not available in standard rule languages like Datalog or Answer Set Programming (ASP), e.g., they are not powerful enough to deal with anonymous values (objects that are not explicitly mentioned in the data but whose existence is implied by the background knowledge). In this paper, we introduce a new rule language based on ASP extended with function symbols, which can be used to reason about anonymous values. In particular, we define *binary frontier-guarded programs (BFG programs)* that allow for disjunction, function symbols, and negation under the stable model semantics. In order to ensure decidability, BFG programs are syntactically restricted by allowing at most binary predicates and by requiring rules to be frontier-guarded. BFG programs are expressive enough to simulate ontologies expressed in popular Description Logics (DLs), capture their recent non-monotonic extensions, and can simulate conjunctive query answering over many standard DLs. We provide an elegant automata-based algorithm to reason in BFG programs, which yields a 3ExpTime upper bound for reasoning tasks like deciding consistency or cautious entailment. Due to existing results, these problems are known to be 2ExpTime-hard.

1 Introduction

Rule-based languages are becoming a major tool to cope with the increasing complexity of available data and knowledge. This is particularly true in applications that query and manage data on the Web. A prime example of a rule-based language is *Datalog*, which was developed as a recursive query language for relational databases. However, it has been acknowledged that emerging applications on the Web require features that are not available in plain Datalog. In particular, Datalog was designed for closed-world reasoning, i.e., each input database is assumed to be a complete description of the application's data. Unfortunately, such assumption is often not appropriate for Web applications, where data is likely to be incomplete, e.g., due to missing values or facts.

A significant extension of plain Datalog is *Answer Set Programming (ASP)*, which allows to partially deal with incompleteness. In particular, ASP features disjunction and *default negation* under the stable model semantics, which enable powerful case-based reasoning and inference based on the lack of information.

© Springer International Publishing Switzerland 2015
N. Bassiliades et al. (Eds.): RuleML 2015, LNCS 9202, pp. 311–327, 2015.
DOI: 10.1007/978-3-319-21542-6_20

The presence of these features allows for intelligent management of domain objects under incomplete information. However, plain Datalog and ASP are not powerful enough to deal with missing values, i.e., objects that are not explicitly mentioned in the data but whose existence is implied the background knowledge.

One of the possible approaches to deal with missing values is to allow some form of existential quantification in rule heads. In the setting of databases and Datalog, this can be formalized using *tuple-generating dependencies*, Datalog with *value invention* (see, e.g., [1,21]), or Datalog±[9]. In ASP, missing values are usually simulated using *function symbols* (see Section 7 for a discussion of such examples and further related work). Allowing rules to create new values causes a lot of difficulties; due to the presence of recursion, naive approaches to allow value creation immediately lead to undecidability (this is true already for Horn rules [2]). A prominent approach to regain decidability is to use special atoms to "guard" variables in rule bodies. Examples of this approach are Datalog± in [9] and the frontier-guarded rules in [4]. Importantly, these restrictions are not geared towards limiting recursion, but rather towards ensuring the semantics of a given program can be finitely represented, e.g., by resorting to tree decompositions of infinite structures.

In this paper we show how frontier-guardedness can be used to ensure decidability of ASP with function symbols. Our contributions are as follows:

- We introduce a new fragment of ASP with function symbols, called *binary frontier-guarded programs* (*BFG programs*). Such programs allow for disjunction, function symbols, and negation under the stable model semantics. The programs are syntactically restricted by allowing at most binary predicates and by requiring rules to be frontier-guarded.

- BFG programs generalize FNDC and *core* BD programs [13,14], and can be used for common-sense reasoning in the presence of a possibly infinite number of domain objects.

- BFG programs allow to simulate ontologies expressed in popular Description Logics (DLs), capture some of their recent non-monotonic extensions, and can simulate conjunctive query answering over many standard DLs.

- We show that BFG programs have the so-called *forest-model property*, also enjoyed by many standard DLs.

- We provide an elegant automata based procedure for reasoning in BFG programs. In addition to the forest-model property, the algorithm employs a two-world characterization of ASP, reminiscent to the *here-and-there* approach in [26].

- The construction yields a 3ExpTime upper bound for reasoning tasks like consistency or cautious entailment. These problems are known to be 2ExpTime-hard, e.g., already for positive normal programs [5].

The paper is organized as follows. In Section 2 we recall ASP with function symbols together with the basic notions of automata over infinite trees, which will be our main technical tool. In Section 3 we formally define BFG programs and discuss their features. In Section 4 we show how the stable models of a BFG program can be seen as forests, and then present an encoding of such forests into trees, on which tree automata can run. In Section 5 and 6 we present our automata-based procedure for reasoning in BFG programs. We discuss related work and conclude in Sections 7 and 8, respectively.

BFG programs were first studied in [27], where they were called $\mathbb{GT}$ programs.

2   Preliminaries

Answer Set Programming. We assume mutually disjoint sets of *constants*, *function symbols, relation (predicate) symbols* and *variables*. Each function and relation symbol σ is a associated with a positive integer $\mathsf{arity}(\sigma)$, called the *arity* of σ. A *term* is either a constant, a variable, or an expression of the form $f(t)$ such that f is an n-ary function symbol and t is an n-tuple of terms. An *atom* is an expression of the form $R(t)$ where R is an n-ary relation symbol and t is an n-tuple of terms. A *(disjunctive) program* P is any set of *rules* r of the form

$$A_1 \vee \ldots \vee A_n \leftarrow A_{n+1}, \ldots, A_m, not\ A_{m+1}, \ldots, not\ A_k, \qquad (1)$$

where each A_j is an atom. If r is of the form $A \leftarrow$, then r is a *fact* (often written simply A). If $n = 0$, then r is a *constraint*. We let $\mathsf{head}(r) = \{A_1, \ldots, A_n\}$, $\mathsf{body}^+(r) = \{A_{n+1}, \ldots, A_m\}$, and $\mathsf{body}^-(r) = \{A_{m+1}, \ldots, A_k\}$. If $\mathsf{body}^-(r) = \emptyset$, then r is *positive*. A program P is *positive*, if all rules of P are positive. A term, atom, rule or program is *ground*, if it contains no variables. Let $\mathcal{HU}^P$ be the *Herbrand universe* of P, i.e. the set of terms that can be built from constants and function symbols occurring in a program P. Similarly, $\mathcal{HB}^P$ is the *Herbrand base* of P, i.e. the set of atoms that can be built from relation symbols of P and terms in $\mathcal{HU}^P$. An *interpretation* I for P is any set $I \subseteq \mathcal{HB}^P$. We use $\mathsf{ground}(P)$ to denote the *grounding* of P, i.e., the set of all ground rules that can be obtained from rules in P by applying some substitution from variables to terms in $\mathcal{HU}^P$. An interpretation I *satisfies* a ground positive rule r, denoted $I \models r$, if $\mathsf{body}^+(r) \subseteq I$ implies $I \cap \mathsf{head}(r) \neq \emptyset$. An interpretation I is a *model* of a ground positive program P, denoted $I \models P$, if I satisfies each rule $r \in \mathsf{ground}(P)$. A model I of P is called *minimal*, if there is no $J \subseteq I$ such that J is a model of P. Assume an interpretation I for a program P. The *GL-reduct* P^I (see [17]) is the program obtained from $\mathsf{ground}(P)$ by

(i) removing all rules r such that $\mathsf{body}^-(r) \cap I \neq \emptyset$, and
(ii) deleting every expression of the form $not\ A$ in the remaining rules.

If I is a minimal model of P^I, then I is called a *stable model* (or *answer set*) of P. A *ground (atomic) query* is any ground atom A. A program P *bravely* (resp., *cautiously*) *entails* a ground query A, denoted $P \models_b A$ (resp., $P \models_c A$), if $A \in I$ holds for some (resp., each) stable model I of P.

Automata over Infinite Trees. We recall here finite state automata over infinite trees, which we will use as a tool to reason in BFG programs. In particular, following [29] closely we define here *2-way alternating tree automata*.

A *(full infinite) tree* T is any set $T \subseteq \mathbb{N}^*$ of words over the set $\mathbb{N}$ of positive integers such that $x \cdot c \in T$, where $x \in \mathbb{N}^*$ and $c \in \mathbb{N}$, implies (i) $x \in T$ and (ii) $x \cdot c' \in T$ for all $0 < c' < c$. Each element $x \in T$ is a *node* of T, where ϵ (the empty word) is the *root* of T. The nodes $x \cdot c \in T$, where $c \in \mathbb{N}$, are the *successors* of x. By convention, $x \cdot 0 = x$ and $(x \cdot i) \cdot (-1) = x$ (note that $\epsilon \cdot (-1)$ is undefined). T is *k-ary* if each node in T has k successors.

An *infinite path in* T is any set $p \subseteq T$ of nodes such that (i) $x \cdot c \in p$ implies $x \in p$, and (ii) for every $i \geq 0$ there is a unique $x \in p$ such that $|x| = i$. A *labeled tree* over an alphabet Σ is a tuple $(T, \mathcal{L})$, where $\mathcal{L} : T \to \Sigma$, i.e., a tree where the nodes are labeled with symbols from Σ.

For a finite set V, let $B(V)$ be the set of formulae that can be built from $V \cup \{\top, \bot\}$ using $\vee$ and $\wedge$ as connectives. We say that $I \subseteq V$ *satisfies* $\varphi \in B(V)$, if I is a model of φ, when elements in V as seen as propositional variables and φ as a propositional formula. Let $[k] = \{-1, 0, 1, \ldots, k\}$. A *two-way alternating tree automaton (2ATA)* over infinite k-ary trees is a tuple $A = \langle \Sigma, Q, \delta, q_0, F \rangle$, where Σ is an input alphabet, Q is a finite set of states, $\delta : Q \times \Sigma \to B([k] \times Q)$ is a transition function, $q_0 \in Q$ is an initial state, and F is an *acceptance condition*.

Assume a 2ATA $A = \langle \Sigma, Q, \delta, q_0, F \rangle$ over k-ary trees. A *run* of A over a k-ary labeled tree $(T, \mathcal{L})$ is a labeled tree (T_r, r) over $T \times Q$ that satisfies the following:

(i) $r(\epsilon) = (\epsilon, q_0)$.

(ii) For each $y \in T_r$, with $r(y) = (x, q)$ and $\delta(q, \mathcal{L}(x)) = \varphi$, there is a set

$$S = \{(c_1, q_1), \ldots, (c_n, q_n)\} \subseteq [k] \times Q$$

such that (i) S satisfies φ, and (ii) for all $1 \leq i \leq n$, we have that $y \cdot i \in T_r$, $x \cdot c_i$ is defined, and $r(y \cdot i) = (x \cdot c_i, q_i)$.

The run (T_r, r) above is *accepting*, if every infinite path $p \subseteq T_r$ satisfies the acceptance condition F as follows. Let $inf(p)$ be the set of states $q \in Q$ that occur infinitely often in p. A *parity* acceptance condition F is given by a tuple $F = (G_1, G_2, \ldots, G_m)$ where $G_1 \subseteq G_2 \subseteq \ldots \subseteq G_m$ and $G_m = Q$. Then p satisfies F, if an even i exists for which $inf(p) \cap G_i \neq \emptyset$ and $inf(p) \cap G_{i-1} = \emptyset$. A *pairs* or a *co-pairs* acceptance condition is given by a set $F = \{(G_1, R_1), \ldots, (G_n, R_n)\}$ of pairs with $(G_i, R_i) \in 2^Q \times 2^Q$ and $G_i \cap R_i = \emptyset$. Then p satisfies a pairs condition F as above if there is $(G, R) \in F$ such that $inf(p) \cap G = \emptyset$ and $inf(p) \cap R \neq \emptyset$. Dually, p satisfies a co-pairs condition F as above if for all $(G, R) \in F$ we have $inf(p) \cap G \neq \emptyset$ or $inf(p) \cap R = \emptyset$. An automaton accepts a labeled tree, if there is a run that accepts it. By $L(A)$ we denote the set of trees that A accepts. Unless stated otherwise, by default automata a *parity automata*, i.e., they have a parity acceptance condition.

We say A is a *nondeterministic one-way tree automaton (1NTA)* if $\delta(q, \sigma)$ is of the form $\delta(q, \sigma) = \left((1, q_0^1) \wedge \ldots \wedge (k, q_0^k) \right) \vee \ldots \vee \left((1, q_n^1) \wedge \ldots \wedge (k, q_n^k) \right)$, for every $q \in Q$ and $\sigma \in \Sigma$. Intuitively, 1NTAs only move down the tree and with each guess the automaton proceeds with exactly one state for each child node.

2ATAs can be translated into 1NTAs while preserving the language.

$$\mathsf{KnownVenuePub}(x) \leftarrow \mathsf{PublishedIn}(x,y), \mathsf{Conference}(y)$$
$$\mathsf{KnownVenuePub}(x) \leftarrow \mathsf{PublishedIn}(x,y), \mathsf{Journal}(y)$$
$$\mathsf{PublishedIn}(x,f(x)) \leftarrow \mathsf{hasISBN}(x,y), not\ \mathsf{KnownVenuePub}(x)$$
$$\mathsf{Published}(x) \leftarrow \mathsf{PublishedIn}(x,y)$$
$$\mathsf{IncompleteProfile}(x) \leftarrow \mathsf{AuthorOf}(x,y), \mathsf{PublishedIn}(y,f(y))$$
$$\mathsf{EditorAuthorship}(x,y) \leftarrow \mathsf{EditorOf}(x,z), \mathsf{AuthorOf}(x,y), \mathsf{PublishedIn}(y,z)$$

Fig. 1. Example BFG program

Theorem 1 ([29]). *Let A be a 2ATA with a parity acceptance condition. Then there is a parity 1NTA A^n such that $L(A) = L(A^n)$. The number of states in A^n is exponential in the number of states in A, but the size of the acceptance condition of A^n is linear in the size of the acceptance condition of A.*

3   Binary Frontier-Guarded Programs

In this section we define *binary frontier-guarded* ASP programs with function symbols (*BFG programs*). Intuitively, they only allow for at most binary relation symbols and at most unary function symbols. In addition, to ensure decidability we require that the rules are *frontier-guarded*. As we shall see, these restrictions are not too severe; e.g., BFG programs allows to capture many standard DLs and some of their recent non-monotonic extensions.

Definition 1. *A* BFG program P *is a program satisfying the next restrictions.*

(1) All ground rules are facts of the form $A(c) \leftarrow$ and $R(c,d) \leftarrow$, where c,d are constants. Constants occur in facts only.
(2) The rules with variables have the following properties:
  (i) atoms have the form $A(x)$, $A(f(x))$, $R(x,y)$, $R(x,f(x))$ or $R(f(x),x)$, where $x \neq y$;
  (ii) (frontier-guardedness) if $r \in P$ and $H \in \mathsf{head}(r)$, then there is $B \in \mathsf{body}^+(r)$ that contains all the variables of H.

We first note that BFG programs subsume FDNC programs and *core* BD programs, which allow for at most two variables in rules [13,14]. Note that the body of a rule in a BFG program may have the shape of an arbitrary graph. This allows, e.g., to pose a binary Boolean conjunctive query over the stable models of a BFG program. Indeed, a constraint $\leftarrow A_1, \ldots, A_n$, where each A_i is as in (2.i) above is frontier-guarded and thus in the syntax of BFG programs.

Example 1. In Figure 1 we present an example of a BFG program. In particular, we consider a publication database, which stores information about publications, authors, editors and venues. The first two rules state that a document x published in a venue y that is known to be a journal or conference is a publication in a known venue. The third rule deals with a possibly miss-ing information about publication venues that are known to exist; for a doc-ument x that has an ISBN number but does not have a known publication venue, the rule creates a fresh value for it. The 4th rule states that every document that has a publication venue is a publication. Using the 5th rule we state an author's profile is incomplete if he/she has a publication in an anonymous venue. Finaly, the 6th rule collects pairs x, y of authors and pub-lications such that x is an editor of the venue in which y is published. Con-sider the program P that consists of the rules in Figure 1 and includes the set of facts $F = \{$PublishedIn(p_1, v), Journal(v), hasISBN(p_2, n), EditorOf(a_1, v), AuthorOf(a_1, p_1), AuthorOf$(a_2, p_2)\}$. It is not difficult to see that P has a single stable model $I = F \cup \{$KnownVenuePub(p_1), PublishedIn$(p_2, f(p_2))$, Published(p_1), Published(p_2), IncompleteProfile(a_2), EditorAuthorship$(a_1, p_1)\}$.

Many standard DLs can be seen as fragment of first-order logic. Moreover, DL knowledge bases can be transformed into theories that are syntactically very close to BFG programs. For example, the DL $\mathcal{ALCHI}$ can be seen as a first order theory consisting of only the following formulae:

(DL1) $\forall x.(A_1(x) \wedge \cdots \wedge A_n(x) \rightarrow A_1'(x) \vee \cdots \vee A_k'(x))$, where $n \geq 1$ and $k \geq 0$;

(DL2) $\forall x.(A(x) \wedge R(x, y) \rightarrow A'(y))$;

(DL3) $\forall x, y.(R(x, y) \rightarrow R'(x, y))$;

(DL4) $\forall x, y.(R(x, y) \rightarrow R'(y, x))$;

(DL5) $\forall x.(A(x) \rightarrow \exists y.(R(x, y) \wedge A'(y)))$;

(DL6) atomic formula of the form $A(c)$ or $R(c, d)$.

More precisely, a general $\mathcal{ALCHI}$ KB can be transformed into a theory of the above shape while preserving satisfiability and answers to conjunctive queries. The above rules (DL1-DL6) can almost immediately be stated as a BFG pro-gram. e.g., (DL1) translates into a rule $A_1'(x) \vee \cdots \vee A_k'(x) \leftarrow A_1(x), \cdots, A_n(x)$. The formula in (DL5) requires *skolemization*, i.e., we capture it by the rules (i) $R'(x, f(x)) \leftarrow A(x)$, (ii) $A'(y) \leftarrow R'(x, y)$, and (iii) $R(x, y) \leftarrow R'(x, y)$, where f is a fresh function symbol and R' is a fresh binary relation symbol. The above translation, which in fact does not employ stable negation, leads to a program that has a model iff the input DL KB has a model. A (constant-free) Boolean conjunctive query over $\mathcal{K}$ can now be expressed by adding a corresponding con-straint to the program. In [18] the authors show how to extend DLs of the DL-Lite and $\mathcal{EL}$ families with stable negation, where the semantics is given by a translation into a normal guarded Datalog$\pm$ program whose existential variables are treated via skolemization. It is easy to see that the target programs used in the translation are a fragment of BFG programs. The presence of disjunction in BFG programs can be used to generalize the proposal of [18] to support DLs that support disjunction, e.g., $\mathcal{ALCHI}$.

In the remainder of this paper we show how consistency of BFG programs can be decided by employing tree automata. We concentrate on the existence of stable models because cautious and brave entailment of atomic queries can be reduced in linear time to checking (non)existence of a stable model. We also note that, similarly as for $\mathbb{FDNC}$ and $\mathbb{BD}$ programs, decidability of BFG programs can be inferred from the decidability of monadic second-order logic over trees (see, e.g., [12] for an overview). However, we provide a direct automata-based algorithm, that allows us to obtain a 3ExpTime upper bound. We build on the method used in [11] for answering (extensions of) conjunctive queries over expressive DLs, but require a non-trivial adaptation to handle frontier-guarded rules and to perform minimality tests as required by the stable model semantics.

4   Forest-Model Property

We show here that stable models of a BFG program can be seen as forests and describe their encoding into labeled trees, on which automata can run. We assume for the rest of the paper an arbitrary BFG program P, and proceed with the following observation:

Proposition 1. *If I is a stable model of P, then every atom in I is of the form $A(t)$, $R(c,d)$, $R(t, f(t))$ or $R(f(t), t)$, where c, d are constants and t is a term.*

Proof. Suppose there exists a stable model I of P that violates the above property. Then we can simply remove from I all atoms W that are *not* of the mentioned forms. Since the rules of P^I are frontier-guarded, removing such a W can not cause a rule in P^I to be violated, hence the resulting interpretation J is a model of P^I. This contradicts the assumption that I is a stable model of P.

If P has only one constant c, then each stable model of P can be seen as a tree, where c is the root and each term $f(t)$ is a child of the term t. If P has more than one constant, then a stable model can be viewed as a forest, i.e., a set of trees, where roots correspond to the constants and may be arbitrarily interconnected.

To obtain an automata-based algorithm, we must encode the above forests-shaped interpretations into labeled trees. To this end, let $a_1, \ldots, a_n, f_{n+1}, \ldots, f_m$ be an enumeration of constants and function symbols that appear in P, where each a_i is a constant and each f_j is a function symbol. We let $\mathbf{C} = \{1, \ldots, n\}$ and $\mathbf{F} = \{n+1, \ldots, m\}$. A word $w \in \mathbf{C} \times \mathbf{F}^*$ is called a *term node*. For a term node $w = i \cdot j_1 \cdots j_k$, we let $\mathsf{term}(w) = f_{j_k}(\ldots f_{j_1}(a_i) \ldots)$. Let L_P be the set of unary relation symbols consisting of:

(T1) each unary A that appears in P;
(T2) fresh unary R_f and R_f^- for each binary R and function f occurring in P;
(T3) a fresh unary $R_{c,d}$ for each binary R and constants c, d occurring in P.

Intuitively, R_f and R_f^- will encode atoms of the form $R(t, f(t))$ and $R(f(t), t)$, respectively, while unary symbols $R_{c,d}$ will encode ground atoms $R(c,d)$.

We let $\Sigma_P = 2^{L_P}$, and call a tree $\mathcal{T} = (T, \mathcal{L})$ over Σ_P *proper*, if the following are true for every $n \in T$:

(P1) if $\mathcal{L}(n)$ contains some relation of type (T3), then $n = \epsilon$;
(P2) if $\mathcal{L}(n)$ contains some relation of type (T1) or (T2), then n is a term node;
(P3) if $\mathcal{L}(n) \neq \emptyset$, then $n = \epsilon$ or n is a term node.

Note that the size of Σ_P is exponential in the size of P. A proper tree $\mathcal{T} = (T, \mathcal{L})$ over Σ_P is a representation of an interpretation for P. Indeed, the root ϵ of $\mathcal{T}$ stores the binary atoms of the form $R(c, d)$. The nodes $1, \ldots, n$ correspond to constants of P, and the $\mathbf{F}^+$ descendants of such nodes correspond to functional terms. The labeling of nodes provides the relations that are satisfied in the interpretation. More formally, given a proper tree $\mathcal{T} = (T, \mathcal{L})$ over Σ_P, we use $\mathsf{int}(\mathcal{T})$ to denote the interpretation consisting of:

(i) $R(c, d)$, for each $R_{c,d} \in \mathcal{L}(\epsilon)$;
(ii) $A(\mathsf{term}(w))$, for each term node $w \in T$ and unary $A \in \mathcal{L}(w)$ of type (T1);
(iii) $R(\mathsf{term}(w), f(\mathsf{term}(w)))$ for each term node $w \in T$ with $R_f \in \mathcal{L}(w)$;
(iv) $R(f(\mathsf{term}(w)), \mathsf{term}(w))$ for each term node $w \in T$ with $R_f^- \in \mathcal{L}(w)$.

Observe that for any interpretation I with atoms of the forms given in Proposition 1, we can find a proper $\mathcal{T}$ with $\mathsf{int}(\mathcal{T}) = I$. Due to Proposition 1, we then know that for any stable model I of P there exists a proper $\mathcal{T}$ with $\mathsf{int}(\mathcal{T}) = I$.

5   Outline of the Algorithm

We present here our algorithm for checking the existence of a stable model for P. To this end, we will build tree automata running on trees that encode interpretations as well as pairs of interpretations.

We say an automaton A with alphabet Σ_P is *proper* if every tree accepted by A is proper. A proper A with alphabet Σ_P *accepts an interpretation* I for P if there is a proper $\mathcal{T}$ such that $\mathsf{int}(\mathcal{T}) = I$ and A accepts $\mathcal{T}$. We also use trees that represent a *pair* of interpretations for P. Let $\mathcal{T} = (T, \mathcal{L})$ be a tree over $\Sigma_P \times \Sigma_P$. We denote by $\mathcal{T}|_1 = (T, \mathcal{L}_1)$ (resp., $\mathcal{T}|_2 = (T, \mathcal{L}_2)$) the tree over Σ_P such that, for each $n \in T$, $\mathcal{L}_1(n)$ (resp., $\mathcal{L}_2(n)$) is the first (resp., second) component of $\mathcal{L}(n)$. We say that $\mathcal{T}$ is *proper* if $\mathcal{T}|_1$ and $\mathcal{T}|_2$ are proper. We say that an automaton A with alphabet $\Sigma_P \times \Sigma_P$ is *proper* if it accepts proper trees only. Such an A *accepts* an intepretation pair (I_1, I_2) if there is a proper $\mathcal{T}$ over $\Sigma_P \times \Sigma_P$ such that A accepts $\mathcal{T}$, $I_1 = \mathsf{int}(\mathcal{T}|_1)$ and $I_2 = \mathsf{int}(\mathcal{T}|_2)$.

To check if P has a stable model, we build an automaton A_P^{sm} that accepts exactly the proper trees $\mathcal{T}$ such that $\mathsf{int}(\mathcal{T})$ is a stable model of P. In other words, the program P has a stable model iff the automaton A_P^{sm} is nonempty, i.e., accepts some tree. We build A_P^{sm} by manipulating the following simpler automata.

Proposition 2. *The following proper parity 1NTA can be constructed:*

(a) $A_P^{\not\models}$ *that accepts exactly the pairs* (I, I') *such that* $I \not\models P^{I'}$. *The number of states in* $A_P^{\not\models}$ *is exponential in the size of* P, *while the acceptance condition is of polynomial size in the size of* P.

(b) $A_P^{\not\subseteq}$ that accepts exactly the pairs (I, I') such that $I \not\subseteq I'$. The automaton $A_P^{\not\subseteq}$ has a fixed number of states and an acceptance condition of fixed size.

(c) $A_P^{=}$ that accepts exactly the pairs (I, I') such that $I = I'$. The automaton $A_P^{=}$ has a fixed number of states and an acceptance condition of fixed size.

The precise construction of $A_P^{\not\models}$, $A_P^{\not\subseteq}$ and $A_P^{=}$ is presented in Section 6. By manipulating these automata we can obtain the desired automaton A_P^{sm}.

(1) We construct an automaton A_1 by complementing $A_P^{\not\models}$ and intersecting the resulting automaton with $A_P^{=}$, i.e., $L(A_1) = L(A_P^{=}) \backslash L(A_P^{\not\models})$. Then A_1 accepts pairs of interpretations (I, I') such that $I = I'$ and $I \models P^{I'}$. We can use the results in [25] for the complementation step. Measured in the size of P, the automaton A_1 has at most double exponential number of states and a co-pairs acceptance condition with exponentially many pairs.

(2) We let A_P^{mods} be an automaton accepting trees obtained by projecting away the first interpretation in the language of A_1. That is, A_P^{mods} accepts a tree T' iff there exists a tree T over $\Sigma_P \times \Sigma_P$ such that $T|_2 = T'$ and A_1 accepts T. Due to the construction of A_1, we then get that A_P^{mods} accepts an interpretation I iff $I \models P^I$. The construction of A_P^{mods} is fairly standard. Assume $A_1 = (\Sigma_P \times \Sigma_P, Q, \delta, q_0, F)$. We simply define $A_P^{mods} = (\Sigma_P, Q, \delta', q_0, F)$, where δ' is as follows. For each $N' \in \Sigma_P$ and each state $q \in Q$, we have $\delta'(N', q) = \bigvee_{N \in \Sigma_P} \delta((N, N'), q)$. Note that this construction does not modify the state set or the co-pairs acceptance condition of A_1.

(3) We construct an automaton A_2 that accepts the language $L(A_2) = L(A_P^{\not\models}) \cup L(A_P^{\not\subseteq})$. In other words, A_2 accepts a pair (I, I') iff $I \subset I'$ implies $I \not\models P^{I'}$. The automaton A_2 requires at most exponentially many states and a parity condition that is of polynomial size in the size of P.

(4) We construct an automaton A_3 that accepts a pair (I, I') iff $I \subset I'$ and $I \models P^{I'}$. This construction simply complements the automaton A_2. Using the results of [25] and measured in the size of P, the automaton A_3 has at most double exponential number of states and a co-pairs acceptance condition with exponentially many pairs.

(5) We let A_4 be an automaton accepting trees obtained by projecting away the first interpretation in the language of A_3. That is, A_4 accepts a tree T' iff there exists a tree T over $\Sigma_P \times \Sigma_P$ such that $T|_2 = T'$ and A_3 accepts T. Due to the construction of A_3, we then get that A_4 accepts an interpretation I' iff there exists $I \subset I'$ such that $I \models P^{I'}$. The construction of A_4 is identical to the construction of A_P^{mods} from A_1 and does not modify the state set or the co-pairs acceptance condition of A_3.

(6) We construct an automaton A_P^{min} that accepts a tree T' over Σ_P iff for all trees T over $\Sigma_P \times \Sigma_P$ with $T|_2 = T'$ we have that A_2 accepts T. In other words, A_P^{min} accepts an interpretation I' iff $I \not\models P^{I'}$ holds for all $I \subset I'$. The automaton A_P^{min} is a 1NTA obtained by employing the complementation of A_3. Again, using the results of [25], A_P^{min} is a 1NTA with at most triple

exponential number of states and a pairs condition with doubly exponentially many pairs, measured in the size of P.

(7) Finally, we construct an automaton A_P^{sm} by intersecting A_P^{min} with the automaton A_P^{mods}. That is, the automaton A_P^{sm} accepts the language $L(A_P^{sm}) = L(A_P^{min}) \cap L(A_P^{mods})$. We have that A_P^{sm} accepts an interpretation I' iff $I' \models P^{I'}$ and there is no $I \subset I'$ with $I \models P^{I'}$. The 1NTA A_P^{sm} requires at most triple exponential number of states and a pairs condition with doubly exponentially many pairs, measured in the size of P.

Due to the above construction, consistency of P can be decided by checking non-emptiness of A_P^{sm}.

Theorem 2. *P has a stable model iff the language of A_P^{sm} is non-empty.*

Overall, the automaton A_P^{sm} has a triple exponential number of states and a pairs acceptance condition with doubly exponentially many pairs in the size of P. Due to [15], testing emptiness of A_P^{sm} is feasible in triple exponential time in the size of P.

Theorem 3. *Checking consistency of BFG programs is in 3ExpTime.*

We do not know whether the above upper bound is worst-case optimal, but we know that the problem is 2ExpTime-hard. This is already true for core $\mathbb{BD}$ programs, which is a fragment of BFG programs [27]. We note that 2ExpTime-hardness already holds for positive normal BFG programs due to [5]. An yet another way to see the lower bound is a straightfoward reduction from the conjunctive query entailment problem in the DL $\mathcal{ALCI}$, which was shown to be 2ExpTime-hard in [22] (the reduction only requires positive disjunctive BFG programs).

6   Automata Constructions

In this section we prove Proposition 2, i.e., show how to build the automata $A_P^{\not\models}$, $A_P^{\not\subseteq}$ and $A_P^{\doteq}$. Before we begin, note that we can easily construct a 1NTA A_P^{prop} that accepts a tree $\mathcal{T}$ over $\Sigma_P \times \Sigma_P$ iff $\mathcal{T}$ is proper. Such an automaton only requires a constant number of states and an acceptance condition of fixed size.

The Automata $A_P^{\doteq}$ and $A_P^{\not\subseteq}$. We now proceed with the construction of the automata $A_P^{\doteq}$ and $A_P^{\not\subseteq}$ for checking the equality or a violation of strict containment between interpretations, respectively. We start by constructing two alternating automata $A_0^=$ and $A_0^{\not\subseteq}$, and then we transform them into the desired 1NTAs. We let

$$A_0^= = (\Sigma_P \times \Sigma_P, \{q^=\}, \delta, q^=, F),$$

where $F = (\emptyset, \{q^=\})$ is a parity acceptance condition, and δ is as follows. For each $(N, N') \in \Sigma_P \times \Sigma_P$, $\delta((N, N'), q^=) = [N = N'] \wedge \bigwedge_{i \in \mathbf{C} \cup \mathbf{F}} (i, q^=)$. Here $[cond]$ stands for $\top$ if $cond$ is true and for $\bot$ if $cond$ is false. We let

$$A_0^{\not\subseteq} = (\Sigma_P \times \Sigma_P, \{q^{\not\subseteq}\}, \delta, q^{\not\subseteq}, F),$$

where $F = (\{q^{\mathbb{Z}}\})$ is a parity acceptance condition, and δ is as follows. For each $(N, N') \in \Sigma_P \times \Sigma_P$, $\delta((N, N'), q^{\mathbb{Z}}) = [N \not\subseteq N'] \vee \bigvee_{i \in \mathbf{C} \cup \mathbf{F}}(i, q^{\mathbb{Z}})$. We construct a union automaton $A_0^{\mathbb{Z}} = A_0^{\mathbb{Z}} \cup A_0^{=}$. The desired automata $A_P^{\mathbb{Z}}$ and $A_P^{\mathbb{Z}}$ are obtained by transforming $A_0^{=}$ and $A_0^{\mathbb{Z}}$, respectively, into proper 2ATAs (i.e., intersecting them with A_P^{prop}) and then into 1NTAs (in fact, it is not hard to see that 2-wayness and alternation are not really needed in these automata). Both automata $A_P^{=}$ and $A_P^{\mathbb{Z}}$ have boundedly many states and a bounded acceptance condition.

The Automaton $A_P^{\not\models}$. The remainder of this section is devoted to constructing the automaton $A_P^{\not\models}$ that accepts a pair (I, I') iff $I \not\models P^{I'}$. This construction is the most involved one. It requires some auxiliary automata and requires the definition of another kind of trees. Let X be the set of variables occurring P. We let $\hat{\Sigma} = 2^X \times \Sigma_P \times \Sigma_P$. Intuitively, a tree T over $\hat{\Sigma}$ represents a pair (I, I') of interpretations where, additionally, the variables of P are assigned to some terms. Our first step is to define an automaton A_P^X that ensures that in a tree $T = (T, \mathcal{L})$ over $\hat{\Sigma}$ every variable is assigned to exactly one node, i.e., the tree encodes a function π from X to T. In the second step we define another automaton A that verifies whether the given variable assignment witnesses $I \not\models P^{I'}$. In the third and final step, we use A_P^X and A to obtain $A_P^{\not\models}$.

Step 1. We define the automaton $A_P^X = (\hat{\Sigma}, Q, \delta, q_0, F)$ to ensure that in a tree $T = (T, \mathcal{L})$ over $\hat{\Sigma}$ every variable is assigned to exactly one node.

The state set Q of A_P^X consists of an initial state q_0 and the states q_x, q_x', $q_x^{\in}$ and $q_x^{\not\in}$ for each variable x of P. Intuitively, the automaton uses q_x to verify that some node is labeled with x, and uses the state q_x' to verify that x is neither in the labeling of the current symbol, nor in the labeling of any descendant. The states $q_x^{\in}$ are $q_x^{\not\in}$ to verify the presence or absence of the variable x is in the labeling of the current node, respectively.

The transition function δ is as follows. From the initial state the automaton switches to states q_x for each variable $x \in X$, i.e., for each $\sigma \in \hat{\Sigma}$, we have $\delta(\sigma, q_0) = \bigwedge_{x \in X}(0, q_x)$.

When in state q_x, the automaton either decides to place the variable in the current node, or chooses a branch where it will be placed. After placing the variable, it enters the state q_x' to ensure that a variable does not occur more than once. This is implemented by the following transition for each $\sigma \in \hat{\Sigma}$ and variable $x \in X$:

$$\delta(\sigma, q_x) = \left((0, q_x^{\in}) \wedge \bigwedge_{i \in \mathbf{C} \cup \mathbf{F}}(i, q_x')\right) \vee \left(\bigvee_{i \in \mathbf{C} \cup \mathbf{F}}\left((i, q_x) \wedge \bigwedge_{j \in \mathbf{C} \cup \mathbf{F}, j \neq i}(j, q_x')\right)\right),$$

$$\delta(\sigma, q_x') = \left((0, q_x^{\not\in}) \wedge \bigwedge_{i \in \mathbf{C} \cup \mathbf{F}}(i, q_x')\right).$$

The transitions for $q_x^{\in}$ and $q_x^{\not\in}$ are simple. We let $\delta(\sigma, q_x^{\in}) = [x \in V]$ and $\delta(\sigma, q_x^{\not\in}) = [x \not\in V]$ for each $\sigma = (V, N, N')$ in $\hat{\Sigma}$ and variable $x \in X$.

Finally, we need to ensure that each variable is eventually placed in the tree by prohibiting the states q_x from occurring infinitely often. For this, we simply take the acceptance condition $F = (\{q_x \mid x \in X\}, Q)$.

Step 2. Now we build the automaton A that verifies whether a given variable assignment π witnesses $I \not\models P^{I'}$. More precisely, we assume a given tree $\mathcal{T} = (T, \mathcal{L})$ over $\hat{\Sigma}$ such that $\mathcal{T}$ represents an assignment π of variables to nodes of the tree (i.e., each query variable x occurs in the label of exactly one node $\pi(x) \in T$) together with a pair of interpretations (I, I'). We construct an automaton A such that A accepts $\mathcal{T}$ iff π *witnesses* $I \not\models P^{I'}$, that is, if under the assignment π the atoms of its positive body are true in I, the atoms of its negative body are false in I', and the atoms in its head are false in I.

The automaton $A = (\hat{\Sigma}, Q, \delta, q_0, F)$ is defined as follows. The state set Q is as follows.

$$Q = \{q_W^t, q_W^f, q_W^{f'}, q_W^{t,\downarrow}, q_W^{f,\downarrow}, q_W^{f',\downarrow} \mid W \text{ is an atom occurring in } P\} \cup$$
$$\{q_A^t, q_A^f, q_A^{f'} \mid A \text{ is a unary predicate name occurring in } P\} \cup$$
$$\{q_{(R,x)}^t, q_{(R,x,y)}^t, q_{(R,x)}^f, q_{(R,x,y)}^f, q_{(R,x)}^{f'}, q_{(R,x,y)}^{f'} \mid R(x,y) \text{ is from } P\} \cup$$
$$\{q_x \mid x \text{ is a variable from } P\}.$$

We next explain how the transition function is defined.

(I) The state set Q contains q_W^t, q_W^f and $q_W^{f'}$ for each atom W occurring in P. Intuitively, A moves to q_W^t, q_W^f or $q_W^{f'}$, to verify that under the assignment π the atom W is true in I, false in I, or false in I', respectively.

From the initial state q_0, the automaton nondeterministically chooses a rule $r \in P$ and verifies that it is violated, by moving to q_W^t for each positive body atom W, to $q_W^{f'}$ for each negative body atom W, and to q_W^f for each head atom W. Hence, for each $\sigma \in \hat{\Sigma}$, we have:

$$\delta(\sigma, q_0) = \bigvee_{r \in P} \left(\bigwedge_{W \in body^+(r)} (0, q_W^t) \wedge \bigwedge_{W \in body^-(r)} (0, q_W^{f'}) \wedge \bigwedge_{W \in head(r)} (0, q_W^f) \right).$$

It only remains to implement the transitions for q_W^t, q_W^f and $q_W^{f'}$.

(II) The transitions for q_W^t use the states $q_W^{t,\downarrow}$ to check that, at the current position in the tree, the atom W is satisfied.

The transitions from the state q_W^t depend on the form of the atom W. For ground atoms they are simple. Recall that we store binary ground atoms $R_{c,d}$ in the label of the root, and that unary atoms $A(c)$ are represented by the symbol A in the label of the term node i with $c = a_i$. Hence, to verify the satisfaction of $R(c,d)$ we simply look for the corresponding symbol at the root. If the atom is unary, we use the auxiliary state q_A^t to check that the labeling of the corresponding term node contains A. For non-ground atoms the automaton non-deterministically navigates to some node of the tree. Then it uses the state $q_W^{t,\downarrow}$ to test there the satisfaction of W.

First, depending on the type of W, we let for each $\sigma = (V, N, N')$ in $2^X \times \Sigma_P \times \Sigma_P$:

$$\delta(\sigma, q_W^t) = \begin{cases} (0, q_W^{t,\downarrow}) \vee \bigvee_{i \in \mathbf{C} \cup \mathbf{F}} (i, q_W^t) & \text{if } W \text{ is not ground,} \\ [R_{c,d} \in N] & \text{if } W = R(c, d), \\ (i, q_A^t) & \text{if } W = A(c) \text{ and } c = a_i, \end{cases}$$

and for all $(V, N, N') \in \hat{\Sigma}$ and unary A of P, we let $\delta(\sigma, q_A^t) = [A \in N]$.
For the case where W is not ground, we also define transitions from the state $q_W^{t,\downarrow}$, which again depend on the form of the atom W. In case W is unary, for each $\sigma = (V, N, N')$ in $\hat{\Sigma}$, we let:

$$\delta(\sigma, q_W^{t,\downarrow}) = \begin{cases} [A \in N \text{ and } x \in V] & \text{if } W = A(x), \\ [x \in V] \wedge (i, q_A^t) & \text{if } W = A(f(x)) \text{ and } f = f_i. \end{cases}$$

If W is binary with a function symbol (i.e., if $W = R(x, f(x))$ or $W = R(f(x), x)$), we define, for each $\sigma = (V, N, N')$ in $\hat{\Sigma}$:

$$\delta(\sigma, q_W^{t,\downarrow}) = \begin{cases} [R_f \in N \text{ and } x \in V] & \text{if } W = R(x, f(x)) \\ [R_f^- \in N \text{ and } x \in V] & \text{if } W = R(f(x), x). \end{cases}$$

For atoms $R(x, y)$ it is a bit more complicated. For all $(V, N, N') \in \hat{\Sigma}$ and $W = R(x, y)$, we have:

$$\delta(\sigma, q_W^{t,\downarrow}) = (0, q_{(R,x,y)}^t) \vee \left([x \in V] \wedge \left(\bigvee_{i \in \mathbf{F}} ([R_{f_i} \in N] \wedge (i, q_y)) \right) \right) \vee$$
$$\left([x \in V] \wedge (-1, q_y) \wedge (-1, q_{(R,x)}^t) \right)$$

Intuitively, the three disjuncts verify the three possible ways in which an atom $R(x, y)$ can be satisfied: (i) x and y are assigned to constants, (ii) y is mapped to a functional successor of $\pi(x)$, and (iii) x is mapped to a functional successor of $\pi(y)$. In the first disjunct, the automaton moves to the auxiliary state $q_{(R,x,y)}^t$ to verify whether there is a pair of constants witnessing the satisfaction of the atom $R(x, y)$, i.e., whether there is a pair c, d such that x is assigned to c, y is assigned to d, and $R(c, d)$ holds; recall that the latter is stored at the label of the root. Hence we have, for each $\sigma = (V, N, N')$ in $\hat{\Sigma}$:

$$\delta(\sigma, q_{(R,x,y)}^t) = \bigvee_{\{i,j\} \subseteq \mathbf{C}} ([R_{a_i,a_j} \in N] \wedge (i, q_x) \wedge (j, q_y))$$

Finally, for q_x and $q_{(R,x)}^t$ we have $\delta(\sigma, q_x) = [x \in V]$ and $\delta(\sigma, q_{(R,x)}^t) = \bigvee_{i \in \mathbf{F}} [R_{f_i}^- \notin N] \wedge (i, q_x)$ for all $\sigma = (V, N, N')$ in $\hat{\Sigma}$.

(III) The transitions for q_R^f are analogous, but tests $[s \in N]$ for a symbol $s \in L_P$, is replaced by the test $[s \notin N]$, and we use the states super-indexed with f instead of their t counterparts (q_W^f instead of q_W^t, $q_W^{f,\downarrow}$ instead of $q_W^{t,\downarrow}$, etc.).

(IV) Similarly, in the transitions for $q_R^{f'}$ we test for $[s \notin N']$ and use the states super-indexed with f'.

In the acceptance condition, we only need to prohibit the states q_W^t, q_W^f and $q_W^{f'}$, which can postpone the tests for the truth or falsity of atoms, from occurring infinitely often. Hence we set $F = (\{q_W^t, q_W^f, q_W^{f'} \mid W$ is an atom in $P\}, Q)$.

Step 3. We can finalize the construction of $A_P^{\not\models}$. First we let $B = (\hat{\Sigma}, Q, \delta, q_0, F)$ be the result of translating the intersection automaton $A \cap A_P^X$ into a 1NTA. The state set of B is exponential in P, and its parity condition is of polynomial size. To obtain $A_P^{\not\models}$, we first obtain B' by projecting away the variable assignment in the first component of the labels. That is, $B' = (\Sigma_P \times \Sigma_P, Q, \delta', q_0, F)$ where for each $(N, N') \in \Sigma_P \times \Sigma_P$ and each state $q \in Q$,

$$\delta'((N, N'), q) = \bigvee_{V \in 2^X} \delta((V, N, N'), q).$$

The automaton B' accepts a tree $\mathcal{T}$ over $\Sigma_P \times \Sigma_P$ iff $\mathcal{T}$ can be decorated with variables in a way that the resulting tree $\mathcal{T}'$ over $\hat{\Sigma}$ is accepted by B. Finally, the automaton $A_P^{\not\models}$ is obtained by transforming B' into a proper automaton, by intersecting it with A_P^{prop}. This involves a linear increase in the number of states, and hence the state set of $A_P^{\not\models}$ remains exponential and the parity condition of polynomial size. The automaton $A_P^{\not\models}$ accepts exactly the pairs (I, I') such that $I \not\models P^{I'}$, as required.

7   Related Work

Since ASP with function symbols is highly undecidable, e.g., checking existence of a stable model lies at the second level of the analytical hierarchy [24], many authors have suggested ways to reduce the complexity of reasoning. To this end, "mild" restrictions were considered in [6,7,10] to obtain fragments that are very expressive and computationally better behaved (e.g., obtaining semi-decidability). Unfortunately, reasoning in these fragments is either not decidable, or checking whether a program belongs to a given fragment is undecidable. Another approach is to consider various acyclicity notions, with ω-*restricted* programs of [28] being one the first approaches. See, e.g., [8,20] and the references therein for the recent works in this direction. They ensure decidability by guaranteeing finiteness (and a relatively small size) of stable models of a program. In contrast, BFG programs may have infinite stable models and thus are in line with [13,14,16], where efficiently verifiable restrictions are used to ensure that the possibly infinite stable models are forest-shaped.

The presence of negation is not the only cause of undecidability: basic reasoning is undecidable already for Horn programs with existentially quantified variables in rule heads [2]. Ensuring decidability by requiring rules to be *guarded* was first proposed by Calì et at. [9]. Here "guarded" means that each rule is required to have a positive body atom that contains all universal variables of a given rule. The authors also relax this condition to "weak guardedness", which excludes from guarding the variables that can be safely assumed to range over constants. The notion of frontier-guarded rules, which generalizes guarded rules, was proposed in [4]. Further generalization of guarded and frontier-guarded rules were considered in [5]. The recent work in [18] adds to guarded rules negation under the stable model semantics. Our BFG programs are incomparable to the fragments of [18] as we consider predicates of arity at most 2, but allow for disjunction and non-guarded rules. Adding stable negation to existential rules in combination with various acyclicity notions was recently considered in [3, 23].

8   Discussion

In this paper we have introduced BFG programs, which is a new decidable fragment of ASP with function symbols. Understanding whether the provided 3EXPTIME upper bound is worst-case optimal is left for future work. We believe that, using word automata instead of tree automata, the 3EXPTIME upper bound for general BFG programs can be recast to show a 2EXPSPACE upper bound BFG programs that allow for a single function symbol.

An important issue for future research is to characterize the data complexity of BFG programs, i.e. the complexity measured in the size of program facts. Unfortunately, automata based techniques, including the one used in this paper, don't seem to be adequate for characterizing data complexity as often too much structure is lost when encoding desired structures into labeled trees. In the future we also plan to investigate the possibility of rewriting BFG programs into ASP programs without function symbols, similarly to the approach of [19] to rewrite existential frontier-guarded rules into plain Datalog.

Acknowledgments. This work has been supported by the Austrian Science Fund (FWF) grants P20840 and P25207, and the Vienna Science and Technology Fund (WWTF) project ICT12-15. The author is grateful to Thomas Eiter for all the inspiring discussions on the topic.

References

1. Abiteboul, S., Vianu, V.: Datalog extensions for database queries and updates. Journal of Computer and System Sciences **43**(1), 62–124 (1991)
2. Andréka, H., Németi, I.: The generalised completeness of Horn predicate logics as programming language. Acta Cybernetica **4**(1), 3–10 (1978)
3. Baget, J., Garreau, F., Mugnier, M., Rocher, S.: Revisiting chase termination for existential rules and their extension to nonmonotonic negation. CoRR abs/1405.1071 (2014)
4. Baget, J., Leclère, M., Mugnier, M., Salvat, E.: On rules with existential variables: Walking the decidability line. Artif. Intell. **175**(9–10), 1620–1654 (2011)
5. Baget, J., Mugnier, M., Rudolph, S., Thomazo, M.: Walking the complexity lines for generalized guarded existential rules. In: Proc. of IJCAI 2011. IJCAI/AAAI (2011)

6. Baselice, S., Bonatti, P.A., Criscuolo, G.: On finitely recursive programs. Theory and Practice of Logic Programming **9**(2), 213–238 (2009)
7. Bonatti, P.A.: Reasoning with infinite stable models. Artificial Intelligence **156**(1), 75–111 (2004)
8. Calautti, M., Greco, S., Molinaro, C., Trubitsyna, I.: Checking termination of logic programs with function symbols through linear constraints. In: Bikakis, A., Fodor, P., Roman, D. (eds.) RuleML 2014. LNCS, vol. 8620, pp. 97–111. Springer, Heidelberg (2014)
9. Calì, A., Gottlob, G., Kifer, M.: Taming the infinite chase: Query answering under expressive relational constraints. J. Artif. Intell. Res. (JAIR) **48**, 115–174 (2013)
10. Calimeri, F., Cozza, S., Ianni, G., Leone, N.: Computable functions in ASP: theory and implementation. In: de la Banda, M.G., Pontelli, E. (eds.) ICLP 2008. LNCS, vol. 5366, pp. 407–424. Springer, Heidelberg (2008)
11. Calvanese, D., Eiter, T., Ortiz, M.: Answering regular path queries in expressive description logics via alternating tree-automata. Inf. Comput. **237**, 12–55 (2014)
12. Courcelle, B., Engelfriet, J.: Graph Structure and Monadic Second-Order Logic - A Language-Theoretic Approach, Encyclopedia of mathematics and its applications, vol. 138. Cambridge University Press (2012)
13. Eiter, T., Šimkus, M.: Bidirectional answer set programs with function symbols. In: Boutilier, C. (ed.) Proc. of IJCAI 2009, pp. 765–771 (2009)
14. Eiter, T., Šimkus, M.: FDNC: decidable nonmonotonic disjunctive logic programs with function symbols. ACM Trans. Comput. Log. **11**(2) (2010)
15. Emerson, E.A., Jutla, C.S.: The complexity of tree automata and logics of programs (extended abstract). In: Proc. of FOCS 1988, pp. 328–337. IEEE (1988)
16. Feier, C., Heymans, S.: Reasoning with forest logic programs and f-hybrid knowledge bases. TPLP **13**(3), 395–463 (2013)
17. Gelfond, M., Lifschitz, V.: Classical negation in logic programs and disjunctive databases. New Generation Computing **9**(3/4), 365–386 (1991)
18. Gottlob, G., Hernich, A., Kupke, C., Lukasiewicz, T.: Stable model semantics for guarded existential rules and description logics. In: Proc. of KR 2014. AAAI Press (2014)
19. Gottlob, G., Rudolph, S., Šimkus, M.: Expressiveness of guarded existential rule languages. In: Proc. of PODS 2014, pp. 27–38. ACM (2014)
20. Greco, S., Molinaro, C., Trubitsyna, I.: Bounded programs: a new decidable class of logic programs with function symbols. In: Proc. of IJCAI 2013. IJCAI/AAAI (2013)
21. Hull, R., Yoshikawa, M.: Ilog: declarative creation and manipulation of object identifiers. In: Proc. of VLDB 1990. Morgan Kaufmann Publishers Inc. (1990)
22. Lutz, C.: Inverse roles make conjunctive queries hard. In: Proc. of DL 2007. CEUR Workshop Proceedings, vol. 250. CEUR-WS.org (2007)
23. Magka, D., Krötzsch, M., Horrocks, I.: Computing stable models for nonmonotonic existential rules. In: Proc. of IJCAI 2013, pp. 1031–1038. AAAI Press/IJCAI (2013)
24. Marek, V.W., Nerode, A., Remmel, J.B.: How complicated is the set of stable models of a recursive logic program? Ann. Pure Appl. Logic **56**(1–3), 119–135 (1992)
25. Muller, D.E., Schupp, P.E.: Simulating alternating tree automata by nondeterministic automata: New results and new proofs of the theorems of rabin, mcnaughton and safra. Theor. Comput. Sci. **141**(1&2), 69–107 (1995)
26. Pearce, D.: A new logical characterisation of stable models and answer sets. In: Dix, J., Przymusinski, T.C., Moniz Pereira, L. (eds.) NMELP 1996. LNCS, vol. 1216, pp. 57–70. Springer, Heidelberg (1997)

27. Šimkus, M.: Nonmonotonic Logic Programs with Function Symbols. Ph.D. thesis, Vienna University of Technology (2010)

28. Syrjänen, T.: Omega-restricted logic programs. In: Eiter, T., Faber, W., Truszczyński, M. (eds.) LPNMR 2001. LNCS (LNAI), vol. 2173, pp. 267–279. Springer, Heidelberg (2001)

29. Vardi, M.Y.: Reasoning about the past with two-way automata. In: Larsen, K.G., Skyum, S., Winskel, G. (eds.) ICALP 1998. LNCS, vol. 1443, pp. 628–641. Springer, Heidelberg (1998)

Graal: A Toolkit for Query Answering
with Existential Rules

Jean-François Baget, Michel Leclère, Marie-Laure Mugnier(✉),
Swan Rocher, and Clément Sipieter

Inria – University of Montpellier, Montpellier, France
mugnier@lirmm.fr

Abstract. This paper presents Graal, a java toolkit dedicated to ontological query answering in the framework of existential rules. We consider knowledge bases composed of data and an ontology expressed by
existential rules. The main features of Graal are the following: a basic
layer that provides generic interfaces to store and query various kinds of
data, forward chaining and query rewriting algorithms, structural analysis of decidability properties of a rule set, a textual format and its
parser, and import of OWL 2 files. We describe in more detail the query
rewriting algorithms, which rely on original techniques, and report some
experiments.

1   Introduction

Existential rules, a.k.a. Datalog+, are increasingly raising interest in the knowledge representation and database communities [CGL09,BLMS11]. Indeed, they
appear to be well suited for representing ontologies, particularly in the Ontology-
Based Data Access framework (OBDA) [PLC+08], which seeks to exploit ontological knowledge when querying data. On the one hand, existential rules extend
(function-free) Horn rules, a.k.a. Datalog rules, by allowing existentially quantified variables in rule heads. This allows for asserting the existence of unknown
entities, a fundamental feature for reasoning on incomplete representations of
data. On the other hand, they generalize lightweight description logics used
in the context of OBDA, like those underpinning the tractable profiles of the
Semantic Web ontological language OWL 2.

While the issue of querying data via existential rule ontologies has been well-
studied from a theoretical viewpoint, there is still a lack of software tools that
would allow to improve and demonstrate the practical usability of the framework.
In this paper, we present such a software, named *Graal*.[1] Graal comes in the
form of a java toolkit dedicated to existential rules and oriented toward query
answering tasks. The objective of Graal is to provide algorithms and utility
tools that can be used as basic blocks to develop applications and carry out
experimental evaluation of new solutions.

---

[1] Graal and related tools are available at www.github.com/graphik-team/graal

© Springer International Publishing Switzerland 2015
N. Bassiliades et al. (Eds.): RuleML 2015, LNCS 9202, pp. 328–344, 2015.
DOI: 10.1007/978-3-319-21542-6_21

We consider knowledge bases composed of data and existential rules, as well as conjunctive queries, all seen at a logical level. The main features of Graal are the following:

1. a basic layer that provides generic interfaces to store and query heterogeneous data without considering the rules; these interfaces define mappings between the logical level and data stored in various systems (currently: main memory, relational databases, triple stores, graph databases);
2. 'saturation' algorithms, which apply rules on the data in a forward chaining manner; the saturated data can then be queried using the basic layer;
3. 'query rewriting' algorithms, which reformulate a conjunctive query into a set (or 'union') of conjunctive queries; the rewritten query can then be evaluated over the data using the basic layer. Furthermore, the set of rules can be partially compiled independently from any query and the rewriting process exploits this compilation to compute compact rewritings, which have a small size in practice;
4. utility tools: a format called dlgp (for 'datalog+') and its parser, decomposition of rules, structural analysis of decidability properties of a rule set, and translation of OWL 2 files into dlgp.

Graal integrates improved versions of the query rewriting algorithm PURE [KLMT15] and the rule base analyser Kiabora [LMR13]. To the best of our knowledge, the only other tool dedicated to ontological query answering with existential rules is IRIS$^{\pm}$ [GOP14], which builds on the query rewriting algorithm Nyaya.

The paper is organized as follows. Section 2 is devoted to fundamental notions on existential rules and the associated ontological query answering problem. Sections 3 to 7 present the main features of Graal as enumerated above. Since our query rewriting algorithms rely on original techniques, we present them in more detail and report experiments that demonstrate the interest of the compilation-based rewriting.

2 Fundamental Notions

We consider logical vocabularies without function symbols, hence a *term* is a variable or a constant. An *atom* is of the form $p(t_1, \ldots, t_k)$ where p is a predicate of arity k, and the t_i are terms.

The Ontological Query-Answering Problem. A *fact base* is an existentially closed conjunction of atoms. Note that variables may occur in the fact base. This allows to encode in a natural way null values in databases or blank nodes in RDF, moreover existential rules may produce new existential variables. A *conjunctive query* (CQ) is an existentially quantified conjunction of atoms (and its free variables are called *answer variables*). When it is a closed formula, it is called a *Boolean* CQ (BCQ). Hence, fact bases and BCQs have the same logical form. It is convenient to see them as sets of atoms. A *union of CQs* is a disjunction of CQs with the same answer variables.

Given existentially closed conjunctions A and B seen as sets of atoms, a *homomorphism* h from A to B is a substitution of the variables in A by terms in B such that $h(A) \subseteq B$. It is well-known that B is logically entailed by A (notation: $A \models B$) if and only if there is a homomorphism from B to A. Hence, homomorphism is a core notion for reasoning. A fact base $\mathcal{F}$ is *redundant* if there is a homomorphism from $\mathcal{F}$ to one of its strict subsets $\mathcal{F}'$ (then $\mathcal{F}$ and $\mathcal{F}'$ are equivalent).

Given a fact base $\mathcal{F}$ and a BCQ Q, the answer to Q in $\mathcal{F}$ is *positive* if $\mathcal{F} \models Q$. If Q is a non-Boolean CQ with answer variables $(x_1 \ldots x_q)$, a tuple of constants $(a_1 \ldots a_q)$ is an answer to Q in $\mathcal{F}$ if there is a homomorphism from Q to $\mathcal{F}$ that maps x_i to a_i for each i. In other words, $(a_1 \ldots a_q)$ is an answer to Q in $\mathcal{F}$ if the answer to the BCQ obtained from Q by substituting each x_i with a_i is positive.

An *existential rule* (hereafter abbreviated to *rule*) R is a formula $\forall \boldsymbol{x} \forall \boldsymbol{y}(B[\boldsymbol{x}, \boldsymbol{y}] \rightarrow \exists \boldsymbol{z} \, H[\boldsymbol{x}, \boldsymbol{z}])$ where B and H are conjunctions of atoms, respectively called the *body* and the *head* of R (as for facts and BCQs, it is convenient to see the *body* and the *head* of a rule as sets of atoms). The variables $\boldsymbol{z}$ which occur only in H are called *existential* variables. The variables $\boldsymbol{x}$, which occur in B and in H are called *frontier* variables. Since there is no ambiguity, we may omit quantifiers in rules and simply denote a rule by $B \rightarrow H$. For example, $p(x, y) \rightarrow q(x, z) \wedge s(z)$ stands for $\forall x \forall y(p(x, y) \rightarrow \exists z(q(x, z) \wedge s(z)))$.

A *fact* is a rule with an empty body, hence it is an existentially closed conjunction of atoms (and not only a ground atom). It follows that a conjunction of facts can be seen as a single fact, which explains the above definition of a fact base.

A *knowledge base* (KB) $\mathcal{K} = (\mathcal{F}, \mathcal{R})$ consists of a fact base $\mathcal{F}$ and a finite set of (existential) rules $\mathcal{R}$. The answer to a BCQ Q in $\mathcal{K}$ is *positive* if $\mathcal{K} \models Q$ (and the definition of the answer to a CQ in $\mathcal{K}$ follows). The *(ontological) query answering problem* we consider takes as input a KB $\mathcal{K} = (\mathcal{F}, \mathcal{R})$ and a CQ Q, and asks for all answers to Q in $\mathcal{K}$. This problem has long been shown undecidable for general existential rules. However, many decidable, and even tractable, classes have been exhibited.

There are two main approaches to query answering in the presence of rules. The first approach is related to forward chaining (a.k.a. *chase* in databases): it triggers the rules to build a finite representation of inferred data such that answers can be computed by evaluating the query against this representation. The second approach, first proposed for the description logic DL-Lite [CDL⁺07], is related to backward chaining: it rewrites the query such that answers can be computed by evaluating the rewritten query against the data. We now define fundamental notions related to these approaches.

Notions related to Forward Chaining. A rule R is *applicable* to a fact base $\mathcal{F}$ if there is a homomorphism h from the body of R to $\mathcal{F}$; the result of the *application of R on $\mathcal{F}$ w.r.t. h* is $\mathcal{F} \cup h^{safe}(head(R))$ where h^{safe} is a substitution of $head(R)$, that replaces each x in the frontier of R with $h(x)$, and each other variable with a "fresh" variable.

Example 1. Let $\mathcal{F} = \{p(a, b), r(b)\}$ and $R = p(x, y) \wedge r(y) \rightarrow q(x, z) \wedge s(z)$. Note that z is an existential variable. R is applicable to $\mathcal{F}$ with homomorphism $\{x \mapsto a, y \mapsto b\}$. This application produces the fact $\exists z_0(q(a, z_0) \wedge s(z_0))$, where z_0 is a fresh variable. Hence, the resulting fact base is $\mathcal{F}_1 = \{p(a, b), r(b), q(a, z_0), s(z_0)\}$.

Given a BCQ Q, it holds that $\mathcal{K} \models Q$ if and only if there is a fact base $\mathcal{F}'$ obtained from $\mathcal{F}$ by a finite sequence of rule applications such that $\mathcal{F}' \models Q$. The *saturation* $\mathcal{F}^*$ of $\mathcal{F}$ with $\mathcal{R}$ is obtained from $\mathcal{F}$ by repeatedly applying rules from $\mathcal{R}$ until no new rule application can be performed. Note that $\mathcal{F}^*$ can be infinite. Given a BCQ Q, it holds that $\mathcal{K} \models Q$ if and only if $\mathcal{F}^* \models Q$. An answer to a CQ Q in $\mathcal{K}$ can thus be seen as an answer to Q in $\mathcal{F}^*$.

Notions related to Backward Chaining. Query rewriting relies on unification between the query and a rule head. Care must be taken when handling existential variables: if a term t of the query is unified with an existential variable in a rule head, all atoms in which t occurs must also be part of the unification, otherwise the result is unsound.

Example 2. Let $Q = \{q(u, v), r(v)\}$. Consider $\mathcal{F}$ and R from the previous example. Note that Q cannot be mapped by homomorphism to $\mathcal{F}_1 = \mathcal{F}^*$, hence Q has no answer in $(\mathcal{F}, \{R\})$. Assume we unify the atom $q(u, v)$ from Q with the atom $q(x, z)$ in the head of R: then, Q is rewritten into $Q_1 = \{r(v), p(u, y), r(y)\}$, which is unsound. Indeed, Q_1 can be mapped to $\mathcal{F}$ by the homomorphism $\{u \mapsto a, y \mapsto b, v \mapsto b\}$. Intuitively, the trouble is that the 'connection' between variables u and v has been lost in Q_1.

Hence, we unify a subset Q' of the query with a subset H' of a rule head. To define such a unifier, it is convenient to use a partition of the set of terms of $Q' \cup H'$. A partition π of a set of terms is said to be *admissible* if no class of π contains two constants; then a substitution σ can be obtained from π by selecting an element e_i in each class C_i of π, with priority given to constants, and setting $\sigma(t) = e_i$ for all $t \in C_i$. A *piece-unifier* of a BCQ Q with a rule $R = B \rightarrow H$ is a triple $\mu = (Q', H', \pi_\mu)$, where $Q' \subseteq Q$, $H' \subseteq H$ and π_μ is an admissible partition on the terms of $Q' \cup H'$ such that:

1. $\sigma(H') = \sigma(Q')$, where σ is a substitution obtained from π_μ;
2. if a class C_i in π_μ contains an existential variable (from H), then the other terms in C_i are variables from Q' that do not occur in $(Q \setminus Q')$.

A *piece* P of Q with respect to μ is a non-empty inclusion-minimal subset of atoms that have to be processed together, i.e., such that: for all $a \in P$ and $a' \in Q$, if a and a' share a variable unified with an existential variable of R by μ, then $a' \in P$. One can easily check that Q' is composed of pieces of Q with respect to μ (hence the name piece-unifier). The *(direct) rewriting* of Q with R with respect to μ is $\sigma(Q \setminus Q') \cup \sigma(B)$ where σ is a substitution obtained from π_μ.

Example 3. Consider again Q, R and $\mathcal{F}$. There is no piece-unifier of Q with R since, z being an existential variable, $q(u, v)$ cannot be unified with $q(x, z)$ without extending the unifier to $r(v)$, which is not possible. Let $Q_2 = \{q(u, v), q(w, v), r(u), t(w)\}$.

A piece-unifier of Q_2 with R is $(\{q(u,v), q(w,v)\}, \{q(x,z)\}, \{\{u,w,x\}, \{v,z\}\})$. The corresponding rewriting is $\{r(u), t(u), p(u,y), r(y)\}$.

Given a BCQ Q, it holds that $\mathcal{K} \models Q$ if and only if there is a BCQ Q' obtained from Q by a finite sequence of (direct) query rewriting steps such that $\mathcal{F} \models Q'$. When CQs (and not only BCQs) are involved, an answer variable cannot be unified with an existential variable from a rule head. In practice, instead of making the piece-unifier definition more complex, we simply transform a CQ Q into a BCQ by adding an atom with a special predicate *ans* that contains all answer variables, which ensures that answer variables are correctly handled, and remove all atoms with predicate *ans* at the end of the rewriting process.

3   Basic Query Answering

The kernel of Graal deals with the following problems: store a fact base and answer conjunctive queries without considering the rules yet. Graal's interface considers sets of atoms (built from predicates of any non-null arity, and whose terms include variables). Answering a query is thus seen as finding homomorphisms from a set of atoms to another. However, Graal may rely upon different storage systems as well as different querying algorithms to implement these basic problems.

Storage. A set of atoms can be stored either in main memory or in secondary memory when it is very large. In main memory, the two implementations proposed are either a list of atoms (smallest memory usage, smallest cost for adding atoms), or a graph-based data structure (a better access to the data required for querying). In secondary memory, the storage systems supported by Graal can be split into three families.

- *Relational Databases* Here, an atom $p(t_1, \ldots, t_k)$ is stored as a line $(t_1, \ldots, t_k)$ in the table. Graal uses JDBC to implement relational database systems, which allows to easily plug any RDBMS that provides a JDBC driver. Graal is currently provided with a choice of MySQL, postgreSQL and SQLite.
- *Triple Stores* Here, a binary atom $p(t_1, t_2)$ is stored as a triple $(t_1 p \, t_2)$. Graal provides an implementation using Jena TDB and another using the SAIL API that allows to use Sesame triple stores, as well as any storage that also implements that API. Note that, to encode a set of arbitrary atoms into a triple store, it is first necessary to binarize these atoms.
- *Graph Databases* Here, atoms, terms and predicates are represented by nodes in a binary graph. An atom $a = p(t_1, \ldots, t_k)$ is represented by $k+1$ labeled edges: one edge labeled `predicate` between the node representing a and the node representing p, and the others labeled `term-i` between the node representing a and the node representing t_i. Currently, Graal provides two implementations of this representation. The first one uses Neo4j, the second uses the Blueprints API through which it is possible to plug in several graph database systems.

Querying. Graal comes with a generic backtrack algorithm that can compute homomorphisms regardless of the storage system used, thanks to Graal's core API. Though this algorithm does not come (yet) with any particular optimization, it allows for the quick deployment of any new storage system. Alternatively, Graal provides translations from a conjunctive query to the native querying languages of the storage mechanisms it handles: SQL queries are used to access RDBMS; SPARQL queries are used to access triple stores; and Cypher query language is used to query data encoded in Neo4j. Note that all those translations, whatever the storage system used, ensure that the same set of answers is obtained from a given CQ.

4 Saturation

Graal provides a forward chaining algorithm for existential rules, as well as several optimizations of this algorithm. The algorithm performs breadth-first saturation. The fact base is initialized with $\mathcal{F} = \mathcal{F}_0$. Then, at each step, considering the fact base $\mathcal{F}_i$, we compute all homomorphisms from all rule bodies to $\mathcal{F}_i$. The fact base $\mathcal{F}_{i+1}$ is obtained by applying the rules following these homomorphisms on $\mathcal{F}_i$. We illustrate the saturation mechanism on the following running example.

Example 4 (Running Example). We start from a quaternary relation *project* (x, y, z, w), which intuitively links a project identifier x, an area y, a scientific manager z and an administrative manager w. Rule R_0 decomposes this relation into binary relations *hasArea*, *hasScManager* and *hasAdmManager*. Rules R_1 to R_3 introduce specializations of the concept *area*, namely *sensitiveArea*, itself specialized into *security* and *innovation*. Rules R_4 and R_5 state that relations *hasScManager* and *hasAdmManager* are specializations of *hasManager*. Rules R_{6a} and R_{6b} state that *hasManager* and *isManagerOf* are inverse relations. Rule R_7 states that 'every manager manages something'. Rules R_{8a} and R_{8b} define the concept *criticalManager* ('a critical manager is someone who manages something in a sensitive area, and reciprocally'). Finally, Rule R_9 partially defines the concept of *accreditedManager*: 'an accredited manager is necessarily someone who manages a project in a security area'.

$R_0 = project(x, y, z, w) \rightarrow hasArea(x, y) \wedge hasScManager(x, z) \wedge hasAdmManager(x, w)$
$R_1 = sensitiveArea(x) \rightarrow area(x)$
$R_2 = security(x) \rightarrow sensitiveArea(x)$
$R_3 = innovation(x) \rightarrow sensitiveArea(x)$
$R_4 = hasScManager(x, y) \rightarrow hasManager(x, y)$
$R_5 = hasAdmManager(x, y) \rightarrow hasManager(x, y)$
$R_{6a} = isManagerOf(y, x) \rightarrow hasManager(x, y)$
$R_{6b} = hasManager(y, x) \rightarrow isManagerOf(x, y)$
$R_7 = manager(x) \rightarrow isManagerOf(x, y)$
$R_{8a} = isManagerOf(x, y) \wedge hasArea(y, z) \wedge sensitiveArea(z) \rightarrow criticalManager(x)$
$R_{8b} = criticalManager(x) \rightarrow isManagerOf(x, y) \wedge hasArea(y, z) \wedge sensitiveArea(z)$
$R_9 = accreditedManager(x) \rightarrow isManagerOf(x, y) \wedge project(y, z, v, w) \wedge security(z)$

Example 5. Let $\mathcal{F} = \{accreditedManager(claire), woman(claire)\}$. The saturation at Step 1 produces the atoms $isManagerOf(claire, y_0)$, $project(y_0, z_0, v_0, w_0)$, $security(z_0)$ (by application of rule). The saturation at Step 2 produces the atom $hasManager(y_0, claire)$ (by application of rule R_{6a}), the atom $sensitiveArea(z_0)$ (by application of rule R_2), and the atoms $hasArea(y_0, z_0)$, $hasScManager(y_0, v_0)$, $hasAdmManager(y_0, w_0)$ (by application of rule R_0).

The optimizations implemented in Graal on the saturation mechanism are twofold. The first one is related to the way we detect that a rule application added new information. The default behavior of Graal is the *restricted chase* [FKMP05]: inferred atoms are not added at step $i + 1$ if there is a folding from those atoms into F_i (*i.e.,* a homomorphism from the head of the rule into F_i that preserves frontier variables according to the homomorphism used to apply the rule).

Example 6. Let $\mathcal{F} = \{manager(tom), isManagerOf(tom, project7)\}$. The application of R_7 on $\mathcal{F}$ would produce the atom $isManagerOf(tom, y_0)$. Since it folds into $\mathcal{F}$, the restricted chase does not add this atom to $\mathcal{F}$.

The second optimization is related to the selection of rules that have to be checked to generate $\mathcal{F}_{i+1}$. The *default* behavior is to check the applicability of *all* rules at each step. We may also rely upon the *graph of rule dependencies* (GRD). The nodes of this graph are the rules. There is an arc from a rule R to a rule R' if there is a piece-unifier of the body of R' (hence, seen as a query) with (the head of) R. Optionally, such an arc can be labeled with all piece-unifiers of the body of R' with R. The essential properties of the GRD are the following:

- R' depends on R (i.e., an application of R may trigger a new application of R') iff there is an arc from R to R';
- when the GRD contains no circuit (including self-loops), then the saturation halts for any fact base.

The GRD can then be used as follows: without loss of completeness, the *dependency behavior* checks for applicability at step $i+1$ solely rules that depend on rules that were successfully applied at step i; the *unifier behavior* improves the previous behavior by considering the (piece-)unifiers between a rule R_1 and a rule R_2: if R_1 was applied at step i according to a homomorphism h, and $\mu_1, \ldots, \mu_k$ are the unifiers of the body of R_2 with R_1, then any homomorphism from the body of R_2 at step $i + 1$ extends a partial homomorphism $\mu_i \circ h$ that can be computed in linear time. This latter improvement not only reduces the number of rules to be checked for applicability, but also the search space for homomorphisms.

Finally, let us point out that by combining different storage methods and querying algorithms (see Section 3), different rule decompositions (see Section 6), different redundancy elimination mechanisms (restricted, core, etc...) and different rule triggering behaviors, we obtain different algorithms that can be more or less efficient for a particular application. These choices not only impact the efficiency of the saturation mechanism, but also the halting of that procedure. It is well known, for instance, that the core chase (which removes all redundancies by computing the smallest equivalent subset of atoms) halts for some instances where the restricted chase does not. Note also that the choice of rule decomposition into atomic heads may lead to the non-termination of the chase, as shown in Section 6.2 (Example 17).

5   Query Rewriting

In this section, we present the 'piece-based' rewriting technique. Two other rewriting techniques applicable to existential rules are known. The first one skolemizes the rule heads, i.e., replaces existential variables by Skolem functions (e.g., REQUIEM [Perez-Urbina et al. 2009]). The second one decomposes the unification step into two steps: factorisation of the query, and unification itself (e.g., PerfectRef [CDL$^+$07] and IRIS   [GOP14]). In both methods, some intermediate queries that will not yield rewritings are generated. This is avoided in piece-based rewriting.

Basic Algorithm (PURE). Given a query Q and a set of rules $\mathcal{R}$, let $\mathcal{Q}$ be the set of all rewritings that can be obtained by a sequence of direct rewritings from Q. This set is (pre-)ordered by subsumption (Q_1 subsumes Q_2 if any answer to Q_2 is an answer to Q_1; this can be decided by a homomorphism test). When $\mathcal{Q}$ is finite, it can be seen as a UCQ. However, it is sufficient to consider $\mathcal{Q}' \subseteq \mathcal{Q}$, such that any element of $\mathcal{Q}$ is covered (i.e., subsumed) by an element of $\mathcal{Q}'$ (we say that $\mathcal{Q}'$ is a cover of $\mathcal{Q}$). All inclusion-minimal covers of $\mathcal{Q}$ have the same cardinality.

The basic query rewriting algorithm in Graal (named PURE) takes as input a CQ and a set of existential rules and outputs a minimal cover of the set of rewritings, if the set of rewritings is finite (equivalently: if there exists a UCQ-rewriting of Q). Otherwise, it may not terminate. Among the main classes of rules ensuring the existence of a UCQ rewriting for *any* CQ, we can cite *linear* rules, which generalize most DL-Lite dialects, the *sticky* family, and classes satisfying conditions expressed on a graph of *rule dependencies* (see in particular [CGL09, CGP10, BLMS11]).

The algorithm PURE starts from the set of rewritings $\mathcal{Q}_F = \{Q\}$ and proceeds in a breadth-first manner. At each step, queries from $\mathcal{Q}_F$ which have been generated at the preceding step are explored; 'exploring' a query consists of computing the set of direct rewritings of this query with all rules. Let $\mathcal{Q}_t$ be the obtained set of new queries. At the end of the step, only a minimal cover of $\mathcal{Q}_F \cup \mathcal{Q}_t$ is kept.

The computation of a minimal cover at *each* step may seem expensive, since each comparison of two queries is a homomorphism check. The point is to ensure the termination of the algorithm whenever a finite set of rewritings exists: since a set of rewritings may be infinite and still have a finite cover, a cover has to be maintained at each step (or computed after a finite number of steps). For some classes of rules, such as linear and sticky rules, this problem does not occur, and the minimal cover could be computed only once at the end of the algorithm. For a detailed presentation of the rewriting algorithm, we refer the reader to [KLMT15].

It is well known that the bottleneck of UCQ-rewriting is the size of the produced UCQ, which can be prohibitively large in practice. Graal proposes an optimized rewriting technique, presented next.

Compilation-Based Algorithm ($PURE_C$). We can observe that some simple rules are an obvious cause of combinatorial explosion. A typical example is that of rules describing hierarchies of concepts (seen as unary predicates), as in the following example.

Example 7. Let $R_1 \ldots R_n$ be rules of the form $R_i : b_i(x) \to b_{i-1}(x)$. These rules express that the concept b_0 is specialized into concept b_1, itself specialized into b_2, etc. Let $Q = \{b_0(x_1) \ldots b_0(x_k)\}$. Each atom $b_0(x_j)$ in Q is rewritten into $b_1(x_j)$, which in turn is rewritten into $b_2(x_j)$, and so on. Thus, there are $(n+1)^k$ rewritings of Q.

Now, assume that we compile the rules from the previous example into an order on predicates $b_n < b_{n-1} < \ldots < b_0$ and embed this order in the homomorphism notion such that a predicate b_i can be mapped to any predicate b_j such that $j \le i$. Then, the only rewriting of Q needed to compute the answers to Q over any fact base is Q itself. We generalize this idea by compiling all rules with an atomic body as long as they do not introduce existential variables. Since the atoms in a rule may have predicates of different arity and arguments in different positions, we compute a relation on *atoms* and not only predicates. Moreover, this relation is not necessarily an order, but a *preorder* (i.e., a reflexive, transitive, but not necessarily antisymmetric relation).

A rule is said to be *compilable* if it has a single body atom, no existential variable and no constant. W.l.o.g. we also assume that a compilable rule has a single head (indeed, if the rule has no existential variable, each atom in the head forms a piece). Let $\mathcal{R}_c$ be the set of compilable rules. We compute the closure of $\mathcal{R}_c$, denoted by $\mathcal{R}_c^*$, which is the set of all rules inferred from $\mathcal{R}_c{}^2$, as illustrated next on the running example.

Example 8 (Running example). The compilable rules are R_0 (decomposed into 3 rules), $R_1 \ldots R_5$, R_{6a}, R_{6b}. The inferred rules are the following:

$project(x, y, z, w) \to hasManager(x, z)$
$project(x, y, z, w) \to hasManager(x, w)$
$security(x) \to area(x)$
$innovation(x) \to area(x)$
$hasScManager(x, y) \to isManagerOf(y, x)$
$hasAdmManager(x, y) \to isManagerOf(y, x)$

---

[2] Let R_1 and R_2 be compilable rules such that $head(R_1)$ and $body(R_2)$ are unifiable by a (classical) most general unifier u. The rule *inferred* from (R_1, R_2) is $u(body(R_1)) \to u(head(R_2))$.

$project(x, y, z, w) \rightarrow isManagerOf(z, x)$
$project(x, y, z, w) \rightarrow isManagerOf(w, x)$

The preorder $\preccurlyeq$ on atoms associated with $\mathcal{R}_c^*$ is as follows: given two atoms A and B, we have $A \preccurlyeq B$ if (i) $A = B$ or (ii) there is a rule $R \in \mathcal{R}_c^*$, with a homomorphism h from $body(R)$ to A such that $h(head(R)) = B$.

Example 9 (Running example). It holds that $security(u) \preccurlyeq area(u)$ by the inferred rule $security(x) \rightarrow area(x)$; and that $project(u, b, a, a) \preccurlyeq isManagerOf(a, u)$ by the rule $project(x, y, z, w) \rightarrow isManagerOf(w, x)$ and the homomorphism $h = \{x \mapsto u, y \mapsto b, z \mapsto a, w \mapsto a\}$.

Homomorphism is the fundamental notion to compute logical entailment on sets of atoms. We extend it to embed the preorder: Given sets of atoms $\mathcal{A}$ and $\mathcal{B}$, a $\preccurlyeq$-homomorphism from $\mathcal{B}$ to $\mathcal{A}$ is a substitution h from $vars(\mathcal{B})$ to $terms(\mathcal{A})$ such that for all $B \in \mathcal{B}$, there is $A \in \mathcal{A}$ with $A \preccurlyeq h(B)$. This allows to answer CQs over a KB composed of a fact base and a set of compilable rules.

Example 10 (Running example). Let $Q(x) = \{hasManager(y, x), hasArea(y, z), sensitiveArea(z)\}$, asking for managers of projects about sensitive areas. Let $\mathcal{F} = \{project(id_1, a_1, m_1, m_2), security(a_1)\}$. The answers to Q are m_1 and m_2. For m_1, we have the $\preccurlyeq$-homomorphism $h_1 = \{x \mapsto m_1, y \mapsto id_1, z \mapsto a_1\}$, with $project(id_1, a_1, m_1, m_2) \preccurlyeq hasManager(id_1, m_1)$, $project(id_1, a_1, m_1, m_2) \preccurlyeq hasArea(id_1, a_1)$ and $security(a_1) \preccurlyeq sensitiveArea(a_1)$; and similarly for m_2.

Now, let $\mathcal{R} = \mathcal{R}_c \cup \mathcal{R}_e$ be a set of existential rules, where $\mathcal{R}_c$ is composed of compilable rules. $\mathcal{R}_c$ is compiled into a preorder $\preccurlyeq$ and query rewriting is performed with $\mathcal{R}_e$. The preorder has to be embedded into the rewriting process, otherwise the rewriting process would not be complete, as shown in the next example.

Example 11 (Running example). Consider again the query Q from the preceding example. There is no rewriting of Q with the non-compilable rules, whereas clearly, using the compilable Rules R_{6a}, R_0 and R_2, Q could be rewritten into $\{isManagerOf(x, y), project(y, z, z_0, w_0), security(z)\}$, which would then allow to obtain the rewriting $\{accreditedManager(x)\}$ with Rule R_9.

Hence, the preorder is embedded into the piece-unifier operation as well. Given a preorder $\preccurlyeq$ on atoms, a $\preccurlyeq$-piece-unifier of Q with R is a triple $\mu = (Q', H', \pi_u)$ defined similarly to a piece-unifier, with Condition 1 ($\sigma(H') = \sigma(Q')$) being replaced by: there is a surjective mapping f from $\sigma(H')$ to $\sigma(Q')$ such that, for all $A \in \sigma(H')$, we have $f(A) \preccurlyeq A$. The direct $\preccurlyeq$-rewriting of Q according to μ is $u(body(R)) \cup u(Q \setminus Q')$.

Example 12 (Running example). Let $Q = \{criticalManager(x), woman(x)\}$. The basic query rewriting algorithm outputs a set of 38 CQs (these CQs are pairwise incomparable w.r.t. logical entailment, hence we cannot do better if the output is a classical UCQ). The direct $\preccurlyeq$-rewriting outputs only the 3 following queries: $Q_1(x) = Q(x)$, $Q_2(x) = \{isManagerOf(x, x_1), hasArea(x_1, x_2),$

$sensitiveArea(x_2), woman(x)$} and $Q_3(x) = \{accreditedManager(x), woman$
$(x)\}$. Q_2 is a direct rewriting of Q with Rule R_{8a} and Q_3 is a direct $\preccurlyeq$-rewriting
of Q_2 with Rule R_9.

The following theorem states that the process is sound and complete: given
a KB $\mathcal{K} = (\mathcal{F}, \mathcal{R})$, where $\mathcal{R} = \mathcal{R}_e \cup \mathcal{R}_c$ and $\mathcal{R}_c$ is a set of compilable rules
with associated preorder $\preccurlyeq$, and a BCQ Q, it holds that $\mathcal{K} \models Q$ iff there is Q'
obtained by a sequence of direct $\preccurlyeq$-rewritings from Q using rules from $\mathcal{R}_e$ such
that $\mathcal{F}, \mathcal{R}_c \models Q'$ (i.e., there is a $\preccurlyeq$-homomorphism from Q' to $\mathcal{F}$). For more
details, the reader is referred to [KLM15].
    Graal's optimized rewriting algorithm (PURE$_C$) is composed of two steps:
(1) it partitions the given rule set $\mathcal{R}$ into $\mathcal{R}_e$ and $\mathcal{R}_c$, computes $\mathcal{R}_c^*$ and encodes
it into a preorder $\preccurlyeq$; (2) given Q, $\mathcal{R}_e$ and $\preccurlyeq$, it outputs a minimal cover of
the set of $\preccurlyeq$-rewritings (with the notion of cover being defined with respect to
$\preccurlyeq$-homomorphism instead of homomorphism). Since Step 1 is independent from
any query, it can be perfomed independently from Step 2. Hence, the algorithm
also accepts as input $\mathcal{R}_e$, $\mathcal{R}_c^*$ and Q.

Query Evaluation. Let $\mathcal{Q}$ be the result of the optimized rewriting algorithm: $\mathcal{Q}$
can be seen as a 'pivotal' representation, in the sense that it can be transformed
into different kinds of queries, depending on the type of data storage and the
applicative context. Obviously, it can be directly evaluated with an adequate
implementation of $\preccurlyeq$-homomorphism in the case the data can be loaded in main
memory.[3]
    Otherwise, the set $\mathcal{Q} \cup \mathcal{R}_c$ can be straightforwardly translated into a Datalog
query, as illustrated in the next example, and passed to a Datalog engine.

Example 13 (Running example). From $\mathcal{Q} = \{Q_1(x), Q_2(x), Q_3(x)\}$ (see the
preceding example), we build 3 Datalog rules with head $ans(x)$ (where ans is
the answer predicate). E.g., from $Q_1(x)$, we obtain `ans(x):-criticalManager(x),`
`woman(x)`. The Datalog query is composed of these 3 rules and compilable rules from
$\mathcal{R}_c$.

A mixed approach can be adopted with $\mathcal{R}_c$ being used to saturate the data,
and $\mathcal{Q}$ being evaluated over the 'semi-saturated' data. One may even assume that
all information that could be inferred by compilable rules is already present in the
data, and delegate the encoding of this information to the database manager.
In particular, if $\mathcal{R}_c$ is composed solely of hierarchical rules and the data are
stored in a RDBMS, semantic index techniques allow to effectively avoid the
computation of saturation [RC12].
    When partial saturation of the data is not feasible, $\mathcal{Q}$ may also be *unfolded*
into a set of CQs (i.e., a UCQ) $\mathcal{Q}'$: $\mathcal{Q}'$ is obtained from $\mathcal{Q}$ by adding, for each $Q \in$
$\mathcal{Q}$, all Q' such that $Q' \preccurlyeq Q$ (then computing a cover). We have experimentally
checked that it is more efficient to unfold $\mathcal{Q}$ than to directly compute $\mathcal{Q}'$.

---

[3] The $\preccurlyeq$-homomorphism is not available yet as a standalone querying operation in the
current version of Graal.

Example 14 (Running example). Queries Q_1 and Q_3 are invariant by unfolding; Q_2 is unfolded into $6 \times 2 \times 3 = 36$ queries. All queries are incomparable, hence $|\mathcal{Q}'| = 38$.

Experiments. We synthetize here experimental results that demonstrate the interest of compilation-based rewriting. Due to space requirements, we cannot provide the detailed results. Since benchmarks dedicated to existential rules are not available yet, we considered rule bases obtained by translation from description logics (DLs). We first carried out experiments about the query rewriting step itself. For these experiments, we considered a widely used benchmark, introduced in [PHM09], composed of DL-Lite$_\mathcal{R}$ ontologies, namely ADOLENA, STOCKEXCHANGE, UNIVERSITY and VICODI. Additionally, we considered very large DL-Lite$_\mathcal{R}$ ontologies proposed in [TSCS13], which respectively contain more than 53k and 34k rules, with 54% and 64% of compilable rules. Each ontology is provided with 5 handcrafted queries. We first evaluated the impact of rule compilation on the rewriting process, w.r.t. the rewriting size and runtime respectively. We found a huge gap between the sizes of the output; the pivotal UCQ is often restricted to a single CQ even when the classical UCQ has thousands of CQs (up to more than 30000 CQs in a case where the pivotal UCQ contains 1 CQ). Unsurprisingly, the results on the query rewriting runtimes lead to similar observations. We found that PURE$_C$ (without or with unfolding) scales well on the large ontologies. We also compared to other query rewriting tools, namely Nyaya (which was the only other tool processing existential rules, before the recent release of IRIS±), as well as some well-known DL tools. We emphasize that these DL tools exploit the particularities of DL-Lite, specially the most recent ones, namely tw-rewriting [RMKZ13] (part of the Ontop OBDA system) and Rapid [CTS11], whereas Graal and Nyaya are designed for general existential rules. Globally, PURE$_C$ behaves similarly to the fastest tools, Rapid and tw-rewriting. If we restrict the comparaison to classical UCQ output, the fastest tools are undeniably tw-rewriting and Rapid, followed by PURE$_C$ with unfolding.

We carried out additional experiments to compare the evaluation of the classical UCQ rewriting on data with the evaluation of the pivotal UCQ on data semi-saturated by compilable rules. For these experiments, we used the DL benchmark LUBM$_{20}^{\exists}$ proposed in [LSTW13], which comes with a data generator. This benchmark is a modification of the well-known benchmark LUBM introduced in [GPH05] (and provided with 14 queries). In particular, it yields more rules with existential variables and adds 6 challenging queries. We consider two fact bases (stored in an RBDMS) of 151 MB (10 universities) and 3266 MB (200 universities). In both cases, the ratio between the initial base and the semi-saturated base is rather small (approx. 1.22). Note that the semi-saturation step is independent from any query, hence it can be computed only once as a preprocessing step (for information, it took 41 seconds and 15 minutes respectively). We rewrote the 20 queries associated with LUBM and LUBM$_{20}^{\exists}$. Results about the rewriting step itself confirmed the conclusions of the first experiments. Table 1 reports the evaluation runtime for each query ('UCQ': evaluation of the classical UCQ on the initial database; 'Pivotal': evaluation of the pivotal query on the semi-saturated database; 'Rew TO' and 'Ans TO': 30 minutes timeout in the rewriting step and in the evaluation step resp.; 'SQL Err.': query too large for the RDBMS). We can see that the pivotal UCQ is evaluated much more efficiently than the classical UCQ (which could even not be produced or passed to the RDBMS in several cases). Note that, despite the pivotal rewriting of q_{18} is a single CQ, it could not be evaluated, even on the smaller fact base, because it requires a large number of joins.

Table 1. Evaluation time over $\text{LUBM}_{20}^{\exists}$ (in seconds)

# univ.	Rew.	q1	q2	q3	q4	q5	q6	q7	q8	q9	q10
10	UCQ	0.62	1.09	0.62	0.91	0.64	13.99	0.74	4.35	3.40	0.78
	Pivotal	0.56	0.56	0.55	0.56	0.55	5.88	0.58	0.57	1.62	0.65
200	UCQ	0.63	1.74	0.66	1.00	0.64	229.23	0.76	4.68	23.37	0.75
	Pivotal	0.58	0.82	0.56	0.58	0.57	85.00	0.58	0.58	6.56	0.66

# univ.	Rew.	q11	q12	q13	q14	q15	q16	q17	q18	q19	q20
10	UCQ	0.65	0.86	0.648	11.27	Rew TO	SQL Err.	SQL Err.	Rew TO	3.31	4.62
	Pivotal	0.66	0.69	0.66	11.29	1.02	0.66	0.69	Ans TO	0.56	1.36
200	UCQ	0.60	0.82	0.68	173.51	Rew TO	SQL Err.	SQL Err.	Rew TO	3.30	17.58
	Pivotal	0.67	0.66	0.65	168.45	4.71	0.95	0.68	Ans TO	0.58	5.58

6   Utility Tools for Existential Rules

In this section, we present utility tools dedicated to existential rules, which allow to exchange, decompose and analyze rule bases.

Datalog+ Format and OWL 2 Translator. We defined a textual format, called *dlgp* (for Datalog+), which extends standard datalog notation. Example 15 shows part of the running example in dlgp format.

In addition to 'pure' existential rules, dlgp allows to encode negative constraints (existential rules with an empty head, interpreted as always false), equality atoms anywhere in the rule bodies and heads (which allows for instance to encode functional dependencies), as well as conjunctive queries and facts. Note that the tools currently implemented in Graal do not process negative constraints and rules with equality in a specific way. For compatiblity with semantic web languages, the use of URIs instead of standard predicates or term names is allowed.

Graal is provided with a dlgp parser and writer. It comes also with a translator of OWL 2, built on the OWL API. This tool processes OWL 2 axioms that can be translated into existential rules and ignores the others.

Example 15 (Rules R_{8a} and R_{8b} in dlgp format).

```
[R8a]criticalManager(X):-isManagerOf(X,Y),hasArea(Y,Z),sensitiveArea(Z).
[R8b]isManagerOf(X,Y),hasArea(Y,Z),sensitiveArea(Z):-criticalManager(X).
```

Decomposition Tools. As already explained, existential variables in rule heads 'glue' atoms into subsets ('pieces') that have to be processed as a whole. Formally, a *piece* P in a rule head H is a non-empty and inclusion-minimal subset of H such that: for all $A \in P$ and A' in H, if A and A' share an existential variable, then $A' \in P$. A rule head is said to be *single-piece* (resp. *atomic*) if it is composed of a single-piece (resp. a single atom).

A piece of a rule R can be seen as a 'unit' of knowledge brought by an application of R. Indeed, R can be decomposed into an equivalent set of single-piece-head rules with the same body; furthermore, a rule with a single-piece-head cannot be decomposed into an equivalent set of atomic-head rules, except by adding a new predicate.

Example 16 (Running example). Rule R_0 has no existential variable, thus each atom forms a piece. It can be decomposed into: $\{R_{0,1} = project(x, y, z, w) \to hasArea(x, y),\ R_{0,2} = project(x, y, z, w) \to hasScManager(x, z),\ R_{0,3} = project(x, y, z, w) \to hasAdmManager(x, w)\}$.

By adding a special predicate, one can always decompose an existential rule into atomic-head rules. Hence, without loss of expressivity one could restrict attention to such rules. However, breaking the rule pieces has several drawbacks. First, it leads to a less accurate analysis of dependencies between rules. Second, it leads to less efficient query rewriting (we refer the reader to the experiments reported in [KLMT15]). Finally, it can even make the forward chaining infinite because it prevents from detecting some redundancies in the saturated facts as shows Example 17.

Example 17. Consider the rule $R = p(x) \to r(x, y) \wedge r(y, y) \wedge p(y)$ and its decomposition into atomic-head rules: $\{\ R_1 = p(x) \to p_R(x, y),\ R_2 = p_R(x, y) \to r(x, y),\ R_3 = p_R(x, y) \to r(y, y),\ R_4 = p_R(x, y) \to p(y)\ \}$. Let $\mathcal{F} = \{p(a)\}$. The restricted chase with R halts on this instance. The first application of R generates $\mathcal{F}_1 = \{p(a), r(a, y_0), r(y_0, y_0), p(y_0)\}$. The next application generates $\mathcal{F}_2 = \{p(a),\ r(a, y_0),\ r(y_0, y_0),\ p(y_0),\ r(y_0, y_1),\ r(y_1, y_1),\ p(y_1)\}$ that folds into $\mathcal{F}_1$ (with both y_0 and y_1 being mapped to y_0).

Graal provides these two transformations of rules for convenience, however only the decomposition into single-piece heads is exploited in reasoning algorithms, since the other one is always less efficient.

Analysis of a Rule Set. Graal also provides a rule base analyser, which was first developed as Kiabora, available online.[4] We briefly explain why such an analysis may be useful. Since ontological query answering is undecidable for general existential rules, neither forward nor backward chaining mechanisms

---

[4] http://www.lirmm.fr/kiabora

may halt. Therefore, some 'abstract' properties of rule sets have been defined, in relation with the kind of algorithm that halts on rule sets satisfying these properties. These properties are the following:

- *FES*. A rule set is a *finite expansion set* when, for any fact base $\mathcal{F}$, $\mathcal{F}^*$ is equivalent to a finite fact base (hence, a forward chaining algorithm able to detect equivalent fact bases halts).
- *FUS*. A rule set is a *finite unification set* when, for any CQ Q, the set of all rewritings that can be obtained by a sequence of direct rewritings from Q has a finite cover (hence, a breadth-first query rewriting algorithm that maintains a minimal cover halts).
- *BTS*. A rule set is a *bounded treewidth set* when, for any fact base $\mathcal{F}$, $\mathcal{F}^*$ has bounded treewidth, even if it may be infinite (see [TBMR12] for an algorithm).

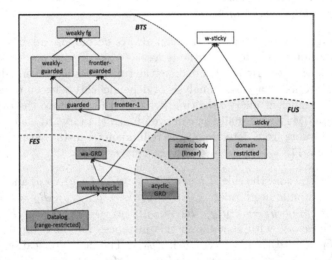

Fig. 1. Decidable classes processed by the analyser

These abstract properties are not recognizable. However, many concrete classes of rules have been exhibited, whose syntactic properties ensure the satisfaction of one or several of the abstract properties. Figure 1 pictures the concrete classes currently recognized by the rule analyser; for an overview of these classes, see, e.g., [Mug11].

Furthermore, the analyser uses the graph of rule dependencies as a tool to improve decidability recognition. Indeed, some global properties on this graph allows one to combine FES, FUS or BTS behaviors to obtain a halting procedure. For instance, if no rule from a subset processed as FES depends on a rule from a subset processed as FUS, one can first saturate the fact base with the FES rules, rewrite the query with the FUS rules, and finally query the partially saturated fact base with the obtained rewritings. For more details on the decidability recognition module, the reader is referred to [LMR13].

7   Conclusion

We presented the main features of Graal, a java toolkit devoted to existential rules and oriented toward ontological query answering. Graal is a modular tool, with minimal dependencies between modules, which allows to embed part of it in another sofware. It is designed to be easily customized or extended. Its core is a set of java interfaces that can be implemented to plug in other storage sytems, input /output formats, or new algorithms. Future work includes processing negative constraints and equality in rules, providing other exchange formats, such as the Datalog+ fragment of RuleML, and implementing other query answering algorithms as well as approaches allowing to combine them, as initiated in Kiabora rule analyser.

References

BLMS11. Baget, J.-F., Leclère, M., Mugnier, M.-L., Salvat, E.: On Rules with Existential Variables: Walking the Decidability Line. Artif. Intell. **175**(9–10), 1620–1654 (2011)

CDL+07. Calvanese, D., De Giacomo, G., Lembo, D., Lenzerini, M., Rosati, R.: Tractable Reasoning and Efficient Query Answering in Description Logics: The DL-Lite Family. J. Autom. Reasoning **39**(3), 385–429 (2007)

CGL09. Calì, A., Gottlob, G., Lukasiewicz, T.: A general datalog-based framework for tractable query answering over ontologies. In: PODS pp. 77–86 (2009)

CGP10. Calì, A., Gottlob, G., Pieris, A.: Query answering under non-guarded rules in datalog+/-. In: Hitzler, P., Lukasiewicz, T. (eds.) RR 2010. LNCS, vol. 6333, pp. 1–17. Springer, Heidelberg (2010)

CTS11. Chortaras, A., Trivela, D., Stamou, G.: Optimized query rewriting for OWL 2 QL. In: Bjørner, N., Sofronie-Stokkermans, V. (eds.) CADE 2011. LNCS, vol. 6803, pp. 192–206. Springer, Heidelberg (2011)

FKMP05. Fagin, R., Kolaitis, P.G., Miller, R.J., Popa, L.: Data exchange: semantics and query answering. Theor. Comput. Sci. **336**(1), 89–124 (2005)

GOP14. Gottlob, G., Orsi, G., Pieris, A.: Query Rewriting and Optimization for Ontological Databases. ACM Trans. Database Syst. **39**(3), 25 (2014)

GPH05. Guo, Y., Pan, Z., Heflin, J.: LUBM: A Benchmark for OWL Knowledge Base Systems. J. Web Sem. **3**(2–3), 158–182 (2005)

KLM15. König, M., Leclère, M., Mugnier, M.-L.: Query rewriting for existential rules with compiled preorder. In: IJCAI (2015)

KLMT15. König, M., Leclère, M., Mugnier, M.-L., Thomazo, M.: Sound, Complete and Minimal UCQ-Rewriting for Existential Rules. Sem. Web J. (2015, to appear)

LMR13. Leclère, M., Mugnier, M.-L., Rocher, S.: Kiabora: an analyzer of existential rule bases. In: Faber, W., Lembo, D. (eds.) RR 2013. LNCS, vol. 7994, pp. 241–246. Springer, Heidelberg (2013)

LSTW13. Lutz, C., Seylan, I., Toman, D., Wolter, F.: The combined approach to OBDA: taming role hierarchies using filters. In: Alani, H., et al. (eds.) ISWC 2013, Part I. LNCS, vol. 8218, pp. 314–330. Springer, Heidelberg (2013)

Mug11. Mugnier, M.-L.: Ontological query answering with existential rules. In: Rudolph, S., Gutierrez, C. (eds.) RR 2011. LNCS, vol. 6902, pp. 2–23. Springer, Heidelberg (2011)

PHM09. Pérez-Urbina, H., Horrocks, I., Motik, B.: Efficient query answering for OWL 2. In: Bernstein, A., Karger, D.R., Heath, T., Feigenbaum, L., Maynard, D., Motta, E., Thirunarayan, K. (eds.) ISWC 2009. LNCS, vol. 5823, pp. 489–504. Springer, Heidelberg (2009)

PLC⁺08. Poggi, A., Lembo, D., Calvanese, D., De Giacomo, G., Lenzerini, M., Rosati, R.: Linking Data to Ontologies. J. Data Semantics **10**, 133–173 (2008)

RC12. Rodriguez-Muro, M., Calvanese, D.: High performance query answering over dl-lite ontologies. In: KR (2012)

RMKZ13. Rodriguez-Muro, M., Kontchakov, R., Zakharyaschev, M.: Query rewriting and optimisation with database dependencies in ontop. In: DL 2013, pp. 917–929 (2013)

TBMR12. Thomazo, M., Baget, J.-F., Mugnier, M.-L., Rudolph, S.: A generic querying algorithm for greedy sets of existential rules. In: KR (2012)

TSCS13. Trivela, D., Stoilos, G., Chortaras, A., Stamou, G.B.: Optimising resolution-based rewriting algorithms for dl ontologies. In: DL 2013, pp. 464–476 (2013)

Legal Rules and Reasoning Track

Input/Output STIT Logic
for Normative Systems

Xin Sun[✉]

Faculty of Science, Technology and Communication,
University of Luxembourg, Walferdange, Luxembourg
xin.sun@uni.lu

Abstract. In this paper we study input/output STIT logic. We introduce the semantics, proof theory and prove the completeness theorem. Input/output STIT logic has more expressive power than Makinson and van der Torre's input/output logic. We show that input/output STIT logic is decidable and free from Ross' paradox.

Keywords: Input/output logic · STIT · Norm

1 Introduction

In recent years, normative multi-agent system [2,7] arises as a new interdisciplinary academic area bringing together researchers from multi-agent system [22], deontic logic [9] and normative system [1,10]. Norms play an important role in normative multi-agent system. They are heavily used in agent cooperation and coordination, group decision making, multi-agent organizations, electronic institutions, and so on.

In the first volume of the handbook of deontic logic and normative systems [9], input/output logic [14–17] appears as one of the new achievement in deontic logic in recent years. Input/output logic takes its origin in the study of conditional norms. Unlike the modal logic framework, which usually uses possible world semantics, input/output logic adopts mainly operational semantics: a normative system is conceived in input/output logic as a deductive machine, like a black box which produces normative statements as output, when we feed it descriptive statements as input.

Boella and van der Torre [6] extends input/output logic to reasoning about constitutive norms. Tosatto *et al.* [8] adapts it to represent and reason about abstract normative systems. For a comprehensive introduction to input/output logic, see Parent and van der Torre [17]. A technical toolbox to build input/output logic is developed in Sun [21].

One limitation of Makinson and van der Torre's input/output logic is that it uses propositional logic as its base logic. Such treatment restricts its expressive power. For example, concepts such as agent, action and ability which are crucial for agent theory and multi-agent system, are unable to be expressed in

© Springer International Publishing Switzerland 2015
N. Bassiliades et al. (Eds.): RuleML 2015, LNCS 9202, pp. 347–359, 2015.
DOI: 10.1007/978-3-319-21542-6_22

input/output logic. To overcome this limitation, we need a more expressive logic to be the base of input/output logic.

STIT theory or STIT logic [5], is one of the most prominent accounts of agency in philosophy of action. It is the logic of constructions of the form "agent i sees to it that ϕ holds". STIT logic has strong expressive power. Notions like agent, action and ability can be expressed in STIT logic. Therefore STIT logic is an ideal candidate to build new input/output logic. But there are various STIT logic: individual STIT and group STIT, achieve STIT and deliberative STIT. In this paper we choose *individual deliberative* STIT logic as the basis to develop input/output logic. We make this choice for the following reasons:

1. Compared to Makinson and van der Torre's input/output logic, this input/output STIT logic has more expressive power.
2. Choosing individual STIT makes our logic decidable, while if we choose group STIT we lose decidability.
3. By choosing deliberative STIT, our logic is free from a well known paradox, Ross' paradox, which is a challenge for lots of deontic logic, including Makinson and van der Torre's input/output logic. If we choose achieve STIT, we are not free from Ross' paradox.

The structure of this paper is as follows: we recap some background knowledge, including some basic concepts and results of STIT logic, in the Section 2. Then in Section 3 and 4 we study the proof theory, semantics, completeness and decidability of input/output STIT logic. We show that input/output STIT logic solves Ross' paradox in Section 5. We discuss research avenues for future work and conclude this paper in Section 6.

2   Background

Given a countable set $\mathbb{P}$ of propositional letters and a finite set Agt of agents, the language of individual STIT logic $\mathfrak{L}$ is defined by the following BNF: for every $p \in \mathbb{P}$ and $i \in Agt$,

$$\varphi ::= p \mid \neg\varphi \mid (\varphi \wedge \varphi) \mid [i^d]\varphi \mid \Box\varphi$$

Intuitively $[i^d]\varphi$ is read as "agent i deliberately sees to it that φ", $\Box\varphi$ is read as "necessary φ". We use $[i]\varphi$, read as "agent i successfully sees to it that φ", as an abbreviation of $[i^d]\varphi \vee \Box\varphi$. We use $\Diamond\varphi$ to represent $\neg\Box\neg\varphi$.

In the literature $[i^d]$ is called "deliberative STIT" and $[i]$ is called "achieve STIT" (or Chellas' STIT). Intuitively, $[i]\varphi$ simply means i sees to it that φ holds, while $[i^d]\varphi$ means i not only sees to it that φ holds, but also φ can be false without the action of i. Deliberative STIT and achieve STIT are inter-definable because $[i]\phi$ is equivalent to $[i^d]\varphi \vee \Box\varphi$, while $[i^d]\phi$ is equivalent to $[i]\varphi \wedge \neg\Box\varphi$. We will introduce the semantics and axiomatic system via achieve STIT, and build our input/output logic on deliberative STIT.

In STIT logic, actions are expressed as relations between agents and effects: $[i]\phi$ is an action which means "agent i ensures the world is among those satisfying

ϕ". Agent's ability is expressed by $\Diamond[i]\varphi$ meaning that agent i has the ability to ensure the world is among those satisfying ϕ.

The semantics of STIT logic is originally defined by the branching-time choice structure. A simpler possible world semantics for group STIT is proposed by Kooi and Tamminga [13]. Here we simplify it for individual STIT.

Definition 1 (Possible world semantics). *A model is a tuple* $M = (W, Choice, V)$, *where*

1. W *is a nonempty set of possible worlds,*
2. $V : \mathbb{P} \mapsto 2^W$ *is the valuation for propositional letters.*
3. *Choice is a choice function which satisfies the following conditions:*
   (a) *for every* $i \in Agt$ *it holds that* $Choice(i)$ *is a partition of* W;
   (b) *for* $Agt = \{1, ..., n\}$, *for every* $x_1 \in Choice(1), ..., x_n \in Choice(n)$,
   $x_1 \cap ... \cap x_n \neq \emptyset$;

Let R_i be the equivalence relation induced by $Choice(i)$. That is, $(w, w') \in R_i$ iff there is $K \in Choice(i)$ such that $\{w, w'\} \subseteq K$. Given a model M and a world $w \in M$, formulas of $\mathfrak{L}$ is evaluated as follows:

- $M, w \models p$ iff $w \in V(p)$ for all $p \in \mathbb{P}$.
- $M, w \models \neg\varphi$ iff not $M, w \models \varphi$.
- $M, w \models \varphi \wedge \psi$ iff $M, w \models \varphi$ and $M, w \models \psi$.
- $M, w \models \Box\varphi$ iff $M, w' \models \varphi$ for all $w' \in W$.
- $M, w \models [i]\varphi$ iff $M, w' \models \varphi$ for all w' such that $(w, w') \in R_i$.

A formula $\phi \in \mathfrak{L}$ is valid iff for all model M and all $w \in M$, if $M, w \models \phi$. ϕ is satisfiable iff there are some model M and some $w \in M$ such that $M, w \models \phi$. ϕ is a logical consequence of a set of formulas Φ if for all model M and all $w \in M$, if $M, w \models \psi$ for all $\psi \in \Phi$, then $M, w \models \phi$. The individual STIT logic is axiomatized by the following axioms [4,5]:

1. all instances of propositional tautologies
2. the axiom schemas of $S5$ for $\Box$
3. the axiom schemas of $S5$ for every $[i]$
4. $\Box\varphi \rightarrow [i]\varphi$
5. $(\Diamond[0]\varphi_0 \wedge ... \wedge \Diamond[k]\varphi_k) \rightarrow \Diamond([0]\varphi_0 \wedge ... \wedge [k]\varphi_k)$

The derivation rules of STIT logic is modus ponens and necessitation for $\Box$. A formula φ is a derivable ($\vdash \varphi$) iff it is derivable via the above axiomatic system. We use $\psi \vdash \varphi$ to represent $\vdash \psi \rightarrow \varphi$.

Theorem 1 ([5]). *For every* $\phi \in \mathfrak{L}$, $\models \phi$ *iff* $\vdash \phi$.

The satisfiability problem of individual STIT logic is the following decision problem: given a formula ϕ, is ϕ satisfiable? Balbiani *et al* [4] show that this problem is solvable in exponential time by a non-deterministic Turing machine.

Theorem 2 ([4]). *The complexity of the satisfiability problem of individual STIT logic is in NEXPTIME.*

3   Input/Output STIT Logic

Input/output logic adopts mainly operational semantics. The procedure of operational semantics is divided into three stages. In the first stage, we have in hand a set of propositions (call it the input) as a description of the current state. We then apply logical operators to this set, say close the set by logical consequence. Then we pass this set to a deductive machine and we reach the second stage. In the second stage, the machine accepts the input and produces a set of propositions as output. In the third stage, we accept the output and apply logical operators to it. A more formal explanation relies on the following terminologies.

A normative system $N \subseteq \mathcal{L} \times \mathcal{L}$ is a set of ordered pairs of formulas. A pair $(\phi, \psi) \in N$, call it a norm, is read as "given ϕ, it ought to be ψ". N is viewed as a function (or a deductive machine) from $2^{\mathcal{L}}$ to $2^{\mathcal{L}}$ such that for a set Φ of formulas, $N(\Phi) = \{\psi \mid (\phi, \psi) \in N \text{ for some } \phi \in \Phi\}$. Let $Cn(\Phi) = \{\phi \in \mathcal{L} : \Phi \models \phi\}$.

3.1   Simple-Minded

Definition 2 (Simple-minded output). *Given a set of norms $N \subseteq \mathcal{L} \times \mathcal{L}$ and a set of formulas $\Phi \subseteq \mathcal{L}$,*

$$O_1(N, \Phi) = Cn(N(Cn(\Phi))).$$

The idea behind simple-minded input/output STIT logic O_1 is: we first take a set of formulas representing facts, then we close it under logical consequence. We further pass this closed set to the deductive machine (*i.e.* the normative system). The deductive machine produces a set of formulas representing obligations. We finally close obligations under logical consequence.

Example 1. Suppose a, b, x, y are propositional letters, i, j are agents. Let $N = \{(a, [i]x), (a, [j]y), (b, x \wedge y)\}$. Then $O_1(N, \{a\}) = Cn(N(Cn(\{a\}))) = Cn(\{[i]x, [j]y\})$. $\qquad\square$

On the proof-theoretical side, input/output STIT logics are characterized by derivation rules about norms. Given a set of norms N, a derivation system is the smallest set of norms which extends N and is closed under certain derivation rules. The following are the rules we will use:

- SI (strengthening the input): from (ϕ_1, ψ) to (ϕ_2, ψ) whenever $\models \phi_2 \rightarrow \phi_1$
- WO (weakening the output): from (ϕ, ψ_1) to (ϕ, ψ_2) whenever $\models \psi_1 \rightarrow \psi_2$
- AND (conjunction of the output): from (ϕ, ψ_1) and (ϕ, ψ_2) to $(\phi, \psi_1 \wedge \psi_2)$
- OR (disjunction of the input): from (ϕ_1, ψ) and (ϕ_2, ψ) to $(\phi_1 \vee \phi_2, \psi)$
- CT (cumulative transitivity): from (ϕ, ψ_1) and $(\phi \wedge \psi_1, \psi_2)$ to (ϕ, ψ_2)

The derivation system of simple-minded input/output STIT logic, $D_1(N)$, is decided by the rules SI, WO and AND. Adding OR to $D_1(N)$ gives $D_2(N)$, the derivation system of basic input/output STIT logic. Adding CT to $D_1(N)$ gives $D_3(N)$, the derivation system of simple-minded reusable input/output STIT logic. All the five rules together gives the derivation system of basic reusable input/output STIT logic.

Example 2. Suppose a, b, x, y are propositional letters, i, j are agents. Let $N = \{(a \vee b, [j]x)\}$, then $([i]b, [j](x \vee y)) \in D_1(N)$ because we have the following derivation

1. $(a \vee b, [j]x)$ Assumption
2. $([i]b, [j]x)$ 1, SI
3. $([i]b, [j](x \vee y))$ 2, WO

Theorem 3. *Given $N \subseteq \mathfrak{L} \times \mathfrak{L}$, $\psi \in O_1(N, \{\phi\})$ iff $(\phi, \psi) \in D_1(N)$.*

Proof. Using technics from Sun [20], the proof is routine and here we omit it. ⊣

3.2 Basic

Simple-minded output O_1 is unable to process disjunctive input intelligently: from input $\Phi = \{\phi_1 \vee \phi_2\}$ and normative system $N = \{(\phi_1, \psi), (\phi_2, \psi)\}$ we don't have $\psi \in O_1(N, \Phi)$. Basic output O_2 strengthens O_1 to make up for such deficiency.

Definition 3 (Basic output). *Given a set of norms $N \subseteq \mathfrak{L} \times \mathfrak{L}$ and a set of formulas $\Phi \subseteq \mathfrak{L}$,*

$$O_2(N, \Phi) = \bigcap \{Cn(N(Cn(\Psi))) : \Phi \subseteq \Psi, \Psi \text{ is disjunctive}\}.$$

Here a set Ψ is disjunctive if for all $\phi \vee \psi \in \Psi$, either $\phi \in \Psi$ or $\psi \in \Psi$.

It can be verified that from input $\Phi = \{\phi_1 \vee \phi_2\}$ and normative system $N = \{(\phi_1, \psi), (\phi_2, \psi)\}$ we have $\psi \in O_2(N, \Phi)$. The following completeness theorem shows that O_2 corresponds to the derivation system D_2 where the rule disjunction of the input is involved.

Theorem 4. *Given $N \subseteq \mathfrak{L} \times \mathfrak{L}$, $\psi \in O_2(N, \{\phi\})$ iff $(\phi, \psi) \in D_2(N)$.*

Proof. ($\Rightarrow$) Assume $(\phi, \psi) \in D_2(N)$, we prove by induction on the length of derivation.

Base step: assume $(\phi, \psi) \in N$. Then $\psi \in N(\{\phi\}) \subseteq N(Cn(\phi)) \subseteq \bigcap \{N(Cn(\Psi)) : \phi \in \Psi, \Psi \text{ is disjunctive}\} \subseteq \bigcap \{ Cn(N(Cn(\Psi))) : \phi \in \Psi, \Psi \text{ is disjunctive}\} = O_2(N, \{\phi\})$.

Inductive step: here we only prove the case (ϕ, ψ) is derived by the OR rule in the last step of derivation. Other cases are easier. Assume there are $(\phi_1, \psi) \in D_2(N)$, $(\phi_2, \psi) \in D_2(N)$ and ϕ is $\phi_1 \vee \phi_2$. By induction hypothesis we know $\psi \in O_2(N, \phi_1)$ and $\psi \in O_2(N, \phi_2)$. Now for every set of formulas E such that $\phi \in E$ and E is disjunctive, we have $\phi_1 \vee \phi_2 \in E$ since ϕ is $\phi_1 \vee \phi_2$. Note that E is disjunctive, so we further have either $\phi_1 \in E$ or $\phi_2 \in E$. If $\phi_1 \in E$, then E is a disjunctive set contains ϕ_1. So we have $\psi \in O_2(N, \phi_1) = \bigcap \{Cn(N(Cn(B)) : \phi_1 \in B, B \text{ is disjunctive}\} \subseteq Cn(N(Cn(E)))$. Hence $\psi \in Cn(N(Cn(E)))$. If $\phi_2 \in E$, we can similarly deduce $\psi \in Cn(N(Cn(E)))$. Therefore no matter $\phi_1 \in E$ or $\phi_2 \in E$, we have $\psi \in Cn(N(Cn(E)))$. Therefore $\psi \in O_2(N, \phi)$.

($\Leftarrow$) Assume $\psi \in O_2(N,\phi)$, then $\psi \in \bigcap\{Cn(N(Cn(B)) : \phi \in B, B$ is disjunctive$\}$. Let $\{B_1, \ldots, B_n\}$ be the set of all minimal disjunctive extensions of $\{\phi\}$. Therefore we have $\psi \in Cn(N(Cn(B_i)))$ for each $i \in \{1, \ldots, n\}$.

Each B_i corresponds to a branch of the disjunctive parsing tree, defined in Definition 4, of ϕ. Note that formulas in B_i can be strictly ordered by their length. Let ϕ_i be the shortest formula of B_i. Then for each $\chi \in B_i$, $\models \phi_i \to \chi$.

Then we know $\psi \in Cn(N(Cn(\phi_i)))$. Hence there are $\psi_{i1}, \ldots, \psi_{ik} \in N(Cn(\phi_i))$ such that $\psi_{i1} \wedge \ldots \wedge \psi_{ik} \models \psi$. Then by SI we know $(\phi_i, \psi_{i1}), \ldots, (\phi_i, \psi_{ik}) \in D_2(N)$. Then by AND and WO we know $(\phi_i, \psi) \in D_2(N)$. Now by Lemma 2 we know $(\phi, \psi) \in D_2(N)$. $\dashv$

Definition 4 (disjunctive parsing tree). *Given a formula $\phi \in \mathfrak{L}$, the disjunctive parsing tree $P(\phi)$ is a tree such that:*

(a) ϕ is the root of $P(\phi)$.
(b) Every node which is not a leaf has arity 2.
(c) A node ψ has daughters ψ_1 and ψ_2 iff ψ is $\psi_1 \vee \psi_2$.
(d) We define the height for each node as follows: every leaf has height 0. If μ is a node with daughters ν_1, ν_2, then the height of μ is $max\{height(\nu_1), height(\nu_2)\} + 1$.

Lemma 1. *For every formula ϕ, every branch of $P(\phi)$ is a disjunctive set.*

Proof. Let B be an arbitrary branch of $P(\phi)$. For every $\phi_1 \vee \phi_2 \in B$, we know ϕ_1 and ϕ_2 are the only daughters of $\phi_1 \vee \phi_2$. Therefore B contains either ϕ_1 or ϕ_2. Hence B is disjunctive. $\dashv$

Lemma 2. *Let (ϕ, ψ) be a norm and N a normative system. If for every B_i which is a branch of $P(\phi)$, there exist $\phi_i \in B_i$ such that $(\phi_i, \psi) \in N$, then $(\phi, \psi) \in D_2(N)$.*

Proof. Since the length of ϕ is always finite, we know $P(\phi)$ is also finite. So we assume $\{B_1, \ldots, B_n\}$ is the set of all branches of $P(\phi)$.

Here we just consider the worst case, other cases are easier. In the worst case we have for every B_i, the element $\phi_i \in B_i$ such that $(\phi_i, \psi) \in N$ is of height 0. Then by applying the OR rule finitely many times we know that for every $\phi_i' \in B_i$ with $height(\phi_i') = 1$, $(\phi_i', \psi) \in D_2(N)$. Similarly we can deduce that for every $\phi_i'' \in B_i$ with $height(\phi_i'') = 2$, $(\phi_i'', \psi) \in D_2(N)$. This progress can go on and on and we will eventually have $(\phi, \psi) \in D_2(N)$ since the height of ϕ is finite. $\dashv$

3.3 Simple-Minded Reusable

In certain situations, it may be appropriate for outputs to be available for recycling as inputs. On the syntactic level, such a principle of reusability is expressed by the rule CT. On the semantic level, we define simple-minded reusable output O_3 to implement reusability.

Definition 5 (Simple-minded reusable output). *Given a set of norms $N \subseteq \mathfrak{L} \times \mathfrak{L}$ and a set of formulas $\Phi \subseteq \mathfrak{L}$, We define a function $f_\Phi^N : 2^\mathfrak{L} \to 2^\mathfrak{L}$ such that $f_\Phi^N(X) = Cn(\Phi \cup N(X))$, for all $X \in 2^\mathfrak{L}$. It can be proved that f_Φ^N is monotonic with respect to the set theoretical $\subseteq$ relation, and $(2^\mathfrak{L}, \subseteq)$ is a complete lattice. Then by Tarski's fixed point theorem there exist a least fixed point of f_Φ^N. Let B_Φ^N be the least fixed point of f_Φ^N,*

$$O_3(N, \Phi) = Cn(N(B_\Phi^N)).$$

We use B_ϕ^N as an abbreviation of $B_{\{\phi\}}^N$. The following theorem shows that the syntactic approach D_3 and the semantics approach O_3 coincide.

Theorem 5. *Given $N \subseteq \mathfrak{L} \times \mathfrak{L}$, $\psi \in O_3(N, \{\phi\})$ iff $(\phi, \psi) \in D_3(N)$.*

Proof. The proof mainly uses technics from Sun [20].
($\Leftarrow$) Assume $(\phi, \psi) \in D_3(N)$, then we prove by induction on the length of derivation.

- (Base step) Assume $(\phi, \psi) \in N$, then by Lemma 4 we have $\phi \in B_\phi^N$. Hence $\psi \in N(B_\phi^N) \subseteq Cn(N(B_\phi^N))$.
- Assume $(\phi, \psi) \in D_3(N)$ and it is derived by using SI from $(\chi, \psi) \in D_3(N)$ and $\models \phi \to \chi$. Then by inductive hypothesis we have $\psi \in Cn(N(B_\chi^N))$. By Lemma 6 we know $B_\chi^N \subseteq B_\phi^N$. Therefore we further have $N(B_\chi^N) \subseteq N(B_\phi^N)$, $Cn(N(B_\chi^N)) \subseteq Cn(N(B_\phi^N))$. Hence $\psi \in Cn(N(B_\phi^N))$.
- Assume $(\phi, \psi) \in D_3(N)$, ψ is $\psi_1 \wedge \psi_2$ and it is derived by using AND from (ϕ, ψ_1) and (ϕ, ψ_2). Then by inductive hypothesis we have $\psi_1 \in Cn(N(B_\phi^N))$ and $\psi_2 \in Cn(N(B_\phi^N))$. Therefore $\psi_1 \wedge \psi_2 \in Cn(N(B_\phi^N))$.
- Assume $(\phi, \psi) \in D_3(N)$ and it is derived by using WO from $(\phi, \psi_1) \in D_3(N)$ and $\models \psi_1 \to \psi$. Then by inductive hypothesis we have $\psi_1 \in Cn(N(B_\phi^N))$. Since $\models \psi_1 \to \psi$, we can prove that $\psi \in Cn(N(B_\phi^N))$.
- Assume $(\phi, \psi) \in D_3(N)$ and it is derived by using CT form $(\phi, \psi_1) \in D_3(N)$ and $(\phi \wedge \psi_1, \psi) \in D_3(N)$. Then by inductive hypothesis we have $\psi_1 \in Cn(N(B_\phi^N))$ and $\psi \in Cn(N(B_{\phi \wedge \psi_1}^N))$. Then by Lemma 8 we have $B_\phi^N = B_{\phi \wedge \psi_1}^N$. Therefore $\psi \in Cn(N(B_\phi^N))$.

($\Rightarrow$) Assume $\psi \in Cn(N(B_\phi^N))$, then there exist $\psi^1, \dots, \psi^n \in N(B_\phi^N)$ such that $\psi^1 \wedge \dots \wedge \psi^n \models \psi$. For each $i \in \{1, \dots, n\}$, from $\psi^i \in N(B_\phi^N)$ we know there is $\phi^i \in B_\phi^N$ such that $(\phi^i, \psi^i) \in N$. From $\phi^i \in B_\phi^N$ we know there exist k such that $\phi^i \in B_{\phi,k}^N$. Now by Lemma 9 we know $(\phi, \psi^i) \in D_3(N)$. Then by applying the AND rule we have $(\phi, \psi^1 \wedge \dots \psi^n) \in D_3(N)$. Then by the WO rule we have $(\phi, \psi) \in D_3(N)$. $\dashv$

Lemma 3. $B_\Phi^N = \bigcup_{i=0}^\infty B_{\Phi,i}^N$, where $B_{\Phi,0}^N = Cn(\Phi)$, $B_{\Phi,i+1}^N = Cn(\Phi \cup N(B_{\Phi,i}^N))$.

Proof. We first prove that $\bigcup_{i=0}^\infty B_{\Phi,i}^N$ is a fixed point of f_Φ^N. We prove by showing the following:

1. $\Phi \subseteq \bigcup_{i=0}^{\infty} B_{\Phi,i}^N$: this is because $\Phi \subseteq Cn(\Phi) = B_{\Phi,0}^N \subseteq \bigcup_{i=0}^{\infty} B_{\Phi,i}^N$.
2. $N(\bigcup_{i=0}^{\infty} B_{\Phi,i}^N) \subseteq \bigcup_{i=0}^{\infty} B_{\Phi,i}^N$: For every $\phi \in N(\bigcup_{i=0}^{\infty} B_{\Phi,i}^N)$, there exist k such that $\phi \in N(B_{\Phi,k}^N) \subseteq B_{\Phi,k+1}^N \subseteq \bigcup_{i=0}^{\infty} B_{\Phi,i}^N$.
3. $Cn(\bigcup_{i=0}^{\infty} B_{\Phi,i}^N) = \bigcup_{i=0}^{\infty} B_{\Phi,i}^N$: the right-to-left direction is obvious; for the other direction: assume $\phi \in Cn(\bigcup_{i=0}^{\infty} B_{\Phi,i}^N)$, then there exist $\phi_1, \ldots \phi_n \in \bigcup_{i=0}^{\infty} B_{\Phi,i}^N$ such that $\models \phi_1 \wedge \ldots \wedge \phi_n \to \phi$. Therefore there exist k such that $\phi_1, \ldots \phi_n \in B_{\Phi,k}^N$. Hence $\phi \in B_{\Phi,k+1}^N \subseteq \bigcup_{i=0}^{\infty} B_{\Phi,i}^N$.

With the above items in hand, we can prove that $f_{\Phi}^N(\bigcup_{i=0}^{\infty} B_{\Phi,i}^N) \subseteq \bigcup_{i=0}^{\infty} B_{\Phi,i}^N$. For the other direction, we prove by induction on i that for every i, $B_{\Phi,i}^N \subseteq f_{\Phi}^N(\bigcup_{i=0}^{\infty} B_{\Phi,i}^N)$. Here we omit the details.

So we have proved that $\bigcup_{i=0}^{\infty} B_{\Phi,i}^N$ is a fixed point of f_{Φ}^N. To prove that it is the least fixed point, we can again prove by induction that for every i, $B_{\Phi,i}^N \subseteq f_{\Phi}^N(B)$, where B is a fixed point of f_{Φ}^N. Here we omit the details.   ⊣

Lemma 4. *For every* $\Phi \subseteq \mathfrak{L}, N \subseteq \mathfrak{L} \times \mathfrak{L}, \Phi \subseteq B_{\Phi}^N$.

Proof. By Lemma 3, the proof is trivial.   ⊣

Lemma 5. *For every* $\phi \in \mathfrak{L}, N \subseteq \mathfrak{L} \times \mathfrak{L}, B_{\phi}^N = Cn(B_{\phi}^N)$.

Proof. By Lemma 3, the proof is easy.   ⊣

Lemma 6. *For every* $\phi, \psi \in \mathfrak{L}, N \subseteq \mathfrak{L} \times \mathfrak{L}$, *if* $\models \phi \to \psi$ *then* $B_{\psi}^N \subseteq B_{\phi}^N$.

Proof. We will prove that for every i, $B_{\psi,i}^N \subseteq B_{\phi,i}^N$. We prove by induction on i.

If $i = 0$, then $B_{\psi,0}^N = Cn(\psi) \subseteq Cn(\phi) \subseteq B_{\phi,0}^N$. Assume $i = k + 1$ and $B_{\psi,k}^N \subseteq B_{\phi,k}^N$. Then $B_{\psi,k+1}^N = Cn(\{\psi\} \cup N(B_{\psi,k}^N))$. From $B_{\psi,k}^N \subseteq B_{\phi,k}^N$ we deduce $N(B_{\psi,k}^N) \subseteq N(B_{\phi,k}^N)$. Now by the monotony of $Cn(\bullet)$ we know $Cn(\{\psi\} \cup N(B_{\psi,k}^N)) \subseteq Cn(\{\phi\} \cup N(B_{\phi,k}^N))$. Hence $B_{\psi,k+1}^N \subseteq B_{\phi,k+1}^N$.

So we have proved for every i, $B_{\psi,i}^N \subseteq B_{\phi,i}^N$. With this result in hand, we can easily deduce that $B_{\psi}^N \subseteq B_{\phi}^N$.   ⊣

Lemma 7. *If* $\psi \in Cn(N(B_{\phi}^N))$, *then* $\psi \in B_{\phi}^N$.

Proof. By Lemma 3, it is easy to verify that $N(B_{\phi}^N) \subseteq B_{\phi}^N$ and $Cn(B_{\phi}^N) \subseteq B_{\phi}^N$. The result then follows.

Lemma 8. *If* $\psi \in Cn(N(B_{\phi}^N))$, *then* $B_{\phi}^N = B_{\phi \wedge \psi}^N$.

Proof. It's easy to prove that $B_{\phi}^N \subseteq B_{\phi \wedge \psi}^N$. For the other direction, we need to prove that for every i, $B_{\phi \wedge \psi,i}^N \subseteq B_{\phi}^N$. We prove this by induction on i.

- Base step: Let $i = 0$, we then have $B_{\phi \wedge \psi,i}^N = Cn(\phi \wedge \psi)$. By Lemma 4 we have $\phi \in B_{\phi}^N$. By Lemma 7 we have $\psi \in B_{\phi}^N$. Then by Lemma 5 we have $\phi \wedge \psi \in B_{\phi}^N$.

- Inductive step: Assume for $i = k$, $B^N_{\phi \wedge \psi, k} \subseteq B^N_\phi$. Then $B^N_{\phi \wedge \psi, k+1} = Cn(\{\phi \wedge \psi\} \cup N(B^N_{\phi \wedge \psi, k}))$. From $B^N_{\phi \wedge \psi, k} \subseteq B^N_\phi$ we know there exist j such that $B^N_{\phi \wedge \psi, k} \subseteq \bigcup_{i=0}^j B^N_{\phi, i}$. Therefore $N(B^N_{\phi \wedge \psi, k})) \subseteq N(\bigcup_{i=0}^j B^N_{\phi, i}) \subseteq \bigcup_{i=0}^{j+1} B^N_{\phi, i} \subseteq B^N_\phi$. So we have proved $N(B^N_{\phi \wedge \psi, k})) \subseteq B^N_\phi$. By the base step we have $\phi \wedge \psi \in B^N_\phi$. Then by Lemma 5 we know $Cn(\{\phi \wedge \psi\} \cup N(B^N_{\phi \wedge \psi, k})) \subseteq B^N_\phi$. That is, $B^N_{\phi \wedge \psi, k+1} \subseteq B^N_\phi$.

Lemma 9. *For all i, if $\chi \in B^N_{\phi, i}$ and $(\chi, \psi) \in N$, then $(\phi, \psi) \in D_3(N)$*

Proof. We prove by induction on i.

- Base step: Let $i = 0$. Then $\chi \in B^N_{\phi, 0} = Cn(\phi)$. Hence $\models \phi \rightarrow \chi$. Therefore we can apply SI to $\models \phi \rightarrow \chi$ and (χ, ψ) to derive (ϕ, ψ).
- Inductive step: Assume for $i = k$, if $\chi \in B^N_{\phi, k}$ and $(\chi, \psi) \in N$, then $(\phi, \psi) \in D_3(N)$. Now let $\chi \in B^N_{\phi, k+1}$. Then $\chi \in Cn(\{\phi\} \cup N(B^N_{\phi, k}))$, and there exist $\chi_1 \cdots \chi_n \in N(B^N_{\phi, k})$ such that $\phi \wedge \chi_1 \wedge \ldots \wedge \chi_n \models \chi$. Then apply SI to $(\chi, \psi) \in N$ and $\phi \wedge \chi_1 \wedge \ldots \wedge \chi_n \models \chi$ we have $(\phi \wedge \chi_1 \wedge \ldots \wedge \chi_n, x) \in D_3(N)$. Note that for each $i \in \{1, \ldots, n\}$, from $\chi_i \in N(B^N_{\phi, k})$ we know there is $\phi_i \in B^N_{\phi, k}$ such that $(\phi_i, \chi_i) \in N$. Now by inductive hypothesis we have $(\phi, \chi_i) \in D_3(N)$. Then applying the AND rule we have $(\phi, \chi_1 \wedge \ldots \wedge \chi_n) \in D_3(N)$. From $(\phi, \chi_1 \wedge \ldots \wedge \chi_n) \in D_3(N)$ and $(\phi \wedge \chi_1 \wedge \ldots \wedge \chi_n, \psi) \in D_3(N)$ we can adopt the CT rule to derive $(\phi, \psi) \in D_3(N)$.

4 Decidability

Concerning the decidability of input/output STIT logic, we study on the following problems:

- Compliance problem: given a finite set of norms N, a finite set of formulas Φ and a formula ψ, is $\psi \in O(N, \Phi)$?
- Violation problem: given a finite set of norms N, a finite set of formulas Φ and a formula ψ, is $\neg \psi \in O(N, \Phi)$?
- Compatibility problem: given a finite set of norms N, a finite set of formulas Φ and a formula ψ, is $\neg \psi \notin O(N, \Phi)$?

Intuitively, the compliance problem asks whether certain proposition complies the normative system. The violation problem asks whether certain proposition violates the normative system and the compatibility problem asks whether the normative system is compatible with certain proposition. Both the violation problem and the compatibility problem can be reduced to the compliance problem, therefore we only study the decidability of the compliance problem.

We prove that all the input/output STIT logic introduced in this paper is decidable by showing that the compliance problem is solvable by oracle Turing machines.

Definition 6 (oracle Turing machine [3]). *An oracle for a language L is a device that is capable of reporting whether any string w is a member of L. An oracle Truing machine M^L is a modified Turing machine that has the additional capability of querying an oracle. Whenever M^L writes a string on a special oracle tape it is informed whether that string is a member of L, in a single computation step.*

4.1 Simple-Minded

Theorem 6. *The compliance problem of simple-minded input/output STIT logic is decidable.*

Proof: We provide the following algorithm on an oracle Turing machine with oracle STIT-$SAT = \{\phi \in \mathfrak{L} : \phi$ is satisfiable$\}$ to solve the compliance problem of simple-minded input/output STIT logic.

Let $N = \{(\phi_1, \psi_1), \ldots, (\phi_n, \psi_n)\}$, $\varPhi$ be a finite set of formulas and ψ be a formula.

1. for each $\phi_i \in \{\phi_1, \ldots, \phi_n\}$, ask the oracle if $\neg(\bigwedge \varPhi \to \phi_i)$ is satisfiable.
   (a) If the oracle answer "no", then mark ψ_i
   (b) Otherwise do nothing.
2. Let $\psi_{i_1}, \ldots \psi_{i_k}$ be all those ψ_i which are marked in step 1.
3. Ask the oracle if $\neg(\psi_{i_1} \wedge \ldots \wedge \psi_{i_k} \to \psi)$ is satisfiable.
   (a) If the oracle answer "no", then return "accept"
   (b) Otherwise return "reject".

It can be verified that $\psi \in Cn(N(Cn(\varPhi)))$ iff the algorithm returns "accept". Therefore simple-minded input/output STIT logic is decidable.   ⊣

Remark 1. Here the decidability of individual STIT logic is crucial for the decidability of input/output STIT logic. If we choose group STIT, of which the satisfiability problem is undecidable [11], as our base logic, then our input/output STIT logic will be undecidable because the satisfiability problem of the base logic can be reduced to the compliance problem by making $N = \emptyset$.

Corollary 1. *The violation problem and compatibility problem of simple-minded input/output STIT logic is decidable.*

4.2 Basic

Theorem 7. *The compliance problem of basic input/output STIT logic is decidable.*

Proof: We provide the following algorithm on an oracle Turing machine with oracle STIT-SAT to solve the compliance problem.

Let $N = \{(\phi_1, \psi_1), \ldots, (\phi_n, \psi_n)\}$, $\varPhi = \{\chi_1, \ldots, \chi_m\}$ be a finite set of formulas and ψ be a formula.

1. Let $B_1, \ldots, B_m$ be the sequence of all minimal disjunctive extension of Φ.
2. Let $i = 1$.
3. Let $\Phi = B_i$.
4. for each $\phi_j \in \{\phi_1, \ldots, \phi_n\}$, ask the oracle if $\neg(\bigwedge \Phi \rightarrow \phi_i)$ is satisfiable.
   (a) If the oracle answer "no", then mark ψ_j
   (b) Otherwise do nothing.
5. Let $\psi_{j_1}, \ldots \psi_{j_k}$ be all those ψ_j which are marked in step 4.
6. Ask the oracle if $\neg(\psi_{j_1} \wedge \ldots \wedge \psi_{j_k} \rightarrow \psi)$ is satisfiable.
   (a) If the oracle answer "no", then let $i = i + 1$.
      i. if $i \leq m$, then goto step 3.
      ii. if $i = m + 1$, then return "accept"
   (b) Otherwise return "reject".

It can be verified that $\psi \in O_2(N, \Phi)$ iff the algorithm returns "accept". Therefore simple-minded input/output STIT logic is decidable.   ⊣

Corollary 2. *The violation problem and compatibility problem of basic input/output STIT logic is decidable.*

4.3   Simple-Minded Reusable

Theorem 8. *The compliance problem of simple-minded reusable input/output STIT logic is decidable.*

Proof: We provide the following algorithm on an oracle Turing machine with oracle STIT-*SAT* to solve the compliance problem of simple-minded reusable input/output STIT logic. The case for simple-minded input/output STIT logic is easier and left to the readers.

Let $N = \{(\phi_1, \psi_1), \ldots, (\phi_n, \psi_n)\}$, Φ be a finite set of formulas and ψ be a formula.

1. Let $X = \Phi, Y = Z = N, U = \emptyset$.
2. for each $(\phi_i, \psi_i) \in Y$, ask the oracle if $\neg(\bigwedge X \rightarrow \phi_i)$ is satisfiable
   (a) if "no", then let $X = X \cup \{\psi_i\}, Z = Z - \{(\phi_i, \psi_i)\}$.
   (b) Otherwise do nothing.
3. If Y equals to Z, goto 4. Otherwise let $Y = Z$, goto step 2
4. for each $(\phi_i, \psi_i) \in N$, ask the oracle if $\neg(\bigwedge X \rightarrow \phi_i)$ is satisfiable
   (a) If "no", then let $U = U \cup \{\psi_i\}$.
   (b) Otherwise do nothing
5. Ask the oracle if $\neg(\bigwedge U \rightarrow \psi)$ is satisfiable.
   (a) If "no", then return "accept".
   (b) Otherwise return "reject".

The correctness of the above algorithm is routine to be proven and we left it to the readers. Therefore simple-minded reusable input/output STIT logic is decidable.   ⊣

Corollary 3. *The violation problem and compatibility problem of simple-minded reusable input/output STIT logic is decidable.*

5   On Ross' Paradox

Ross' paradox [18] originate from the logic of imperatives, and is a well-known puzzle in deontic logic. Ross' paradox says that the inference rule WO cannot be valid, since if it were, then from

(1) You ought to post the letter

we could conclude that

(2) You ought to post the letter or burn it

and we obviously cannot.

Both Makinson and van der Torre's input/output logic and deontic STIT logic [12,13,19] are not free from this paradox.

Ross' paradox relies on the rule $Ought(\phi) \to Ought(\phi \vee \psi)$ of deontic logic. In our input/output STIT logic, we choose deliberative STIT as our base logic. Therefore we don't have $\models [i^d]\phi \to [i^d](\phi \vee \psi)$ because it might be $\models \Box(\phi \vee \psi)$. Therefore $(\top, [i^d](\phi \vee \psi))$ is not derivable from $(\top, [i^d]\phi)$, which means Ross' paradox is solved.

6   Conclusion

In this paper we study input/output STIT logic. We introduce the semantics, proof theory and prove the completeness theorem. Input/output STIT logic has stronger expressive power than Mankinson and van der Torre's input/output logic. We show that input/output STIT logic is decidable and free from Ross' paradox.

Directions of future work are manifold. Two natural directions includes: (1) What is the semantics for basic reusable input/output STIT logic? (2) What is the complexity of input/output STIT logic?

References

1. Ågotnes, T., van der Hoek, W., Rodríguez-Aguilar, J.A., Sierra, C., Wooldridge, M.: On the logic of normative systems. In: Veloso, M.M. (ed.) Proceedings of the 20th International Joint Conference on Artificial Intelligence, IJCAI 2007, Hyderabad, India, pp. 1175–1180, January 6–12, 2007
2. Andrighetto, G., Governatori, G., Noriega, P., van der Torre, L.W.N. (eds.): Normative Multi-Agent Systems. Dagstuhl Follow-Ups, vol. 4. Schloss Dagstuhl - Leibniz-Zentrum fuer Informatik (2013)
3. Arora, S., Barak, B.: Computational Complexity: A Modern Approach. Cambridge University Press, New York (2009)
4. Balbiani, P., Herzig, A., Troquard, N.: Alternative axiomatics and complexity of deliberative stit theories. Journal of Philosophical Logic 37(4), 387–406 (2008)
5. Belnap, N., Perloff, M., Xu, M.: Facing the future: agents anc choice in our inderterminist world. Oxford (2001)

6. Boella, G., van der Torre, L.W.N.: A logical architecture of a normative system. In: Goble, L., Meyer, J.-J.C. (eds.) DEON 2006. LNCS (LNAI), vol. 4048, pp. 24–35. Springer, Heidelberg (2006)
7. Boella, G., van der Torre, L., Verhagen, H.: Introduction to the special issue on normative multiagent systems. Autonomous Agents and Multi-Agent Systems **17**(1), 1–10 (2008)
8. Colombo, S., Guido, T., van der Torre, B.L., Villata, S.: Abstract normative systems: semantics and proof theory. In: Proceedings of the Thirteenth International Conference on Principles of Knowledge Representation and Reasoning, pp. 358–368 (2012)
9. Gabbay, D., Horty, J., Parent, X., van der Meyden, R., van der Torre, L. (eds.): Handbook of Deontic Logic and Normative Systems. College Publications (2014)
10. Herzig, A., Lorini, E., Moisan, F., Troquard, N.: A dynamic logic of normative systems. In: Walsh, T. (ed.) Proceedings of the 22nd International Joint Conference on Artificial Intelligence, IJCAI 2011, barcelona, Catalonia, Spain, July 16–22, 2011, pp. 228–233. IJCAI/AAAI (2011)
11. Herzig, A., Schwarzentruber, F.: Properties of logics of individual and group agency. In: Areces, C., Goldblatt, R. (eds.) Advances in Modal Logic, pp. 133–149. College Publications (2008)
12. Horty, J.: Agency and Deontic Logic. Oxford University Press, New York (2001)
13. Kooi, B., Tamminga, A.: Moral conflicts between groups of agents. Journal of Philosophical Logic **37**, 1–21 (2008)
14. Makinson, D., van der Torre, L.: Input-output logics. Journal of Philosophical Logic **29**, 383–408 (2000)
15. Makinson, D., van der Torre, L.: Constraints for input/output logics. Journal of Philosophical Logic **30**(2), 155–185 (2001)
16. Makinson, D., van der Torre, L.: Permission from an input/output perspective. Journal of Philosophical Logic **32**, 391–416 (2003)
17. Parent, X., van der Torre, L.: I/O logic. In: Horty, J., Gabbay, D., Parent, X., van der Meyden, R., van der Torre, L. (eds.) Handbook of Deontic Logic and Normative Systems. College Publications (2014)
18. Ross, A.: Imperatives and logic. Theoria, **7**(5371) (1941)
19. Sun, X.: Conditional ought, a game theoretical perspective. In: van Ditmarsch, H., Lang, J., Ju, S. (eds.) LORI 2011. LNCS, vol. 6953, pp. 356–369. Springer, Heidelberg (2011)
20. Sun, X.: How to build input/output logic. In: Bulling, N., van der Torre, L., Villata, S., Jamroga, W., Vasconcelos, W. (eds.) CLIMA 2014. LNCS, vol. 8624, pp. 123–137. Springer, Heidelberg (2014)
21. Sun, X., van der Torre, L.: Combining constitutive and regulative norms in input/output logic. In: Cariani, F., Grossi, D., Meheus, J., Parent, X. (eds.) DEON 2014. LNCS, vol. 8554, pp. 241–257. Springer, Heidelberg (2014)
22. Wooldridge, M.J.: An Introduction to MultiAgent Systems. Wiley (2009)

Towards Formal Semantics for ODRL Policies

Simon Steyskal[1,2(✉)] and Axel Polleres[1]

[1] Vienna University of Economics and Business, Vienna, Austria
simon.steyskal@wu.ac.at, {simon.steyskal,axel.polleres}@siemens.com
[2] Siemens AG, Vienna, Austria

Abstract. Most policy-based access control frameworks explicitly model whether execution of certain actions (read, write, etc.) on certain assets should be permitted or denied and usually assume that such actions are disjoint from each other, i.e. there does not exist any explicit or implicit dependency between actions of the domain. This in turn means, that conflicts among rules or policies can only occur if those contradictory rules or policies constrain the same action. In the present paper - motivated by the example of ODRL 2.1 as policy expression language - we follow a different approach and shed light on possible dependencies among actions of access control policies. We propose an interpretation of the formal semantics of general ODRL policy expressions and motivate rule-based reasoning over such policy expressions taking both explicit and implicit dependencies among actions into account. Our main contributions are (i) an exploration of different kinds of ambiguities that might emerge based on explicit or implicit dependencies among actions, and (ii) a formal interpretation of the semantics of general ODRL policies based on a defined abstract syntax for ODRL which shall eventually enable to perform rule-based reasoning over a set of such policies.

1 Introduction

ODRL (Open Digital Rights Language) [7] is a comprehensive policy expression language that aims to develop and promote an open international specification for interchangeable policy expressions. As shown in [1,12], ODRL has proven to be suitable to express fine-grained access restrictions, access policies, as well as licensing information for Linked Data. It was recently published as version 2.1 and allows to not only model permission or prohibitions of actions over assets, but also to define (optional) obligations for permission rules which need to be fulfilled in order for associated permissions to become active.[1] By using

---

Simon Steyskal has been partially funded by the Vienna Science and Technology Fund (WWTF) through project ICT12-015 and by the Austrian Research Promotion Agency (FFG) grant 845638 (SHAPE).

[1] We note that the specification so far does not define obligations in the form of contractual debts referring to the future upon using the permission, which may be a potential extension.

© Springer International Publishing Switzerland 2015
N. Bassiliades et al. (Eds.): RuleML 2015, LNCS 9202, pp. 360–375, 2015.
DOI: 10.1007/978-3-319-21542-6_23

obligations, data owners would be able to define preconditions for using their data, e.g. paying a certain amount of money, which might in turn serve as an incentive to publish their data in the first place as well as duties to be fulfilled when re-sharing the data. Obviously, if there is no possibility to protect or regain some of the expenses made during creating and curating a dataset, data owners might not see any benefit from publishing it.

In order to be able to use ODRL in an automated environment where requests against a set of control policies can be automatically processed and inconsistencies/conflicts among policies automatically detected, a formal specification of the semantics of policies expressed in ODRL is necessary. Unfortunately, there does not exist such an official formal specification, which is primarily caused by the fact that ODRL claims to follow an open design approach which shall allow applications using ODRL to each impose their own concrete interpretation of its semantics [8]. This, however, leads to difficulties when trying to process and consume ODRL policies automatically (i.e. perform reasoning over them), especially because natural language definitions usually leave a margin for interpretation.

Another issue we want to address within the present paper came up during our work on defining the formal semantics of ODRL policies. Most policy-based access control frameworks (e.g. PROTUNE [2]) consider conflicts among policies to only occur between ones that constrain the same action(s) contradictorily (e.g. by prohibiting and permitting a specific action at the same time), but do not take potential dependencies among different actions into account when checking for conflicts. Such dependencies can occur in different manifestations (cf. Section 3) and should be taken into account appropriately when processing requests.

In the present paper we aim to close those gaps of (i) a missing formal specification of ODRL and (ii) resolving ambiguities when handling explicit or implicit dependencies among actions. In particular, our contributions can be summarized as follows:

1. Definition of an abstract syntax for expressing ODRL policies.
2. Formalization of a possible interpretation of ODRL policy semantics.
3. Discussion of a solution proposal for handling implicit dependencies between ODRL actions.

The remainder of this paper is structured as follows: Section 2 provides a brief introduction into ODRL and defines an abstract syntax for expressing ODRL policies. Section 3 discusses the relationship between explicit and implicit dependencies among ODRL actions, and their impact on processing potential query requests, while Section 4 introduces a possible formal interpretation of ODRL policy semantics and Section 5 discusses proposed extended semantics of ODRL conflict resolution strategies. Finally, we discuss related work in Section 6 before we conclude our paper in Section 7.

2   Abstract Syntax of ODRL

The Open Digital Rights Language (ODRL) was invented to provide an open standard for defining policy expressions for digital content and media.

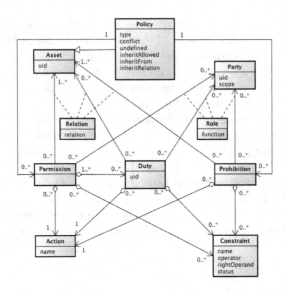

Fig. 1. ODRL Core Model Version 2.1 taken from http://www.w3.org/community/odrl/model/2.1/

The ODRL Core Model (cf. Figure 1) contains all major components of an ODRL policy expression.

To the best of our knowledge, there exists no officially agreed on abstract syntax of ODRL that covers all main concepts of the ODRL core model. In the following, we will introduce such an abstract syntax of ODRL that covers its main concepts and continue with utilizing this concise representation to propose a potential interpretation of the formal semantics of ODRL.

Table 1 represents the abstract syntax of ODRL, which was inspired by an approach to formalize XACML used in [9] and can be read as follows:

- text in **bold** represents non-terminal symbols
- text in `typewriter` represents terminal symbols
- text in *italic* represents functions and identifiers
- A^* indicates zero or more occurrences of symbol A
- A^+ indicates one or more occurrences of symbol A
- $A?$ indicates zero or one occurrence of symbol A

A *Policy* contains at least one *PermissionRule* or *ProhibitionRule* and has an associated ODRL *ConflictResolutionStrategy* which is either *permit overrides* (`perm`), *prohibition overrides* (`prohibit`), or *no conflicts allowed* (`invalid`). A *Policy* is applicable, if at least one of the *Rules* it contains matches with the request.

A *ProhibitionRule* defines the prohibition of performing an *Action* on an asset by a particular party which are both declared in the *RuleMatch* component of the *ProhibitionRule*. When its *RuleMatch* and *Action* components match a particular

Table 1. Abstract Syntax of ODRL

		ODRL Policy Components
Policy	$\mathcal{P}$	$::= \mathcal{P}_{id} = [\langle(\mathcal{PRR}_{id}|\mathcal{PER}_{id})^+\rangle, \mathcal{ALG}]$
ProhibitionRule	$\mathcal{PRR}$	$::= \mathcal{PRR}_{id} = [\mathcal{RM}, \mathcal{A}, \mathcal{CONS}]$
PermissionRule	$\mathcal{PER}$	$::= \mathcal{PER}_{id} = [\mathcal{RM}, \mathcal{A}, \langle\mathcal{DUR}^*_{id}\rangle, \mathcal{CONS}]$
DutyRule	$\mathcal{DUR}$	$::= \mathcal{DUR}_{id} = [\mathcal{RM}, \mathcal{A}, \mathcal{CONS}]$
ConstraintSet	$\mathcal{CONS}$	$::= \mathcal{CONS}_{id} = \langle\mathcal{CON}^*_{id}\rangle$
Constraint	$\mathcal{CON}$	$::= \mathcal{CON}_{id} = f^{bool}(status(a), operator(o), bound(a))$
RuleMatch	$\mathcal{RM}$	$::= \mathcal{RM}_{id} = \langle\mathcal{M}^+\rangle$
Match	$\mathcal{M}$	$::= \mathcal{M}_{id} = \phi(a)$
Action	$\mathcal{A}$	$::= \mathcal{A}_{id} = action(a)$
	$\phi(a)$	$::= party(a) \mid asset(a)$
	a	$::= value$
	o	$::= \texttt{eq} \mid \texttt{neq} \mid \texttt{lt} \mid \texttt{lteq} \mid \texttt{gt} \mid \texttt{gteq}$
ConflictRes.Strat.	$\mathcal{ALG}$	$::= \texttt{perm} \mid \texttt{prohibit} \mid \texttt{invalid}$
		Query & Proof
QueryRequest	$\mathcal{Q}$	$::= \mathcal{Q}_{id} = \langle party(a)?, action(a), asset(a)\rangle$
DutyTarget	$\mathcal{DT}$	$::= \mathcal{DT}_{id} = \langle party(a)?, action(a), asset(a)?\rangle$
DutyProof	$\mathcal{DPF}$	$::= \mathcal{DPF}_{id} = [\mathcal{DT}, \mathcal{CON}_{id}, status(a)]$
Proof	$\mathcal{PF}$	$::= \mathcal{PF}_{id} = [\mathcal{CON}_{id}, status(a)]$
ProofSet	$\mathcal{PFS}$	$::= \langle(\mathcal{DPF}_{id}|\mathcal{PF}_{id})^*\rangle$

request, the applicability of the *ProhibitionRule* can be further constrained by a set of *Constraints*. *Constraints* are represented as boolean formulas that compare a *status* according to an *operator*[2] with a respective *bound*. The *status* of a particular *Constraint* is provided by a respective *Proof* or *DutyProof* that serve as input for the *Constraint*.

PermissionRules are similarly defined as *ProhibitionRules*, but instead of prohibiting the execution of an *Action* they permit it. Furthermore, a sequence of *DutyRules* can be associated with *PermissionRules*. All associated *DutyRules* must be fulfilled in order for the respective *PermissionRule* to become valid.

A *QueryRequest* contains a particular access request that consists of an action and the respective asset it should be performed on, as well as optional information about the party which shall be performing the action.

3 Explicit and Implicit Dependencies among Actions in ODRL

Policy-based access control frameworks allow to explicitly model whether the execution of certain actions on certain assets should be permitted or prohibited and usually consider those actions to be disjoint from each other, i.e. there does

---

[2] Note, that we do not take set operators into account, but see them as a potential extension for further work.

not exist any explicit or implicit dependency between actions of the domain. Which in turn means, that conflicts among rules or policies can only occur if those contradictory rules or policies constrain the same action. However, in some situations there might indeed be interferences between different actions which have to be taken into account. Therefore, we have identified two different types of dependencies among actions of ODRL policies, namely: (i) *implicit dependencies*, and (ii) *explicit dependencies*.

In the following, we will discuss those dependencies in more detail.

3.1   Implicit Dependencies among ODRL Actions

The first dependency we discuss, defines a part-of relationship between actions which is related to Aggregations in UML [3].

Definition 1. *Let A_1 and A_2 be two arbitrary ODRL actions, then A_1 requires the permission of A_2 for its execution,* requires(A_1,A_2), *if the execution of A_1 involves the execution of A_2.*

That means, if the execution of an action A_1 implies, that an action A_2 must be executable (i.e. execution of A_2 is not denied), then requires(A_1,A_2) holds. To illustrate this relationship, consider the definition of odrl:share given in Figure 2, where its natural language semantics definition is taken from the official ODRL 2.0 specification [6].

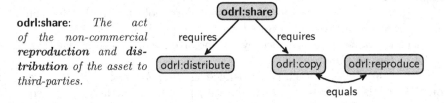

odrl:share: *The act of the non-commercial reproduction and distribution of the asset to third-parties.*

Fig. 2. Implicit dependencies of **odrl:share** (ODRL 2.0)

According to its semantics, odrl:share defines the non-commercial reproduction and distribution of an asset to third-parties. Which obviously would lead to a conflict when considering a policy as defined in Listing 1 which generally permits to share dataset :dataset1 but at the same time denies Assignee :alice to distribute it. A naive evaluation approach would allow :alice to share :dataset1 because there does not exist any rule that prohibits her from performing odrl:share on :dataset1. But since odrl:share defines the non-commercial reproduction (odrl:reproduce) and distribution (odrl:distribute) of an asset, it requires their execution permission to become valid itself, i.e. requires(odrl:share,odrl:reproduce) and requires(odrl:share,odrl:distribute) hold.

```
@prefix odrl: <http://w3.org/ns/odrl/2/>.
@prefix : <http://www.example.com/>.

:sharePolicy a odrl:Set;
        odrl:permission [
                a odrl:Permission;
                odrl:action odrl:share;
                odrl:target :dataset1];
        odrl:prohibition [
                a odrl:Prohibition;
                odrl:assignee :alice;
                odrl:action odrl:distribute;
                odrl:target :dataset1].
```

Listing 1. Prohibition of action **odrl:distribute** causes a conflict with permission of **odrl:share**.

Furthermore, some actions are defined to be equal according to the ODRL 2.0 specification [6] which means that they can be used interchangeably[3].

Definition 2. *Let A_1 and A_2 be two arbitrary ODRL actions, then A_1 is equal to A_2, equals(A_1,A_2), if A_1 and A_2 represent the same functionality according to the official ODRL specification.*

For the example of odrl:share given in Figure 2, this means that odrl:share depends not only on the explicitly mentioned action odrl:reproduce but also on its equivalent action odrl:copy, i.e. equals(odrl:reproduce,odrl:copy) and requires(odrl:share,odrl:copy) hold both.

3.2 Explicit Dependencies among ODRL Actions

In contrast to the aforementioned implicit part-of dependencies among actions in ODRL which are based on their natural language description, there also exist explicit relationships which are indicated by a subsumption hierarchy in the ODRL specification.

Definition 3. *Let A_1 and A_2 be two arbitrary ODRL actions, then broader(A_1,A_2) holds, if A_1 represents a broader term for A_2,*

In contrast to the previous defined part-of dependency, this explicit dependency imposes different semantics for the evaluation of ODRL policy expressions. Whenever broader(A_1,A_2) holds and both A_1 and A_2 have different access rights (i.e. permission or prohibition), then either A_1 or A_2 has to adapt its rights, according to the respective conflict resolution strategy in place.

Consider the excerpt of the subsumption hierarchy between actions illustrated in Figure 3. Based on the chosen conflict resolution strategy, if e.g. action

---

[3] Note that one of each pair of equivalent terms was defined as deprecated in ODRL 2.1.

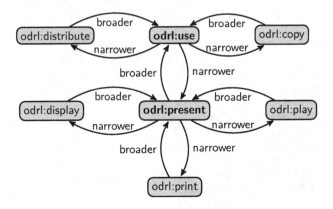

Fig. 3. Excerpt of explicit subsumption hierarchy between actions

odrl:use is prohibited then there cannot exist any other action that represents a narrower term of odrl:use and is permitted (cf. Section 5 for a more detailed discussion).

4   Basic Semantics of ODRL Policies

The following section proposes a possible interpretation of the formal semantics of ODRL which differs from earlier approaches defined in [5,10]. Starting from a potential request that was issued against a system, we first evaluate which rules are triggered by the request, and then check whether those rules hold according to potential duties or constraints they might have attached[4]. Eventually, all policies that contain rules which have matched are evaluated by following one of the three proposed ODRL conflict resolution strategies.

Match and RuleMatch. Let $\mathcal{MRM}$ be either a *Match* or a *RuleMatch* component and let $\boldsymbol{\mathcal{QDT}}$ either be a set of all possible *QueryRequests* or *DutyTargets*. A match semantic function is a mapping $[[\mathcal{MRM}]] : \boldsymbol{\mathcal{QDT}} \rightarrow \{m, nm\}$, where m and nm denote match and no match respectively.

A certain *Match* component $\mathcal{M}$ (i.e. the attribute value it represents) matches, whenever it is part of a particular *Query* or *DutyTarget*.

$$[[\mathcal{M}]](\mathcal{QDT}) = \begin{cases} m & \text{if } \mathcal{M} \in \mathcal{QDT} \\ nm & \text{if } \mathcal{M} \notin \mathcal{QDT} \end{cases} \tag{1}$$

A *RuleMatch* component $\mathcal{RM}$ (i.e. a set of *Match* components defined as $\langle \mathcal{M}_1, \ldots, \mathcal{M}_n \rangle$) only matches, if all of its *Match* components are evaluated to m.

---

[4] For now, we assume to have evidence of the fulfillment or violation of constraints/obligations available denoted as *proofs*. Future work will tackle the issue of actually generating or providing those evidences.

$$[[\mathcal{RM}]](\mathcal{QDT}) = \begin{cases} \mathsf{m} & \text{if } \forall i : [[\mathcal{M}_i]](\mathcal{QDT}) = \mathsf{m} \\ \mathsf{nm} & \text{if } \exists i : [[\mathcal{M}_i]](\mathcal{QDT}) = \mathsf{nm} \end{cases} \qquad (2)$$

Action. Let $\mathcal{A}$ be an *Action* component and let $\boldsymbol{\mathcal{QDT}}$ either be a set of all possible *QueryRequests* or *DutyTargets*. An action semantic function is a mapping $[[\mathcal{A}]] : \boldsymbol{\mathcal{QDT}} \to \{\mathsf{m}, \mathsf{broadm}, \mathsf{narm}, \mathsf{reqm}, \mathsf{partm}, \mathsf{nm}\}$, where m denotes match, broadm match of broader action, narm match of narrower action, reqm match of requiring action, partm match of required action, and nm denotes no match.

A certain *Action* component (i.e. the action it represents) matches, whenever it is part of a particular *QueryRequest* or *DutyTarget* or if an equivalent action is part of a particular *QueryRequest* or *DutyTarget*. Otherwise, it evaluates to broadm if it is related to a broader action that is part of the *QueryRequest* or *DutyTarget*, or to narm if it is related to a narrower action that is part of the *QueryRequest* or *DutyTarget*, or to partm if it is related to an action that is part of the *QueryRequest* or *DutyTarget* and this action requires the *Action* component for its execution, or to reqm if it requires another action for its execution and this required action is part of the *QueryRequest* or *DutyTarget*, or to nm otherwise.

$$[[\mathcal{A}]](\mathcal{QDT}) = \begin{cases} \mathsf{m} & \text{if } \mathcal{A} \in \mathcal{QDT} \text{ or} \\ & \exists i : \mathsf{equals}(\mathcal{A}, \mathcal{A}_i) \wedge \mathcal{A}_i \in \mathcal{QDT} \\ \mathsf{narm} & \text{if } \exists i : \mathsf{broader}(\mathcal{A}_i, \mathcal{A}) \wedge \mathcal{A}_i \in \mathcal{QDT} \\ \mathsf{broadm} & \text{if } \exists i : \mathsf{broader}(\mathcal{A}, \mathcal{A}_i) \wedge \mathcal{A}_i \in \mathcal{QDT} \\ \mathsf{partm} & \text{if } \exists i : \mathsf{requires}(\mathcal{A}_i, \mathcal{A}) \wedge \mathcal{A}_i \in \mathcal{QDT} \\ \mathsf{reqm} & \text{if } \exists i : \mathsf{requires}(\mathcal{A}, \mathcal{A}_i) \wedge \mathcal{A}_i \in \mathcal{QDT} \\ \mathsf{nm} & \text{otherwise} \end{cases} \qquad (3)$$

Constraint and ConstraintSet. Let $\mathcal{CON}$ be a *Constraint* component, $\mathcal{CONS} = \langle \mathcal{CON}_1, \ldots, \mathcal{CON}_n \rangle$ a *ConstraintSet* component, and let $\boldsymbol{\mathcal{PFS}} = \langle \mathcal{DPF}_1, \ldots, \mathcal{DPF}_m, \mathcal{PF}_1, \ldots, \mathcal{PF}_n \rangle$ represent all possible *ProofSets*. A constraint semantic function is a mapping $[[\mathcal{CON}]] : \boldsymbol{\mathcal{PFS}} \to \{\mathsf{t}, \mathsf{f}\}$, where t and f indicate whether the boolean formula represented by $\mathcal{CON}$ holds, given a *ProofSet* $\mathcal{PFS}$ as input.

This boolean formula is evaluated, if the provided *ProofSet* $\mathcal{PFS}$ contains a *Proof* $\mathcal{PF}$ that is associated with the respective *Constraint* of the formula. If no associated *Proof* exists, it is evaluated to f.

$$[[\mathcal{CON}]](\mathcal{PFS}) = \begin{cases} f^{bool}(\mathcal{PF}_i, operator(o), bound(a)) & \text{if } \exists i : \mathcal{PF}_i \wedge i = id \\ \mathsf{f} & \text{otherwise} \end{cases} \qquad (4)$$

A *ConstraintSet* component only evaluates to t, if all of its *Constraint* components are evaluated to t or the *ConstraintSet* is empty, i.e. there do not exist any associated *Constraints* at all.

$$[[\mathcal{CONS}]](\mathcal{PFS}) = \begin{cases} \mathsf{t} & \text{if } \forall i : [[\mathcal{CON}_i]](\mathcal{PFS}) = \mathsf{t} \text{ or} \\ & \quad \mathcal{CONS} = \emptyset \\ \mathsf{f} & \text{if } \exists i : [[\mathcal{CON}_i]](\mathcal{PFS}) = \mathsf{f} \end{cases} \tag{5}$$

DutyRule. Let $\mathcal{DUR} = [\mathcal{RM}, \mathcal{CONS}]$ be a *DutyRule* component and let $\mathcal{PFS} = \langle \mathcal{DPF}_1, \ldots, \mathcal{DPF}_m, \mathcal{PF}_1, \ldots, \mathcal{PF}_n \rangle$ represent all possible *ProofSets*. A duty rule semantic function is a mapping $[[\mathcal{DUR}]] : \mathcal{PFS} \to \{\mathsf{t}, \mathsf{f}\}$, where t represents the fulfillment of $\mathcal{DUR}$, and f the opposite.

$\mathcal{DUR}$ evaluates to t, if there exists at least one *DutyProof* $\mathcal{DPF}$ in the provided *ProofSet* $\mathcal{PFS}$ whose *DutyTarget* $\mathcal{DT} \in \mathcal{DPF}$ matches with the *RuleMatch* component of $\mathcal{DUR}$, and its *ConstraintSet* returns true. It evaluates to f in any other case.

$$[[\mathcal{DUR}]](\mathcal{PFS}) = \begin{cases} \mathsf{t} & \text{if } \exists i : \mathcal{DPF}_i \in \mathcal{PFS} \wedge [[\mathcal{RM}]](\mathcal{DT}) = \mathsf{m} \wedge \\ & \quad [[\mathcal{A}]](\mathcal{DT}) = \mathsf{m} \wedge [[\mathcal{CONS}]](\mathcal{PFS}) = \mathsf{t} \\ \mathsf{f} & \text{otherwise} \end{cases} \tag{6}$$

PermissionRule. Let $\mathcal{PER}$ be a *PermissionRule* component of the form $\mathcal{PER} = [\mathcal{RM}, \mathcal{A}, \mathbf{\mathcal{DUR}}, \mathcal{CONS}]$ where $\mathbf{\mathcal{DUR}} = \langle \mathcal{DUR}_1, \ldots, \mathcal{DUR}_n \rangle$, let $\mathcal{Q}$ be a set of all possible *QueryRequests*, and let $\mathcal{PFS}$ denote all possible *Proof-Sets*. A permission rule semantic function is a mapping $[[\mathcal{PER}]] : \mathcal{Q}, \mathcal{PFS} \to \{\mathsf{permission, cper, cpro, na, nm}\}$, where given $\mathcal{PFS}$ as input, permission represents permission of $\mathcal{Q}$, cper denotes conditional permission of $\mathcal{Q}$, cpro indicates conditional prohibition of $\mathcal{Q}$, and na, nap represent that $\mathcal{PER}$ is not active or not applicable respectively.

$\mathcal{PER}$ evaluates to permission, if its *RuleMatch* component matches with provided *QueryRequest* Q, its *ConstraintSet* component returns true, and if it has no associated duties. It evaluates to cpro if its *RuleMatch* component matches with Q, its *ConstraintSet* component returns true, but it has at least one associated *DutyRule* component that evaluates to false given a specific *ProofSet* $\mathcal{PFS}$ as input. It evaluates to cper if its *RuleMatch* component matches with Q, its *ConstraintSet* component returns true, and all associated *DutyRule* components evaluate to true given $\mathcal{PFS}$ as input. Finally, a *PermissionRule* component evaluates to na if its *RuleMatch* component matches with Q but its *ConstraintSet* component returns false, and it evaluates to nap if its *RuleMatch* component does not match with Q.

$$[[\mathcal{PER}]](\mathcal{Q}, \mathcal{PFS}) = \begin{cases} \text{permission} & \text{if } [[\mathcal{RM}]](\mathcal{Q}) = \text{m, } [[\mathcal{A}]](\mathcal{Q}) \neq \text{nm,} \\ & [[\mathcal{CONS}]](\mathcal{PFS}) = \text{t and } \boldsymbol{DUR} = \emptyset \\ \text{cpro} & \text{if } [[\mathcal{RM}]](\mathcal{Q}) = \text{m, } [[\mathcal{A}]](\mathcal{Q}) \neq \text{nm,} \\ & [[\mathcal{CONS}]](\mathcal{PFS}) = \text{t and } \exists i : [[\mathcal{DUR}_i]](\mathcal{PFS}) = \text{f} \\ \text{cper} & \text{if } [[\mathcal{RM}]](\mathcal{Q}) = \text{m, } [[\mathcal{A}]](\mathcal{Q}) \neq \text{nm,} \\ & [[\mathcal{CONS}]](\mathcal{PFS}) = \text{t and } \forall i : [[\mathcal{DUR}_i]](\mathcal{PFS}) = \text{t} \\ \text{na} & \text{if } [[\mathcal{RM}]](\mathcal{Q}) = \text{m, } [[\mathcal{A}]](\mathcal{Q}) \neq \text{nm and} \\ & [[\mathcal{CONS}]](\mathcal{PFS}) = \text{f} \\ \text{nap} & \text{otherwise} \end{cases}$$

(7)

ProhibitionRule. Let $\mathcal{PRR}$ be a *ProhibitionRule* component of the form $\mathcal{PRR}$ = $[\mathcal{RM}, \mathcal{A}, \mathcal{CONS}]$, let $\boldsymbol{\mathcal{Q}}$ be a set of all possible *QueryRequests*, and let $\boldsymbol{\mathcal{PFS}}$ denote all possible *ProofSets*. A prohibition rule semantic function is a mapping $[[\mathcal{PRR}]] : \boldsymbol{\mathcal{Q}}, \boldsymbol{\mathcal{PFS}} \rightarrow \{\text{prohibition, na, nm}\}$, where given $\boldsymbol{\mathcal{PFS}}$ as input, prohibition represents the prohibition of $\boldsymbol{\mathcal{Q}}$, na denotes that $\mathcal{PRR}$ is not active, and nap states that $\mathcal{PRR}$ is not applicable.

$\mathcal{PRR}$ evaluates to prohibition, if its *RuleMatch* component matches with the *QueryRequest* $\mathcal{Q}$ and its *ConstraintSet* component returns true given a specific *ProofSet* $\mathcal{PFS}$ as input. It evaluates to na if its *RuleMatch* component matches with $\mathcal{Q}$ but its *ConstraintSet* component returns false, and it evaluates to nap if its *RuleMatch* component does not match with $\mathcal{Q}$ (i.e. the rule is not applicable).

$$[[\mathcal{PRR}]](\mathcal{Q}, \mathcal{PFS}) = \begin{cases} \text{prohibition} & \text{if } [[\mathcal{RM}]](\mathcal{Q}) = \text{m, } [[\mathcal{A}]](\mathcal{Q}) \neq \text{nm and} \\ & [[\mathcal{CONS}]](\mathcal{PFS}) = \text{t} \\ \text{na} & \text{if } [[\mathcal{RM}]](\mathcal{Q}) = \text{m, } [[\mathcal{A}]](\mathcal{Q}) \neq \text{nm and} \quad (8) \\ & [[\mathcal{CONS}]](\mathcal{PFS}) = \text{f} \\ \text{nap} & \text{otherwise} \end{cases}$$

Policy. Let $\mathcal{P}$ be a *Policy* component of the form $\mathcal{P} = [\mathcal{R}, \boldsymbol{ALG}]$, where $\mathcal{R} = \langle \mathcal{R}_1, \ldots, \mathcal{R}_n \rangle$ is the set of all *Rules* of $\mathcal{P}$ with $\mathcal{R}_i, \mathcal{R}_j \in \mathcal{R}$ representing either a *ProhibitionRule* or a *PermissionRule*, and $\boldsymbol{ALG}$ is denoting the conflict resolution strategy of the *Policy*. Further, let $\boldsymbol{\mathcal{Q}}$ be a set of all possible *QueryRequests*, and let $\boldsymbol{\mathcal{PFS}}$ denote all possible *ProofSets*. A policy semantic function is a mapping $[[\mathcal{P}]] : \boldsymbol{\mathcal{Q}}, \boldsymbol{\mathcal{PFS}} \rightarrow \{\text{permission, prohibition, cpro, na, nm}\}$, where given $\boldsymbol{\mathcal{PFS}}$ as input, permission represents permission of $\boldsymbol{\mathcal{Q}}$, prohibition represents prohibition of $\boldsymbol{\mathcal{Q}}$, cpro indicates conditional prohibition of $\boldsymbol{\mathcal{Q}}$, and na, nap represent that $\mathcal{P}$ is not active or not applicable respectively.

A *Policy* $\mathcal{P}$ is not active, if all $\mathcal{R}$ in $\mathcal{P}$ are evaluated to na. $\mathcal{P}$ is not applicable (nap), if all $\mathcal{R}$ in $\mathcal{P}$ are evaluated to nap. If there is at least one $\mathcal{R}$ in $\mathcal{P}$ which is neither evaluated to na nor nap, $\mathcal{P}$ is evaluated to the result returned by the respective conflict resolution strategy $\mathcal{ALG}$ that takes $\mathcal{I} = [\mathcal{R}, \mathcal{Q}, \mathcal{PFS}]$ as input.

$$[[\mathcal{P}]](\mathcal{Q}, \mathcal{PFS}) = \begin{cases} \mathsf{na} & \text{if } \forall i : [[\mathcal{R}_i]](\mathcal{Q}, \mathcal{PFS}) = \mathsf{na} \\ \mathsf{na} & \text{if } \exists i : \neg([[\mathcal{R}_i]](\mathcal{Q}, \mathcal{PFS}) = (\text{permission}|\text{prohibition})) \\ & \quad \wedge \exists j : [[\mathcal{R}_j]](\mathcal{Q}, \mathcal{PFS}) = \mathsf{na} \\ \mathsf{nap} & \text{if } [[\mathcal{RM}]](\mathcal{Q}) = \mathsf{nm} \text{ and } [[\mathcal{A}]](\mathcal{Q}) = \mathsf{nm} \\ \otimes_{\mathcal{ALG}(\mathcal{I})} & \text{otherwise} \end{cases} \tag{9}$$

5 Proposed Semantics of ODRL Conflict Resolution Strategies

Sometimes, it may be the case that an unambiguous answer to a certain query request cannot be computed. Which is usually the case, if two or more mutually exclusive rules are triggered and thus produce multiple (possibly mutually exclusive) answers. Such a potential conflict is illustrated in Listing 2 where execution of action odrl:use on asset :dataset1 is both permitted and prohibited at the same time.

```
@prefix odrl: <http://w3.org/ns/odrl/2/> .
@prefix : <http://www.example.com/> .

:policy1 a odrl:Set ;
        odrl:permission [
                a odrl:Permission ;
                odrl:action odrl:use ;
                odrl:target :dataset1 ] ;
        odrl:prohibition [
                a odrl:Prohibition ;
                odrl:action odrl:use ;
                odrl:target :dataset1 ] .
```

Listing 2. Two conflicting rules of a policy.

To deal with this issue, the official ODRL specification defines an optional attribute for policies called conflict, that represents the conflict resolution strategy a policy must adhere to. There are three different conflict resolution strategies defined, namely:

perm: Permissions always take precedence over prohibitions.
prohibit: Prohibitions always take precedence over permissions.
invalid: Any conflicts cause invalidity of the policy.

In case attribute conflict is omitted, the default conflict resolution strategy is set to invalid.

Apart from their rather concise natural language description listed above, there does not exist any detailed definition of the semantics of ODRL conflict resolution strategies. Although, they all might seem quite straightforward to realize, there are some specific scenarios where a more elaborate semantics definition is necessary. For example, consider the policy illustrated in Listing 3, where actions odrl:use and odrl:delete are prohibited and action odrl:give is permitted to be performed on :dataset1.

```
@prefix odrl: <http://w3.org/ns/odrl/2/> .
@prefix : <http://www.example.com/> .

:policy2 a odrl:Set ;
        odrl:prohibition [
                a odrl:Prohibition ;
                odrl:action odrl:use ;
                odrl:target :dataset1 ] ;
        odrl:permission [
                a odrl:Permission ;
                odrl:action odrl:give ;
                odrl:target :dataset1 ] .
        odrl:prohibition [
                a odrl:Prohibition ;
                odrl:action odrl:delete ;
                odrl:target :dataset1 ] .
```

Listing 3. Two conflicting rules of a policy.

In the following, we will propose and explain suitable semantics for each ODRL conflict resolution strategy.

Note, that we (i) value evaluation results obtained by duties, i.e. cper or cpro higher than any conflict resolution strategy, and (ii) do not treat *Rules* assigned to a specific party different from those having no associated party. Furthermore, we abbreviate *QueryRequests* with $\mathcal{Q}$, *Rules* with $\mathcal{R}$, and *Actions* with $\mathcal{A}$.

5.1 Permission Overrides (perm)

First conflict resolution strategy values permissions more than prohibitions thus, whenever there are two *Rules* in conflict with each other, the one granting permission to execute an action a on a particular asset cannot be overwritten. Nevertheless, there are some exceptions:

1. If there exists a rule which constrains an action that is either (i) equal to the one contained in the query request, (ii) a broader term for the action contained in the query request, or (iii) an action which is required to be executable in order to perform the one contained in the query request, and this rule evaluates to cpro, return cpro.

2. If 1. does not hold and there exists a rule which constrains an action that is either (i) equal to the one contained in the query request, (ii) a broader term for the action contained in the query request, or (iii) an action which requires the one contained in the query request to be executable, and this rule evaluates to cper or permission, return permission.
3. If all rules contain the same or equal actions to the ones queried and all rules evaluate to the same result r, then return r.
4. Otherwise, return na.

$$\bigotimes_{perm}(\mathcal{I}) = \begin{cases} \text{cpro} & \text{if } \exists i : [[A_i]](\mathcal{Q}) = (\text{m|broadm|partm}) \wedge [[R_i]](\mathcal{Q}, \mathcal{PFS}) = \text{cpro} \\ \text{permission} & \text{if } \exists i : [[A_i]](\mathcal{Q}) = (\text{m|broadm|reqm}) \wedge [[R_i]](\mathcal{Q}, \mathcal{PFS}) = (\text{permission|cper}) \\ & \text{and } \neg \exists j : [[A_j]](\mathcal{Q}) = (\text{m|broadm|partm}) \wedge [[R_j]](\mathcal{Q}, \mathcal{PFS}) = \text{cpro} \\ r & \text{if } \forall i : [[A_i]](\mathcal{Q}) = \text{m} \wedge [[R_i]](\mathcal{Q}, \mathcal{PFS}) = r \\ \text{na} & \text{otherwise} \end{cases}$$

$$(10)$$

5.2 Prohibition Overrides (prohibit)

Second conflict resolution strategy values prohibitions more than permissions thus, whenever there are two *Rules* in conflict with each other the one prohibiting the execution of an action a on a particular asset cannot be overwritten. Again, there are some exceptions:

1. If there exists a rule which constrains an action that is either (i) equal to the one contained in the query request, (ii) a broader term for the action contained in the query request, or (iii) an action which is required to be executable in order to perform the one contained in the query request, and this rule evaluates to cpro, return cpro.
2. If 1. does not hold and there exists a rule which constrains an action that is either (i) equal to the one contained in the query request, (ii) a broader term for the action contained in the query request, or (iii) an action which requires the one contained in the query request to be executable, and this rule evaluates to cper, return permission.
3. If 1. and 2. does not hold and there exists a rule which constrains an action that is either (i) equal to the one contained in the query request, (ii) a broader term for the action contained in the query request, or (iii) an action which is required to be executable in order to perform the one contained in the query request, and this rule evaluates to prohibition, return prohibition.
4. If all rules contain the same or equal actions to the ones queried and all rules evaluate to the same result r, then return r.
5. Otherwise, return na.

$$\bigotimes_{prohibit} (\mathcal{I}) = \begin{cases} \text{cpro} & \text{if } \exists i : [[A_i]](\mathcal{Q}) = (\text{m}|\text{broadm}|\text{partm}) \wedge [[R_i]](\mathcal{Q}, \mathcal{PFS}) = \text{cpro} \\ \text{permission} & \text{if } \exists i : [[A_i]](\mathcal{Q}) = (\text{m}|\text{broadm}|\text{reqm}) \wedge [[R_i]](\mathcal{Q}, \mathcal{PFS}) = \text{cper} \\ & \text{and } \neg\exists j : [[A_j]](\mathcal{Q}) = (\text{m}|\text{broadm}|\text{partm}) \wedge [[R_j]](\mathcal{Q}, \mathcal{PFS}) = \text{cpro} \\ \text{prohibition} & \text{if } \exists i : [[A_i]](\mathcal{Q}) = (\text{m}|\text{broadm}|\text{partm}) \wedge [[R_i]](\mathcal{Q}, \mathcal{PFS}) = \text{prohibition} \\ & \text{and } \neg\exists j : [[A_j]](\mathcal{Q}) = (\text{m}|\text{broadm}|\text{reqm}) \wedge [[R_j]](\mathcal{Q}, \mathcal{PFS}) = \text{cper} \\ & \text{and } \neg\exists k : [[A_k]](\mathcal{Q}) = (\text{m}|\text{broadm}|\text{partm}) \wedge [[R_k]](\mathcal{Q}, \mathcal{PFS}) = \text{cpro} \\ r & \text{if } \forall i : [[A_i]](\mathcal{Q}) = \text{m} \wedge [[R_i]](\mathcal{Q}, \mathcal{PFS}) = r \\ \text{na} & \text{otherwise} \end{cases}$$

$$(11)$$

5.3 No Conflicts Allowed (invalid)

Third conflict resolution strategy does not allow any conflicting *Rules*, therefore whenever there are two *Rules* returning inconsistent answers, no results can be provided.

1. All rules must evaluate to the same result. If two rules evaluate to different results, those results must be one of cper or permission.
2. Otherwise, return an error.

$$\bigotimes_{invalid} (\mathcal{I}) = \begin{cases} r_i & \forall i \forall j : ([[R_i]](\mathcal{Q}, \mathcal{PFS}) = r_i \wedge [[R_j]](\mathcal{Q}, \mathcal{PFS}) = r_j) \rightarrow (r_i = r_j \vee \\ & r_i \neq r_j \rightarrow (r_i = (\text{cper}|\text{permission}) \wedge r_j = (\text{cper}|\text{permission}))) \\ \text{error} & \text{otherwise} \end{cases}$$

$$(12)$$

6 Related Work

Over the last couple of years, very little research has been conducted into the formal semantics for ODRL. While in [10] the authors propose formal semantics to a fragment of ODRL based on First-Order Logic and limit themselves to a very small subset of supported actions, the authors of [5] use finite-automata like structures to model permissions and their respective actions they permit. In contrast to both of those approaches, we defined an abstract syntax for all basic concepts of ODRL and formalized their semantics together with the semantics of conflict resolution strategies accordingly. Other approaches try to capture the semantics of ODRL in terms of ontologies [4,8] which is very similar to the semantics definition of our approach but differs in terms of treatment of implicit dependencies between actions as well as the proposed abstract syntax. Complementary our work, there has been work to formalize licence compatibility [11], which though was not embedded in the framework of ORDL, but might be an interesting direction to look into for formally grounding our semantics likewise into Deontic logic.

7   Conclusion

In the present paper, we defined an abstract syntax for expressing ODRL policies which served as a foundation for formalizing a possible interpretation of basic ODRL policy semantics. We furthermore discussed the impact of explicit and implicit dependencies among ODRL actions on the evaluation of policy expressions. While the former is explicitly defined in the ODRL specification and modeled as subsumption hierarchy between actions, the latter can only be implicitly derived from the natural language semantics definition of actions and expressed as part-of relationship among actions. Which we both took into account when formalizing ODRL's semantics.

First point to be addressed is to introduce the concept of *PolicySets* as container for policies which allows to combine the evaluation results of policies independently of their respective chosen conflict resolution strategy. Second, we want to formalize and extend the mapping between ODRL policies and logic programs, which enables basic, rule-based reasoning tasks and was omitted in the present paper because of page restrictions. Finally, we will address the elaborate provision of proofs for constraints and duties which are currently assumed to be provided by the requester itself. Especially addressing the latter point, offers interesting new research directions and allows for possible collaborations with other research fields like Business Process Management, where correct completion of a business process that was automatically generated based on a constraint or duty serves as a proof of their fulfillment.

References

1. Cabrio, E., Palmero Aprosio, A., Villata, S.: These are your rights - a natural language processing approach to automated RDF licenses generation. In: Presutti, V., d'Amato, C., Gandon, F., d'Aquin, M., Staab, S., Tordai, A. (eds.) ESWC 2014. LNCS, vol. 8465, pp. 255–269. Springer, Heidelberg (2014)
2. De Coi, J.L., Olmedilla, D., Bonatti, P.A., Sauro, L.: Protune: a framework for semantic web policies. In: International Semantic Web Conference (Posters & Demos), vol. 401, p. 128 (2008)
3. Fowler, M., Scott, K.: UML distilled - a brief guide to the Standard Object Modeling Language, 2nd edn. Addison-Wesley-Longman (2000)
4. García, R., Gil, R., Gallego, I., Delgado, J.: Formalising ODRL semantics using web ontologies. In: Proc. 2nd Intl. ODRL Workshop, pp. 1–10 (2005)
5. Holzer, M., Katzenbeisser, S., Schallhart, C.: Towards formal semantics for ODRL. In: Proceedings of the First International Workshop on the Open Digital Rights Language (ODRL), Vienna, Austria, April 22–23, pp. 137–148 (2004)
6. Iannella, R., Guth, S.: Odrl version 2.0 common vocabulary. W3C ODRL Community Group (2012). http://www.w3.org/community/odrl/two/vocab/
7. Iannella, R., Guth, S., Pähler, D., Kasten, A.: Odrl: Open digital rights language 2.1. W3C ODRL Community Group (2012). http://www.w3.org/community/odrl/
8. Kasten, A., Grimm, R.: Making the semantics of ODRL and URM explicit using web ontologies. In: Virtual Goods, pp. 77–91 (2010)

9. Kencana Ramli, C.D.P., Nielson, H.R., Nielson, F.: XACML 3.0 in answer set programming. In: Albert, E. (ed.) LOPSTR 2012. LNCS, vol. 7844, pp. 89–105. Springer, Heidelberg (2013)

10. Pucella, R., Weissman, V.: A Formal Foundation for ODRL. CoRR, abs/cs/0601085 (2006)

11. Rotolo, A., Villata, S., Gandon, F.: A deontic logic semantics for licenses composition in the web of data. In: Int'l Conf. on Artificial Intelligence and Law ICAIL, pp. 111–120 (2013)

12. Steyskal, S., Polleres, A.: Defining expressive access policies for linked data using the ODRL ontology 2.0. In: Proceedings of the 10th International Conference on Semantic Systems, SEMANTICS 2014, Leipzig, Germany, September 4–5, pp. 20–23 (2014)

Representing Flexible Role-Based Access Control Policies Using Objects and Defeasible Reasoning

Reza Basseda[1]([✉]), Tiantian Gao[1], Michael Kifer[1],
Steven Greenspan[2], and Charley Chell[2]

[1] Computer Science Department, Stony Brook University,
Stony Brook, NY 11794, USA
{rbasseda,tiagao,kifer}@cs.stonybrook.edu
[2] CA, Inc., 520 Madison Avenue, New York, NY 10022, USA
{steven.greenspan,charley.chell}@ca.com

Abstract. Access control systems often use rule based frameworks to express access policies. These frameworks not only simplify the representation of policies, but also provide reasoning capabilities that can be used to verify the policies. In this work, we propose to use defeasible reasoning to simplify the specification of role-based access control policies and make them modular and more robust. We use the Flora-2 rule-based reasoner for representing a role-based access control policy. Our early experiments show that the wide range of features provided by Flora-2 greatly simplifies the task of building the requisite ontologies and the reasoning components for such access control systems.

Keywords: Access control policy · Object oriented logic programming · Ontology

1 Introduction

Administering and maintaining access control systems is a challenging task, especially when the environments are complex and the authorization requirements are subject to frequent change. Policy languages play an important role in designing and implementing flexible access control systems. There are a number of role-based policy specification languages that can express access control policies, including XACML [14], X-RBAC [8], Rei [9], Common Policy [18], and Ponder [4]. These languages simplify management of access control by factoring the authorization policy out of the hard-coded resource guard. For example, XACML defines a general XML role-based policy language. X-RBAC is another XML role-based access control language for specifying RBAC policies [8]. Common Policy provides a framework for authorization policies controlling access to application-specific data. Although they have been applied to a broad domain of enterprise environments, it is difficult to use them at the semantic level. To mitigate this problem, some approaches inject RDF [2] and OWL [6] into the mix.

© Springer International Publishing Switzerland 2015
N. Bassiliades et al. (Eds.): RuleML 2015, LNCS 9202, pp. 376–387, 2015.
DOI: 10.1007/978-3-319-21542-6_24

Rei [9] is an example of this approach, which uses OWL-Lite and RDF. Ponder is a declarative policy language, which is designed based on object-oriented principles. It can be used to specify both security and management policies. Ontologies are also used to develop hybrid distributed access control systems [19]. Another access control policy specification language based on OWL and SWRL has been proposed in [13].

Clearly, representation of domain classes and objects is a key component of an access control system because such representation facilitates the development and changing of policies. Although all of the above mentioned access control policy specification languages are able to represent domain classes and objects, none is a *rule*-based language and none is as expressive as a rule based policy specification language can be.

One of the key challenges in role-based access control is that policies are subject to frequent changes, which calls for hierarchical structure of policy components and roles. However, none of the above mentioned languages can matches the flexibility for defining such hierarchies that is provided by object-oriented rule-based languages based on F-logic [11,12], such as Flora-2 [10,22]. The use of such an expressive knowledge representation and reasoning language lets us both to integrate hierarchies between policy components into policy rules and encapsulate different components of rule based policies in different modules. This gives us the necessary machinery to localize the changes initiated by the clients. The reasoning capabilities that come with object-oriented rule languages like Flora-2 also allows one to make policies more concise, clearer, easier to specify, analyze, and change. Modularity also helps with certain security issues. For instance, in many applications, especially in distributed systems, rules and facts used for access control decision making are ranked and grouped by their trust levels. The reasoning mechanism that understands encapsulation can take into account the different levels of trust when it responds to access requests.

In this paper, we show that by using an elegant defeasible reasoning system we can build a rule based access control policy in terms of separate, encapsulated modules based on the application semantics and security requirements. We use *Logic Programming with Defaults and Argumentation Theories* (LPDA) [20] to define different groups of rules and facts and use this logic to make our access control decision. Together with the higher-order features of Hilog [3] and object-oriented nature of F-Logic [12], great flexibility is provided to the access control policy developers.

The rest of the paper is organized as follows. Section 2 provides a brief overview of logic programming with defaults and argumentation theories. Section 3 illustrates our methodology for building a flexible access control system and its corresponding architecture. Section 4 gives a practical example of defining different components in the rule based access control policy, and Section 5 concludes the paper.

2   Overview of Defeasible Reasoning

Defeasible reasoning is a type of non-monotonic reasoning where conclusions may have priorities and be *defeated* by other conclusion. Such theories are usually conducive to specifying general defaults and conclusions can be easily, modularly, and incrementally altered when new information becomes available. This contrasts with monotonic logic where any previously inferred information remains valid with the addition of new knowledge. For example, given the access control policy stating that *typically, a student is authorized to use a device unless the student has abused the device before,* and the facts that *John is a student and a printer is a device,* we might conclude that John is authorized to use the printer. However, if later it becomes known that *John has abused the printer,* the previous conclusion can be defeated without making any modifications to the policy. Defeasible reasoning is intended to model this kind of scenarios in modular and natural fashion.

General non-monotonic resoning frameworks, such as circumscription, default logic, and autoepistemic logic, can also model the above scenarios, but their languages are not attuned to making changes modular and simple. In this work, we use Logic programming with defaults and argumentation theories (LPDA), a unifying defeasible reasoning framework that uses *defaults* and *exceptions* with prioritized rules, and argumentation theories. LPDA is based on the three-valued well-founded semantics [17]. Here we briefly review LPDA. Defails can be found in [20].

A *literal* has one of the following forms:

- An atomic formula.
- *neg A*, where A is an atomic formula.
- *not A*, where A is an atom.
- *not neg A*, where A is an atom.
- *not not L* and *neg neg L*, where L is a literal.

Let A be an atom. A *not-free* literal refers to a literal that can be reduced to A or *neg A*. A *not*-literal refers to a literal that can be reduced to *not A* or *not neg A*. LPDA has two types of rules: *strict* and *defeasible*, where *strict* rules generate non-defeasible conclusions and *defeasible* rules generate defeasible conclusions that can be defeated by some exceptions. A strict rule is of the form:

$$L \leftarrow Body$$

where L is a *not-free* literal and *Body* is a conjunction of literals. A defeasible rule is of the form:

$$@r\ L \leftarrow Body$$

where r is a *term* that denotes the label of the rule.

Each LPAD program is accompanied by an argumentation theory that specifies when a defeasible rule is defeated. An argumentation theory is a set of definite rules with four special predicates: \defeated, \opposes, \overrides, and \cancel where \defeated denotes the defeatedness of a defeasible rule, \opposes indicates the literals that are incompatible with each other, \overrides denotes a binary relation between defeasible rules indicating priority, and \cancel cancels a defeasible rule. There can be several different argumentation theories that can be used simultaneously for different modules. Users can select one of the predefined ones and use it as is or modify it, as appropriate. A rule is defeated if it is *refuted, rebutted,* or *disqualified.* The meaning of *refuted, rebutted,* and *disqualified* depends on the chosen argumentation theory. Generally, a rule is *refuted* if there is another rule that draws an incompatible conclusion with higher priority. A rule is *rebutted* if there is another rule that draws an incompatible conclusion and there is no way to resolve the conflict based on the relative priorities. A rule is disqualified if it is *cancelled,* self-defeated, etc. An example is shown in Figure 1.

```
@{id1} authorized(?Principal,?Dev) :- device(?Dev),
                                      principal(?Principal).

@{id2} \neg authorized(?Principal,?Dev) :- abused(?Principal,?Dev).

\overrides(id2,id1).
\opposes(authorized(?Principal,?Dev), \neg authorized(?Principal,?Dev)).

principal(Mary).
principal(John).
device(printer).
abuse(John,printer).
```

Fig. 1. An example of a simple LPDA program

In the figure, rule id1 says that if there is a person and a device, then the person is authorized to use the device. Rule id2 says that if a person has abused the device, then the person is not authorized to use the device. The predicate \overrides(id2,id1) indicates that rule id2 has higher priority than id1. The statement \opposes(authorized (?Persn, ?Dev), *neg* authorized(?Persn,?Dev)) says that one can be either authorized or not, but not both. Taking into account the facts person(Mary) and device(priter), we can conclude authorized(Mary,printer) from rule id1. From the facts person(John), device(printer), and abuse(John,printer), rules id1 and id2 derive *contradictory* conclusions that both authorized(John,printer) and *neg* authorized(John, printer) hold. Since rule id2 has a higher priority than rule id1, authorized(John,printer) is defeated.

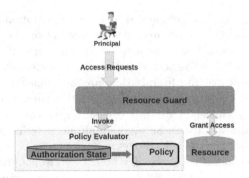

Fig. 2. A typical architecture of an access control system

3   Methodology and Architecture

Although several architectures have been proposed for access control systems [15,16], none of them has gained the status of a standard. To explain different access control policy representation languages, we assume a simple architecture in Figure 2, borrowed from [1]. However, the discussion below applies to more complex architectures as well. To keep our technique as general as possible, we also do not limit our framework to any specific classic access control model, such as Role-Based Access Control [5] or Attribute-Based Access Control [7] Models.

As shown in Figure 2, the authorization *policy* is not hard-coded as a *resource guard* but instead appears as a list of declarative rules. When a principal requests access, the resource guard issues an authorization query to the policy evaluator. Access is granted only if the policy evaluator succeeds in proving that the request complies with the local policy and a set of facts describing the *authorization state*, i.e., with a set of relevant facts, including the knowledge obtained from submitted or fetched credentials. For instance, the history of locations of a principal can be reflected in the authorization state and used by policy evaluator.

This approach greatly increases the maintainability of access control systems, as modifying the declarative policy rules is much simpler than rewriting and recompilation of the code embedded in the resource guard. In fact, resource guards are usually designed to take care of the low-level security considerations while policies are expected to be high-level descriptions of security requirements. Therefore, imperative programming languages (e.g. C or C++) are used to implement resource guard, while higher-level declarative languages are preferred for security policies. There are several reasons why policies should be formally verifiable. For one, the declarative nature of policy languages and the formal framework required for query evaluation make logic programming languages the top candidates for policy specification.

In accordance with this architecture, we assume that the policy evaluator is completely separate from the resource guard. To issue an authorization query to the policy evaluator, the resource guard uses a predicate of form $grantAccess(t_1, \ldots, t_n)$ as a query. Given a set $\mathbb{R}$ of policy rules, the policy evaluator returns *true* or *false* answer, thereby allowing or disallowing the access. Next, we will show how using an object oriented logic programming and defeasible rules can make an access control system much simpler and more flexible.

3.1 Resilience to Changes

Access control policies are not usually considered as a fixed component of an access control system and they are often modified on the request of non-technical policy makers. Therefore, it is very important to make policies as flexible as possible and to minimize the cost of changes. The following features are therefore very desirable:

- Prevention of introduction of bugs through modification via semantic constraints.
- A robust patching mechanism for expansion of policies.

We will now explain how object oriented features in Flora-2 [10,22] and defeasible reasoning via LPDA [20,21] solve these issues.

Classes and Objects: We use a set of classes to represent different resources and roles used by the policy. These classes serve both as semantic integrity constraints and as a policy development guide. The classes are typically identified by IRIs pointing to the actual resources, which is useful for standardization and portability. Figure 3 shows two sample classes in a typical policy represented in Flora-2.

```
Person[|
    firstName => string,
    lastName  => string |].

Employee::Person[|
    employmentYear => integer,
    department     => Department,
    profession     => string,
    rank           => Rank,
    loc(?)         => Location |].
```

Fig. 3. An example of ontology for access control systems in Flora-2

Modification via Patching: To provide a patching mechanism, we use defeasible reasoning to override default rules of a policy with new rules. Consider a policy $\mathbb{P}$ consisting of n rules of the form @r_i $L_i \leftarrow Body_i$ where $1 \leq i \leq n$. Suppose that we need to change $\mathbb{P}$ to $\mathbb{P}'$ such that for some $1 \leq j \leq n$, a new rule of the form $@r'_j \; L_j \leftarrow Body'_j$ derives L_j, L_j conflicts with L_i, and the new rule has higher priority if condition $Cond$ holds. To obtain $\mathbb{P}'$ out of $\mathbb{P}$, one needs to simply add the following rules to $\mathbb{P}$.

$$
\begin{aligned}
&@r'_j \; L_j \leftarrow Body'_j. \\
&\backslash overrides(r'_j, r_j) \leftarrow Cond. \\
&\backslash opposes(L_i, L_j).
\end{aligned}
\tag{1}
$$

We can also use a similar technique also to disable a rule under certain circumstances. Suppose that for some $1 \leq j \leq n$, we need to disable the rule $@r_j \; L_j \leftarrow Body_j$ from $\mathbb{P}$ when condition $Cond$ is true. To this end, one can simply add

$$
\backslash cancel(r_j) \leftarrow Cond.
\tag{2}
$$

Note that $Body'_j$ may have literals that are defined by other rules in which case those rules would be added as well. The following example illustrates how this patching mechanism works.

Example 1 (Access Control Based on Time and Location). Consider the policy shown in Figure 4. A policy evaluator can use this policy to answer queries of the form $grantAccess(?E, ?R, ?T, ?D)$ where the variables $?E$, $?R$, $?T$, $?D$ range over the members of the classes Employee, Resource, TimeOfAccess, and DateOfAccess, respectively. The first rule defines the predicate $hasmoved(?E, ?D1, ?D2)$ which is true if the location of employee $?E$ is different on day $?D1$ and day $?D2$. The second and third rules define the predicate $moved(+?E, +?D1, +?D2, -?M)$,[1] which binds $?M$ to 1 if the employee $?E$ has moved between days $?D1$ and $?D2$. The predicate $locRisk(+?E, +?D, -?K)$ specifies the security risk if employee $?E$ is known to have moved in each of the four days preceding day $?D$. Finally, the predicate $grantAccess(+?E, +?R, +?T, +?D)$, if true, indicates that the employee $?E$ is allowed to access the resource $?R$ at time $?T$ of day $?D$. This rule just checks if the departments of the employee $?E$ and of resource $?R$ are the same and the risk assessment of the employee is below the threshold.

Suppose that now it is required to use a new parameter called *access time risk*, which computes the risk based on the access hour with respect to $13:00$, *if* the employee is away from the home department. To this end, we construct a patch that enforces the new policy, as shown in Figure 5. The second rule in the figure defines $timeRisk(+?R, +?T, -?TD)$ as the difference between the access time and $13:00$ (this number may indicate the risk of unauthorized accesses). For example an access request at $14:00$ is more reasonable than at at $21:00$ or $03:00$. The third rule says that access is prohibited if the employee is traveling and $timeRisk$ exceeds the threshold. The first fact in Figure 5 states that atom $grantAccess/4$ resulted from rule `locAccess` is defeated by the same atom resulted from rule $timeAccess$. Note that the rule `locAccess` is not completely disabled: it still holds sway if the employee is not traveling.

---

[1] $+$ indicates that the variable is used as input and must be bound before calling the predicate; $-$ means that the variable is an output and will be bound after calling the predicate produces an answer.

```
hasmoved(?E,?D1,?D2) :-
    ?E:Employee[loc(?D1) -> ?L1],
    ?E[loc(?D2) -> ?L2],
    ?L1 != ?L2.

moved(?E,?D1,?D2,1) :- hasmoved(?E:Employee,?D1,?D2).

moved(?E,?D1,?D2,0) :-
    ?E:Employee,
    \naf hasmoved(?E,?D1,?D2).

locRisk(?E,?D,?K) :-
    ?E:Employee,
    moved(?E,?D,?D1,?M1),
    moved(?E,?D1,?D2,?M2),
    moved(?E,?D2,?D3,?M3),
    moved(?E,?D3,?D4,?M4),
    nextDay(?D4,?D3),
    nextDay(?D3,?D2),
    nextDay(?D2,?D1),
    nextDay(?D1,?D),
    ?K \is ?M1 + ?M2 + ?M3 + ?M4.

@{locAccess}
grantAccess(?E,?R,?,?D) :-
    ?E:Employee[department-> ?DE],
    ?R:Resource[owner-> ?DE],
    locRisk(?E,?D,?K),
    ?K < 3.
```

Fig. 4. An example of a simple policy in Flora-2

```
\overrides(timeAccess,locAccess).

timeRisk(?T,?TD) :- ?TD \is abs(?T - 13).

@{timeAccess}
\neg grantAccess(?E,?R,?T,?D) :-
    ?E:Employee,
    ?R:Resource,
    ?E.department.location != ?E.loc(?D),
    ?E[timeWorked(?D) -> ?T],
    timeRisk(?T,?K),
    ?K > 5.
```

Fig. 5. The first modification of the policy

Now suppose that policy makers suddenly realize that time is different in different time zones, so they decide to calculate access times based on employee's local time rather than resource's local time. This means that the rule timeAccess will now be defeated by a new rule, flexAccess, if the locations of the resource $?R$ and the employee $?E$ are different. Figure 6 shows the rules of this patch. The third rule defines $timeRisk(+?E, +?T, +?D, -?TD)$, which gets an employee $?E$ and a GMT time id $?T$, computes the actual time in the time zone of the employee, and then assesses the risk according to the employee's local time zone. The flexAccess rule for $grantAccess(+?E, +?R, +?T, +?D)$ now says that the employee $?E$ can access resource $?R$ at time $?T$ on day $?D$, if the access happens within the local normal working hours. Other than that, the conditions are the same as for locAccess.   □

```
\overrides(flexAccess,timeAccess).

timeRisk(?E,?T,?D,?TD) :-
    ?E:Employee[loc(?D) -> ?L],
    ?L[timeZone -> ?TZR],
    ?TD \is abs(?T + ?TZR - 13).

@{flexAccess}
grantAccess(?E,?R,?T,?D) :-
    ?E[department-> ?DE],
    ?R[owner-> ?DE],
    ?E.loc(?D) != ?R.location,
    timeRisk(?E,?T,?D,?TR),
    ?TR < 5.
```

Fig. 6. The second modification of the policy

As shown in in our example, defeasible reasoning can simplify the process of changing policies. Figure 7 shows the difference between the architectures of policies with and without using defeasible reasoning and object oriented logic programming. The architecture shown in Figure 7(b) is more modular than the one in Figure 7(a).

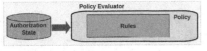

(a) Without defeasible reasoning and object orientation.

(b) With defeasible reasoning and object orientation.

Fig. 7. Possible architectures of policies

3.2   Virtual Hierarchies

In many cases, policy rules may conflict and be considered with regard to the position of the policy makers in the organizational hierarchy. For instance, suppose that policy makers x and y introduce policy rules $@r_x\ L_x \leftarrow Body_x$ and $@r_y\ L_y \leftarrow Body_y$ whose conclusions may conflict in some cases. If the organizational position of x is higher than y's, we can set the priority of rule r_x higher than that of r_y. There are two choices to apply such organizational hierarchies to policy rules: (1) the organizational hierarchy can be encoded in policy evaluator; or (2) we can use defeasible reasoning to allow policy rules of a lower-ranked actor to be defeated. Clearly, the second choice is more flexible than the first.

To represent organizational hierarchies of policy developers, we can assume that every rule in a policy is of the form $@r(x)\ L \leftarrow Body$ where x identifies the maker of the rule. We can represent the institutional hierarchy as a transitively closed set of facts of the form boss(X,Y) and then define the priorities of the policy rules as follows:

$$\backslash\text{override}(\text{r}(\text{u}_i), \text{r}(\text{u}_j)) : - \text{boss}(\text{u}_i, \text{u}_j). \tag{3}$$

4   Conclusion

In this paper, we argue that the use of defeasible reasoning can yield significant benefits in the area of role-based access control systems. As an illustration, we show that complex modifications to access control policies can be naturally represented in a logic programming framework with defeasible reasoning and they can be applied in modular fashion. The use of logic programming also easily supports various extensions such as institutional hierarchies. The same technique can be used to capture even more advanced features, such as distributed access control policies, Team-Based Access Control, and more.

There are several promising directions for future work. One is to investigate other access control models and, hopefully, accrue similar benefits. Other possible directions include incorporation of advanced features of object oriented logic programming, such as inheritance.

Acknowledgments. This work was supported, in part, by the Center for Dynamic Data Analysis (CDDA),[2] and NSF grant 0964196. We also thank Paul Fodor for his collaboration.

References

1. Becker, M.Y., Nanz, S.: A logic for state-modifying authorization policies. ACM Trans. Inf. Syst. Secur. **13**(3), 20:1–20:28 (2010). http://doi.acm.org/10.1145/1805974.1805976

---

[2] CDDA was supported by NSF award IIP1069147 and CA Technologies.

2. Brickley, D., Guha, R.: Rdf schema 1.1. Tech. rep., W3C (2014)
3. Chen, W., Kifer, M., Warren, D.S.: Hilog: A foundation for higher-order logic programming. The Journal of Logic Programming **15**(3), 187–230 (1993). http://www.sciencedirect.com/science/article/pii/074310669390039J
4. Damianou, N., Dulay, N., Lupu, E.C., Sloman, M.: The ponder policy specification language. In: Sloman, M., Lobo, J., Lupu, E.C. (eds.) POLICY 2001. LNCS, vol. 1995, p. 18. Springer, Heidelberg (2001). http://dl.acm.org/citation.cfm?id=646962.712108
5. Ferraiolo, D.F., Kuhn, R.D., Chandramouli, R.: Role-Based Access Control, 2nd edn. Artech House Inc, Norwood (2007)
6. Hitzler, P., Krtzsch, M., Parsia, B., Patel-Schneider, P.F., Rudolph, S.: Owl 2 web ontology language primer (second edition). Tech. rep., W3C (2012)
7. Jin, X., Krishnan, R., Sandhu, R.: A unified attribute-based access control model covering DAC, MAC and RBAC. In: Cuppens-Boulahia, N., Cuppens, F., Garcia-Alfaro, J. (eds.) DBSec 2012. LNCS, vol. 7371, pp. 41–55. Springer, Heidelberg (2012). http://dx.doi.org/10.1007/978-3-642-31540-4_4
8. Joshi, J., Bhatti, R., Bertino, E., Ghafoor, A.: An access control language for multi-domain environments. IEEE Internet Computing **8**(6), 40–50 (2004)
9. Kagal, L.: Rei1: A policy language for the me-centric project. Tech. rep., HP Laboratories (2002)
10. Kifer, M.: FLORA-2: An object-oriented knowledge base language. The FLORA-2 Web Site. http://flora.sourceforge.net
11. Kifer, M.: Rules and ontologies in F-logic. In: Eisinger, N., Małuszyński, J. (eds.) Reasoning Web. LNCS, vol. 3564, pp. 22–34. Springer, Heidelberg (2005)
12. Kifer, M., Lausen, G., Wu, J.: Logical foundations of object-oriented and frame-based languages. J. ACM **42**(4), 741–843 (1995). http://doi.acm.org/10.1145/210332.210335
13. Li, H., Zhang, X., Wu, H., Qu, Y.: Design and application of rule based access control policies. In: Proceedings of 7th Semantic Web and Policy Workshop (2005)
14. Parducci, B., Lockhart, H.: extensible access control markup language (xacml) version 3.0. Tech. rep., OASIS Standard (2013)
15. Park, J.S., Ahn, G.J., Sandhu, R.: Role-based access control on the web using ldap. In: Proceedings of the Fifteenth Annual Working Conference on Database and Application Security, Das 2001, pp. 19–30 Kluwer Academic Publishers, Norwell (2002). http://dl.acm.org/citation.cfm?id=863742.863745
16. Park, J.S., Sandhu, R., Ahn, G.J.: Role-based access control on the web. ACM Trans. Inf. Syst. Secur. **4**(1), 37–71 (2001). http://doi.acm.org/10.1145/383775.383777
17. Przymusinski, T.: Well-founded and stationary models of logic programs. Annals of Mathematics and Artificial Intelligence **12**(3–4), 141–187 (1994)
18. Schulzrinne, H., Tschofenig, H., Morris, J.B., Cuellar, J.R., Polk, J., Rosenberg, J.: Common policy: A document format for expressing privacy preferences. Internet RFC 4745, February, 2007
19. Sun, Y., Pan, P., Leung, H., Shi, B.: Ontology based hybrid access control for automatic interoperation. In: Xiao, B., Yang, L.T., Ma, J., Muller-Schloer, C., Hua, Y. (eds.) ATC 2007. LNCS, vol. 4610, pp. 323–332. Springer, Heidelberg (2007). http://dl.acm.org/citation.cfm?id=2394798.2394840

20. Wan, H., Grosof, B., Kifer, M., Fodor, P., Liang, S.: Logic programming with defaults and argumentation theories. In: Hill, P.M., Warren, D.S. (eds.) ICLP 2009. LNCS, vol. 5649, pp. 432–448. Springer, Heidelberg (2009)
21. Wan, H., Kifer, M., Grosof, B.: Defeasibility in answer set programs with defaults and argumentation rules. Semantic Web Journal (2014)
22. Yang, G., Kifer, M., Zhao, C.: FLORA-2: a rule-based knowledge representation and inference for the semantic web. In: Meersman, R., Schmidt, D.C. (eds.) CoopIS 2003, DOA 2003, and ODBASE 2003. LNCS, vol. 2888, pp. 671–688. Springer, Heidelberg (2003)

Explanation of Proofs of Regulatory (Non-)Compliance Using Semantic Vocabularies

Sagar Sunkle[(✉)], Deepali Kholkar, and Vinay Kulkarni

Tata Research Development and Design Center, Tata Consultancy Services, 54B,
Industrial Estate, Hadapsar, Pune 411013, India
{sagar.sunkle,deepali.kholkar,vinay.vkulkarni}@tcs.com

Abstract. With recent regulatory advances, modern enterprises have
to not only comply with regulations but have to be prepared to provide
explanation of proof of (non-)compliance. On top of compliance checking,
this necessitates modeling concepts from regulations and enterprise operations so that stakeholder-specific and close to natural language explanations could be generated. We take a step in this direction by using
Semantics of Business Vocabulary and Rules to model and map vocabularies of regulations and operations of enterprise. Using these vocabularies and leveraging proof generation abilities of an existing compliance
engine, we show how such explanations can be created. Basic natural
language explanations that we generate can be easily enriched by adding
requisite domain knowledge to the vocabularies.

Keywords: Regulatory compliance · Proof of compliance · Explanation
of proof · SBVR

1 Introduction

Regulatory compliance is a unique change driver that modern enterprises *have
to* face. Enterprises find complying to regulations in a cost effective manner
extremely difficult. This can be attributed to the fact that regulations and
changes therein tend to impact enterprises' operational practices substantially.
With spend on compliance slated to rise to many billions of dollars in next 10
years, the need for improving the state of practice in regulatory compliance is
all the more evident [1,2].

With regards the state of the practice in compliance, one of the most sought
after features is the ability to prove and explain (non-)compliance, preferably in
a way tailored to specific stakeholders' requirements [2,3]. It should be possible
to produce an explanation which compliance officers/internal auditors can use
in a legally defensible way. It should also be possible to produce an explanation
that business stakeholders may use to find out how (non-)compliance is affecting
business goals that are currently operationalized.

In spite of a number of formal techniques suggested for compliance checking [4–8], proof explanation has received less attention in general [10,11]. While

© Springer International Publishing Switzerland 2015
N. Bassiliades et al. (Eds.): RuleML 2015, LNCS 9202, pp. 388–403, 2015.
DOI: 10.1007/978-3-319-21542-6_25

the diagnostic information available in given formal techniques can be leveraged, at least two additional functionalities need to be provided for creating stakeholder-specific explanations that are purposive: a) concepts from legal and operational practices from regulations and business processes need to be modeled and mapped [12] and b) additional domain knowledge need to be modeled other than knowledge expressed in compliance rules [11] to enrich explanations and increase their value to the stakeholders.

We take a step in this direction by presenting an approach in which we use Semantics of Business Vocabulary and Rules (SBVR) to model concepts from regulations and enterprise operations. While we leverage proof generation ability of a formal compliance engine [10], our specific contribution is *generation of close to natural language explanation of proof of (non-)compliance using SBVR vocabularies*. We also substantiate our approach with a work-in-progress case study of banking regulations applicable to a bank's account opening business process. We believe that our approach shows how requirement a) can be satisfied and also paves way for satisfying requirement b) stated above.

The paper is arranged as follows. In Section 2, we motivate the use of SBVR vocabularies for modeling regulations and operations of enterprise and present an outline of our approach. We elaborate our approach for proof explanation in Section 3. Section 4 presents an ongoing case study where we implement our proof explanation approach for a bank's compliance to account opening regulations. We discuss related and future work in Section 5. Section 6 concludes the paper.

2   Motivation and Outline

Industry compliance reporting trends reveal that auditors increasingly expect consistent evidence of compliance whereas enterprise management expects an accurate and succinct assessment of risks associated with compliance [2]. Furthermore, explanations of proofs of (non-)compliance are increasingly expected to include which regulations a given operational practice of enterprise is subject to and what parts of a regulation does the practice depart from and why [3]. The latter functionality is especially relevant for shareholders since it forces an enterprise to give business reasons for (non-)compliance.

Industry governance, risk, and compliance (GRC) solutions tend to take semi-/in-formal approach to compliance checking. In comparison, formal logic-based compliance techniques seem to be better positioned to produce more elaborate explanation of proof of (non-) compliance than document-based evidence. As stated in Section 1, this necessitates modeling and mapping of concepts in regulations and operational practices on top of proof generation abilities.

In our approach, we leverage the proof generation ability of a formal compliance engine DR-Prolog [10]. We use SBVR to model and map vocabularies of regulations and enterprises' operations. While DR-Prolog provides a formal model of regulatory rules and operational facts, SBVR provides a semantic model for a formal terminology. SBVR provides a cohesive set of interconnected concepts, with behavioral guidance in terms of policies and rules to govern the

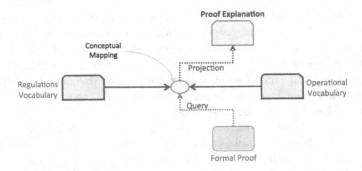

Fig. 1. Outline of Our Approach for Proof Explanations

actions of subject of the formal terminology. We first generate the proof of (non-)compliance using DR-Prolog and then query the formal terminology for concepts in the proof. The projection of results from queries to formal terminology model achieves close to natural language explanation of the proof. This is illustrated in Figure 1.

We elaborate our approach in the next section. First, we show how proofs are generated from DR-Prolog models of regulatory rules and operational facts. We then show how SBVR can be used to model and map regulations and operations. Finally, we show how concepts from proofs are queried and how results are projected to obtain explanation.

3   Proof Generation and Explanation

Proof generation and explanation in DR-Prolog is based on a translation of a defeasible theory into a logic metaprogram and describes a framework for defining different versions of defeasible logics, following different intuitions [10,14,15]. This approach uses tracing mechanism of XSB[1] which is a logic programming and deductive database system. Proof generation is tailored to preprocessing XSB trace to obtain a defeasible logic search tree that is subsequently transformed into a proof. It is clarified in [14], that since knowledge is represented using defeasible reasoning, the explanation of a proof is at the level of defeasible logics. An implication of choice to stay at the level of defeasible logics is that the explanation takes the form of chain of predicates that led to success or failure.

3.1   Generating Proof of (Non-)Compliance

We differ from the proof generation approach in [10,14,15] in our choice of arriving at the specific rules and facts that imply success or failure instead of obtaining chain of defeasible predicates. Instead of XSB, we use trace producing meta-interpreter from[16].

---

[1] See http://xsb.sourceforge.net/

Algorithm 1. GET SUCCESS RULE AND FACTS FROM SUCCESS TRACE

Input: Texts of success trace and theory
Output: Success rules and success facts

1 Trace $trace \leftarrow read(successTrace.txt)$,Theory $theory \leftarrow read(theory.txt)$
2 **procedure** processTrace (*Trace trace*)
3 | **while** $trace.hasFail()$ **do**
4 | | $depth \leftarrow computeMaxDepth(trace)$
5 | | **if** $depth \neq 0$ **then**
6 | | | $trace.tag(get\_CALL\_FAIL\_Pairs())$
7 | | $depth \leftarrow depth - 1$
8 | | $trace.remove(get\_CALL\_FAIL\_Pairs())$
10 | | processTrace (*trace*)
12 | **return**

13 **procedure** matchRules (*Trace t, Theory theory*)
14 | **if** $t.predicate.startsWith(\text{``}defeasible\text{''}~or~\text{``}strict\text{''})$ **then**
15 | | **for** $n = 0$ **to** $theory.length()$ **do**
16 | | | $th \leftarrow theory.line()$
17 | | | **if** $match(t.ruleIdenfier(), th)$ **then**
18 | | | | $successRules.add(th)$

19 **procedure** matchFacts (*Trace t, Theory theory*)
20 | **if** $t.predicate.startsWith(\text{``}fact\text{''})$ **then**
21 | | **for** $n = 0$ **to** $theory.length$ **do**
22 | | | $th \leftarrow theory.line$
23 | | | **if** $match(t, th)$ **then**
24 | | | | $successFacts.add(th)$

25 processTrace (*trace*)
   // Only CALL EXIT pairs left in the trace.
26 **for** $n = 0$ **to** $trace.length() - 1$ **do**
27 | $t \leftarrow trace.line()$
28 | matchRules (*trace, theory*)
29 | matchFacts (*trace, theory*)
30 **return** $successRules, successFacts$

This meta-interpreter produces trace that minimally contains three pieces of information: depth of predicate invocation, the invocation type which is one of CALL, EXIT, FAIL, and REDO, and the current predicate being processed. An example of trace is shown below.

0'CALL 'defeasibly(client_account_data(17,open_account),obligation)
1'CALL 'strictly(client_account_data(17,open_account),obligation)
2'CALL 'fact(obligation(client_account_data(17,open_account)))
2'FAIL 'fact(obligation(client_account_data(17,open_account)))
. . .

To arrive at specific successful or failed rules and facts, we exploit the procedure box abstraction [17] that is represented in the trace by the depth of invocation. CALL, EXIT, FAIL, and REDO essentially indicate the time when predicate is entered/invoked, successfully returned from, completely failed, or failed but backtracked respectively. The meta-interpreter can be used to produce trace that can be saved as a text file where each line indicates one invocation with three pieces of information each.

Algorithm 1 shows how a success trace is processed to recursively remove successive CALL and FAIL pairs. These pairs indicate failed invocations and are not relevant for obtaining success rules and facts. These pairs may occur at various depths bound by maximum depth that recursive invocations led to. Algorithm 1 first tags the CALL FAIL pairs at the maximum current depth for removal indicating innermost procedure box and then proceeds till the lowest depth indicating outermost procedure box.

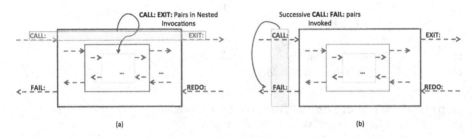

Fig. 2. Exploiting Procedure Box Representation for Proof Generation in Success (a) and Failure (b).eps

Recursive calls in Algorithm 1 are needed to ensure that all CALL FAIL pairs at various depths are removed as illustrated in Figure 2 (a). Once all CALL FAIL pairs are removed, the successive CALL EXIT pairs in the remaining trace indicate successful invocation of rules and facts.

In contrast, to find specific failed rules and facts, instead of removing successive CALL FAIL pairs, we need to *retain* only these pairs while removing rest of other kinds of invocations. Because we are interested only in successive CALL FAIL pairs in case of failed rules and facts, we do not need to recurse as in Algorithm 1. Figure 2 (b) illustrates this.

For Algorithm 1 used to obtain success rules and facts and a similar algorithm to obtain failure rules and facts not shown here for the want of space, we take as input the trace of successful query and failed query respectively. The calls to match*() methods in both algorithms indicate that rules and facts are sought to match with the theory of the problem which is stored line by line itself. Since the trace contains intermediate substitutions by the inference engine, the strings of invocations of rules and facts from trace are attempted to match partially with the rules and facts from theory. The output of both algorithms is sets of matched rules and facts from the theory rather than the trace.

The successful or failed rules and facts are used to generate explanation via vocabularies. In the next section, we present how vocabularies are modeled, mapped, and used in generating the explanation.

3.2   Generating Explanation

Modeling and Mapping Regulations and Operations Vocabularies.
SBVR vocabularies for regulations and operations are defined in terms of four sections. First, vocabulary to capture the business context is created, consisting of the semantic community and sub-communities owning the regulation and to which the regulation applies. Each semantic community is unified by shared understanding of an area, i.e., body of shared meanings. This in turn can comprise smaller bodies of meanings, containing a body of shared concepts that captures concepts and their relations, and a body of shared guidance containing business rules. These concepts are shown as *Business Vocabulary* in SBVR metamodel in Figure 3.

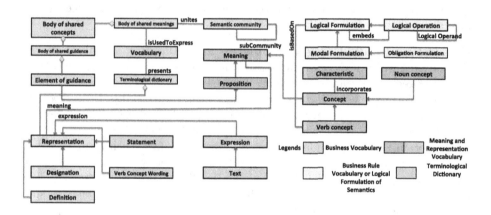

Fig. 3. SBVR Metamodel For Creating and Mapping Regulations and Operations Vocabularies

Second, the body of concepts is modeled by focusing on key terms in regulatory rules. Concepts referred in the rule are modeled as noun concepts. A general concept is defined for an entity that denotes a category. Specific details about an entity are captured as characteristics. Verb concepts capture behavior in which noun concepts play a role. Binary verb concepts capture relations between two concepts. Characteristics are unary verb concepts. The SBVR metamodel for modeling regulation body of concepts are shown as *Meaning and Representation Vocabulary* in Figure 3.

Third, we build the body of guidance using policies laid down in the regulation. This includes logical formulation of each policy (an obligation formulation for obligatory rules) based on logical operations such as conjunctions, implications and negation. At the lowest level are atomic formulations based on verb concepts from the body of concepts. This is shown in *Business Rules Vocabulary* in Figure 3.

Fourth and lastly, we model the terminological dictionary that contains various representations used by a semantic community for its concepts and rules defined above. These consist of designations or alternate names for various concepts, definitions for concepts and natural language statements for policies stated in the regulation. We also use the terminological dictionary to capture the vocabulary used by the enterprise in its business processes. Each activity in the process becomes a verb concept wording in the terminological dictionary. SBVR concepts for modeling terminological variations are shown as *Terminological Dictionary* in Figure 3.

SBVR defines verb concept wordings as representations of verb concepts in their most general form. Every verb concept in the regulation body of concepts is *mapped to corresponding verb concept wording from the process terminological dictionary*. This mapping is used to look up consequent terms of rules and the corresponding process entity is treated as a placeholder for compliance implementation of the rule.

Elaborating Proofs Using Vocabularies and Mapping. At this stage, on the one hand we have success/failure rules and facts and on the other, the vocabularies of regulations and operations. The mapping between concepts defined using the *Business Vocabulary*, rules defined using the *Business Rules Vocabulary*, and the terminological variations of concepts defined using the *Terminological Dictionary* is used as the source of the proof explanation.

To obtain the explanation for a success or failure fact, each term/keyword in the fact is looked up in the *Business Vocabulary* body of concepts and its corresponding terminological representation in *Terminological Dictionary*. For rules, logical formulation of rule is fetched from *Business Rules Vocabulary* and it natural language representation is obtained from its corresponding mappings in the *Terminological Dictionary*.

To substantiate our approach, we present a case study in the next section. This case study concerns Reserve Bank of India' (RBI) Know Your Customer (KYC) regulations for Indian banks.

4 Case Study

RBI's KYC regulations are aimed at identifying *different types of customers*, accepting them as customers of given bank when they fulfill certain *identity and address documentation* criteria laid out in various regulations and annexes in the most recent RBI KYC master circular[2], and categorizing them into various risk profiles for periodic KYC reviews.

---

[2] See RBI KYC 2014 Master Circular http://www.rbi.org.in/scripts/BS_ViewMas Circulardetails.aspx?id=9074#23.

The following shows how KYC regulations characterize a salaried employee working at a private company and which documents are acceptable for opening a new account by such individual.

KYC Regulation for Salaried Employees [RBI KYC Customer Identification 2014 §2.5 (vii)]

[... <u>for opening bank accounts of salaried employees</u> some banks rely on a certificate / letter issued by the employer as the only KYC document ..., banks <u>need to rely on such certification only from corporates and other entities of repute</u> and should be aware of the competent authority designated by the concerned employer to issue such certificate/letter. Further, <u>in addition to the certificate from employer, banks should insist on at least one of the officially valid documents</u> as provided in the Prevention of Money Laundering Rules (viz. passport, driving licence, PAN Card, Voters Identity card etc.) or utility bills for KYC purposes for opening bank account of salaried employees of corporates and other entities.]

The business process (BP) model of BankA where individuals of the kind *private salaried employee* desire to open account is shown in Figure 4. A general bank official interacts with a client while KYC documents are managed by content management official. The compliance official is in charge of compliance function. This BP model is traversed to generate BankA *Terminological*

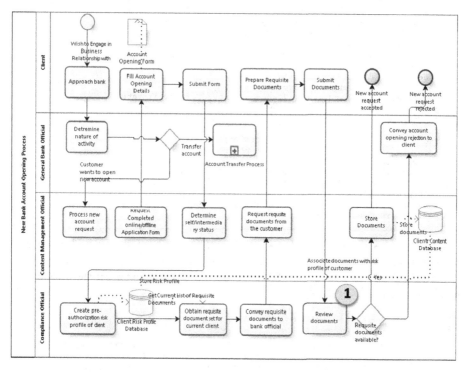

Fig. 4. Business Process of BankA with PSE Regulation Annotation

Dictionary which is in the form of a list of verb concept wordings corresponding to a) each Task/ SubProcess from the process, e.g., *Approach Bank, Process New account Request* and b) each object and condition label in the process, e.g., *Client Risk Profile Database, Self, and Intermediary* etc.

Vocabularies for the KYC regulations and specifically regulation §2.5 (vii), and the account opening business process, are modeled and mapped as described below.

Business vocabulary consists of the semantic community banking industry, with sub-communities RBI and BankA. The RBI semantic community is unified by body of shared meanings RBI_Regulations. It contains the body of meanings RBI_KYCRegulation which comprises body of shared concepts RBI_KYCRegulationConcepts and body of shared guidance RBI_KYCRules. Process concepts such as ReviewDocuments are captured as verb concept wordings in *Terminological Dictionary* of BankA. Finally, *Terminological Dictionary* RBI_Terminological_Reference contains natural language representation of various KYC concepts.

Listing 1.1 shows a DR-Prolog formulation of a rule for *private salaried employee* from KYC regulation stated above. Three different cases are captured in Listing 1.1. The regulation is complied with for individual 17 whereas conditions for individuals 18 and 19 result in non-compliance.

Listing 1.1. Case Theory in DR-Prolog

```
1  defeasible(r3,obligation,client_account_data(Client_ID,
2  open_account),[client_data(Client_ID,ind,pse),pse_data(
3  Client_ID, approvedCorporate),pse_KYC_document_data(
4  Client_ID,acceptApprovedCorpCertificate,pse_kyc_document_set)]).
5  /* Everything is OK, so account can be opened.*/
6  fact(client_data(17,ind,pse)).
7  fact(pse_data(17,approvedCorporate)).
8  fact(pse_KYC_document_data(17,acceptApprovedCorpCertificate,
9  pse_kyc_document_set)).
10 /* Corporate is not approved, account cannot be opened*/
11 fact(client_data(18,ind,pse)).
12 fact(pse_data(18,not(approvedCorporate))).
13 fact(pse_KYC_document_data(18,acceptApprovedCorpCertificate,
14 pse_kyc_document_set)).
15 /* Requisite documents not submitted, account cannot be opened*/
16 fact(client_data(19,ind,pse)).
17 fact(pse_data(19,approvedCorporate)).
18 fact(pse_KYC_document_data(19,acceptApprovedCorpCertificate,
19 not(pse_kyc_document_set))).
```

For the theory shown in Listing 1.1, queries such as shown in Listing 1.2 are executed. The traces are collected and input to the program implementing Algorithm 1 and also to obtain failure rules and facts along with the theory for generating proofs.

Listing 1.2. Queries about Private Salaried Employees in DR-Prolog

```
1  trace(defeasibly(client_account_data(17,open_account),obligation)).
2  trace(defeasibly(client_account_data(18,open_account),obligation)).
3  trace(defeasibly(client_account_data(19,open_account),obligation)).
```

The success/failure rules and facts are then parsed to obtain terms. These terms are then used in a manner illustrated in Figure 5.

Business Vocabulary with Characteristics on top left of Figure 5 shows regulation body of concepts, containing the concept hierarchy with client at its root, specialized by general concept individual, specialized by concept pse denoting private salaried employee. Concept pse_KYC_document denotes the documents submitted by a private salaried employee. Characteristics of private salaried employee are whether employer is an approvedCorporate or notApprovedCorporate. Verb concepts client_is_ind, client_is_pse and pse_has_pse_KYC_document capture relations between concepts.

Business Rules Vocabulary on the bottom left of Figure 5 is the body of guidance containing a section of regulation policy denoted by rule r3 in Listing 1.1. Rule r3 is defined as an obligation formulation based on an implication, with antecedent list client_is_ind, client_is_pse, approvedCorporate and acceptApproved-CorpCertificate and consequent open_account.

The *Terminological Dictionary* contains alternate names client_data, pse_data, pse_KYC_document_data for concepts client, pse and pse_KYC_document respectively. It also contains the descriptions Customer, Private salaried employee and KYC document details for private salaried employee and definitions such as Employer is a corporate approved by the bank and Certificate from approved corporate can be accepted for characteristics approvedCorporate and acceptApproved-CorpCertificate respectively.

Each concept is mapped to its corresponding representation in the *Terminological Dictionary*. Similarly, each rule in *Business Rules Vocabulary* is mapped to its natural language statement in the *Terminological Dictionary*. This mapping leads to attaching the rule r3 in Listing 1.1 at the activity *Review Documents* indicated by (1) in the BP model shown earlier in Figure 4.

Various XML fragments shown in Figure 5 can be treated as tables with mapping concepts as foreign keys. Upon querying specific terms from respective tables/XML fragments, projecting the natural language expressions including the rule statements, and performing textual processing including removing _ underscore characters; for case (1) in Figure 5 of success rules and facts we obtain the following explanation:

> As per rule r3, it is obligatory for bank to obtain requisite documents including approved employer certificate and additionally at least one valid document from individual who is a private salaried employee in order to open account for this individual. For current individual that is private salaried employee; Employer is a corporate approved by the bank and KYC documents required for private salaried employee submitted. Therefore **compliance is achieved** for current individual with *Client_ID 17*.

Similarly for case (2) of failure rules and facts, we obtain the following explanation:

> For current individual that is private salaried employee; Employer is NOT a corporate approved by the bank and KYC documents required

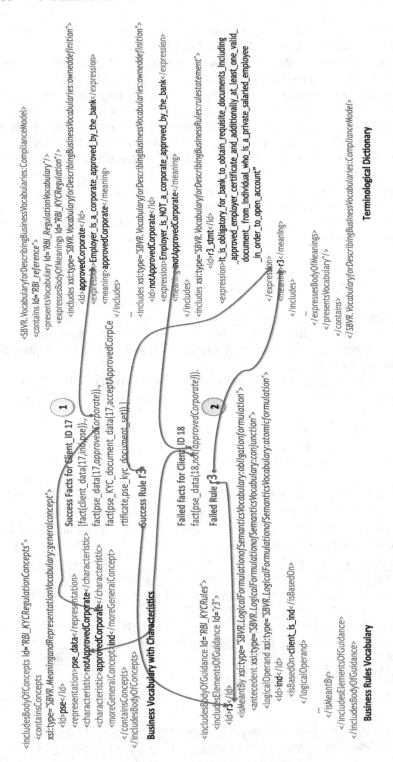

Fig. 5. Generating Proof Explanation By Querying Vocabularies and Projecting Results

for private salaried employee submitted. As per rule r3, it is obligatory for bank to obtain requisite documents including approved employer certificate and additionally at least one valid document from individual who is a private salaried employee in order to open account for this individual. Therefore **compliance is NOT achieved** for current individual with *Client_ID 18*.

The underlined parts of the explanation are blanks in a textual template filled in with the results of projection. Note that the explanations above can be made to contain additional information such as regulation number (RBI KYC Customer Identification 2014 §2.5 (vii)), risks identified by regulatory body for given case ("... accepting documents from an unapproved corporate is fraught with risk...") by modeling this information in the *Terminological Dictionary*.

Implementation Details. To implement vocabulary artifacts, we imported elements shown in Figure 3 from the consumable XMI of SBVR meta-model available at OMG site[3] into Eclipse Modeling Framework Ecore model. The BP model is created and traversed using an in-house tool that we described in [18]. We implemented DR-Prolog programs using TuProlog.[4] Algorithm 1 and also similar algorithm for capturing failure rules and facts are implemented in Java. For loading and querying XML fragments shown in Figure 5, and projecting results into templates we used Apache Metamodel[5] which takes as input the XML representation of vocabularies modeled with standard Ecore editor. It provides SQL like query API to query XML data. Results of queries are substituted into textual template(s) using FreeMarker[6] Java template engine.

Implementation Evaluation. The case study presented here is an ongoing case study with a private bank. RBI's 2014 KYC regulations contains 11 main categories of customers of which we have modeled 5 categories so far including private salaried employees for which we have shown an exemplar in this section. While we have not conducted an empirical evaluation of efforts involved in building vocabularies, experiments so far have shown that this effort results in reusable vocabulary artifacts such as KYC regulation vocabulary components. Further scalability studies are part of our future work.

In the next section, we review related work and also describe future work.

5   Related and Future Work

Proof Explanation. A compliance checking approach presented in [21] uses information in the *event log* and a *labeling function* that relates Petri net-based

---

[3] See under *Normative Machine Consumable Files* at http://www.omg.org/spec/SBVR/20130601/SBVR-XMI-Metamodel.xml

[4] See http://apice.unibo.it/xwiki/bin/view/Tuprolog/

[5] See http://metamodel.apache.org/

[6] See http://freemarker.org/

compliance patterns to the transitions of events to indicate violations. Similar to [10,14,15], we use inference trace as a diagnostic knowledge base, but in comparison to [10,14,15] and [21], we model the vocabularies of regulatory and operations domains which enables us to generate close to natural language explanations. In another approach presented in [22], whenever a rule is violated by the process model, temporal logic querying techniques along with BPMN-Q queries extended with data aspects are used to visually explain violations in the process model. Similarly, approach in [23] annotates BP models with predicates from regulations and uses them in creating status reports of violations. These approaches lack an explicit modeling of domain concepts, which means that explanations in these approaches are not expressive enough and they require knowledge of formal technique to interpret the violations explained. The explanation we generate are natural language statements which are easy to understand and can be extended to include other stakeholder-specific information.

Explicit Mapping of Concepts. The need for an explicit mapping between concepts of regulations and business processes has been identified in [12]. Formal compliance checking approaches in contrast implicitly assume that a terminological mapping already exists between regulations and the BP models. The locations where regulations become applicable are then found by constructing an execution trace as in [4], finding paths in process structure tree as in [11], or placed manually on a business property specification language diagram as in [5]. Labels from business process in such traces, paths, or other representations are often presumed to map to labels of formal models of regulations. In comparison to approaches that assume same labels, we take similar stance as in [12,13] and map concepts from regulations and business process as described in Section 3.2.

SBVR in Regulatory Compliance. SBVR has been used in the context of regulatory compliance in [24–26]. These approaches use SBVR to describe process rules, transform SBVR process vocabulary to a formal compliance language, and represent legal rules using SBVR respectively. In comparison to these approaches, our approach *applies* the vocabularies toward proof explanation. The general mechanism we presented in this paper can accommodate purposive vocabularies that can be queried for stakeholder-specific interpretations and explanations.

Future Work- Elaborating Business Reasons in Proof Explanation. In order to explicate business reasons in proof explanation, business reasons must be modeled. An approach is presented in [27] which extracts legal requirements from regulations by mapping the latter to the Legal Profile for Goal-oriented Requirements Language. This approach hints at creating models of legal goals at the same level of abstraction as business goals. Similarly, business motivation model by OMG [28] treats regulations as external directives which affect the current courses of action being used to support business motivations. If business objectives which the existing operational practices serve can be modeled using mechanisms as in [27,28], then they can be used in proof explanations with models of operations/business processes as the common point of confluence.

In [29], we showed how to incorporate directives such as internal policies and external regulations into enterprise to-be architecture. Our approach in [29] enables querying directives given operational details such as business process specifics and also querying business process specifics given directives. If the high level motivations of enterprise were expressed in the *Terminological Dictionary*, it might be possible to relate these to terms in the proof explanation. This is part of our future work.

6   Conclusion

We presented an approach in which we use SBVR to model and map concepts from regulation and operations and leverage proof generation ability of DR-Prolog to generate elaborate explanation of proofs of (non-)compliance. Our approach can accommodate additional information from domain under consideration which can be included in the explanations. We are currently working on combining our approach for modeling business motivations presented in [29] with our proof generation approach to include business reasons behind (non-)compliance. We believe that with our current and ongoing work we take a solid step toward purposive and stakeholder-specific explanations of proofs of (non-)compliance.

References

1. French Caldwell, J.A.W.: Magic quadrant for enterprise governance, risk and compliance platforms (Gartner) (2013)
2. English, S., Hammond, S.: Cost of compliance 2014 (Thomson Reuters Accelus) (2014)
3. FRC: What constitutes an explanation under 'comply or explain'? Report of discussions between companies and investors (February 2012)
4. Sadiq, W., Governatori, G., Namiri, K.: Modeling Control Objectives for Business Process Compliance. In: Alonso, G., Dadam, P., Rosemann, M. (eds.) BPM 2007. LNCS, vol. 4714, pp. 149–164. Springer, Heidelberg (2007)
5. Liu, Y., Müller, S., Xu, K.: A static compliance-checking framework for business process models. IBM Systems Journal 46(2), 335–362 (2007)
6. El Kharbili, M., Stein, S., Markovic, I., Pulvermüller, E.: Towards a framework for semantic business process compliance management. In: The Impact of Governance, Risk, and Compliance on Information Systems (GRCIS), June 17. CEUR Workshop Proceedings, vol. 339, Montpellier, France, pp. 1–15 (2008)
7. Ly, L.T., Rinderle-Ma, S., Knuplesch, D., Dadam, P.: Monitoring business process compliance using compliance rule graphs. In: Meersman, R. (ed.) OTM 2011, Part I. LNCS, vol. 7044, pp. 82–99. Springer, Heidelberg (2011)
8. Hashmi, M., Governatori, G.: A methodological evaluation of business process compliance management frameworks. In: Song, M., Wynn, M.T., Liu, J. (eds.) AP-BPM 2013. LNBIP, vol. 159, pp. 106–115. Springer, Heidelberg (2013)

9. Fellmann, M., Zasada, A.: State-of-the-art of business process compliance approaches. In: Avital, M., Leimeister, J.M., Schultze, U. (eds.) 22st European Conference on Information Systems, ECIS 2014, June 9–11, Tel Aviv, Israel (2014)

10. Bikakis, A., Papatheodorou, C., Antoniou, G.: The DR-Prolog tool suite for defeasible reasoning and proof explanation in the semantic web. In: Darzentas, J., Vouros, G.A., Vosinakis, S., Arnellos, A. (eds.) SETN 2008. LNCS (LNAI), vol. 5138, pp. 345–351. Springer, Heidelberg (2008)

11. Awad, A., Smirnov, S., Weske, M.: Resolution of compliance violation in business process models: a planning-based approach. In: Meersman, R., Dillon, T., Herrero, P. (eds.) OTM 2009, Part I. LNCS, vol. 5870, pp. 6–23. Springer, Heidelberg (2009)

12. Boella, G., Janssen, M., Hulstijn, J., Humphreys, L., van der Torre, L.: Managing legal interpretation in regulatory compliance. In: Francesconi, E., Verheij, B. (eds.) International Conference on Artificial Intelligence and Law, ICAIL 2013, pp. 23–32. ACM. Rome (2013)

13. Becker, J., Delfmann, P., Eggert, M., Schwittay, S.: Generalizability and applicability of modelbased business process compliance-checking approaches – a state-of-the-art analysis and research roadmap. BuR – Business Research 5(2), 221–247 (2012); Publication status: Published

14. Antoniou, G., Bikakis, A., Dimaresis, N., Genetzakis, M., Georgalis, G., Governatori, G., Karouzaki, E., Kazepis, N., Kosmadakis, D., Kritsotakis, M., Lilis, G., Papadogiannakis, A., Pediaditis, P., Terzakis, C., Theodosaki, R., Zeginis, D.: Proof explanation for a nonmonotonic semantic web rules language. Data & Knowledge Engineering 64(3), 662–687 (2008)

15. Kontopoulos, E., Bassiliades, N., Antoniou, G.: Visualizing semantic web proofs of defeasible logic in the DR-DEVICE system. Knowl.-Based Syst. 24(3), 406–419 (2011)

16. Bratko, I.: PROLOG Programming for Artificial Intelligence, 2nd edn. Addison-Wesley Longman Publishing Co. Inc., Boston (1990)

17. Tobermann, G., Beckstein, C.: What's in a trace: The box model revisited. In: Fritzson, P.A. (ed.) AADEBUG 1993. LNCS, vol. 749, pp. 171–187. Springer, Heidelberg (1993)

18. Kholkar, D., Yelure, P., Tiwari, H., Deshpande, A., Shetye, A.: Experience with industrial adoption of business process models for user acceptance testing. In: Van Gorp, P., Ritter, T., Rose, L.M. (eds.) ECMFA 2013. LNCS, vol. 7949, pp. 192–206. Springer, Heidelberg (2013)

19. Antoniou, G., Dimaresis, N., Governatori, G.: A modal and deontic defeasible reasoning system for modelling policies and multi-agent systems. Expert Syst. Appl. 36(2), 4125–4134 (2009)

20. Antoniou, G., Dimaresis, N., Governatori, G.: A System for modal and deontic defeasible reasoning. In: Orgun, M.A., Thornton, J. (eds.) AI 2007. LNCS (LNAI), vol. 4830, pp. 609–613. Springer, Heidelberg (2007)

21. Ramezani, E., Fahland, D., van der Aalst, W.M.P.: Where did i misbehave? diagnostic information in compliance checking. In: Barros, A., Gal, A., Kindler, E. (eds.) BPM 2012. LNCS, vol. 7481, pp. 262–278. Springer, Heidelberg (2012)

22. Awad, A., Weidlich, M., Weske, M.: Specification, verification and explanation of violation for data aware compliance rules. In: Baresi, L., Chi, C.-H., Suzuki, J. (eds.) ICSOC-ServiceWave 2009. LNCS, vol. 5900, pp. 500–515. Springer, Heidelberg (2009)

23. Governatori, G., Hoffmann, J., Sadiq, S., Weber, I.: Detecting regulatory compliance for business process models through semantic annotations. In: Ardagna, D., Mecella, M., Yang, J. (eds.) Business Process Management Workshops. LNBIP, vol. 17, pp. 5–17. Springer, Heidelberg (2009)

24. Goedertier, S., Mues, C., Vanthienen, J.: Specifying process-aware access control rules in SBVR. In: Paschke, A., Biletskiy, Y. (eds.) RuleML 2007. LNCS, vol. 4824, pp. 39–52. Springer, Heidelberg (2007)

25. Kamada, A., Governatori, G., Sadiq, S.: Transformation of SBVR compliant business rules to executable FCL rules. In: Dean, M., Hall, J., Rotolo, A., Tabet, S. (eds.) RuleML 2010. LNCS, vol. 6403, pp. 153–161. Springer, Heidelberg (2010)

26. Abi-Lahoud, E., Butler, T., Chapin, D., Hall, J.: Interpreting regulations with SBVR. In: Fodor, P., Roman, D., Anicic, D., Wyner, A., Palmirani, M., Sottara, D., Lévy, F. (eds.) Joint Proceedings of the 7th International Rule Challenge, the Special Track on Human Language Technology and the 3rd RuleML Doctoral Consortium. CEUR Workshop Proceedings, vol. 1004. CEUR-WS.org, Seattle (2013)

27. Ghanavati, S., Amyot, D., Rifaut, A.: Legal goal-oriented requirement language (legal GRL) for modeling regulations. In: Proceedings of the 6th International Workshop on Modeling in Software Engineering, MiSE 2014, pp. 1–6. ACM, New York (2014)

28. OMG: Business Motivation Model - Version 1.2 (May 2014)

29. Sunkle, S., Kholkar, D., Rathod, H., Kulkarni, V.: Incorporating directives into enterprise TO-BE architecture. In: Grossmann, G., Hallé, S., Karastoyanova, D., Reichert, M., Rinderle-Ma, S. (eds.) 18th IEEE International Enterprise Distributed Object Computing Conference Workshops and Demonstrations, EDOC Workshops 2014, September 1–2, Ulm, Germany, pp. 57–66. IEEE (2014)

Rule Learning Track

Rule Generalization Strategies in Incremental Learning of Disjunctive Concepts

Stefano Ferilli[1,2]([✉]), Andrea Pazienza[1], and Floriana Esposito[1,2]

[1] Dipartimento di Informatica, Università di Bari, Bari, Italy
{stefano.ferilli,andrea.pazienza,floriana.esposito}@uniba.it
[2] Centro Interdipartimentale per la Logica e sue Applicazioni,
Università di Bari, Bari, Italy

Abstract. Symbolic Machine Learning systems and applications, especially when applied to real-world domains, must face the problem of concepts that cannot be captured by a single definition, but require several alternate definitions, each of which covers part of the full concept extension. This problem is particularly relevant for incremental systems, where progressive covering approaches are not applicable, and the learning and refinement of the various definitions is interleaved during the learning phase. In these systems, not only the learned model depends on the order in which the examples are provided, but it also depends on the choice of the specific definition to be refined. This paper proposes different strategies for determining the order in which the alternate definitions of a concept should be considered in a generalization step, and evaluates their performance on a real-world domain dataset.

1 Introduction

The use of symbolic knowledge representations is mandatory for applications that need to reproduce the human inferential behavior and/or that may be required to explain their decisions in human-understandable terms. These representations must embed suitable definitions for the concepts (entities or relationships) that may come into play in the given application domain, in order to check their occurrence and suitably combine them to carry out their reasoning task. Concepts can be classified as *conjunctive* and *disjunctive*, depending on how they are defined. The former allow a single definition to account for all possible instances of the concept, while the latter require several alternate definitions, each of which covers part of the full concept extension. Psychological studies have established that capturing and dealing with the latter is much harder for humans than it is with the former [4]. Unfortunately, the latter are pervasive and fundamental in any sufficiently complex real-world domain.

A well-known problem in setting up automatic knowledge-based systems is the so-called 'knowledge acquisition bottleneck', by which it is very hard and costly to extract from human experts and/or formalize the knowledge they need to carry out their task. The solution proposed by Artificial Intelligence relies on the use of symbolic Machine Learning systems, that may acquire autonomously

© Springer International Publishing Switzerland 2015
N. Bassiliades et al. (Eds.): RuleML 2015, LNCS 9202, pp. 407–421, 2015.
DOI: 10.1007/978-3-319-21542-6_26

such knowledge. In the supervised setting, concept definitions are inferred starting from descriptions of valid (positive) or invalid (negative) instances (examples) thereof. Of course, the problem of dealing with disjunctive concepts is still present, and even harder to face, in Machine Learning (ML for short).

In turn, ML systems can be classified as *batch* or *incremental*, depending on their learning concept definitions by having available the whole set of examples when the learning task is started, or by allowing new examples to be provided after a tentative definition has already been learned. In the former case, which is the classical setting in ML, the definitions can be learned by considering all the examples, and are immutable; if additional examples are provided later, the learned definitions must be withdrawn and a new learning session must start from scratch considering the whole (extended) set of examples now available. Disjunctive definitions have been classically learned, in this setting, by adopting *progressive coverage* strategies: a conjunctive definition is learned that accounts for a subset of available examples, then these examples are removed and another conjunctive definition is learned to account for a subset of the remaining examples, and so on until all the examples are covered by the learned conjunctive definitions. We call a *component* each such conjunctive definition; a disjunctive definition consists of the set of components referred to the same concept. In this approach, the *components* automatically emerge and are fixed as long as they are found.

The incremental approach, instead, assumes that at any given moment in time a set of examples, and a (possibly disjunctive) definition that accounts for them, are available, and that new examples may become available in the future. If the available concept definition cannot properly account for them, it must be 'refined' (i.e., revised, changed, modified) so that the new version properly accounts for both the old and the new examples. In this setting the progressive covering strategy is not applicable, and the issue of disjunctive definitions becomes particularly relevant. Indeed, when the partial definition is disjunctive, and many of its components can be refined so that the whole definition properly accounts for the whole set of examples, there is no unique way for determining which component is most profitably refined. However, refining different components results in different updated definitions, that become implicit constraints on how the definition itself may evolve when additional examples will become available in the future. Thus, in incremental systems, not only the learned model depends on the order in which the examples are provided, but it also depends on the choice of the specific definition component to be refined at each step.

This paper proposes different strategies for determining the order in which the alternate definition components of a disjunctive concept should be considered in a refinement step, and evaluates their performance on a real-world domain dataset. The next Section recalls useful background information, including related works and the specific system used in our study. Then, Section 3 introduces and motivates the proposed strategies. Section 4 evaluates and discusses the performance of the different strategies, and Section 5 concludes the paper and outlines future work issues.

2   Background and Related Work

In the logic-based ML setting, the learned concept definitions are called *theories*. Automatic revision of logic theories is a complex and computationally expensive task. In fact, most systems for theory revision deal with propositional logic. They can integrate different reasoning methods and learning strategies. Among these systems we find RTLS [10], DUCE [14], DUCTOR [5]. The system proposed in [12] and EITHER [13] explicitly use a deductive-inductive method for modifying a given domain theory.

There are also systems that can revise first-order theories. Most of them try to limit the search space by exploiting information and, generally, require a wide, although incomplete, domain theory or a deep knowledge acquired (possibly in an interactive manner) from the user. Some others, such as MIS [21] and CLINT [7], strongly rely on the interaction with the user to reduce the search space. Others, such as WHY [19], TRACEY [2] and KBR [3], do not require any interaction with the user during the induction process and adopt sophisticated search strategies or more informative search structures. Still others, such as FORTE [18] and AUDREY [23], do not allow the use of negation in the theories because of computational complexity considerations. As a consequence, half of the whole search space is not explored. Aleph [22] is a very flexible system: its settings can be customized to modify the search strategy and allow randomized search, incremental learning and learning constraints, modes and features. InTheLEx [8] is a noteworthy system in this landscape. While the generalization strategy we will present is general, for reasons that will be explained in the following we will use InTheLEx for implementing and testing it.

2.1   InTheLEx

InTheLEx (INcremental THEory Learner from EXamples) can learn *hierarchical* (i.e., non-recursive) theories from positive and negative examples. It is particularly suited for our purposes because it is *fully incremental*: it is able not only to refine existing theories, but also to start learning from an empty theory and from the first available example. This is necessary when incomplete information is available at the time of initial theory generation, as in most real-world application domains. Incrementality is obtained by means of a *closed loop* learning behavior [1], according to which the validity of the learned theory is checked on any new example and, in case of failure, a revision process is activated on it, in order to restore completeness and consistency.

InTheLEx works on Datalog representations interpreted under the Object Identity (OI) assumption[1]. *Datalog* [6] is a simplified version of General Logic Programming [11], and from a syntactic viewpoint can be considered as a sublanguage of Prolog where terms can only be variables or constants (functions are

---

[1] "Within a rule, terms denoted with different symbols must be distinct." While there is no loss in expressive power [20], this has interesting consequences, both from a practical point of view (see next section) and from an intuitive one.

not permitted). Accordingly, the concept definitions in the learned theory are expressed as Horn clauses, i.e. rules whose conclusion represents the concept and whose premise reports a conjunctive definition for it. Disjunctive concepts are defined using several rules with the same predicate in the head. So, for instance:

ball(A) :- weight_medium(A), air_filled(A), has_patches(A),
        horizontal_diameter(A,B), vertical_diameter(A,C), equal(B,C).
ball(A) :- weight_medium(A), air_filled(A), has_patches(A,B),
        horizontal_diameter(A,B), vertical_diameter(A,C), larger(B,C).
ball(A) :- weight_heavy(A), has_holes(A),
        horizontal_diameter(A,B), vertical_diameter(A,C), equal(B,C).
ball(A) :- weight_light(A), regular_shape(A),
        horizontal_diameter(A,B), vertical_diameter(A,C), equal(B,C).

is a theory that defines the disjunctive concept 'ball' using 4 components. E.g., the 'etrusco' 1990 World Cup soccer ball, described as follows:

ball(e) :- weight_medium(e), has_patches(e), air_filled(e), made_of_leather(e),
        horizontal_diameter(e,he), vertical_diameter(e,ve), equal(he,ve).

fits the first component; conversely, negative examples such as a snowball and a spitball are not recognized by any component:

neg(ball(s1)) :- weight_light(s1), made_of_snow(s1), irregular_shape(s1),
        horizontal_diameter(s1,hs1), vertical_diameter(s1,vs1), smaller(hs1,vs1).
neg(ball(s2)) :- weight_light(s2), made_of_paper(s2),
        horizontal_diameter(s2,hs2), vertical_diameter(s2,vs2), larger(hs2,vs2).

InTheLEx adopts a *full memory storage* strategy [17] —i.e., it retains all the available examples— and guarantees the learned theories to be valid on all of them. It incorporates two refinement operators, one for generalizing definitions that reject positive examples, and the other for specializing definitions that explain negative examples. To carry out the process of logic theory revision, InTheLEx exploits a previous theory (optional), and a historical memory of all the past (positive and negative) examples that led to the current theory. Whenever a new example is taken into account, it is recorded in the processed examples list and the 'Tuning' phase, in charge of the possible revision of the current theory, is started. It has no effect on the theory if the new example is negative and not covered (i.e., it is not predicted by the theory to belong to the concept) or positive and covered (i.e., it is predicted by the theory to belong to the concept); in all the other cases, the theory needs to be revised. When a positive example is not covered, a generalization of the theory is needed. When, on the other hand, a negative example is covered, a specialization of the theory must be performed. The candidate refinements (generalizations or specializations) of the definitions are required to preserve correctness with respect to the entire set of currently available examples. If no candidate refinement fulfills this requirement, the specific problematic example is stored as an exception.

The process of identifying the part of the theory that causes the wrong classification of the example, and that needs to be refined, is called *abstract diagnosis*. For conjunctive definitions this process is quite trivial, because the only available definition is obviously in charge of the faulty classification. The question becomes more tricky in the case of disjunctive concepts, for which several alternate conjunctive definitions are available in the theory. Indeed, in this case, if a negative example is covered, the system knows exactly which components of the definition erroneously accounts for it (it is a case of *commission* error). Those components must necessarily be refined (specialized), so that the overall definition does no more account for that example (while still accounting for all the known positive examples —a property known as 'completeness'). Conversely, when a positive example is not covered, this means that no component of the current definition accounts for it, and several such components might be refined (generalized) so that they will account for that example (while still not accounting for any known negative example —a property known as 'consistency').

Thus, abstract diagnosis of an incorrect theory is performed at different levels of granularity, according to the type of error found: while for commission errors it identifies specific faulty conjunctive components to be specialized, for omission errors the scope of the diagnosis process is limited to the coarser level of the disjunctive definition, i.e. of several conjunctive components that are candidate to generalization. Specifically, for our current purposes we are interested in the generalization procedure. Clearly, one might generalize all the candidate components so that they are able to correctly classify the positive example. This contrasts with the general assumption, made in incremental learning, that the learned theories must represent as tight as possible a coverage of the available positive examples. Indeed, over-generalization would make the theory more prone to covering forthcoming negative examples. This problem is not present in batch learning, since the set of examples is assumed to be immutable, and thus any definition whose coverage boundary is able to account for all positive examples and no negative example is considered as equally good in principle (of course, other quality parameters than simple coverage may determine a more detailed ranking). Taking to the extreme the approach of generalizing many components of the definition, one might generalize *all* components, but then each conjunctive component would account alone for all positive examples, yielding the contradiction that the concept is conjunctive (while we are assuming that it is not).

2.2 Generalization and Disjunctive Concepts

So, a single component is to be generalized, and a strategy is needed to decide which is to be tried first. If the selected component cannot be generalized (in principle, or within the available computational cost allowed to the refinement operator) so that completeness is restored while still preserving consistency, generalization of the next best component can be attempted, and so on, until either a generalization is found that ensures correctness of the theory, or all attempts fail. The latter case requires the application of different kinds of refinements

---

Algorithm 1. Generalization in InTheLEx

```
Procedure Generalize
(E: positive example, T: theory, M: negative examples);
L := list of the rules in the definition of E's concept
while not generalized and L ≠ ∅ do
    Select from L a rule C for generalization
    L' := generalize(C, E) (* list of generalizations *)
    while not generalized and L' ≠ ∅ do
        Select next best generalization C' from L'
        if (T \ {C} ∪ {C'} is consistent wrt M then
            Implement C' in T
    Remove C from L
if not generalized then
    C' := E with constants turned into variables
    if (T \ {C} ∪ {C'} is consistent wrt M then
        Implement C' in T
    else
        Implement E in T as an exception
```

---

than generalization of a conjunctive component. While some incremental systems do not provide such additional kinds of refinement, the solution adopted by InTheLEx to deal with these cases consists in introducing in the theory a new alternate conjunctive definition of the concept. In fact, it is this very step that yields disjunctive definitions in the theory.

Algorithm 1 describes the generalization strategy in InTheLEx. Starting from the current theory, the misclassified example and the set of processed examples, it ends with a revised theory. First of all, the system chooses a rule to be generalized among those that define the example concept (the purpose of this paper is exactly to propose and compare useful strategies for performing this step). Then, the system tries to compute the generalization of this rule and the example. Due to the theoretical and implementation details of the generalization operator used, several incomparable generalizations might be obtained [20]. If one of such generalizations is consistent with all the past negative examples, then it replaces the chosen rule in the theory, or else a new rule is chosen to compute the generalization. Moreover, an implementation of the theoretical definition of the generalization operator would be clearly infeasible, since the system would run out of the available resources even for relatively small rules. Thus, an approximation of the theoretical operator is computed, exploiting a similarity-based strategy. Experiments have shown that such an approximation comes very close, and often catches, least general generalizations [9].

If all generalization attempts fail on all available rules (i.e., no rule in the theory can be generalized so that the resulting theory is consistent), the system checks if a new rule, obtained by reproducing exactly the same pattern of the example, but with its constants properly turned into variables, is consistent with the past negative examples. If so, such a rule is added to the theory, extending the disjunctive definition so that other examples, having the same shape as the current problematic one, can be recognized by the theory. When starting from an empty theory, this is the only available option, that introduces the initial tentative conjunctive definition of the concept. The second time this option is executed, the conjunctive definition turns out to be insufficient and, by adding a second rule, the concept becomes disjunctive. All subsequent executions of this option extend the 'disjunctiveness' of the concept. When even the new definition cannot be added, because it covers a previous negative example, the specific new example is added as an exception. Such an exception does not concur to the definition of the concept, but just contributes to make up a list of specific cases that must be checked in addition to the normal definition application.

3   Clause Selection Strategy for Generalization

Let us now focus on the case in which a disjunctive concept definition is available in the current theory, and a new positive example becomes available that is not covered by such a definition. As said, the problem with this situation is that none of the definition components is specifically guilty for not covering the new example, and still one of them must be generalized. The issue is relevant because in incremental learning each refinement introduces implicit constraints on how it will be possible to further refine the theory in the future. Thus, the learned theory depends not only on the order in which examples are provided to the system, but also on the choice of the elements to be refined. For this reason, incremental learning systems should be careful in determining the order in which the various components are to be considered for generalization. So, although a random strategy might well be exploited as long as the formal correctness of the refined definition is guaranteed, guided solutions may improve the overall outcome as regards effectiveness and efficiency.

We will try in the following to answer some questions that arise in this context: what sensible strategies can be defined for determining the order in which disjunctive concept definition elements are to be considered for generalization? what are their expected pros and cons? what is the effect of different ordering strategies on the quality of the theory? what about their consequences on the effectiveness and efficiency of the learning process? InTheLEx is a suitable candidate for experimentation because it is fully incremental, it is able to learn disjunctive concept definitions, and its refinement strategy can be tuned to suitably adapt its behavior. We propose the following five strategies for determining the order in which the components of a disjunctive concept definition are to be considered for generalization. A discussion follows of the motivations for each of these options, of its features and expected impact on the learned theory. Note that lower components in the ranking are considered only after generalization attempts have failed on all higher-ranking components. So, higher-ranked components will be tried first, and will have more chances to be generalized than lower-ranked ones. Also note that there is no direct connection between the age and length of a rule, except that older rules might have had more chances of refinement. Whether this means that they are also shorter (i.e., more general) mainly depends on the ranking strategy, and on the specific examples that are encountered and on their order (which is not controllable in a real-world setting).

Older elements first. The components are considered in the same order as they were added to the theory. This can be considered as the most straightforward way of considering the components: each new component is appended to the definition, and the definition is processed by scanning top-down its elements. In this sense, this is a sort of baseline for our study. This is a static ordering, because the position of each component in the processing order is fixed once and for all when that component is created and added to the definition. Since each generalization refines a component, making it converge toward its ideal final form (generalizations are monotonic, because they progressively remove constraints from a component), we expect this strategy to yield very refined (i.e., short) components toward the top of the rank, and very raw (i.e., long) ones toward the bottom. This means that the components at the top will be more human-readable and understandable. After several refinements, it is likely that the components at the top have reached a nearly final and quite stable form, for which reason all attempts to further refine them will be likely to fail, leading to inconsistent solutions. The computational time spent in these useless attempts, albeit presumably not huge (because the rules to be generalized are short, and generalizing shorter rules requires less time) will just be wasted, and thus runtimes for this option are expected to grow as long as the life of the theory proceeds.

Newer elements first. The components are considered in the reverse order as they were added to the theory. Also this option can be considered quite straightforward. Each new component is simply stacked ontop of the others, pushing them down the ranking. Again this is a static ordering, but in this case it is not so obvious to foresee what will be the shape and evolution of the components. Immediately after the addition of a new component, one can be sure that it will undergo a generalization attempt as soon as the first non-covered positive example will be processed. So, compared to the previous option, there should be no completely raw components in the definition, but the 'average' level of generality in the definition is expected to be less than in the previous option. Also, there are many chances that a newly added component can be generalized successfully at the first attempt against any example, but the resulting generalization might leverage strange and unreliable features that might be not very related to the correct concept definition.

Longer elements first. The components are considered in descending order of the number of conjuncts of which they are made up. This strategy specifically addresses the level-of-refinement issue of the various definition components. This strategy can be considered as an evolution of the previous one, in which not just the most recently added component is favored for generalization. Intuitively, the more conjuncts that make up a component of the disjunctive definition, the more specialized the component. This intuition is backed under Object Identity, where a strict subset of conjuncts necessarily yields a more general definition. This is another reason why InTheLEx is particularly suited for our research. So, trying to generalize longer elements first should ensure that the level of generalization of the different components is somehow comparable. The components on which generalization is tried first are those that, being longer, provide more room for generalization, which should avoid waste of time trying to generalize very refined rules that would hardly yield consistent generalizations. On the other hand, generalizing a longer rule is expected to take more time than generalizing shorter ones. Experiments will allow to discover whether the time gained in avoiding unpromising generalization is comparable to, significantly more or significantly less than the time spent on computing harder single generalizations.

Shorter elements first. The components are considered in ascending order of the number of conjuncts of which they are made up. This strategy adopts the opposite behavior compared to the previous one, trying to generalize first the components that are already more refined. Accordingly, it can be considered as an evolution of the first one. As a consequence, compared to all other strategies the resulting disjunctive definition is expected to show the largest variance in degree of refinement (i.e., of number of conjuncts in the rule premise) among its components. This opposite perspective may provide confirmation of the possible advantage of spending time in trying harder but most promising generalization versus spending time in trying easier but less promising ones first.

More similar elements first. The components are considered in descending order of similarity with the new uncovered example. Differently from all the previous options, that were based on purely syntactic/structural features, this is a content-based strategy. It is motivated by the consideration that the length or age of a definition component are not directly, nor necessarily, related to their aptitude for generalization against a specific example. In fact, if the concept is inherently disjunctive, its components should capture very different actualizations thereof. In turn, each instance of the concept (i.e., each example) should in principle belong to one of these actualizations, and not belong to the other. Each example may be covered by different components, but it is intuitively fair to expect that the sets of examples covered by different components have a very small intersection in practice. In this perspective, generalizing a component with an example that refers to the concept actualization ideally captured by another component, while possibly succeeding, might result in a refined component that is odd, and may pose coverage and generalization problems in the future, causing bad theory and inefficient refinements. Thus, it would be desirable that the generalization strategy is able to identify which is the appropriate component for a given example. One way in which this can be obtained is ranking the candidate components to be refined by similarity to the given example. While widespread for attribute-value representations, similarity measures for first-order logic descriptions are rare and hard to define. Here we will use the approach proposed in [9], which is the same exploited in the generalization operator used by

InTheLEx. As a consequence of this choice, one might expect that the generalized components maintain some specificity, and that the generalization operator is likely to find a solution that is also consistent with negative examples, because over-generalization is avoided. However, if the generalization is more easily computed, this strategy involves an overhead to compute the similarity of the given example with respect to all the definition components, which is not required in all the previous options. It will be interesting to see if the improvement is sufficiently significant as to compensate this increase in runtime.

4   Evaluation

An experiment was run to check how using the proposed strategies in the generalization process affects the performance of the learning system. We focused on a real-world dataset[2] that includes 353 layout descriptions of first pages of scientific papers belonging to 4 classes: Elsevier journals, Springer-Verlag Lecture Notes series (SVLN), Journal of Machine Learning Research (JMLR) and Machine Learning Journal (MLJ). Each paper provides examples to learn definitions for these classes (a task known as *classification*) and and for the significant components in the papers (a task known as *understanding*), such as Title, Author and Abstract. The page descriptions express several kinds of spatial relationships among the page components, thus requiring a first-order logic representation formalism, and a learning system that can deal with this kind of representations.

This dataset is complex for several reasons, which prevents us from giving short samples. First, some layout styles are quite similar, so that it is not easy to grasp the difference when trying to group them in distinct classes. 67920 atoms are used to describe the documents, with an average description length of more than 192 atoms and some descriptions made up of more than 400 atoms. Last, the description language is heavily based on a membership relation (of layout components to pages) that increases indeterminacy and thus the complexity of the task. In the experiments, the layout description of each document is considered as a positive example for the class it belongs and as a negative example for all other classes. Different qualitative and quantitative evaluation parameters were used to assess both the quality of the learned theories and the computational cost spent to obtain them:

- number of components in the disjunctive concept definition (**# comp**): indicates how compact is a theory (less components yield a more compact theory, which does not necessarily provide for greater accuracy).
- average number of conjuncts per component (**avg length**): this is an indicator of the degree of refinement that the concept definition has reached (the more conjuncts, the more specific —and thus the less refined— the concept).
- number of negative exceptions (**# exc**): this is a quality indicator because exceptions highlight weaknesses of the theory rather than contributing to its formation and refinement; the more exceptions, the worse the theory.

---

[2] Available at http://lacam.di.uniba.it/~ferilli/ufficiale/ferilli.html

- accuracy (**acc**): indicates the prediction capabilities of the theory on test examples.
- runtime needed to carry out the learning task (**time**): this is a measure of efficiency for the different ranking strategies.

The incremental approach is justified in this domain because in many real-world document collections new instances of documents are continuously available in time. We compare all strategies: older (O), newer (N), longer (L), shorter (S), and similarity ($\sim$). Random is not tried because O or N are somehow random (they just append definitions as long as they are generated, without any insight). We ran a 10-fold cross-validation procedure. The classification task was used to check in detail the behavior of the different strategies, while the understanding task was used to assess the statistical significance of the difference in performance between different strategies.

On the classification task, InTheLEx always returned single-rule definitions for Elsevier and JMLR, to which the ranking approach is not applicable. So, Tables 1 and 2 show the results only for the other classes, MLJ and SVLN. However, examples for Elsevier and JMLR still played a role as negative exam-

Table 1. Results for SVLN class

	Fold	1	2	3	4	5	6	7	8	9	10	Avg	Rank	Overall
	# comp	3	3	3	2	4	3	3	3	2	3	2.9	1	
	avg length	27	60	35	31	30	29	29	41	37	67	38.6	1	
O	# exc	3	0	1	4	1	3	1	0	1	0	1.4	2	8
	acc (%)	100	97	97	94	97	97	94	100	94	100	97	2	
	time (sec.)	58	20	27	67	50	68	22	30	28	27	39.7	2	
	# comp	3	3	3	2	4	3	3	3	2	3	2.9	1	
	avg length	27	60	35	31	30	29	28	42	37	67	38.6	1	
N	# exc	3	0	1	4	1	3	1	0	1	0	1.4	2	6
	acc (%)	100	97	97	94	97	97	97	100	94	100	97.3	1	
	time (sec.)	56	20	27	66	48	67	23	34	28	27	39.6	1	
	# comp	3	3	3	2	4	3	3	3	2	3	2.9	1	
	avg length	27	59	35	31	30	29	29	42	37	67	38.6	1	
L	# exc	3	0	1	4	1	3	1	0	1	0	1.4	2	10
	acc (%)	100	97	97	94	97	97	94	100	94	100	97	2	
	time (sec.)	57	27	26	69	43	64	46	32	28	28	42	4	
	# comp	3	3	3	2	4	3	3	3	2	3	2.9	1	
	avg length	27	60	35	31	30	29	29	41	37	67	38.6	1	
S	# exc	3	0	1	4	1	3	1	0	1	0	1.4	2	9
	acc (%)	100	97	97	94	97	97	94	100	94	100	97	2	
	time (sec.)	58	20	26	67	51	69	23	30	28	27	39.9	3	
	# comp	3	3	3	2	4	3	3	3	2	3	2.9	1	
	avg length	29	60	35	31	30	29	29	42	37	67	38.9	2	
$\sim$	# exc	1	0	1	4	1	3	1	0	1	0	1.2	1	11
	acc (%)	100	97	97	94	97	97	94	100	94	100	97	2	
	time (sec.)	46	38	35	74	59	71	52	49	36	38	49.8	5	

Table 2. Results for MLJ class

Fold	1	2	3	4	5	6	7	8	9	10	Avg	Rank	Overall
# comp	3	7	6	4	6	7	4	5	5	4	5.1	2	
avg length	26	45	56	37	51	46	65	37	50	39	45.2	2	
O # exc	3	1	7	0	0	1	10	10	0	9	4.1	4	13
acc (%)	97	97	91	94	97	94	88	82	97	94	93.1	1	
time (sec.)	178	355	1236	260	349	291	236	303	221	351	378	4	
# comp	3	7	5	4	6	7	4	5	6	4	5.1	2	
avg length	25	44	42	36	43	71	65	46	54	33	45.9	3	
N # exc	3	1	2	0	0	0	10	10	0	9	3.5	3	12
acc (%)	97	97	97	94	97	97	88	82	97	94	94	3	
time (sec.)	176	316	197	247	301	436	220	277	196	353	271.9	1	
# comp	3	7	6	4	6	8	4	6	6	4	5.4	5	
avg length	25	41	57	36	42	56	237	43	47	33	61.7	5	
L # exc	3	1	1	0	0	0	10	9	0	8	3.2	1	19
acc (%)	97	97	97	94	97	97	88	94	97	94	95.2	5	
time (sec.)	172	472	223	241	526	446	246	435	221	635	361.7	3	
# comp	3	7	6	4	6	6	4	5	5	4	5	1	
avg length	25	44	56	36	43	83	65	72	50	39	51.3	4	
S # exc	3	1	7	0	0	1	10	10	0	9	4.1	4	13
acc (%)	97	97	91	94	97	97	88	82	97	94	93.4	2	
time (sec.)	178	339	1207	254	337	211	232	294	219	343	361.4	2	
# comp	3	7	5	4	6	8	4	6	6	4	5.3	4	
avg length	25	41	39	36	42	55	37	43	47	33	39.8	1	
~ # exc	3	1	1	0	0	0	10	9	0	8	3.2	1	15
acc (%)	97	97	97	94	97	94	88	94	97	94	94.9	4	
time (sec.)	288	588	256	320	628	650	354	479	283	711	455.7	5	

ples for the other classes, which is why they were not dropped from the dataset. Some expectations are confirmed: for runtime, in both classes the 'newer' approach yields the best runtime (because often the first generalization attempt succeeds), and the 'similarity' approach yields the worst (due to the need for computing the similarity of each component and the example). However, the 'similarity' approach always yields the least number of exceptions, due to the improved selection of components for generalization, and also the 'shorter' approach performs good on this parameter. Considering an aggregated indicator that assigns to each approach the sum of ranking positions for the different parameters (so that the smaller, the better), the 'newer' wins for both classes.

For the rest, the behavior is somehow mixed for the two classes. In SVLN there is much less variance than in MLJ, possibly indicating that the definition of this class is quite clear and that the examples are quite significant for it. The impact of the different ranking strategies is much clearer in MLJ. Here we can see a substantial agreement between the quality-related indicators (average component length, accuracy and, partly, number of components), so that, for each approach, either they all tend to be good (as in 'similarity') or they all tend

Table 3. Statistical significance of the difference between strategies

	MLJ				Abstract				Author				Keywords				Title			
	N	L	S	~	N	L	S	~	N	L	S	~	N	L	S	~	N	L	S	~
acc L	+				+				-				-				-			
S	-	-			+	-			+	+			+	+			-	-		
~	+	-	+		-	-	-		+	+	-		+	+	-		+	+	+	
O	-	-	-	-	=	-	-	+	+	+	-	+	-	+	-	-	-	+	+	-
avg length L	+				-				-				-				-			
S	-	-			-	+			-	+			-	-			-	+		
~	-	-	-		-	+	+		-	+	+		+	+	+		-	+	-	
O	-	-	-	+	+	+	+	+	-	+	-	-	+	+	+	+	-	-	-	-
# comp L	+				+				+				=				+			
S	-	-			-	-			-	-			-	-			-	-		
~	+	-	+		+	+	+		+	-	+		+	+	+		+	+	+	
O	=	-	+	-	-	-	+	-	-	-	-	-	-	-	+	-	-	-	+	-
# exc L	-				+				-				+				=			
S	+	+			+	+			+	+			+	+			-	-		
~	-	=	-		+	+	+		+	+	+		+	-	-		+	+	+	
O	+	+	=	+	-	-	-	-	+	+	+	+	+	-	-	-	-	-	-	-
time L	+				+				+				+				-			
S	+	-			-	-			+	-			+	+			-	+		
~	+	+	+		+	+	+		+	+	+		+	+	+		-	+	-	
O	+	+	+	-	-	-	+	-	-	-	-	-	+	+	-	-	-	+	+	+

to be bad (as in 'shorter' and 'older'). Also the figures of single folds provide interesting indications. Fold 3 shows a peak in runtime and number of exceptions for 'shorter' and 'older' (the runtime being a consequence of the unsuccessful search for specialization, that in turn may have some connection with the quality of the theory). Indeed, we had already pointed out that 'shorter' is in some sense an evolution of 'older'. In fold 8 shows accuracy increases from 82% to 94% for 'similarity' and 'longer', which shows how in difficult situations the quality of the theory is improved by the content-based approach.

The understanding task, albeit run on the same data, is quite different. We assessed the statistical significance of the difference in performance between different strategies using Friedman's nonparametric test, that compares three or more matched or paired groups. It first ranks the values in each matched set (each row) from low to high. Each row is ranked separately. It then sums the ranks in each group (column). If the sums are very different, the null hypothesis can be rejected, and the conclusion can be drawn that at least one of the treatments (columns) differs from the rest. When this happened, the Nemenyi post-hoc test was applied to decide which groups are significantly different from each other, based upon the mean rank differences of the groups, obtaining a grade of similarity between each ordering strategy expressed in percentage. Due to space constraints, here we report only the results of learning definitions for Abstract, Authors, Keywords and Title blocks in papers of class MLJ, along with those of the classification task. Table 3 specifies whether the strategy on the row is equal (=), better (+) or worse (−) than the one on the column. The best strategy is in bold. When the difference is significant, the behavior of 'longer' and 'similarity' is in general analogous for degree of accuracy (which is greater), number of disjunctive definitions and number of negative exceptions. As expected, the latter requires longer runtime. Also 'older' and 'shorter' have in general an analogous behavior, but do not reach as good results as the previous ones. Finally, 'newer' is not outstanding for good performance, but is better than 'older' (the standard strategy) for all parameters except runtime. Note that, on the classification task, the average length of the disjunctive definition components using 'longer' is significantly larger than all the others (due to the fact that this strategy returns more balanced components), but ensures more accuracy and less negative exceptions.

5   Conclusions

Disjunctive concept definitions are necessary when a single conjunctive definition is insufficient to characterize all available positive examples and discriminate them from all negative ones. Each component of the disjunctive definition covers a subset of positive examples for the concept, while ensuring consistency with all negative examples [15]. In incremental learning, when a new positive example is not recognized by the current theory, one component must be generalized. Since this is an omission error, there is no specific element of the disjunctive definition that is responsible for the omission. So, the system must decide the order in which the elements are to be considered for trying a generalization. This paper proposed five strategies for determining such an order, and evaluates their impact on the learning system's effectiveness and efficiency using a real-world dataset concerning document classification. The outcomes confirm some of the expectations for the various strategies, but more extensive experimentation must be carried out to have confirmations and additional details. This will be the subject of our future work, in addition to the identification of further strategies and the refinement of the proposed ones.

Acknowledgments. The authors would like to thank Immacolata Incantalupo for her help in running the experiments. This work was partially funded by the Italian PON 2007-2013 project PON02_00563_3489339 'Puglia@Service'.

References

1. Becker, J.M.: Inductive learning of decision rules with exceptions: Methodology and experimentation. B.s. diss., Dept. of Computer Science, University of Illinois at Urbana-Champaign, Urbana. UIUCDCS-F-85-945 (1985)
2. Bergadano, F., Gunetti, D.: Learning clauses by tracing derivations. In: Wrobel, S. (ed.) Proceedings of the 4th International Workshop on Inductive Logic Programming, pp. 1–29 (1994)

3. Botta, M.: Learning first order theories. In: Raś, Z.W., Zemankova, M. (eds.) ISMIS 1994. LNCS, vol. 869, pp. 356–365. Springer, Heidelberg (1994)
4. Bruner, J.S., Goodnow, J.J., Austin, G.A.: A Study of Thinking. John Wiley & Sons (1956)
5. Cain, T.: The ductor: a theory revision system for propositional domains. In: Proceedings of the 8th International Workshop on Machine Learning [16], pp. 485–489
6. Ceri, S., Gottlöb, G., Tanca, L.: Logic Programming and Databases. Springer-Verlag, Heidelberg (1990)
7. de Raedt, L.: Interactive Theory Revision - An Inductive Logic Programming Approach. Academic Press (1992)
8. Esposito, F., Semeraro, G., Fanizzi, N., Ferilli, S.: Multistrategy theory revision: Induction and abduction in inthelex. Machine Learning Journal 38(1/2), 133–156 (2000)
9. Ferilli, S., Basile, T.M.A., Biba, M., Di Mauro, N., Esposito, F.: A general similarity framework for horn clause logic. Fundamenta Informaticae Journal 90(1–2), 43–66 (2009)
10. Ginsberg, A.: Theory reduction, theory revision, and retranslation. In: Proceedings of the 8th National Conference on Artificial Intelligence, pp. 777–782 (1990)
11. Lloyd, J.W.: Foundations of Logic Programming, 2nd edn. Springer-Verlag, Berlin (1987)
12. Matwin, S., Plante, B.: A deductive-inductive method for theory revision. In: Proceedings of the International Workshop on Multistrategy Learning, pp. 160–174. Harper's Ferry (1991)
13. Mooney, R.J., Ourston, D.: A multistrategy approach to theory refinement. In: Michalski, R.S., Tecuci, G. (eds.) Machine Learning: A Multistrategy Approach, vol. 4, pp. 141–164. Morgan Kaufman, San Mateo (1994)
14. Muggleton, S.: Duce, an oracle based approach to constructive induction. In: Proceedings of the 5th International Joint Conference on Artificial Intelligence, pp. 287–292 (1987)
15. Murray, K.S.: Multiple convergence: an approach to disjunctive concept acquisition. In: Proceedings of the 10th international joint conference on Artificial intelligence (IJCAI 1987), vol. 1, pp. 297–300. Morgan Kaufmann (1987)
16. Proceedings of the 8th International Workshop on Machine Learning. Morgan Kaufmann, San Mateo (1991)
17. Reinke, R.E., Michalski, R.S.: Incremental learning of concept descriptions: a method and experimental results. In: Michie, D. (ed.) Machine Intelligence, vol. 11. Edinburgh University Press (1985)
18. Richards, B.L., Mooney, R.J.: Refinement of first-order horn-clause domain theories. Machine Learning Journal 19(2), 95–131 (1995)
19. Saitta, L., Botta, M., Neri, F.: Multistrategy learning and theory revision. Machine Learning Journal 11, 153–172 (1993)
20. Semeraro, G., Esposito, F., Malerba, D., Fanizzi, N., Ferilli, S.: A logic framework for the incremental inductive synthesis of datalog theories. In: Fuchs, N.E. (ed.) LOPSTR 1997. LNCS, vol. 1463, pp. 300–321. Springer, Heidelberg (1998)
21. Shapiro, E.Y.: Algorithmic Program Debugging. MIT Press (1983)
22. Srinivasan, A.: The aleph manual. Technical report (2001)
23. Wogulis, J.: Revising relational domain theories. In: Proceedings of the 8th International Workshop on Machine Learning [16], pp. 462–466

Using Substitutive Itemset Mining Framework for Finding Synonymous Properties in Linked Data

Mikołaj Morzy, Agnieszka Ławrynowicz(✉), and Mateusz Zozuliński

Institute of Computing Science, Poznan University of Technology, Poznan, Poland
{Mikolaj.Morzy,Agnieszka.Lawrynowicz}@put.poznan.pl

Abstract. Over the last two decades frequent itemset and association rule mining has attracted huge attention from the scientific community which resulted in numerous publications, models, algorithms, and optimizations of basic frameworks. In this paper we introduce an extension of the frequent itemset framework, called substitutive itemsets. Substitutive itemsets allow to discover equivalences between items, i.e., they represent pairs of items that can be used interchangeably in many contexts. In the paper we present basic notions pertaining to substitutive itemsets, describe the implementation of the proposed method available as a RapidMiner plugin, and illustrate the use of the framework for mining substitutive object properties in the Linked Data.

1 Introduction

With the proliferation of knowledge bases and knowledge graphs, especially those published within the Linked Open Data cloud[1], the number of available datasets represented in RDF [1] has grown rapidly over last years. At the same time, the problem of improving the quality of Linked Data has become a major issue. One aspect of the quality deals with inherent redundancy in the Linked Data. It is common to find overlaps between ontologies, to find identical real-world objects described using different vocabulary, or to employ many synonyms when designing and populating RDF stores. Thus the task of finding links between similar or matching ontological terms is one of the major topics in the field [2] of semantic technologies.

In this paper we present *substitutive itemsets*, an extension of the frequent itemset framework, which allows to discover pairs of items that are mutually exchangeable. When searching for such pairs we make sure that substitutive items can be used interchangeably, which means that the items must appear in similar contexts. In order to model the context we analyze the relationships between meta-data (patterns discovered in the RDF triple store) and we discover pairs of items which appear within the same frequent itemsets, yet the pairs almost never appear themselves in the data store.

The rest of the paper is structured as follows. We begin by showing recentpapers that are relevant to our work in Section 2. In Section 3 we present

---

[1] http://linkeddata.org

© Springer International Publishing Switzerland 2015
N. Bassiliades et al. (Eds.): RuleML 2015, LNCS 9202, pp. 422–430, 2015.
DOI: 10.1007/978-3-319-21542-6_27

basic definitions used throughout the paper. Section 4 introduces substitutive itemsets. Section 4 describes the use case in DBpedia. We conclude in Section 6 with a brief summary and a future work agenda.

2   Related Work

Since its introduction in [3] association rule mining has attracted huge attention from the scientific community. Many extensions of the basic association rule mining have been proposed in the literature (cf. [4–6]). Specialized models of correlated association rules, class association rules, maximal association rules, dissociation rules, (onto-)relational association rules (cf. [7–11]) are just a few examples. The work that is most similar to our approach has been presented in [12], although there are very significant differences. Tang *et al.* base their method on the correlation analysis and they generate substitution rules if a negative association between items exists. We, on the other hand, consider primarily the context in which items forming a substitutive itemset appear. To model the context we explore the set of frequent patterns discovered in the database and we measure the amount of overlap between patterns which contain items.

Though various approaches for ontology classes and property matching have been researched in the past mining exchangeable (object) properties has not received focus. The related approaches were concentrated on instance matching [2], class mappings [13], matching of RDF data properties [14] and largely on the task of matching two input ontologies [15, 16].

To summarize, the difference between previous works and our approach is the fact that we ground our method on the analysis and mining of the meta-data represented as frequent patterns appearing in the dataset. Importantly, ontology matching methods mostly concentrate on the task of matching (two) different ontologies, and not on the deduplication of terms within one ontology. Our method works on the level of the schema rather than the level of individual instances that also differentiates it from approaches in the field of entity resolution (deduplication from a database perspective). From this perspective, we are not trying to recognize all instances of a particular entity, but we are discovering pairs of attributes which share the same semantics.

3   Preliminaries

3.1   Frequent Itemset Mining

Given a set of elements $I = \{i_1, i_2, \ldots, i_m\}$, where each element i_k is referred to as an *item*. Given a database of transactions $D_T = \{t_1, t_2, \ldots, t_n\}$, where $\forall i \; t_i \subseteq I$. The *support* of an item i is the percentage of database transactions that contain the item i:

$$support(i) = \frac{|\{t \in D_T : i \in t\}|}{|D_T|}$$

The support of an itemset X is the percentage of database transactions that contain all elements of X:

$$support(X) = \frac{|\{t \in D_T : X \subseteq t\}|}{|D_T|}$$

Given a user-defined threshold of minimum support, called *minsup*. An itemset X is said to be a *frequent itemset* if the support of the itemset X exceeds the minimum support threshold. Let L_k denote the collection of all frequent itemsets of the size k discovered in the database D_T for a given value of the *minsup* parameter.

$$L_k = \{X \subseteq I : support(X) \geqslant minsup \wedge |X| = k\}$$

Let $L = \bigcup_k L_k$ denote the collection of all frequent itemsets discovered in the database D_T for a given value of the *minsup* parameter. For any frequent item i the *covering set* of the item is the collection of all frequent itemsets discovered in the database D_T, with which the given item i forms a frequent itemset. In other words, a frequent itemset X belongs to the covering set of i if $\{X \cup \{i\}\}$ is frequent:

$$CS(i|L) = \{X \in L : \{i\} \cup X \in L\}$$

We will refer to the size of the covering set of the item i as its *coverage*.

3.2   RDF

Resource Description Framework (RDF) is a framework that can be used to represent information on any resources (e.g., documents, people, objects). RDF data model is based on graphs. It allows to represent statements on resources on the Web in the form of subject–predicate–object triples. An *RDF triple* is a tuple $\tau = (s, p, o) \in (\mathbf{U} \cup \mathbf{B} \cup \mathbf{L}) \times \mathbf{U} \times (\mathbf{U} \cup \mathbf{B} \cup \mathbf{L})$, where s is the subject, p is the predicate, and o is the object of the tuple, and $\mathbf{U}$, $\mathbf{B}$, and $\mathbf{L}$ are pairwise disjoint infinite sets that denote, respectively, URI references, blank nodes and literals. An *RDF dataset* is a set of RDF triples.

4   Substitutive Sets

The method for generating substitutive itemsets uses, as its starting point, the collection L of frequent itemsets discovered in the transactional database D_T. A two-element itemset $\{x, y\}$ is a *substitutive itemset*, if:

- $x \in L_1$, $y \in L_1$,
- $support(\{x\} \cup \{y\}) < \varepsilon$, where ε is a user-defined threshold representing the highest amount of noise in the data allowed,
- $\frac{|CS(x|L) \cap CS(y|L)|}{\max\{|CS(x|L)|,|CS(y|L)|\}} \geqslant mincommon$, where *mincommon* is a user-defined threshold of context similarity between items x and y.

The above definition requires a brief explanation. A substitutive itemset consists of two interchangeable items, i.e., items, which appear in the collection of frequent itemsets in very similar contexts. The context in which an item appears is simply the collection of its covering sets. We are interested in finding pairs of items which share a large proportion of their covering sets, and yet almost never appear together in database transactions. By definition, the necessary condition for an item x to have a covering set is that the item x itself is frequent. In order to capture the fact that items from the substitutive itemset should almost never appear together, we have introduced an additional frequency threshold ε, which prunes pairs of items which appear together too often. Such situation might arise for example in case of pairs of items which are partially functionally dependent (the item x induces the purchase of the item y). Here we use an analogy from the database theory where the existence of a functional dependency between attributes X and Y represents the fact that a given value of the attribute X in a tuple t determines the value of the attribute Y in the tuple t (or makes it highly probable in case of partial functional dependency). Similarly, the appearance of a particular item x might increase the probability of the the item y in the same transaction. In data mining parlance this would be tantamount to high confidence of an association rule $x \rightarrow y$. On the other hand, for items $\{x, y\}$ to form a substitutive set we require that these items share common contexts, i.e., that their covering sets are similar. One simple way to measure the similarity of contexts of two items is to measure the overlap of their coverage sets using a slightly modified Jaccard's coefficient of set similarity. The second frequency threshold of *mincommon* guarantees that the overlap of contexts of both items is significant enough to consider the two items to be mutually substitutive.

Let us consider a real-world example of a retail database and customer transactions, where each transaction represents grocery purchases made by a customer during a single visit to the supermarket. Furthermore, let us assume that the pair of items {*nachos,salsa*} was found to be frequent, i.e., that these two items appear in more than *minsup* percentage of transactions. Although both individual items are frequent and the overlap of their covering sets is significant (probably these items appear in very similar contexts), since this itemset is itself frequent this means that *nachos* and *salsa* are not mutually substitutive. A closer inspection would reveal that *salsa* is a popular supplement for *nachos*, not a replacement for *nachos*. On the other hand, consider the relationship between *coca-cola* and *pepsi*. These two items are frequent, and they appear in very similar contexts in the customer database. However, there is a very tiny fraction of customers who purchase *coca-cola* and *pepsi* together. Since most probably the itemset {*coca-cola,pepsi*} satisfies the *mincommon* threshold of maximal support, these two items can be regarded as mutually substitutive.

Finally, let us discuss the usability of the substitutive itemsets framework for the Linked Data. In case of the Linked Data the database of customer transactions is replaced with the RDF triple store. Thus, all transactions consist of three items, namely, the subject, the predicate, and the object of the triple. Each such transaction supports three individual items, three two-element itemsets, and a single three-element itemset. Suppose that a certain pair of items is found to be a substitutive itemset. What this means in the context of the RDF data model is that both items are frequent in the database, often occur with the same concepts in triples, yet almost never appear in a single tuple. From these properties we may conclude that the items comprising a substitutive itemset in an RDF data store are simply synonymous terms.

The method for generating substitutive itemsets has the following input and output:

- *input data*
    - the collection L of frequent itemsets in the database D_T
- *input parameters*
    - ε: floating point number in the range $[0, 1]$
    - *mincommon*: floating point number in the range $[0, 1]$
- *output result*
    - the collection L_S of all substitutive itemsets in the database D_T

Of course, there is no single rule for setting the values of parameters such as *minsup*, *mincommon* or ε, because the values strongly depend on the characteristics of the dataset being mined. However, a general rule of thumb is that the ε parameter should be an order of magnitude smaller than *minsup*, and *mincommon* should probably exceed 75% in order to capture a true overlap of covering sets of itemsets regarded as mutually substitutive. Setting a too low value of ε results in excessive pruning of substitutive itemsets, in particular, in pruning substitutive itemsets for which its constituent items may appear together by chance. Also, it is possible that an item y is a true substitute for an item x, but at the same time the item y may have a very specific use independent of x. Such scenario would artificially increase the support of the itemset $\{x, y\}$. A similar argument can be formulated with respect to the *mincommon* parameter. If this threshold is set too low, the method may produce substitutive itemsets consisting of items that are actually not related to each other. Setting of the *mincommon* parameter too high will perform a very strong pruning and will produce very little results.

5   Use Case: DBpedia

In this section, we demonstrate the use of substitutive itemsets for deduplication (matching) of object properties in Linked Data. Many large Linked Data use relatively lightweight schemas with a high number of object properties. For instance, the DBpedia 2014 ontology[2] has 1310 object and 1725 data properties. The DBpedia ontology is manually created by a community effort, based on the most often used infoboxes in Wikipedia. The infobox extraction method is available that is based on these manual mappings of Wikipedia infoboxes to the DBpedia ontology. A public wiki is also available [3] for editing infobox mappings,

---

[2] http://wiki.dbpedia.org/Ontology2014
[3] http://mappings.dbpedia.org/index.php/How_to_edit_the_DBpedia_Ontology

```
PREFIX rdf: <http://www.w3.org/1999/02/22-rdf-syntax-ns#>
PREFIX dbo: <http://dbpedia.org/ontology/>

SELECT ?c1 ?p ?c2
WHERE {
?s rdf:type dbo:$name_of_the_class$ .
?s ?p ?o .
?s rdf:type ?c1 .
?o rdf:type ?c2 .
FILTER(?p != dbo:wikiPageWikiLink) .
FILTER(?p != rdf:type) .
FILTER(?p != dbo:wikiPageExternalLink) .
FILTER(?p != dbo:wikiPageID) .
FILTER(?p != dbo:wikiPageInterLanguageLink) .
FILTER(?p != dbo:wikiPageLength) .
FILTER(?p != dbo:wikiPageOutDegree) .
FILTER(?p != dbo:wikiPageRedirects) .
FILTER(?p != dbo:wikiPageRevisionID) }
```

Fig. 1. SPARQL query for generating transactions

as well as editing the DBpedia ontology. In this way, external contributors may define mappings for the infoboxes that are interesting from their point of view and they may extend the DBpedia ontology by adding new classes and properties. A problem may arise, for instance, when a contributor adds new classes and/or properties, without carefully checking the existing ones for possibly re-using them. This may lead to the existence of redundant properties.

5.1   Experimental Setup

We used the DBpedia knowledge base version 2014 that describes 4.58 million things (4.22 million out of them are classified in the DBpedia ontology), and 583 million facts [17]. We generated sets of three–item transactions for the classes, using the SPARQL query presented in Fig. 1. Thus each transaction has the form of a set $\{c_1, p, c_2\}$, where c_1 and c_2 denote items being the classes of, respectively, a subject and an object of an RDF triple from the DBpedia dataset, and p being a property connecting s and o. Additionally, we appended to the URIs of the classes a prefix indicating whether it is a class describing the object or a class describing the subject in the resulting transactions. Subsequently, we selected a sample of 100K results per each query.

For the computation of the substitutive itemsets we used our Market Basket Analysis plugin[4] for the popular data mining environment RapidMiner[5] (community edition). The plugin has been published using the AGPL licence, it can be easily downloaded from the website and installed as an extension inside Rapid-Miner. The parameter values for the RapidMiner operators were as follows. Frequent itemsets were discovered using the FP-Growth algorithm [18] with the minimum number of itemsets set to 500 and the *minsup* threshold set to 0.001.

---

[4] http://www.e-lico.eu/marketbasket.html

[5] https://rapidminer.com

Table 1. Sample substitutive properties generated for the class `Organisation`

item x	item y	*common*
dbpprop:parentOrganization	dbo:parentOrganisation	1.000
dbpprop:owner	dbo:owner	1.000
dbpprop:origin	dbo:hometown	1.000
dbpprop:headquarters	dbpprop:parentOrganization	1.000
dbpprop:formerAffiliations	dbo:formerBroadcastNetwork	1.000
dbo:product	dbpprop:products	1.000
dbpprop:keyPeople	dbo:keyPerson	0.910
dbpprop:commandStructure	dbpprop:branch	0.857
dbo:schoolPatron	dbo:foundedBy	0.835
dbpprop:notableCommanders	dbo:notableCommander	0.824
dbo:recordLabel	dbpprop:label	0.803
dbo:headquarter	dbo:locationCountry	0.803
dbpprop:country	dbo:state	0.753

Our method is independent of a particular frequent itemset mining algorithm, we could have used the popular Apriori algorithm [19]

For the `Create Substitutive Sets` operator we set *mincommon* $= 0.7$ and $\varepsilon = 0.0001$. We performed computation for the classes from the first level of the DBpedia ontology (from the DBpedia namespace) and the remaining notable DBpedia classes (listed at http://wiki.dbpedia.org/Datasets/DatasetStatistics). The computations were performed on the desktop computer with 12GB RAM and CPU Intel(R) Core(TM) i5-4570 3.20GHz. A single run of mining substitutive sets (for one class and 100k transactions) took several seconds on average (ranging from 2s to 12s).

5.2   Results

For the classes from the first level of the DBpedia ontology, we have obtained 31 non-empty result sets by running the query from Figure 1. We have used transactions associated with these classes to mine substitutive itemsets. For the computed sample of transactions (query results limited to maximum 100K results), no substitutive itemsets containing properties were discovered for many classes. From among 31 of the above-mentioned transaction sets, we have obtained substitutive itemsets for each, but only 4 of them contained pairs of properties within substitutive sets. These resulting sets for the first level of DBpedia ontology are published at http://www.cs.put.poznan.pl/alawrynowicz/substitutive together with a description of a preliminary user study.

We discuss the selected results below. Table 1 presents sample substitutive properties generated for the class `Organisation`. We present both properties constituting a substitutive itemset and the overlap of their covering sets (column *Common*). The result includes frequent cases where the substitutes are adequate properties from property (`dbpprop:`) and ontology (`dbo:`) namespaces[6]. Sometimes, in these discovered cases, different naming scheme is used (e.g., dbpprop:keyPeople and dbo:keyPerson), different spelling (e.g., dbpprop:parentOrganization and dbo:parentOrganisation) or singular vs. plural form (e.g., dbo:product and dbpprop:products). There are also pairs of truly substitutive properties, for instance dbpprop:headquarters and dbpprop:parentOrganization (*common*=1.0). Such information might be useful to track and resolve redundancies from the DBpedia ontology. Other pairs, such as dbpprop:country and dbo:state or dbo:recordLabel and dbpprop:label might indicate inconsistent usage of the properties for indicating similar relations in particular context.

6 Conclusions

In this paper, we have introduced a model for substitutive itemset mining, that is itemsets that can be used interchangeably as substitutes since they appear in the transactional database in very similar contexts. We have performed preliminary tests of this model within the task of deduplication of object properties in RDF datasets. The preliminary experiment provides promising results. In future work, we plan to conduct an extended experimental evaluation.

Acknowledgments. This work was partially supported by the EC 7th framework ICT-2007.4.4 (No 231519) e-LICO. Agnieszka Ławrynowicz acknowledges the support from the PARENT-BRIDGE program of Foundation for Polish Science, co-financed from European Union, Regional Development Fund (Grant No POMOST/2013-7/8). We thank Ewa Kowalczuk for debbuging the plugin.

References

1. Manola, F., Miller, E.: RDF primer. W3C recommendation, W3C (February 2004). http://www.w3.org/TR/2004/REC-rdf-primer-20040210/
2. Ngomo, A.C.N., Auer, S.: Limes: a time-efficient approach for large-scale link discovery on the web of data. In: Proceedings of the Twenty-Second International Joint Conference on Artificial Intelligence. IJCAI 2011, vol. 3, pp. 2312–2317. AAAI Press (2011)
3. Agrawal, R., Imieliński, T., Swami, A.: Mining association rules between sets of items in large databases. SIGMOD Rec. **22**(2), 207–216 (1993)
4. Rauch, J.: Classes of association rules: an overview. In: Lin, T., Xie, Y., Wasilewska, A., Liau, C.J. (eds.) Data Mining: Foundations and Practice, pp. 315–337. Springer, Heidelberg (2008)
5. Fürnkranz, J., Gamberger, D., Lavrac, N.: Foundations of Rule Learning. Cognitive Technologies. Springer (2012)
6. Aggarwal, C.C., Han, J., eds.: Frequent Pattern Mining. Springer (2014)
7. Zimmermann, A., De Raedt, L.: CorClass: correlated association rule mining for classification. In: Suzuki, E., Arikawa, S. (eds.) DS 2004. LNCS (LNAI), vol. 3245, pp. 60–72. Springer, Heidelberg (2004)

---

[6] http://dbpedia.org/property/ and http://dbpedia.org/ontology/

8. Kliegr, T., Kuchař, J., Sottara, D., Vojíř, S.: Learning business rules with association rule classifiers. In: Bikakis, A., Fodor, P., Roman, D. (eds.) RuleML 2014. LNCS, vol. 8620, pp. 236–250. Springer, Heidelberg (2014)

9. Morzy, M.: Efficient mining of dissociation rules. In: Tjoa, A.M., Trujillo, J. (eds.) DaWaK 2006. LNCS, vol. 4081, pp. 228–237. Springer, Heidelberg (2006)

10. Józefowska, J., Lawrynowicz, A., Lukaszewski, T.: On reducing redundancy in mining relational association rules from the semantic web. In: Calvanese, D., Lausen, G. (eds.) RR 2008. LNCS, vol. 5341, pp. 205–213. Springer, Heidelberg (2008)

11. Lisi, F.A.: Building rules on top of ontologies for the semantic web with inductive logic programming. TPLP 8(3), 271–300 (2008)

12. Teng, W.G., Hsieh, M.J., Chen, M.S.: On the mining of substitution rules for statistically dependent items. In: Proceedings of the 2002 IEEE International Conference on Data Mining, 2002. ICDM 2003, pp. 442–449. IEEE (2002)

13. Janssen, F., Fallahi, F., Noessner, J., Paulheim, H.: Towards rule learning approaches to instance-based ontology matching. In: Proc. of the First International Workshop on Knowledge Discovery and Data Mining Meets Linked Open Data, pp. 13–18 (2012)

14. Nunes, B.P., Caraballo, A.A.M., Casanova, M.A., Fetahu, B., Leme, L.A.P.P., Dietze, S.: Complex matching of RDF datatype properties. In: Proceedings of the 24th International Conference on Database and Expert Systems Applications, DEXA 2013, Part I, pp. 195–208 (2013)

15. Zapilko, B., Mathiak, B.: Object property matching utilizing the overlap between imported ontologies. In: Presutti, V., d'Amato, C., Gandon, F., d'Aquin, M., Staab, S., Tordai, A. (eds.) ESWC 2014. LNCS, vol. 8465, pp. 737–751. Springer, Heidelberg (2014)

16. Pavel, S., Euzenat, J.: Ontology matching: State of the art and future challenges. IEEE Trans. on Knowl. and Data Eng. 25(1), 158–176 (2013)

17. Lehmann, J., Isele, R., Jakob, M., Jentzsch, A., Kontokostas, D., Mendes, P.N., Hellmann, S., Morsey, M., van Kleef, P., Auer, S., Bizer, C.: Dbpedia - A large-scale, multilingual knowledge base extracted from wikipedia. Semantic Web 6(2), 167–195 (2015)

18. Han, J., Pei, J., Yin, Y., Mao, R.: Mining frequent patterns without candidate generation: A frequent-pattern tree approach. Data Min. Knowl. Discov. 8(1), 53–87 (2004)

19. Agrawal, R., Srikant, R.: Fast algorithms for mining association rules in large databases. In: Proceedings of the 20th International Conference on Very Large Data Bases, pp. 487–499. Morgan Kaufmann Publishers Inc., San Francisco (1994)

Learning Characteristic Rules in Geographic Information Systems

Ansaf Salleb-Aouissi[1]([✉]), Christel Vrain[2], and Daniel Cassard[3]

[1] Center for Computational Learning Systems (CCLS), Columbia University,
475 Riverside Drive, New York, NY 10115, USA
ansafsalleb@columbia.edu
[2] Laboratoire D'Informatique Fondamentale D'Orléans (LIFO),
Université D'Orléans, BP 6759, 45067 Orléans Cedex 2, France
Christel.Vrain@univ-orleans.fr
[3] French Geological Survey (BRGM) 3, Avenue Claude Guillemin, BP 6009,
Orleéans Cedex 2, France
d.cassard@brgm.fr

Abstract. We provide a general framework for learning characterization rules of a set of objects in Geographic Information Systems (GIS) relying on the definition of distance quantified paths. Such expressions specify how to navigate between the different layers of the GIS starting from the target set of objects to characterize. We have defined a generality relation between quantified paths and proved that it is monotonous with respect to the notion of coverage, thus allowing to develop an interactive and effective algorithm to explore the search space of possible rules. We describe GISMiner, an interactive system that we have developed based on our framework. Finally, we present our experimental results from a real GIS about mineral exploration.

1 Introduction

Characterization is a descriptive learning task which aims at extracting concise and compact descriptions of a set of objects, called the *target set*. It consists in discovering properties that characterize these objects, taking into account their own properties but also properties of the objects linked to them. In comparison to classification and discrimination, characterization is interesting since it does not require negative examples. This is an important feature for many applications where it is difficult to collect negative examples.

We are interested in the task of characterization in the context of geographic databases. Geographic Knowledge Discovery (GKD) has been recognized as one of the most important applications of Knowledge Discovery in Databases [20]. Recent years have witnessed the extension of a number of Knowledge Discovery tasks to spatial and geographic databases. These tasks include association rule analysis [2,14,24], subgroup discovery [13], classification [15], clustering [21]. Few prototypes such as GeoMiner [11], have been implemented and usually include basic data mining tasks extended to geographic data.

© Springer International Publishing Switzerland 2015
N. Bassiliades et al. (Eds.): RuleML 2015, LNCS 9202, pp. 431–444, 2015.
DOI: 10.1007/978-3-319-21542-6_28

Although the number of potential applications is very high, this application domain is more challenging to the Data Mining community, because of the complexity of the task, which must manage spatial data and spatial relations between objects: either the data mining system must be embedded in the Geographic Information System (GIS), as [11,13], or spatial data and spatial relations must be preprocessed [2,24]. In this last case, either data is flattened into a single table and aggregation operators are applied to summarize the links with other objects or data is still represented by several tables (usually a table by type of objects) and relations such as *intersect* between objects are computed. The authors in [3,17,18] propose a web-based system named INGENS that integrates a multi-hierarchy association rule mining and an inductive logic programming approach to a GIS [20]. For a review of the state of progress of GKD, we refer the reader to [20]. Important differences exist between the forms of the learned rule: attribute-value pairs, possibly extended by some link relations as in [13] or multi-relational languages inspired by works in Inductive Logic Programming.

In this paper, we propose an intermediate language, which is less expressive than full first order logic, but more expressive than traditional multi-relational languages. Usually multi-relational languages are restricted to the existential quantifier, thus being able to model that a spatial object is spatially linked to another object satisfying some property. But they are not able to express the fact that several (e.g. more than one) or all the objects linked by this relation satisfy this property. In [25] we have introduced a representation language allowing universal and existential quantifiers.

We introduce here a representation language allowing flexible universal and existential quantifiers: $\exists_e$ ($\exists_e$ p is true when p is satisfied by at least e objects) and $\forall_f$ p ($\forall_f$ is true when p is satisfied by at least $f\%$ of the objects).

We introduce a generalization relation in our language and we show that the $\exists_e$ quantifier has a much more interesting behavior than the $\forall_f$ from the viewpoint of generality. Moreover, quantifiers are parameterized by a distance parameter, thus allowing to handle the notion of distance between objects.

Finally, characterization rules are mined with an interactive approach, involving the user in the building of rules of interest. The user in this case is asked to construct the rules by selecting first a target set of geographic objects in a given layer, and then by choosing a quantifier, selecting its parameters (namely the buffer distance and the number or percentage of objects associated with the quantifier $\exists$ or $\forall$ respectively), selecting another layer and so on. At each step, the set of properties that fulfill the minimum coverage requirement and that are interesting using other statistical measures are mined and presented to the user. To be interesting, a characteristic rule must at least be true for a number of target examples, higher than a given threshold. Other criteria can also be introduced.

The outline of this paper is as follows: in Section 2, we provide a brief description of Geographic Information Systems (GIS) illustrated by a GIS on mineral deposits. Section 3 provides the details of our framework and describes the GIS-Miner algorithm. Section 4 contains experimental results. In Section 5, we discuss the related work and finally we conclude in Section 6.

2   Geographic Information Systems

A Geographic Information System (GIS) is a system designed to handle geographic, spatially referenced data, i.e. data having a position and a shape in the space. Practically, such kind of data is most often organized into *thematic layers* linked by geography. Along with geographical information, a GIS handles other kinds of information such as the descriptions of the geographical objects, often maintained in attribute-value tables. In addition of being a mean for visualizing and storing geographical data, a GIS offers a set of tools for an efficient data exploration and querying on the objects and their descriptions.

One can distinguish two kinds of thematic layers: *vector* and *raster*. In the vector representation, each geographical object is a set of point coordinates (x, y). Thus a point object, such as a town or a mineral deposit, is a simple point in the geographical layer. A linear object, as for instance a river or a geological fault, is a succession of coordinates while a polygonal object, such as a lake, is represented by a succession of coordinates constituting the boundary of a closed area. In the raster representation, a layer is a grid or a matrix of cells, where each cell is a numerical value. This kind of representation is useful to model continuous data such as elevation or heat maps. We will focus in the following on the vector representation.

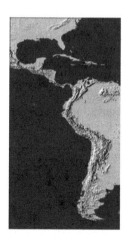

Example 1. Our approach is illustrated throughout this paper with a real-life Geographic Information System about mineral exploration in South America [5]. It is a homogeneous GIS covering an area of 3.83 million km and extending for some 8,500 km long, from the Guajira Peninsula (northern Colombia) to Cape Horn (Tierra del Fuego). Conceived as a tool for mineral exploration and development, this GIS handles many kinds of layers including geographic, geologic, seismic, volcanic, mineralogy, gravimetric layers. These layers store more than 70 thousands geographic objects. We aim at finding characterization rules of a given set of geographic objects as for example mineral ore deposits using geological information, faults, volcanos and nearby objects.

Fig. 1. USGS-GTOPO30 Numerical Model Terrain of the Andes Cordillera

We consider that we have knowledge about geographic objects that are typed and relationships between them. We consider also a subset of objects with the same type, called in the following the *target set*. We aim at learning characteristic rules describing this target set, taking into account the properties of the target objects but also the properties of the objects in relations with them. We first define the notion of characteristic rules to handle distance along objects and relaxing the quantifiers to have a more flexible representation language.

More formally, let $\mathcal{E}$ be a set of geographic objects on a same thematic layer, $\mathcal{E} = \mathcal{E}_1 \cup \mathcal{E}_2 \cdots \cup \mathcal{E}_n$, where each $\mathcal{E}_i$ represents a set of objects with the same type T_i. A set of attributes is defined for each type of objects, and objects are described by attribute-value pairs. Let $\mathcal{R}$ be a set of binary relations. We can have two kinds of relations between objects, classical relations such as *intersect* and distance-based relations expressing that two objects are at a distance less than a given parameter. In the following, r_{ij} denotes a binary relation on $\mathcal{E}_i \times \mathcal{E}_j$. In order to take into account the notion of distance between objects, which is fundamental in GIS, we introduce a parameter λ and a new relation r_{ij}^{λ} for each type of objects E_i and E_j. The relation r_{ij}^{λ} is true for each pair (o_i, o_j) of objects, $o_i \in \mathcal{E}_i$ and $o_j \in \mathcal{E}_j$ such that $d(o_i, o_j) \leq \lambda$.

Example 2. For instance, if $\mathcal{E}_1$ represents mineral deposits and $\mathcal{E}_3$ represent volcanoes, the relation $r_{1,3}^{100km}$ represents a binary relation between mineral deposits and volcanoes at a distance less or equal than 100 kilometers.

In the case of geographic objects, this parameter denotes the distance between objects, but it could also be used in other applications, as for instance in temporal data to represent time between two events.

3   Framework

3.1   Distance Quantified Path and Geographic Characteristic Rule

We define the notion of Distance Quantified Path, considering the parameter λ used in binary relations. Moreover, in order to make the quantifiers used in our previous framework more flexible, we associate with the universal quantifier a percentage that can be less than 100%. Likewise, the existential quantifier is associated with a number that can exceed 1.

Definition 1. *A* Distance Quantified Path *(denoted in the following by $\mathcal{QP}$) on X_0 is a formula:*

$$X_0 - Q_1\ X_1 \ldots Q_n\ X_n$$

where

- $n \geq 0$
- X_0 *represents the target set of objects to characterize,*
- *for each $i \neq 0$, X_i is a type of objects,*
- *for each $i \neq 0$, Q_i can take one of the 4 following forms: $\forall_{r_{ij}}^{f}$, $\exists_{r_{ij}}^{e}$, $\forall_{\lambda}^{f}$ or $\exists_{\lambda}^{e}$, where f is a percentage with $f \neq 0$, and e is a natural number with $e \neq 0$: in the case where the quantifiers are indexed by λ, the binary relation between objects X_{i-1} and objects X_i is the distance relation $r_{(i-1)i}^{\lambda}$. Note that $\forall^{100\%}$ (resp. $\exists^1$) stands for $\forall_{\lambda}$ (resp. $\exists_{\lambda}$).*

A $\mathcal{QP}$ has a length n that is the number of its quantifiers. It is denoted by $length(\mathcal{QP})$. The final type of the quantified path, denoted by $ftype(\mathcal{QP})$, is defined as the type of X_n. The initial type of the quantified path, denoted by $itype(\mathcal{QP})$, is defined as the type of X_0.

Example 3. For instance, $Mines - \forall_{10km}Faults\forall_{5km}Volcanos$ is a distance quantified path where the target set of objects to characterize is mines, and where the path denotes all the volcanoes that are at less than 5 kilometers than faults that are at less than 10 kilometers than mines.
$Mines - \forall_{10km}^{75\%} Faults \exists_{5km}^3 Volcanoes$ denotes the existence of at least 3 volcanoes that are at less than 5 kilometers than 75% of all faults that are at less than 10 kilometers than mines. The length of these paths is equal to 2, their initial type is *mine* and their final type is *volcano*.

Let T_i be a type of objects and let A_j be the attributes used to describe the objects of type T_i. Many kinds of properties can be considered such as: $A = v$, $A \in \{v_1, \ldots, v_n\}$, $A \geq V$, etc. To remain as general as possible in this framework, we suppose that for each type T_i we have a language $\mathcal{L}_i$ specifying the properties that can be built. We also assume that there exists a boolean function $\mathcal{V}$, such that for each object o of type T and for each property p in $\mathcal{L}_i$ $\mathcal{V}_p(o) = true$ or $\mathcal{V}_p(o) = false$, expressing whether the property is satisfied by o or not.

We define two basic properties $True$ and $False$ such that for any object o, $\mathcal{V}_{True}(o) = true$ and $\mathcal{V}_{False}(o) = false$.

Definition 2. *We define a* geographic characteristic rule *on a target set X_0 as the conjunction of a distance quantified path δ and a property* p *, denoted by:* $X_0 - \delta \rightarrow p$.

Example 4. The rule $Mines - \exists_{5km}^3 Faults \rightarrow True$ expresses that there exist at least 3 Faults within 5km of the target (mineral deposits).
The rule $Mines - \exists_{1km}^1 Volcano \rightarrow$ (active=yes) expresses that there exist at least one active volcano within 1km of the target (mineral deposits).

3.2   Generality Order

Definition 3. *We define a generality order between quantified path as follows: We say that a distance quantified path δ_1 is* more general than *a distance quantified path δ_2 (denoted by $\delta_1 \succeq \delta_2$) iff $length(\delta_1) = length(\delta_2))$, $1 \leq i \leq length(\delta_1)$, either:*

- $Q_i^1 \equiv Q_i^2$, *or*
- $Q_i^1 = \exists_{r_{ij}}$ *and* $Q_i^2 = \forall_{r_{ij}}$
- $Q_i^1 = \exists_\lambda$ *and* $Q_i^2 = \forall_\lambda$
- $Q_i^1 = \exists_{r_{ij}}^e$ *and* $Q_i^2 = \exists_{r_{ij}}^{e'}$, *with* $e \leq e'$
- $Q_i^1 = \exists_\lambda^e$ *and* $Q_i^2 = \exists_{\lambda'}^{e'}$, *with* $\lambda \geq \lambda'$ *and* $e \leq e'$

We say that a geographic characteristic rule r_1 ($\delta_1 \to p_1$) is more general than a rule r_2 ($\delta_2 \to p_2$) (denoted by $r_1 \succeq r_2$) iff

- *either $\delta_1 \succeq \delta_2$ and $p_1 \succeq p_2$,*
- *or $length(\delta_1) < length(\delta_2)$, δ_1 is more general than the prefix of δ_2 with length equal to $length(\delta_1)$ and $p_1 = True$.*

It is worth noting that the parameterized universal quantifiers ($Q_i^1 = \forall_\lambda^f$ and $Q_i^2 = \forall_{\lambda'}^{f'}$, with $\lambda \leq \lambda'$ and $f \geq f'$) do not satisfy an interesting generality relation, in the sense that a property satisfied by $f\%$ of the objects in a buffer of size λ may not be satisfied by $f'\%$ of the objects in a buffer of size λ', and vice versa.

The second case in the definition of the generality of a geographic characteristic rule expresses that the property $True$ satisfied by all the objects is more general than a property expressed in terms of a quantified path and a property. For instance $True$ is more general than $\exists_{10Km}^2 F$.

Example 5. $\exists_{10Km}^2 Faults \succeq \exists_{5Km}^2 Faults \succeq \exists_{3Km}^3 Faults$
Intuitively, this means that if there exist three faults at less than 3km from a mine with a given property, than there exists 2 faults at less than 5km and at less than 10km with the same property.

$\forall_{3Km} Faults \succeq \forall_{5Km} Faults \succeq \forall_{10Km} Faults$
Vice-versa, if a property holds for all faults at a distance less than 10km from a mine, then this property also holds for all faults at less than 5km and 3km from this mine.
On the other hand, we have no relation between $\forall_{5Km}^{40\%} Faults$ and $\forall_{10Km}^{20\%} Faults$.

3.3   Evaluation Measures

The notion of coverage is defined for a property p relatively to a quantified path δ. It measures the number of objects that have this property.
For a rule $r = X_0 \text{ - } \delta \to p$ and an object $o \in X_0$, we define $\mathcal{V}_{\delta \to p}(o)$ recursively as follows:
Let $o_1, \ldots o_n$ be the objects of type X at a distance less than λ from o.

- If $n = 0$ (i.e., there are no objects of X at a distance less than λ from o)
  $\mathcal{V}_{\forall_\lambda^f X. \delta' \to p}(o) = \mathcal{V}_{\exists X_\lambda^e. \delta' \to p}(o) = False$
- $\mathcal{V}_{\forall_\lambda X. \delta' \to p}(o) = \mathcal{V}_{\delta' \to p}(o_1) \wedge \cdots \wedge \mathcal{V}_{\delta' \to p}(o_n)$
- $\mathcal{V}_{\forall_\lambda^f X. \delta' \to p}(o) = True$ if $\frac{|\{o_i | \mathcal{V}_{\delta' \to p}(o_i) = True\}|}{n} \geq f$, $False$ otherwise
- $\mathcal{V}_{\exists_\lambda X. \delta' \to p}(o) = \mathcal{V}_{\delta' \to p}(o_1) \vee \cdots \vee \mathcal{V}_{\delta' \to p}(o_n)$
- $\mathcal{V}_{\exists X_\lambda^e. \delta' \to p}(o) = True$ if $|\{o_i | \mathcal{V}_{\delta' \to p}(o_i) = True\}| \geq e$, $False$ otherwise.

The same definition easily extends to a relation r_{ij} by considering the objects $o_1, \ldots o_n$ linked to o by the relation r_{ij}.

Definition 4. *For a given target set of objects $\mathcal{E}_{target}$, coverage is given by the following:*

$$coverage(r, \mathcal{E}_{target}) = \frac{|\{o | o \in \mathcal{E}_{target}, \; \mathcal{V}_r(o) = true\}|}{|\mathcal{E}_{target}|}$$

Proposition. Let r_1 $(\delta_1 \rightarrow p_1)$ and r_2 $(\delta_2 \rightarrow p_2)$ be two geographic rules then

$$r_1 \succeq r_2 \Rightarrow coverage(r_1, \mathcal{E}_{target}) \geq coverage(r_2, \mathcal{E}_{target})$$

Definition 5. *We define the notion* link-coverage *of a rule r, denoted by $\mathcal{L}$-coverage, as follows:*

$$\mathcal{L} - coverage(\mathcal{E}_{target} - \delta \rightarrow p, \mathcal{E}_{target}) = coverage(\mathcal{E}_{target} - open(\delta) \rightarrow True, \mathcal{E}_{target})$$

where $open(\delta)$ is obtained by setting all the quantifiers of δ to $\exists$ (with no constraint on the number of elements).

Intuitively, link coverage measures the number of target objects for which there exists at least an object linked to them through δ, and we have the following relation:

$$coverage(\mathcal{E}_{target} - \delta \rightarrow p, \mathcal{E}_{target}) \geq \epsilon \Rightarrow \mathcal{L} - coverage(\mathcal{E}_{target} - \delta \rightarrow p, \mathcal{E}_{target}) \geq \epsilon$$

For a rule $\mathcal{E}_{target} - \delta \rightarrow p$, coverage measures the number of objects in the target set having the property p. We would like to estimate whether this property is really characteristic of $\mathcal{E}_{target}$ or not. This can be achieved by verifying if the property covers *enough* objects in the target set, while covering *few* objects outside the target set.

In [16], the authors analyze some rule evaluation measures used in Machine Learning and Knowledge Discovery. They propose the *novelty* measure, which can be considered as a measure of novelty, precision, accuracy, negative reliability, or sensitivity. It is defined by: (P represents a probability)

$$novelty(H \longleftarrow B) = P(HB) - P(H) * P(B)$$

where H and B represent the head and the body of the rule respectively. For a characteristic rule r, for each object $o \in \mathcal{E}$, we can consider the objects o belonging to $\mathcal{E}_{target}$ and the objects satisfying $\mathcal{V}_r(o) = true$. We are looking for a strong association between these two facts, which can be estimated by the novelty measure. In our framework, it is defined by:

$$novelty(r) = \frac{|\{o | o \in \mathcal{E}_{target}, \; \mathcal{V}_r(o) = true\}|}{|\mathcal{E}|}$$

$$- \frac{|\mathcal{E}_{target}|}{|\mathcal{E}|} \cdot \frac{|\{o | o \in \mathcal{E}, \; \mathcal{V}_r(o) = true\}|}{|\mathcal{E}|}$$

According to [16], we have $-0.25 \leq novelty(r) \leq 0.25$. A strongly positive value indicates a strong association between the two facts.

We can also use other measures such as entropy, purity, or Laplace estimate. See [9] for more details about evaluation measures. In our framework, we define a function *Interesting* that can filter the rules relying on such heuristics in order to keep only characteristic ones. An example of such a function relying on the novelty metric is given below. A minimum novelty threshold $min\_novelty$ is chosen by the user.

Function Interesting (r): boolean
  If $|novelty(r)| \geq min\_novelty$ then return True
  else return False

Algorithm 1. GISMiner

Input:
- $\mathcal{E}_{target}$
- $\mathcal{E}_i$, $\mathcal{P}_i$, $i \in \{1..n\}$
- R_{ij} set of binary relations between $\mathcal{E}_i$ and $\mathcal{E}_j$, $i,j \in \{1..n\}$
- $MinCov$.

Output:
- Set of characterization rules $\mathcal{R}$
- A tree representing the rules.

1   $\mathcal{QP}$ =empty string
2   response=T
3   **while** $response=T$ **do**
4 | Choose a quantifier $q \in \{\forall, \exists\}$
5 | Choose a buffer λ or a relation $r_{i,j}$
6 | Choose a parameter k for the quantifier
7 | Choose a set of objects $\mathcal{E}_j \in \{\mathcal{E}_i, i \in \{1..n\}\}$
8 | $\mathcal{QP} = \mathcal{QP}.Q_\lambda^k\ \mathcal{E}_j$
9 | **if** $\mathcal{L}\text{-}coverage(\mathcal{E}_{target} - \mathcal{QP} \to True) \geq MinCov$ **then**
10 | | **foreach** *property* $p \in \mathcal{P}_j$ **do**
11 | | | **if** $coverage(\mathcal{E}_{target} - \mathcal{QP} \to p, \mathcal{E}_{target}) \geq MinCov$ **then**
12 | | | | **if** $interesting(\mathcal{E}_{target} - \mathcal{QP} \to p)$ **then**
13 | | | | | $\mathcal{R}=\mathcal{R} \cup \{\mathcal{E}_{target} - \mathcal{QP} \to p\}$
14 | **if** *user wishes no longer to extend* QP **then**
15 | | response=F
16 **return** $\mathcal{R}$

3.4   Algorithm

In [25], we have proposed 𝕮𝖆𝖗𝖆𝖈𝖙𝖊𝖗𝖎𝖃, a general framework for mining characteristic rules relying on the notion of quantified paths, and we have given a level-wise algorithm to explore the space of all possible characterization rules. Here we propose an interactive algorithm for mining such rules in geographic information systems without exploring the space of all possible rules. The pseudo-code of our interactive algorithm named *GISMiner* is given in Algorithm 1. The algorithm has as input (1) a target set of objects $\mathcal{E}_{target}$ belonging to a given thematic layer chosen by the user, (2) the GIS itself, that is all the layers $\mathcal{E}_i$ that are available along with their properties $\mathcal{P}_i$ built from their attribute tables, (3) a set of binary relations between $\mathcal{E}_i$ and $\mathcal{E}_j$, $i, j \in \{1..n\}$, (4) a user-defined minimum coverage threshold $MinCov$.

Starting from the target set, the user chooses a quantifier ($\forall$ or $\exists$), its parameter k (a percentage for $\forall$ and a number of objects for $\exists$) and a buffer λ. The user selects also a thematic layer $\mathcal{E}_j$. The quantified path $\mathcal{QP}$ initially empty is thus extended by the chosen quantifier and set of objects. Using the $\mathcal{L}$-coverage, the algorithm checks the number of target objects for which there exists at least an object linked to them through $\mathcal{QP}$. If there are enough target objects w.r.t. the minimum coverage, then the algorithm will check the coverage of the rules with all the possible properties of the related objects $\mathcal{E}_j$ and keeps the ones with enough coverage that are interesting w.r.t. statistical measures chosen by the user.

Table 1. Some examples of *interesting* rules extracted by GISMiner for GIS Andes. Only rules with $|novelty| \geq 0.05$ are kept by GISMiner.

Rule	Coverage
$Mines \rightarrow Mines.Era \in \{Mesozoic, Cretacious\}$	4%
$Mines \rightarrow Mines.Era \in \{Mesozoic, Jurassic, Cretacious\}$	6%
$Mines \rightarrow Mines.Lithology = sedimentary\ deposits$	5%
$Mines \rightarrow Mines.Lithology = volcanic\ deposits$	64%
$Mines \rightarrow Mines.Distance\_Benioff \in [170..175]$	67%
$Mines_{gold} \rightarrow substance = Gold/Copper$	12%
$Mines_{gold} \rightarrow Country = Peru$	31%
$Mines_{gold} \rightarrow Country = Chile$	16%
$Mines_{gold} \rightarrow Country = Argentina$	22%
$Mines_{gold} \rightarrow Morphology = Present - dayorrecentplacers$	16%
$Mines_{gold} \rightarrow Morphology = Discordantlodeorvein(thickness > 50cm), \cdots$	30%
$Mines_{gold} \rightarrow Gitology = Alluvial - eluvialplacers$	14%
$Mines_{gold} - \exists^1_{10km} Geology \rightarrow True$	95%
$Mines_{gold} - \exists^1_{10km} Geology \rightarrow Geology.Age \in \{Cenozoic, Tertiary\}$	58%
$Mines_{gold} - \forall^{75\%}_{10km} Geology \exists^1_{20km} Fault \rightarrow True$	58%
$Mines_{gold} - \exists^1_{10km} Geology \rightarrow Geology.Age \in \{Cenozoic, Quaternary\}$	40%
$Mines_{gold} - \exists^1_{10km} Geology \rightarrow Geology.Age \in \{Mesozoic, Cretacious\}$	42%
$Mines_{gold} - \exists^1_{10km} Geology \rightarrow Geology.Age = Paleozoic$	38%
$Mines_{gold} - \exists^1_{10km} Geology \rightarrow Geology.System = Neogene$	41%
$Mines_{gold} - \exists^1_{10km} Geology \rightarrow Geology.GeolType = Sedimentary$	35%
$Mines_{gold} - \exists^1_{15km} Faults \rightarrow True$	63%
$Mines_{gold} - \exists^2_{15km} Faults \rightarrow True$	51%
$Mines_{gold} - \exists^3_{15km} Faults \rightarrow True$	43%

4 Experiments

We have implemented GISMiner in Java. In addition to the geographical layers in the GIS, we pre-compute the relation tables that link the thematic layers by pairs. Given two layers, each entry in a relation table linking those two layers contains three fields: the identifier of a geographic object in the first layer, the identifier of a geographic object in the second layer and the distance between them. In order to do this pre-processing just once, we choose a large distance between the objects to allow the user to choose big buffers around the objects. Note that relation tables between objects in a same thematic layer are also computed.

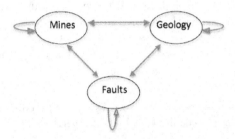

Fig. 2. Database schema of GIS Andes. Links represent an "is_distant" relationship.

Example 6. The model that we have proposed and the system GISMiner have been experimented on a real geographic database. Consider the three thematic layers: Mines, Geology and Faults. The relations computed between the layers are represented in Figure 2.

A tree is constructed during the interactive process of learning characterization rules. The process allows to select a target set of examples from a given table, such as gold mines and explore the GIS through a graph constructed by the user. Figure 3 (a) gives the tree as built in GISMiner. Starting from the target set of gold mines (614 objects selected among 2923 mines), four quantified paths are created by the user:

1. $\forall_{10km}^{75\%} Geol,$
2. $\forall_{10km}^{75\%} Geol \exists_{20km}^{1} Faults,$
3. $\exists_{10km}^{1} Faults$ and
4. $\forall_{10km}^{25\%} Mines.$

Note that quantified path 2 is an extension of quantified path 1. At each node including the target set node, the system extracts the set of properties thus completing the characterization rule built so far. Also at each node, the user can add additional nodes by extending the quantified path. At each node a set of rules is then discovered. Figure 3 (b) explains the content of the nodes. Figure 3

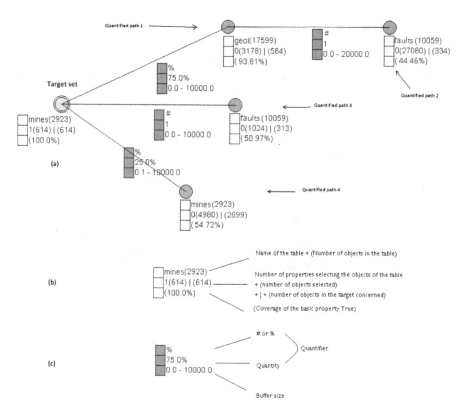

Fig. 3. Example of tree exploration in GISMiner

(c) details the quantifiers present on the edges of the tree, the example shown represents $\forall_{10km}^{75\%}$.

Depending on the length of the quantified paths in a tree and the size of the database, the time needed to build a complete tree can vary from seconds to several minutes. However, a tree built by the user can be saved and recovered any time.

Some examples of rules are given in Table 1. The rules that have been learned have been evaluated by a geologist expert. All these rules were consistent with previous knowledge regarding this GIS. Our tool can be seen as an exploratory data analysis tool that can help navigate into large and complex GIS data.

5   Related Work

The work that we present here belongs to a family of problems, called descriptive induction that aims at discovering patterns satisfied by data. Although the most studied tasks are certainly mining frequent patterns and mining association rules, there has been a growing interest for new tasks, such as subgroup discovery [12,26,27], mining contrast set [4], mining emergent patterns [7,8]. It has been shown in [23] that these three tasks, although formulated differently are quite comparable. In all the approaches, a population Π described by data is given. The settings differ according that the target objects are the whole population Π (frequent pattern mining), a subset Π_1 of the population the behavior of which is compared to the whole population (subgroup discovery), a subset of the population Π_1 the behavior of which is compared to another subset Π_2 (contrast set, emerging pattern, subgroup discovery).

We can also consider that characterization is close to the task of mining frequent properties on the target set. This task has already long been studied [1,10,19], since in many systems, it is the first step for mining association rules. Nevertheless, most works suppose that data is stored in a single table, and few algorithms [6,22] really handle multi-relational databases. Moreover, the frequency (also called the support) is not sufficient to characterize the objects of the target set, because it is also important to determine whether a property is truly a characteristic feature by considering also the frequency of that property outside the target set.

6   Conclusion

In this paper we have addressed the problem of learning rules from Geographic Information Systems. We have focused on characterization rules, viewed as an exploratory task. Therefore instead of automatically mining all the interesting characteristic rules, which is time-consuming and which leads to too many rules, we have developed GISMiner an interactive tool for mining Geographic Information Systems: in such a system, the user iteratively builds the quantified paths, specifying the relations and the properties. We propose a language for characteristic rules, which allows taking into account the structure of the GIS. Moreover, in this language, we can specify properties like "for the object o, a given proportion of objects o_i at a distance less than λ from o satisfy a property p".

This work has proven to be useful in a real-life application and we plan on testing it on other GIS. In the future we would like to study whether our approach could be useful for other kinds of data such as temporal and social media data.

Knowledge discovery in geographic databases is still an open research area for which new scalable, efficient and interactive algorithms that can deal with large numbers of geo-referenced objects yet need to be developed. One of the main frontiers of GKD is to see ultimately intelligent methods and discoveries integrated to Geographic Information Systems [20].

References

1. Agrawal, R., Imielinski, T., Swami, A.N.: Mining association rules between sets of items in large databases. In: Proc. of the ACM SIGMOD International Conference on Management of Data, pp. 207–213 (1993)
2. Appice, A., Ceci, M., Lanza, A., Lisi, F.A., Malerba, D.: Discovery of spatial association rules in geo-referenced census data: A relational mining approach. Intell. Data Anal. **7**(6), 541–566 (2003)
3. Appice, A., Ciampi, A., Lanza, A., Malerba, D., Rapolla, A., Vetturi, L.: Geographic knowledge discovery in INGENS: an inductive database perspective. In: ICDM Workshops, pp. 326–331 (2008)
4. Bay, S.D., Pazzani, M.J.: Detecting group differences: Mining contrast sets. Data Min. Knowl. Discov. **5**(3), 213–246 (2001)
5. Cassard, D.: GIS andes: a metallogenic GIS of the andes cordillera. In: 4th Int. Symp. on Andean Geodynamics, pp. 147–150. IRD Paris, October 1999
6. Dehaspe, L., De Raedt, L.: Mining association rules in multiple relations. In: Džeroski, S., Lavrač, N. (eds.) ILP 1997. LNCS, vol. 1297, pp. 125–132. Springer, Heidelberg (1997)
7. Dong, G., Li, J.: Efficient mining of emerging patterns: discovering trends and differences. In: KDD, pp. 43–52 (1999)
8. Fan, H.: Efficiently mining interesting emerging patterns. In: Dong, G., Tang, C., Wang, W. (eds.) WAIM 2003. LNCS, vol. 2762, pp. 189–201. Springer, Heidelberg (2003)
9. Furnkranz, J.: Separate-and-conquer rule learning. Technical Report OEFAI-TR-96-25, Austrian Research Institute for Artificial Intelligence Schottengasse (1996)
10. Gouda, K., Zaki, M.J.: Efficiently mining maximal frequent itemsets. In: 1st IEEE International Conference on Data Mining, November 2001
11. Han, J., Koperski, K., Stefanovic, N.: Geominer: a system prototype for spatial data mining. In: SIGMOD 1997: Proceedings of the 1997 ACM SIGMOD International Conference on Management of Data, pp. 553–556. ACM, New York (1997)
12. Klösgen, W.: Explora: a multipattern and multistrategy discovery assistant. In: Advances in Knowledge Discovery and Data Mining, pp. 249–271 (1996)
13. Klösgen, W., May, M.J.: Spatial subgroup mining integrated in an object-relational spatial database. In: Elomaa, T., Mannila, H., Toivonen, H. (eds.) PKDD 2002. LNCS (LNAI), vol. 2431, pp. 275–286. Springer, Heidelberg (2002)
14. Koperski, K., Han, J.: Discovery of spatial association rules in geographic information databases. In: Egenhofer, M., Herring, J.R. (eds.) SSD 1995. LNCS, vol. 951, pp. 47–66. Springer, Heidelberg (1995)
15. Koperski, K., Han, J., Stefanovic, N.: An efficient two-step method for classification of spatial data. In: Proc. International Symposium on Spatial Data Handling SDH 1998, pp. 45–54 (1998)
16. Lavrač, N., Flach, P.A., Zupan, B.: Rule evaluation measures: a unifying view. In: Džeroski, S., Flach, P.A. (eds.) ILP 1999. LNCS (LNAI), vol. 1634, pp. 174–185. Springer, Heidelberg (1999)
17. Malerba, D., Esposito, F., Lanza, A., Lisi, F.A.: Discovering geographic knowledge: the INGENS system. In: Ohsuga, S., Raś, Z.W. (eds.) ISMIS 2000. LNCS (LNAI), vol. 1932, pp. 40–48. Springer, Heidelberg (2000)
18. Malerba, D., Esposito, F., Lanza, A., Lisi, F.A., Appice, A.: Empowering a GIS with inductive learning capabilities: the case of INGENS. Computers, Environment and Urban Systems **27**(3), 265–281 (2003)

19. Mannila, H., Toivonen, H.: Levelwise search and borders of theories in knowledge discovery. Data Mining and Knowledge Discovery **1**(3), 241–258 (1997)
20. Miller, H.J., Han, J.: Geographic Data Mining and Knowledge Discovery. Taylor & Francis Inc., Bristol (2001)
21. Raymond, T.Ng., Han, J.: Efficient and effective clustering methods for spatial data mining. In: VLDB 1994: Proceedings of the 20th International Conference on Very Large Data Bases, pp. 144–155. Morgan Kaufmann Publishers Inc., San Francisco (1994)
22. Nijssen, S., Kok, J.N.: Efficient frequent query discovery in FARMER. In: Lavrač, N., Gamberger, D., Todorovski, L., Blockeel, H. (eds.) PKDD 2003. LNCS (LNAI), vol. 2838, pp. 350–362. Springer, Heidelberg (2003)
23. Novak, P.K., Lavrac, N., Webb, G.I.: Supervised descriptive rule discovery: A unifying survey of contrast set, emerging pattern and subgroup mining. Journal of Machine Learning Research **10**, 377–403 (2009)
24. Salleb, A., Vrain, C.: An application of association rules discovery to geographic information systems. In: Zighed, D.A., Komorowski, J., Żytkow, J.M. (eds.) PKDD 2000. LNCS (LNAI), vol. 1910, pp. 613–618. Springer, Heidelberg (2000)
25. Turmeaux, T., Salleb, A., Vrain, C., Cassard, D.: Learning characteristic rules relying on quantified paths. In: Lavrač, N., Gamberger, D., Todorovski, L., Blockeel, H. (eds.) PKDD 2003. LNCS (LNAI), vol. 2838, pp. 471–482. Springer, Heidelberg (2003)
26. Wrobel, S.: An algorithm for multi-relational discovery of subgroups. In: Komorowski, J., Żytkow, J.M. (eds.) PKDD 1997. LNCS, vol. 1263, pp. 78–87. Springer, Heidelberg (1997)
27. Zelezný, F., Lavrac, N.: Propositionalization-based relational subgroup discovery with rsd. Machine Learning **62**(1–2), 33–63 (2006)

Industry Track

Rule-Based Data Transformations in Electricity Smart Grids

Rafael Santodomingo[1(✉)], Mathias Uslar[1], Jose Antonio Rodríguez-Mondéjar[2],
and Miguel Angel Sanz-Bobi[2]

[1] OFFIS – Institute for Information Technology, Oldenburg, Germany
{santodomingo,uslar}@offis.de
[2] Comillas Pontifical University, Madrid, Spain
{mondejar,masanz}@iit.upcomillas.es

Abstract. The systems that will control future electricity networks (also referred to as Smart Grids) will be based on heterogeneous data models. Expressing transformation rules between different Smart Grid data models in well-known rule languages – such as Semantic Web Rule Language (SWRL) and Jena Rule Language (JRL) – will improve interoperability in this domain. Rules expressed in these languages can be easily reused in different applications, since they can be processed by freely available Semantic Web reasoners. In this way, it is possible to integrate heterogeneous Smart Grid systems without using costly ad-hoc converters. This paper presents a solution that leverages SWRL and JRL transformation rules to resolve existing mismatches between two of the most widely accepted standard data models in the Smart Grids.

Keywords: Interoperability · Rule languages · Rule-based data transformations · Semantic web · Smart Grids · SWRL · Jena

1 Business Case

The term "Smart Grid" refers to a modernization of the electricity delivery system so it monitors, protects and automatically optimises the operation of its interconnected elements [1]. Numerous Smart Grid systems will have to co-operate over complex control tasks in order to make this modernisation possible. For instance, substation automated systems, which locally control electric facilities, will exchange data (e.g. voltage and current measurements) with energy management systems, which manage transmission networks from remote control centres [2]. Smart metering systems, for its part, will exchange data about customer consumptions with the distribution management systems that operate distribution networks [3]. Therefore, interoperability is seen as a key enabler of future electricity Smart Grids.

Standardisation is an established approach adopted to address interoperability issues [4]. Initially, standardisation activities in electricity networks were focussed on the definition of protocols for transporting data [5]. More recently, the focus of standardisation efforts has shifted to interoperability at semantic level [6]. This means that

© Springer International Publishing Switzerland 2015
N. Bassiliades et al. (Eds.): RuleML 2015, LNCS 9202, pp. 447–455, 2015.
DOI: 10.1007/978-3-319-21542-6_29

Smart Grid systems do not only have to exchange data, but they must also be able to correctly "understand" and use the data they receive.

The main standardisation body in the electricity sector, the International Electrotechnical Commission (IEC), has created standard data models defining the semantics of the data that is exchanged within this domain. Given the numerous vendors, applications and benefits associated with different approaches, in practice it is not possible to define one single standard data model which is valid for all Smart Grid systems [7]. Consequently, it is mandatory to carry out transformations between heterogeneous data models in order to achieve interoperability in Smart Grids [8].

Expressing transformation rules in well-known rule languages improves their reusability. Rule languages defined within the Semantic Web initiative [9], such as Semantic Web Rule Language (SWRL) [10] and Jena Rule Language (JRL) [11], are particularly interesting for the sake of reusability, since they can be processed by inference engines (reasoners) freely available in the Web. This paper presents a converter based on SWRL and JRL reasoners that performs translations between IEC data models. It enables utilities (e.g. transmission or distribution system operators) to manage data about their own electricity power networks without carrying out time-consuming manually transformations and without using costly ad-hoc converters.

2   Technological Challenges

The *Common Information Model (CIM)* and the *Substation Configuration Language (SCL)* are highlighted in the literature as two of the most relevant standard data models within the scope of electricity Smart Grids [5]. This study focuses on the need for communicating applications based on these two data models.

2.1   Heterogeneous Data Models in Smart Grids: CIM and SCL

The *CIM* is defined in the IEC 61970/61968/62325 standard series. It standardises the semantics to achieve interoperability in a broad range of energy management functionalities, such as: network operations, asset management and electricity markets [12]. Several extensions have been proposed in order to adopt the CIM for further applications, such as the operation of electrified railway systems [13].

Hundreds of classes organised in packages are included in this data model. Among all the CIM packages, *Core*, *Wires* and *Topology* packages contain classes to represent electricity networks. For instance, cim:Substation, cim:Breaker, and cim:Disconnector are the CIM classes to represent substations, circuit breakers, and disconnectors, respectively. Electrical connections are represented in CIM with the classes cim:Terminal and cim:ConnectivityNode. As shown in Fig. 1, each piece of conducting equipment has one or more terminals, which are linked to each other by connectivity nodes within the facility.

The *SCL* is defined in the IEC 61850 standard series. It includes the concepts required for configuring the automation systems that locally control electricity networks. The SCL defines terms to represent automation systems and electric facilities. For instance, `scl:tSubstation` is the SCL class for representing substations. Meanwhile, pieces of conducting equipment are represented in SCL as instances of the class `scl:tConductingEquipment`. The specific type of conducting equipment is determined by the attribute `scl:type`. For example, the values "CBR" and "DIS" are used to represent circuit breakers and disconnectors, respectively. As in the CIM, electrical connections between pieces of conducting equipment are represented in SCL by means of terminals (instances of the class `scl:tTerminal`) and connectivity nodes (instances of the class `scl:tConnectivityNode`) (Fig. 1).

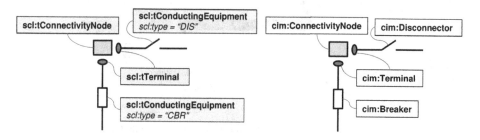

Fig. 1. Electrical connections in SCL and in CIM

2.2   CIM-SCL Communication with Traditional Technologies

Previous studies identified several use cases of information exchanges between CIM-based and SCL-based applications [14]. However, the working groups of experts that created these data models had different objectives and requirements, which resulted in heterogeneities or mismatches between the data models hindering CIM-SCL communications [5, 15].

Traditionally, utilities address mismatches between heterogeneous data models by carrying out time-consuming and inaccurate manual transformations or by means of costly ad-hoc converters [16], which are only valid for a specific case and cannot be easily upgraded for working with new versions of the evolving data models.

Therefore, with the aim of enabling a seamless integration among Smart Grid systems, it is necessary to express the transformation rules between the standard data models in formal languages that can be processed by freely available reasoners. This will enable utilities to directly reuse previously tested transformation rules among several applications and will make it possible to perform automatic data transformations without investing in costly ad-hoc converters.

3   Rule-Based Solution

This work presents a rule-based converter to carry out bi-directional translations between CIM and SCL automatically. The converter is based on SWRL and JRL transformation rules (Fig. 2).

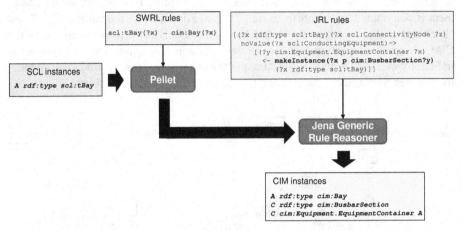

Fig. 2. Rule-based data transformation from SCL into CIM

The *Semantic Web Rule Language (SWRL)* combines the OWL ontology language with the Unary/Binary Datalog RuleML sublanguages of the Rule Markup Language [10]. As explained in [17], SWRL rules are Description Logic (DL)-safe rules when they are applied to only named individuals in the ontology. SWRL DL-safe rules can be processed by DL reasoners, such as Pellet [18], which guarantee the completeness and soundness of the inferences carried out from the rules.

The *Jena Rule Language (JRL)* enables to express inference rules within the Jena Semantic Web programming framework and can be processed by the Jena Generic Rule Reasoner [11]. The inference process in this reasoner does not guarantee completeness and soundness. However, given its expressiveness and level of maturity, JRL was utilised in this work for representing complex transformation rules that cannot be expressed as SWRL DL-safe rules. By using the *makeInstance* built-in term, JRL can represent transformation rules that infer new instances in the consequent that are not defined in the antecedent. In this way, JRL rules, unlike SWRL DL-safe rules, enable to express one-to-many transformations between two data models.

What follows describes by means of illustrative examples how SWRL and JRL transformation rules resolve mismatches between CIM and SCL data models. The complete list of the transformation rules developed in this study is available in [19].

3.1   Resolving Naming Mismatches

Naming mismatches occur when the same real entity is represented in two data models with two modelling elements (classes, properties, attributes) that have different names. For example, substations are represented in SCL as instances of the class `scl:tSubstation` and in CIM as instances of the class `cim:Substation`. Fig. 3 shows how these mismatches can be resolved with SWRL transformation rules.

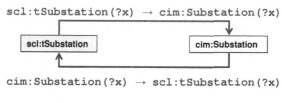

```
scl:tSubstation(?x)  →  cim:Substation(?x)
```

```
cim:Substation(?x)  →  scl:tSubstation(?x)
```

Fig. 3. Resolving naming mismatches with SWRL rules

3.2 Resolving Multilateral Correspondences

Multilateral correspondences occur when an element of a model is represented in the other model with multiple modelling elements. For instance, CIM represents circuit breakers with a single element (an instance of the class `cim:Breaker`), whereas in SCL, these entities are represented with the combination of two modelling elements: an instance of the class `scl:tConductingEquipment` and the enumerated value "CBR" in the attribute `scl:type`. Fig. 4 shows the SWRL rules that were created in this study to overcome this mismatch.

```
scl:tConductingEquipment(?x) ∧ scl:type(?x, "CBR")
→ cim:Breaker(?x)
```

```
scl:tConductingEquipment
scl:type = "CBR"
```
```
cim:Breaker
```

```
cim:Breaker(?x) →
scl:tConductingEquipment(?x) ∧ scl:type(?x, "CBR")
```

Fig. 4. Resolving multilateral correspondences with SWRL rules

3.3 Resolving Covering Mismatches

Covering mismatches occur when two models describe different regions of a domain. This means that these mismatches stand for the fact that one model cannot represent an entity that can be represented in the other model. For example, bus bar sections can be represented in CIM with the class `cim:BusbarSection`. However, SCL does not include specific modelling elements to represent these entities. Fig. 5 shows the JRL transformation rule created in this work to resolve this mismatch.

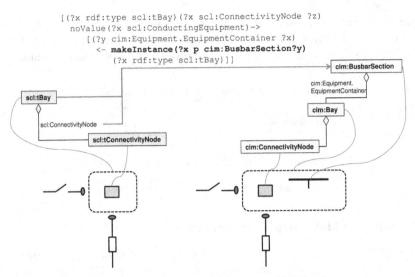

```
[(?x rdf:type scl:tBay)(?x scl:ConnectivityNode ?z)
 noValue(?x scl:ConductingEquipment)->
    [(?y cim:Equipment.EquipmentContainer ?x)
     <- makeInstance(?x p cim:BusbarSection?y)
        (?x rdf:type scl:tBay)]]
```

Fig. 5. Resolving coverage mismatches with JRL rules

4   Results

Three case studies were taken to evaluate the rule-based converter presented in this work. The objective of these case studies was to prove that the converter is able to enable interoperability between two applications belonging to different systems within a utility: a SCL-based control application at the substation automation system and a CIM-based supervisory application located at the remote energy management system (Fig. 6). In each case study, the converter was supposed to perform bi-directional translations between CIM and SCL files describing the power system model of a particular electricity substation. The three representative substations used in the cases studies are those defined by the main Spanish electricity companies in reference [20].

The case studies were evaluated for three key performance indicators: *Runtime*, *Cost*, and *Accuracy*. *Runtime* refers to the runtime in seconds required to perform the data transformations. *Cost* indicates the costs associated with the data transformations. Finally, *Accuracy* is a function of *Recall* and *Precision* (1); with *Recall* being the ratio of correct instances that were translated (true positives) to the total number of instances that had to be translated, and with *Precision* being the ratio of true positives to the total number of instances that were translated. An *Accuracy* greater than 0 means that the automatic data transformation is useful, that is, it is easier for users to correct the incorrect transformations obtained by the system than to manually transform all the instances from scratch.

$$Accuracy = Recall \times \left(2 - \frac{1}{Precision} \right) \tag{1}$$

Given that the rule-based solution performed the data transformations without any false or missing translation, the *Accuracy* was 1 for both the three case studies. This therefore proves that the proposed rule-based solution is better in terms of accuracy than the manual process and, at least, as good as an ad-hoc converter specifically designed for that purpose.

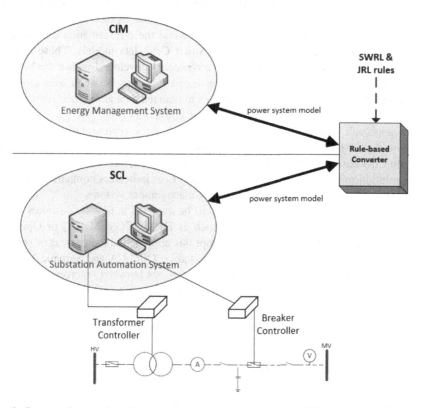

Fig. 6. Case studies: exchanging power system models between SCL-based and CIM-based systems within a utility

In order to measure the *Runtime* of the data transformations, the tests were carried out on a 2.70 GHz Intel Core Duo CPU with 8.00 GB of RAM, running Windows 7. The average *Runtime* obtained for the three case studies with the rule-based solution presented in this work was 1.472 seconds, which is considerably less than the time required for the manual transformations.

As explained previously, one of the main advantages of the data transformations based on SWRL and JRL is that they can be processed by freely available inference engines. Therefore, on the contrary to what happens in the ad-hoc converters traditionally used within energy management systems, the data transformations performed by the rule-based solution presented in this study are not associated with any direct costs. That is, the rule-based solution improves also the *Cost* indicator compared with traditional technologies. In addition to this, it should be noted that the SWRL and JRL transformation rules can be easily reused in other applications, since they are written in external files, instead of hardcoded within a converter.

5   Importance and Impact

In order to achieve interoperability in Smart Grids it is mandatory to facilitate information exchanges between systems based on heterogeneous data models. This paper showed how SWRL and JRL rule languages enable these information exchanges by overcoming existing mismatches between Smart Grid data models. These rule languages can be processed by freely available reasoners developed within the Semantic Web initiative. Hence, expressing the transformation rules between data models in SWRL and JRL makes it possible for utilities to manage data about their own electricity power networks without using costly ad-hoc converters.

Our approach was evaluated in this work with three representative case studies based on one of the main interoperability issues within this domain: the interactions between CIM-based and SCL-based systems. The tests showed that the proposed rule-based solution improves *Runtime, Accuracy,* and *Cost* indicators compared with traditional technologies commonly used in energy management systems.

In future work, the proposed approach will be assessed in new case studies involving additional Smart Grid data models, such as DLMS/COSEM [21] or OpenADR [22]. Moreover, we will analyse how to adopt this approach in the context of semantic enabled Smart Grid middleware platforms based on OPC UA and Sematic Web Services [2], [23] in order to enable run-time interactions between heterogeneous Smart Grid systems. In addition to this, we will enhance ontology matching techniques to automatically find the transformation rules between two data models [24], [25].

References

1. Report to NIST on the Smart Grid Interoperability Standards Roadmap. Electronic Power Research Institute. Technical report (2009)
2. Sučić, S., Dragicevic, T., Havelka, J.: A Device-Level Service-Oriented Middleware Platform for Self-Manageable DC Microgrid Applications Utilizing Semantic-Enabled Distributed Energy Resources. International Journal of Electrical Power & Energy Systems **54**, 576–588 (2014)
3. Rodriguez-Mondejar, J.A., Santodomingo, R., Brown, C.: The ADDRESS energy box: design and implementation. In: IEEE International Energy Conference and Exhibition (ENERGYCON), pp.629-634 (2012)
4. Uslar, M., Specht, M., Dänekas, C., Trefke, J., Rohjans, S., González, J.M., Rosinger, C., Bleiker, R.: Standardization in Smart Grids - Introduction to IT-Related Methodologies, Architectures and Standards. Springer-Verlag, Berlin Heidelberg (2013)
5. IEC TC 57 Architecture – Part 1: Reference Architecture for TC 57, Draft IEC TC 57 WG 19. Technical Report (2009)
6. Uslar, M.: Semantic interoperability within the power systems domain. In: Proc. ACM first international workshop on Interoperability of heterogeneous information systems, pp. 39–46 (2005)
7. Haslhofer, B., Klas, W.: A survey of techniques for achieving metadata interoperability. ACM Comput. Surv **42**(2), 71–737 (2010)

8. Uslar, M.: Ontologiebasierte Integration heterogener Standards in der Energiewirtschaft. Ph.D. Thesis, Oldenburger Verlag für Wirtschaft, Informatik und Recht (2010)
9. Berners-Lee, T., Hendler, J., Lassila, O.: The Semantic Web. Scientific American **284**(5), 34–43 (2001)
10. Horrocks, I., Patel-Schneider, P.F., Boley, H., Tabet, S., Grosof, B., Dean, M.: SWRL: A Semantic Web Rule Language Combining OWL and RuleML. World Wide Web Consortium; National Research Council of Canada, Network Inference, and Stanford University (2004). URL: http://www.w3.org/Submission/SWRL/
11. Jena Programming Framework for the Semantic Web – the general purpose engine. URL: http://jena.apache.org/documentation/inference/index.html#rules
12. Uslar, M., Specht, M., Rohjans, S., Trefke, J., Gonzalez, J.M.V.: The Common Information Model CIM IEC 61968/61970 and 62325 - A practical introduction to the CIM (Power Systems). Springer-Verlag, Berlin, Heidelberg (2012)
13. Santodomingo, R., Pilo, E., Rodríguez-Mondéjar, J.A., Garcia-Vaquero, M.A.: Adapting the CIM model to describe electrified railway systems. In: Eleventh International Conference on Computer System Design and Operation in the Railway and Other Transit Systems (COMPRAIL) (2008)
14. Falk, H., Saxton, T.: Harmonizing the International Electrotechnical Commission Common Information Model (CIM) and 61850 Standards via a Unified Model: Key to Achieve Smart Grid Interoperability Objectives. EPRI, Palo Alto, CA. 1020098 (2010)
15. Preiss, O., Kostic, T.: Unified information models in support of location transparency for future utility applications. In: Proc. 39th Hawaii Int. Conf. System Sciences (HICSS), 2006, pp. 242–251 (2006)
16. IEEE P2030™ - Guide for Smart Grid Interoperability of Energy Technology and Information Technology Operation with the Electric Power System (EPS), and End-Use Applications and Loads, IEEE Standards Association Department (2011)
17. Motik, B., Sattler, U., Studer, R.: Query Answering for OWL-DL with Rules. In: McIlraith, S.A., Plexousakis, D., van Harmelen, F. (eds.) ISWC 2004. LNCS, vol. 3298, pp. 549–563. Springer, Heidelberg (2004)
18. Sirin, E., Parsia, B., Grau, B.C., Kalyanpur, A., Katz, Y.: Pellet: A practical OWL-DL reasoner. Web Semantics **5**(2), 51–53 (2007)
19. SWRL & JRL alignments between CIM and SCL data models, May 2015. URL: http://www.iit.upcomillas.es/santodomingo/Thesis.html
20. Minimum common specification for substation protection and control equipment in accordance with the IEC 61850 standard. E3 Group of Spanish Electricity Companies for Studies on IEC 61850 (2010)
21. Berganza, I., Sendin, A., Arzuaga, A., Sharma, M., Varadarajan, B.: PRIME on-field deployment - First summary of results and discussion. In: IEEE International Conference on Smart Grid Communications (SmartGridComm), pp. 297–302 (2011)
22. Kim, J.J., Yin, R., Kiliccote, S.: Automated Demand Response Technologies and Demonstration in New York City using OpenADR. Ernest Orlando Lawrence Berkeley National Laboratory (2013)
23. Rohjans, S., Uslar, M., Appelrath, H.J.: OPC UA and CIM: Semantics for the smart grid. In: IEEE PES Transmission and Distribution Conference and Exposition (2010)
24. Santodomingo, R., Rohjans, S., Uslar, M., Rodríguez-Mondéjar, J.A., Sanz-Bobi, M.A.: Facilitating the automatic mapping of IEC 61850 signals and CIM measurements. IEEE Transactions on Power Systems **28**(4), 4348–4355 (2014)
25. Santodomingo, R., Rohjans, S., Uslar, M., Rodríguez-Mondéjar, J.A., Sanz-Bobi, M.A.: Ontology matching system for future energy smart grids. Eng. Appl. Artif. Intel. (2014). http://dx.doi.org/10.1016/j.engappai.2014.02.005

Norwegian State of Estate: A Reporting Service for the State-Owned Properties in Norway

Ling Shi[1(✉)], Bjørg E. Pettersen[1], Ivar Østhassel[1], Nikolay Nikolov[2],
Arash Khorramhonarnama[3], Arne J. Berre[2], and Dumitru Roman[2]

[1] Statsbygg, Pb. 8106 Dep 0032, Oslo, Norway
{ling.shi,bjorg.pettersen,ivar.osthassel}@statsbygg.no
[2] SINTEF, Pb. 124 Blindern 0314, Oslo, Norway
{nikolay.nikolov,arne.j.berre,dumitru.roman}@sintef.no
[3] University of Oslo, Pb. 1072 Blindern 0316, Oslo, Norway
arashk@ifi.uio.no

Abstract. Statsbygg is the public sector administration company responsible for reporting the state-owned property data in Norway. Traditionally the reporting process has been resource-demanding and error-prone. The State of Estate (SoE) business case presented in this paper is creating a new reporting service by sharing, integrating and utilizing cross-sectorial property data, aiming to increase the transparency and accessibility of property data from public sectors enabling downstream innovation. This paper explains the ambitions of the SoE business case, highlights the technical challenges related to data integration and data quality, data sharing and analysis, discusses the current solution and potential use of rules technologies.

Keywords: Property data · Data integration · Data quality · Data sharing · Rules

1   Business Case

The public sector owns a significant amount of property data. Re-use of public sector information is required by both the EU and the Norwegian government. EU's DIRECTIVE 2013/37/EU OF THE EUROPEAN PARLIAMENT AND OF THE COUNCIL of 26 June 2013 amending Directive 2003/98/EC on the re-use of public sector information [1] establishes a set of rules on the re-use of the public information to meet the challenges caused by increasing data volumes, varying data formats and technological advancements in the last decades. The Norwegian government follows closely this EU-directive. One of the demands and regulations from the Norwegian government requires that "The agencies shall make appropriate and existing raw data available in machine-readable formats. This applies to information that has value to society, which can be further used, which is not confidential and where the costs of publication are believed to be modest (loss of income from the sale of data considered an expense).[1]" The Norwegian public sector is obliged to follow the government

---

[1] https://www.regjeringen.no/nb/dokumenter/fellesforinger-2012/id665965/

© Springer International Publishing Switzerland 2015
N. Bassiliades et al. (Eds.): RuleML 2015, LNCS 9202, pp. 456–464, 2015.
DOI: 10.1007/978-3-319-21542-6_30

regulation. For example, Statistics Norway[2] shares the statistical data through an online service – StatBank Norway.[3] The Norwegian Agency for Public Management and eGovernment (Difi)[4] provides a data sharing portal[5] for Open Data in Norway. Though many government agencies began to use the Difi platform, further efforts are needed to enlist more government agencies and improve the platform.

Statsbygg[6] is a public sector administration company responsible to the Ministry of Local Government and Modernisation[7] (KMD). It is the Norwegian government's key advisor in construction and property affairs, building commissioner, property manager and property developer. Statsbygg has been responsible for reporting real estate properties owned by the public sector in Norway. The latest report is distributed both as a hard copy of 314 pages and as a PDF file.[8] It takes in average 6 Person-Months of Statsbygg to create the report, excluding the time spent on answering surveys by the involved organizations. The data has been collected and aggregated predominantly by using spreadsheet software. Quality assurance is implemented through e-mails and phone correspondence. Evidently, the current manual data collection process is re-source-demanding and error-prone. Furthermore, there are other property related data that have not been covered by the earlier surveys and reports, although the data can provide valuable analysis results (for example, accessibility of buildings (BFA)[9] and statistical market price of real estates from Statistics Norway (SSB)[10]).

Statsbygg is in the process of creating and exploiting a new SoE reporting service based on integrated cross-sectorial property data. Fig. 1 below shows a high-level view of an integrated open property dataset accessible as Web services – the "State of the Estate (SoE)" Service. The datasets used as input to the service include national cadastral data, buildings' universal design data, statistical data, data from the Norwegian register for legal entities and business enterprises (BR[11]). BR gathers organizational information of the public sector, such as the organization's identification number, name, address and its registered sub-units. The national cadastral dataset includes owner information of properties and the owner is identified by the organization's identification number if properties are owned by organizations. Thus, a complete state-owned properties list can be generated if the cadastral data and the legal entity register are shared and integrated based on identification numbers of the organizations in public sector. Data such as addresses and areas of the buildings are already included in the list since the data are part of the cadastral dataset. The Statsbygg's property dataset adds additional information such as administrative grouping of buildings

---

[2] https://www.ssb.no/
[3] https://www.ssb.no/en/statistikkbanken
[4] http://www.difi.no/
[5] http://data.norge.no/
[6] http://www.statsbygg.no
[7] https://www.regjeringen.no/en/dep/kmd/id504/
[8] https://www.regjeringen.no/contentassets/f4346335264c4f8495bc559482428908/no/sved/state igedom.pdf
[9] https://byggforalle.no/
[10] http://www.ssb.no
[11] http://www.brreg.no/english/

and other administrative information of the buildings. Any data mismatch, deviation, or conflicts are identified by comparing Statsbygg's datasets with the cadastral data. In that way, the survey can be redesigned as a checklist for the involved organizations to confirm their portfolio of real properties, rather than a manual data gathering job. As a result, also data quality will be improved, since data from the respective owners are made visible, accessible and comparable. In summary, the new SoE service will significantly reduce the workload of data collection and later processing and analysis by following the approach as described in this section.

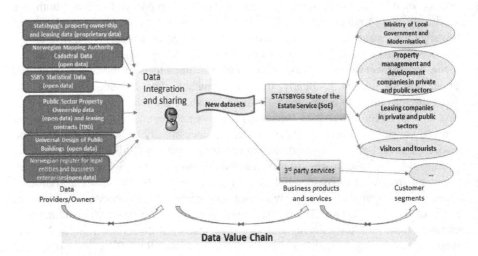

Fig. 1. Data Value Chain of the SoE Business Case

SoE has been designed to support scenarios such as:

- Reporting the state-owned properties in Norway
- Analysis of accessibility of office locations in the public sectors (by integrating property data with accessibility data of buildings).
- Risk and vulnerability analysis of real estate properties (by integrating property data with geographical datasets such as flooding zones, landslide zones, soil contamination areas, etc). This is meant to support a better regime of planning and maintenance of the buildings within the area by foreseeing and reducing the risks.
- Analysis of leasing prices against statistical market leasing price in the same area (by integrating property data with statistical market leasing prices).
- 3rd party services by integrating property data with other relevant 3rd party property datasets

The impact of the approach described above will affect several groups of stakeholders. Firstly, users from the public sectors will both benefit from, and contribute to this new service. The public administration offices are providing data on their portfolios of owned or leased properties. When property-related data from other domains and sectors are added, the report and support will be enriched with new possibilities to analyze and present the data. For example, some government agencies own or lease real estate properties abroad, e.g. embassies. Thus, corresponding datasets from other countries can be used to further append and enrich the service. Moreover, the result of analysis will present the status of the estates and help identify any unnecessary spending of resources, which can be reallocated where they are needed most. At the same time this will help reduce the cost of the government's estates which aligns well with the government's efficiency and reform agenda.

The new SoE service is meant to be open to the public and the integrated dataset will be shared under specified conditions. Therefore, another beneficiary group is private persons and users from the private sector. One example use of the SoE service is as an overview of the state-owned properties in a given city or area. In such an example, the SoE service will provide detailed information such as the accessibility of a state-owned building, which is important information for visitors with impairments. Additionally, real estate broker companies can reuse the service to enrich their portfolio databases. Finally, architects or the real estate development and management companies can take advantage of the risk and vulnerability analysis result in the design and construction phases of their building projects.

Value Proposition. The focus of the SoE business case is on integrating property data from several sources into a multi-sectorial property dataset which is the key to establish a service to support and enhance the whole data collection, analysis and reporting lifecycle of the State of the Estate service. The goal is to increase efficiency and optimize the resource allocation of government estate data management.

2   Technological Challenges

One of the main challenges related to integrating data in the context of SoE is data distribution. Property data reside in different source systems owned both by public and private sectors. For example, the Norwegian Mapping Authority[12] administrates and stores land register and cadaster including ownership of estates. On the other hand, Statsbygg administrates 2350 state-owned buildings making a total of around 2.8 million square meter area. The Norwegian government requires the public sector to open and share data to increase the transparency of government administration.[13] This applies also to the property data.

Another challenge related to implementing the SoE service is the complexity of property data. The property data are rich in attributes and relations and also are location-based. A real estate property is associated with horizontal and vertical dimensions such as ground, land, road, air and neighborhood. Apart from spatial aspects, this type of data has also a time dimension that records the changes of a property throughout the years. Therefore, sharing of property data requires much more effort in aggregating and association than simply publishing a static tabular list of values.

---

[12] http://www.kartverket.no/en/About-The-Norwegian-Mapping-Authority/
[13] http://www.difi.no/sites/difino/files/veileder-i-tilgjengeliggjoring-av-offentlig-data-web.pdf

Challenges in Data Integration and Data Quality

Since property data are managed by several cross-sectorial organizations and companies, they are stored and provisioned in different formats. Data are often shared in the original format, for example, the cadastral data in Norway are open and shared in a searchable map-based web application.[14] It is difficult to integrate data from a map-based web application with other property data provided in different formats, and, thus difficult to achieve automated analysis covering multiple properties. On the other hand, when the data are exported and shared in alternative formats (i.e., other than the original format), some of the essential characteristics may be lost in the transition. In this context, rule-based validation techniques are appealing, as they enable a more automated process for integrity checking and thus reduce the possible data loss after conversion to a new data format.

There are exceptions and mismatches in the different registers because each register has its own domain focus and scope. For example, as described in [2], the national cadastral system does not register buildings less than 15 square meters, whereas Statsbygg's property management system does. There is also often no unique identifier to connect the datasets since the unique identifier in one dataset may be missing or incomplete in the other dataset. In these cases rule-based techniques could be applied in enabling filtering out any known exceptions during integration, and through supporting conditional integration, whereby the integration action turns on or off depending on certain conditions [3].

Ensuring data consistency is also a significant challenge of integrating property data. Firstly, some attributes, such as the building's name, area and address information, are stored across several different systems with deviations or even conflicts. Furthermore, property data evolve and may not be updated in all the systems at the same time. For example, a building can be extended during renovation, which would alter its original area. It is up to the data owner to report the changes to the Norwegian Mapping Authority office. However, if the change is not reported the data become inconsistent. In this context, rules can be used to automatically identify inconsistencies between different data sources and thereby make suggestions for improving data quality in the respective source systems and, subsequently, of the SoE service.

Challenges in Data Sharing and Data Security

Data security, which data to share and with whom are some of the key aspects in this business case. Firstly, some of the cadastral data involves personal identifiable information such as owner name and national ID, which is subject to the EU Data Protection Directive (Directive 95/46/EC)[15] and the Norwegian personal information law.[16] Secondly, some data providers such as Statsbygg have special restrictions on the information and data security of some types of properties (for example, prison facilities and King's properties). In this context, data sharing rules can be applied to ensure appropriate access control to sensitive information. Such data sharing rules are a useful input to form the access rights and security policy in the business case requirements.

---

[14] http://www.seeiendom.no/

[15] http://eur-lex.europa.eu/legal-content/EN/TXT/HTML/?uri=CELEX:31995L0046

[16] https://lovdata.no/dokument/NL/lov/2000-04-14-31

Challenges in Data Analysis
Data analysis (for example, the risk and vulnerability analysis of properties owned by public sector) based on the integrated data is a demanding task when data come from different sources with different quality, especially when data from both authorized and non-authorized sources are integrated. To address this, it is important to set up a trustworthiness scale mechanism for data sources for the purposes of data analysis. Using the scale as an input we can thus set up rules on how the integrated data shall be used or manipulated in the analysis process.

3   Rule-Based Solution

As already pointed out in the previous section, rule technologies can be used to meet the challenges of the SoE business case by assisting the processes of property data integration, quality control, data sharing and analysis in the business case. In order to achieve that, first, a set of business rules need to be collected. However, business rules cannot be easily applied for data processing directly, and therefore machine-readable rules need to be created in order to automate rule processing. RuleML, SWRL [4], R2ML (Reverse Rule Markup Language) and F-logic (Frame Logic) [5] are examples of rule languages with different expressiveness and features relevant for encoding rules in this business case.

Rules for Data Integration and Data Quality
To meet the challenges in the data integration process, a collection of definitions, vocabularies, ontology models and business rules from different sectors are needed. Definitions, vocabularies and ontology models describe how the data should be integrated, whereas the rules describe under what conditions. In particular, rules must check the possible data loss after conversion to other data formats, filter out the known exceptions and support conditional integration.

Another application of rules in this business case is for creating flexible data quality validation processes [6]. Machine-readable rules can be formed based on the business rules to automatically identify the deviations and conflicts among different data sources.

Rules for Data Sharing and Data Security
The work in [7] proposes an approach for integrating data from diverse sources, for gathering user preferences for what data to share and when to share it, and a policy management infrastructure in the network for enforcing those preferences. Following that approach, for each dataset in the SoE business case, we are collecting the laws, regulations and business restrictions that apply to the data ownership and data security. Thereafter rules will be defined on what to share, whom to share with and how and what to share. Those rules will be applied to the access and security control of the integrated data to achieve the desired security and privacy levels.

Rules for Data Analysis
To help data consumers justify their respective output analyses, a trustworthiness scale of the data is needed. The integrated property data from the SoE service are

based on authorized sources in the public sector where the trustworthiness is relatively high. Another application of such rules in this context is related to controlling the manipulation of the integrated data in order to avoid misuse by other stakeholders. For example, let's assume that an external company plans to develop a new service based on the integrated property data from the SoE service and data gathered through crowdsourcing. In this case, even though it is based on SoE, the new service would have a relatively low trustworthiness as the final result should be presented with trustworthiness, which is not higher than the lowest of the data sources.

4   Results

Statsbygg has developed a software procedure for integrating data from its internal property management system and the Norwegian national cadastral system. The procedure is executed on input data on a nightly basis, and the result is connected to the internal GIS portal, shown as a map layer for visualization and analysis of the real estate properties owned by Statsbygg.

Several integration challenges were identified and analyzed, and concrete integration rule-based solutions were suggested and implemented in the software procedure. Integration rules have been extracted, for example, based on the heterogeneity analysis in an SBVR integration hub as reported in [2].

An example of business rule for data integration is "the address of a building in different source systems should be identical or with known spell variations". Thus, buildings are firstly integrated by the national cadastral building number, and after that the building's addresses from different source systems are compared to generate a mismatch-list. The above rule is used as a quality control of the first step. The mismatch-list is used both as a reference for address updates in the Statsbygg's property management system, and to identify possible errors in the registered national cadastral building numbers. The national cadastral building identification ID is missing for around 15% of the buildings in the Statsbygg's property management system due to e.g. buildings being situated abroad or being less than 15 square meters. In a third and final step, an address search is executed on the buildings missing cadastral numbers against the national cadastral system in order to discover a possible cadastral building number based on the address. During this process, normal address variations are taken into consideration to increase the address matching percent. This implemented three-step method has improved the integration quality and numbers of matched buildings have been increased by more than 7%.

Nevertheless, the goal of the SoE business case is to extend the existing procedure into an interactive reporting service for properties data. The end product of this business case is expected to be an authoritative portal of state-owned properties, consisting of comprehensive, accurate, and timely updated data about state-owned properties in Norway. Statsbygg and other government agencies (in the role of data providers) are meant to submit and control their own property data online and easily generate the national SoE reports or region- and sector-based reports. The portal will be freely accessible and will be available to the public and other user groups such as property development companies, the media and property service providers.

The SoE business case is developed as part of the H2020 European funded innovation action project proDataMarket,[17] which aims to create a data marketplace for property-related data and disrupt the property-related data market across Europe. It focuses on innovation across sectors, where property-related data value chains are relevant, and leverages and transfers technologies from the emerging Data-as-a-Service and Linked Data domains (see for example [8] and the DaPaaS project[18] which provides cost-effective technologies for publishing and consuming Open Data).

5   Importance and Impact

Collecting ownership of real estate property data from the government agencies has been a resource-demanding and error-prone survey process. The SoE business case described in this paper is evolving the data collection process and reducing the scope of data collection by providing a prefilled checklist, instead of manually collecting already available data from source systems. This is expected to improve the data quality significantly and make it more cost-effective, since it will help identify a uniform "master" dataset from data that currently are being duplicated in several systems. For example, buildings' addresses are duplicated in several systems, but the cadastral system has been identified as the "master" dataset of address information.

The SoE service makes the property data from the public sector in Norway easily accessible and usable for analysis thereby providing opportunities for downstream innovation related to property data. The SoE service is expected to have following impacts and outcomes:

- Sharing of Statsbygg's internal property datasets in novel ways
- Exploitation of cadastral data and other cross-sectorial data
- A pilot SoE web service using Statsbygg's data and the integrated cross-sectorial data
- Data collection survey for ownership and, possibly, leasing of property data from government agencies
- Sharing the survey data results in novel ways
- An extended pilot to include survey result, i.e., the public sector's owned and, possibly, leased properties
- Reporting function based on SoE web service
- Internationalization process

The main customer group for this improved service is the current Statsbygg's client base: KMD and other governmental agencies. These users from the public sector will continue to be an important group. Nonetheless, private individuals, companies and 3rd-party organisations will also benefit from the service. These could be public media, building architects, property development and management companies, leasing companies, and even tourists.

---

[17] http://prodatamarket.eu/
[18] http://dapaas.eu/

The opportunities to internationalize this service will also make it possible to cover the Norwegian government property abroad. SoE capabilities are commonly needed by the governments in other countries, such as the U.K. which has already started publishing the report[19] in the last few years but has not connected it to the open property data, as suggested in this business case.

Acknowledgements. The work on the State of Estate (SoE) business case is partly supported by the EC funded project proDataMarket (Grant number: 644497).

References

1. Schultz, M., Shatter, A.: Directive 2013/37/EU of the European Parliament and of the Council of 26 June 2013 amending Directive 2003/98/EC on the re-use of public sector information. Official Journal of the European Union, Brussels (2013)
2. Shi, L., Roman, D., Berre, A.J.:SBVR as a Semantic Hub for Integration of Heterogeneous Systems. RuleML2013@ Challenge, Human Language Technology and Doctoral Consortium, 7 (2013)
3. Bohn, C., Atherton, D.P.: An analysis package comparing PID anti-windup strategies. IEEE Control Systems 15(2), 34–40 (1995)
4. Horrocks, I., Patel-Schneider, P.F., Boley, H., Tabet, S., Grosof, B., Dean, M.: SWRL: A semantic web rule language combining OWL and RuleML. W3C Member submission 21, 79 (2004)
5. Kifer, M., Lausen, G.: F-logic: a higher-order language for reasoning about objects, inheritance, and scheme. ACM SIGMOD Record 18(2), 134–146 (1989)
6. Scheppers, J.: Creating flexible data quality validation processes using Business Rules (2009). http://purl.utwente.nl/essays/60714
7. Hull, R., Kumar, B., Lieuwen, D., Patel-Schneider, P.F., Sahuguet, A., Varadarajan, S., Vyas, A.: Enabling context-aware and privacy-conscious user data sharing. In: 2004 Proceedings, IEEE International Conference on Mobile Data Management, pp. 187–198. IEEE (2004)
8. Roman, D., Pop, C.D., Roman, R.I., Mathisen, B.M., Wienhofen, L., Elvesæter, B., Berre, A.J.: The Linked Data AppStore. In: Prasath, R., O'Reilly, P., Kathirvalavakumar, T. (eds.) MIKE 2014. LNCS, vol. 8891, pp. 382–396. Springer, Heidelberg (2014)

---

[19] https://www.gov.uk/government/collections/state-of-the-estate

Ontology Reasoning Using Rules in an eHealth Context

Dörthe Arndt[1]([✉]), Ben De Meester[1], Pieter Bonte[2], Jeroen Schaballie[2],
Jabran Bhatti[3], Wim Dereuddre[3], Ruben Verborgh[1], Femke Ongenae[2],
Filip De Turck[2], Rik Van de Walle[1], and Erik Mannens[1]

[1] Ghent University – IMinds – Multimedia Lab, Ghent, Belgium
{doerthe.arndt,ben.demeester}@ugent.be
[2] IBCN Research Group, INTEC, Ghent University – IMinds, Ghent, Belgium
[3] Televic Healthcare, Izegem, Belgium

Abstract. Traditionally, nurse call systems in hospitals are rather simple: patients have a button next to their bed to call a nurse. Which specific nurse is called cannot be controlled, as there is no extra information available. This is different for solutions based on semantic knowledge: if the state of care givers (busy or free), their current position, and for example their skills are known, a system can always choose the best suitable nurse for a call. In this paper we describe such a semantic nurse call system implemented using the EYE reasoner and Notation3 rules. The system is able to perform OWL-RL reasoning. Additionally, we use rules to implement complex decision trees. We compare our solution to an implementation using OWL-DL, the Pellet reasoner, and SPARQL queries. We show that our purely rule-based approach gives promising results. Further improvements will lead to a mature product which will significantly change the organization of modern hospitals.

Keywords: Notation3 · eHealth · OWL 2 RL

1 Business Case

Our business case is a nurse call system in a hospital. The system is aware of certain details about personnel and patients. Such information can include: personal skills of a staff member, staff competences, patient information, special patient needs, and/or the personal relationship between staff members and patients. Furthermore, there is dynamic information available, as for example the current location of staff members and their status (busy or free). When a call is made, the nurse call system should be able to assign the best staff member to answer that call. The definition of this "best" person varies between hospitals and can be quite complex. Our system should thus be easily adjustable, but also very fast in taking a decision. The system additionally controls different devices. If for example staff members enter a room with a patient, a decent light should be switched on; if they log into the room's terminal, they should have access to the medical lockers in the room. Especially hospitals are interested in that kind of system as it enables them to organize their work in a more efficient way:

© Springer International Publishing Switzerland 2015
N. Bassiliades et al. (Eds.): RuleML 2015, LNCS 9202, pp. 465–472, 2015.
DOI: 10.1007/978-3-319-21542-6_31

- Busy nurses get distracted less. They only receive a call if everyone else is also occupied or if the new task is more important than the task they are currently performing.
- The system allows giving preference to staff members who are close to the caller. This prevents nurses from covering unnecessary big distances in their anyhow stressful and physically exhausting daily work.
- If the system is aware of the reason for a call, it can immediately assign nurses with the required skills. Thus, no time is lost by first calling other staff members who then would have to ask for additional help.
- The system can prefer staff members who already know the patient and have a trust relationship with him. This increases the satisfaction of the patient. At the same time, it also saves time for the caregiver, who is in such cases already familiar with the patient's needs and condition.
- The system is universal, i.e., electronic devices in the hospital can be controlled as well.
- The system is adaptable, i.e., hospitals can add their own requirements and priorities.

2   Technological Challenges

An event-driven system as described above has to fulfill certain requirements. The system should:

Scalability cope with data sets ranging from 1000 to 100 000 relevant triple (i.e., triples necessary to be included for the reasoning to be correct);

Semantics be able to draw conclusions based on the information it is aware of;

Functional complexity implement deterministic decision trees with varying complexities;

Configuration have the ability to change these decision trees at configuration time; and

Real-time return a response within 5 seconds to any given event.

There are several options to implement a nurse call system as described above. Following a more classical approach, the system could be written in an object-oriented programming language such as Java or C++. An implementation like this can easily fulfill the real-time and scalability constraints. But such systems are traditionally hard-coded: they are implemented for a specific use case, and even though they might be able to support the required functional complexity, this implementation would be static. The possibility to configure complex decision trees as postulated by the complexity requirement is rather hard to fulfill using traditional programming. Even more difficult to satisfy is the semantic requirement: most object oriented languages do not support enough logic to "understand" the available information. Knowledge must be stated explicitly, as even simple connections between statements such as *"nurse x has location y"* and *"y is location of nurse x"* cannot be found easily.

Especially the last argument motivates us to solve the described problem using semantic web technologies as they natively fulfill the semantics requirement. Knowledge can be represented in an OWL ontology which is understood by OWL-DL reasoners such as for example Pellet [6]. Complex decision trees can be handled by subsequent SPARQL queries. It is easy to add new queries or to change the order of existing queries and to thereby accommodate for the configuration constraint. But our tests have shown that such systems inherently are not fast and reliable enough to fulfill the scalability and real-time requirements. For bigger amounts of data or too complex decision trees, the reasoning times of traditional OWL-DL reasoners grow exponentially, which is not scalable.

To keep the benefits of an OWL-DL based implementation in a scalable and real-time way, we propose a rule-based solution. By using OWL 2 RL rules and resolution instead of classical tableaux reasoning, we can significantly decrease reasoning times and still cover a major subset of OWL 2. This approach benefits from the high performance of rule based reasoners. Even for bigger datasets the reasoning times are still faster than with the OWL-DL based approach. Also, complex decision trees can directly be implemented in rules. As rules are the most natural representations of such trees, it is easy for a user to understand and change certain priorities or to configure new rules. A further advantage of our approach is that all logic is represented in one single way. Instead of OWL plus SPARQL, we can implement the business case by only employing Notation3 Logic (N3). With the aforementioned system, we can meet all necessary requirements.

3 Rule-Based Solution

In this section, we further explain our solution in three parts. First, we focus on the technical background and the technologies used. In the second part we describe how we could improve reasoning times for our use case by employing OWL 2 RL rules written in N3. In the third part we show example rules from our decision trees and discuss options to change these rules.

3.1 Background

Our solution improves on a more classical implementation which employs the OWL 2 reasoner Pellet [6], and where the decision tree was implemented via SPARQL queries. All knowledge was represented using the ACCIO ontology, which is described by Ongenae et al. [5]. Knowledge could either be fixed or dynamic, and updated via an event. Fixed knowledge is, for example, information about skills of staff members, or patients' preferences. Dynamic knowledge is, for example, the movement of a nurse to a certain location, or a new call which is made by a patient.

Our new implementation keeps the knowledge representation of the first attempt but replaces SPARQL and OWL by Notation3 Logic (N3) [1]. This logic forms a superset of RDF and extends the RDF data model by formulas (graphs),

```
1  @prefix rdfs: <http://www.w3.org/2000/01/rdf-schema#>.
2  @prefix rdf: <http://www.w3.org/1999/02/22-rdf-syntax-ns#>.
3
4  {?C rdfs:subClassOf ?D. ?X a ?C} => {?X a ?D}.
```

Listing 1. OWL-RL rule for `rdfs:subClassOf` class axiom in N3.

functional predicates, universal variables and logical operators, in particular the implication operator. These last two features enable the user to express rules. As reasoner we use EYE [7], a semibackward reasoning engine enhanced with Euler path detection. The main reason for our choice is the high performance of the reasoner. Existing benchmarks and results are listed on the EYE website [3].

3.2 OWL 2 RL in N3

To be able to support OWL 2 RL reasoning in N3 we used the OWL 2 RL/RDF rules as listed on the corresponding website [2]. Where possible, we made use of existing N3-translations of these rules as provided by EYE [4]. Missing concepts were added. Although the ACCIO ontology is designed for OWL-DL reasoning, the limitation to OWL RL had no impact for our specific use case.

To illustrate the idea of using rules for OWL reasoning, we give a small example: Listing 1 shows the class axiom rule[1] which is needed to deal with the rdfs concept `subclassOf`. For convenience we omit the prefixes in the formulas below. The empty prefix refers to the ACCIO ontology, `rdf` and `rdfs` have the same meaning as in Listing 1. Consider that we have the following T-Box triple stating that the class `:Call` is a subclass of the class `:Task`:

$$:\texttt{Call rdfs:subClassOf :Task.} \tag{1}$$

If the A-Box contains an individual which is member of the class `:Call`

$$:\texttt{call1 a :Call.} \tag{2}$$

an OWL DL reasoner would make the conclusion that the individual also belongs to the class `Task`

$$:\texttt{call1 a :Task.} \tag{3}$$

Our rule in Listing 1 does exactly the same: as Formula 1 and Formula 2 can be unified with the antecedence of the rule, a reasoner derives the triple in Formula 3. Other concepts can be handled similarly.

3.3 Decision Trees

The ACCIO ontology [5] provides the user with a huge variety of concepts which can, e.g., be used to describe patients (social background, needs, disease), staff

---

[1] The rule is the N3 version of the cax-sco rule in Table 7 on the OWL 2 Profiles website [2].

```
 1  @prefix : <http://ontology/Accio.owl#>.
 2  @prefix rdf: <http://www.w3.org/1999/02/22-rdf-syntax-ns#>.
 3
 4  {
 5    ?c rdf:type :Call.
 6    ?c :hasStatus :Active.
 7    ?c :madeAtLocation ?loc.
 8    ?p :hasRole [rdf:type :StaffMember].
 9    ?p :hasStatus :Free.
10    ?p :closeTo ?loc.
11  }
12  =>
13  {
14    (?p ?c) :assigned 200.
15  }.
```

Listing 2. Rule assigning a preference value to a staff member with status "free" who is close to the call-location.

members (skills, relationships to patients), and situations (locations of persons, states of devices). If all this information is actually available, decision trees can use all of it and be therefore quite complex. In this section we provide two simple rules which could be part of such a tree and we explain how these rules can be modified depending on the needs of an individual hospital.

Listing 2 shows a rule which, given an active call, assigns a staff member with a certain preference to that call. The EYE reasoner works with filter rules (queries), it is easy to search for the assignment of a staff member with the lowest or highest number. In our example, lower numbers mean higher preferences. The antecedence of the given rule contains certain constraints: the active call is made on a certain location and there is a staff member, who is currently free and close to that location. In such a case, our rule assigns the number 200 to the combination of call and staff member.

Listing 3 displays another rule: here, the reason of the active call is known. We have a staff member who has the required skills to answer that kind of calls, but this staff member is currently busy. Our rule assigns the number 100 to this combination of call and staff member. This means, in our current decision tree, we prefer this assignment to the one described by Listing 2.

Now, it could be, that another hospital has different priorities. Imagine for example that in this new hospital, no busy staff should be called if there is still a free staff member available, regardless of the reason of the call. We could easily adapt our decision tree by simply changing the assignment number of one of the rules. If we replace the triple

$$(?p\ ?c)\ :assigned\ 100.$$

in line 16 of Listing 3 by the triple

$$(?p\ ?c)\ :assigned\ 300.$$

```
 1  @prefix : <http://ontology/Accio.owl#>.
 2  @prefix rdf: <http://www.w3.org/1999/02/22-rdf-syntax-ns#>.
 3
 4  {
 5    ?c rdf:type :Call.
 6    ?c :hasStatus :Active.
 7    ?c :hasReason [rdf:type :CareReason].
 8    ?p rdf:type :Person.
 9    ?p :hasStatus :Busy.
10    ?p :hasRole [rdf:type :StaffMember].
11    ?p :hasCompetence [rdf:type :AnswerCareCallCompetence].
12  }
13  =>
14  {
15    (?p ?c) :assigned 100.
16  }.
```

Listing 3. Rule assigning a preference value to a busy staff member who has the needed skills to answer the call.

the reasoner would prefer the assignment expressed by Listings 2 to 3.

Similarly, we can add extra conditions to the rules. Currently, the rule in listing 3 does not take the location of the staff member into account. We can change that by only adding the triples

```
?c :madeAtLocation ?loc. ?p :closeTo ?loc.
```

to the antecedence of the rule. To give this new rule a higher priority than the existing one, we would again only have to change the assigned number in the consequence. Rules with the same number are treated equally.

4   Results

We compared the reasoning times of our implementation with the results of our former implementation using the Pellet reasoner and subsequent SPARQL-queries. As a joint test set up we ran a sequence of events, which we list below, the expected reasoning result is indicated in brackets.

1. A patient launches a call (*assign nurse and update call status*)
2. The assigned nurse indicates that she is busy (*assign other nurse*)
3. The newly assigned nurse accepts the call task (*update call status*)
4. The nurse moves to the corridor (*update location*)
5. The nurse arrives at the patients' room (*update location, turn on lights and update nurse status*)
6. The nurse logs into the room's terminal (*update status call and nurse, open lockers*)
7. The nurse logs out again (*update status call and nurse, close lockers*)
8. The nurse leaves the room (*update location and call status and turn off lights*)

We tested this set-up for two datasets, one dataset consisting of the nurses, hospital rooms and patients of one single ward, the other one for 10 wards. Figure 1a shows the difference in reasoning times of this use case on the same hardware settings[2], using two different technology stacks: the Pellet+SPARQL installation vs. the EYE installation[3]. The timings shown are the sum of all reasoning cycles.

As the figure shows, the reasoning times of EYE are almost one order of magnitude better than the reasoning times of Pellet+SPARQL. When we review the reasoning times per call for one ward (Figure 1b), we see that the EYE installation has far more predictable reasoning times, as it is more robust against more complex decision trees (e.g., the decision trees of the first two events are notably more complex than the other events' decision trees). Pellet+SPARQL is much faster than EYE in the third event, because this event does not trigger any reasoning for Pellet+SPARQL, however, a full reasoning cycle is performed by EYE. With an average reasoning time of about 2 seconds, the real-time constraint is achieved within small-scale datasets.

No. of	Time in sec.	
wards	EYE	Pellet
1	18	79
10	288	2 124

(a) Sum of reasoning times.

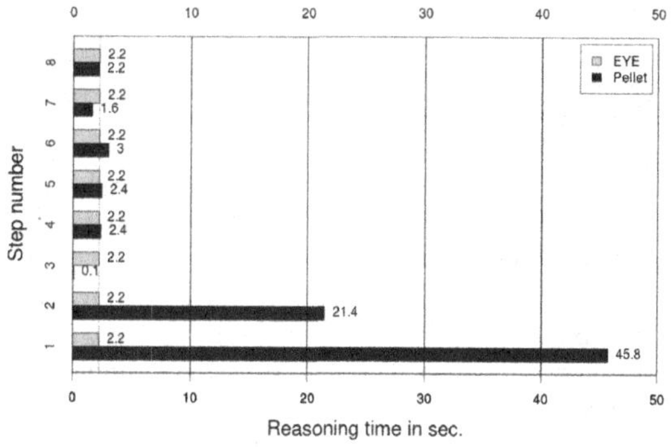

(b) 1 ward, reasoning time per event.

Fig. 1. Comparison of reasoning times. EYE is generally faster, and more predictable.

5 Importance and Impact

By using rule based reasoning instead of description logic based reasoning, we create a more performant system that is more easily configurable. The evaluation shows that the current version does not meet the performance requirements to be applied for larger datasets, however, it can already meet the constraints in a small-scaled setting, it is on average faster than more traditional approaches such as Pellet+SPARQL, and it has more robust and predictable reasoning times.

---

[2] Debian "'Wheezy", Intel(R) Xeon(R) CPU E5620@2.40GHz, 12GB RAM.
[3] Pellet 3.0 and OWL-API 3.4.5 vs. EYE 7995 and SWI-Prolog 6.6.6.

The analysis of converting a decision tree into rules shows how a rule based reasoning method is more suited to implement decision trees, and how it is as such easier configurable to make changes to the implemented decision trees. The described analysis, being generic, can be used as a guideline for converting decision trees into rules for other use cases as well.

The results of this research are being supervised by Televic Healthcare, the leading eHealth electronics company in Belgium. This way, the chances that the findings of this research will be commercialized are quite high, and as such, potentially improve the workload of the nurses in a hospital significantly, as elaborated on in 1.

Further research will involve improving the automatic selection of relevant OWL-RL concepts. This way, reasoning over unused concepts is avoided, which, as we believe, will drastically improve average reasoning times, and more importantly, will make sure that the system will scale a lot better than it does now.

Acknowledgments. The research activities described in this paper were funded by Ghent University, iMinds, the IWT Flanders, the FWO-Flanders, and the European Union, in the context of the project "ORCA", which is a collaboration of Televic Healthcare, Internet-Based Communication Networks and Services (IBCN), and Multimedia Lab (MMLab).

References

1. Berners-Lee, T., Connolly, D., Kagal, L., Scharf, Y., Hendler, J.: N3Logic: A logical framework for the World Wide Web. Theory and Practice of Logic Programming **8**(3), 249–269 (2008)
2. Calvanese, D., Carroll, J., Di Giacomo, G., Hendler, J., Herman, I., Parsia, B., Patel-Schneider, P.F., Ruttenberg, A., Sattler, U., Schneider, M.: OWL 2 Web Ontology Language Profiles. W3C Recommendation, December 2012. www.w3.org/TR/owl2-profiles/
3. De Roo, J.: Euler yet another proof engine (1999–2015). http://eulersharp.sourceforge.net/
4. De Roo, J.: EYE and OWL 2 (1999–2015). http://eulersharp.sourceforge.net/2003/03swap/eye-owl2.html
5. Ongenae, F., Bleumers, L., Sulmon, N., Verstraete, M., Van Gils, M., Jacobs, A., De Zutter, S., Verhoeve, P., Ackaert, A., De Turck, F.: Participatory design of a continuous care ontology (2011)
6. Parsia, B., Sirin, E.: Pellet: An OWL DL reasoner. In: Proceedings of the Third International Semantic Web Conference (2004)
7. Verborgh, R., De Roo, J.: Drawing conclusions from linked data on the web. IEEE Software **32**(5), May 2015. http://online.qmags.com/ISW0515?cid=3244717&eid=19361&pg=25

Author Index

Printed in the United States
By Bookmasters